THE LENS OF TIME

NORMA 2008

Enjoy your hikes in nature!

Love

PAM

THE LENS OF TIME

A repeat photography of landscape change in the Canadian Rockies

CLIFF WHITE AND E.J. (TED) HART

UNIVERSITY OF CALGARY PRESS

University of Calgary Press
2500 University Drive NW
Calgary, Alberta
Canada T2N 1N4
www.uofcpress.com

LIBRARY AND ARCHIVES CANADA CATALOGUING IN PUBLICATION

White, Cliff
The lens of time : a repeat photography of landscape change in the Canadian Rockies / Cliff White and E.J. (Ted) Hart.

Includes bibliographical references and index.
ISBN 978-1-55238-237-0

1. Rocky Mountains, Canadian (B.C. and Alta.)–Historical geography. 2. Rocky Mountains, Canadian (B.C. and Alta.)–Historical geography–Pictorial works. 3. Landscape–Rocky Mountains, Canadian (B.C. and Alta.)–Pictorial works. 4. Repeat photography–Rocky Mountains, Canadian (B.C. and Alta.) I. Hart, E. J. (Edward John), 1946– II. Title.

FC219.W44 2007 971.1 C2007-905735-7

The University of Calgary Press acknowledges the support of the Alberta Foundation for the Arts for our publications. We acknowledge the financial support of the Government of Canada through the Book Publishing Industry Development Program (BPIDP) for our publishing activities. We acknowledge the financial support of the Canada Council for the Arts for our publishing program.

This book has been published with the aid of a grant from Parks Canada.

Alberta Foundation for the Arts   Canada   Canada Council for the Arts   Conseil des Arts du Canada

Printed and bound in Canada by Houghton Boston
This book is printed on Starbrite Dull 80 lb paper

Cover design, page design and typesetting by Melina Cusano

CONTENTS

ACKNOWLEDGMENTS

This book grew from the authors' strong contention that Rocky Mountain ecosystems, past and present, can only be understood by integrating many disciplines including archaeology, history, ecology, and traditional knowledge. We recognize the essential contribution of the managers of Parks Canada and the Board of Directors of the Whyte Museum of the Canadian Rockies for guiding these organizations to gain understanding of both our cultural and ecological heritage. This knowledge is essential to conserve national park ecosystems for the benefit and enjoyment of future generations.

We thank the archivists who guided us through their fonds and photograph collections: Miles Zarowny, Craig Richards, Lena Goon, and Don Bourdon (Whyte Museum of the Canadian Rockies), Mae Boriss (Library and Archives of Canada), Pat Molesky and Doug Cass (Glenbow Museum), Terry Smith, Bob Stevenson, Peter Murphy (Dominion Department of Forestry Collection) and Meghan Power (Jasper Yellowhead Museum). Other assistance in locating and processing photographs was provided by Richard Brown, Birch Howard, Charles Kay, Miles Patterson, Mark Sherrington, and Rob Watt.

Walter Hildebrandt, past director of University of Calgary Press, was instrumental in getting this work into print. Charles Kay and Doug Leighton kindly read early versions of some chapters. Rob Storeshaw and Alison Buckingham from Parks Canada assisted with graphs and maps. We appreciate the efforts of Dave Brown, Melina Cusano, Mieka West, Alexandra White, and two anonymous reviewers in assisting in assembling the manuscript.

On behalf of all readers, we recognize the committed efforts of the photographers, past and present, whose work made this book possible, including but not limited to the Byron Harmon, the Vaux family, Bruno Engler, and Douglas Leighton.

Most of all, we thank our spouses, Johanne and Pat, for making this book possible, and more importantly, for making it an enjoyable task.

1

INTRODUCTION

For millennia the change in the Rocky Mountain landscape was inexorably slow. It was an evolution drawn incrementally onward by climatic modifications and developing populations of people, plants, and animals. At times there were isolated catastrophic events – earthquakes, landslides, fires, and floods, but the more widespread processes of change moved at a slow rate, barely noticeable in a primitive person's lifetime. Even as the human presence expanded into the more rugged recesses of the world, the land was usually not rapidly altered. Populations increased only slowly, and tools and implements were primitive. In the Swiss Alps prior to the nineteenth century, small villages changed little from century to century as a balance was struck between landscape and humans.[1] In the Canadian Rockies, First Nations peoples occupied the valleys for thousands of years, and although evidence of their presence is pervasive in mountain ecology, it was so subtle as to not even be recognizable to many early European observers.[2]

More recently, landscape change has been revolutionary, the product of modern man's exploding population and fast-paced technological society. In western Canada, as in most parts of the world, what was here yesterday is gone tomorrow. Within one brief century virgin prairies dotted with bison were displaced by farms and fences and are now often becoming the suburbs of an expanding metropolis.[3] In less than one hundred years remote mountain valleys have likewise been roaded, logged, mined, and often drowned by lakes from dams and hydro-electric projects. Alteration of the land, while essential to maintaining our standard of living and lifestyle, has been incredibly rapid and invasive.

Nonetheless, our propensity for reshaping the environment is not total. Through nostalgia for the past, or perhaps uncertainty about the future, Canadians value the "natural" landscape and have sought to protect its vestiges in parks and wilderness areas. The National Parks Act stipulates that parks "shall be left unimpaired for the use and enjoyment of future generations." It was in the Rockies that Canadian dedication to saving the land first gained public acceptance with the establishment of Rocky Mountains (later Banff) National Park in 1887.[4] To preserve these rugged landscapes was a noble endeavour, and it has been well supported by the people of Canada and the world. But how successful has this effort been?

Perhaps one of the best measures of success in preserving the landscape of the parks, and one easily judged by all, lies not in detailed scientific studies but rather in the simplicity of the photograph. This is appropriate, as it was the photograph that did much to stimulate the creation of the parks in the first place by framing scenes of spectacular grandeur that were immediately appreciated equally by politicians, businessmen, and the public at large. At the same time as the Canadian Pacific Railway (CPR) was being constructed between 1881 and 1885, a scientific breakthrough in photography allowed the former "wet plate" process, requiring photographers to immediately develop their plates in a tent using chemicals carried along for the purpose, to be replaced with a "dry plate" technique, allowing views to be taken, carefully packed away, and developed at a later time. This leap forward made the camera both a tool to record the natural world for the scientists associated with the Geological Survey of Canada and the Dominion Topographic Survey and a device for entrepreneurs eager to market images of the building of the line and the land it was opening up to eastern audiences.[5]

As early as 1881 the CPR contracted the Montreal firm of William Notman and Son to accompany survey parties exploring the proposed route of the line. In 1884, William McFarlane Notman toured westward taking a series of photographs as far as the "end of steel" in the Kicking Horse Pass, and within months CPR General Manager William C. Van Horne was incorporating some of them into the company's first advertising piece, *The Canadian Pacific, The New Highway to the East Across the Mountains, Prairies & Rivers of Canada*, aimed at attracting passengers to the soon-to-be-completed line. Other itinerant photographers quickly began to ply the rails, and the railway made a special photographer's car available to Notman, his Montreal competitor Alexander Henderson, and touring lecturer Professor Otto B. Buell.[6] Growth of settlements along the line, such as Calgary, Canmore, and Banff along the Canadian Pacific, and later Jasper and Edmonton along the Canadian National, provided a headquarters for more permanent commercial photographers to set up shop, and so began a unique and sometimes profitable trade supplying the seemingly insatiable demands of the postcard, viewbook, and print-buying public.[7] Quickly, more portable versions of their cameras were developed, and by the turn of the century the "Kodak" hand-held folding camera, utilizing cellulose nitrate sheet film, had become the constant companion of the tourist, resulting in an exponential growth in images of the mountains and those experiencing them.

Perhaps the popularity of the camera had come at a very fortuitous time to stimulate legislated preservation of the western mountain landscape. In the United States, early journalists submitting articles describing the marvels of the Yellowstone valley were rejected by reviewers with such comments as "champion liar" or "thank you but we do not print fiction."[8] It was not until William Henry Jackson's and F. Jay Haynes's impressive photographs of Yellowstone's landscapes, waterfalls, and geysers were published in popular magazines that Americans believed in the uniqueness of the world's first national park.[9] In Canada, there is little doubt that the public and government officials were also strongly influenced by the engravings reproduced from photographs in Van Horne's brochure and by other photographic and artistic representations being published in popular journals of the day, such as *The Dominion Illustrated* in Canada and *The Illustrated London News* in Great Britain.[10]

But we are not only indebted to these early photographers for their influence in the preservation of parks. Their works have also provided us with an easily visualized benchmark from which to judge the results of the preservation effort. Prior to the clearing for the railroad, the Banff area may not have been greatly altered by European influence. Hostile plains First Nations had forced fur traders to cross the mountains by more northerly routes; mineral-poor rock of the mountains had not drawn in a rush of prospectors.[11] Thus, the first photographers captured a landscape in the first stages of being rolled over by a wave of change, one of the first times in Canadian history when the camera caught up to the advancing frontier. In the lands that were to form Jasper National Park further north, it was a somewhat different story, as here the camera, in this case in the 1871 photographs by Charles Horetzky, documented the last days of the fast-disappearing fur trade.[12]

In this book we continue the more than a century-long use of photography to document Canadian Rockies landscapes by reproducing retakes made from approximately the same locations as the earliest photographers and the second generation photographers following in their footsteps. This allows not only an appreciation of the earlier scene but also an evaluation of the changes that have occurred during more than a century of intensifying human land use.[13] The repeat photography technique in interpreting landscape and cultural change in the Canadian mountains has a long tradition. After 1894, the Vaux family, during their studies of retreating glaciers, began taking wonderfully detailed views each year from fixed points. Later, renowned photographers such as Byron Harmon routinely took pictures from the same favoured locations to capture rapidly changing hotels and streetscapes as the tourism industry grew in the Bow River valley. In the 1960s, researchers from the University of Calgary again used repeat photography to document human effects on Banff National Park's landscape. As well, famed mountain guide and photographer Bruno Engler periodically received federal government contracts for repeat photography documenting highway building and landscape changes during the period 1950 through 1990. Most recently, the re-discovery of archival negatives from a splendid set of mountain summit photographs made by early government cartographers such as Morrison Bridgland have provided material for a new generation of avid repeat photographers.[14]

The book is the product of a unique collaboration between two observers who have, for more than a quarter-century, been examining these matters – national park biologist Cliff White, who has collected these historic photographs and assiduously retraced the steps of the photographers performing retakes to inform his scientific work, and Canadian Rockies historian E. J. (Ted) Hart, who has equally investigated the stories of the people and places involved. Because the landscape is the most visual component of the ecological whole, or ecosystem, that today's parks attempt to preserve, we have arranged the photographs generally on the basis of ecological regions moving west from Calgary, Alberta, and the foothills, ascending through the low elevation montane zone of Banff National Park, upwards into the lower and upper subalpine. We then follow the historic photographers for brief forays onto the west slopes of the Rockies in the Columbia River watershed of British Columbia, and east into the Front Ranges along the Red Deer and North Saskatchewan rivers. Returning to the main chain, the photographs move northward to show the high windswept alpine zone and glacial ice of the Columbia Icefield, before passing through Jasper National Park and turning eastward to descend to the parkland region at Edmonton, Alberta. For the most part, the early views come from the collections of the most well-known of the commercial and amateur photographers who made it their task to photograph the mountains – Boorne and May, the Vaux family, Byron Harmon, and Bruno Engler – but where material from them was not available, other images were used. The majority of the photographs are from areas either historically or presently in national parks, as the boundaries have been continually adjusted by industrial developments and changing government philosophies.

Join us now as we take our journey of rediscovery and examine landscape change in this glorious mountain world through "the lens of time."

2.1 CHIEF CROWFOOT SPEAKS TO TREATY 7 DELEGATION (BRUCE STAPLETON, GLENBOW NA 40-1).

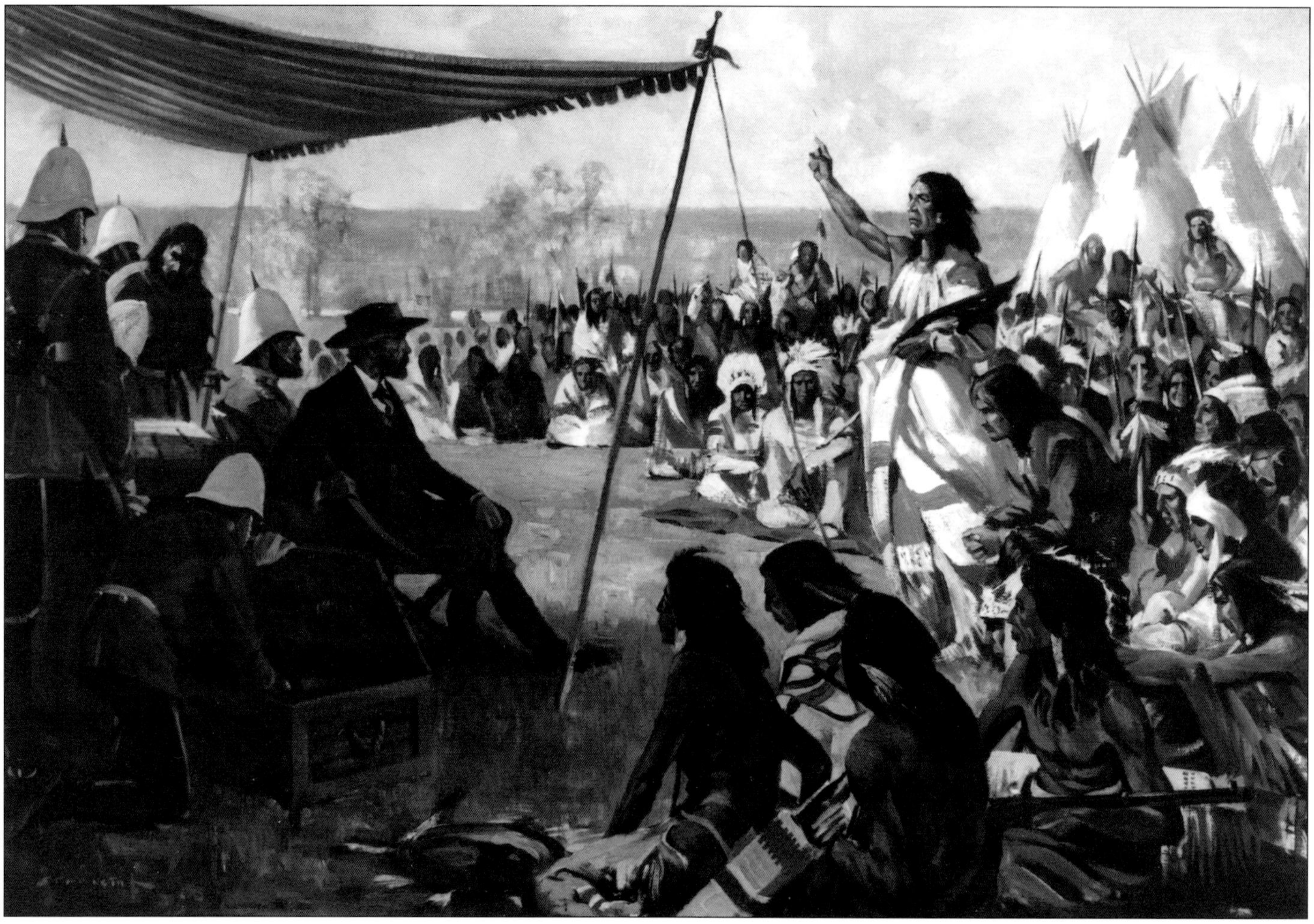

2

INTO THE MOUNTAINS

Blackfoot Crossing to Canmore

Anthony Henday was likely the first European explorer to see the Rocky Mountains. Viewing the peaks from a hill near modern-day Innisfail, Alberta, in September 1754, he called them the "Shining Mountains" – a seemingly impenetrable wall of rock and snow.[1] But of course the foothills and mountain valleys had been the homelands of First Nations for over ten millennia. Trails long trod by moccasins and later the hooves of horses crossed nearly every pass. Traditional campsites and hunting grounds occupied every valley. First Nations passed the names of mountains, rivers, passes, and trails from generation to generation, a legacy of how to live in a rugged environment.[2]

Henday was the advance guard of a culture that by 1900 would come to dominate western Canada. But for a time, the "Blackfoot Confederacy," a loose federation of war-like plains tribes, would block European access to the Bow River country on the east slope of the Rockies.[3] But it was here, with the coming of the railroad, that the Rocky Mountain landscape and its original occupants would first experience the massive, human-caused changes of the Industrial Revolution.

2.2A BLACKFOOT CAMP, GATHERED FOR VISIT OF GOVERNOR-GENERAL AT BLACKFOOT CROSSING, LITHOGRAPH, 1881 (MARQUESS OF LORNE, GLENBOW NA 843-3).

2.2B CAMP AT BLACKFOOT CROSSING, 1930S (W. J. OLIVER, GLENBOW NA 1698-2)

2.2C TREATY FLATS NEAR BLACKFOOT CROSSING, SEPTEMBER 2003 (CW 2003-09C-11)

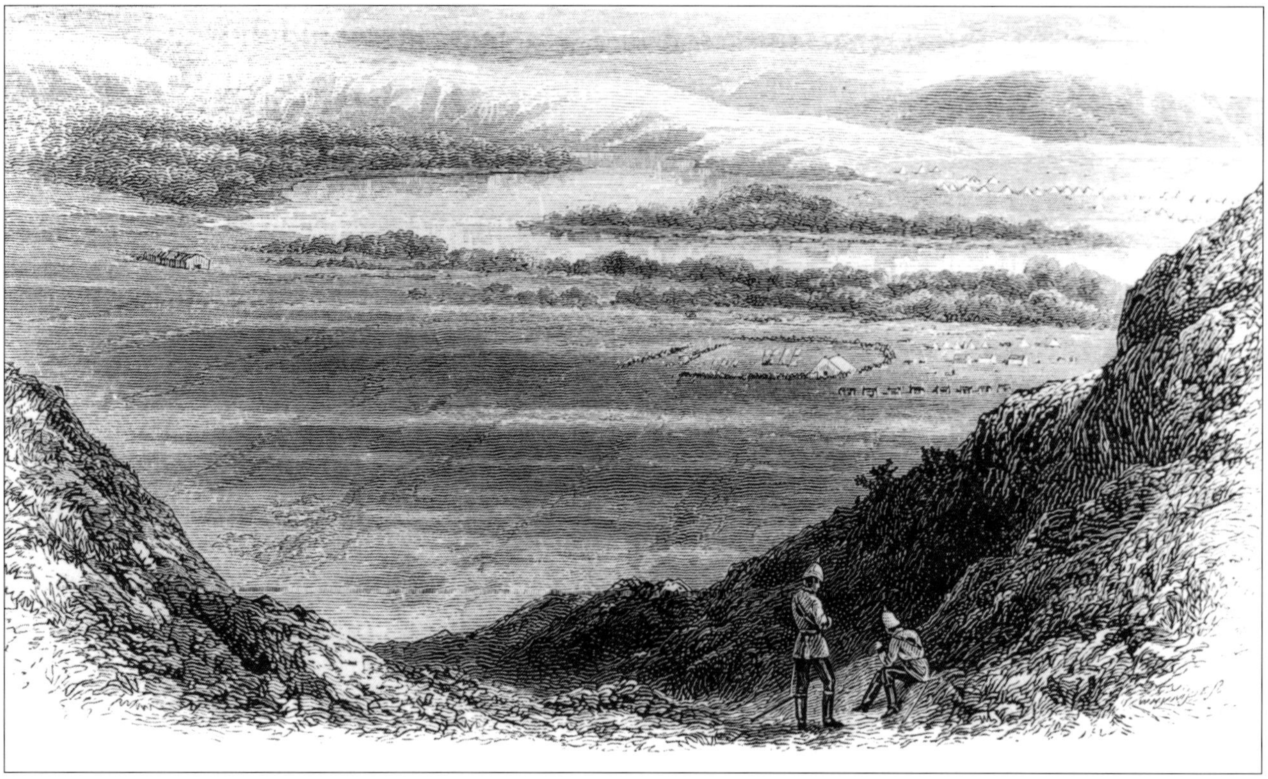

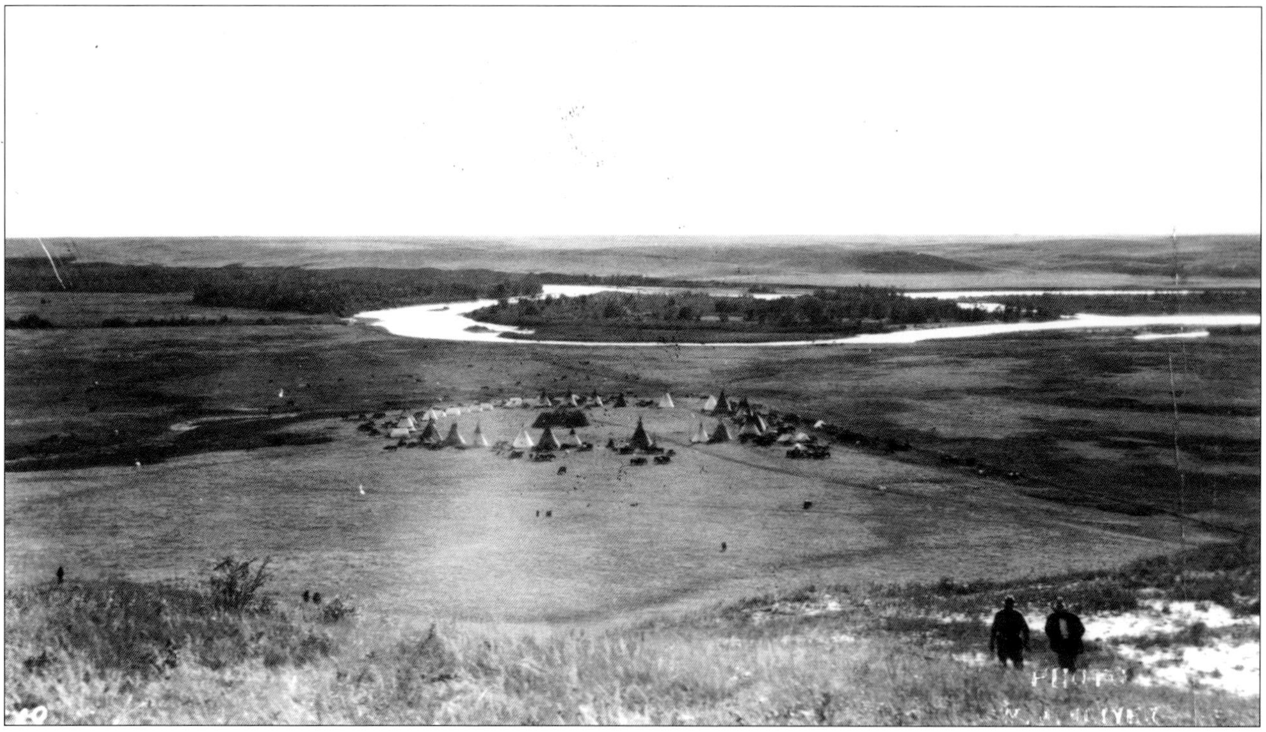

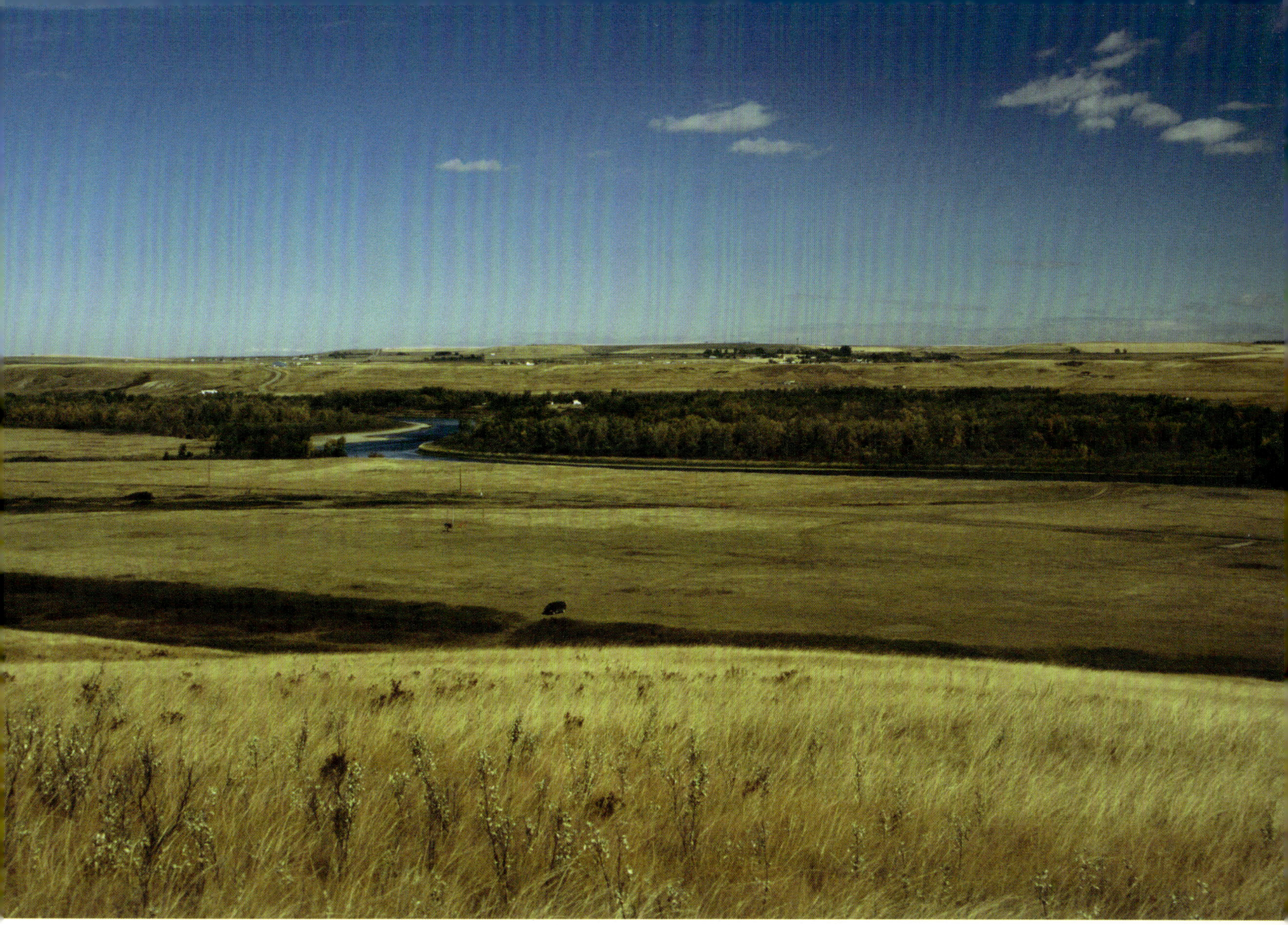

The signing of Treaty 7 at Blackfoot Crossing symbolized the replacement of a long-standing hunter-gatherer culture of First Nations with an industrially based culture from Europe. In September 1877 the Siksika, Blood, Tsuu T'ina, Stoney Nakoda, and Peigan First Nations and officials of the recently confederated country of Canada gathered at a traditional ford of the Bow River downstream from Fort Calgary to arrange a peaceable sharing of the prairies, foothills, and east slopes of the southern Canadian Rocky Mountains.[4] No one – native or government emissary – could have anticipated the massive changes that would occur during the next century. But the signs were ominous. The once great bison populations were dwindling towards near extinction,[5] and railroad construction would soon proceed towards the plains from both the west and the east.[6]

Ironically, despite the massive human alterations that have occurred across most of the prairies and foothills since the signing of Treaty 7 over a century ago, the traditional campsite area on Treaty Flats, on the Siksika Nation lands near Cluny, appears little changed today. However, a closer look at the riparian zone along the Bow River shows an invasion by several Eurasian weed species. Moreover, upstream dams on the Bow River have reduced peak June flows by over 30 per cent, stabilizing the formerly meandering river channel. Balsam poplar and plains cottonwood forests, adapted to disturbed soils for regeneration, are declining in health.[7]

2.3A CALGARY FROM SCOTCHMAN'S HILL, 1885 (P. HIGINBOTHOM, GLENBOW NA 670-53)

2.3B CALGARY FROM SCOTCHMAN'S HILL, 1895 (J. M. LOWNDES, GLENBOW NA 615-1)

2.3C CALGARY FROM SCOTCHMANS' HILL, SEPTEMBER 2003 (CW 2003-09B-35)

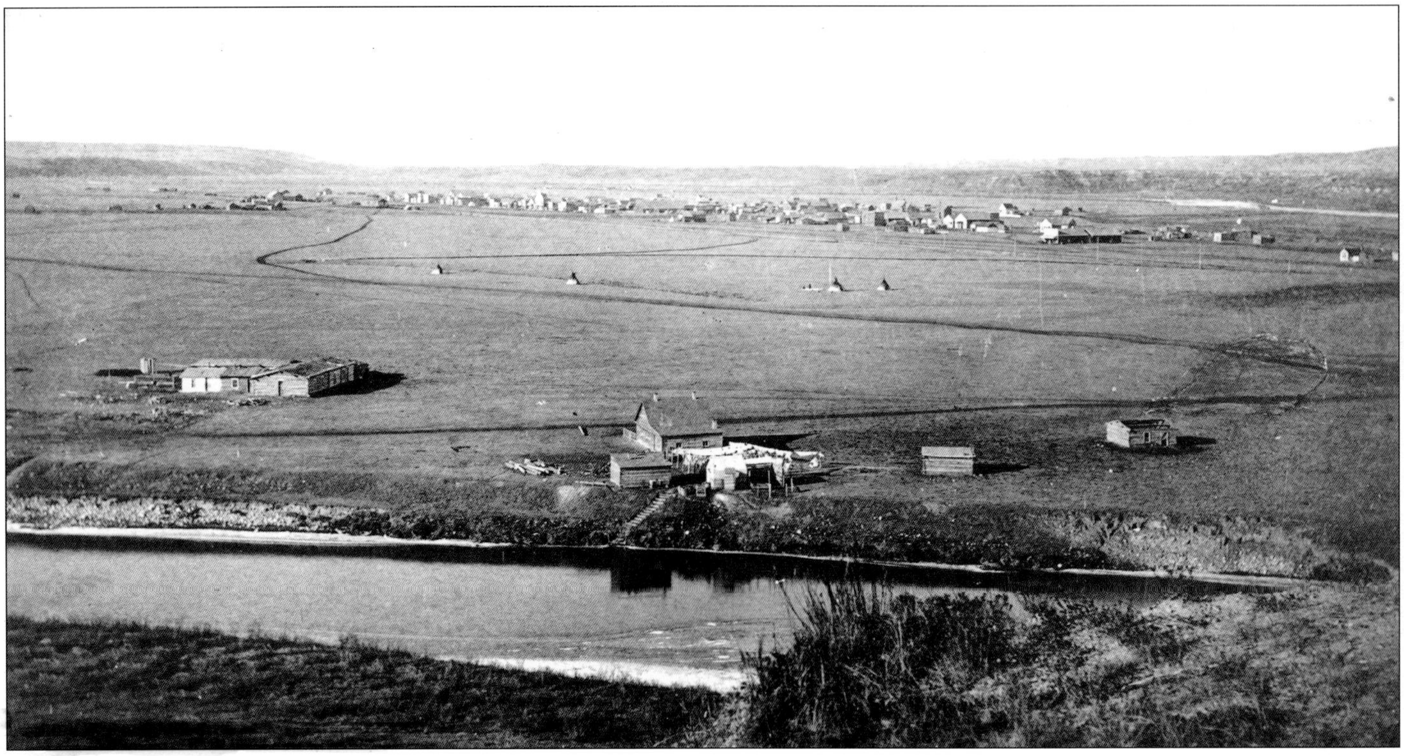

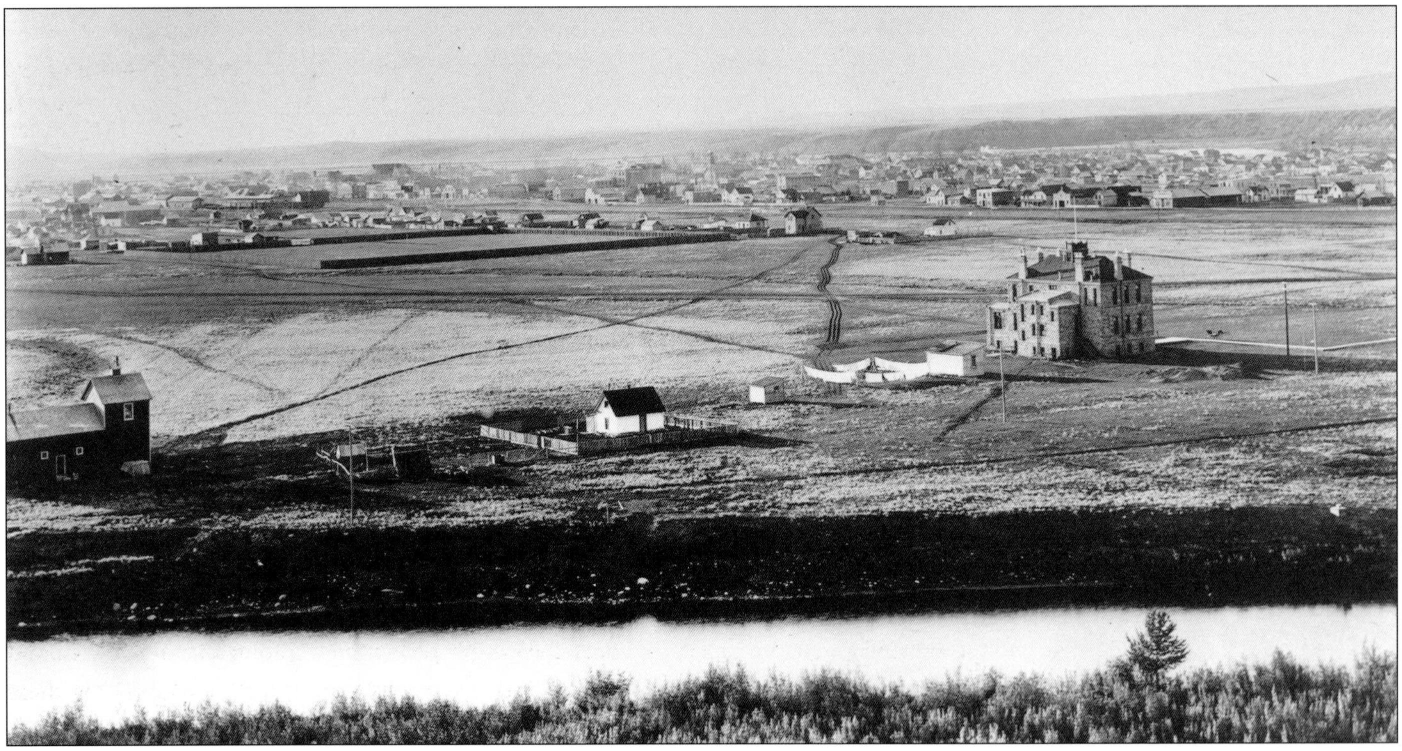

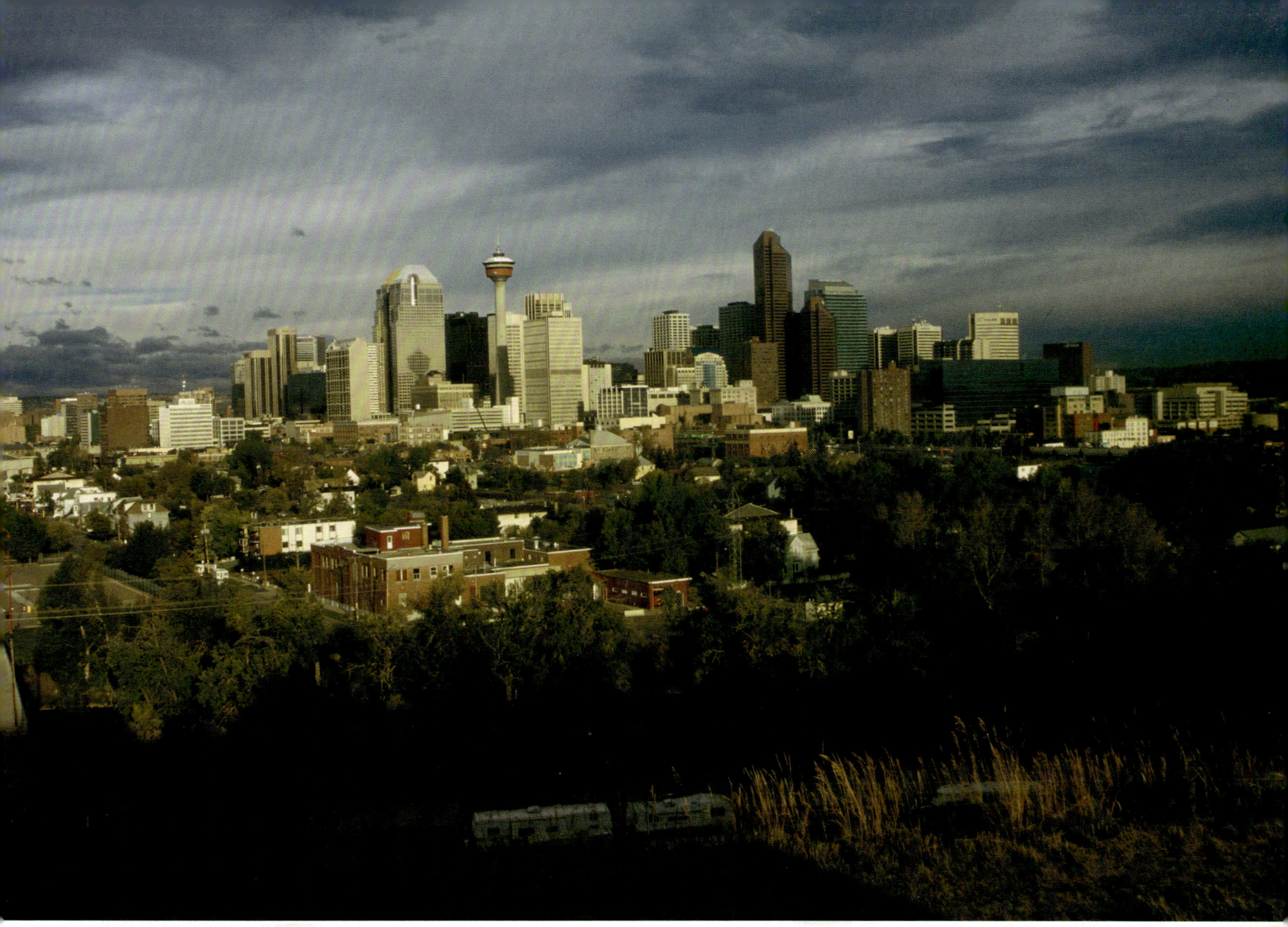

In the fall of 1875 the Northwest Mounted Police established Fort Calgary at the confluence of the Bow and Elbow rivers. The police had been sent by the Canadian government to shut down a series of "whisky forts" on the southern prairies where Americans traded liquor for buffalo hides from the First Nations.[8] On August 23, 1883, the first CPR train reached Calgary and by August 28 the newly initiated *Calgary Herald* reported "track laying is being vigorously proceeded by the C.P.R. ten miles west of Calgary." Construction up the Bow River valley advanced at a record pace, reaching Siding 27 (Canmore) and Siding 29 (Banff) in October and progressing to "end of steel" for the season at Kicking Horse Pass shortly afterwards, an amazing feat of human labour.[9]

Lying within sight of the Rockies, which it quickly began to regard as its "back yard," Calgary grew rapidly, first through cattlemen's stockyards, then propelled on by the exploitation of Alberta's oil and natural gas resources. Its population grew from 4,091 in 1901 to 129,060 in 1951 to a million by 2006. Over this period its citizens were an important element in mountain tourism, from supporting Banff's Winter Carnival and Indian Days celebrations early in the century to being the major users of its ski resorts in the post-war period. Calgarians also plied well their own tourism and convention business, first through the famous Calgary Stampede rodeo and culminating in the 1988 Winter Olympics. Today, Calgary's international airport acts as a gateway for millions of mountain-bound international tourists, and Calgarians themselves are frequent mountain visitors, with many of them keeping recreation homes in the mountain valleys at Canmore, Invermere, and Golden.[10]

2.4A COCHRANE FROM EAST, 1972 (TERRY CIONI, GLENBOW NA 2864-205-28-16)

2.4B COCHRANE FROM EAST, JANUARY 2004 (CW 2004-01A-2)

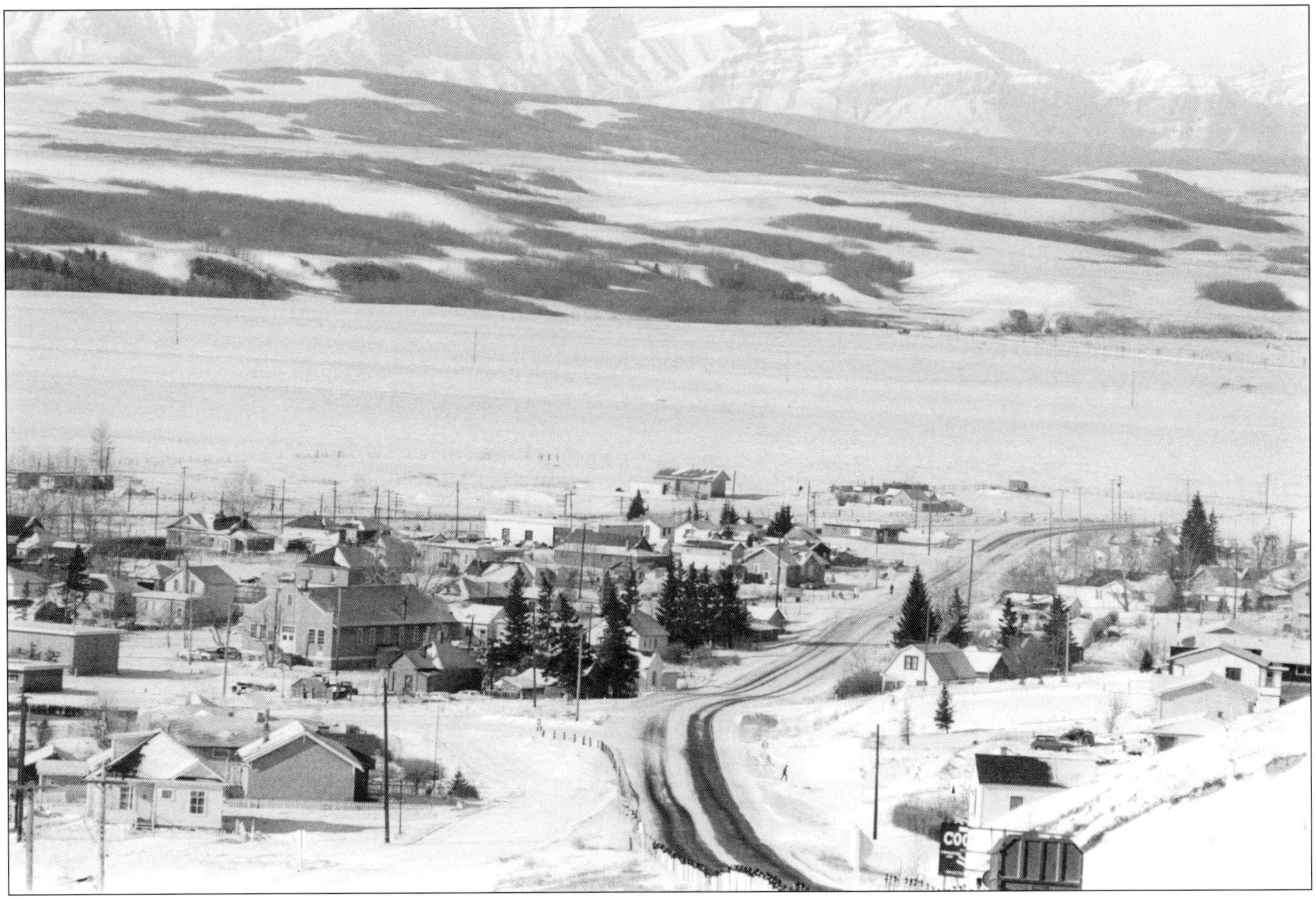

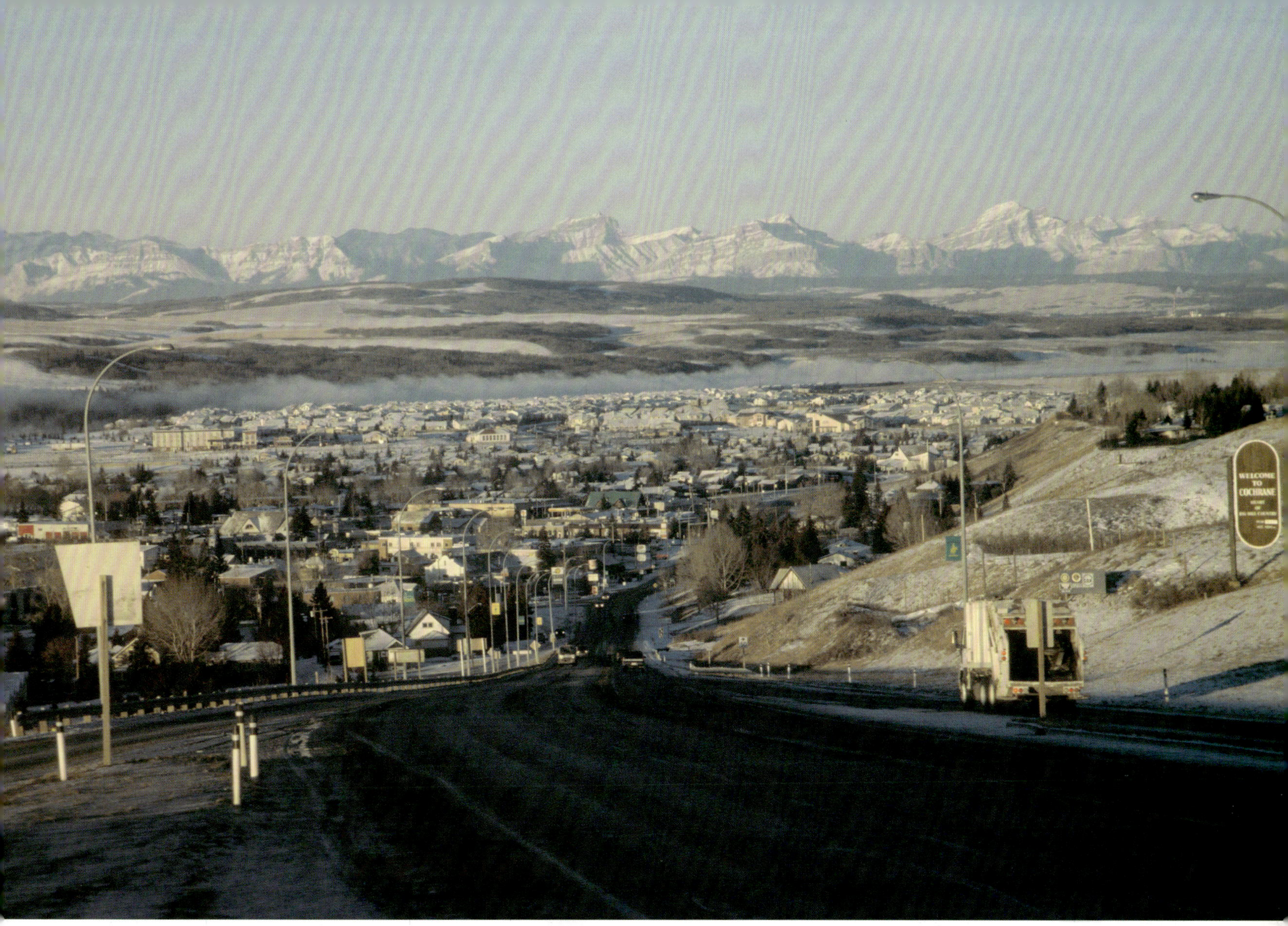

Cochrane lies along the Bow River approximately twenty kilometres upstream from downtown Calgary. It began as a settlement supporting the pioneer cattle ranches during the 1880s, and until the 1970s served as a service community for the farms and ranches of the Rocky Mountain foothills. Today, Cochrane is a bedroom community for Calgary and will within a few decades likely become engulfed as the city spreads westward.[11]

2.5A MCDOUGALL'S STORE, MORLEY, 1885 (O. B. BUELL, GLENBOW NA 4697-59)

2.5B STONEY NAKODA FIRST NATION AND GHOST RESERVOIR, JULY 2001 (CW 2001-07D-17)

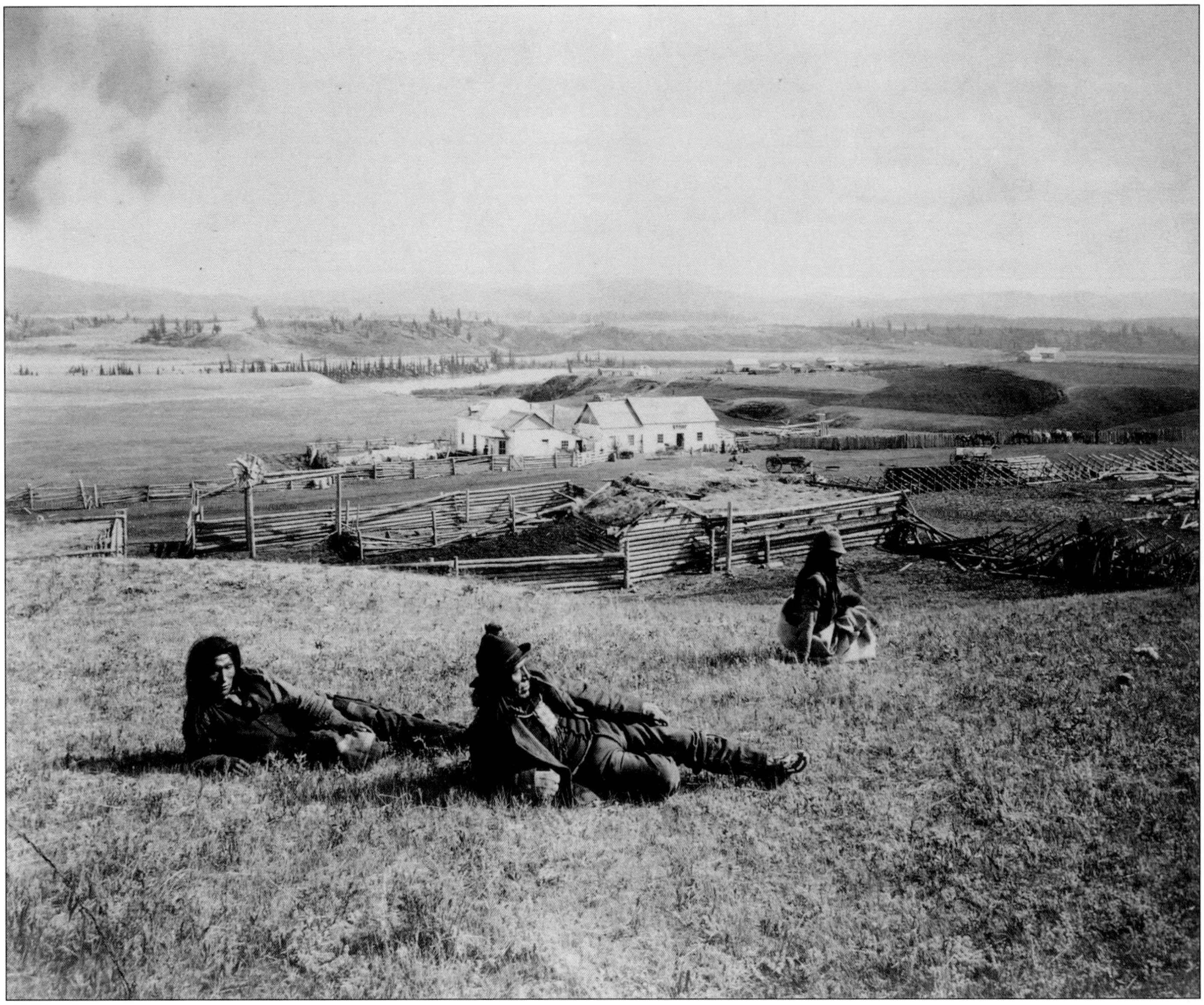

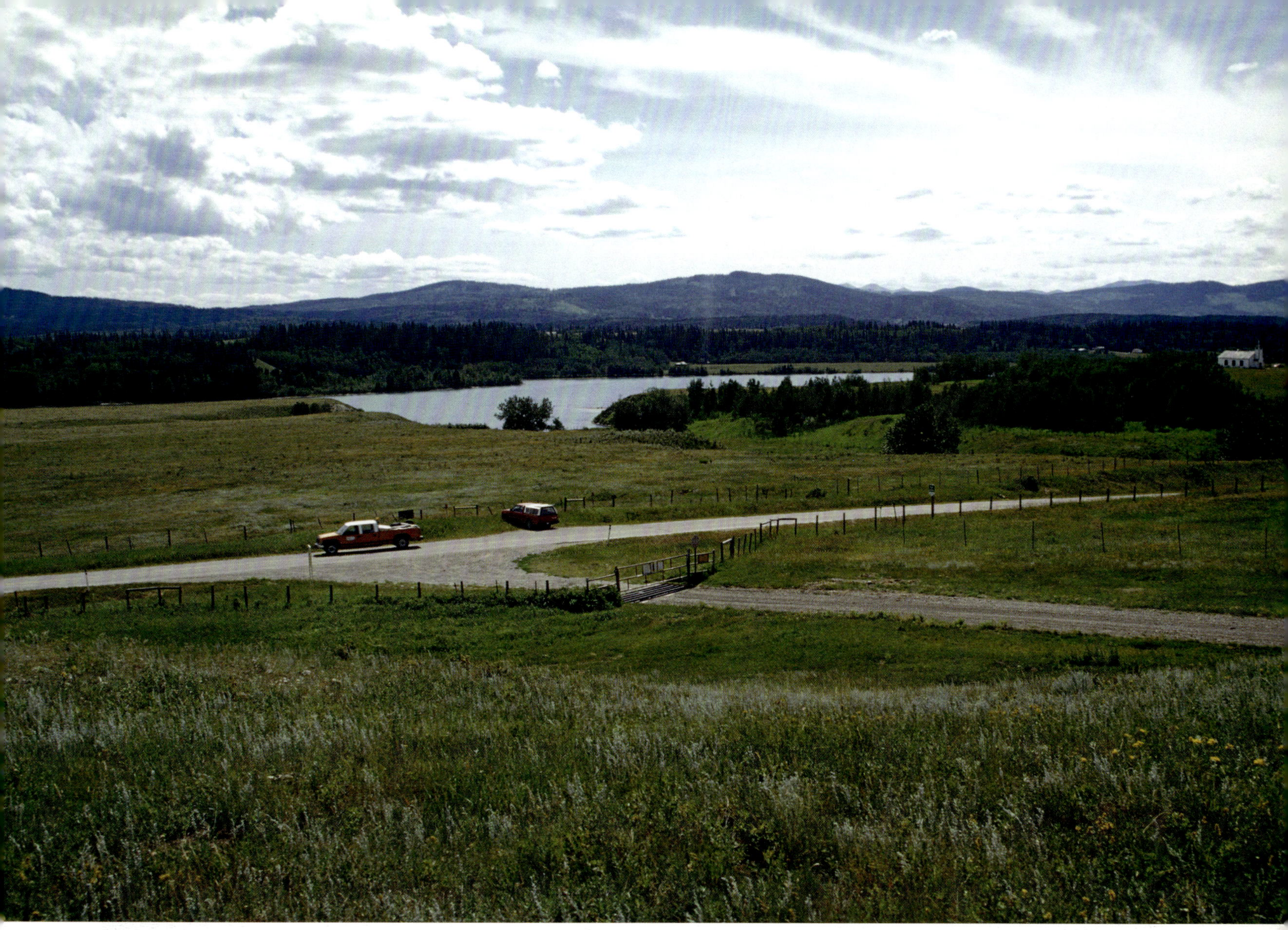

The Reverend John McDougall and his trader brother David built a Methodist mission and store at Morley in 1875. In the Treaty 7 negotiations of 1877, the Stoney Nakoda First Nation chose a large land reserve around the mission, a traditional tribal wintering area.[12] Although it was the government's intention that the Stoney become farmers and ranchers, their customary hunting grounds were in the Rockies and, combined with insufficient rations from the Morley agency, this led them to continue to roam and hunt throughout the region. The passage of national park's legislation prevented them from hunting inside Rocky Mountains (Banff) Park boundaries, and by the turn of the century, they were even being actively discouraged from passing through park lands. Thereafter, their appearance at an annual festival known as Banff Indian Days, staged by the CPR for the benefit of their guests, was the only time that their camping at a traditional ground near Cascade Mountain was allowed.[13]

Today, the village of Morley lies a few kilometres west of its original location, moved closer to the railway, and the Bow River lies impounded in a lake behind the Ghost Dam. The McDougall Church remains on the right side of the recent photograph. With the elimination of the frequent fires of earlier times, the cover of aspen, Douglas fir, and white spruce has increased, particularly on the more moist, north-facing slopes beyond the river.

2.6A GATHERING HORSES ON BAR U RANCH, 1930S (LANE STUDIO, GLENBOW NA 67-8)

2.6B EDEN VALLEY, STONEY NAKODA FIRST NATION, MAY 2003 (CW 2003-05B-24)

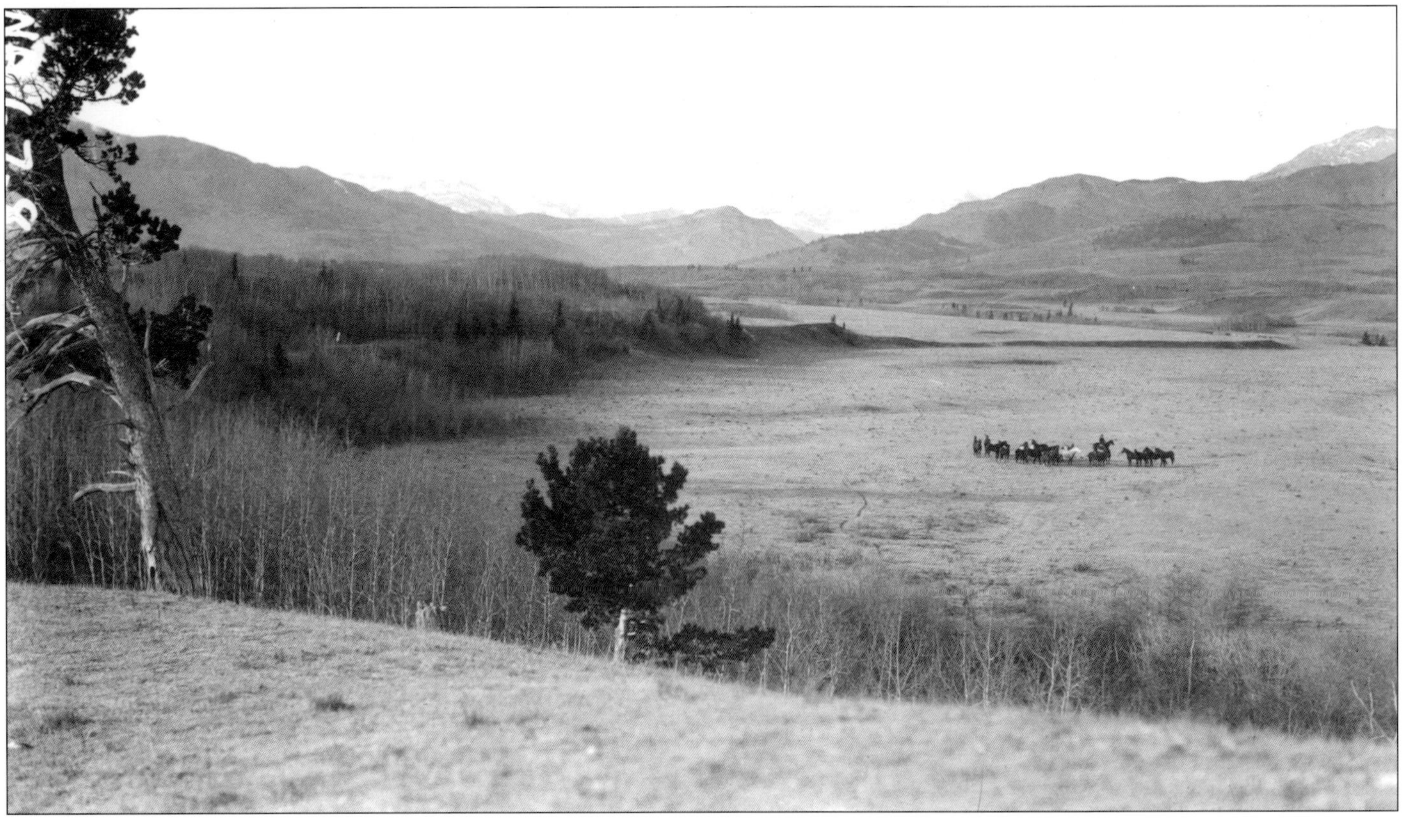

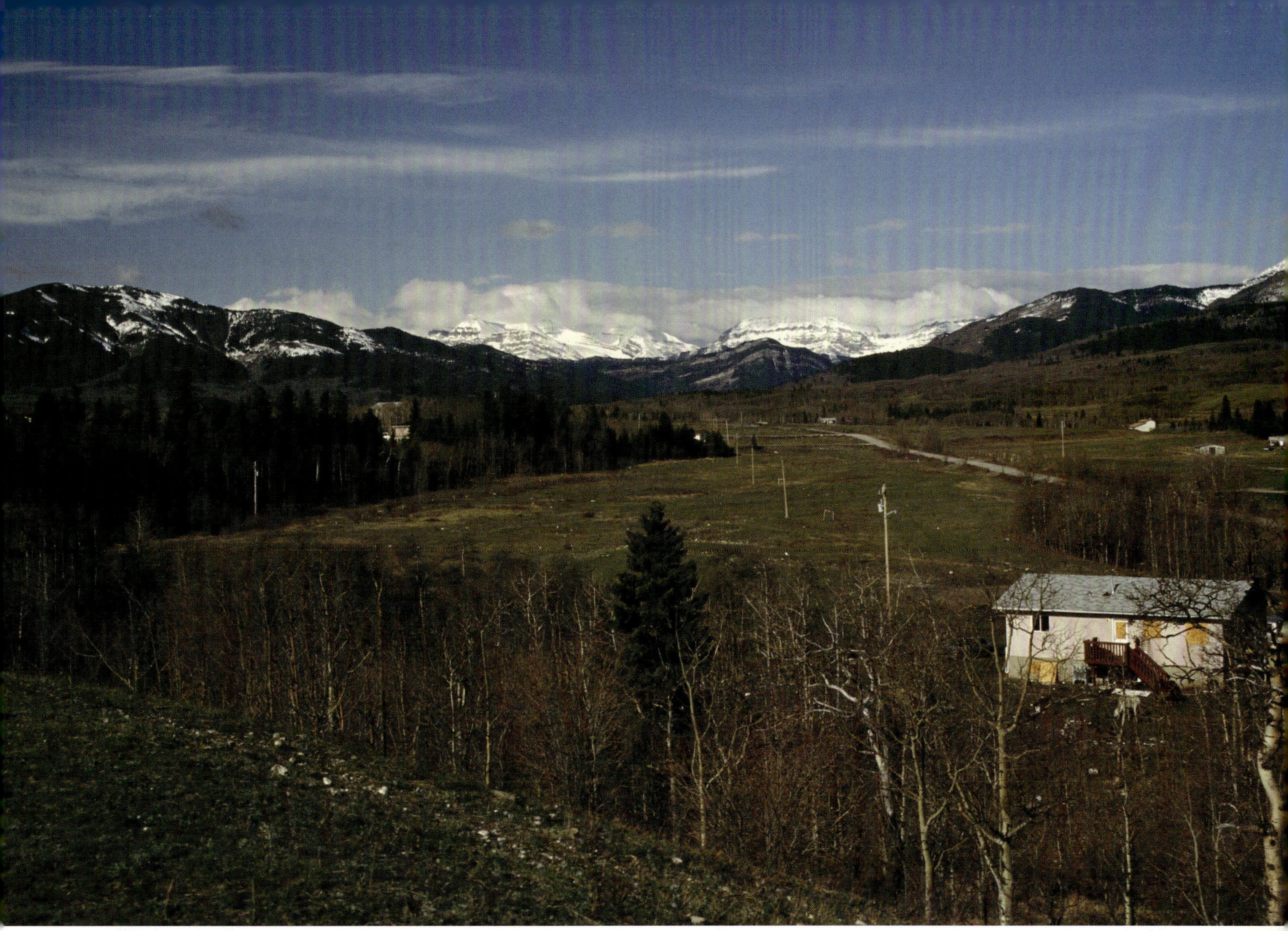

Throughout the period of recorded history, the lands used by different First Nations varied considerably. Near the Rocky Mountains there were expansions to the north and east in the 1600s by tribes obtaining horses from the Spanish. In the 1700s tribes from the east expanded to the north and south after obtaining guns from British and French traders. As well, epidemics of Eurasian diseases from which they had little immunity, such as smallpox, measles, dysentery, meningitis, and tuberculosis, reduced their populations dramatically. The K'tunaxa (Kootenay) frequently hunted bison on the east slope of the Rockies until the great smallpox epidemic of 1781–82, after which they were displaced by a coalition of Blackfoot and Stoney Nakoda in the late 1700s.[14] After Treaty 7 small bands of Stoneys roamed widely from their designated reserve at Morley to continue traditional hunting on the headwaters of many tributaries to the North and South Saskatchewan rivers. The Stoney Nakoda people eventually obtained additional lands, including, in the 1940s, a portion of the Bar U Ranch, at Eden Valley along the Highwood River. By 2003, this area of the Eden Valley had numerous houses and roads.[15]

2.7A NORTH-WEST CATTLE COMPANY RANCH, CA. 1896 (S. A. SMYTH, GLENBOW NA 2084-4)

2.7B GEORGE LANE'S BAR U RANCH, 1930S (R. A. BIRD, GLENBOW NC 26-360)

2.7C PARKS CANADA BAR U NATIONAL HISTORIC SITE, OCTOBER 2007 (CW 20071013-228)

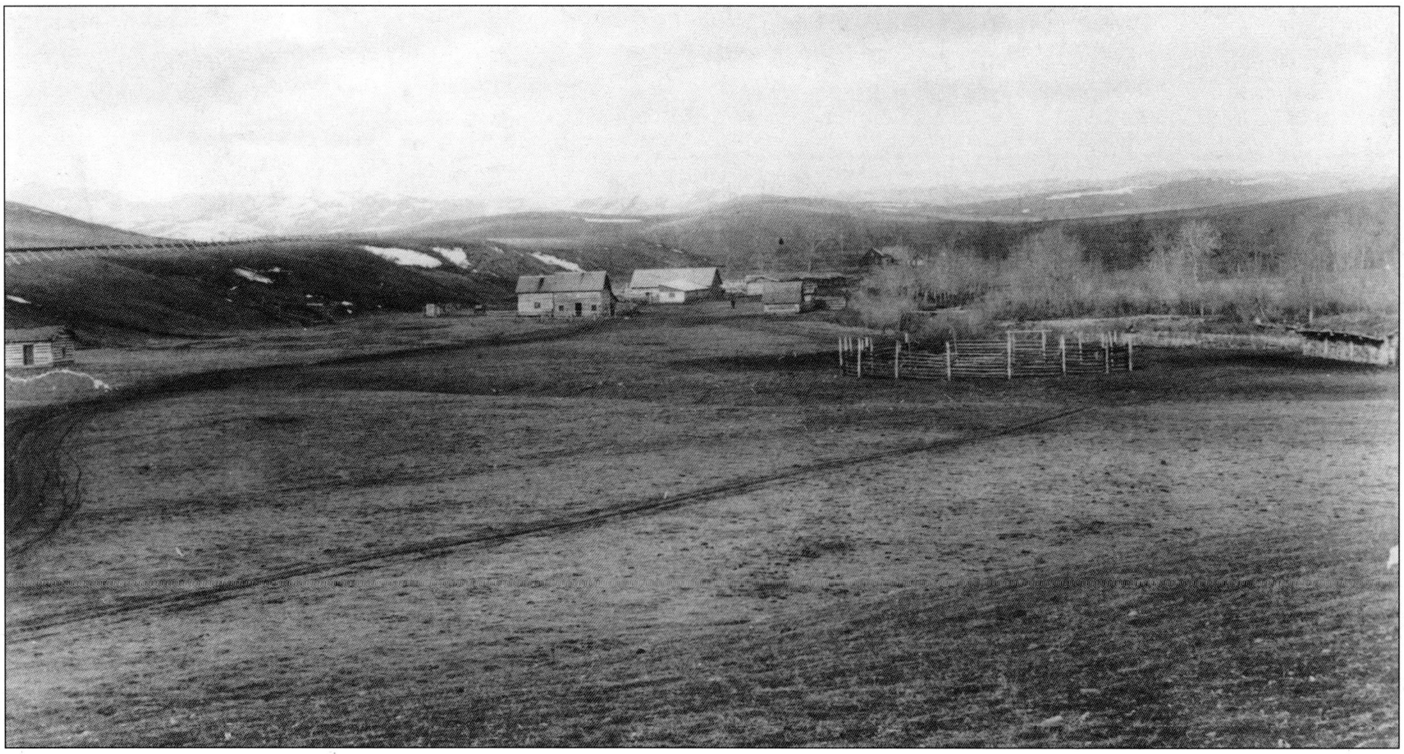

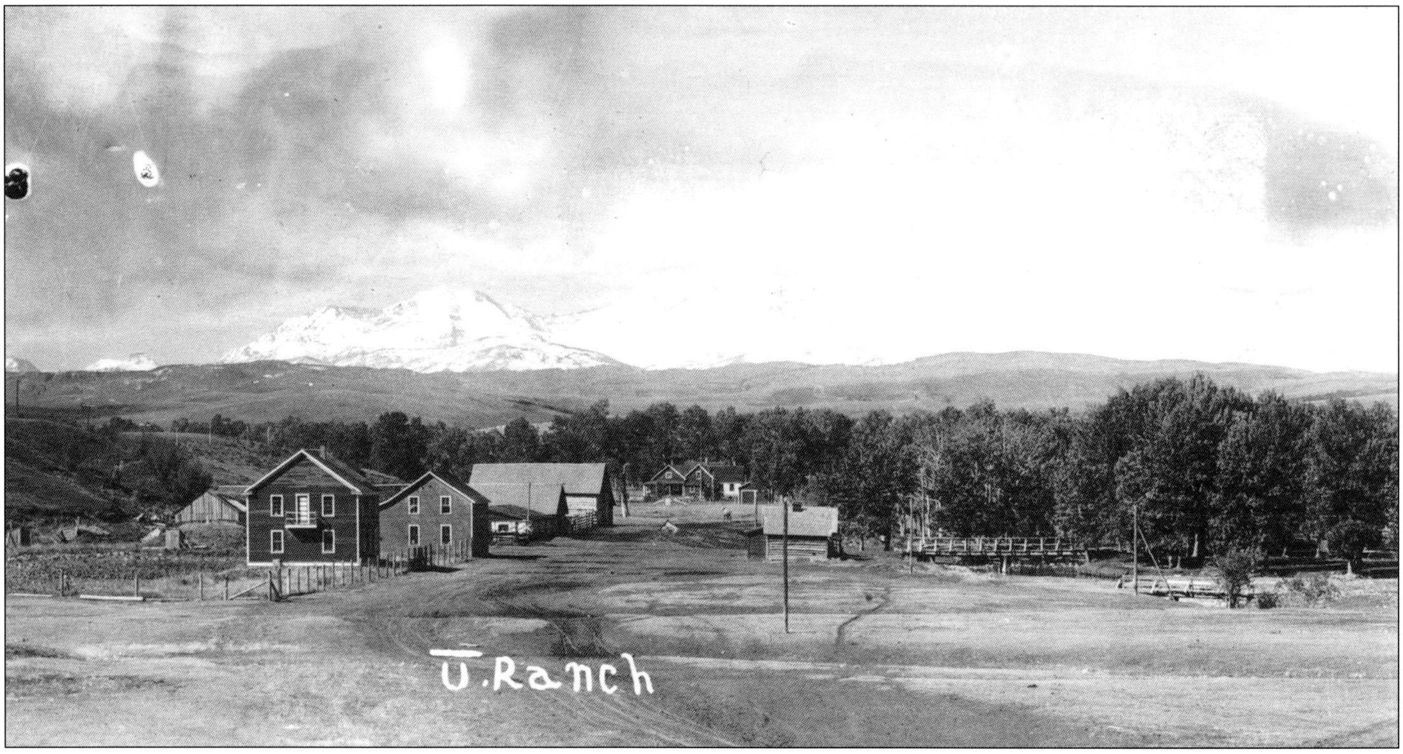

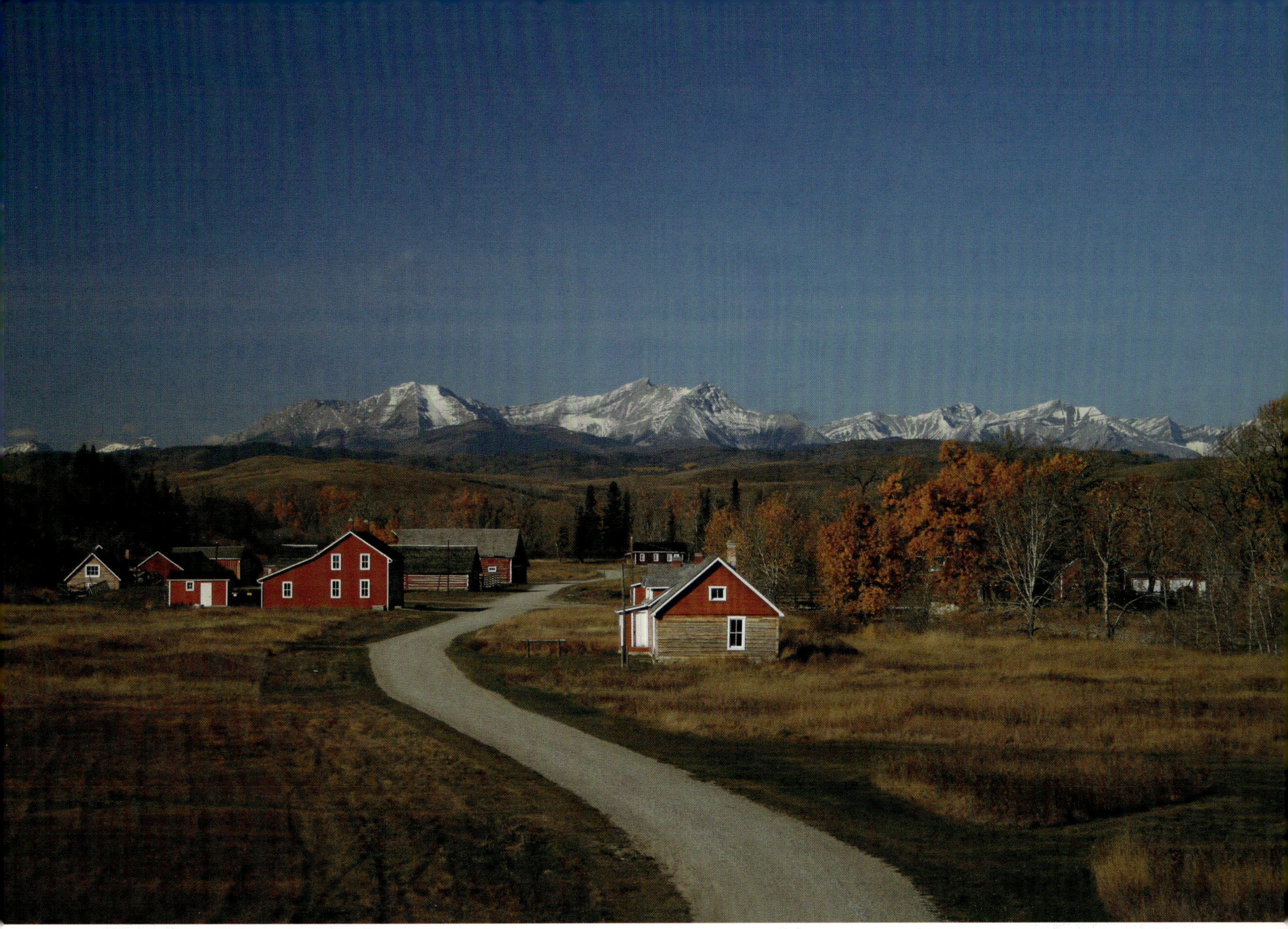

With the signing of the treaties, the demise of the bison, and the ending of the fur trade, Canada's Northwest Territory was a vacant sea of grass. The federal government moved quickly to put the land to work and encourage eastern Canadian and British investors. An Order-in-Council passed in 1881 allowed a person or company to lease up to a hundred thousand acres of grazing land for a penny an acre, the only requirement being that the lessee hold one cow on every ten acres. The North-west Cattle Company, later known as the Bar U Ranch, drove its founding herd of three thousand Durham-Shorthorn cattle across the Canadian border from Montana in August 1881. The next quarter-century would become the classic period of the foothills cowboy – no fences, rounding up free-ranging cattle across the whole of southwest Alberta, and the founding of a "proudly-western tradition" of rodeos and free-wheeling, yet fiscally conservative, thinking.[16]

However, in the 1890s the government began closing out leases, raising annual rents and selling the land to dry-land farmers. These new settlers would provide a greater profit to the railroad, and a broader agricultural economy. During bad winters, cattle bunched up and died in droves against newly strung barbed-wire fences. In 1902 Bar U owner George Lane began diversifying the ranch, making it an international breeding centre for cattle and Percheron horses. In recognition of its historic place in the early ranching period and the changing western economy, in 1991 Parks Canada acquired the ranch headquarters area to establish a National Historic Site.[17]

2.8A VIEW OF TURNER VALLEY, 1930s (LANE STUDIO, GLENBOW NA 67-67)

2.8B TOWN OF TURNER VALLEY, JUNE 2003 (CW 2003-06A-25)

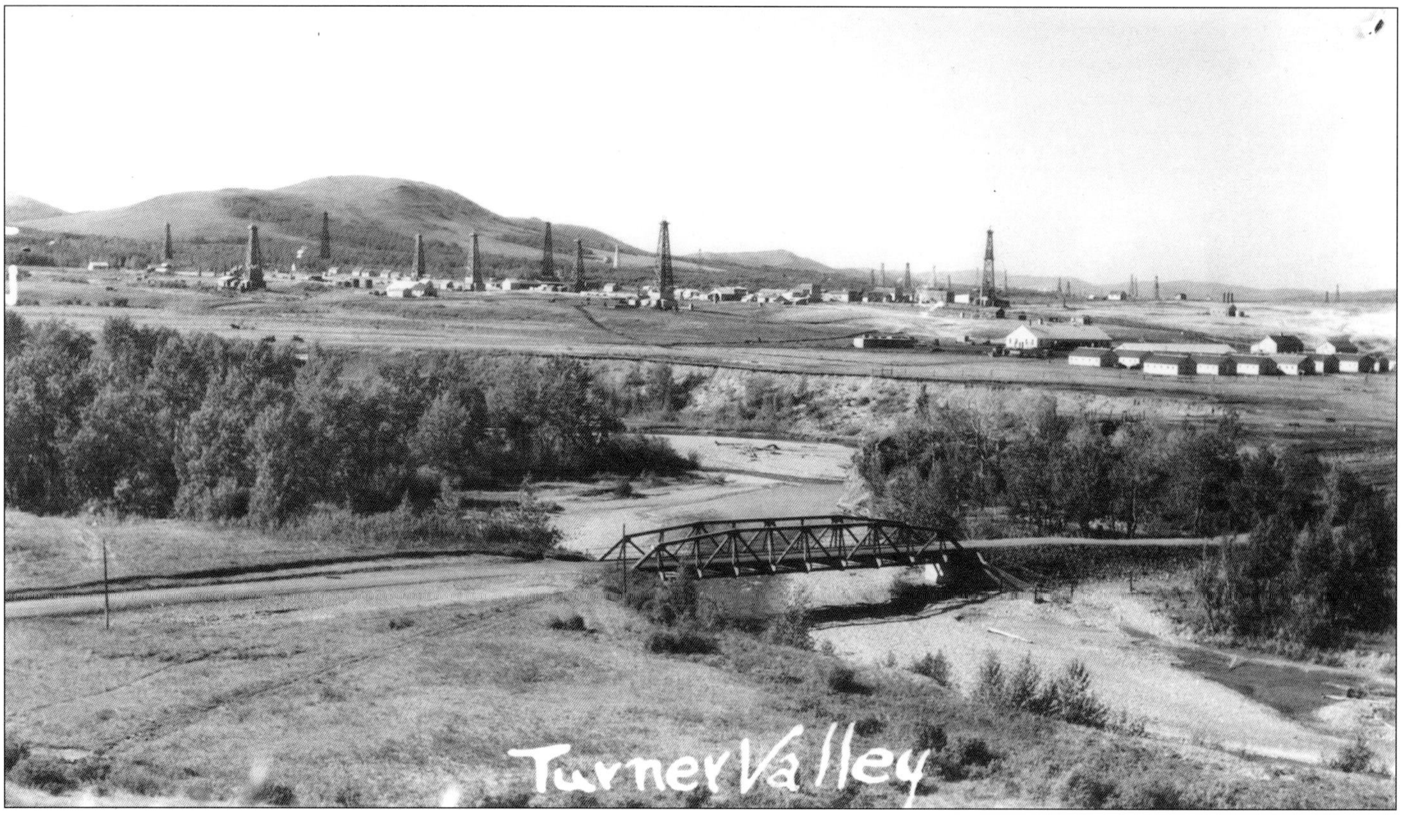

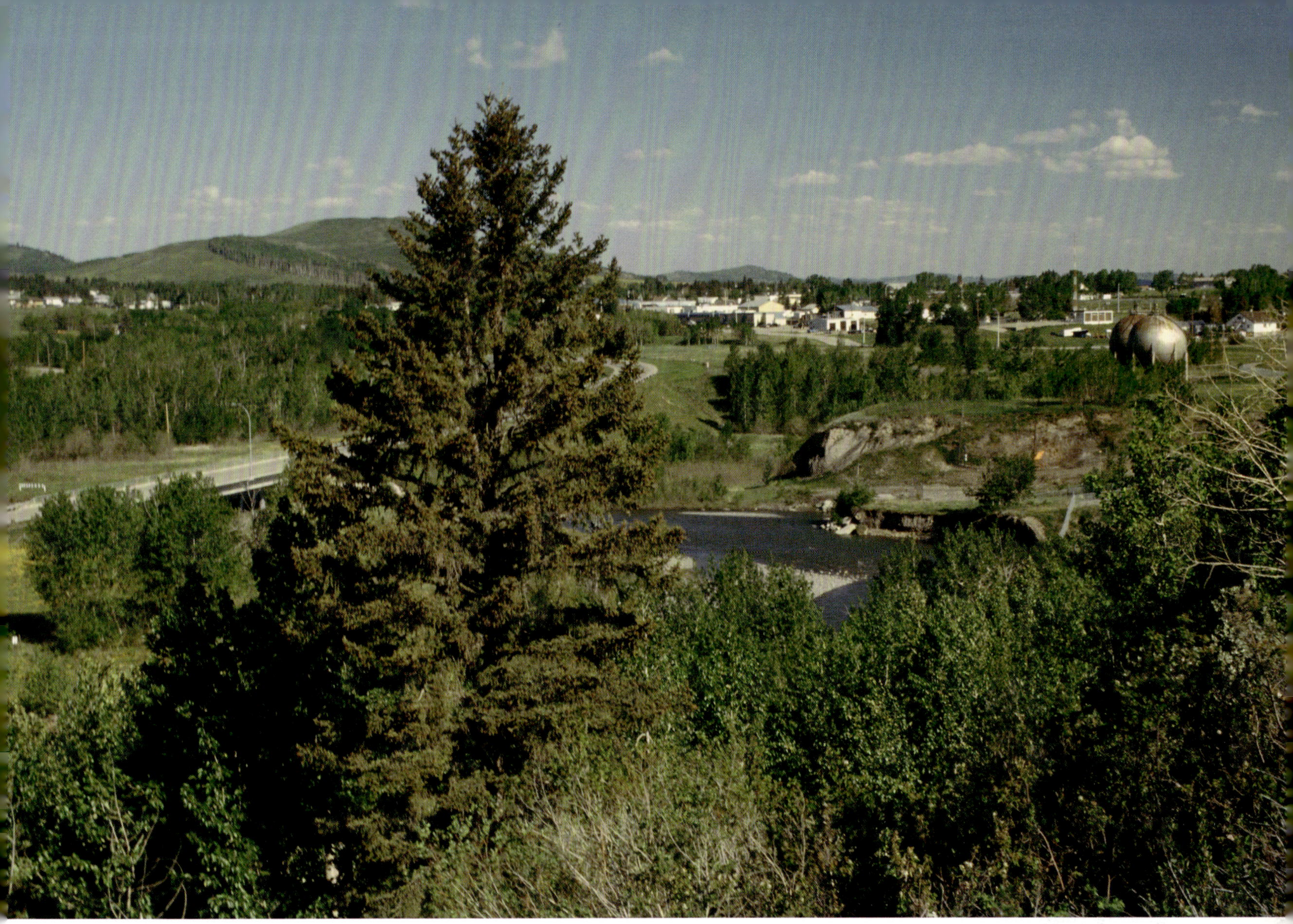

In 1913 William M. Herron, an Okotoks farmer, and Archibald Dingman formed the Calgary Petroleum Products Company and began drilling wells in an area where natural gas bubbled up near the Sheep River in Turner Valley. When "Dingman No. 1" proved productive, Calgary speculators established over a hundred companies, virtually overnight. But early development of the gas field was slow – American money and expertise was needed to build refineries and pipelines to markets. In 1936 further drilling discovered oil beneath the gas and another boom hit the valley, with over seventy wells in production by 1939. Oil and gas fields were discovered across the province, and Alberta, having finally received ownership of its own resources in the Natural Resources Act of 1930, went from one of Canada's poorest provinces to one of its richest in a few decades. The continuing appearance of American oilmen, their families, and their money in connection with the development of the fields profoundly transformed Calgary and Alberta, with the city becoming an international centre for the oil business. The petroleum reservoirs under the Turner Valley townsite area were depleted by the 1970s, and by the time of the 2003 view, the town was quickly growing as a bedroom community for Calgary commuters.[18]

2.9A KANANASKIS FALLS ON THE BOW RIVER AT KANANASKIS, 1885 (O. B. BUELL, GLENBOW NA 4697-62)

2.9B KANANASKIS DAM ON THE BOW RIVER, JULY 1997 (CW 1997-07C-14)

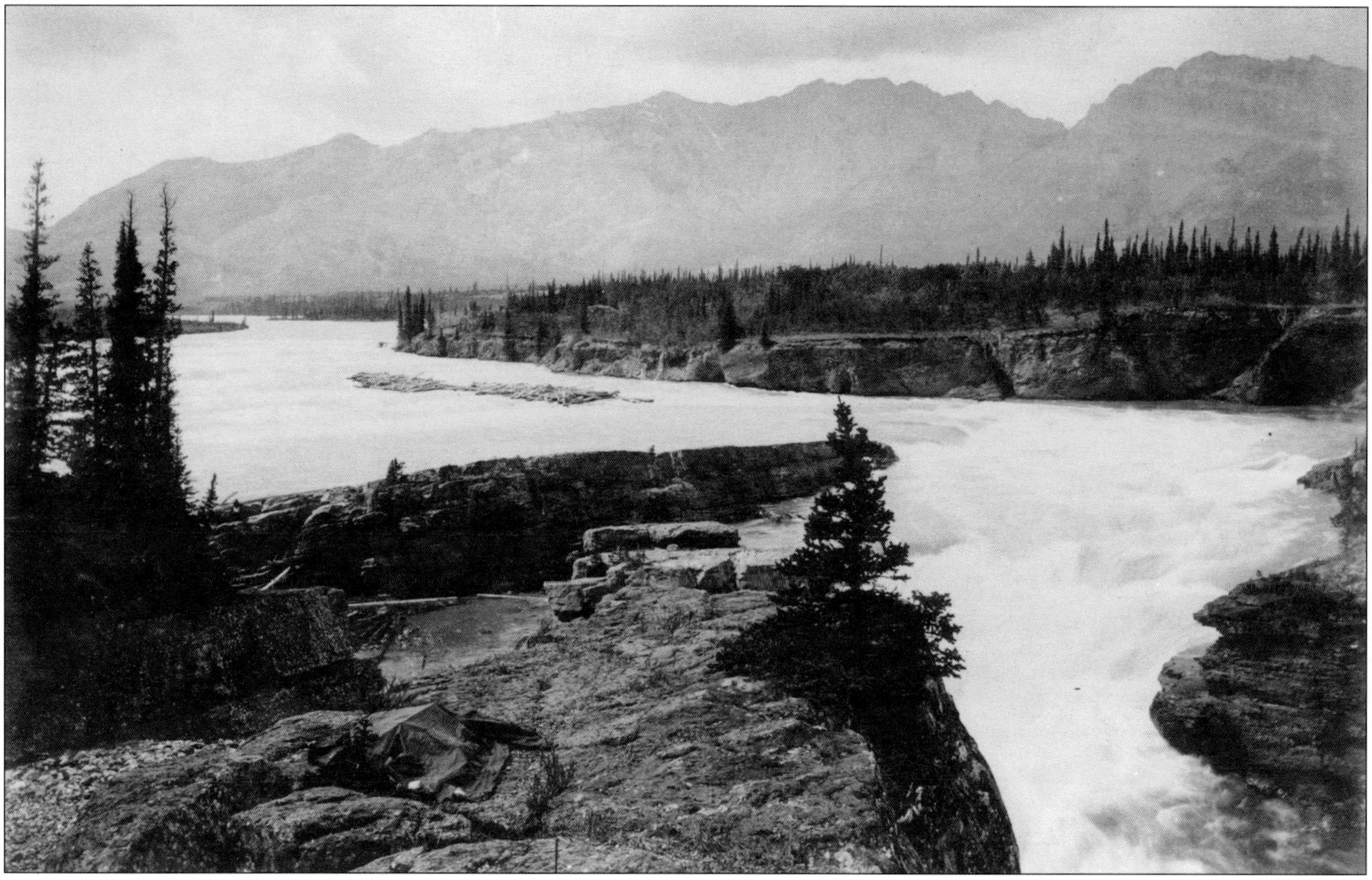

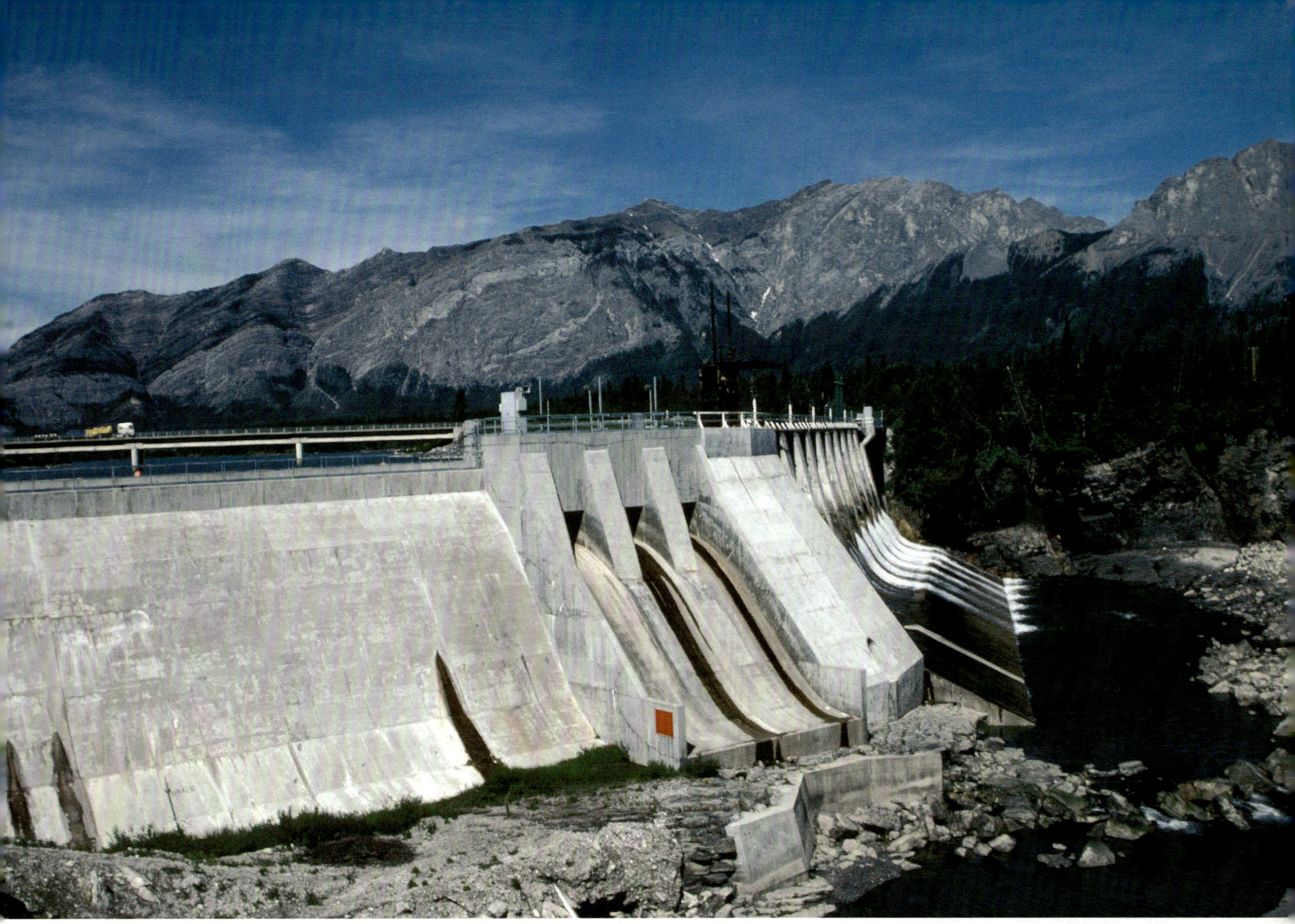

The rapid growth of Calgary in the first decade of the new century made it one of the fastest developing markets for power in Canada. Beginning in 1907 the newly incorporated Calgary Power and Transmission Company began surveying the Bow River to the west for potential sites for dam and hydro-electric generating facilities, the first being planned for Horseshoe Falls below the confluence of the Bow and Kananaskis rivers. Even before it was completed, low seasonal flow in the river had identified a need for a second plant and the Kananaskis Falls site, located about three kilometres upstream from Horseshoe and thought to be the last commercially developable site on the Bow, was chosen. The falls were actually a series of four cascades falling ten metres in a gorge about a hundred metres long, but a dam at this point could raise the water level twenty metres and generate about eleven thousand horsepower.[19]

The construction of these plants became the first of many times that hydro-electric development would become a contentious issue in the foothills and mountains west of Calgary and ultimately shape Rocky Mountain land use. The reservoirs created behind the dams would flood a small portion of Rocky Mountains (Banff) Park, enlarged to over twelve thousand square kilometres in a boundary revision of 1902, and were also partially on the lands of the Stoney Nakoda Reserve at Morley. In 1913 the tribe threatened an armed attack on the construction works if compensation was not provided. Eventually, Ottawa granted $16,500 (or $25 per person) to deal with their claims and the plant was completed.[20] However, by that time the ongoing problem with low winter flow had already resulted in the 1912 impoundment of water in Lake Minnewanka in the heart of national park lands.

2.10A OLD GATEWAY TO ROCKY MOUNTAINS (BANFF) PARK AT THE GAP, 1921 (BYRON HARMON, WHYTE NA 71-3436)

2.10B HIGHWAY 1A WEST OF SEEBE, AUGUST 2001 (CW 2001-08A-23)

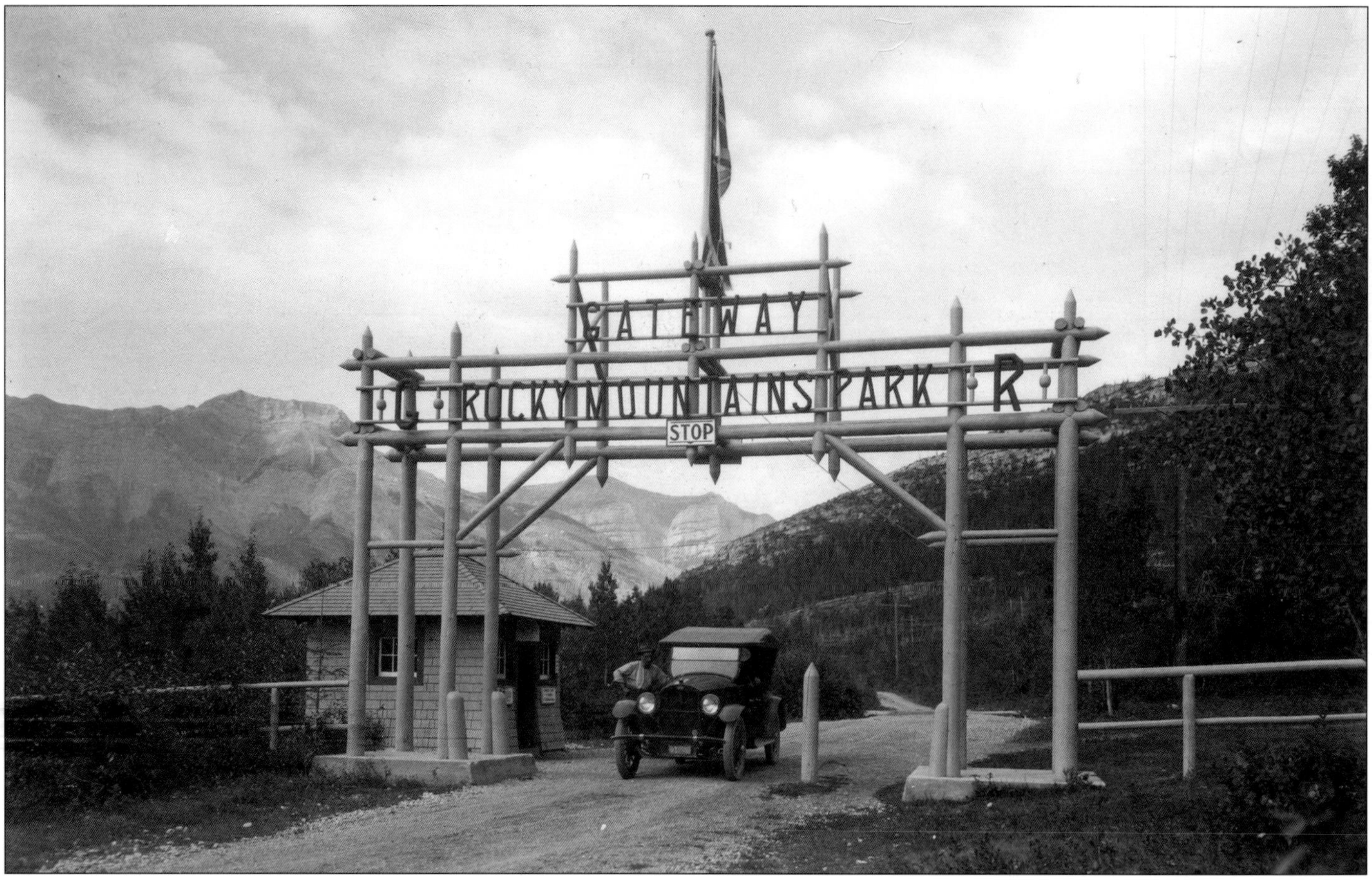

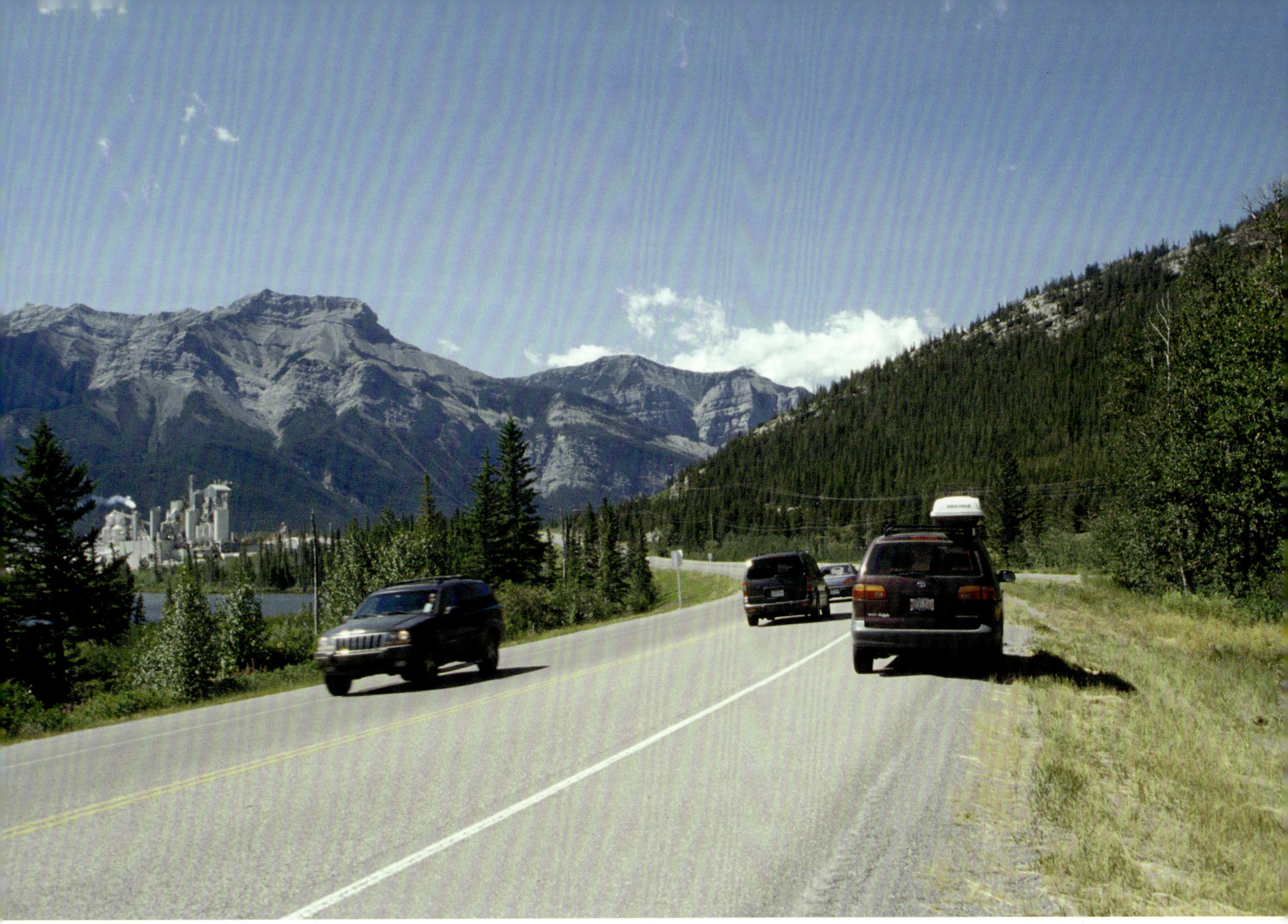

The 1902 enlargement to the size of Rocky Mountains Park resulted in a boundary that lay nearly twenty kilometres to the east of its present location, and until 1930 the park incorporated the villages of Kananaskis, Exshaw, and Canmore as well as the windy "gap" where the Bow Valley leaves the Front Ranges.[21] The development of the Calgary-Banff Coach Road, completed in 1911, required the construction of an entrance gate, and for many years Annie Staple, a widowed warden's wife, was its sole keeper. Living with her four children in a nearby house, she provided twenty-four-hour-a-day service, stringing a chain across the gate at night and marking it with a lantern to warn late-arriving motorists (the "G" and "R" on either side of the gate signify "George Rex," King George V).[22]

The National Parks Act of 1930 marked an important step towards the inviolability of park lands from major commercial resource development, requiring a further boundary revision to remove mining and quarrying activities at Canmore and Exshaw.[23] In June 1930 the gate was moved close to its present location west of Canmore, and Annie Staple continued to work here until retiring in 1948. In the contemporary photograph, a lime and calcium processing plant is visible, while a rock quarry to supply it is out of sight further west.

2.11A TRAIL TO KANANASKIS LAKES, ROCKY MOUNTAINS PARK, 1925 (BYRON HARMON, WHYTE NA 66-1761)

2.11B HIGHWAY 40 AND BARRIER LAKE RESERVOIR, KANANASKIS COUNTRY, JULY 2003 (CW 2003-07C-17)

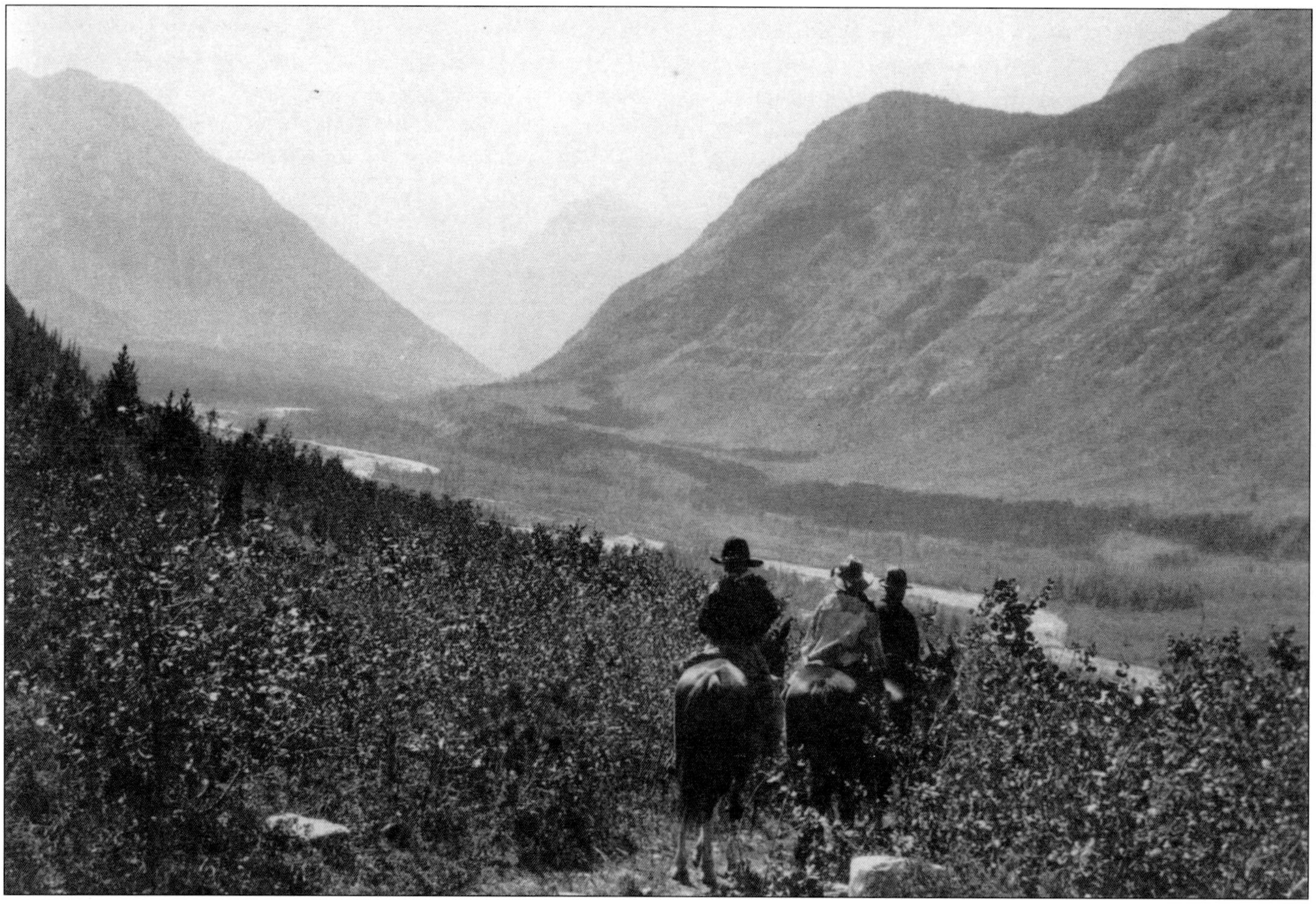

Many generations of First Nations used the old trail in the Kananaskis Valley, and in 1854 the Cree chief Maskepetoon (Broken Arm) led the first group of white travellers, a colonizing party headed for the Oregon territory under the direction of Red River Metis leader James Sinclair, up the valley and through South Kananaskis Pass. Four years later Captain John Palliser followed much the same route and recorded, "this pass I have called the Kananaskis pass, after the name of an Indian, of whom there is a legend, giving an account of his wonder recovery from a blow of an axe which had stunned but had failed to kill him, and the river which flows through this gorge bears his name."[24]

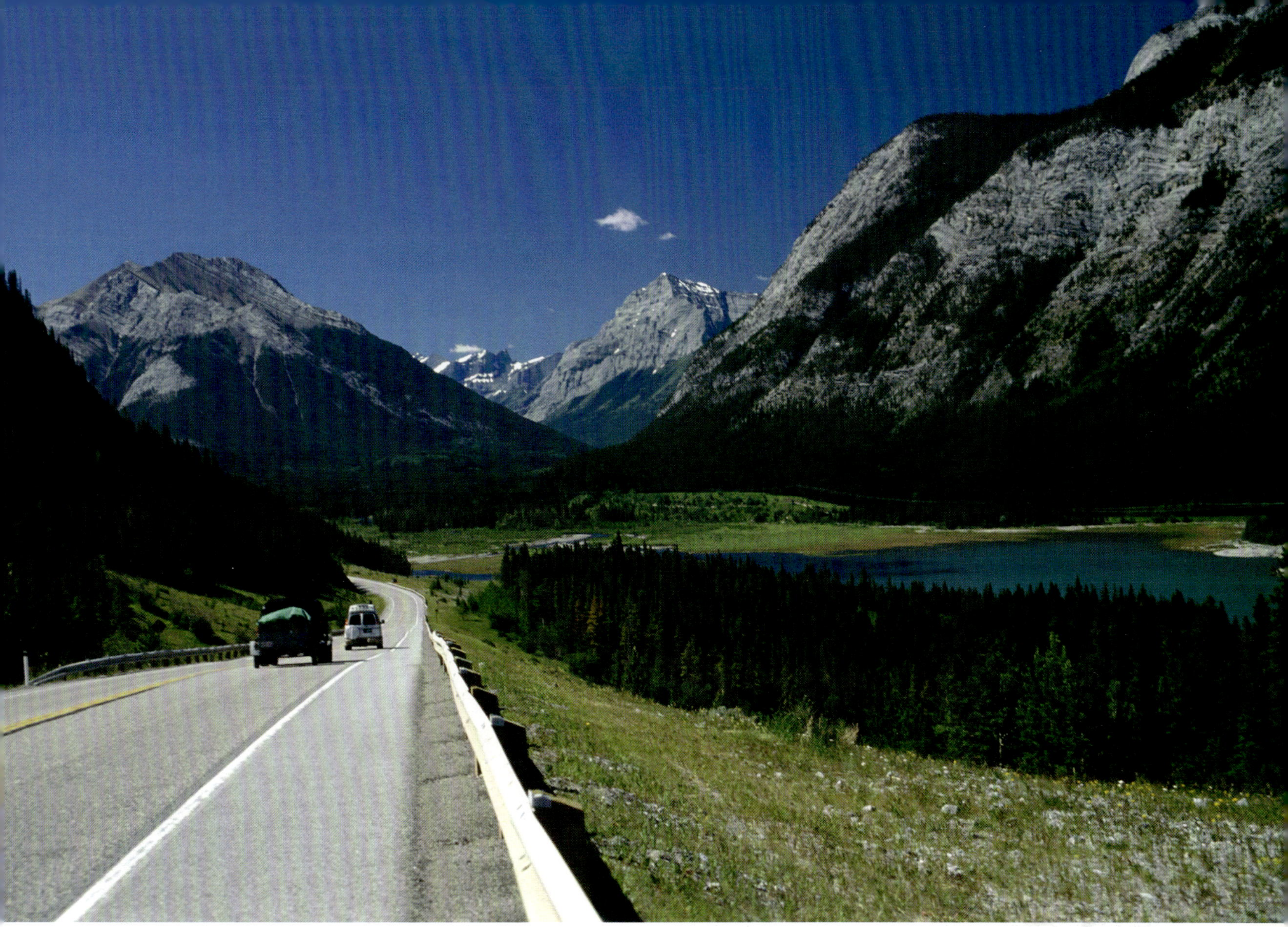

The Kananaskis was to become an area that would reflect a multiplicity of uses over the next century and a half. From the earliest days of resource development with the coming of the CPR, it was a focal point for timber operations, first with a small sawmill operated in 1883 by Colonel James Walker of Calgary and in 1886, at a site near its mouth, for one of the two largest logging camps of the Eau Claire and Bow River Lumber Company. In the early days of the tourist trade, beginning in the 1890s, it was also popular as a destination for trail parties from Banff, as its lakes were renowned for offering the best trout fishing in the Rockies. The valley became part of Rocky Mountains (Banff) National Park in 1902. Beginning in 1910 other entrepreneurs, including Italian immigrant George Pocaterra and German industrial representative Martin Nordegg, began staking coal lands in the valley on Elpoca Mountain and Mount Allan. In 1930 the valley was excised from the national park, and by the time the Kananaskis Lakes were dammed in 1942 to provide power for Calgary, the next step in harnessing the river's power potential was already underway further downstream with the development of a dam, power plant, and reservoir (pictured in the modern view) at Barrier Lake.[25]

It is only in the period since the 1970s that the Kananaskis has taken on its guise as one of Alberta's prime recreational areas. In 1936 a gravel road replaced the trail being used by the riders in the earlier photograph, and this was itself replaced by a paved highway built in 1974, after the Alberta government held hearings on the eastern slopes and determined its future as an area of multiple use. In 1977 the government created a provincial park around the Kananaskis Lakes as well as a huge recreational "buffer zone" around the park, known as Kananaskis Country.[26]

2.12A GEORGE POCATERRA'S CAMP ON WHITEMAN FLAT, 1911 (GEORGE POCATERRA, GLENBOW NA 695-52)

2.12B HELICOPTER LANDING PAD, PETER LOUGHEED PROVINCIAL PARK, JULY 2001 (CW 2001-06C-01)

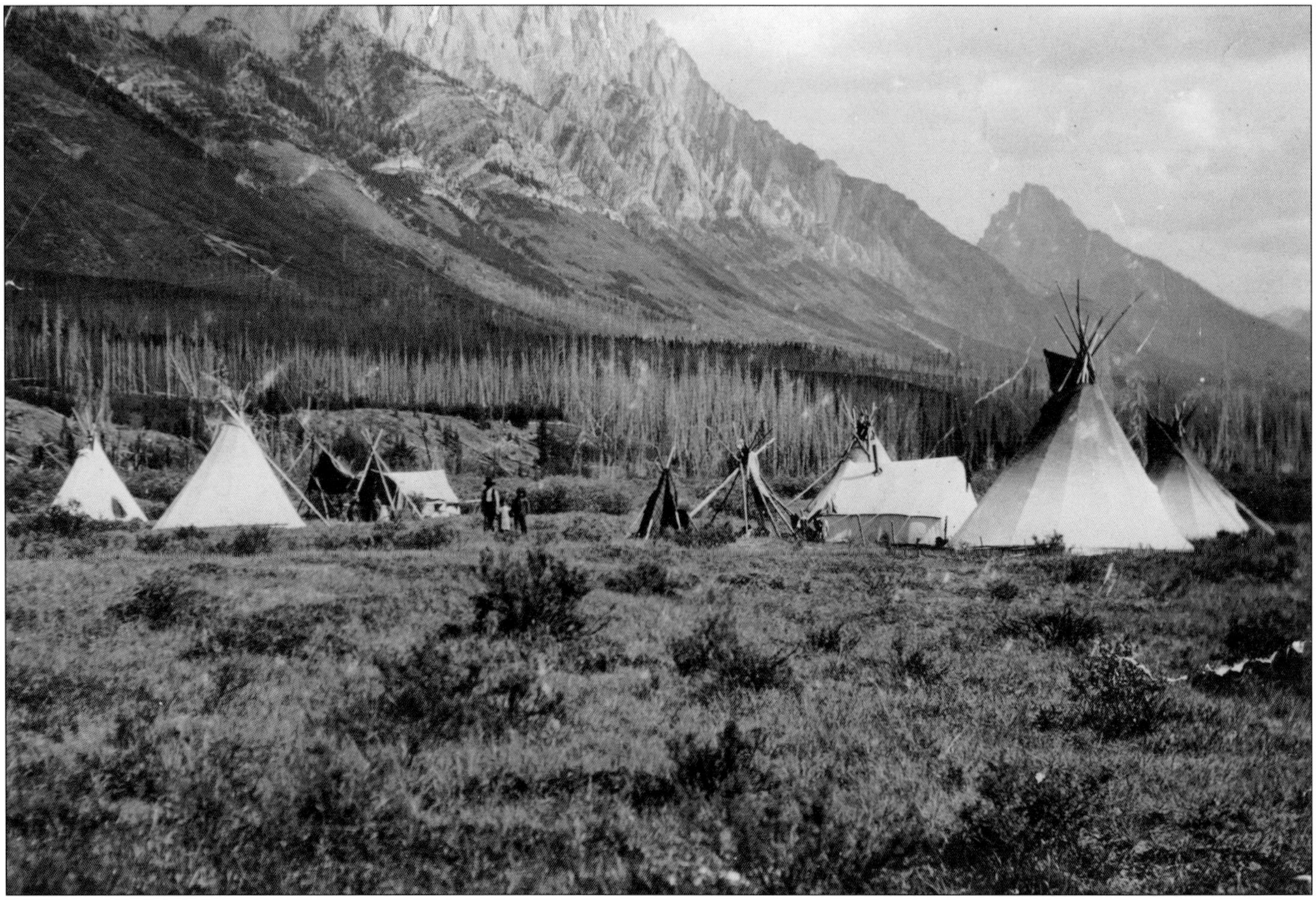

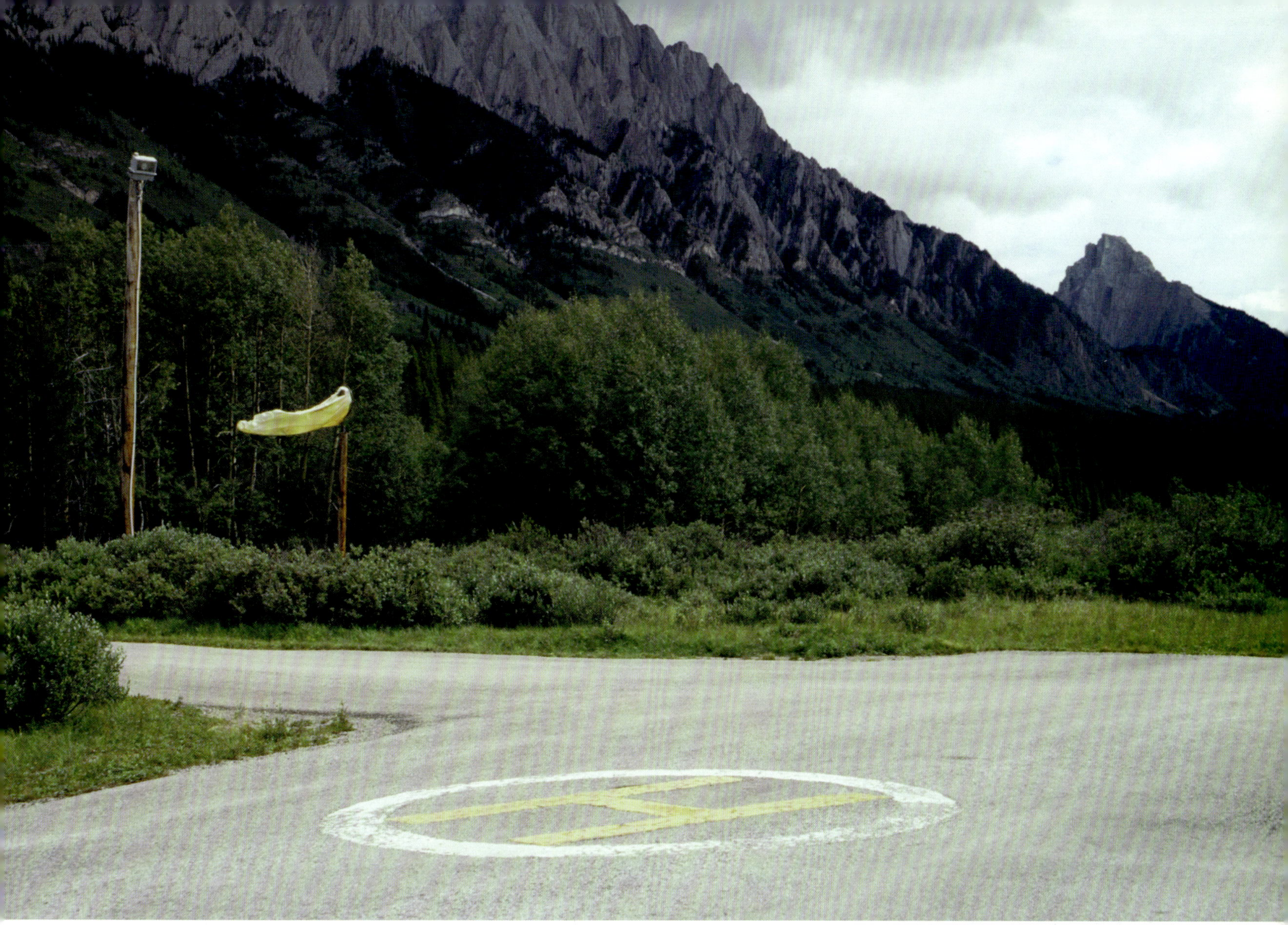

One of the areas that continued to be utilized by the Stoney Nakoda for hunting in the reserve period after 1877 was near the site that became one of George Pocaterra's camps on Whiteman Flat. The tribe, while formerly relying to some degree on bison like other plains groups, had traditionally hunted mountain wildlife species such as elk, bighorn sheep, deer, and mountain goat in isolated valleys. Hunting camps were usually based on small family groups who continued to use the same watersheds over long periods of time, and they likely also regularly burned these valleys to improve wildlife habitat.[27] Their dependence on these food resources in a period when white European visitors and hunters were also putting pressure on wildlife resources aggravated an already serious depletion of game. By 1900, bison had already been long absent from the east slope foothills and mountains, the easily accessible bighorn sheep populations were decimated, and elk had all but disappeared.[28]

For the majority of the period from 1902 through 1930, the Kananaskis Valley was part of Rocky Mountains (Banff) National Park. However, during the early years there was no organized fire and game warden service, and hunting and burning by both whites and First Nations continued unabated. The 1911 photograph shows a traditional Stoney campsite that was frequently burned, maintaining it as grassland with a surrounding shrubfield of trembling aspen and willow. Nearby tree-ring counts have shown that fires in 1765, 1803, 1858, and 1890 spread from the valley bottom up the nearby mountain slopes.[29] After one last major fire in 1920, governments successfully stopped burning in the area, mostly by preventing human-caused ignitions. By 2001, the campsite was a heliport for the nearby headquarters of Peter Lougheed Provincial Park. Grassland cover has declined, aspen has grown to tree-height, and a dense forest of aging lodgepole pine sweeps up in the background slope.

2.13A UPPER KANANASKIS LAKE AND SCHOONER ISLAND, CA. 1910 (BYRON HARMON, WHYTE NA 71-571)

2.13B UPPER KANANASKIS LAKE RESERVOIR, JULY 2003 (CW 2003-07B-19)

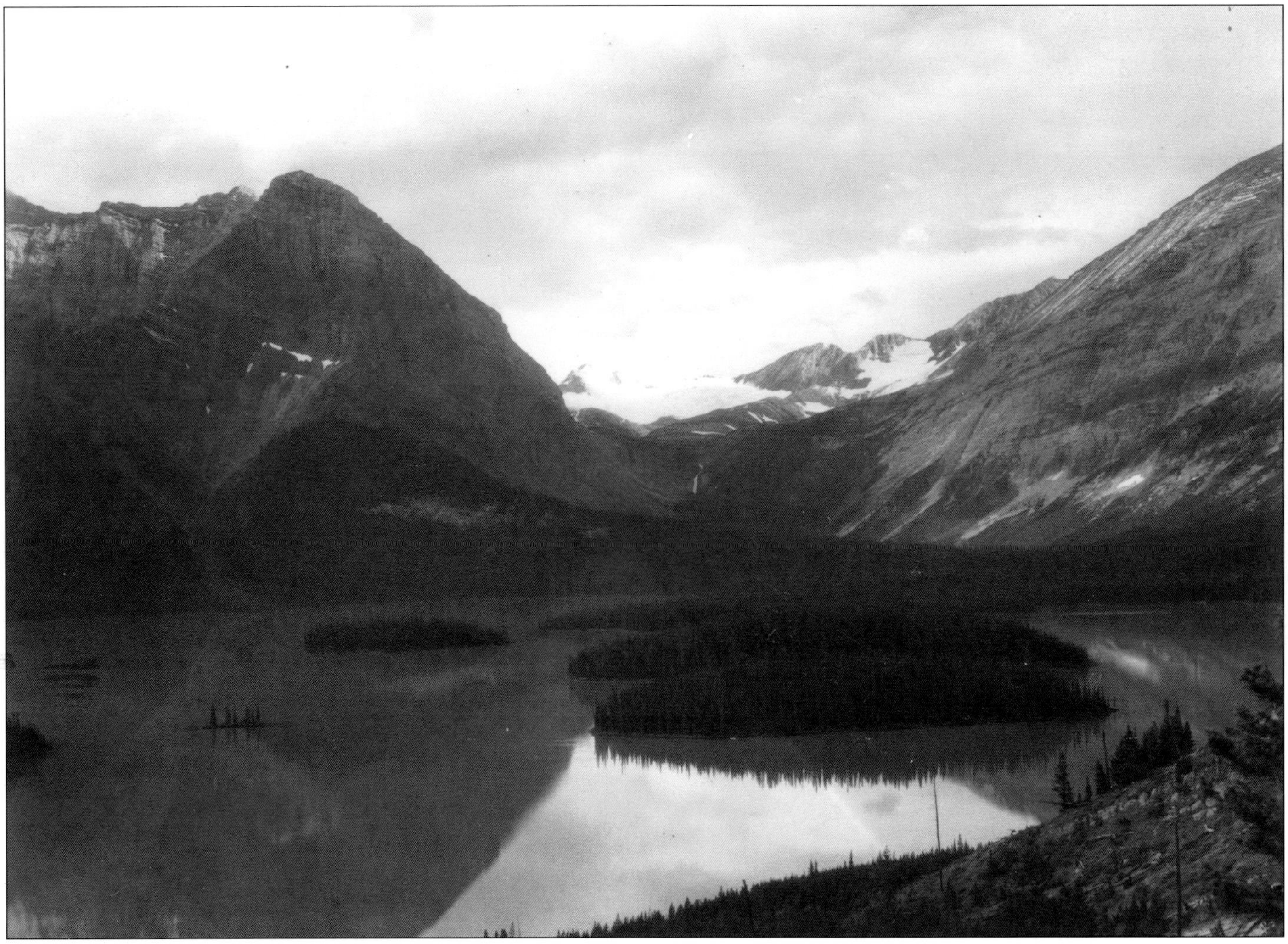

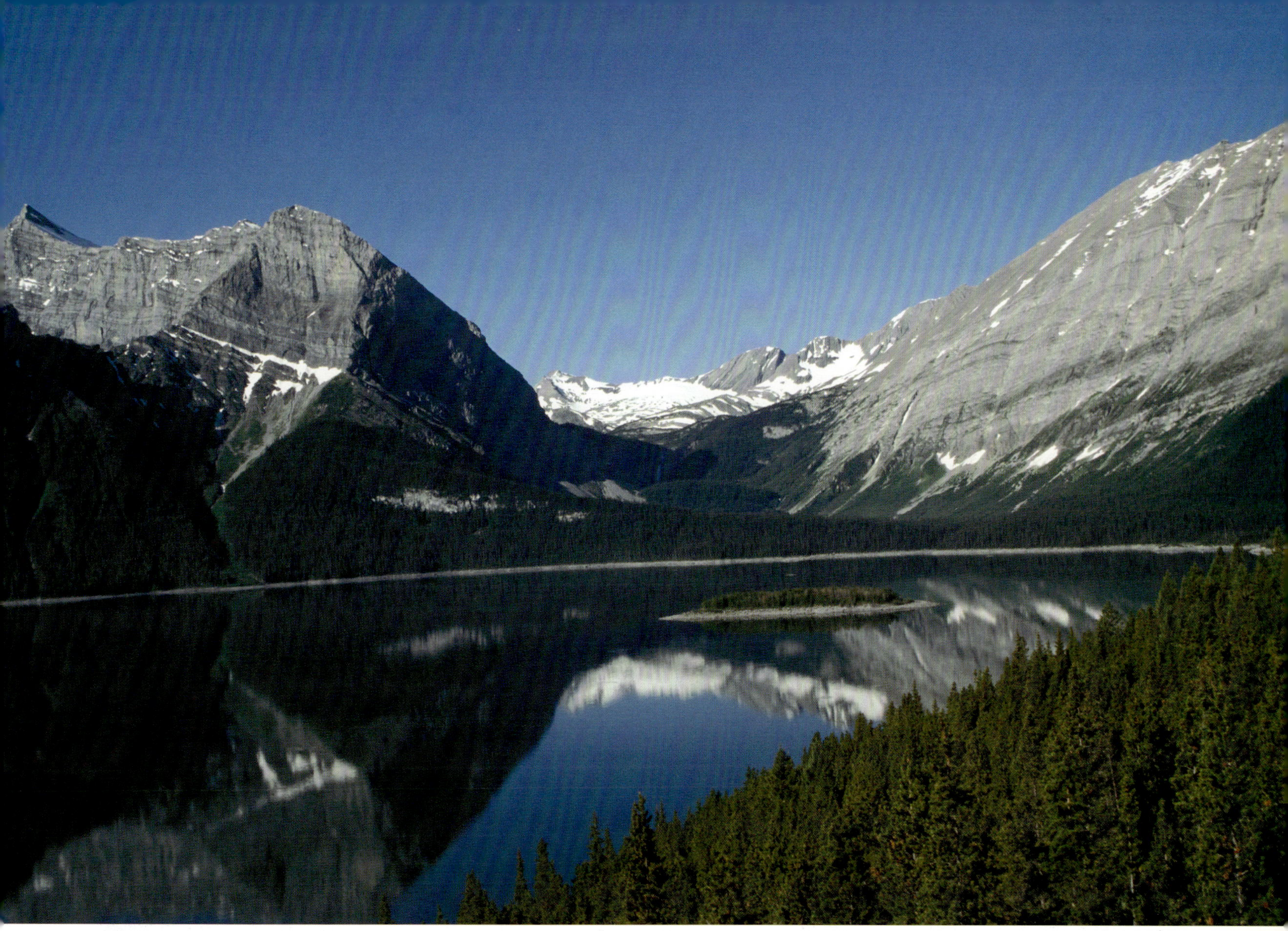

In his penetration of the Kananaskis Valley in August 1858, Captain John Palliser reached what would subsequently be known as Upper Kananaskis Lake, recording in his journal his awed impression: "We came upon a magnificent lake, hemmed in by mountains, and studded by numerous islets thickly wooded. This lake was about 4 miles long, and 1 mile wide, receives its water from the glacier above, and is a favourite place of resort of the Kootanie Indians."[30]

The completion of the Horseshoe and Kananaskis Falls hydro-electric dams on the Bow River resulted in the upper lake becoming part of a reservoir in 1942 and in 1955 a further hydro-electric project was completed placing dams and plants on both the upper and lower lake.[31] In 1975 the lakes were incorporated into the provincial park created by the Alberta government, later named Peter Lougheed in honour of the popular premier who created it, and were used for recreational activities. The view across the upper lake retains many of its scenic qualities, although the unique Schooner Island (lower left in the historic photograph) and most of the other islands have disappeared under the waters of the reservoir.

2.14A CANMORE, NORTHWEST TERRITORY, 1889 (W. NOTMAN AND SON, GLENBOW NA 3740-5)

2.14B CANMORE, ALBERTA, 1981 (BRUNO ENGLER, CW-BE-FM-1981-13)

2.14C CANMORE, ALBERTA, AUGUST 1996 (CW 1996-08A-33)

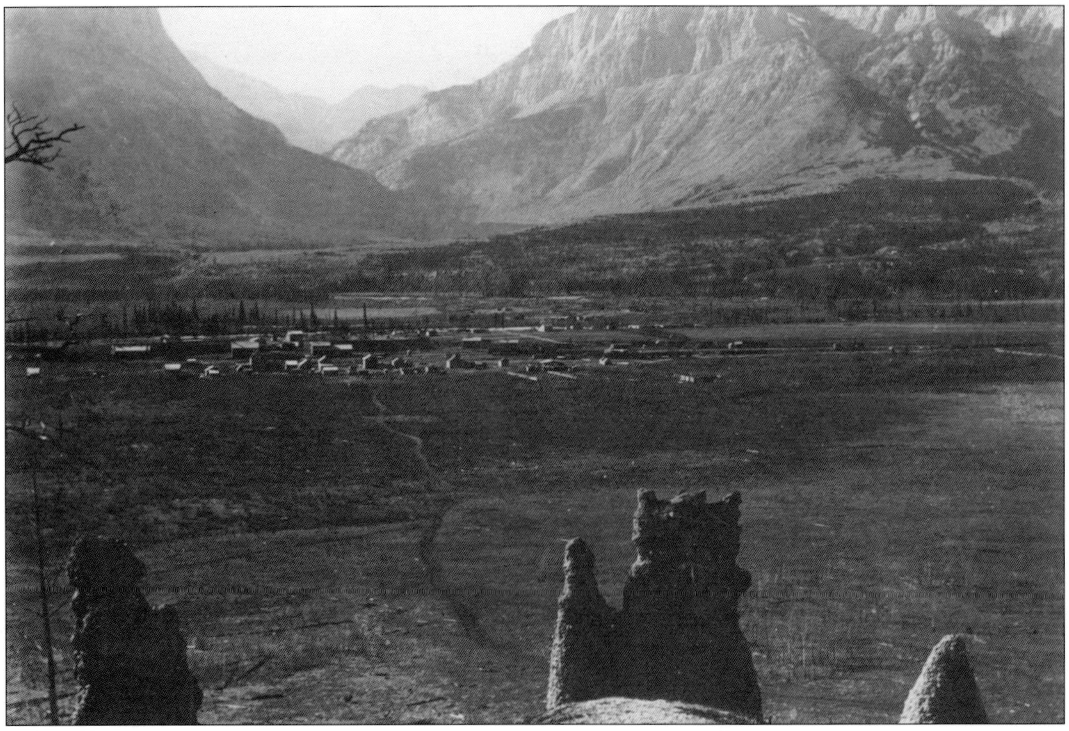

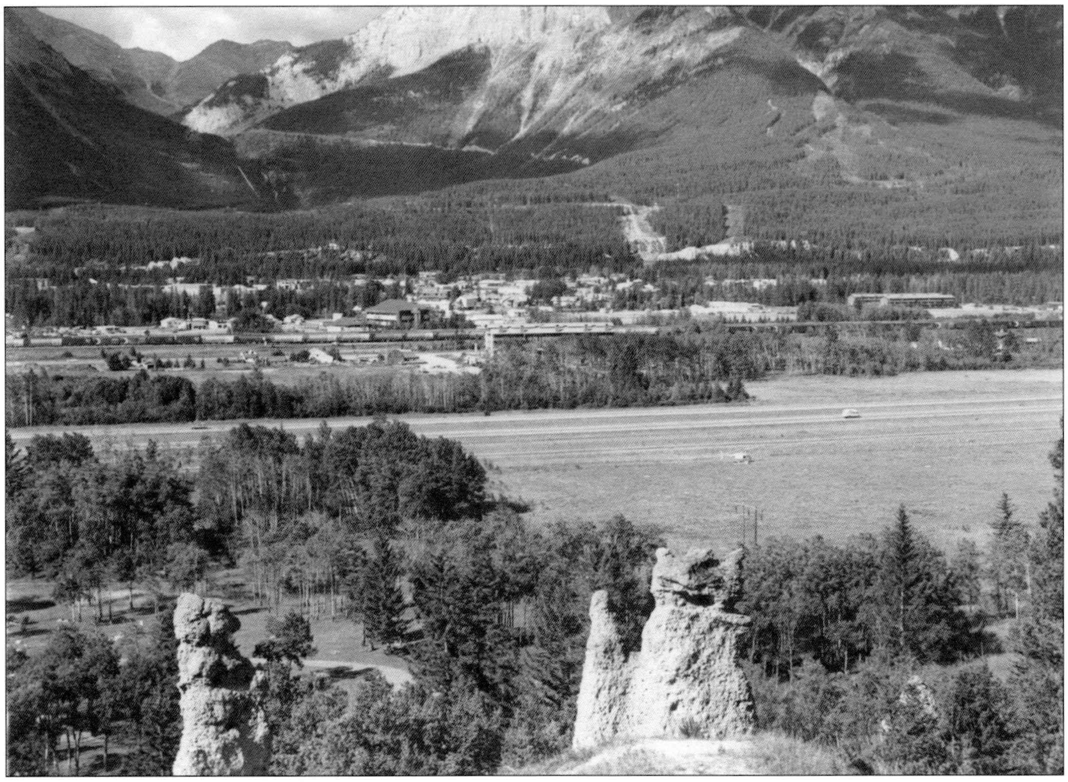

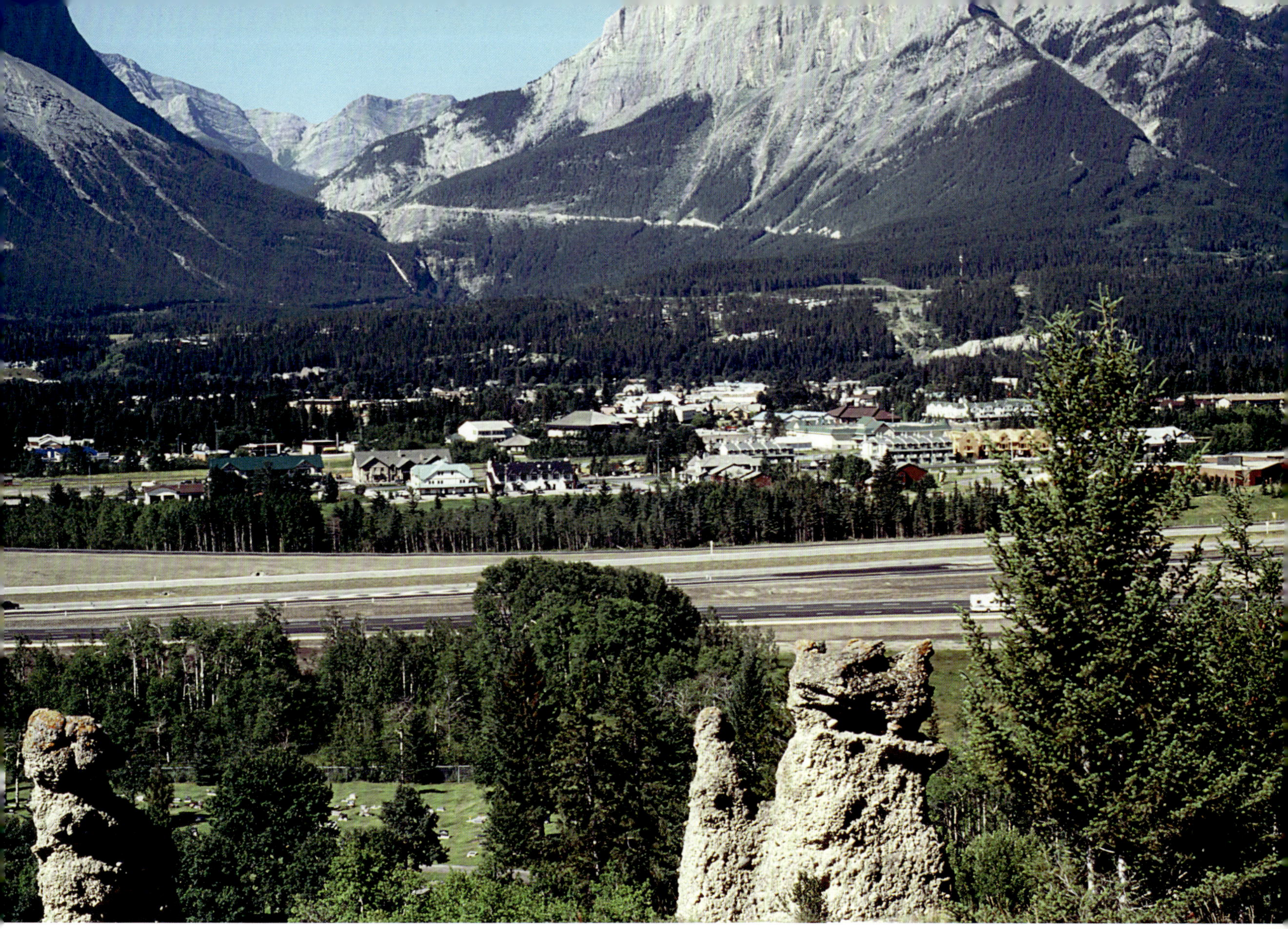

Canmore has exhibited an ability to constantly re-invent itself over its 120-year history. First established as a railroad siding (Siding 27) on October 17, 1883, it was then used as a divisional point by the CPR, resulting in the building of a round-house and a depot, named in honour of Scottish King Malcolm of Canmore. The original town hugged the railway line on the north side of the river in the area of today's Railway Avenue, with Main Street and its four hotels extending southward from the Mounted Police barracks on what became known as Policeman's Creek. But beginning in 1887 things started to change when coal discovered on the south side of the river was mined at what became known as No. 1 Mine. A second operation, the Cochrane Mine, went into production the following year and this activity led to the creation of another townsite on the south side of the river, originally known as "Oskaloosa town" after its first hotel, and until 1892 the two communities were not even joined by a bridge. Due to technological changes the CPR's requirements of having divisional points every 125 miles was soon eliminated, and by 1898 Canmore's divisional status was removed and the repair shops transferred to Calgary.[32]

2.15A CANMORE NO. 1 MINE, 1903 (GEOLOGICAL SURVEY OF CANADA, LIBRARY ARCHIVES CANADA PA 38305)

2.15B CANMORE CREEK, AUGUST 2001 (CW 2001-08C-16)

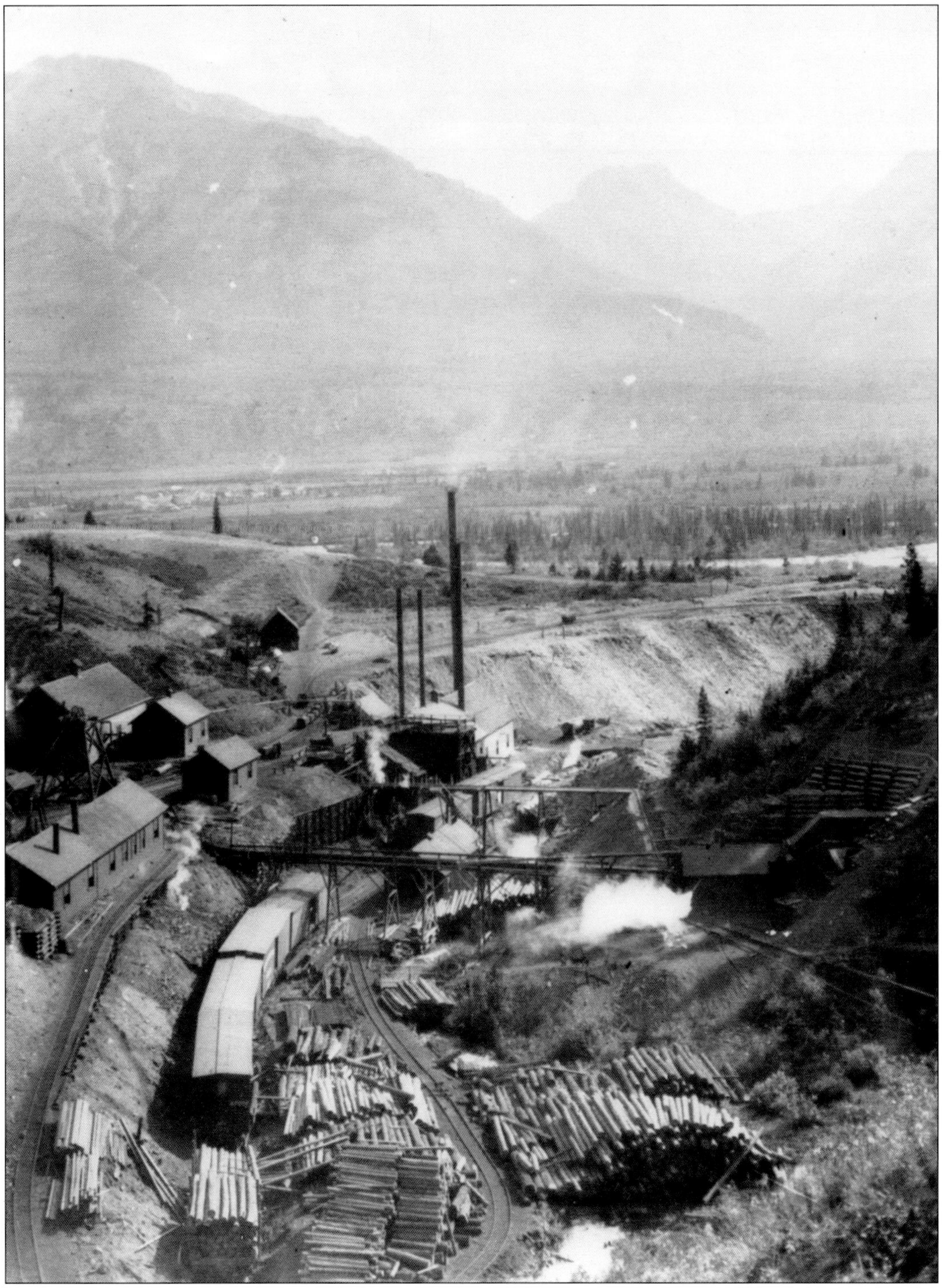

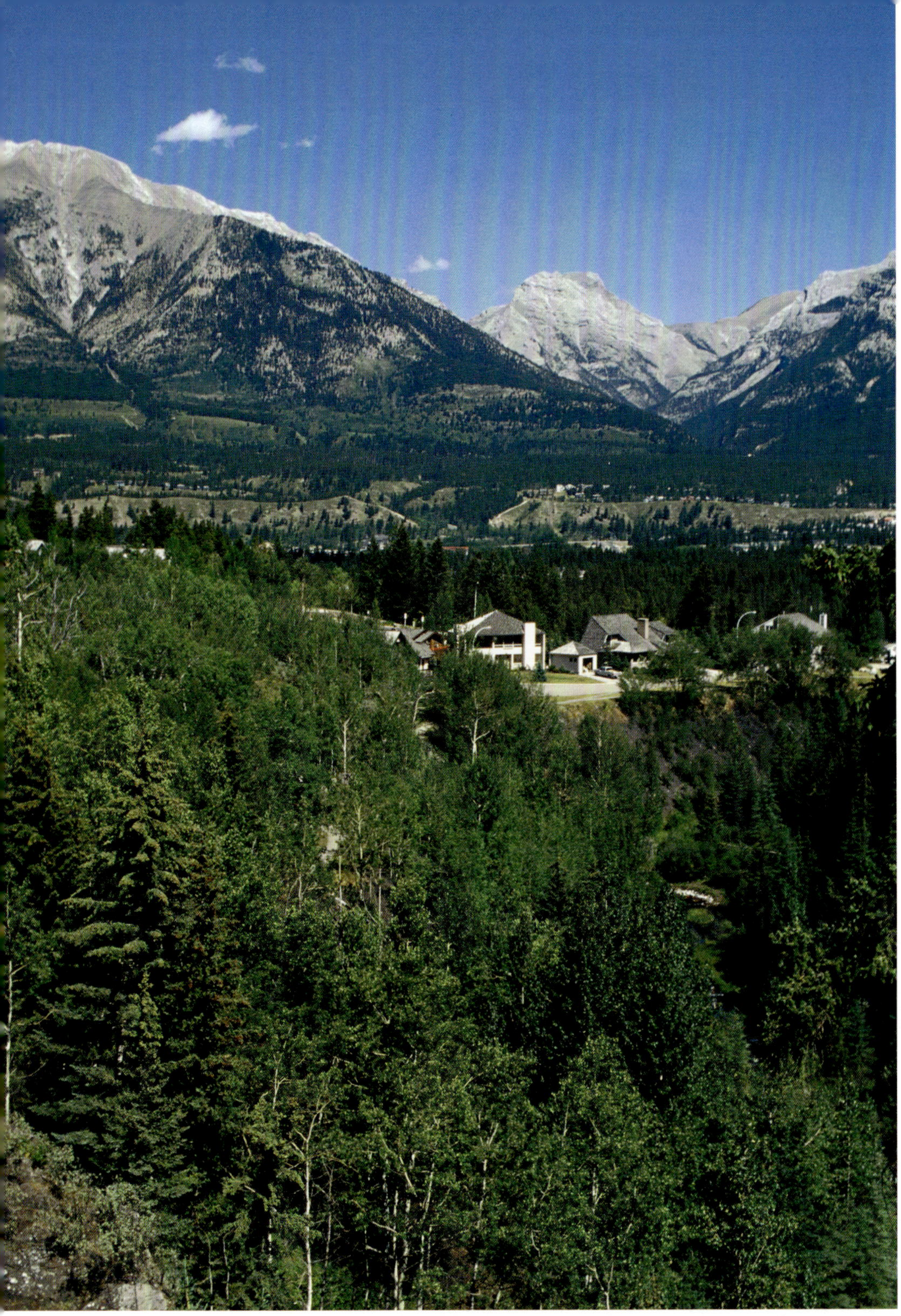

For its first seventy years Canmore's economy was based almost entirely on coal mining, and for much of that time the two communities, which became known as "townside" and "mineside," each had their own infrastructure of stores, hotels, and a post office. Although the town was subsumed into Rocky Mountains Park from 1902 to 1930, tourism was not encouraged, possibly due to competition and political pressure from nearby Banff merchants.[33] Coal production waxed and waned, being negatively affected by the Depression and positively influenced by the Second World War and always subject to the vagaries of the CPR. In the 1960s the town began to undergo its next metamorphosis when the first motels were built along a strip adjoining the new Trans-Canada Highway. Incorporated as a village in 1965 and a town in 1967, Canmore became the subject of numerous studies by the Calgary Regional Planning Authority, and in 1977 it issued a five-volume report that foresaw the future of the community as a service centre for rapidly developing recreational facilities and an administrative headquarters for the recently announced Kananaskis Country. In 1978 "mineside," or "West Canmore," was annexed to the town and a year later the mines closed permanently, marking the end of the town's colourful coal-mining era.[34]

Lands formerly owned by Canmore Mines were soon under development as recreational properties for Calgary's burgeoning population and in 1988 Canmore's transformation to an international tourist destination was marked by the construction of a Nordic Centre and the hosting of the cross-country and biathlon ski events at the Winter Olympics. Today, Canmore is one of Alberta's fastest- growing communities as recreational home buyers from around the world continue to seek an opportunity found in few places. Here they can live in a spectacular mountain environment an hour from an international airport.

2.16A AIR PHOTOGRAPH OF CANMORE, ROCKY MOUNTAINS (BANFF) NATIONAL PARK, 1921 (NATIONAL AIR PHOTOGRAPH LIBRARY CA 114-84)

2.16B CANMORE, ALBERTA, FROM HELICOPTER, OCTOBER 2001 (CW 2001-10A-10)

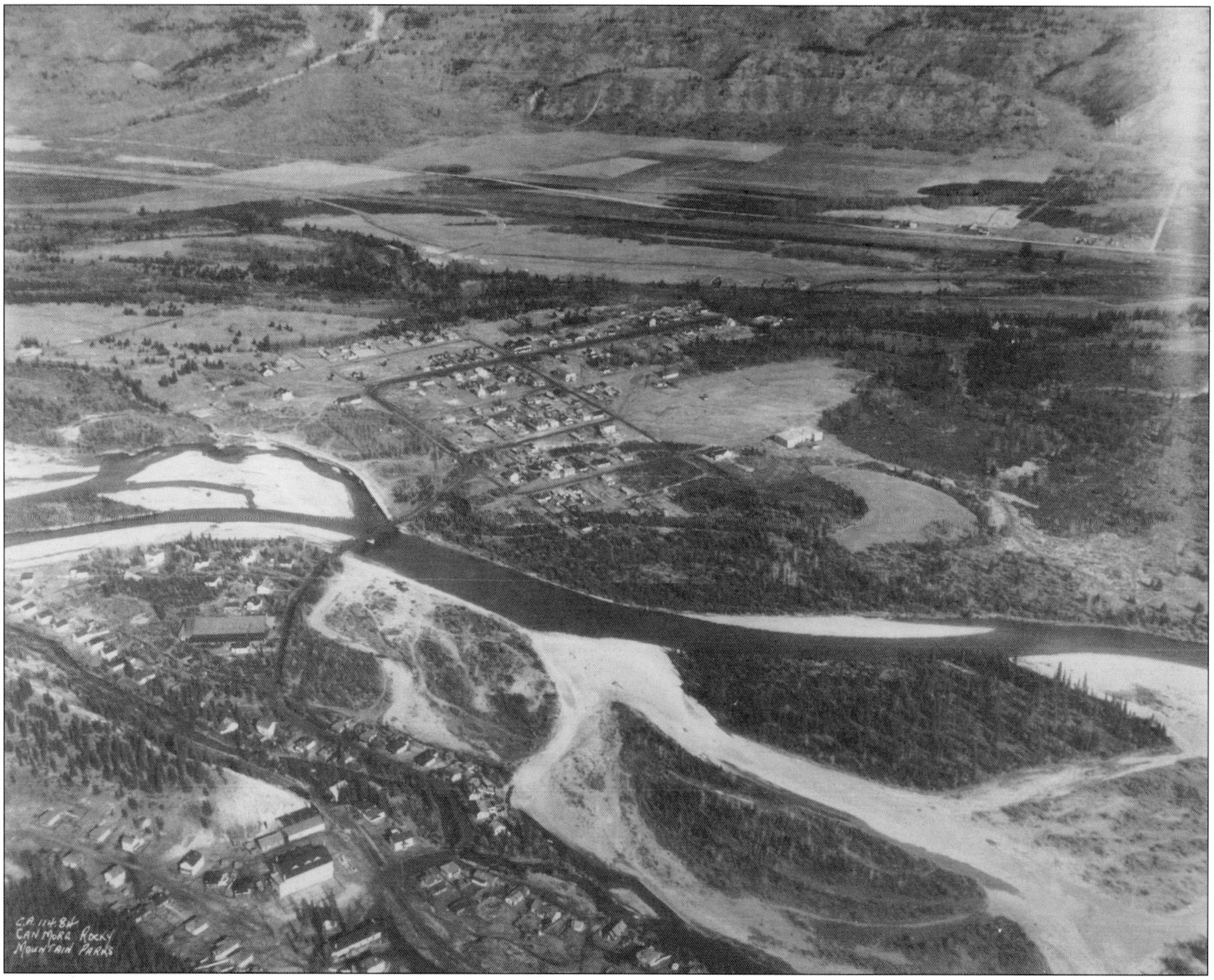

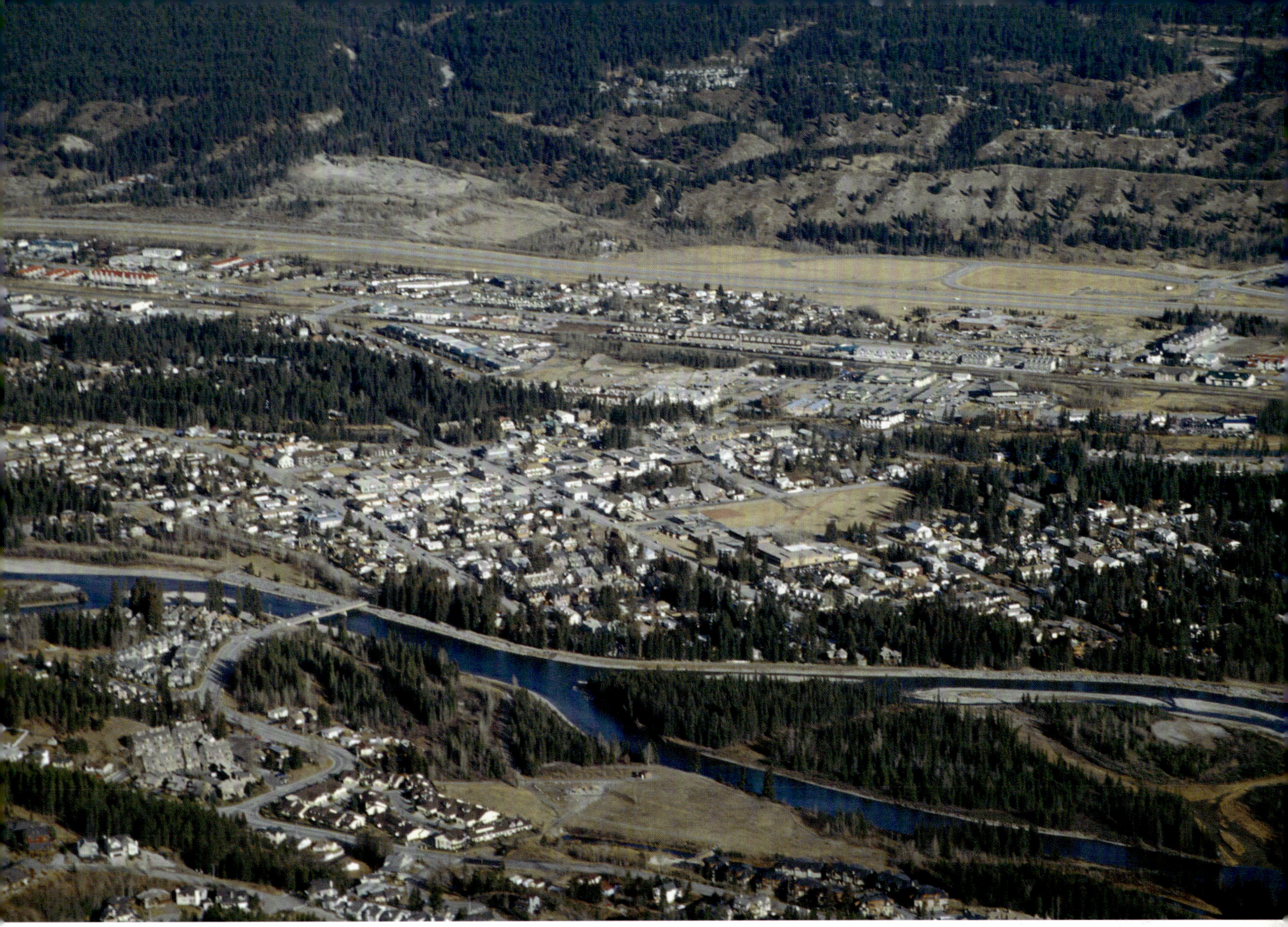

Canmore has expanded up both sides of the Bow Valley with the Rundleview subdivision (bottom left) built in the 1980s, and Silvertip (top right) started in 1992. However, the 1993 Alberta Natural Resources Conservation Board decisions for the Three Sisters Development on the east boundary of the town made provisions for corridors to allow movement of wildlife around the town. These corridors have largely been included within provincial parks or have municipal zoning to ensure their long-term protection.[35] Also evident in the recent photograph is that the Bow River's channels have become constrained on the valley bottom. This has occurred due to upstream dams on the Spray and the Cascade rivers reducing peak flows and levees built along the edge of the floodplain after the 1974 flood.[36]

3

A KEYSTONE SPECIES?

The Role of Mountain Peoples in the Historic Ecosystem

> The popular concept of wilderness as pristine wildland free of any human influence is largely a psycho-cultural myth, springing more from an uplifting version of the proverbial garden of Eden that from any historical reality. For charting the future, there will be no substitute for understanding the dynamics of varied ecosystems and the rules of landscape evolution well enough to be able to judge in advance the results of any specific actions that we are able to control. – William R. Dickenson, 2000[1]

In returning southward from an unsuccessful attempt to find Maligne Lake in the fall of 1907, intrepid Philadelphia tourist explorer Mary T. S. Schäffer made a revealing comment while riding towards the famous Kootenay Plains on the North Saskatchewan River: "The distance from Pinto Lake via Cataract Creek to the Saskatchewan River is about 25 miles; it has been a favourite highway for centuries, as the well-worn trails show, and the fine fishing at the lake still brings a small band of Stoneys there year by year. The red hunter's campsites, many teepee poles, and bones galore lined the route; fires for years had swept hither and yon."[2] Some sixty years later, in 1969, when writing the first complete survey history of the Canadian Rockies, another well-known woman recorder of the Rockies, historian Esther Fraser, wrote, "For eons these valleys had known no human intrusion; when scattered bands of native people began to come, they barely rippled the tranquility of the centuries."[3]

History is a relatively subjective discipline. It can often tell as much about the observer as what was observed. The two quotes come from women with great knowledge of the Canadian Rockies, but separated by over a half century of rapid social change. In that time, historic North America, the long-time homeland of the native peoples encountered by early European visitors had, in the collective mind of most North Americans, become a mythical and pristine wilderness.[4] Today, researchers from the varied disciplines of archaeology, history, anthropology, and ecology are attempting to recover lost knowledge of past Rocky Mountain ecosystems and their human inhabitants. The central focus of these diverse viewpoints is humankind's long-term role in ecosystems. Is the role of people past and present a relatively insignificant part of mountain landscapes? Or, have people long been a "keystone species," a term biologists give to a species whose numbers may be few but whose presence shapes ecosystems in pervasive ways? And, if native peoples were a keystone species, has the recent change from a hunter-gatherer to industrial cultures therefore resulted in a major ecological upheaval, even in the backcountry areas of national parks?[5]

Archaeologists carefully sifting through the layers of ancient campsites have contributed much to our understanding of past human activities in the mountain valleys. Research has shown that people entered the Rockies almost immediately after the retreat of the great Ice Age glaciers. For example, a Clovis-point spearhead, indicative of one of the earliest cultures to occupy North America over eleven thousand years ago, was found on a high alpine pass near Lake Louise.[6] Most significantly, it is a wilderness-myth that humans only infrequently visited the mountain valleys. Instead, dated remains from numerous ancient campsites, such as one near Vermilion Lakes in Banff, show that First Nations peoples have been living and hunting here continuously for as long as 10,800 years.[7] Archaeologists now believe that major valleys in the Rocky Mountains were often occupied year-round – the high diversity of the mountain and foothills ecosystems provided food and other resources that were, perhaps, more predictably located in comparison to the plains to the east. Through the millennia, evidence left in these prehistoric sites shows that cultures shifted back and forth from those with an affinity to the plains bison hunters from the east, to evidence of mountain dwellers and fishermen from the Columbia and Fraser valleys to the west.[8] Possibly there were periods when the mountains of what are now Banff and Jasper were a buffer zone, or cultural tension line, between these different human lifeways.[9]

What lines of evidence lead modern researchers to propose that humans, past and present, are a keystone species? First, there is the relative abundance of different wildlife species' bone fragments in archaeological sites. On the east slope, these are dominated by bison and bighorn sheep, and on the west slope, sheep and deer. Bones from elk, the most abundant ungulate in mountain valley bottoms today, are rarely found. An early interpretation of these findings was that people could not, or would not, hunt elk, and thus the bones are not common in the archaeological digs. However, recent research by wildlife ecologists shows that a favoured prey species will be rapidly depleted by predators and can be held at low densities if alternative prey is available to sustain them. Accordingly, the low numbers of elk bones are now thought to be evidence of this predation pattern. Humans, wolves, bears, and cougars are the predominant hunters of the mountain valleys, and although sustained by migratory bison from the east, or the more difficult-to-hunt bighorn sheep and thicket-dwelling deer, both people and wolves preferred elk. Thus, elk populations were quickly hunted to low numbers but not entirely extirpated, and few elk bones are therefore found in old campsites. When David Thompson and other early explorers followed the trails of First Nations into the mountains, they quickly discovered that this was a well-hunted land with widely dispersed and wary game. Their journals show that elk, in particular, were only rarely observed or killed.[10]

The process of human hunting causing dramatic reductions in the number of large-sized animal species, particularly in locations where they are easily hunted and there is alternative prey, is now thought to have been the primary determinant in the prehistoric ranges of at least two important Rocky Mountain species – moose and bison. Early explorers seldom saw moose, and almost never saw bison, west of the continental divide in the Canadian Rocky Mountains. Bones from these species are extremely rare in west slope archaeological sites. Yet today, moose are common throughout British Columbia, and bison thrive wherever they are ranched or reintroduced. Past explanations for the surprisingly rapid shifts in distribution and survival of these species have included climate change or habitat alterations due to increased burning by settling Europeans. However, there appears to be no linkage between climate change and these species, and no evidence that early Europeans burned the land more frequently than native peoples. A more plausible explanation is that fish, deer, and plants supported dense populations of First Nations along the Columbia and Fraser rivers. In the circumstances, early peoples preferentially hunted moose and bison as an alternative food source whenever possible, and thus, for many millennia, limited their distribution across the mountain west.[11]

More fascinating evidence of past human impacts comes from traditional First Nations knowledge of fire effects. Early peoples appear to have frequently burned the mountain valleys for several purposes, ranging from improving wildlife habitat to regenerating vigorous berry crops. This knowledge was sophisticated and judiciously applied in many western mountain ecosystems.[12] To appreciate the magnitude of this burning, it is useful to observe that, due to weather patterns, the frequency of lightning ignitions on Alberta's east slope side of the Rockies is less than one-hundredth of lightning ignitions on the British Columbia side. However, studies of fire scars in tree-rings show that in the past, ecosystems on both sides of the divide burned with relatively similar frequencies. It seems likely that humans were the source of ignition that balanced this large inequity in nature's burning pattern.[13] The timing of historic fires also gives us an appreciation of these human influences. The majority of the area burned by lightning-caused fire occurs largely from midsummer fires, but the burning practices of First Nations were oriented towards fall and spring seasons when fire was more controllable.[14] Preliminary research looking at the position of fire scars in the annual tree-ring growth cycle appears to validate this pattern of burning in forests near valley bottom meadows in Alberta's Rockies. Scars most commonly occur in the "earlywood" and dormant portions of the tree rings – outside the midsummer lightning fire season. Further, the frequency of historic fire-scarring of trees begins to decline as early as 1800 in some remote valleys, perhaps related to the decimation of native peoples by smallpox.[15]

This evidence of the long-term role of people as an important and pervasive part of Rocky Mountain ecosystems makes us appreciate the potential implications of a recent massive cultural and land use change. The resource harvesting and burning patterns of First Nations are now almost completely forgotten. On the other hand, the most recent wave of humans occupies the landscape in near stupendous numbers. We live in permanent structures, wish to observe almost tame wildlife, and have a deep and abiding fear of fire. However, there is hope. We are slowly rediscovering the long-term "keystone" importance of our species, and, if we pay heed, through that traditional knowledge, we can adjust our practices to maintain the diversity of Rocky Mountain ecosystems.

4.1 “CAMP IN THE MOUNTAINS” (H. J. WARRE, *SKETCHES IN NORTH AMERICA AND THE OREGON TERRITORY* (NEW YORK: IMPRINT SOCIETY, 1970))

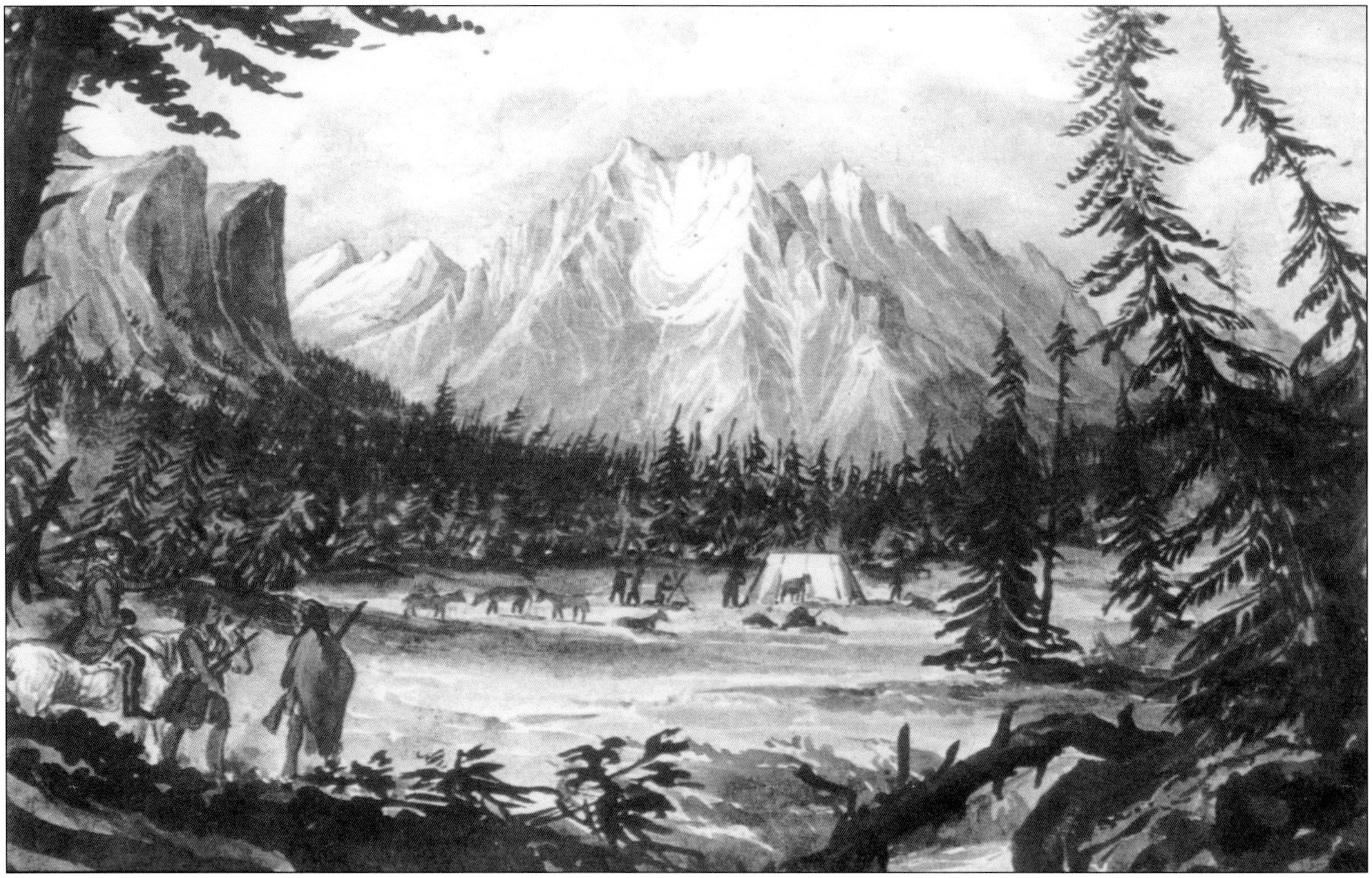

4

BIRTHPLACE OF PARKS

Banff Environs

In 1845 a military reconnaissance party organized by Hudson's Bay Company Governor Sir George Simpson camped near present-day Canmore on a trip across the Rocky Mountains. Although the journal account of Lieutenants Henry J. Warre's and Mervin Vavasour's mountain crossing is sparing, Warre's sketches of the Bow Valley would become important documents. Not only were they the first real artistic depiction showing identifiable scenes and the grandeur of the Rockies, they also spoke to the importance that transportation, in this case on horseback, was going to play in the future history of the mountains.

Warre's sketching was the beginning of an important tradition of art and artists in the Canadian Rockies, but within a few decades the rapidly developing technologies of photography would allow even much more accurate recording of places and people. The scenes in the Bow Valley near Banff became a focal point for this new invention as professional photographers and tourists took the newly completed CPR across Canada. And, ironically, Warre's depiction of this location, where the Bow River winds between Cascade Mountain and Mount Rundle, would be the site of another first – part of the lands of Rocky Mountains (Banff) Park, Canada's first national park.[1]

4.2A OILED ROAD ALONG THE RUNDLE RANGE, ROCKY MOUNTAINS (BANFF) PARK, 1920 (J. S. MACKINNON, WHYTE V428 PD1-33)

4.2B TRANS-CANADA HIGHWAY OUTSIDE OF BANFF NATIONAL PARK EAST GATE, JULY 2003 (CW 2003-7A-11)

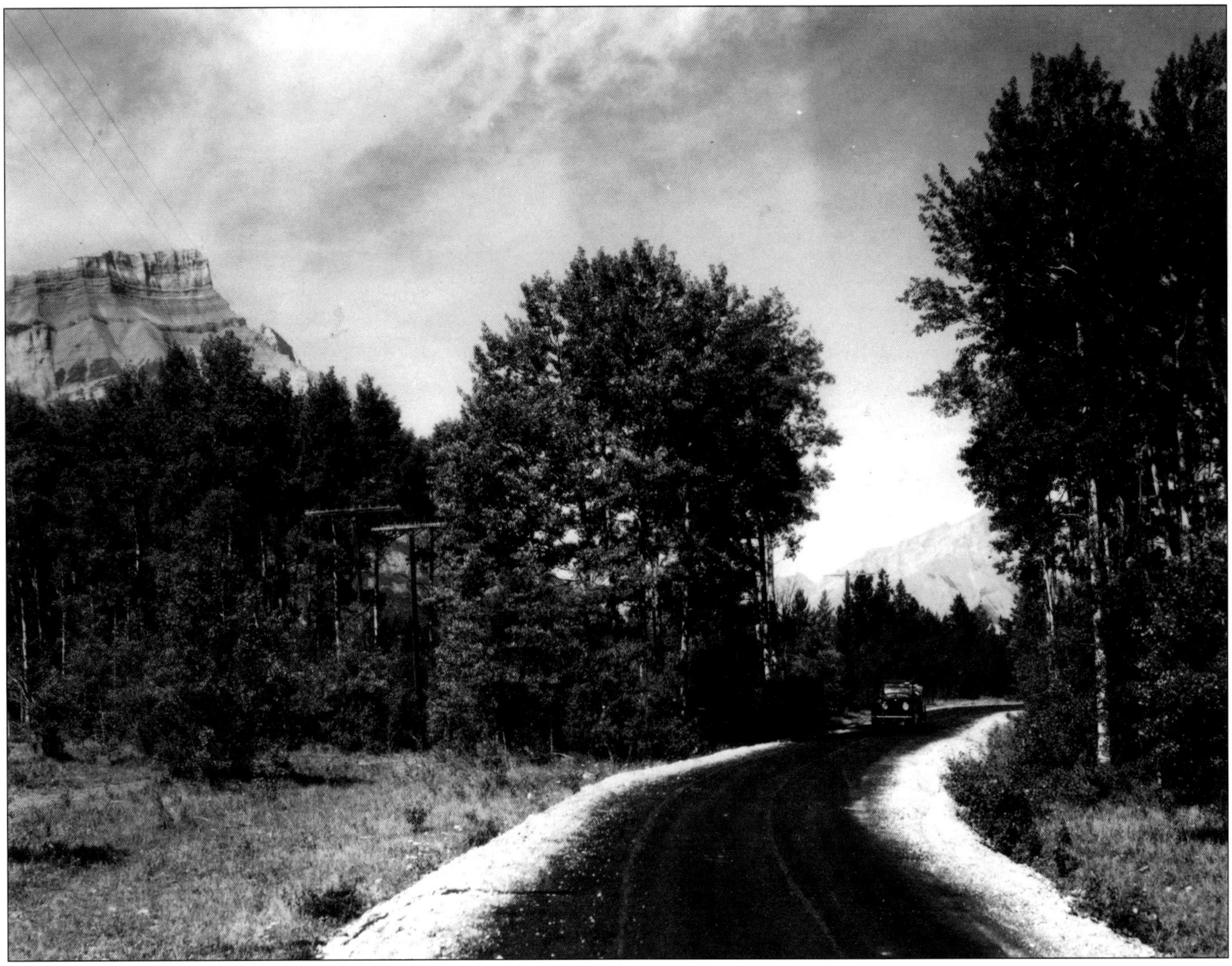

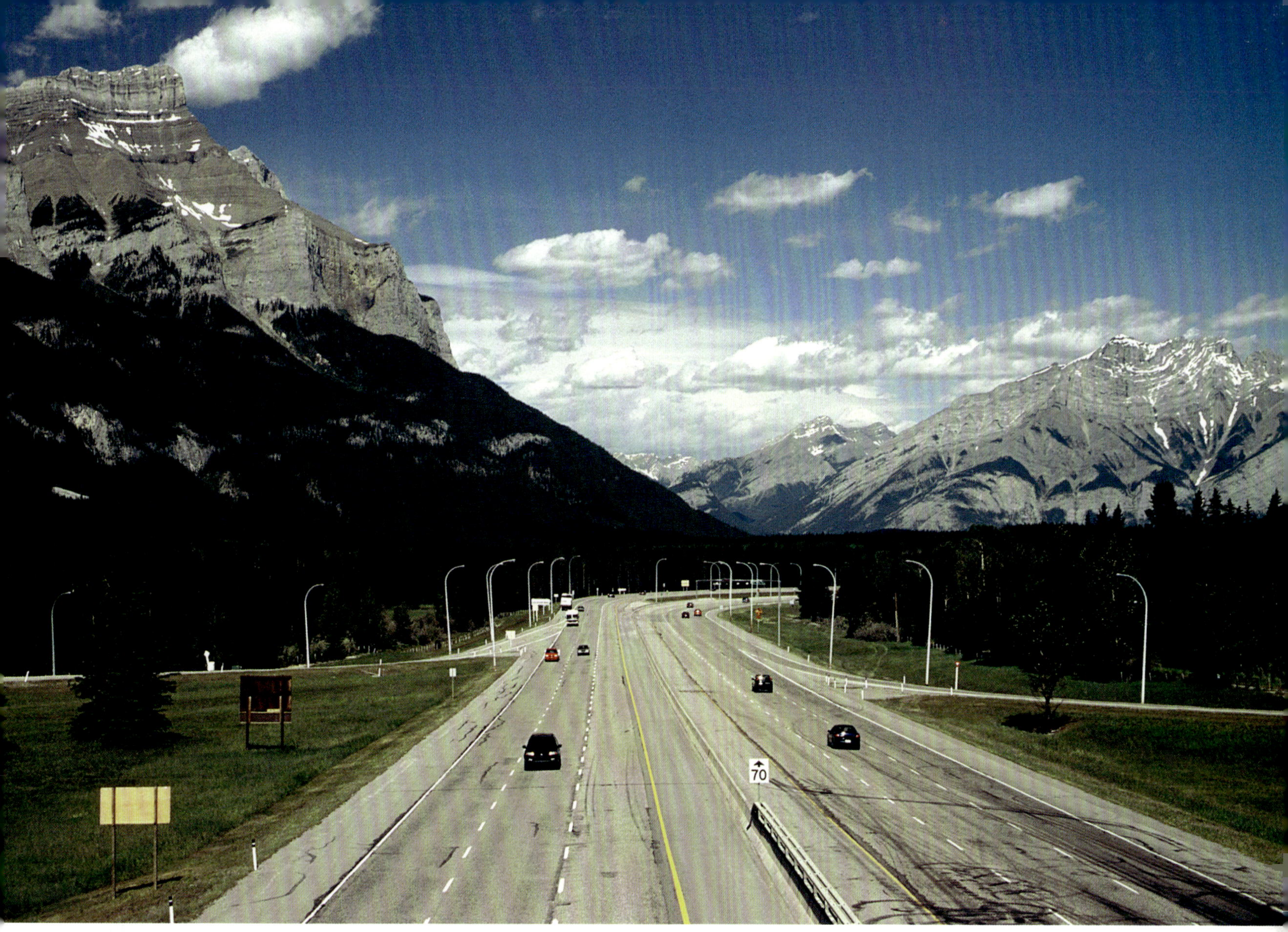

Roads have been one of the most fundamental agents of landscape change in the mountain west over the past ninety years. Initially, Dominion government regulations banned automobiles from Rocky Mountains (Banff) Park, a needless prohibition since there were no roads connecting the park with the outside world. However, carriage roads to allow tourists to be taken by buggy to local beauty spots were gradually constructed, and one of these connected the village of Banff to the east park boundary near modern-day Exshaw. In 1905 the Alberta government built a road from Calgary to join with it. By the time the link was nearing completion in 1909, the whole route from Calgary to Banff was already being used by a few intrepid motorists. By 1915 all restrictions had been lifted, and the Calgary-Banff Coach Road, as it had become known, was being pushed westward as part of the Banff-Windermere Highway project, linking the park with B.C.'s Columbia Valley at Radium and thence by other trunk roads to Vancouver and the western United States. When this road was completed in 1923, it unlocked the American tourism potential formerly confined to the railways, changing forever the way the majority of visitors would arrive in and see the mountain parks.[2]

In 1962, the road from Calgary to Banff became part of the new Trans-Canada Highway, providing a paved, all-weather road to Vancouver through the rugged Rogers Pass. Unrelenting increases in commercial and recreational traffic soon made even this inadequate, and in the early 1980s, expansion of the highway to four lanes began westward through Banff National Park.[3] For the first time in Canada measures such as animal underpasses and fencing were employed in road building to reduce the numbers of animal kills on park highways. Despite this, on a busy summer day over 20,000 vehicles pass through the east gate into Banff National Park, making the highway and its environs one of the most heavily impacted landscapes in the Rockies.[4]

4.3A ENGINE 146, SIDING 29, 1885 (O.B. BUELL, GLENBOW NA 4967-30)

4.3B CANADIAN PACIFIC RAILROAD TRACKS EAST OF BANFF, 2007 (CW 2007-08A-2)

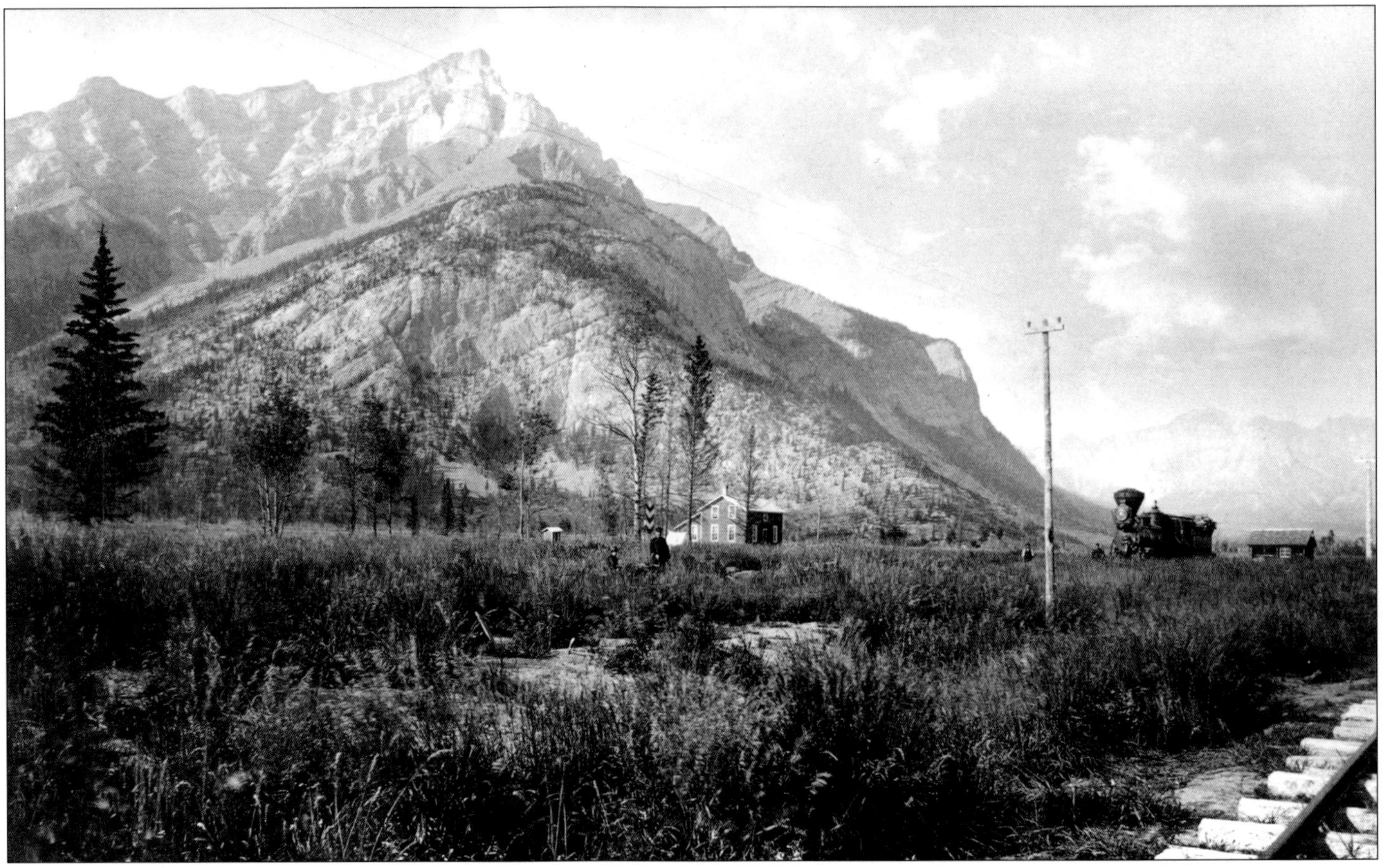

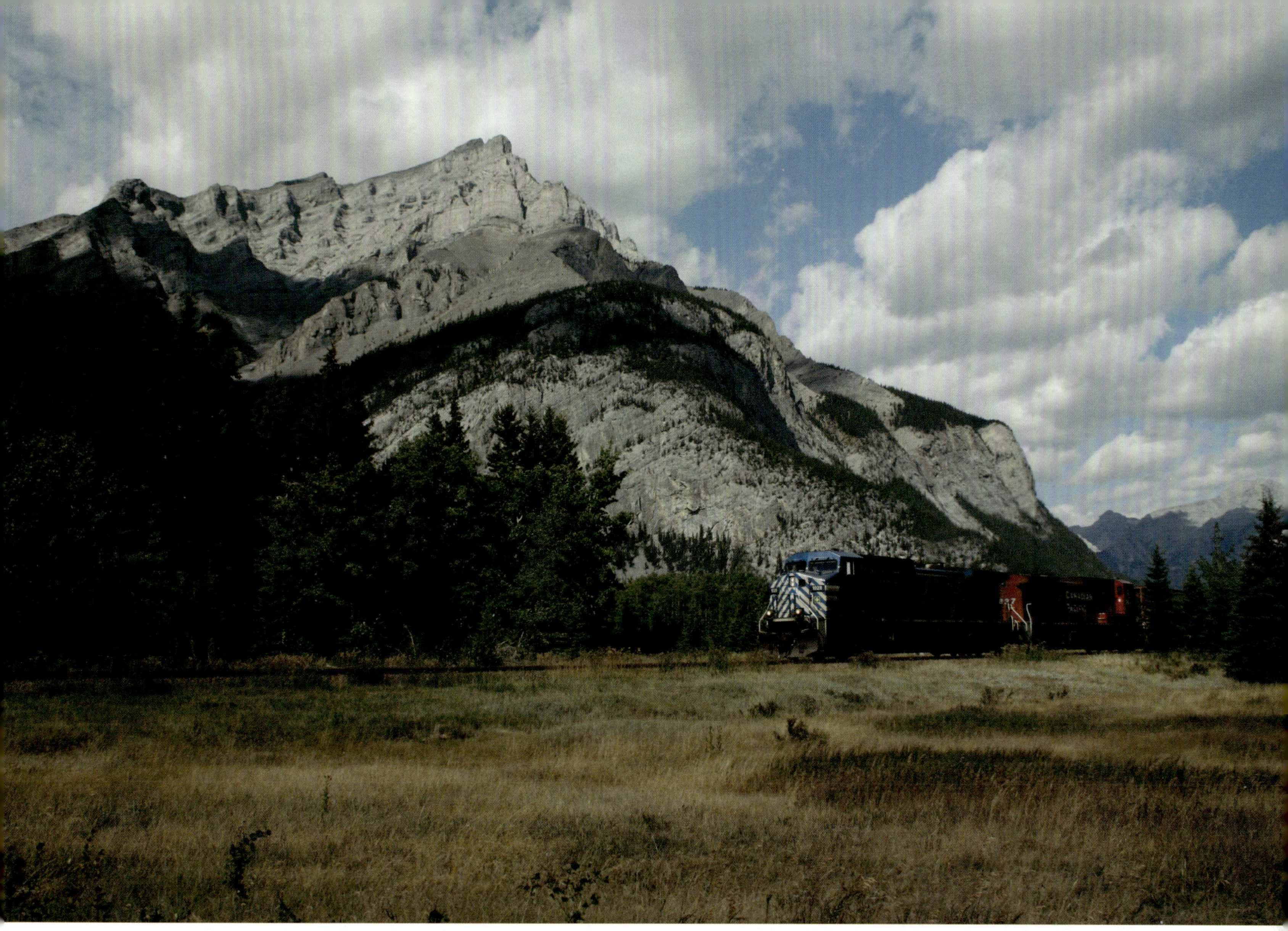

In October 1883, track-laying for the CPR railroad reached the meadows below Cascade Mountain. Siding 29, as it was called to identify it as the twenty-ninth siding west of Medicine Hat, was constructed to allow trains to be pulled off the main line, but it also contained a small depot, a section house, a privy, and at least one other associated structure.

Henry Sandison of Winnipeg, who had been born at Banff, Scotland, upon hearing that a CPR board meeting in Montreal was about to discuss the establishment of a resort in conjunction with the recently reserved Sulphur Mountain hot springs, suggested to CPR Land Commissioner John McTavish that he propose the name "Banff" and then watch for the reactions of CPR President George Stephen and his shareholder cousin Donald Smith. McTavish did bring up the idea, and later reported:

> As soon as the word "Banff" was mentioned, Donald Smith looked at Mr. Stephen and went over to him and whispered. They both seemed quite excited and [General Manager] Mr. Van Horne wondered what it was all about. Donald Smith then explained that he knew Banff very well, as he had been born close to there. Then Mr. Stephen said he had been born within twelve miles of Banff, and had known it ever since he was a boy and that it was a famous watering place. It was now Mr. Van Horne's turn to say something. "I like the name 'Banff,'" he said, "It's a short, snappy name. Suppose we call it Banff." And Banff it was.[5]

In 1888 a new log station was built further west closer to the new townsite and the name went with it. Thereafter "Old Banff," as it became known, quickly disappeared. In the 1885 view, a locomotive on the main line, the section house and related buildings are pictured, with photographer O. B. Buell standing on the siding, likely at the site of the depot. Recently, the site of this depot has been identified by archaeologists, located immediately south of the CPR mainline east of Banff's government and industrial compound road.[6]

4.4A WOODWORTH RANCH AND CASCADE MOUNTAIN, 1888 (ALICE FULMER, WHYTE NA 71-3530)

4.4B MINNEWANKA INTERCHANGE, TRANS-CANADA HIGHWAY, JULY 2001 (CW 2001-07C-6)

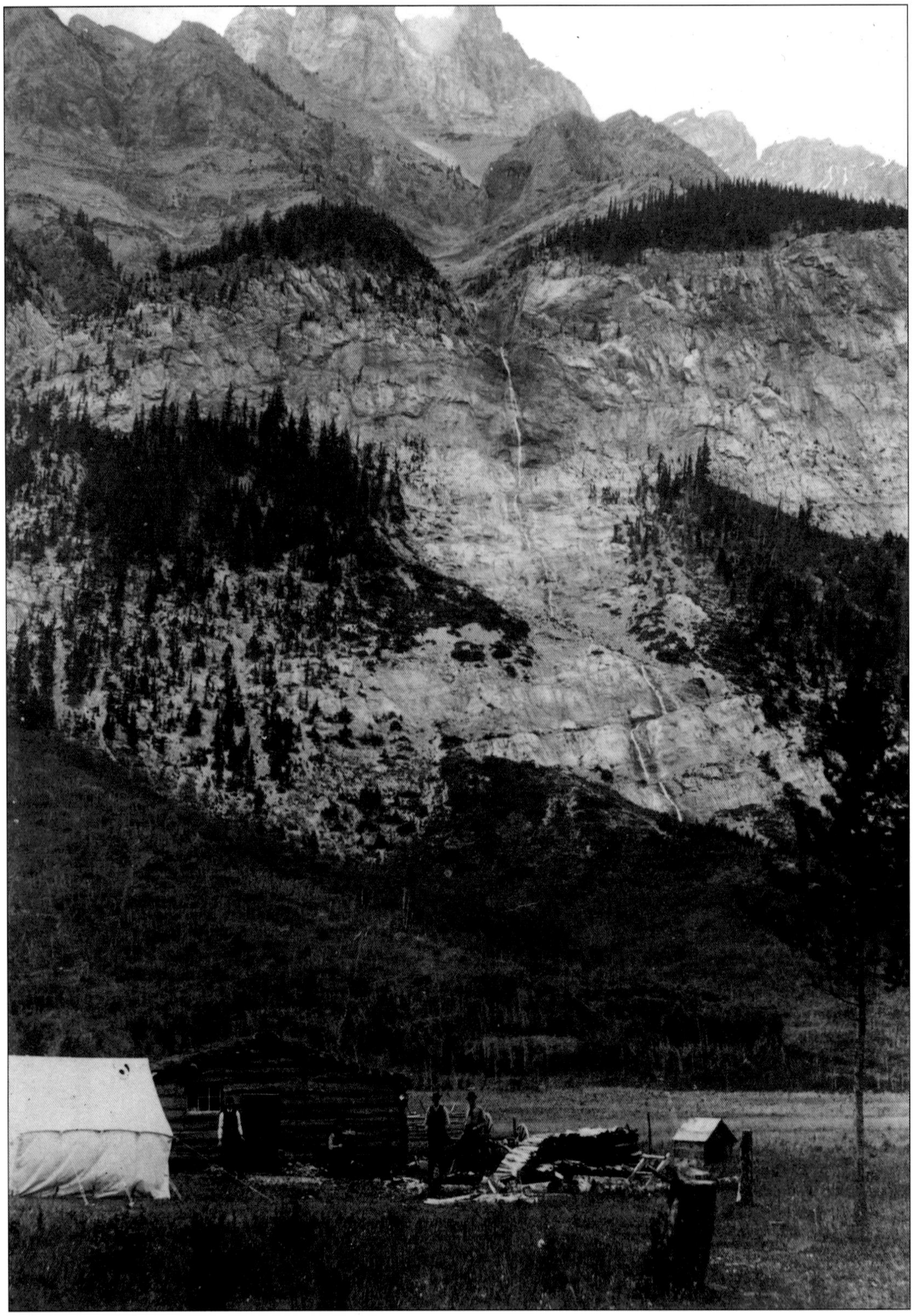

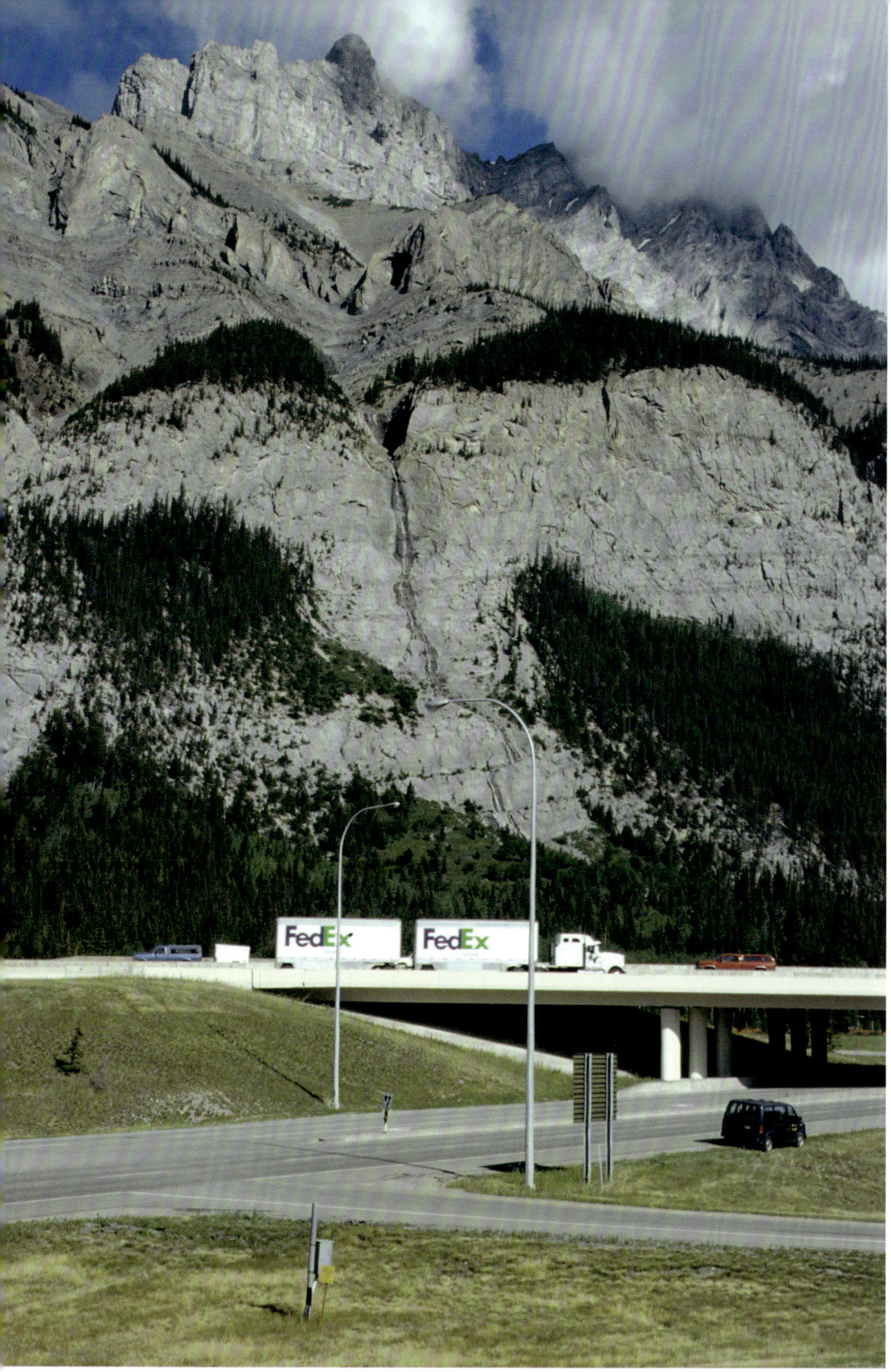

Although the hot springs on Sulphur Mountain are often touted as Banff's most famous landmark, early explorers more often mentioned the waterfall on Cascade Mountain as the area's most prominent feature. Sir George Simpson referred to passing the "spout" in August 1841; Sir James Hector of the Palliser Expedition described camping at the "little prairie" at the foot of "the mountain where the water falls" in August 1858; and James Carnegie, Earl of Southesk, also stayed at this location at the end of an epic hunting trip through the mountains one month later.[7] The Woodworth cabin, shown in the historic photograph, was one of the first buildings constructed at the site to the north and east of Siding 29 in 1883 and when Dominion Land Surveyor George Stewart arrived in 1886 to lay out the new townsite nearer the springs, he set up his tent close by.[8]

After the railway depot was officially moved west to the new location of Banff in 1888, this area continued to be a focus for human use. Upon becoming park superintendent, George Stewart chose the unique grassland as a site for a tree nursery to be irrigated by water from the falls, in 1939 it was developed as the nine-hole Cascade Golf and Country Club, and in 1946 it became a landing field to accommodate the rapidly growing post-war interest in aviation.[9] By the 1990s the meadow was intensively developed – the landing strip was still in operation, an interchange associated with the twinning of the Trans-Canada Highway occupied part of it, and a baseball diamond for a nearby military cadet camp covered another area.

The shrubby aspen forest visible below the falls in 1886 is likely the result of many fires that swept up the hillside from the meadow during the 1800s, some of them probably started by the explorers themselves. Today, as part of the system of wildlife movement corridors created around the Banff townsite, the landing field has been decommissioned, the baseball diamond and the cadet camp are gone, and, having escaped a serious fire for over eighty years, the trembling aspen have matured and are beginning to be replaced by a dense forest of white spruce.

4.5A HOT SPRINGS NEAR SIDING 29, 1885 (O. B. BUELL, GLENBOW NA 4697-22)

4.5B CAVE AND BASIN, 1892 (PHOTOGRAPHER UNKNOWN, GLENBOW NA 529-9)

4.5C CAVE AND BASIN NATIONAL HISTORIC SITE, JUNE 2006 (CW 2006-06B-35)

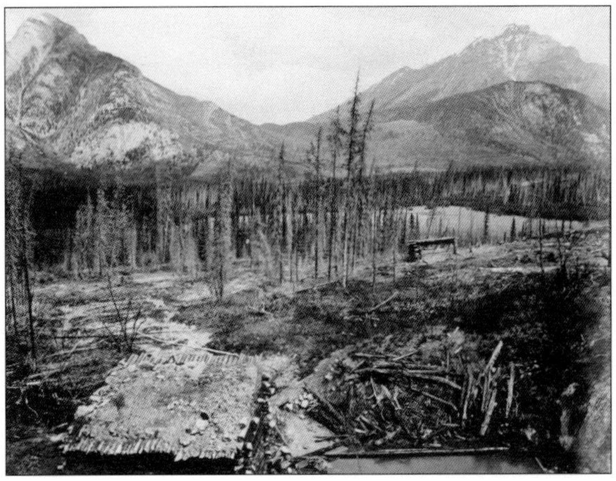

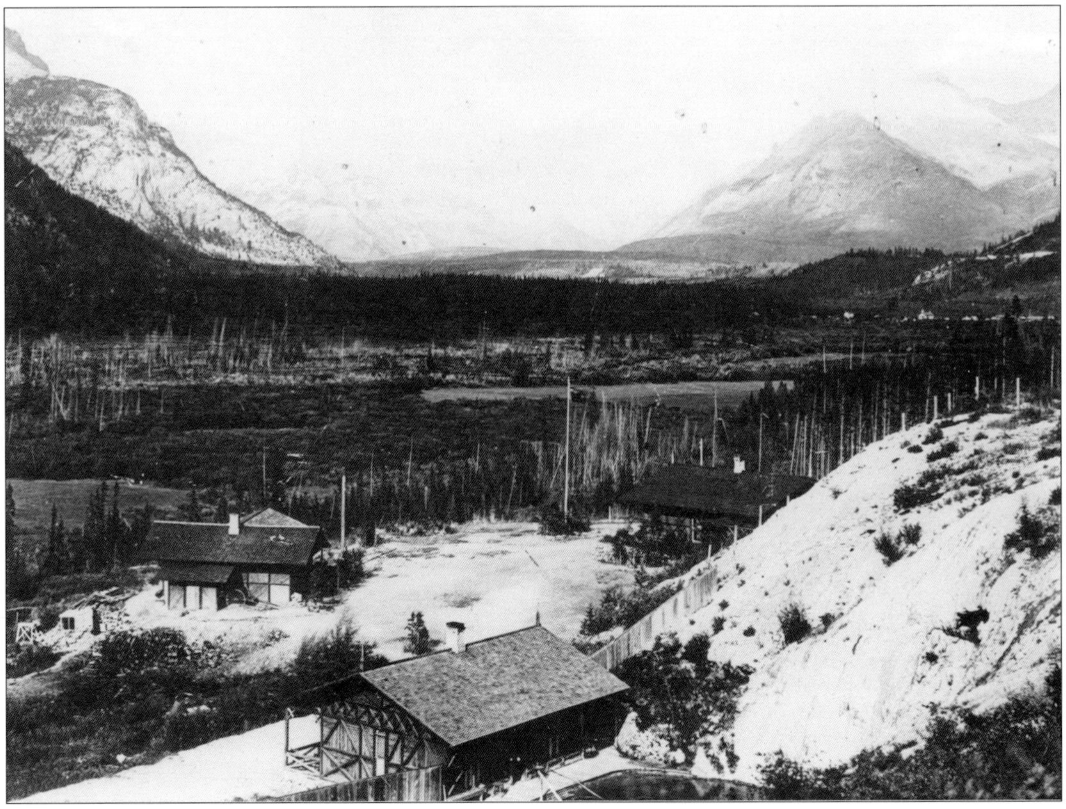

The hot springs in the flanks of Sulphur Mountain, discovered by railway workers Frank McCabe and Bill and Tom McCardell in 1883, became the birthplace of Canada's national park system. Ramshackle development, visible in the 1885 photograph by one of the first commercial photographers to ply the CPR line, Professor O. B. Buell, greeted Deputy Minister of the Interior A. M. Burgess when he visited to inspect the area. Burgess took steps leading to the passage of an Order-in-Council of November 25, 1885, reserving a twenty-six-square-kilometre area around the springs, which promised "to be of

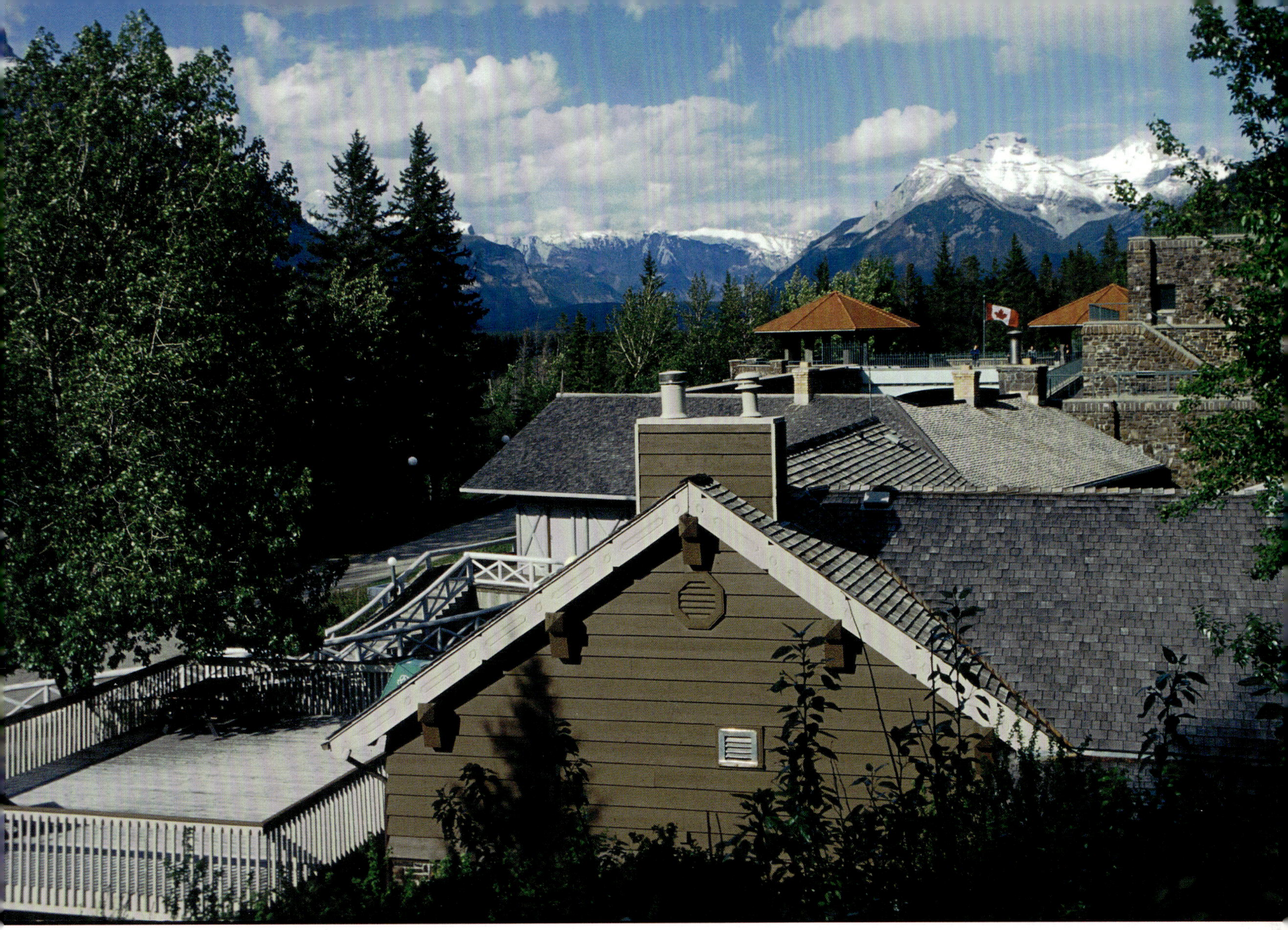

great sanitary advantage to the public." In 1887 with the enactment of the Rocky Mountains Park Act, an enlarged area of 670 square kilometres was "set apart as a public park and pleasure ground for the benefit, advantage and enjoyment of the people of Canada."[10]

By the early 1890s, when the second view was taken, the Dominion government had already built a rustic log bathhouse and caretaker's residence, had lined the porous rock of the pools with masonry and had equipped them with pipes and valves, providing proper bathing facilities. Soon the Cave and Basin was linked with the new Banff townsite by carriage road, and it rapidly became the main attraction for thousands of tourists arriving on the CPR to enjoy the sublime scenery and, as was popular in European spas, to "take the waters." Over the years various improvements were carried out as the crowds grew, the major one being the 1914 construction of a complete new pool and bathing facility designed by Banff Springs Hotel architect Walter Painter.

After some sixty years of use, the pools fell into disrepair due to deterioration from chemicals in the water. In preparation for the centennial of Canada's national parks in 1985, a "Save the Cave and Basin Committee" convinced Parks Canada to undertake a rehabilitation and reconstruction of the Painter buildings as well as the re-creation of the original log bathhouse, and the new facility was dedicated by HRH the Duke of Edinburgh as part of the centenary celebrations.[11] In the 1990s, deterioration problems had reappeared and again led to the discontinuation of the use of the pools. However, the site remains one of Banff's most popular tourist destinations for those wishing to gain an understanding of the history of Banff and Canada's national parks in interpretive displays mounted as part of the centennial renovations.

4.6A CANADIAN PACIFIC RAILROAD HOTEL AT BANFF, CA. 1890 (BOORNE AND MAY, WHYTE NA 66-1942)

4.6B BANFF SPRINGS HOTEL FROM PLAYING FIELD, JUNE 2003 (CW 2003-05C-26)

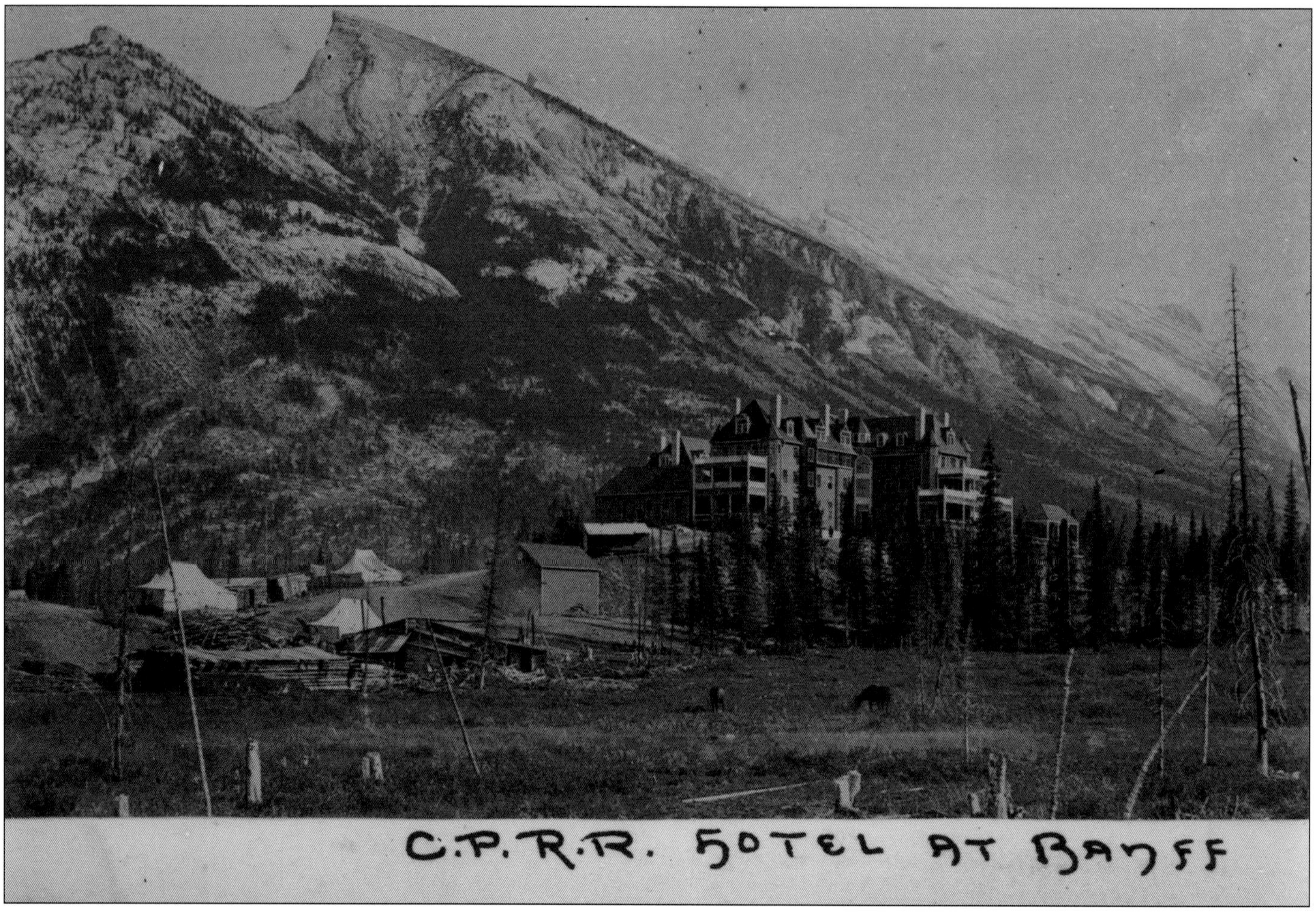

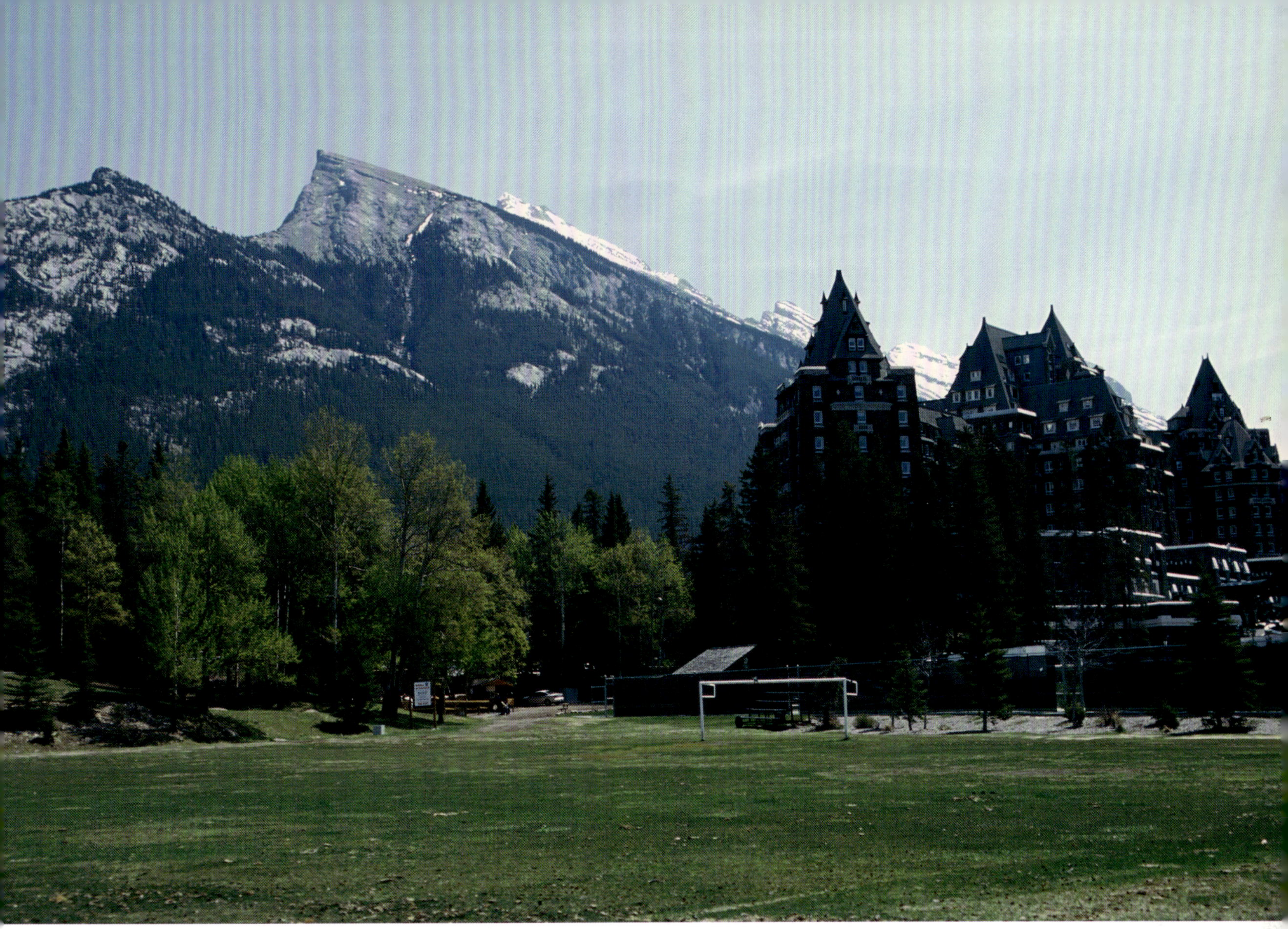

In the early years of Banff's development the relationship formed between the CPR and the Dominion government led to the building of public facilities, such as the Cave and Basin, and major private accommodation, such as the Banff Springs Hotel. After finding a scenic location above the confluence of the Bow and Spray rivers with a majestic view towards the Fairholme Range, CPR General Manager William C. Van Horne set out to build what he described as "the finest hotel on the North American continent." Using the talents of prominent American architect Bruce Price, who took his inspiration from the chateaux of France's Loire Valley, the hotel was designed and under construction when Van Horne arrived to find the plan had been turned 180 degrees so that the kitchen faced the beautiful view of the Bow Valley. Employing his not inconsiderable skills, he immediately sketched out a new rotunda pavilion and saved the view for the guests rather than the kitchen staff. Opened to the public in 1888 with rooms being offered at $3.50 and upwards, the quarter-million-dollar edifice consisted of two frame wings, each of four storeys, with the top floor contained within a dormer roof and Van Horne's pavilion jutting out towards the river.

Over the years the Banff Springs was to undergo many changes, the most noteworthy being the replacement of the original frame hotel with a new eleven-storey concrete and rundlestone centre tower designed by Walter Painter and completed in 1912. In 1928 similarly clad wings buttressing the centre tower were completed, visible in the modern photograph taken from what is today the hotel's playing field and tennis court area.[12]

4.7A BANFF SPRINGS HOTEL AND BOW VALLEY, CA. 1905 (BYRON HARMON, WHYTE V263 NG-11-7)

4.7B BANFF SPRINGS HOTEL AND BOW VALLEY, CA. 1920 (GEORGE NOBLE, WHYTE V469-1701)

4.7C BANFF SPRINGS HOTEL AND BOW VALLEY, CA. 1930 (BYRON HARMON, WHYTE V263 NA 71-3737)

4.7D HELICOPTER VIEW OF THE BANFF SPRINGS HOTEL AND PRESCRIBED BURN ON THE FAIRHOLME BENCHES, JUNE 2003 (CW 2003-06E-13)

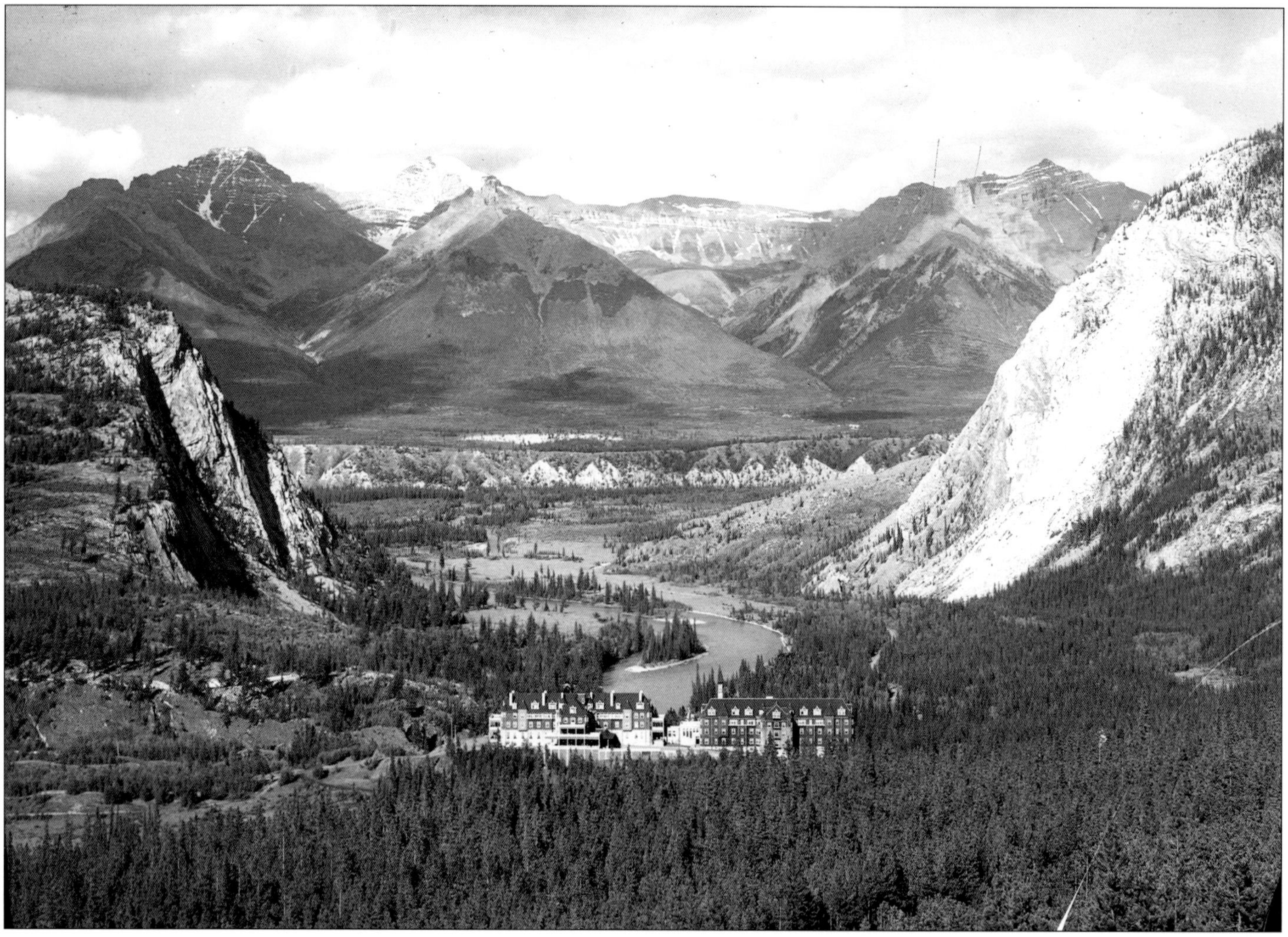

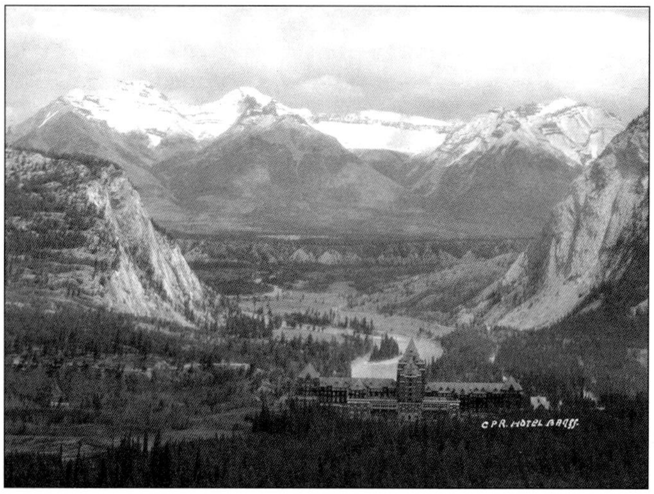

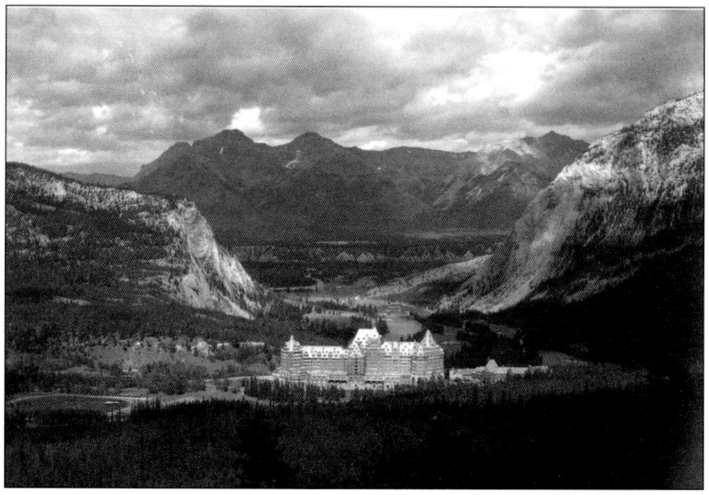

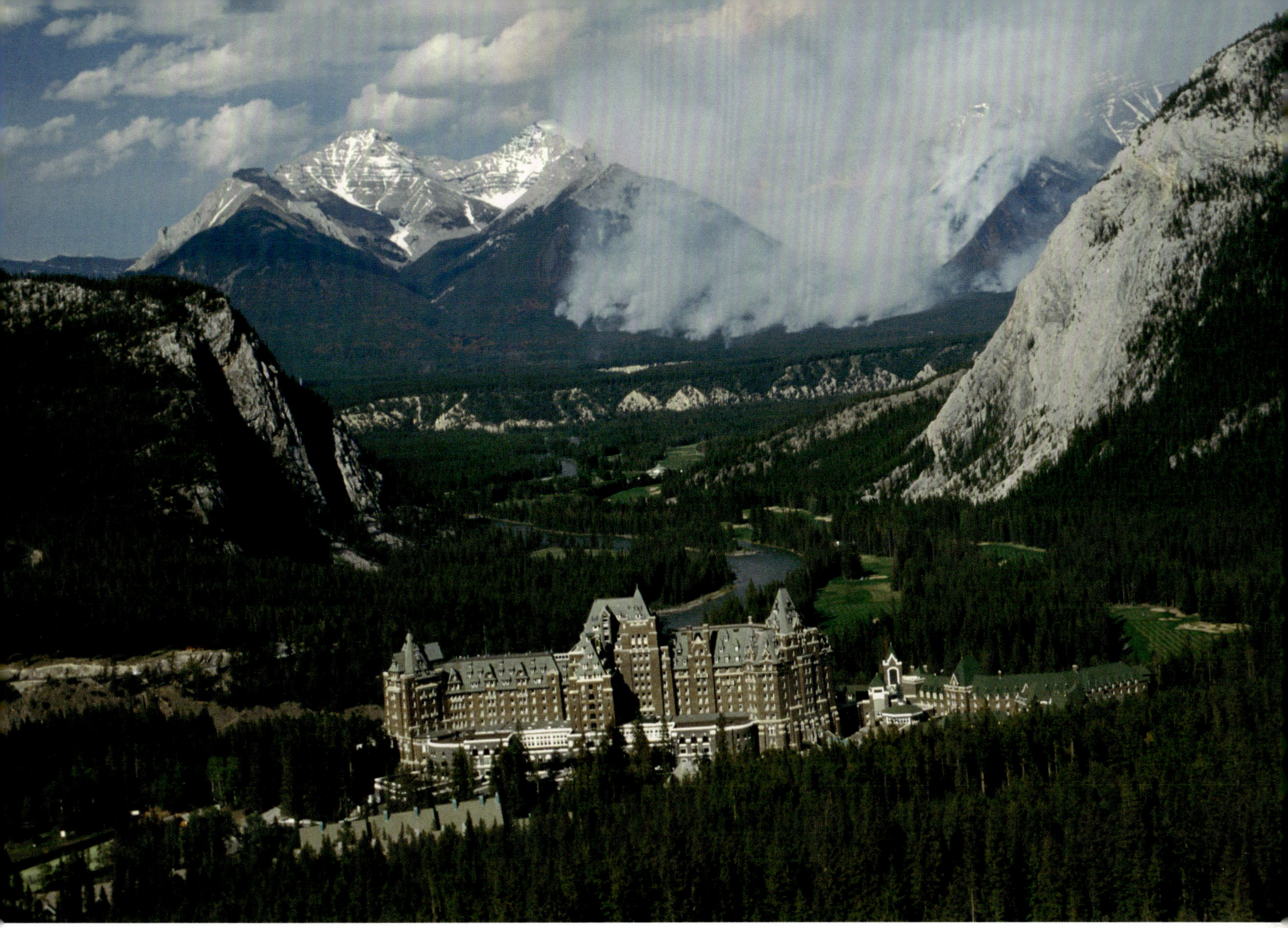

The view from Sulphur Mountain down the Bow Valley towards the Fairholme Range, incorporating the Banff Springs Hotel, was favoured by photographers until tree growth blocked visibility from the ground, necessitating rephotography from a helicopter. This series of images well illustrates the many changes in the historic hotel. In the early view by Byron Harmon shortly after the turn of the century, the original single wing frame hotel has just been doubled in size with the completion of a second wing in 1903. In George Noble's view, some fifteen years later, the transformation of the hotel had begun with the completion of the Painter centre tower situated between the original frame wings, and a decade later at the time of Harmon's second view, the "new" concrete and rundlestone hotel stands completed. It would be the 1980s before the next major addition was undertaken, including an extensive conference centre facility, and in the 2003 view, with a prescribed burn visible on the Fairholme benches in the background, the modern hotel, now operated by Fairmont Hotels & Resorts, had just been completed with the addition of a new lobby and main entrance on the building's west façade.

4.8A CASCADE MOUNTAIN FROM MAIN STREET, BANFF, CA. 1886 (A. B. THOM, GLENBOW NA 673-27)

4.8B BANFF AVENUE, CA. 1928 (BYRON HARMON, WHYTE NA 71-3392)

4.8C BANFF AVENUE, JUNE 2003 (CW 2003-05L-36)

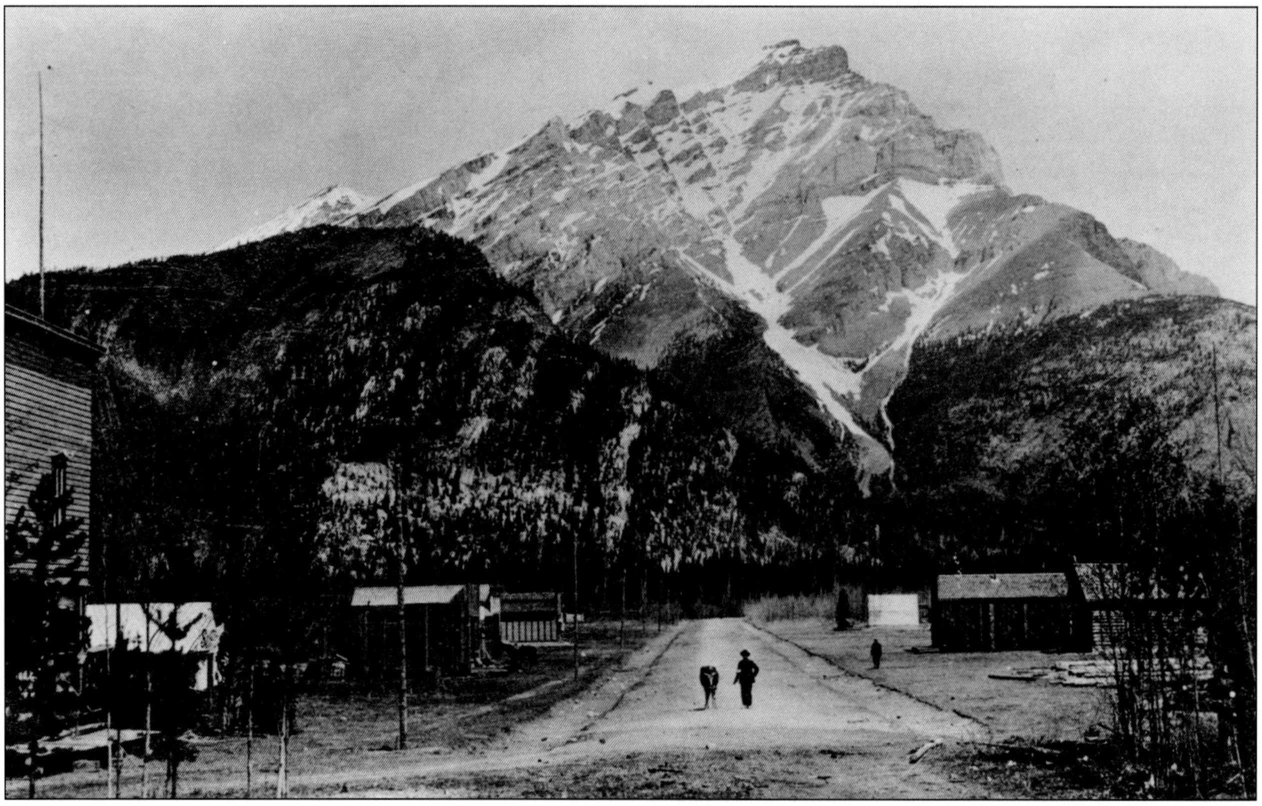

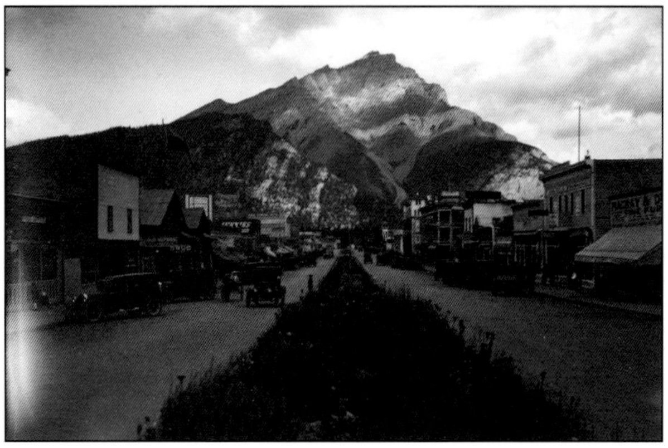

A man stands with a cow on a dirt street, a few false-front buildings surrounding him and a beautiful mountain forming a distant backdrop. This image, taken by professional photographer A. B. Thom shortly after George Stewart had laid out the main street of the new Banff townsite, is the oldest known to exist of Banff Avenue, but it would be only one of millions ultimately capturing this famous view. The village of Banff was at the time of its creation unique in North America, for in the earlier Yellowstone National Park in the United States and in subsequent American parks, such townsites were not allowed. As other urban centres appeared in later Canadian parks, such as Jasper and Waterton,

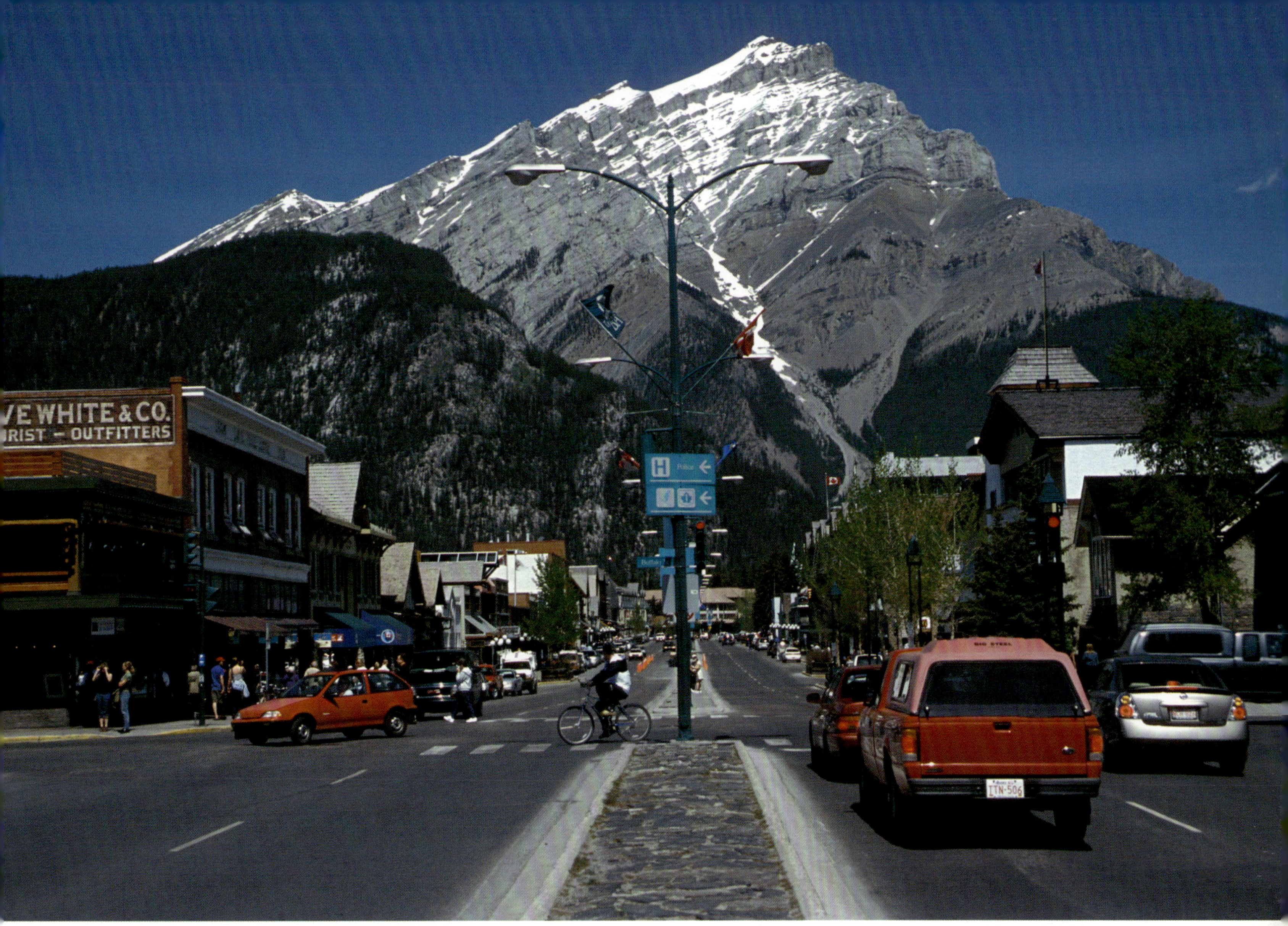

this aspect would provide one of the defining differences between the Canadian and American park systems.[13]

Banff quickly became the economic engine of Rocky Mountains Park, supporting the resort development activities of both the CPR and the government. Small businessmen built tourist outfitting and souvenir shops, restaurants and hotels affording a less expensive option to the palatial Banff Springs Hotel. All such businesses, as well as the residences of those who operated them, were on lands leased from the government, meaning that there was no municipal authority to provide Banffites with a voice in the way the village was administered or developed. Dominion control was exemplified in 1935 when a new Administration Building, built as a depression relief project, replaced the old Bretton Hall Hotel (originally "The Sanitarium") that had dominated the south end of Banff Avenue, much as those who worked within its confines dominated town and park affairs.[14]

Nonetheless, Banff grew and prospered, as evident in Byron Harmon's photograph of the late 1920s, when it had become a bustling community welcoming both those who came in the traditional way on the railroad and those who, in ever-increasing numbers, chose to visit in automobiles accessing the village over the Calgary-Banff Coach Road, completed in 1910. Over the succeeding years the dress of the tourists and style of the vehicles they rode in would continue to change and, as the modern view shows, the stores and hotels would evolve too, but during the same period the economy and function of Banff as the largest town in a North American national park would change very little. However, eventually its residents did get the voice they had so long sought when in 1990 the Town of Banff again illustrated its uniqueness by becoming the first self-governing municipality in a national park.[15]

4.9A MEADOWS BELOW TUNNEL MOUNTAIN, JUNE 1900 (VAUX FAMILY, WHYTE NG 4-626)

4.9B CLUBHOUSE, FAIRMONT BANFF SPRINGS GOLF COURSE, JUNE 2004 (CW 2004-06D-03)

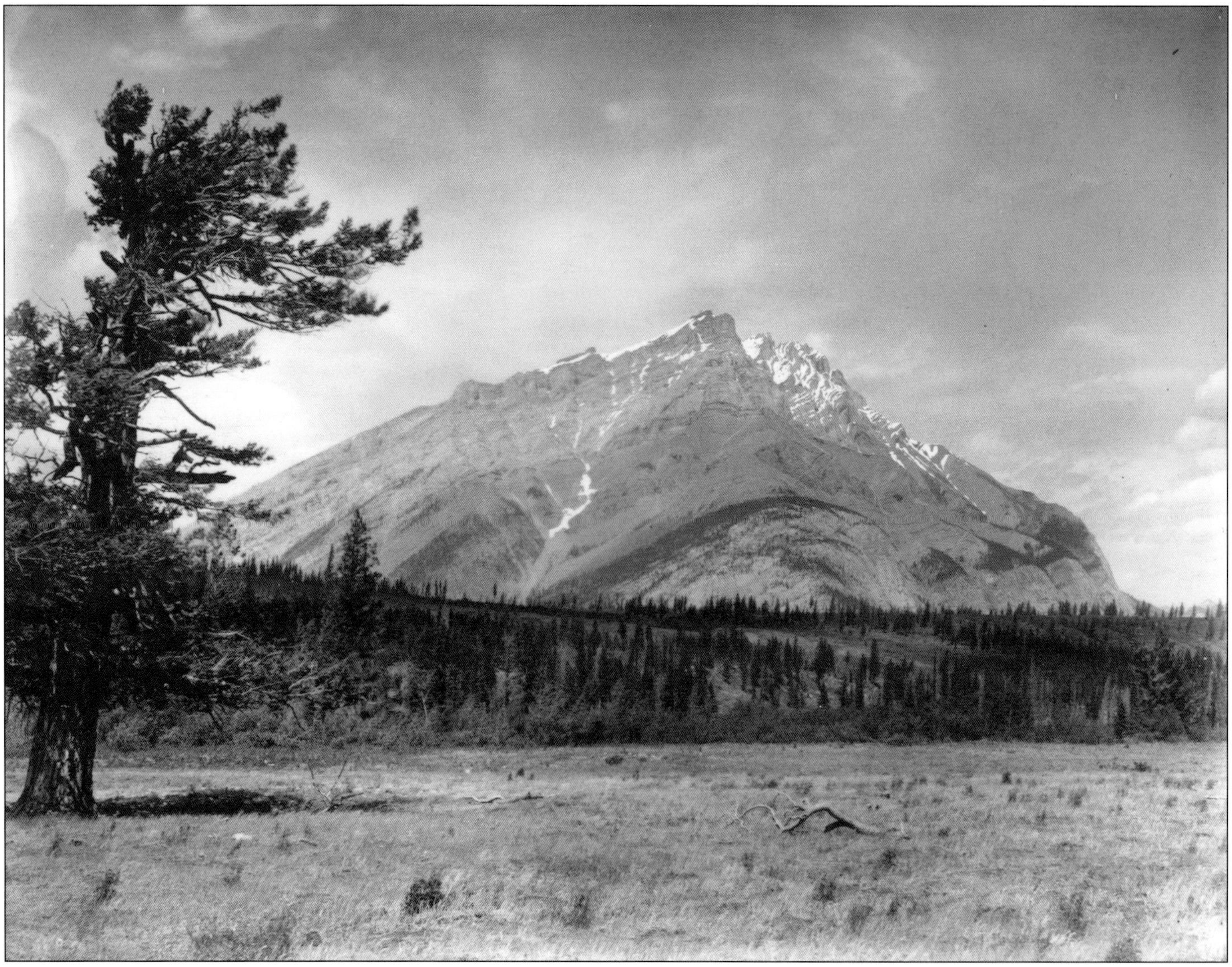

When early parks administrators were looking for locations to provide scenic drives, the flats at the foot of Mount Rundle were among the first areas to fall under their gaze, and by 1889 Superintendent Stewart had constructed the "Loop Drive." It quickly became a tourist favourite, and many stopped to photograph the ancient Douglas firs dotting the dry montane landscape as foreground in the vistas up and down the Bow Valley. Above the bridge over the Spray River connecting the Loop to the Banff

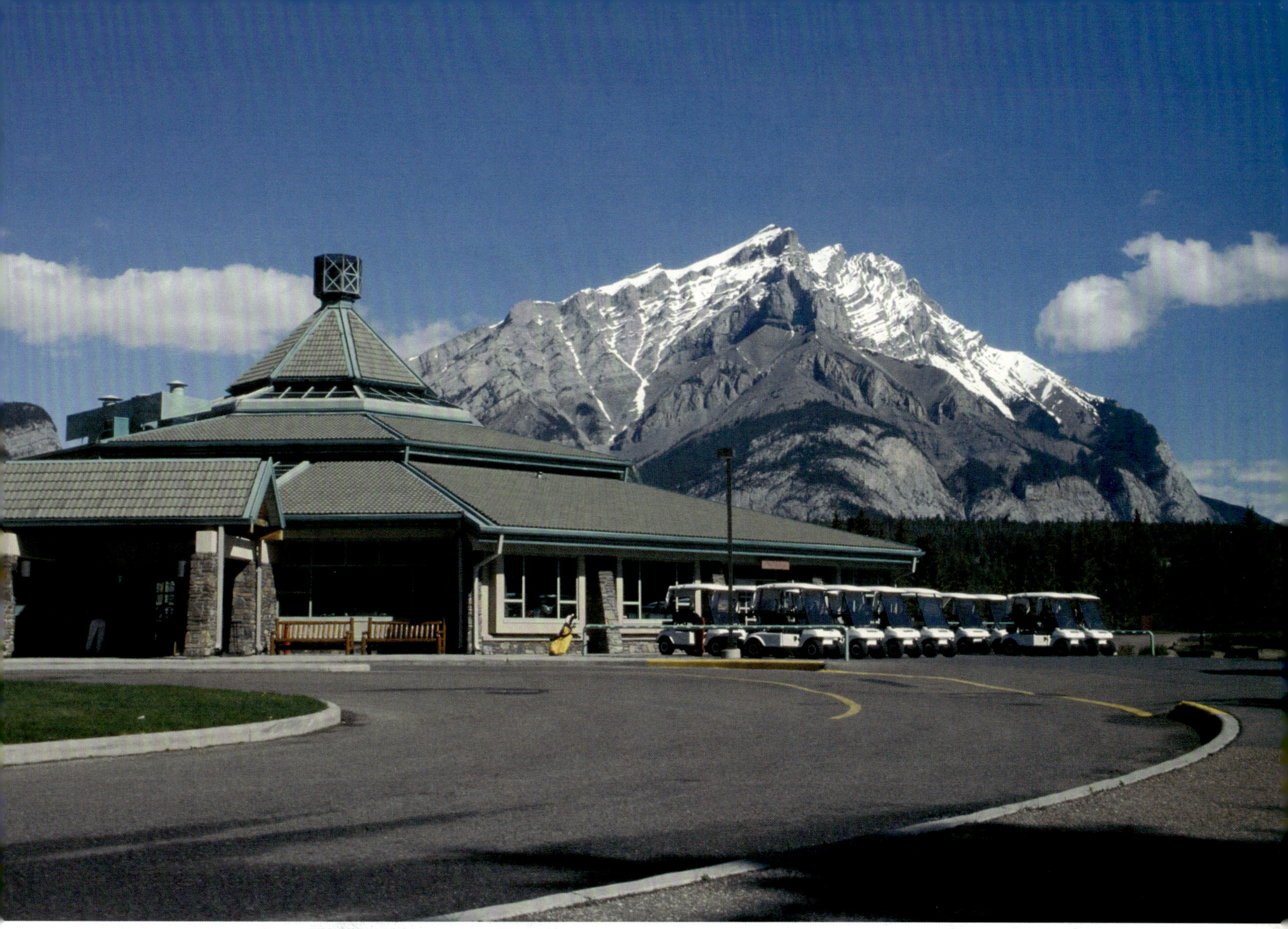

townsite stood the grand Banff Springs Hotel, and in 1911, in an attempt to provide a recreational diversion to its well-heeled guests, it received government approval to build a nine-hole golf links on the meadows adjacent to the drive. Originally consisting of fairways simply mowed in the native fescues and a small clubhouse (now serving as the course greenskeeper's residence), the course was improved and grew over time. In 1919 North America's most famous golf architect, Donald Ross of Pinehurst, North Carolina, was contracted by the Parks Branch to expand the course to eighteen holes, and in 1927 it was redesigned again by the CPR, which had regained ownership, utilizing the skills of Canada's most-famed landscape architect, Stanley Thompson.

Thompson's design placed fairways in the area at the foot of the hotel near the Spray bridge, including grounds that had been in use as the government tent campground since 1917, requiring their relocation to a new site on Tunnel Mountain. Later modifications included the 1989 addition of the "Tunnel Mountain Nine" layout inside the ring created by the original course, a project that included the construction of the new clubhouse pictured in the 2004 image and a requirement to improve wildlife movement by the removal of a 10-kilometre-long, 2.5 metre-high 'elk fence' erected in the 1930s to keep wildlife off the course. Over the years the Thompson course was modified on several occasions and in 1997 a rebuilding to recapture its historic golf shot values was undertaken under the guidance of famed mountain course designer Les Furber. Upon its completion in 1999 as the "Stanley Thompson Eighteen," it was registered under the Audubon Cooperative Sanctuary System, a program "dedicated to enhancing and improving the environment through protecting wildlife habitats, education, research and stewardship action."[16]

4.10A STONEY INDIAN CAMP, BANFF, 1920S (DAN MCCOWAN, GLENBOW NA 714-236)

4.10B 17TH FAIRWAY, FAIRMONT BANFF SPRINGS GOLF COURSE, JUNE 2003 (CW 2003-05L-33)

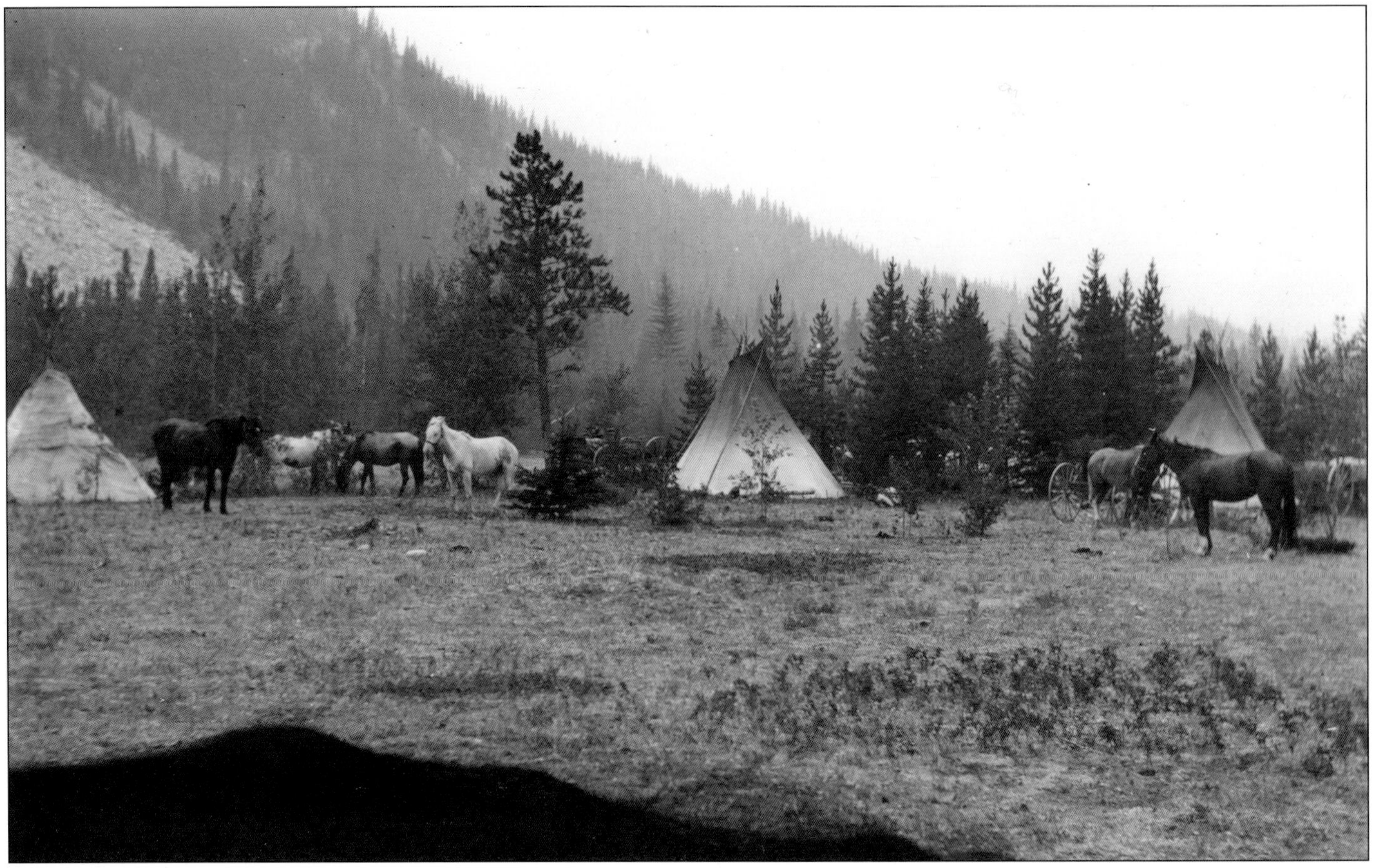

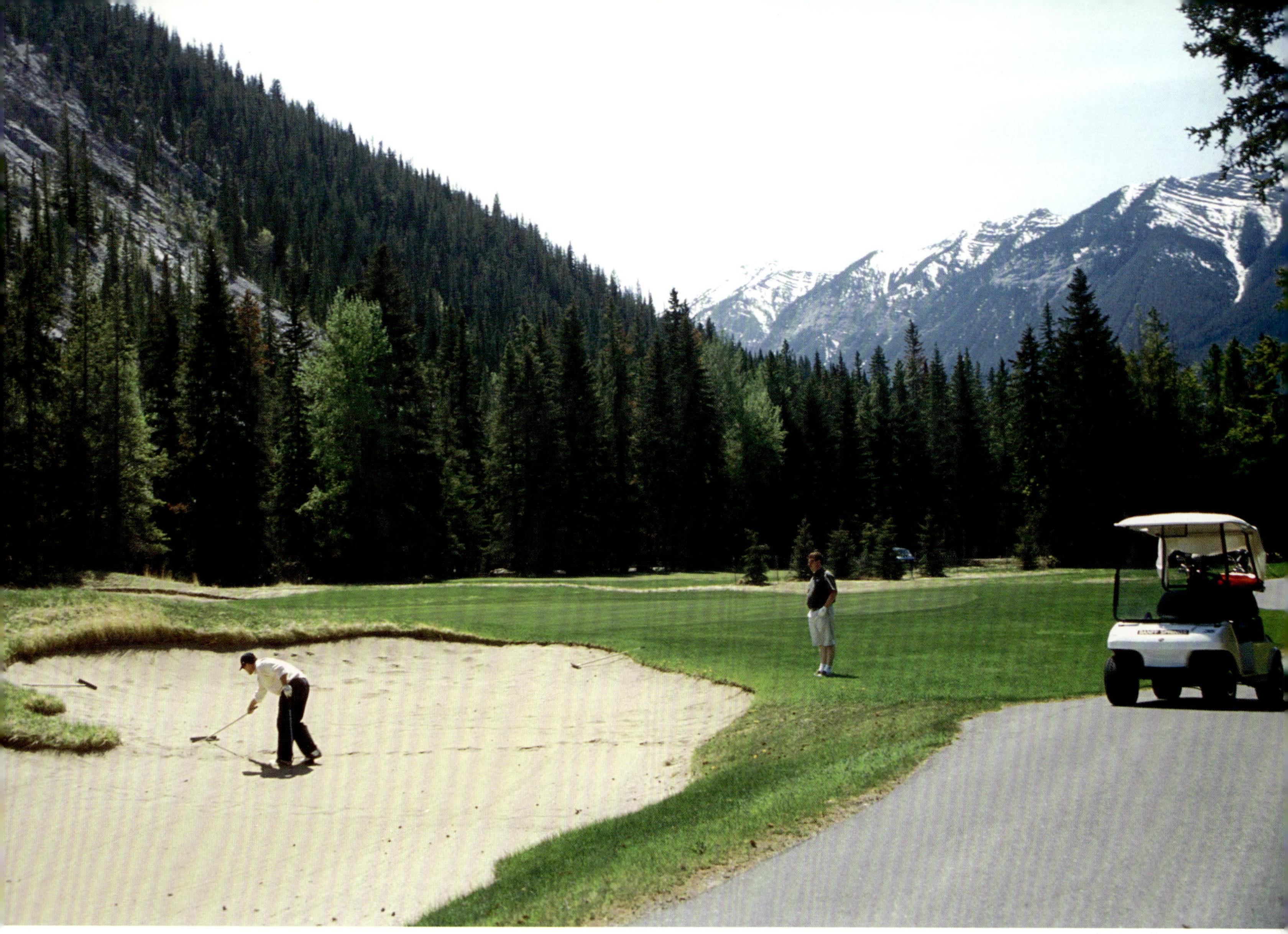

Golf course fairways are not the place where one might expect to consider changes in human occupation and native vegetation and wildlife, but such is the case with the Banff Springs Golf Course. In the rugged mountain topography, it was only in the alluvial valleys of the lower montane life-zone that suitable flat land, soil, growing conditions, and accessibility were combined with the aesthetic qualities that early course designers looked for. These attributes were many of the same that attracted ungulates for winter range and with them earlier hunter-gatherers seeking food close to good camping, wood, and water. Consequently, the banks of the Bow River below Mount Rundle and Tunnel Mountain plied by golf carts today were actually witness to more human and wildlife use and vegetation manipulation than almost any other area in the mountains.[17]

Prehistoric peoples, thought to be related to the Interior Salish of British Columbia, constructed pit house dwellings in the area some 2,800 years ago to use as shelters on their way to hunt bison on the neighbouring plains, leading the Canadian government to make the area the country's first officially designated archaeological site in 1913. As illustrated by the 1920s photograph, it was favoured as a camping ground by native peoples for millennia, and Parks Canada archaeologists have found some of the oldest elk remains in Banff nearby. In the 1920s when the original Banff Springs Golf Course was being expanded eastward, this same spot was incorporated into the new design.[18]

4.11A BOW FALLS, 1889 (ALICE FULMER, GLENBOW NA 636-16)

4.11C LOG RUN AT BOW FALLS, CA. 1890 (JOHN WOODRUFF, WHYTE NA 66-1348)

4.11B BOW FALLS, AUGUST 2001 (CW 2001-08D-11)

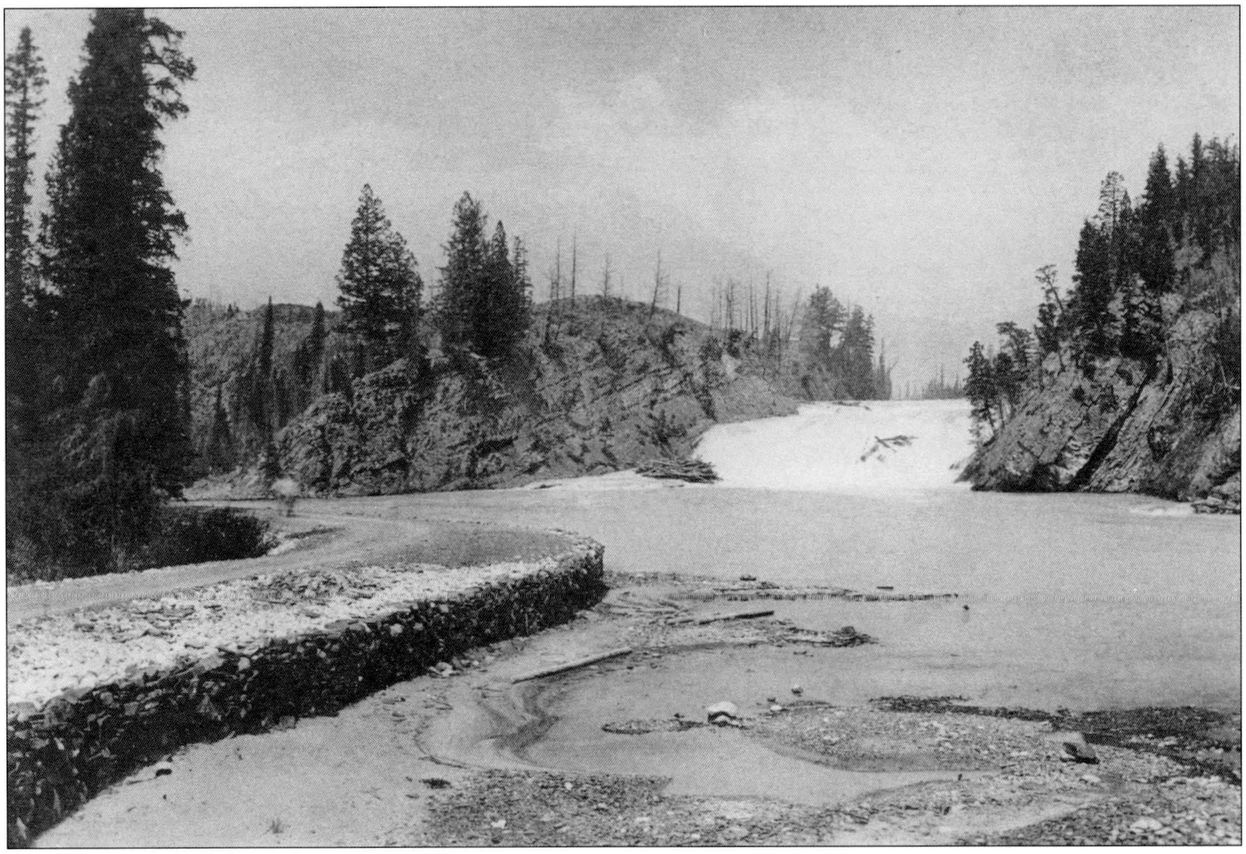

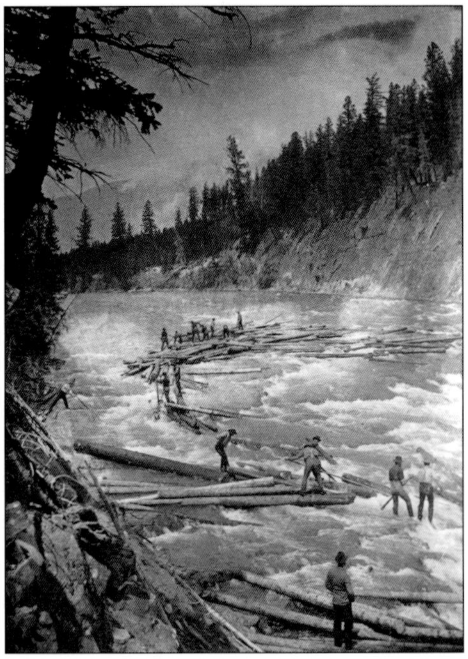

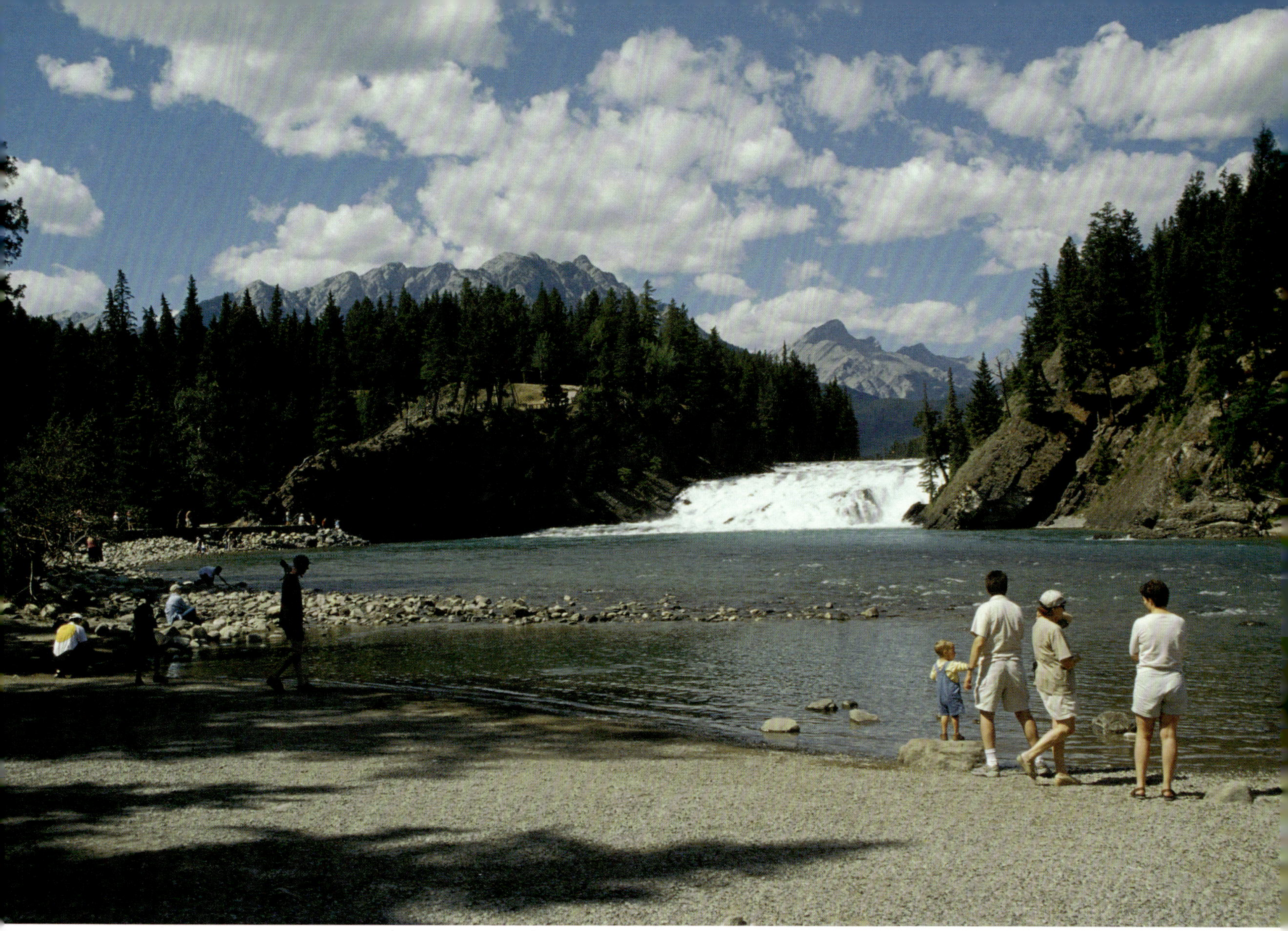

Even before the establishment of Rocky Mountains Park in 1887, logging was being carried out on the lands that would form the park in line with the Department of the Interior's task of making western Canada's resources productive, and it would continue long after the creation of the mountain parks. In 1883–84 the Department inventoried timber supplies in the Bow River watershed and surveyor Louis B. Stewart laid out timber berths along the Bow, Kananaskis, and Spray rivers. Most of these were reserved by the Eau Claire and Bow River Lumber Company of Eau Claire, Wisconsin, which built a mill in what is now the Eau Claire district of Calgary and began actively logging the area in 1886. Timber was cut in the winter and floated down the Bow and its tributaries in huge spring drives that were both exciting and dangerous for the men involved. In 1887 six loggers were drowned when one of the huge rafts that had been brought down the Kananaskis jammed at Kananaskis Falls.[19] In the 1890 view, drivers are moving logs, likely cut on the company's berth near Castle Mountain, through Bow Falls at spring high-water, while the photograph taken a year earlier shows logs left stranded in the summer when the water levels had declined. The last of the log drives in the Kananaskis occurred in 1944 and commercial timber cutting was discontinued in Banff National Park in the 1950s, although Parks Canada continues to harvest timber to create fuel breaks for fire management and to restore more natural forest structure conditions.

4.12A ANTHRACITE, NWT, AND BLACK DIAMOND MINE, CA. 1895 (PHOTOGRAPHER UNKNOWN, WHYTE NA 66-713)

4.12B TRANS-CANADA HIGHWAY AND CALGARY POWER SURGE TOWER, 1981 (BRUNO ENGLER, CW-BE-FM-1981-14B)

4.12C SITE OF ANTHRACITE, JUNE 2003 (CW 2003-06A-08)

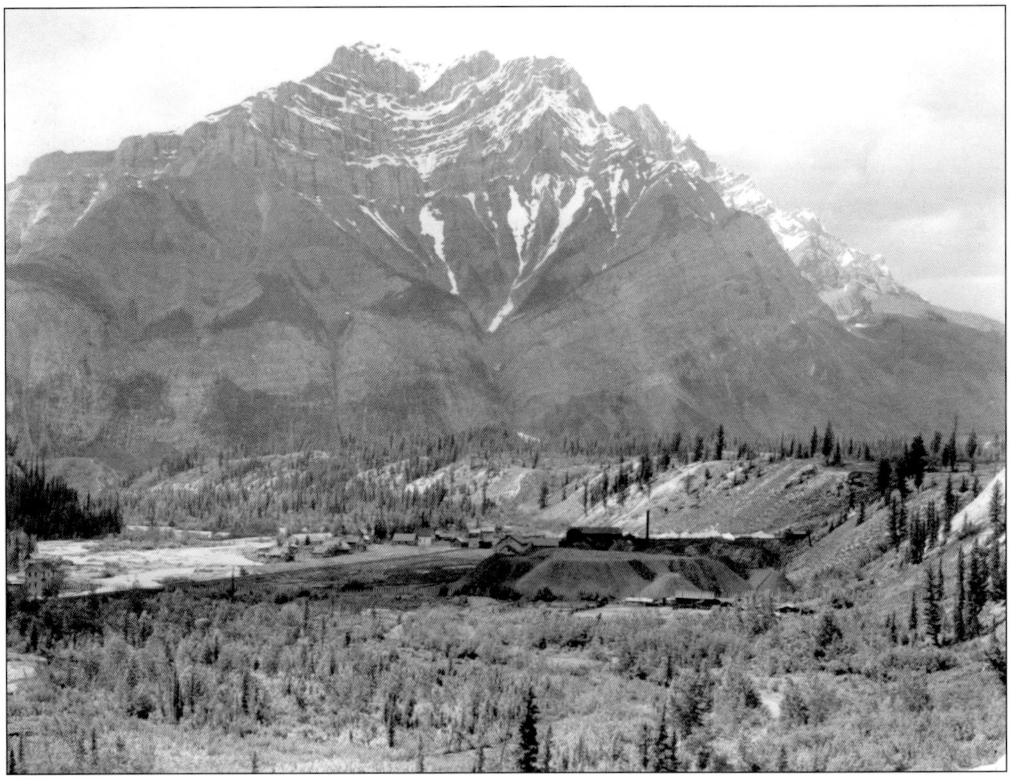

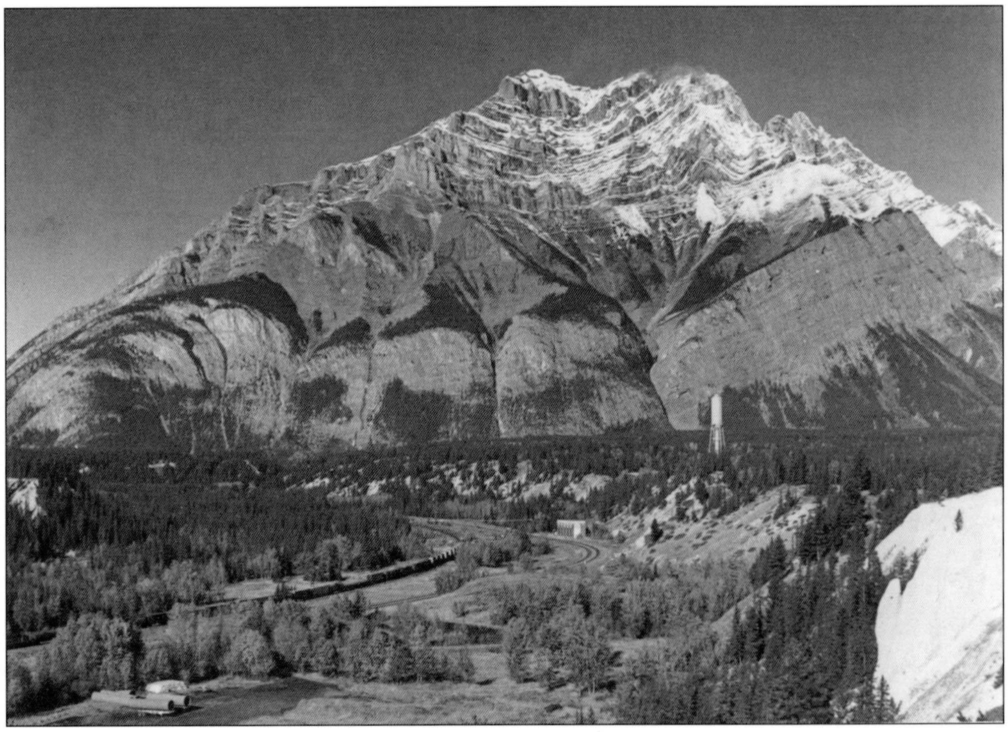

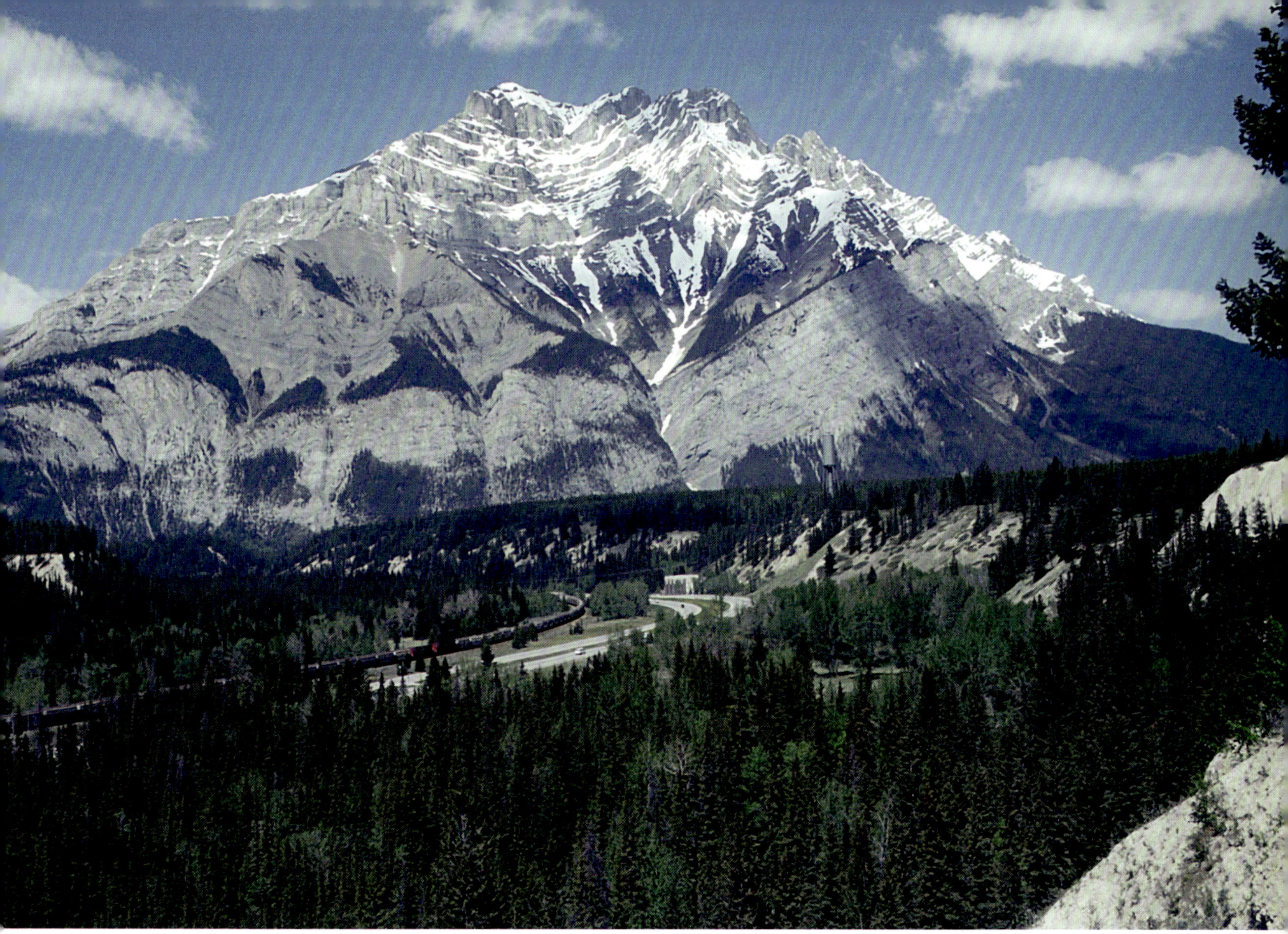

Even as the railroad was being built, officials with the Geological Survey of Canada were sizing the Rocky Mountain's natural resource potential, and by 1886 George M. Dawson had completed a geological map of the Bow Valley region identifying important coal deposits near the confluence of the Cascade and Bow rivers. By 1885 leases were being issued in the ninety-four-square-kilometre Cascade Coal Basin, and one of the first companies to begin operations was the Canadian Anthracite Coal Company.[20] The village of Anthracite was founded in 1886 and two years later it had been surveyed into 337 lots, boasted three hotels, a boarding house for up to three hundred miners, stores, and a church.[21] Mining operations were carried out in the Black Diamond Mine, located at the right in the early photograph, in a ravine leading up towards Johnson's Lake. By 1904 better quality coal at Canmore, losses on operations, and frequent flooding led to the closing of the mines, and many of the buildings and their occupants were moved to more productive mines at Bankhead and Canmore.

Beginning in 1938 the federal government began to try to extinguish various freehold "inholdings" dating to the original town, but in the meantime they had been acquired by a Banff real estate developer, who attempted to subdivide them into lots to be sold as recreational property. The planned construction of the Trans-Canada Highway lent new urgency to their acquisition, and in 1955 the government began expropriation proceedings that were to carry on as late as 1971.[22] In 1942 the Calgary Power hydro-electric development at Lake Minnewanka changed the course of the Cascade River and regulated its flow, modifying the ecology of the area. Visible in the 1981 photograph is the surge tower for the Cascade Power Plant with the two-lane Trans-Canada Highway passing near its base. By the time the 2003 view was taken the vegetation cover had increased, obscuring most of the old river channels, and the highway has been twinned to carry increased commercial and tourist traffic.

4.13A BANKHEAD, ALBERTA, CA. 1908 (PHOTOGRAPHER UNKNOWN, WHYTE NA 66-2446)

4.13B BANKHEAD INTERPRETIVE SITE, BANFF NATIONAL PARK, FEBRUARY 2003 (CW 2003-02A-08)

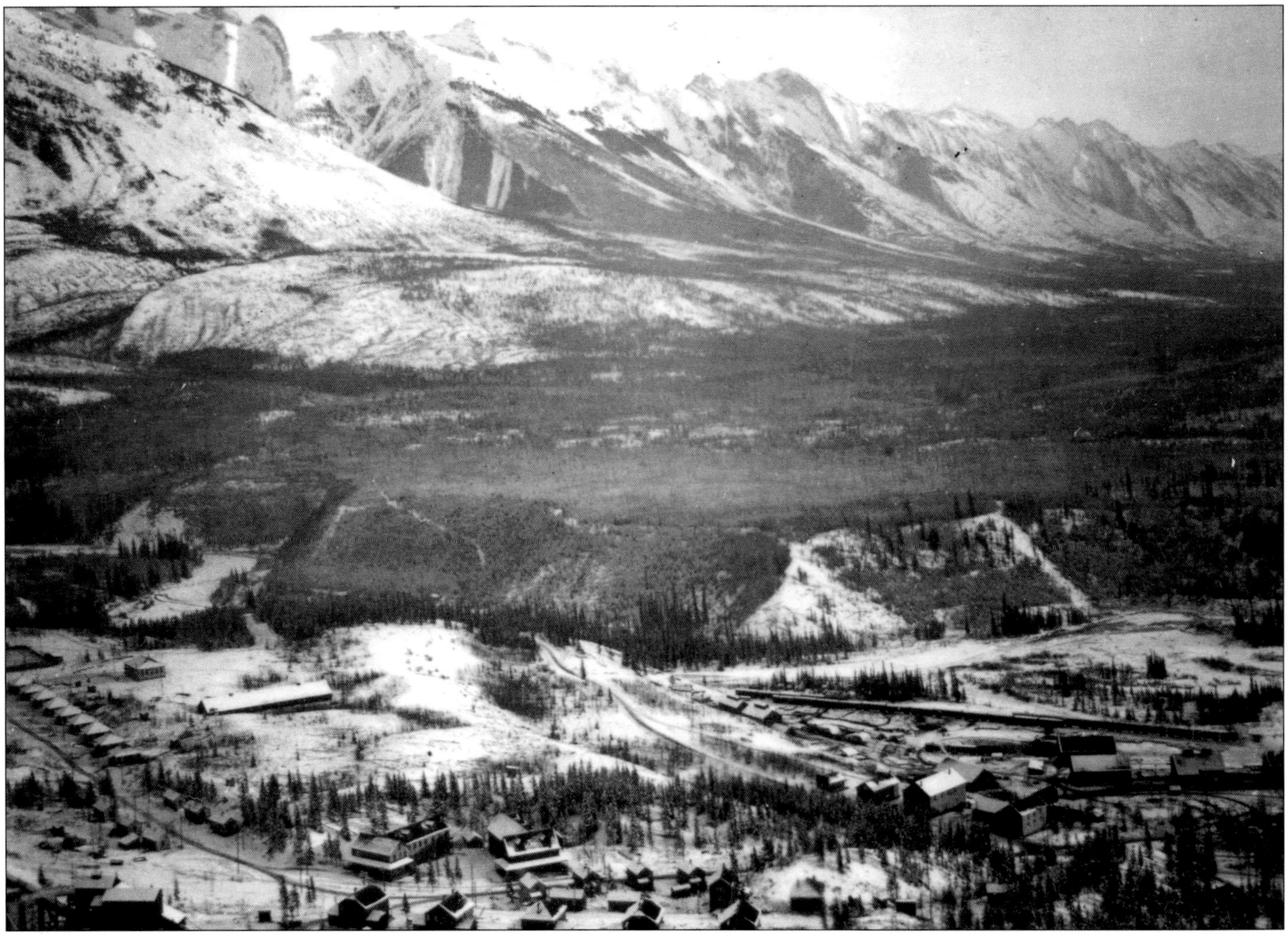

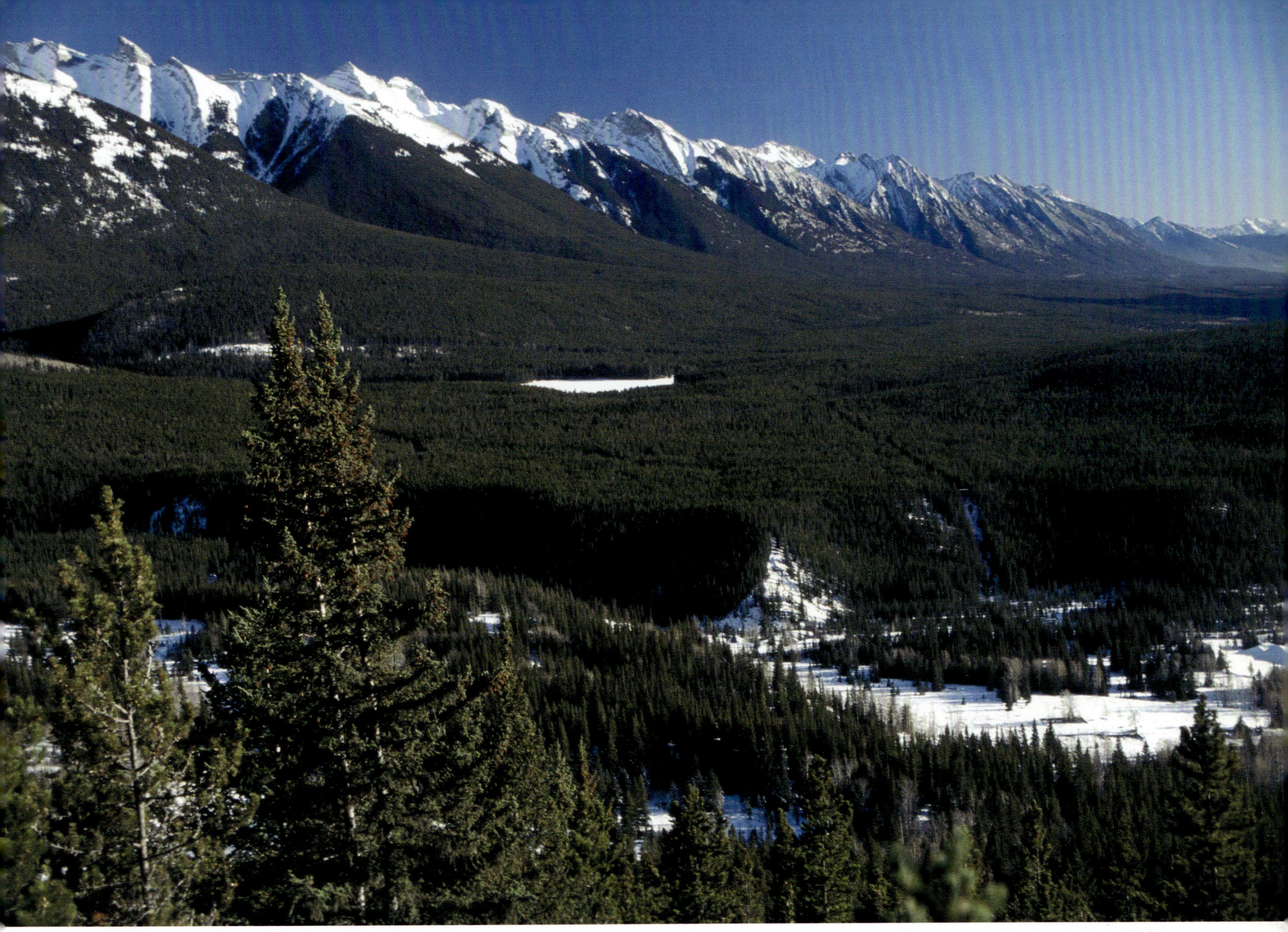

In 1904 the CPR subsidiary Pacific Coal Mines Ltd. began developing its own mining operations along the Cascade River upstream from Anthracite. Named Bankhead after a coal-mining area in Scotland, the townsite was intended to be a model community to illustrate the farsightedness and efficiency of the company. For a time the town did fulfill this goal, housing over twelve hundred residents of British, Italian, and east-European origin in a well-designed community that could boast electric lighting and a municipal sewage system long before the neighbouring villages of Banff and Canmore had such amenities. By 1911 its population was greater than that of nearby Banff. The mine works penetrated under Cascade Mountain at three intervals: "A level" on the river flats near the tipple (bottom right in the 1908 view), "B level" on a grassy bench where many of the miners' homes were also located (bottom right) and "C level" higher up the slope. This configuration and the great pressure the coal was under made mining difficult and produced a friable coal that had to be briquetted before it could be used commercially. Not particularly suitable for railway locomotives, it was used mainly for domestic purposes and for heating CPR passenger depots across western Canada.

Labour unrest resulted in frequent strikes, and when the miners walked out in 1922 the company threatened to close the mines if they did not return, a threat that was made good when the operations were permanently closed down that June. Many of the houses were sold at $200 each and moved to Banff and Canmore, but the company, after officially abandoning the property in 1935, advised the government they were "under no obligation to demolish or remove any remaining buildings, or to clean up the site." Over the succeeding years the parks department carried out much of the work itself, and in 1983 construction of an interpretive trail through the remains, the first human history interpretive unit in Banff, was undertaken to provide visitors with information on the days when such activities were thought to be compatible with national parks.[23]

4.14A LAKE MINNEWANKA, ROCKY MOUNTAINS NATIONAL PARK, 1888 (BOORNE AND MAY, WHYTE NA 66-634)

4.14B LAKE MINNEWANKA RESERVOIR, BANFF NATIONAL PARK, 1981 (BRUNO ENGLER, CW-BE-FM-1981-48)

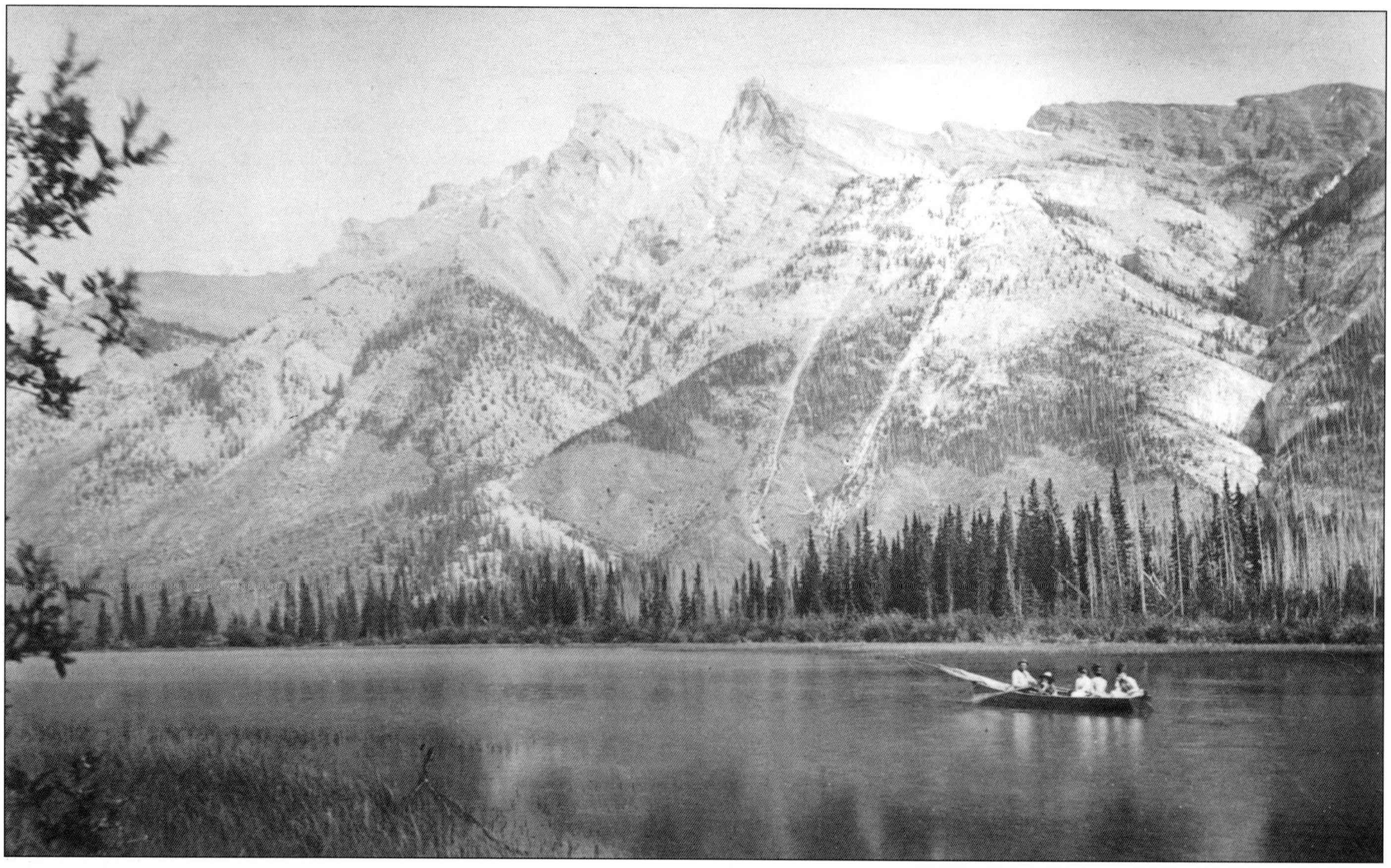

Lake Minnewanka, known to early explorers as Devil's Lake due to its proximity to Devil's Head Mountain to the east, has always played an important role in Canadian Rockies' history. Early First Nations peoples provided the name "Minnewanka," meaning "water of the spirits," because of many legends concerning the spirits inhabiting it. The lake was visited frequently, as it was a favourite camping spot on their travels from the plains by way of the Ghost River-Devil's Gap-Minnewanka route to the "Bow River traverse" near modern-day Banff and then over the mountains by Simpson or Vermilion pass. The first white party reporting on the lake was led by Governor Sir George Simpson of the Hudson's Bay Company, who passed it on his way to the Columbia River during his whirlwind trip around the world in 1841.[24]

In 1887 the lake was incorporated into Rocky Mountains Park, and when connected by a carriage road to Banff, it quickly became a popular tourist destination. Messrs. Astley and Disbrowe

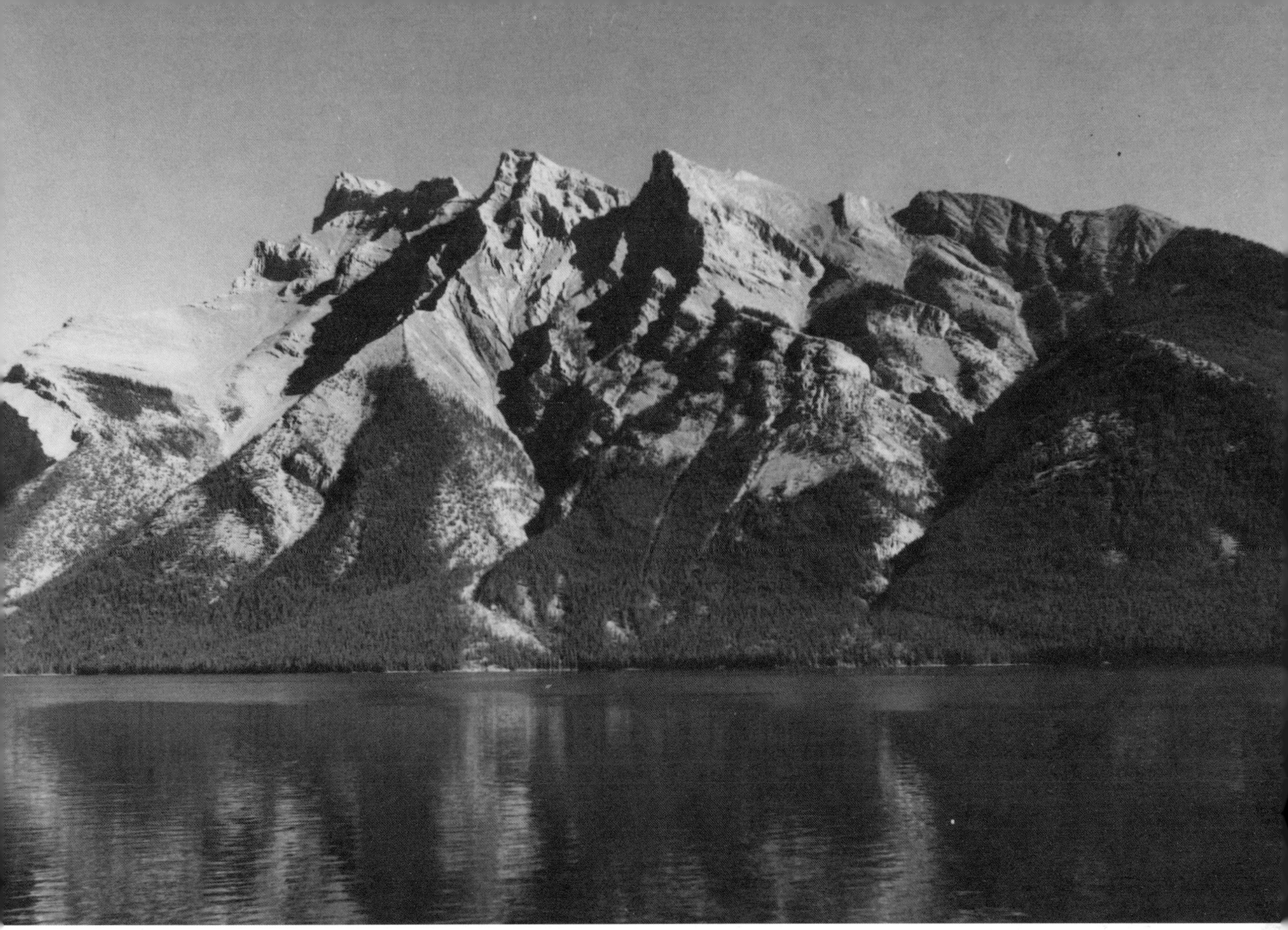

built the log "Beach House" chalet and began renting out boats, which before long were joined by several small steam-powered tour launches and numerous fishermen angling the waters for their giant lake trout. A small cottage subdivision was laid out by Stewart in 1894 and was expanded in 1909 with the expectation that wealthy Calgarians would acquire lots in the summer village. However, beginning in 1895, the lake had begun to undergo a series of modifications that would interrupt these plans and make the next half-century in its story a controversial one. The first was the construction of a control dam on the small creek connecting the lake with the Cascade River flooding the tree-covered estuary at its western end, followed by the 1912 erection of a small concrete dam by Calgary Power after it convinced the Dominion government of the need for storage capacity to provide winter flow for their new hydro-electric dams at Horseshoe and Kananaskis Falls in the Bow River.

By the 1920s Calgary Power was pressing the government to allow further damming of the lake, incorporating power generating facilities to supply Alberta's burgeoning electrical needs, an action that was resisted by Commissioner Harkin and the Parks Branch and a new public conservation lobby, the Canadian National Parks Association, who saw in the proposal threats to the inviolability of park lands.[25] Continuing throughout the decade, this controversy played an important part in the 1930 passage of the National Parks Act, guaranteeing the sanctity of national parks from major industrial development. Unfortunately, in the face of wartime conditions, this principle was violated under the auspices of the War Measures Act in 1942 when Calgary Power received permission to build a twenty-one-metre-high earth-fill dam and associated generating facilities extending through Two Jack Lake and down a penstock to a power-house at Anthracite.[26]

4.15A OBLIQUE AIR PHOTOGRAPH OF THE CASCADE VALLEY AT STONEY CREEK, JUNE 1931 (NATIONAL AIR PHOTOGRAPH LIBRARY A 3412-38)

4.15B CASCADE VALLEY AT STONEY CREEK, VIEW FROM HELICOPTER, JUNE 2003 (CW 2003-06C-18)

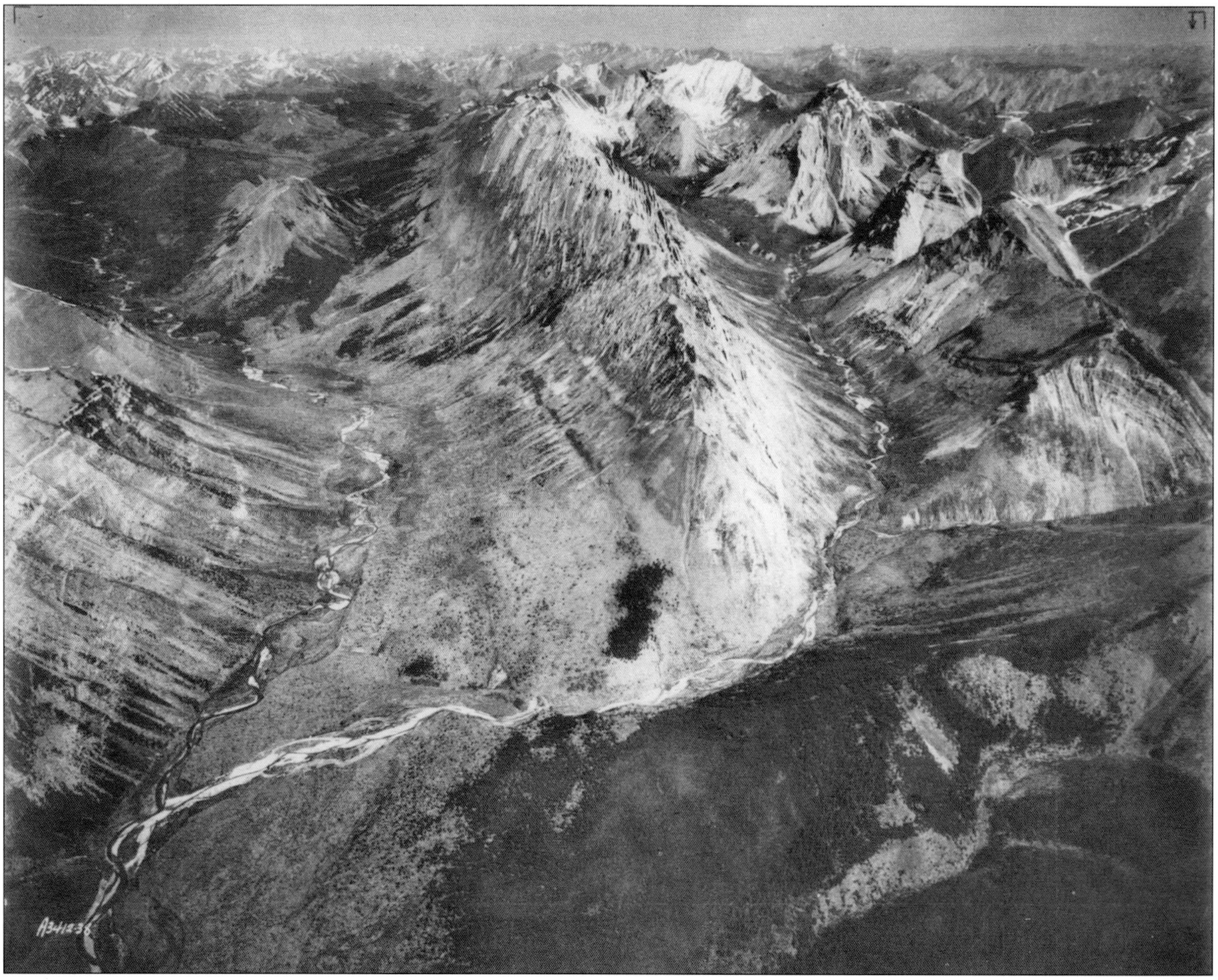

The west-facing grasslands of the Palliser Range, only ten kilometres north of Lake Minnewanka, are one of the ecological "hotspots" of Banff National Park. Four major forest fires swept through this area in the park's first century. In June 1889 strong southwest winds pushed a large fire in the Bow Valley over Elk Lake Pass, burning out the middle Cascade Valley and Stoney Creek (centre right). Then in 1914 a fire swept across the area in the centre of the photograph, burning the brûlé left from

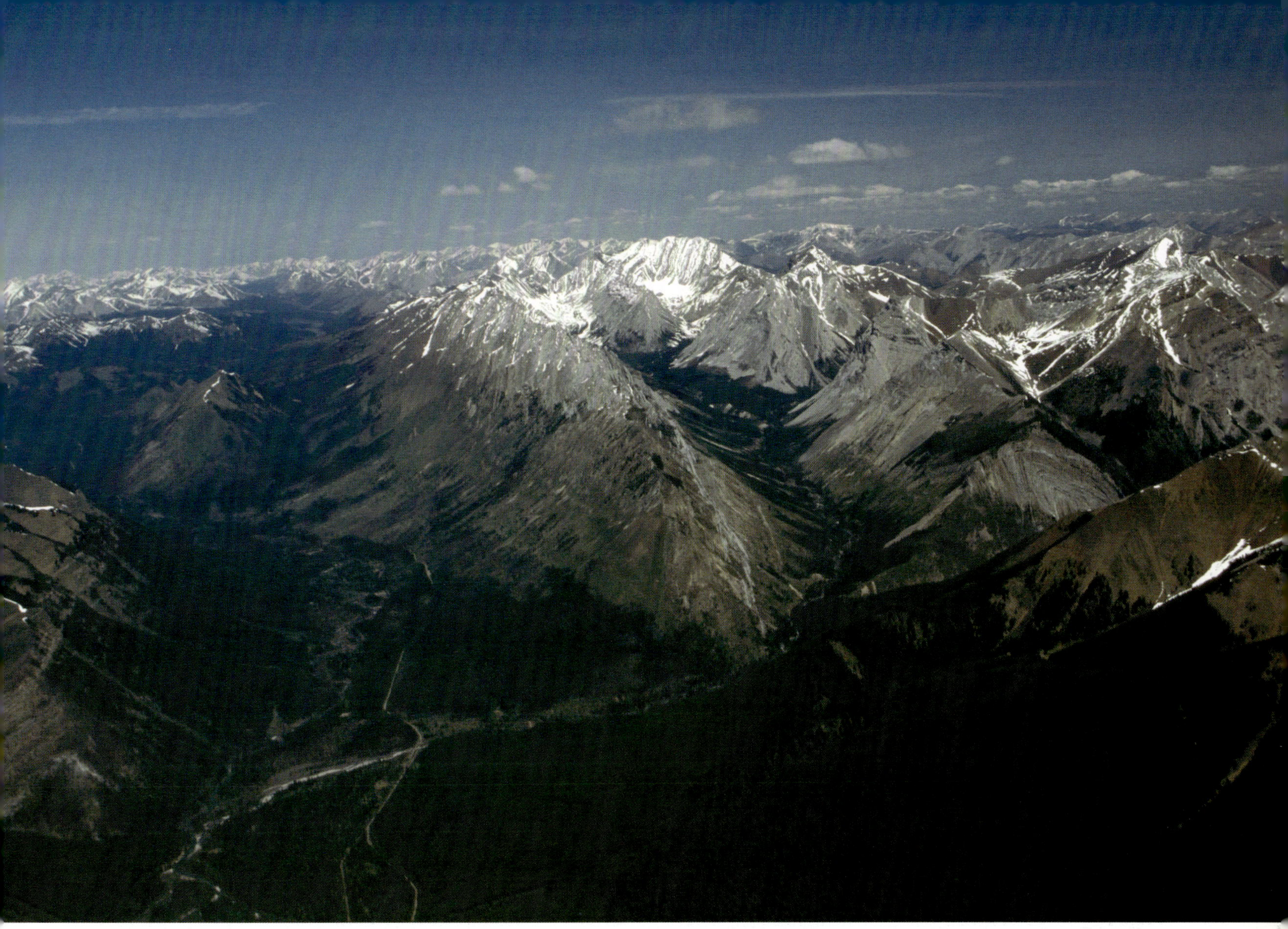

the first fire. Further up the valley, two human-caused fires, one in August 1929 and another massive blaze in August 1936, removed a large area of old forest in the upper Cascade Valley (upper left of photographs). All this burning created high-quality habitat for bighorn sheep, grizzly bears, elk, and wolves, and over the years many researchers used the narrow fire road (visible in the lower left of the 2003 photograph) to access the valley by vehicle to study wildlife.[27]

The valley was also the focal point for one of Banff's major environmental controversies. In 1969 the federal government released provisional master plans for the mountain parks that featured several new scenic roads. The proposed Cascade-Pipestone Loop Road would leave the Trans-Canada Highway on the Minnewanka Road, proceed northwards along the Cascade Fire Road, and eventually rejoin the main highway at Lake Louise via the remote Red Deer and Pipestone valleys.[28] Opposition to increased road development in Banff's backcountry areas was intense, and after a series of public hearings in 1971, then Minister of Indian and Northern Affairs Jean Chrétien made decisions on Banff National Park zoning and development that, in essence, have guided Parks Canada ever since.[29]

The scenic road up the Cascade Valley was never built. The 1988 Banff National Park Management Plan required that all park fire roads be closed to vehicular traffic.[30] By 1992 park staff had removed all automobile bridges along the road, and by the time of the 2003 photograph the road had reverted to a horse and hiking trail. Park wardens set several prescribed burns on the west-facing slopes of the Palliser Range between 1985 and 2003, but most were only low-intensity fires that killed few trees. Winter snow avalanches, sweeping off the steep spine of the Palliser Range (centre), maintain most of the remaining grassland and shrubland areas.

4.16A TALLYHO IN THE BUFFALO PADDOCK, CA. 1910 (BYRON HARMON, WHYTE NA 71-3711)

4.16B TRANS-CANADA HIGHWAY AND ELK, APRIL 2003 (CW 2004-04F-01)

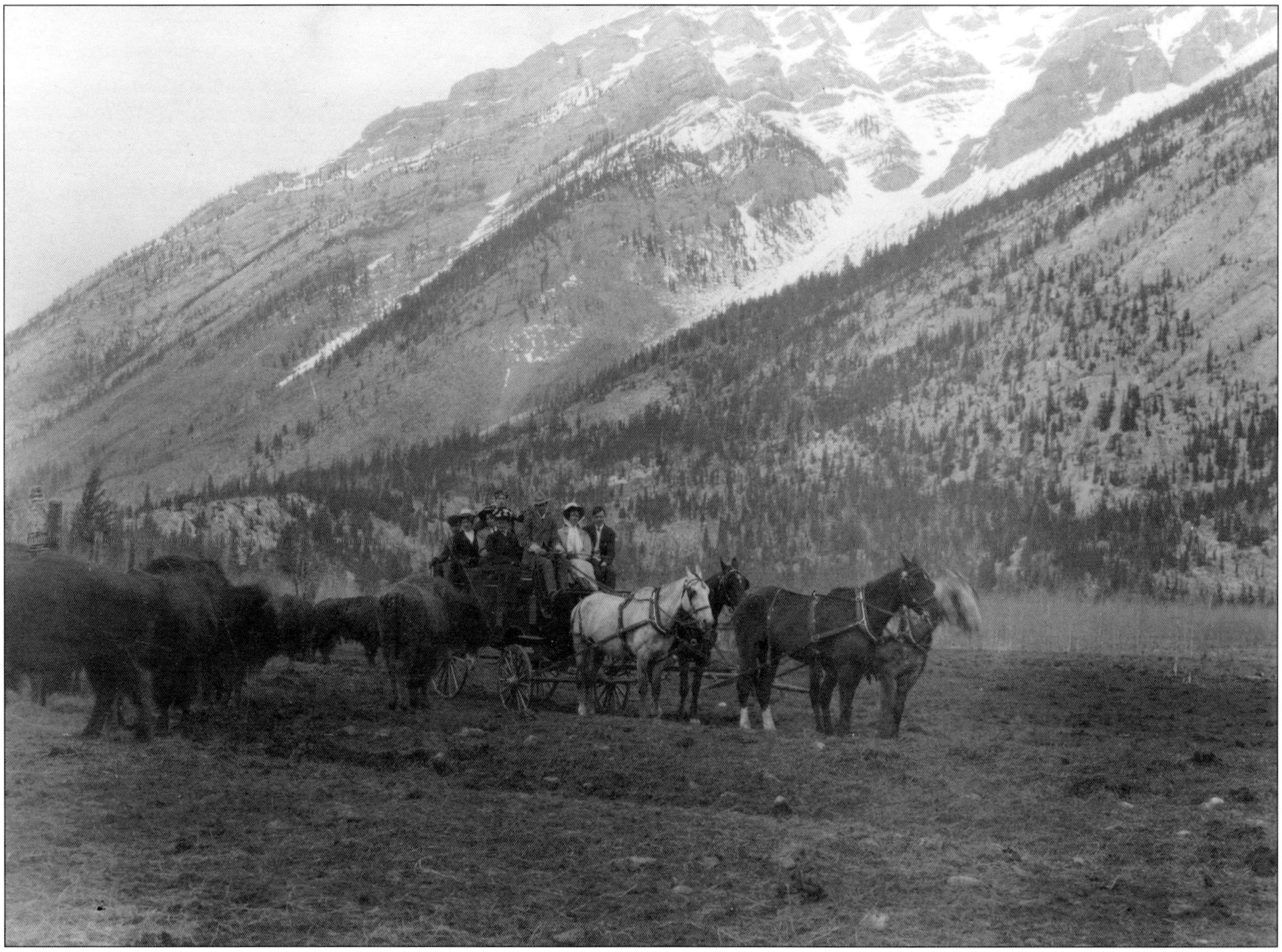

While it was the therapeutic wonders of hot springs, sublime mountain scenery, and the opportunity to engage in mountain recreation that first drew tourists to Banff, in the years around the turn of the century, park officials began to realize that visitors also enjoyed seeing wildlife in their native habitat. This would lead to a policy of controlling predators so that "good" animals, such as elk, deer, and moose, would thrive and provide the perfect foreground to a beautiful mountain scene, but it also led to some of the first steps in Canadian wildlife preservation. The first move in this direction occurred in 1897 when Toronto lawyer T. G. Blackstock purchased three bison from a remnant Texas herd and donated them for display at Banff. Since plains bison, or buffalo, were nearing extinction, this action

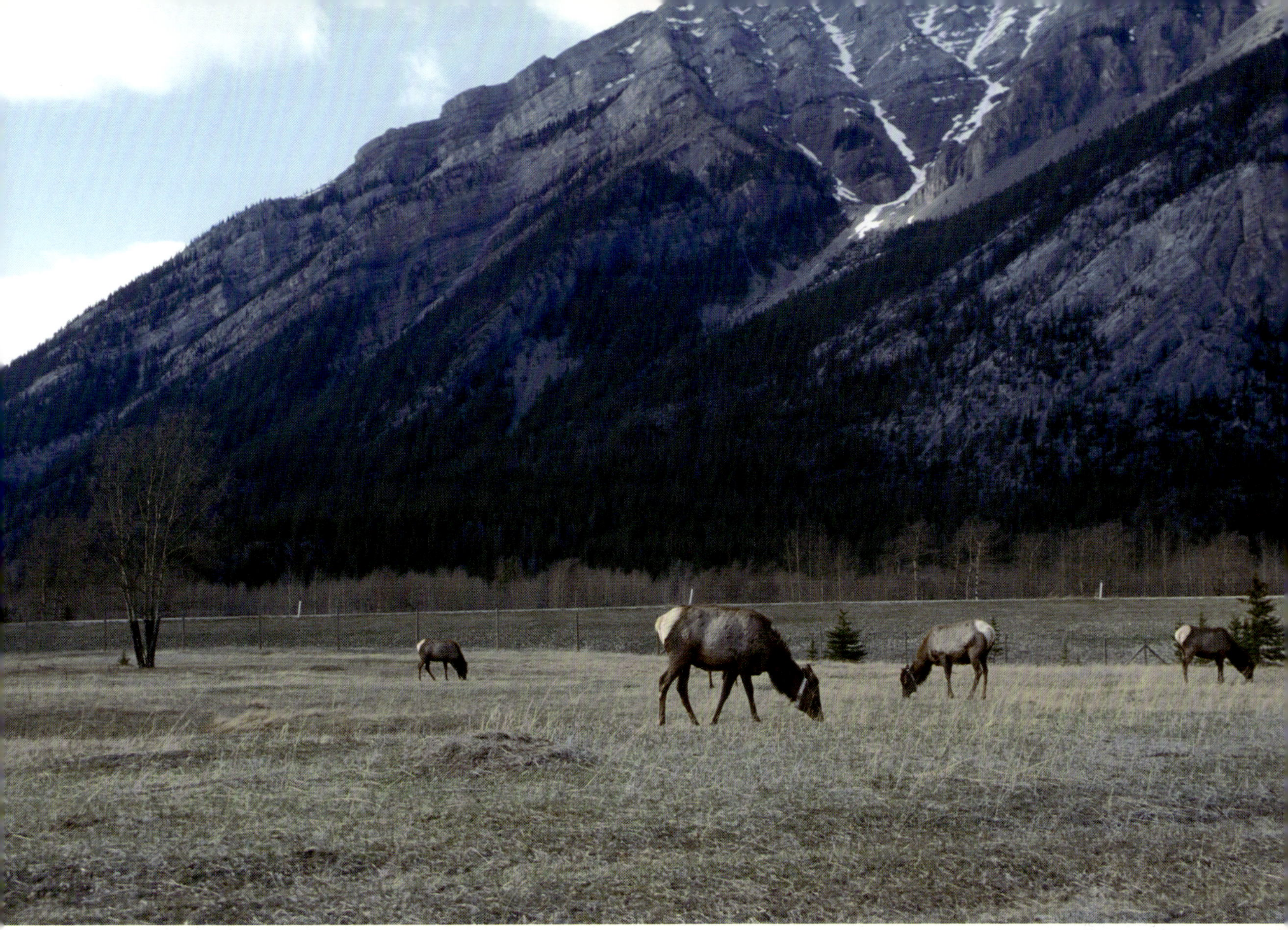

focused considerable public attention on the herd, and in 1899 it was bolstered by a donation of thirteen head by Donald Smith (Lord Strathcona) from his herd at Silver Heights, near Winnipeg. Seeing both the necessity of housing the original three head and an opportunity to promote the restoration of park animal populations decimated during the railroad construction period, Superintendent Howard Douglas convinced his superiors to build an animal enclosure in the vicinity of Banff's Indian Grounds in 1898. The 'Buffalo Paddock' quickly became such a popular tourist attraction that Douglas added other native species such as mountain goats, elk, and deer as well as exotics including angora goats.[31]

In time, it became apparent that an enclosure was not the proper place in a park to observe wildlife, and eventually it was restricted to bison. Banff kept a display of bison for a century, including a small herd of wood bison after 1975, and the paddock remained a popular sightseeing destination for bus tours and individuals driving their own vehicles. In the 1990s parks wildlife researchers recognized that increasing development that had spread across the breadth of the Bow Valley near Banff townsite had partially blocked natural movement routes for wide-ranging and wary carnivores such as cougars, wolves, and grizzly bears. As a result, some five hundred human-habituated elk had learned to escape predators by staying in and near the town. In 1997 Parks Canada spent several million dollars to restore the Cascade Wildlife Corridor by removing the paddock and other nearby facilities, such as the community horse corrals and the Banff Army Cadet Camp. Predator use of the area began to increase and the number of elk decreased. In the final analysis, the paddock area has been a laboratory for wildlife conservation in Banff, evolving from simply providing paddocks for threatened species to attempting to restore a fully functioning ecosystem that incorporates the long-term roles of predator and prey.[32]

4.17A HOODOOS NEAR BANFF, CA. 1890 (GEORGE PARIS, WHYTE NG 5-22)

4.17B HOODOOS, BANFF NATIONAL PARK, 1981 (BRUNO ENGLER, CW-BE-FM-1981-18)

4.17C HOODOOS, BANFF NATIONAL PARK, JULY 1996 (CW 1996-07H-30)

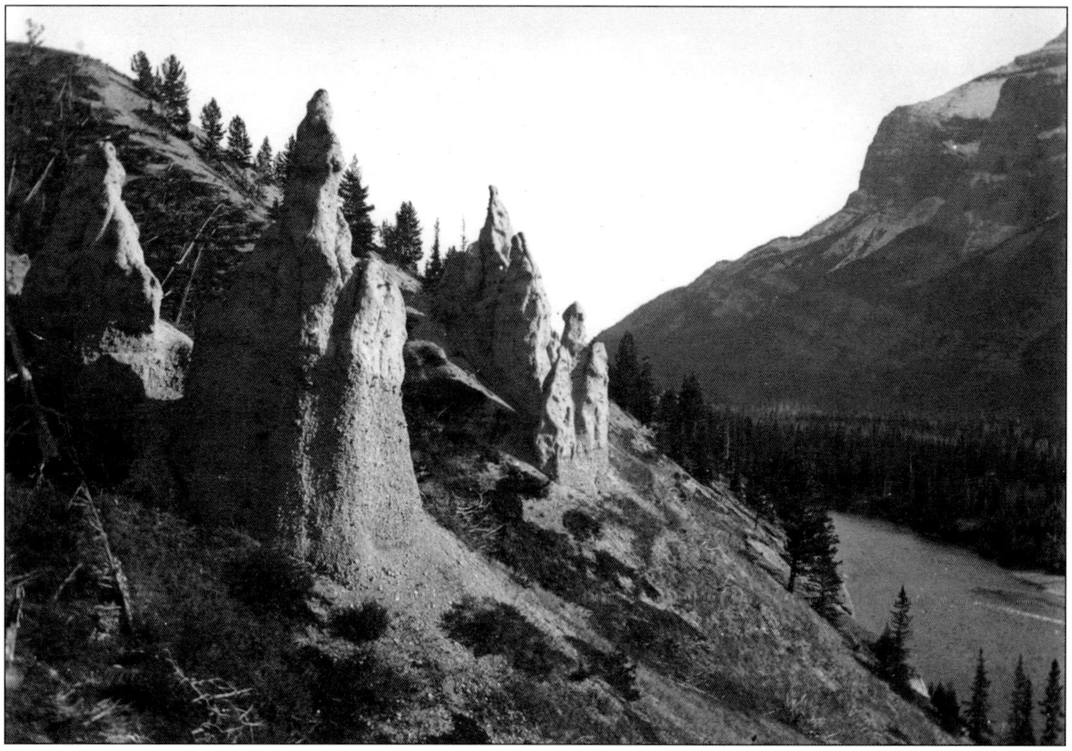

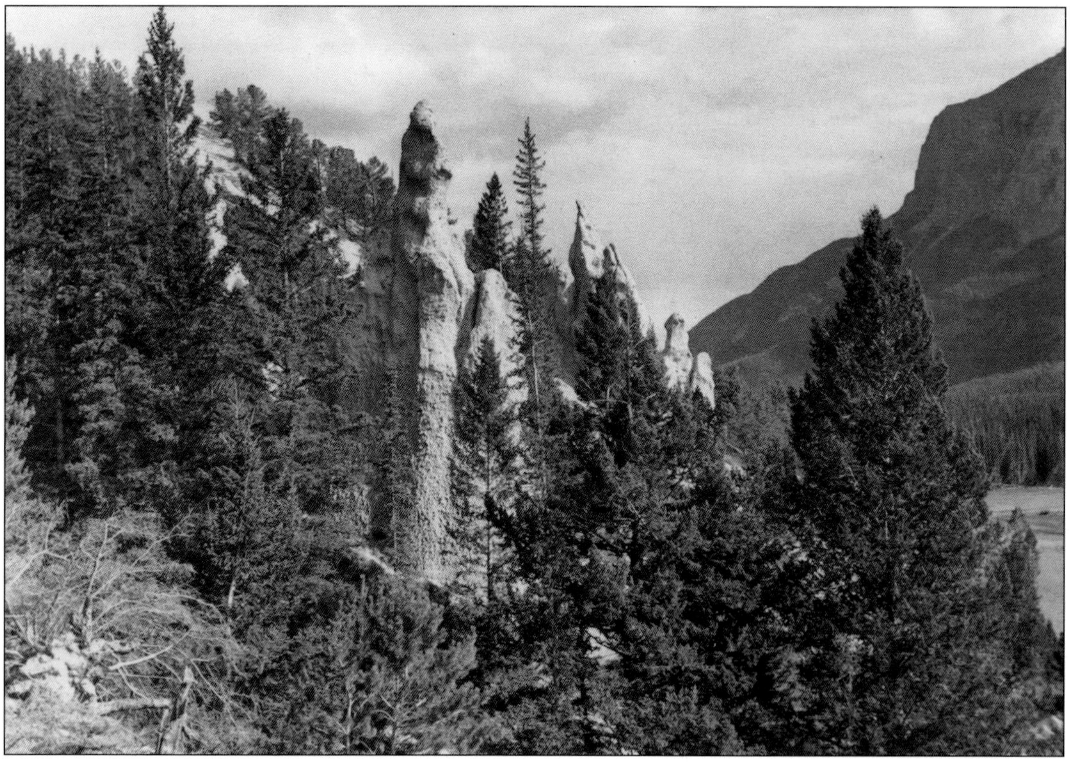

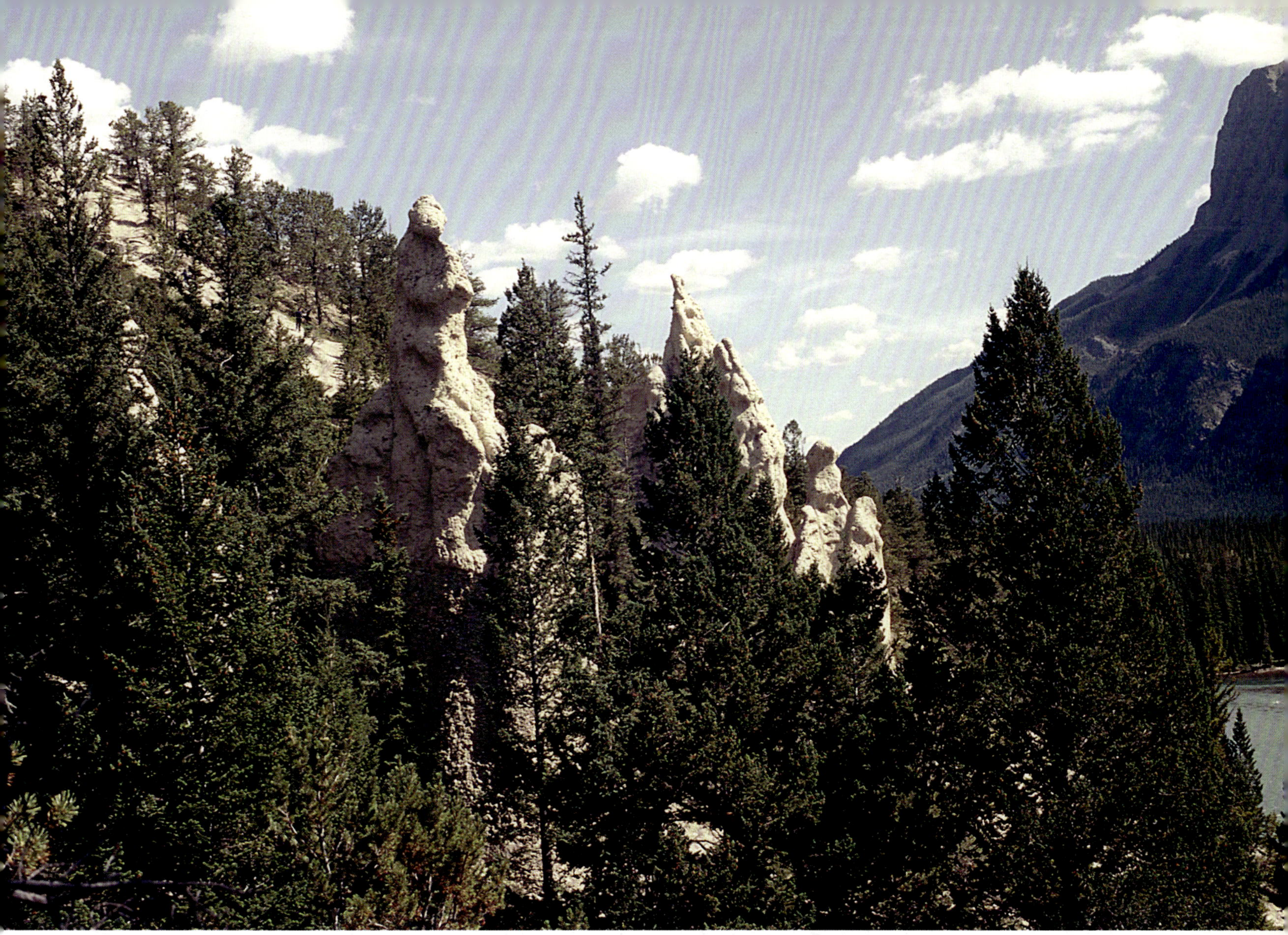

Rising out of the north bank of the Bow River less than two kilometres from Banff townsite, the "hoodoos" were the object of many walks by early Banff tourists seeking to examine the interesting formations and to gain a view of the Bow River valley. In 1927 the nearby slopes of Tunnel Mountain were chosen as the new site for a campground to replace the Rundle Campground at the confluence of the Spray and Bow rivers, bringing many more sightseers to the area. These unique landforms, found at several locations in the Rockies, are carved by water from erosion-resistant materials. Geologists originally thought hoodoos were composed of a unique type of glacial till cemented with lime, but it is now believed they were deposited by debris flows when lakes dammed up behind retreated glaciers broke free and flooded down mountain valleys.[33]

The escarpments near the hoodoos are some of the warmest and driest in Banff National Park, and consequently the area burned frequently prior to 1890. Fires dated to approximately 1845, 1851, 1860, 1867, and 1876 were primarily low-intensity blazes that only scorched the lower branches of some trees or missed them entirely. However, one fire, possibly in 1867, was severe enough to kill many trees immediately above the hoodoos. The area has only burned once since the park's establishment, in 1897 when an abandoned campfire near the railway depot swept eastward over the ridge to the north. Today a dense conifer forest of Douglas fir, limber pine, white spruce, and lodgepole pine covers the slopes.[34]

4.18A BANFF TOWNSITE FROM TUNNEL MOUNTAIN, CA. 1889 (BOORNE AND MAY, WHYTE NA 66-624)

4.18B BANFF AT HEIGHT OF FLOOD, JUNE 1923 (BYRON HARMON, WHYTE NA 66-1280)

4.18C TOWN OF BANFF AND VERMILION LAKES WETLANDS, MAY 2004 (CW 2004-05A-14)

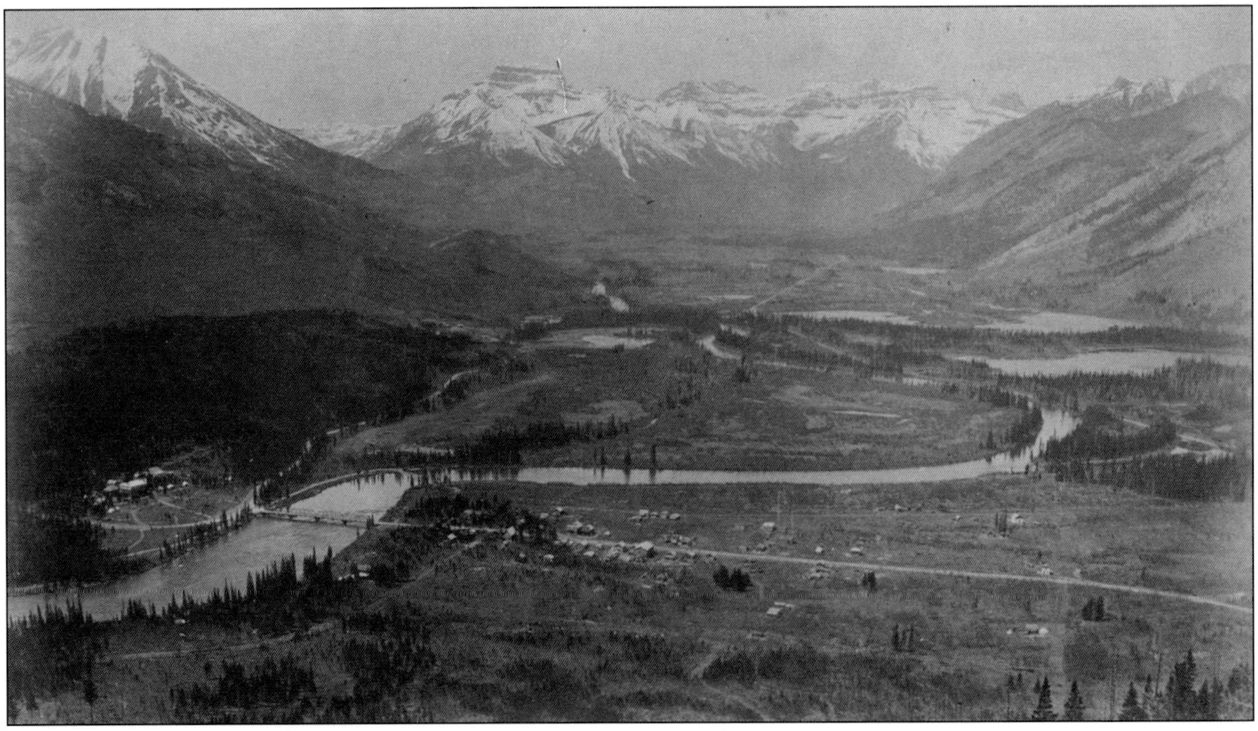

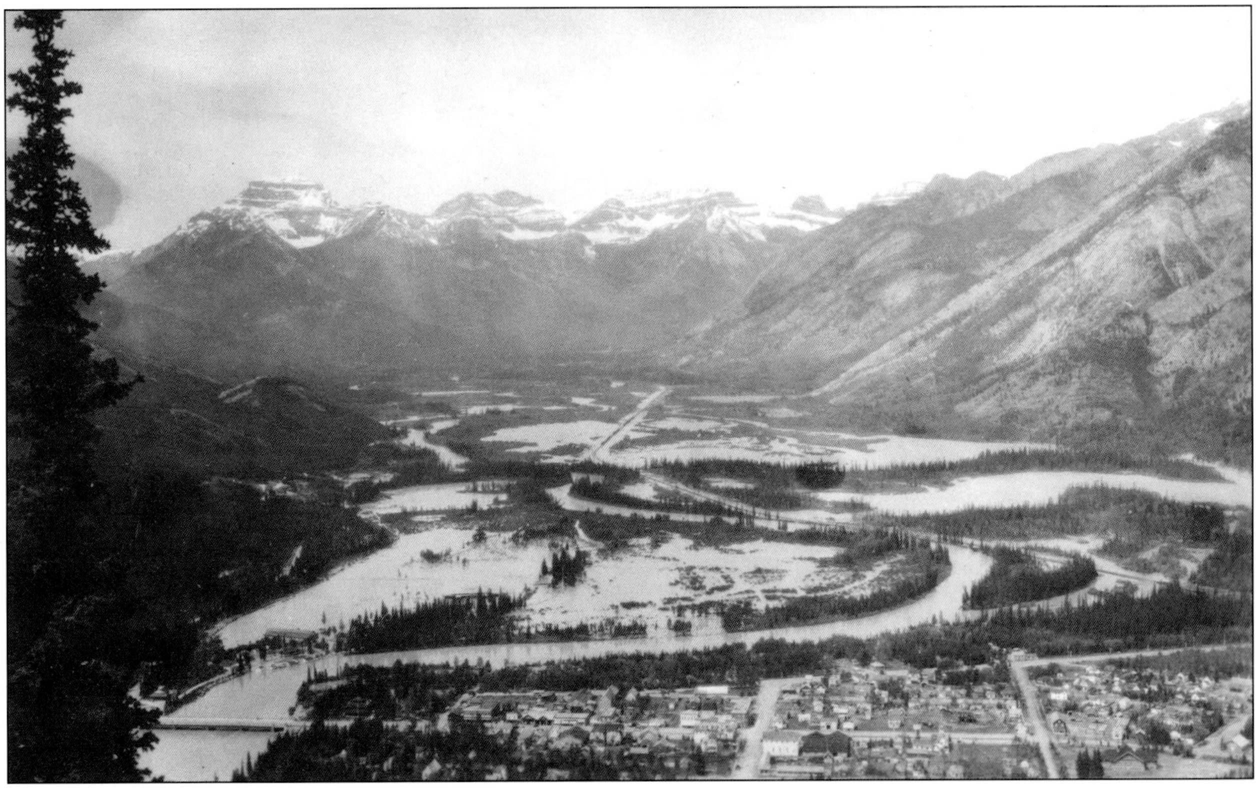

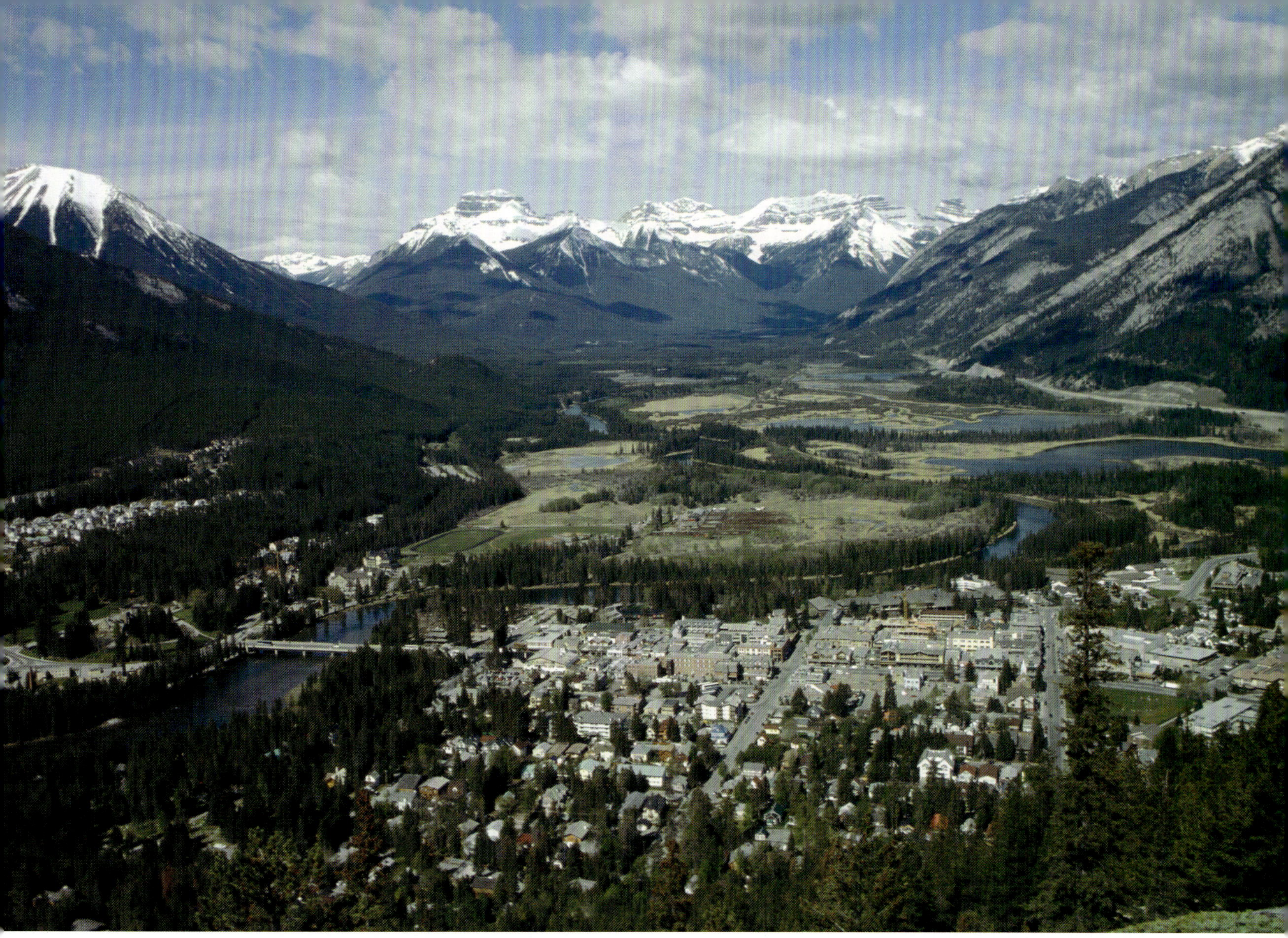

One of the best locations for gaining an appreciation for the ecological and human history of Banff is from the slopes of Tunnel Mountain, a favoured viewpoint for generations of photographers. In Boorne and May's image from the 1880s, the fledgling village is seen huddled along the recently created Banff Avenue, connecting the new townsite with "Old Banff" at Siding 29. The first wave of development is evident in the complex of buildings forming "The Sanitarium," just completed by Dr. R. G. Brett on the south side of the Bow and connected to the main village by the government's new steel bridge, and mere trails that would soon become Beaver, Muskrat, Buffalo, and Bear streets are faintly visible. Also apparent is the low-lying nature of the landscape as Tunnel Mountain in conjunction with alluvial fans created by the Cascade River and Forty Mile Creek have partially blocked the Bow River to create a unique set of wetlands, one of the largest on the southeastern slopes of the Rocky Mountains. Finally, evidence of recent forest fires likely associated with the railroad is everywhere, with aspen, willow and seedling lodgepole pine just beginning to regenerate in the valley bottom.

The early fire regime in the Bow Valley likely played a role in the tendency for the Vermilion Lake wetlands to flood in the early part of the twentieth century, as the lack of forest cover upstream encouraged rapid runoff during the spring snow melt. In Byron Harmon's photograph taken during the spring 1923 flood, the largest on record, we see the now fully developed Banff townsite virtually marooned with the overflowing of the river. By this time, re-vegetation of both the valley bottom and the surrounding slopes is also becoming more apparent. This tendency would continue over the next eighty years so that, by the time the modern view was taken, forest cover had so modified the spring-melt cycle that some Banff development, visible in the lower left of the photograph, had been allowed to spread across the floodplain area.[35]

4.19A MOUNT RUNDLE AND ECHO CREEK, CA. 1918 (BYRON HARMON, WHYTE NA 71-6244)

4.19B FORTY MILE CREEK, 1981 (BRUNO ENGLER, CW-BE-FM-1981-35)

4.19C FORTY MILE CREEK, MAY 1996 (CW 1996-05A-29)

4.19D FORTY MILE CREEK, SEPTEMBER 2005 (CW 2005-09B-05)

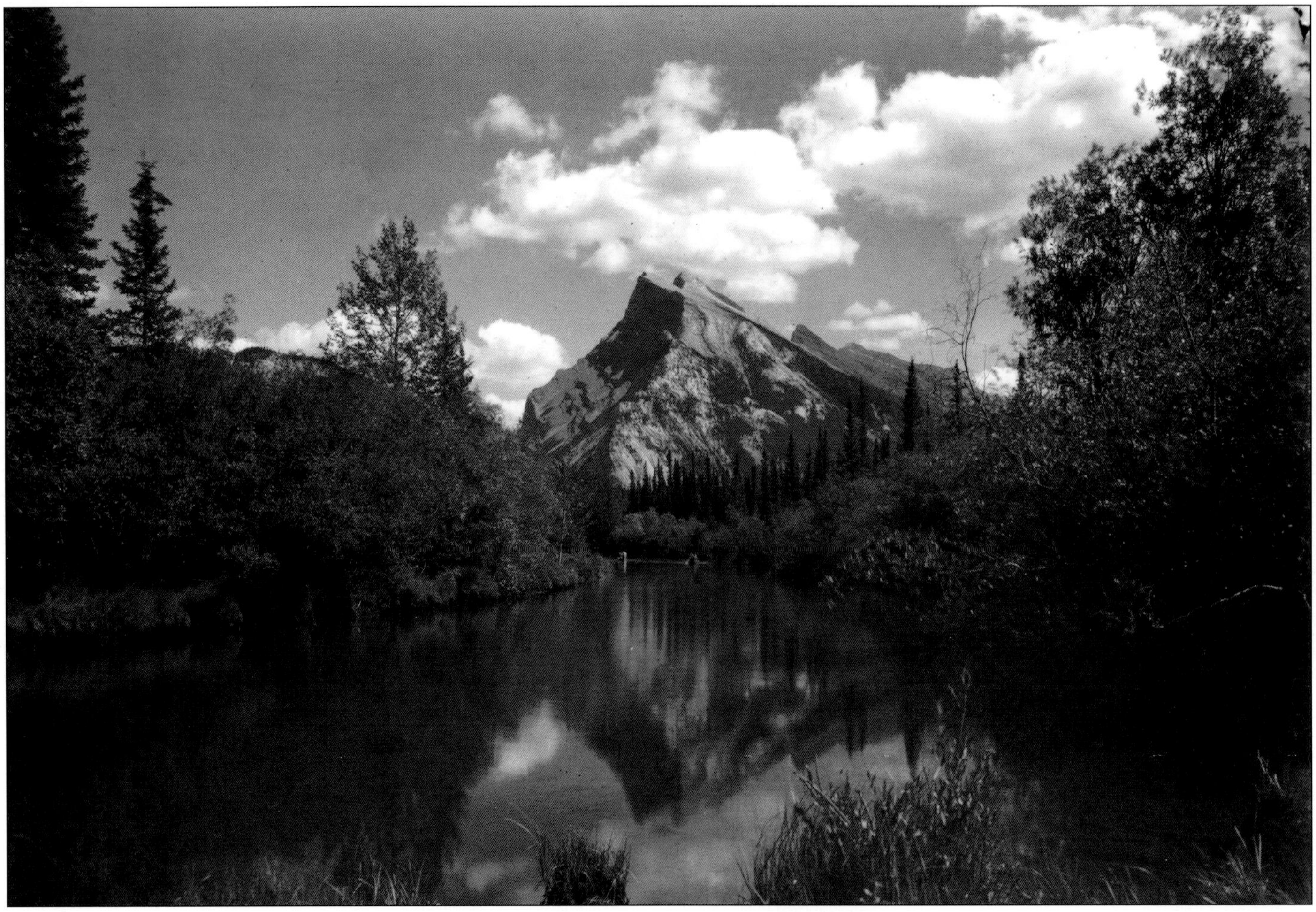

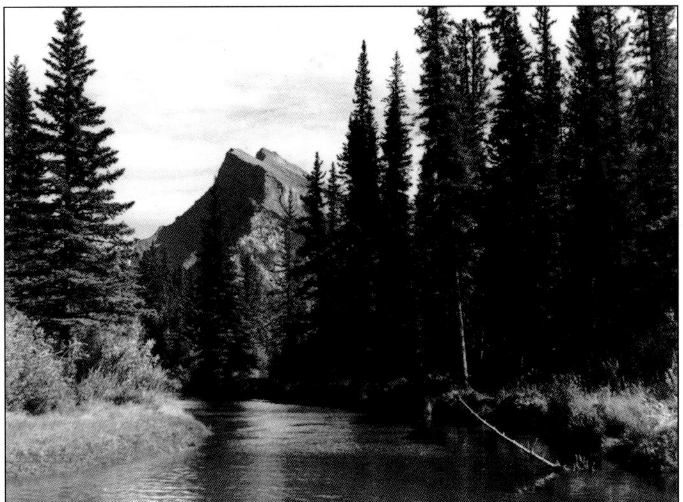

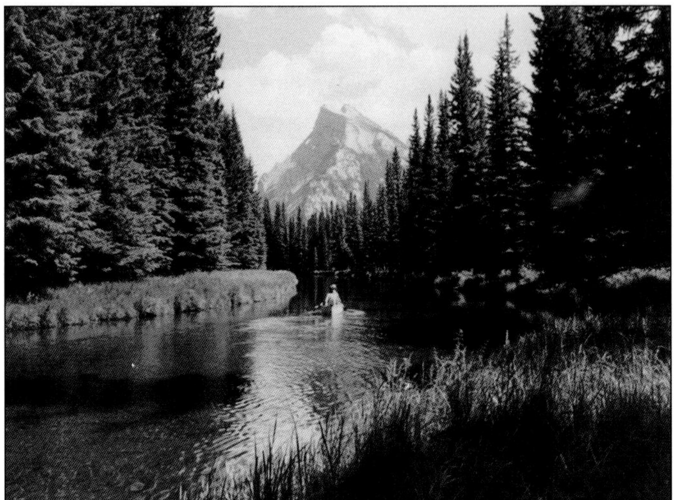

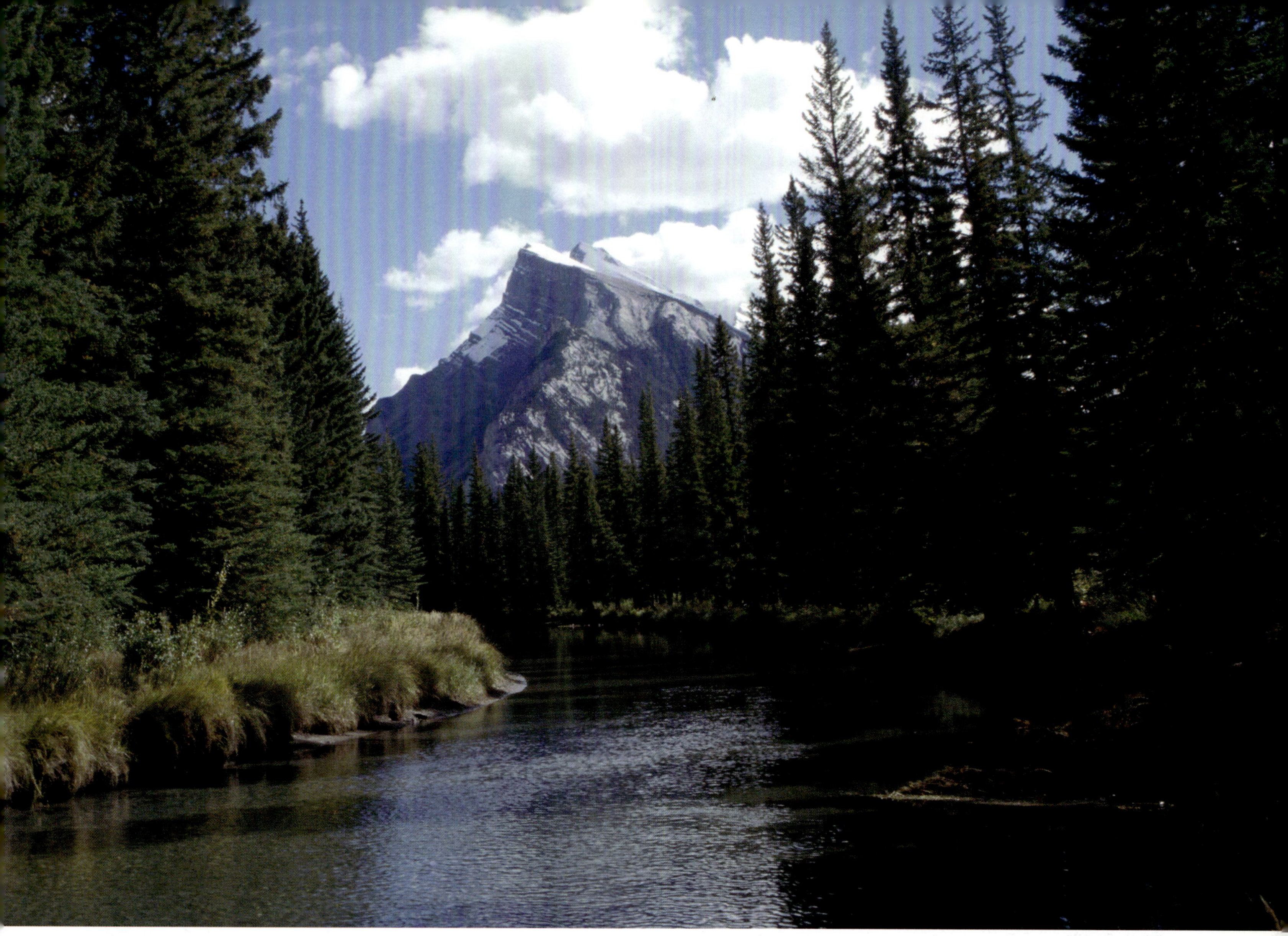

The meandering stretch of Forty Mile Creek joining Vermilion Lakes to the Bow River was known as "Echo Creek," due to the sound effects created by a wall of dense willow, balsam poplar, and red-osier dogwood that historically lined the stream. The most recent photograph shows that the tall streamside shrubs have disappeared in modern times, a result of several ecological changes. First of all, an abundance of beaver appearing in the creek cut down the shrubs for food and lodge building. With the decline in shrub abundance, beaver numbers declined in the 1970s. But by that time a high number of elk avoiding predators by staying near the Banff townsite browsed off young shrub sprouts, preventing the usual cycle of tall shrub regeneration. Furthering these impacts was the ongoing elimination of fire, resulting in the growth of tall white spruce that further suppressed shrub growth.[36] After 1994 Parks Canada began restoring more natural predator-prey and vegetation browsing patterns by relocating developments on the periphery of the town to open wildlife movement corridors for carnivores and by moving human-habituated elk away from the town. While such actions may eventually encourage a return to historic vegetation and wildlife species abundance on the margins of Echo Creek, it is unlikely they will be fully restored without the influence of fire.[37]

4.20A DEMOCRAT AT THE END OF SUNDANCE CANYON ROAD, 1902 (J. SMITH, GLENBOW NA 4654-2)

4.20B SUNDANCE CANYON TRAIL, MAY 2003 (CW 2003-051-15)

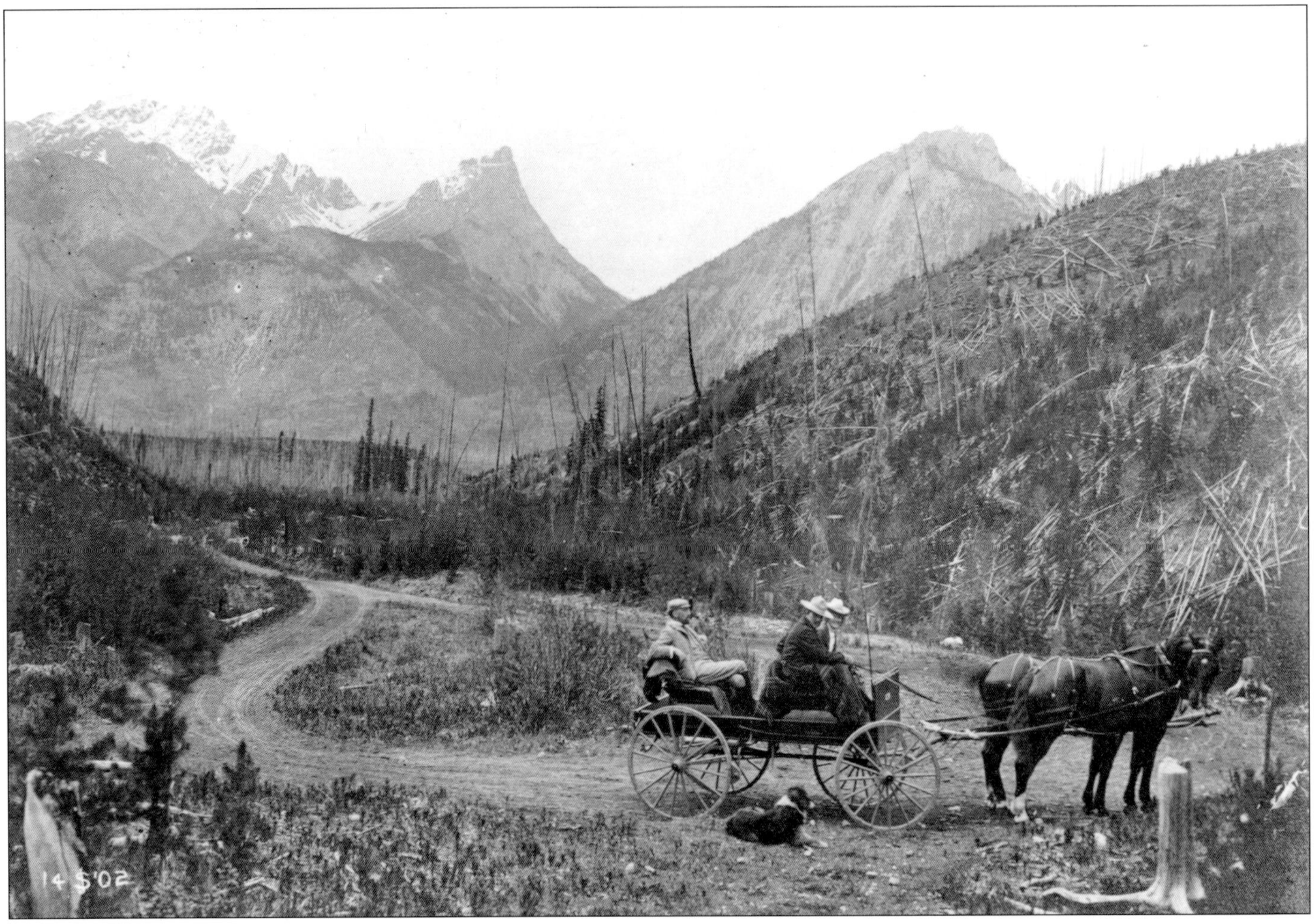

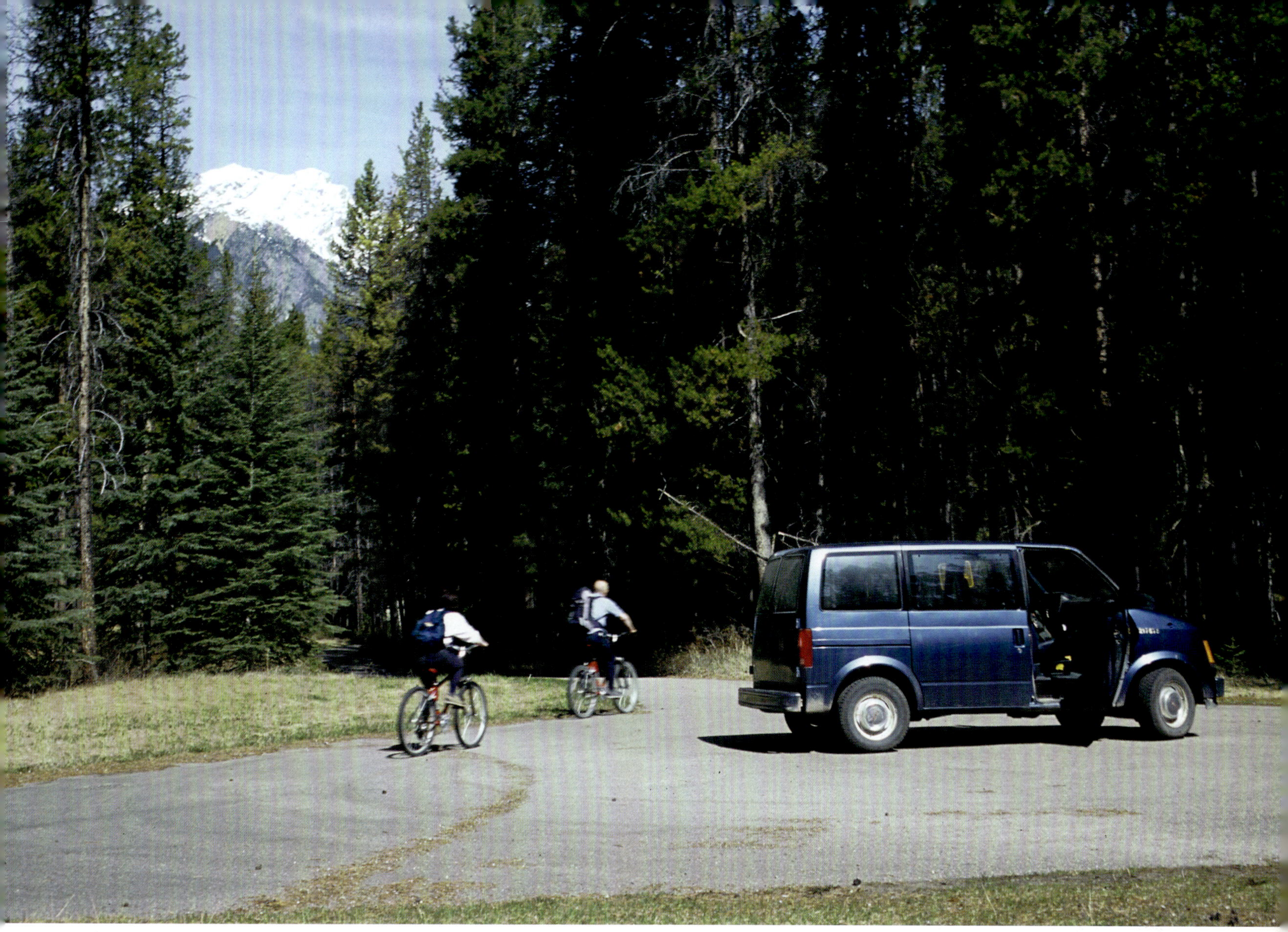

The Dominion government's early focus on opening up new trails and drives for tourist use resulted in an extension of the Cave and Basin road westward into Sundance Canyon. This drive was, for obvious reasons, not among the most popular, as the route wound through an open, young forest burned most recently about 1883 and probably every fifty to one hundred years previously. Fires in steep, constricted areas such as this usually burned extremely hot, killing almost all the trees, and within a decade or two most of the dead hulks fell to the ground and created mazes of logs visible in the 1902 view. However, such conflagrations also created the conditions for forest generation to begin anew, in particular the appearance of lodgepole pine. Already by 1902 seedling lodgepole pine and a few Douglas fir and white spruce have grown from two to five metres in height in the approximately twenty years since the valley burned.

Due to government policy of eliminating fire which prevailed until the 1980s, the recent view shows that the forest has grown undisturbed, creating a dense, mature canopy with almost all the old dead logs having rotted away. While current policy fosters prescribed burns to re-establish a more natural fire and vegetation regime, and to supply habitat for wildlife, forests such as this one in Sundance Canyon cannot be burned easily due to the close proximity to the Town of Banff. When it is determined that they have reached a dangerous state, mechanical thinning is often used near townsites to reduce the risk of high intensity wildfires.

4.21A IVAND NELSON, CHAMPION SKI JUMPER, 1921 (BYRON HARMON, WHYTE NA 71-3967)

4.21B MAIN POWERLINE EAST OF BANFF TOWNSITE, FEBRUARY 2004 (CW 2004-02A-12)

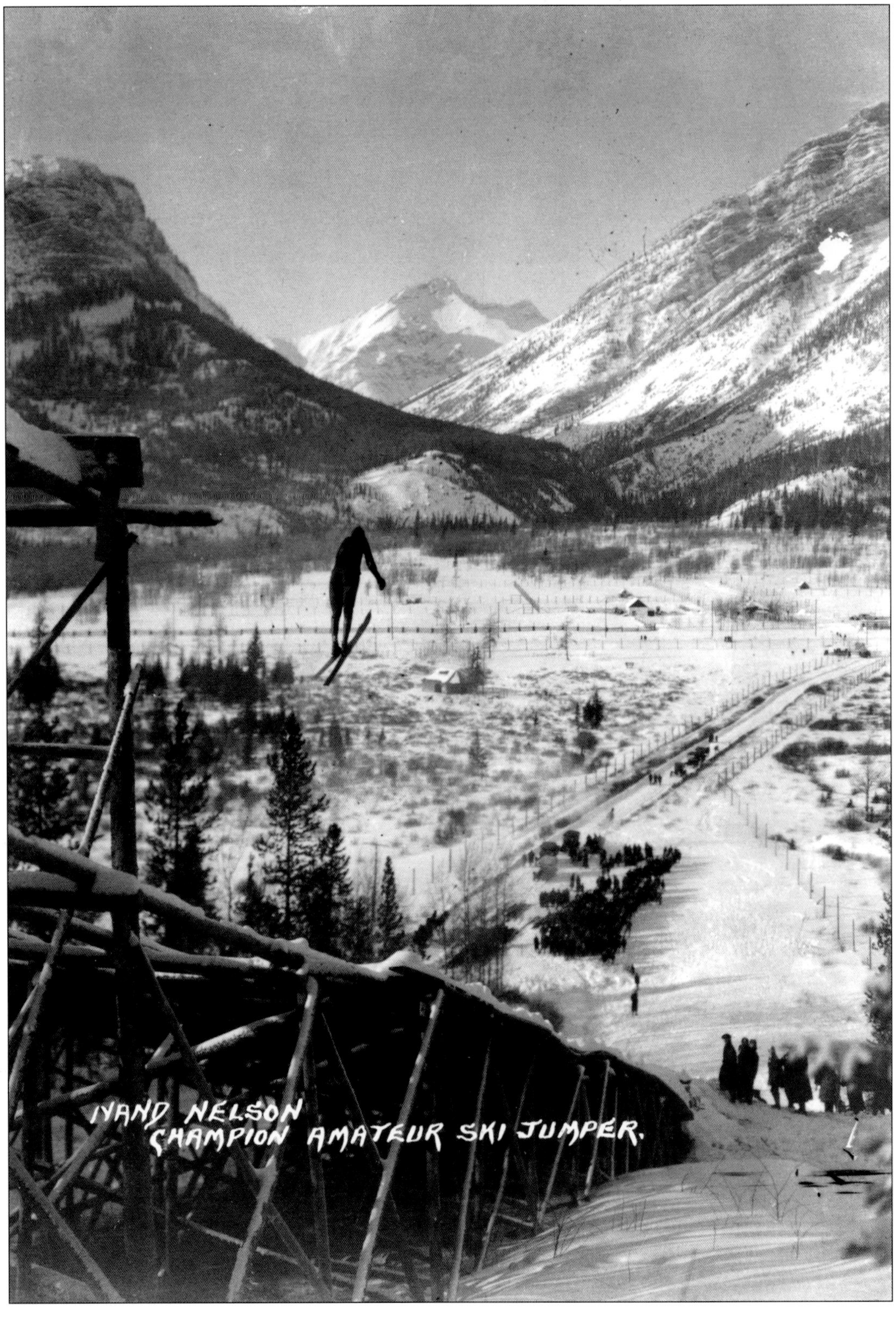

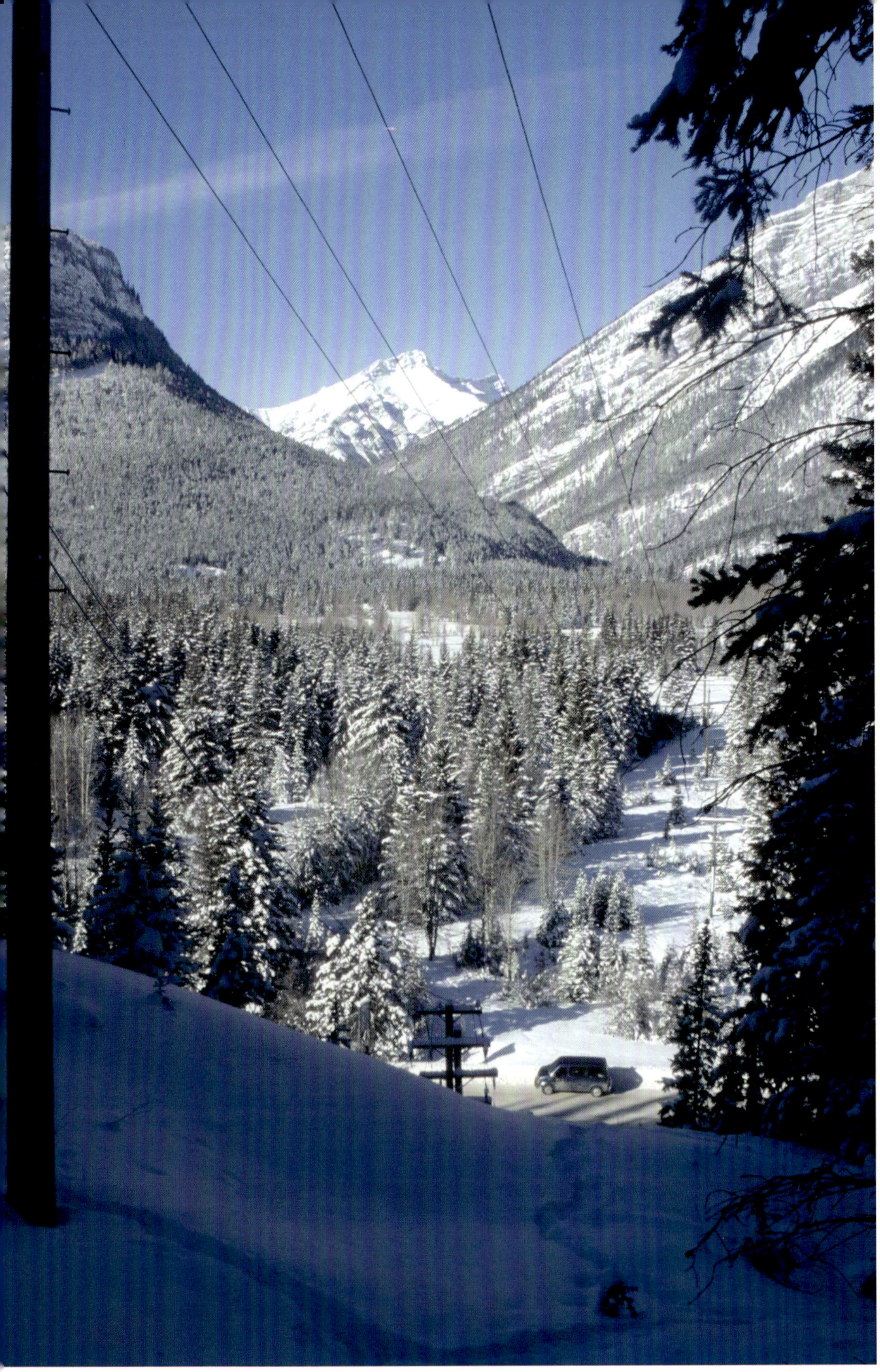

For the first thirty years of the tourism business in the Canadian Rockies, the season began on the Empire Day weekend in May and ended some four months later with the departure of the Banff Springs Hotel staff at the end of September. Eventually, Banff businessmen realized that with eight months of off-season the delights of winter in the mountains could be used to advantage, and in 1917 they decided to add a winter carnival to the annual curling bonspiel. The cooperation of groups and organizations in town was announced in the local *Crag and Canyon* newspaper in early January: "… the Banff Winter Sports club, the Banff curling club and the Banff citizens have joined hands and united their interests and for two weeks … they will enact the role of hosts to the people of Manitoba, Saskatchewan, Alberta and British Columbia. Skiing, tobogganing, ice-boating, hockey, snowshoeing, speed and fancy skating, trap-shooting, swimming contests in the hot pools, etc., will each and all be staged."[38]

One of the most important offshoots of the Carnival was the support it provided to the budding sport of skiing in Banff. In 1911 Austrian guide Conrad Kain had created a ski club for some of the local lads, including Cyril Paris and Cliff and Peter White, and they had soon built a small ski jump on Buffalo Street. The inaugural Winter Carnival attracted a thousand spectators to the jumping event, spurring the 1919 development of a new, larger hill known as the "Buffalo Paddock Jump" on the side of Tunnel Mountain, built to a standard able to host competitions on a western Canadian circuit featuring professional jumpers.[39] The site, just east of the village on the north-facing slopes overlooking the animal enclosure, easily retained its snow until the February carnival date and was accessible to townsfolk and visitors attracted to the competition. Just such a crowd has gathered in the 1921 shot to watch professional jumper Ivand Nelson headed for a landing on the outrun beside the road originally connecting the new Banff townsite with "Old Banff." As the modern image shows, the jump site later became the route for a power line from the east supplying Banff's electricity.

4.22A ON THE SLOPES OF MT. NORQUAY, CA. 1932 (BYRON HARMON, WHYTE NA 71-3614)

4.22B CASCADE CHAIRLIFT AND SNOWBOARD TERRAIN PARK, MT. NORQUAY, FEBRUARY 2003 (CW 2003-02A-13)

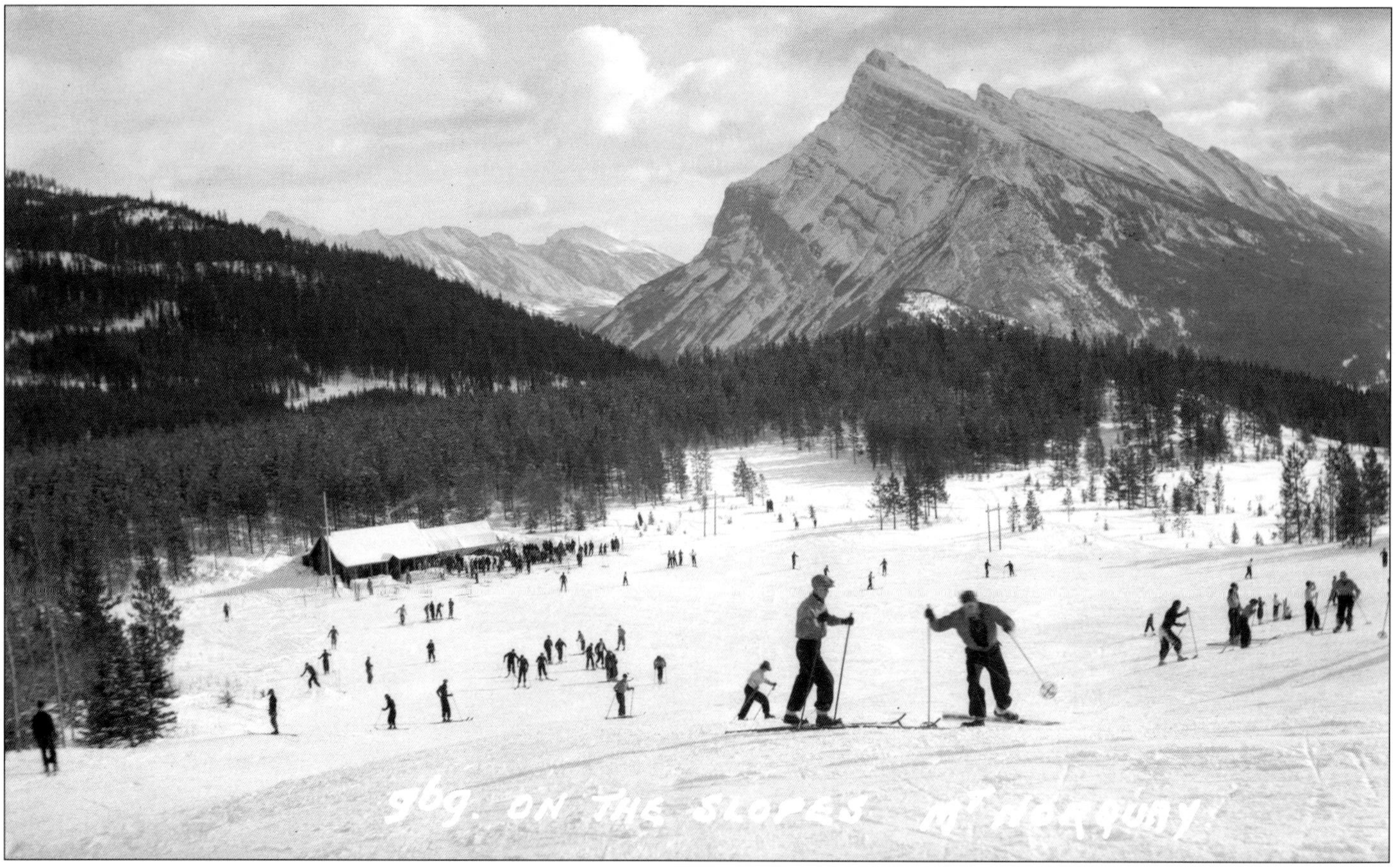

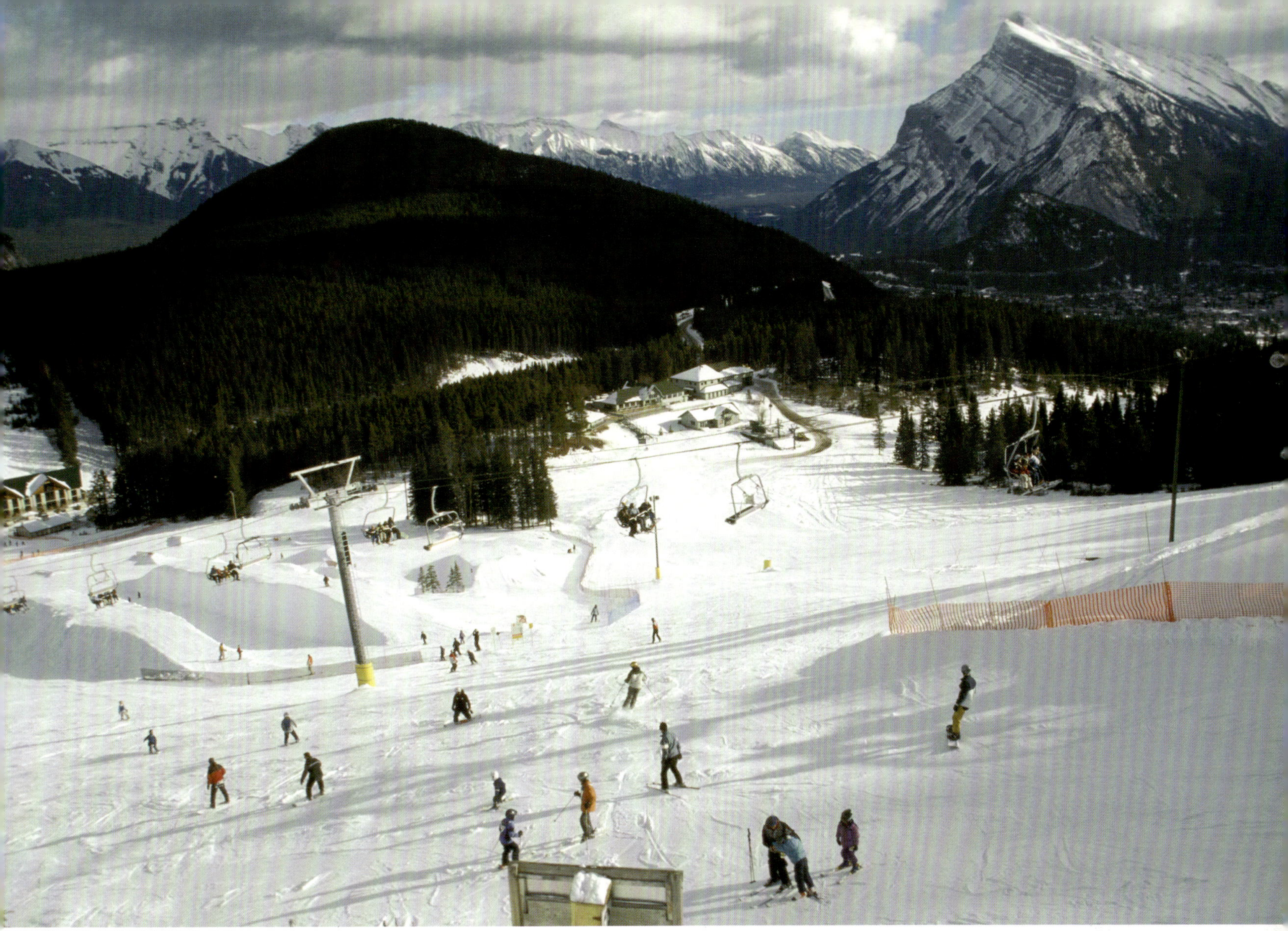

With the focus of skiing in the early 1920s becoming professional jumping, the boys of the Banff Ski Club soon turned their attention to "sliding," or what today we would call downhill skiing. In the late 1920s this led to the clearing of some suitable slopes on Mount Norquay and the building of a rough log ski lodge by club members. The popularity of downhill skiing increased so quickly that by the early 1930s Norquay's slopes were packed on weekends with both local enthusiasts and those visiting from Calgary on special "ski trains." In 1949 the construction of the first chairlift in the Canadian Rockies by Norquay owner George Encil revolutionized the sport and led to years of further development, much of it aimed at gaining first the 1968 and later the 1972 Olympic Winter Games for Banff. These efforts were unsuccessful, at least partially due to the appearance of environmental concerns about such an event being held in a national park, and in 1988 the Games were awarded to Calgary and Canmore instead.[40] Nevertheless, the development of Norquay and other ski areas in Banff National Park provided a major attraction and soon increasing winter visitation encouraged redevelopment and winterization of Banff's hotels and motels. On December 5, 1969, after eight decades of summer-only operations, the Banff Springs Hotel opened for the winter and Banff became an internationally acclaimed four-season tourist resort.[41]

Byron Harmon's 1930s photograph shows the Norquay hill crowded with weekend skiers, many of them undoubtedly trying the sport for the first time, with the original log lodge at the foot of the slope. This burned to the ground in 1938 and was replaced with the lodge visible on the right in the 2003 view, built in 1940 by a consortium of Calgary and Banff businessmen known as the Canadian Rockies Winter Sports Association. The modern lodge (far left) was constructed in 1996 and supports skiers and the new generation of snowboarders using the terrain park on "Banff's ski hill."[42]

4.23A GRAND VIEW HOTEL NEAR BANFF, ALBERTA, 1905 (PHOTOGRAPHER UNKNOWN, GLENBOW NA 2126-15)

4.23B RIMROCK HOTEL, FEBRUARY 2003 (CW-2003-02A-21)

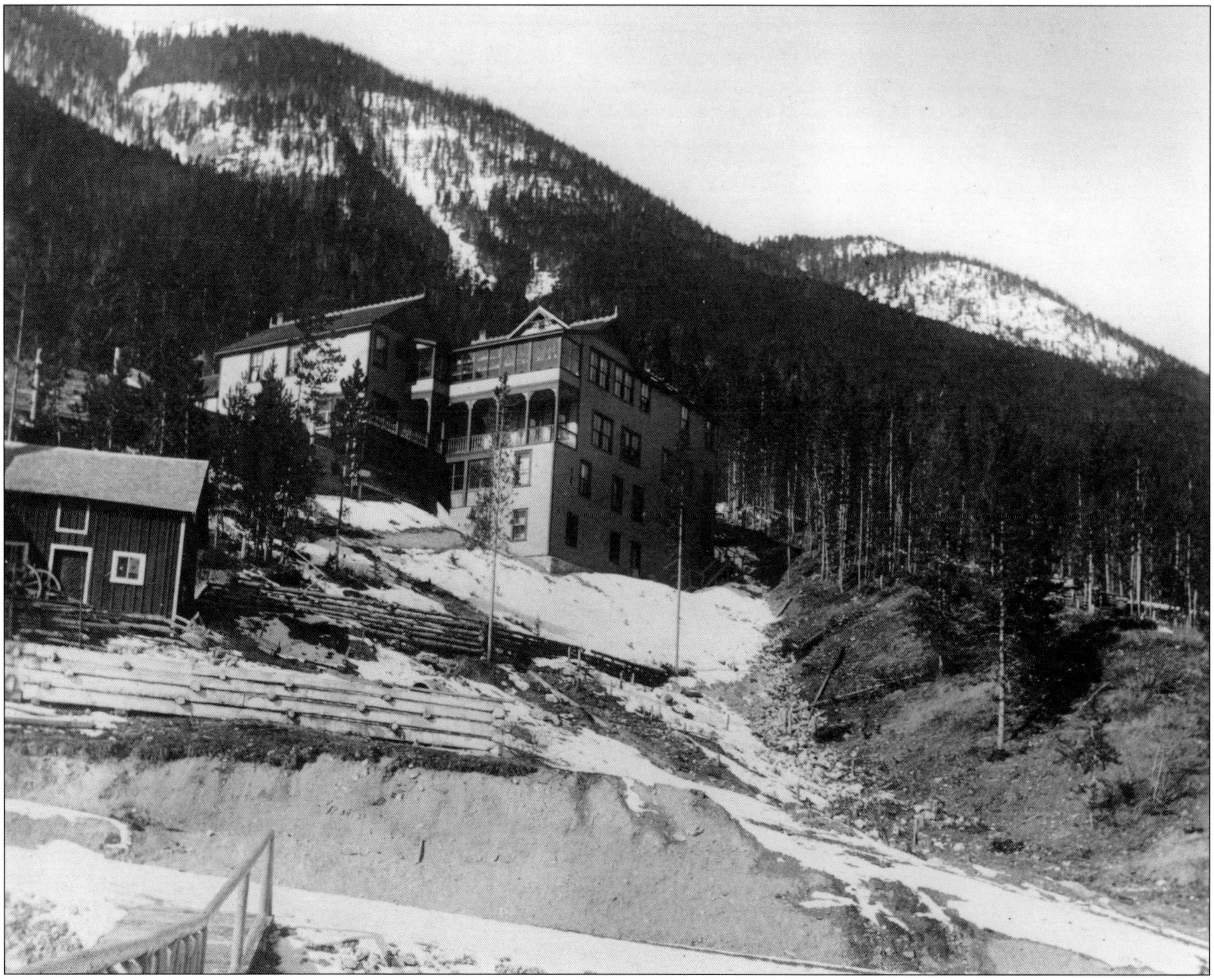

The Cave and Basin springs, although the first to be developed, were not the only hot springs at Banff to be made available to the public. The Upper Hot Springs, higher on the slope of Sulphur Mountain, were likewise improved with public facilities, but the environs were also available for private commercial exploitation. Early on, access to the water and the impressive views of the Bow Valley led to hotel development on the bench immediately below the springs. The Hydro Hotel operated briefly in

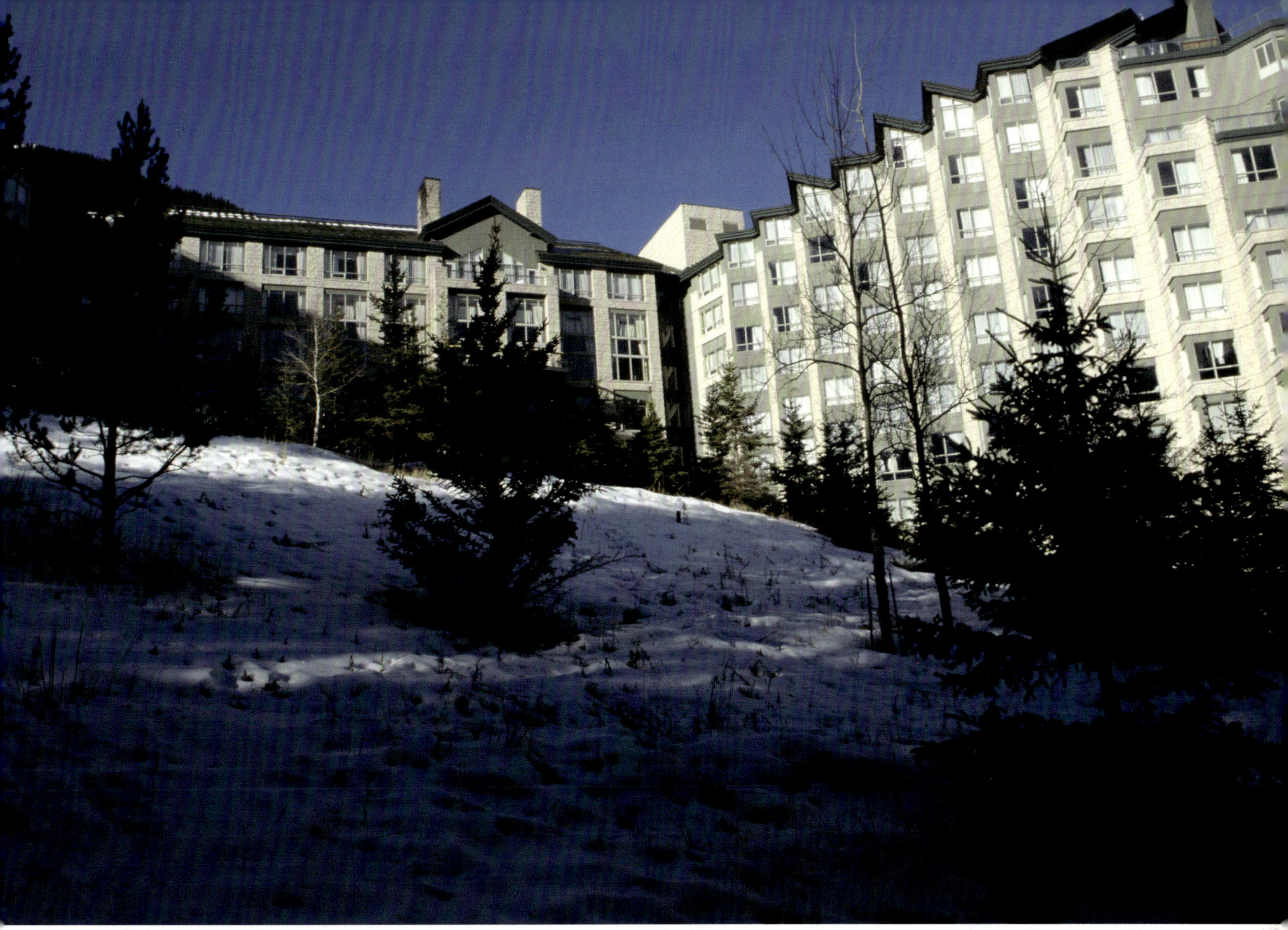

1886–87 and at the same time Dr. R. G. Brett began construction of what would become the Grand View Villa, pictured in 1905 after a major addition two years previously to prepare for the opening of the new government baths.[43] Other hotels joined the Grand View at the springs, the adjacent Upper Hot Springs Hotel being built in 1911, and in 1931, the same year as the Grand View burned down, the rather basic public bathing facilities began to undergo a major improvement with the construction of a new bathhouse and pool as a depression unemployment relief project.

The Upper Hot Springs Hotel was operated by the Ashton family until the early 1960s when it was acquired by John Pawluk, who moved the original structure to the south end and erected the first Rimrock Inn on the old site. A Japanese investor purchased the property in 1989. Despite three-storey height restrictions in the Town of Banff, the Rimrock lay just outside the town boundary and when a new $50 million project was planned in the early 1990s it proposed a ten-storey-high design. The redevelopment became controversial. Despite opposition from those believing that Parks Canada should be holding leaseholders outside the Town to the same standards as those inside, and concerns about the ecological effects and park policy implications, federal government approval was given, and the 307-room structure in the 2003 view was opened in 1993.[44] In 1994 the minister responsible for national parks commissioned the Banff–Bow Valley Study to examine the increasingly serious conflicts between human use and conservation in the valley. The study recommended that the hotel might be considered for future removal if monitoring indicated that it blocked wildlife movements. Although this effect has not been observed to date, the Rimrock Hotel will likely be one of Banff's last major hotel expansions if current park policies favouring ecological maintenance and restoration are retained.[45]

4.24A BANFF FROM SULPHUR MOUNTAIN, 1898 (GEORGE PARIS, WHYTE NG 5-97)

4.24B BANFF FROM TOP OF SULPHUR MOUNTAIN GONDOLA, SEPTEMBER 2005 (CW 2005-09C-29)

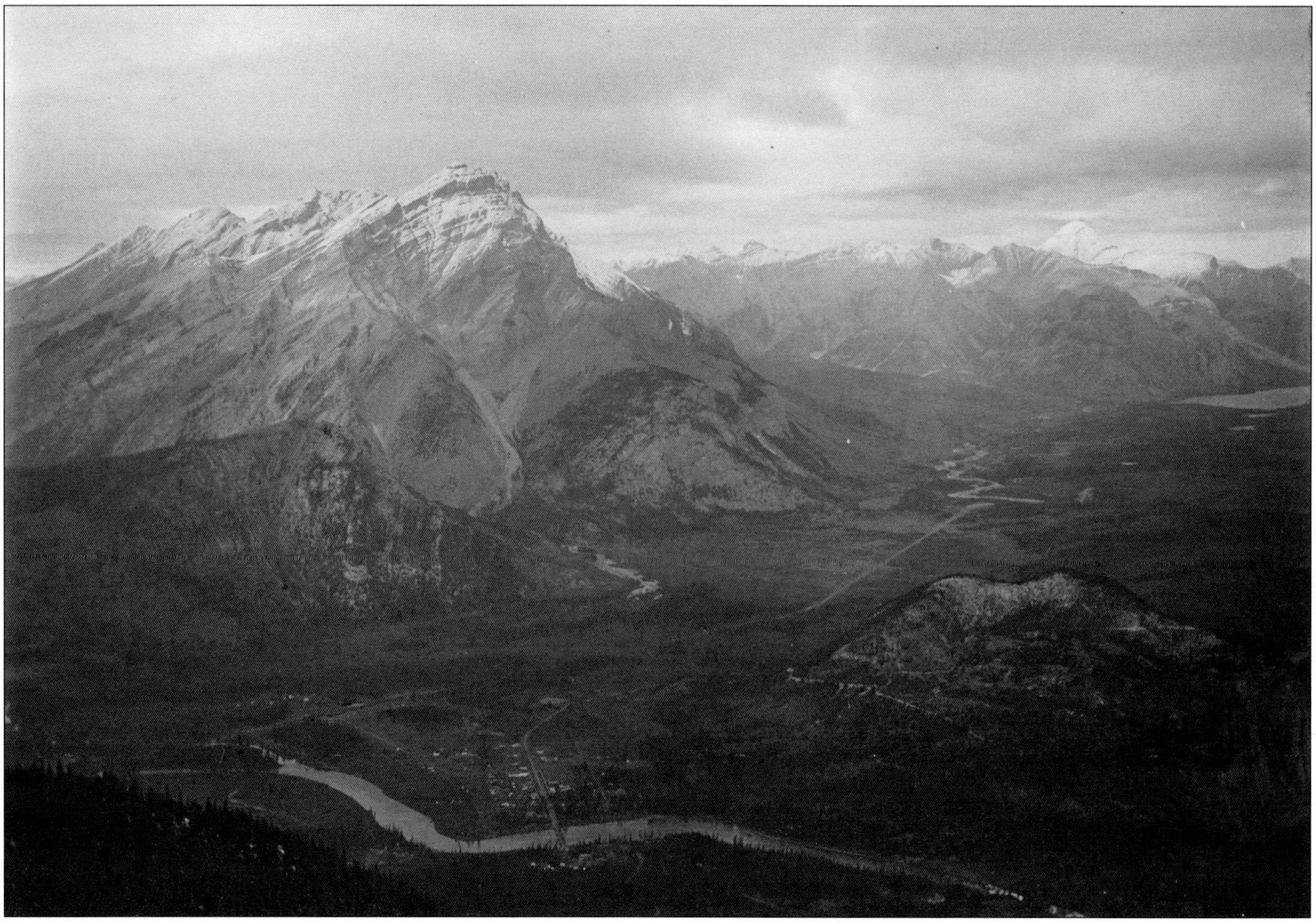

The top of Sulphur Mountain has always been a popular viewpoint for those wishing to photograph the panorama of Banff and the Bow Valley. As early as 1902 the government built a switch-backed walking trail leading to the peak, in preparation for the opening of the Banff Meteorological Observatory in 1903. Guides provided horseback transport for those unwilling or unable to ascend the steep incline on foot, and over the years various other commercial ventures were attempted to get tourists to the finest view in the valley. A particularly interesting one was Swiss native John Jaeggi's "Sulphur Mountain Transport," established in 1947 using a tractor pulling a wheeled platform with handrails that departed from the Upper Hot Springs and took passengers two-thirds of the way to the summit on a road he had cleared himself. In time technology solved the problem of restricted access; in 1959

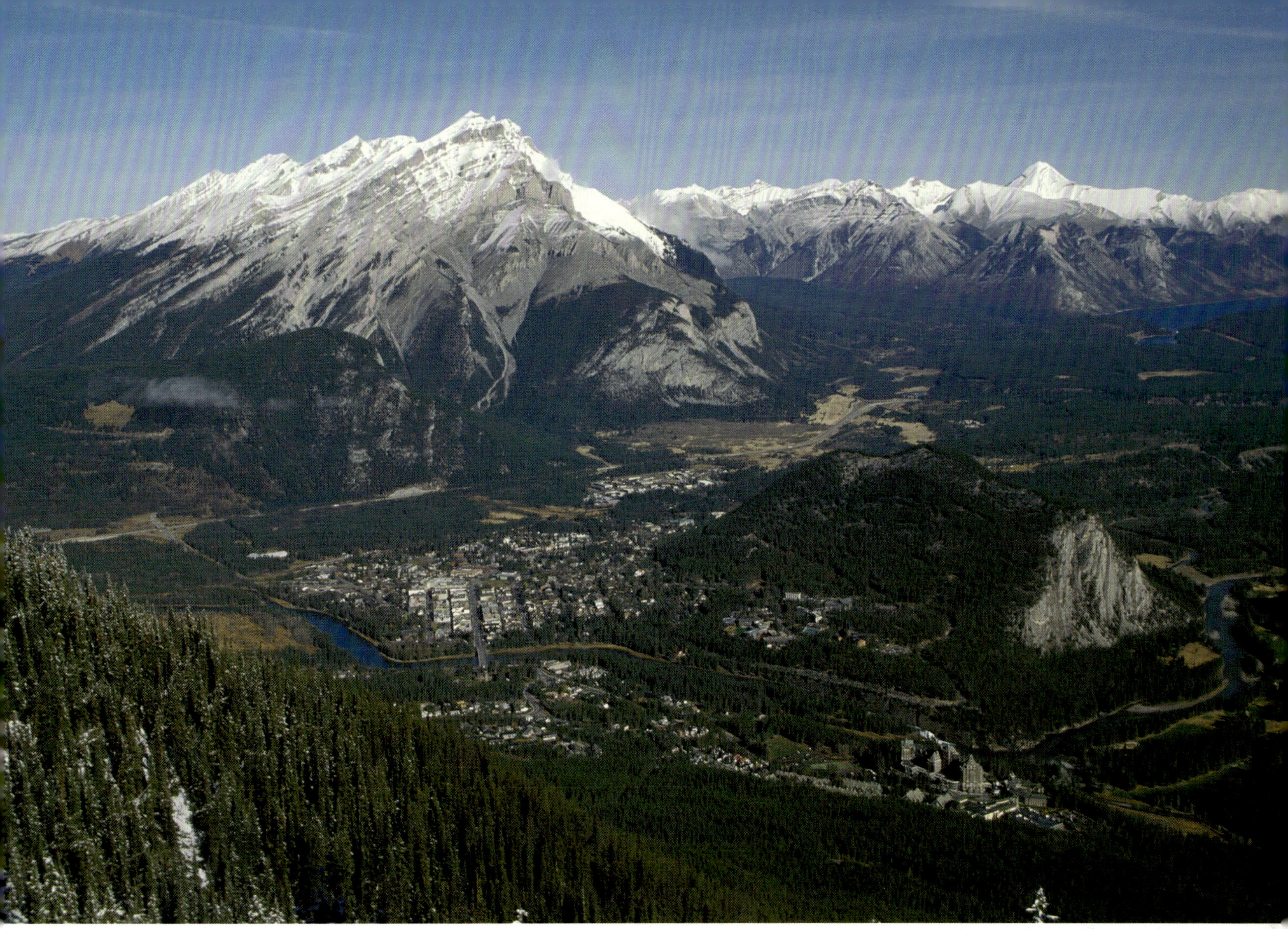

a consortium of Swiss investors put together by Jaeggi constructed a 1,500-metre aerial gondola lift rising over 700 metres from an area adjacent to the Upper Hot Springs to a summit teahouse, and capable of carrying thousands of tourists a day to the top in a mere eight minutes.[46]

Over the years that tourists have enjoyed photographing the vista over Banff to the Fairholme Range, Lake Minnewanka, and the Palliser Range beyond. In George Paris's turn-of-the-century shot, the early growth pattern along the axis of Banff Avenue is plainly visible, as is the route of the CPR heading northeastward through the Cascade Trench to its crossing of the substantial Cascade River flowing from Lake Minnewanka in the upper right. Over a century later when the second image is taken, much has changed. The Town of Banff is shown as reaching its full maturity, particularly noticeable being the development of the Banff Centre on the slopes of Tunnel Mountain beginning in the late 1940s, and the Valleyview–Middle Springs residential area on the south side of the river beginning in the 1970s. The railroad line is still visible, but it is now paralleled for part of its route by the Trans-Canada Highway, and the Cascade River is no more, disappearing with the development of the Calgary Power Lake Minnewanka project in 1942. Equally evident is the fact that the community and related infrastructure have spread out across a key intersecting point of the Bow and Spray valleys, creating a bottleneck for animals moving through historic wildlife corridors. The Banff–Bow Valley Study's final report recommended removal of many facilities adjacent to the community to restore wildlife connectivity. The 1997 Park Management Plan placed a legislative cap on commercial development and the residential footprint of the town, requiring removal of several non-commercial facilities in the corridors.[47]

5

"IF WE CAN'T EXPORT THE SCENERY ... "

Railways and Park Establishment

An axiom attributed to William Cornelius Van Horne, the builder and general manager of the Canadian Pacific Railway line, succinctly summed up the relationship of the railway with the mountain landscape. Faced with huge construction obstacles in forcing the line through the rugged Rockies and Selkirks in the early 1880s, he met the prospect of having several hundred miles of the costliest section having no identifiable product to support its operation by doing what was, in railway terms, a paradigm shift – "If we can't export the scenery, we'll import the tourists." With the stating of this goal, the entire future of Canada's mountain west, hitherto essentially the sole preserve of First Nations peoples, was set on an inexorable new course. The railways – the Canadian Pacific in the south and the Canadian National in the north – stand in the period between the 1880s and the 1920s as one of the primary agents effecting change in the mountains. No other creation or activity in this period was to have such an impact on the landscape and how, when, and where the public experienced it. For most people in the early twentieth century, it was the view of the mountains that these companies created that was to embody their vision of Canada's alpine playground.[1]

The construction of the CPR through what was to become Banff National Park occurred in 1883–84, while the lines that would in 1923 be nationalized into the Canadian National Railways (the Canadian Northern and Grand Trunk Pacific railways) were pushed through the lands of Jasper National Park between 1911 and 1913. In both cases the construction period was one where the only concern was building the line in the most rapid and cost-efficient manner possible, with no consideration to the impact on the landscape. In the early historic period (beginning in the late eighteenth century) when, as pointed out, fewer First Nations hunters traversed the old trails than their prehistoric forebears, mountain vegetation may have been less affected than previously. But this was to instantaneously change in the Bow Valley with the appearance of large railway locating and construction crews who had little regard for their natural surroundings. The first party to provide a written description of the progress of railway construction in the valley, the 1883 expedition of former engineer-in-chief Sandford Fleming and the Reverend George Grant of Queen's University, mentioned forest fires running up the sides of mountains at night "that gleam with a weird light" and described the country beyond Castle Mountain as having a "desolate appearance" because of "the blackened poles, that the fires had left as grim monuments of their fury."[2] That winter, construction shut down near the Great Divide after having established sidings at modern-day Banff and Canmore, and a force of five hundred men remained in the area to cut half a million ties and twenty thousand cords of wood to fuel construction locomotives the next summer. One of those working on the line in 1884 was British novelist Morley Roberts, and upon arriving at the end of steel near Lake Louise he described the scene: "Round me I saw the primeval forest torn down, cut and hewed and hacked. The brute power of man's organized civilization had fought with Nature and had vanquished her."[3]

More devastation was to follow, as superintendent of construction James Ross had announced that some twelve thousand men were to work in the mountains that summer. This situation was duplicated twenty-five years later when the surveyors, navvies, and construction crews building the lines towards Yellowhead Pass wrought their havoc on the Athabasca Valley. Intrepid Philadelphia explorer Mary Schäffer, travelling over the route to be taken by the Grand Trunk Pacific in 1911, noted upon reaching the site of a ferry across the Athabasca, which she had visited during a previous trip, that "to me, who had stood on those banks only three years before, who had looked across the wild body of water to the fair, unbroken prairies beyond, where only the Indian trail marked the way, it was an ugly sight. The great, picturesque bluffs that hung above our heads were scarred and maimed by dynamite to make way for the 'python,' the wreckage of camp-life strewed the near-by forest and there before us came creeping an ugly scow, clinging to a wire stretched overhead, trundling her way through the Athabaska's rebellious waters."[4]

Many of the earliest images in this book were taken by itinerant photographers who, like Professor O. B. Buell, wished to photograph the construction and initial operation of the lines because they felt their photographs would be of interest to a public curious about the new land they were opening up. These provide a benchmark for much of the change in the mountain west that would become evident in the following century. However, even after the initiation of passenger service on the Canadian Pacific in 1886, the railway was responsible for ongoing destruction of neighbouring forests, particularly because early wood- and coal-burning locomotives were not equipped with spark arresters. Reports of fires burning in the Bow Valley were common until the turn of the century when more care began to be taken, partly, at least, because such scenes of desolation did not fit well with the sublime vision of the mountains that the CPR had begun to sell to a burgeoning tourist audience.[5] Van Horne, intent on realizing his precept, made sure he had the best passenger equipment on the continent available, employing a battery of travelling passenger agents and foreign representatives and, most importantly, launching a clever international advertising campaign that made his company's name one and the same with the idea of grand scenery and the excitement of Victorian travellers experiencing the delights of the mountains. He did this by designing his own tourist promotional material and illustrating it with depictions brought back by a battery of the best artists and photographers of the day as well as by utilizing slogans certain to appeal to the Englishman's propensity for touring the continent by invoking the 'Canadian Alps' and 'Switzerland in America.' Indeed, he went further, making sure the comforts of railroad travel were matched by 'luxury in the wilderness' for those who wished to stop over. In the process, the resort-style tourism industry that remains a hallmark of the Canadian Rockies to this day began to emerge.[6]

While it was the building and operations of the railways that had a large initial impact on the landscape, it was this ongoing development of tourist facilities and services that would ultimately bear sustained consequences. The need to build hotel accommodation for those travelling the line or wishing to sojourn in the mountains had already led to the construction of rough railroad inns at Rogers Pass, Field, and Fraser Canyon by the time passenger service began, and they were joined in 1888 by what was to become the focal point of the CPR's mountain tourism services – the Banff Springs Hotel. Choosing a commanding location with a view of the Fairholme Range down the Bow Valley adjacent to the fledgling national park capital of Banff, Van Horne directed the construction of a three-storey frame and wood structure topped with a dormered roof modelled by architect Bruce Price on the chateaux of France's Loire Valley. Pronouncing it "the finest hotel on the North American Continent," he not only ensured the comfort of his guests while in its confines but saw to it that they would have diversions and entertainments to make their stay memorable. In the process, the CPR provided, through contractors such as young Bill and Jim Brewster, buggies and tally-hos to take guests on excursions to visit local beauty spots such as Lake Minnewanka or to view 'wild' park animals in the animal paddock, as well as guides for those wishing horseback outings, either on nearby bridle paths or 'off the beaten track' where they could fish, hunt, explore, or climb some of the challenging peaks.[7] By such means, a symbiotic relationship was formed with the federal government, which provided recreations and diversions such as the Cave and Basin pools and built the roads and trails in the expectation that the CPR would attract the visitors, house them comfortably, and provide the wherewithal for them to participate in tourist offerings.

Over time, the CPR would build on this strong foundation. By the end of the first decade of the new century, the company had established its own Atlantic steamship service and could offer around-the-world excursions linking Liverpool with Hong Kong, generating large numbers of new visitors to Canada. This required additional amenities, in particular hotel facilities, and some of its basic hostelries began to be upgraded and expanded, creating impacts on surrounding lands. An example was development connected with the Lake Louise Chalet, originally built as a rough log lodging in 1890 to house those hardy enough to take on the rugged trail to its location. To make it more convenient for these adventurous individuals, the company soon hacked out a bumpy wagon road connecting it with the station at Laggan (Lake Louise townsite), and thereafter the original chalet's popularity increased so rapidly that after it burned down in 1893, the CPR had to quickly re-assess the situation. Replacing the first small structure was a frame one, more in the mode of a hotel, the company's first tourist development away from its main line. It quickly grew as the lake's fame spread, a design generated by noted Canadian architect F. M. Rattenbury being undertaken in 1899 and constantly being added to until 1908. At the same time, services such as hiking and climbing guides, horseback guides, boatmen, and upgraded roads and trails complemented the growth. In 1912 a concrete wing containing 350 rooms was designed by CPR architect Walter Painter and, with carriage service being inadequate to handle the burgeoning house count, the company soon inaugurated a unique, narrow-gauge tramway on a six-kilometre bed paralleling much of the old roadway. Before long, outlying facilities, such as tea houses at Lake Agnes and the Plain of Six Glaciers and a climbing hut in Abbot Pass, were introduced to add to the comforts of those venturing away from the luxurious surroundings of what was by then being referred to as the Chateau Lake Louise. As a consequence of these activities, the untouched wilderness surrounding the lake that had only first been reported on by guide Tom Wilson in 1882 had, within a period of a mere thirty years, been turned into one of Canada's most popular international tourist destinations visited by thousands each year.[8]

Equally rapid development took place at Banff, where the attempt to attract an aristocratic audience had been so successful that, despite various additions to the original Banff Springs, by 1910 many customers were being turned away or had to stay in sleeping cars at the Banff siding. Consequently, a decision was made to begin construction of a 'new' hotel, designed by Painter in the Scottish baronial tradition in what was, perhaps, a bow in the direction of the homeland of the CPR's founders. It featured an eleven-storey rock and concrete centre tower completed in 1914, incorporating both hot and cold swimming pools on its three exterior terraces, and complemented with two sympathetic wings designed by J. W. Orrock and constructed between 1926 and 1928. The whole edifice was clad with rugged Rundle limestone quarried nearby and its spacious interior halls were decorated, in keeping with its feudal atmosphere, with stone floors, ancient armour, Medici prints, Leonardo tapestries, and furniture replicating period pieces from European castles and manor houses. By the time it was completed, it was being promoted not as a place where guests merely stayed overnight, but where they would remain many weeks and return year after year. This was in keeping with the CPR's increasing promotion of its mountain facilities as resorts rather than simply as hotels, backed by a new slogan featuring the 'Canadian Pacific Rockies,' speaking to the overwhelming confidence the company felt in having achieved Van Horne's vision.[9]

While emerging somewhat later, the dominant position held by Canadian Pacific in the tourism business in Banff's mountains was challenged by the Canadian National in Jasper, creating equally important impacts on its development. Both the Grand Trunk Pacific and the Canadian Northern that were nationalized to form Canadian National Railways in 1923 had initiated tourist promotion campaigns similar to the CPR's during the years of the First World War. Although they sought to back these up with the construction of grand hotels on the scale of the Banff Springs and Lake Louise Chalet, the difficult economic times required a more modest approach. The Grand Trunk Pacific worked out an arrangement with the Edmonton Tent and Mattress Company in 1915 to construct a basic camp on the shore of Lac Beauvert on the road connecting the town of Fitzhugh (Jasper) with the scenic Maligne Canyon. Assisted by Fred and Jack Brewster, brothers of the Brewster transportation interests in Banff, the company erected ten large tents with wooden floors and walls, one which was a main dining room also doubling as a lounge. By the early 1920s, this rough camp would blossom into Jasper Park Lodge under the direction of president Sir Henry Thornton of the CNR, a serious competitor for the CPR's mountain hotel business. One of Thornton's most successful innovations was the creation of a golf course with a reputation for excellence, a goal achieved by hiring Canada's most famous golf architect, Stanley Thompson, to lay out a links around the lodge and adjoining lake.[10] It was so successful that CPR president Sir Edward Beatty immediately responded by hiring Thompson in 1927 to rebuild the earlier course set out along the banks of the Bow River below the Banff Springs. In both cases, the construction of these courses would create unique issues with wildlife and vegetation on the montane grasslands on which they were built.[11]

The heyday of the railway hotels, amenities, and services in both Banff and Jasper began to come to an end with the onset of the Great Depression of the 1930s. Combined with changes brought on by the construction of roads, campgrounds, and other attractions aimed at the burgeoning middle-class tourists beginning to visit the parks, their influence would never again be as great. Nevertheless, they would continue to be important agents impacting the lands of the mountain west. In the modern age, they have been joined by other interests, in particular the park service and smaller private developers, who would soon begin to dominate mountain landscape change.

6.1 BANFF TO WINDERMERE HIGHWAY, 1923 (NATIONAL PARKS PHOTOGRAPH, LIBRARY ARCHIVES CANADA PA-123211)

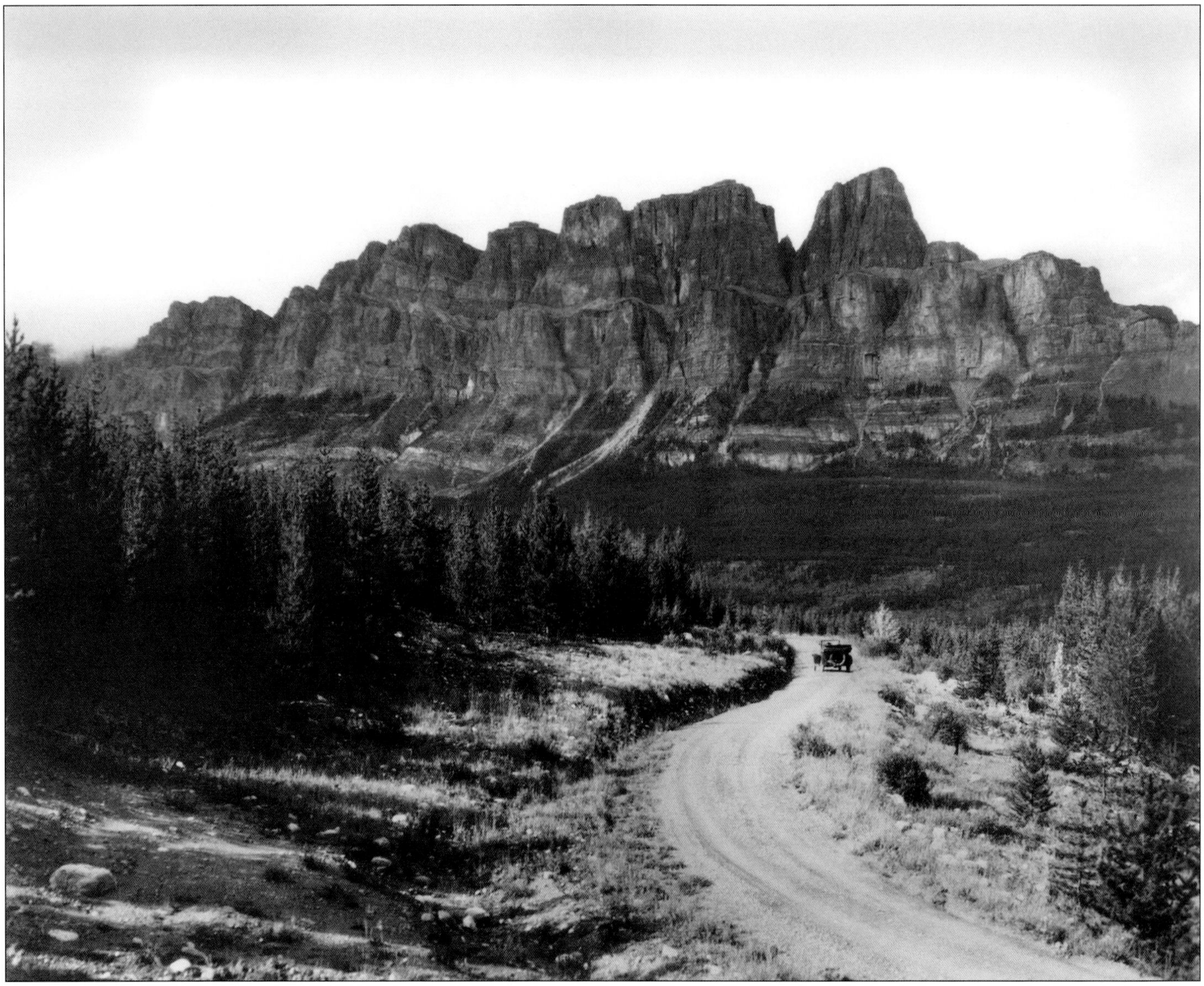

6

THE CALIFORNIA-BANFF BEELINE

Banff to Windermere

For Banff's first quarter-century, tourists arrived by train and were shuttled around by horse-drawn carriages and tally-hos on sightseeing tours and to visit attractions. But the automobile age changed everything; people could travel farther, faster, and more independently. In the same way the railway had connected parks to urban centres, the impetus was now to build roads to the people. With Banff accessible from the east by automobile after 1910, the next link would be to the west and south. A road through Vermilion Pass to Windermere could link Banff to vast tourism markets in the United States, and west to Vancouver, opening the Rocky Mountain parks to a huge new tourism market.

6.2A ROCKY MOUNTAIN TOURS AND TRANSPORT SIGHTSEEING CARS AT VERMILION LAKES, 1924 (BYRON HARMON, WHYTE V263 NA-3472)

6.2B EVENING STROLL ALONG VERMILION LAKES ROAD, SEPTEMBER 2003 (CW 2003-09B-18)

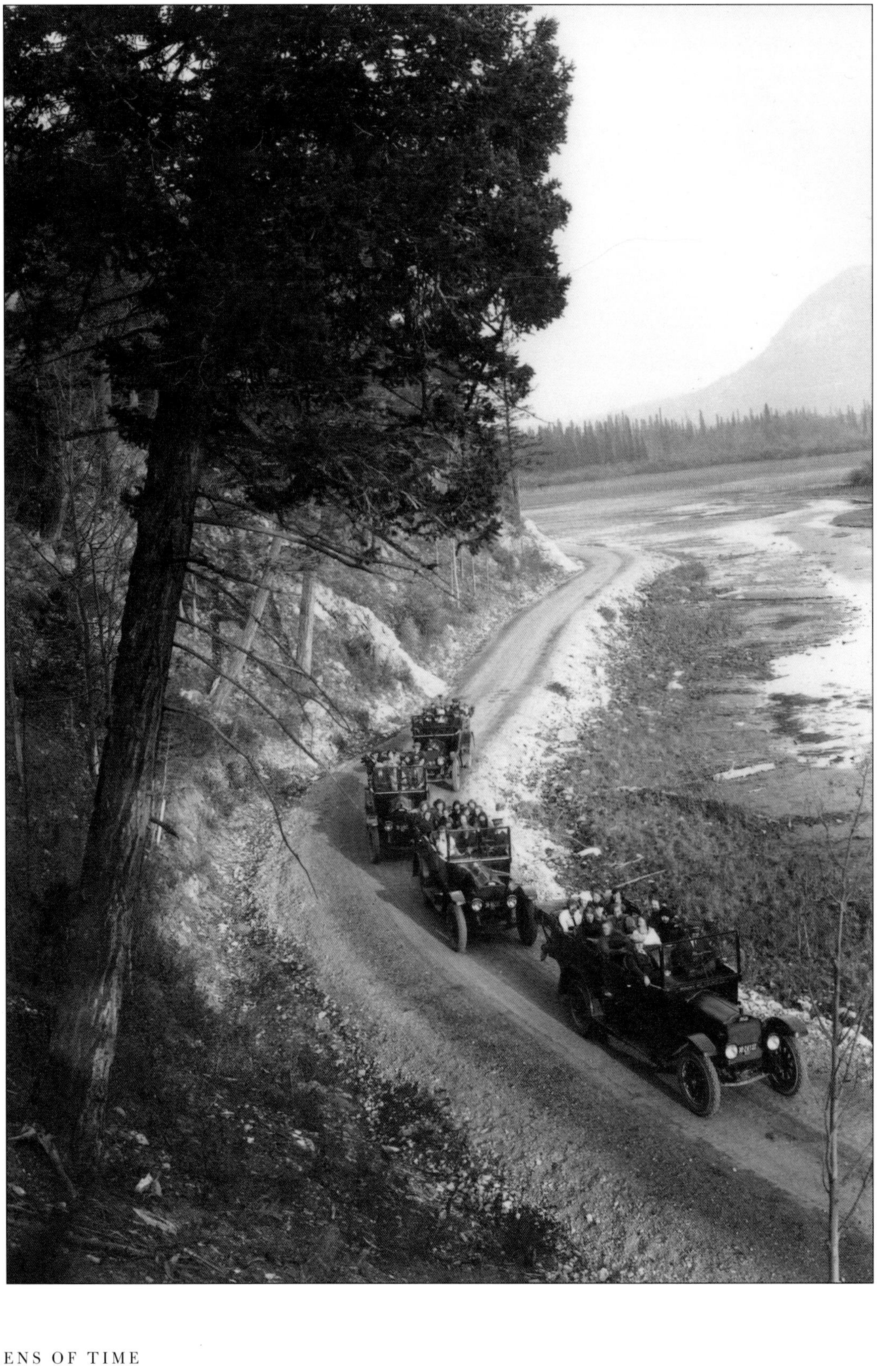

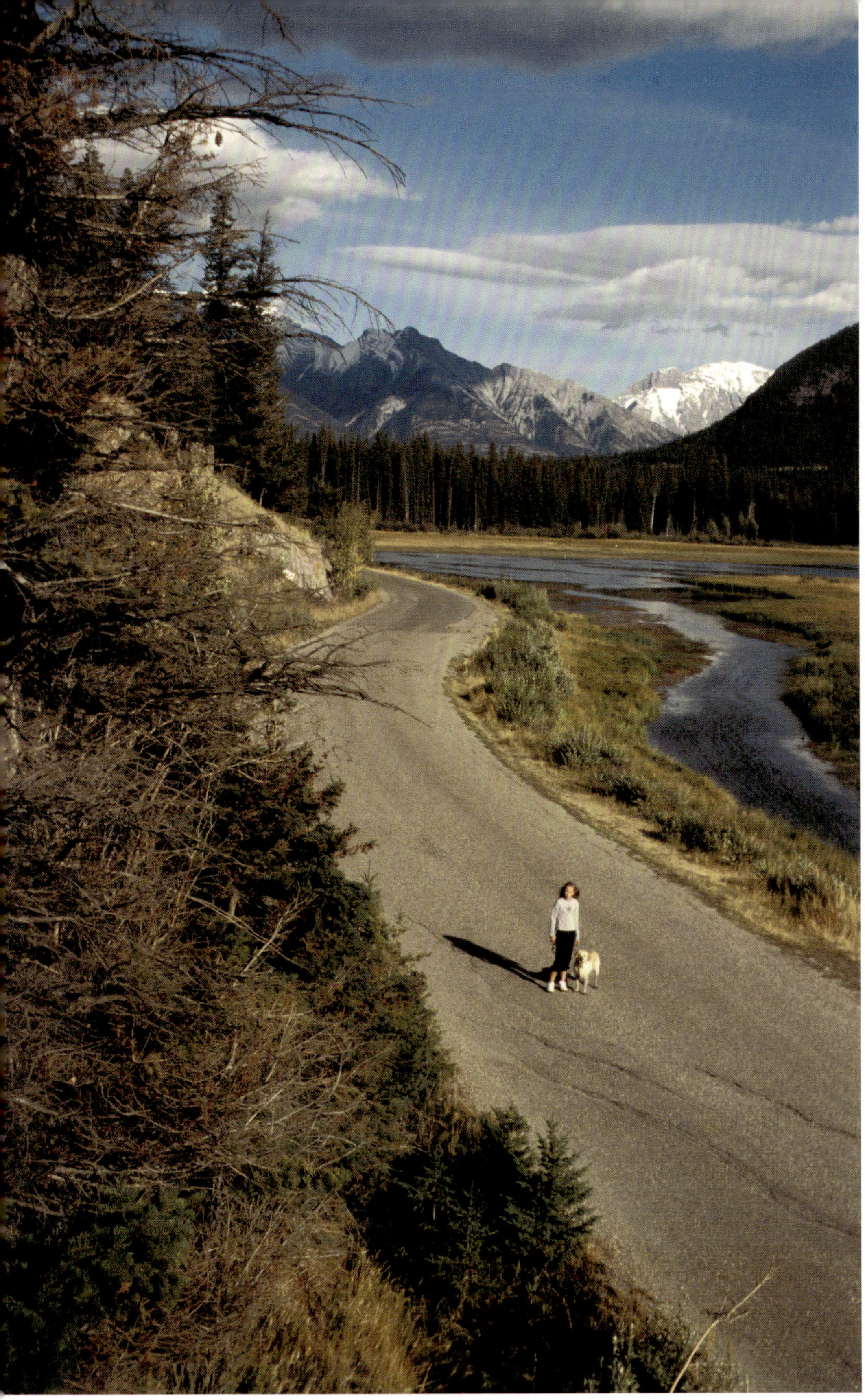

Construction on the motor road west from Banff began in 1911, following the "tote road" that had been used to transport railroad construction materials around Vermilion Lakes. The rapid transition from horses to horseless carriages provided some interesting challenges to Banff's transportation companies. Brewster Transfer, Banff's largest carriage business, solved its problem of surplus horse-drawn tally-hos by removing their tops and welding them onto the stripped-down chassis of used Kissell delivery trucks. In the spring of 1917, three "auto tally-hos" became Banff's first buses. In 1922, Brewster's competitor, Rocky Mountain Tours and Transport, bought the first of several eleven-passenger White buses, touted as the "finest motor car manufactured on the American continent." The 1924 photograph shows the companies' fleet of Whites headed west, likely on a tour to Johnston Canyon.[1]

The road along the Vermilion Lakes carried all Banff's through traffic until the 1959 opening of the Trans-Canada Highway. It remains as a short, scenic road, often used by bikers, joggers, and hikers. The stately Douglas firs that once lined the road's uphill side have been thinned by widening of the road from below, and from tree-cutting and rock-blasting associated with the modern Trans-Canada, constructed immediately uphill from the old road.

6.3A CONSTRUCTING THE TRANS-CANADA HIGHWAY ABOVE VERMILION LAKES, 1956 (BRUNO ENGLER, PARKS CANADA BANFF – NOT NUMBERED)

6.3B TRANS-CANADA HIGHWAY LOOKING EAST TOWARDS MOUNT NORQUAY EXIT TO BANFF, JULY 2003 (CW 2003-07D-05)

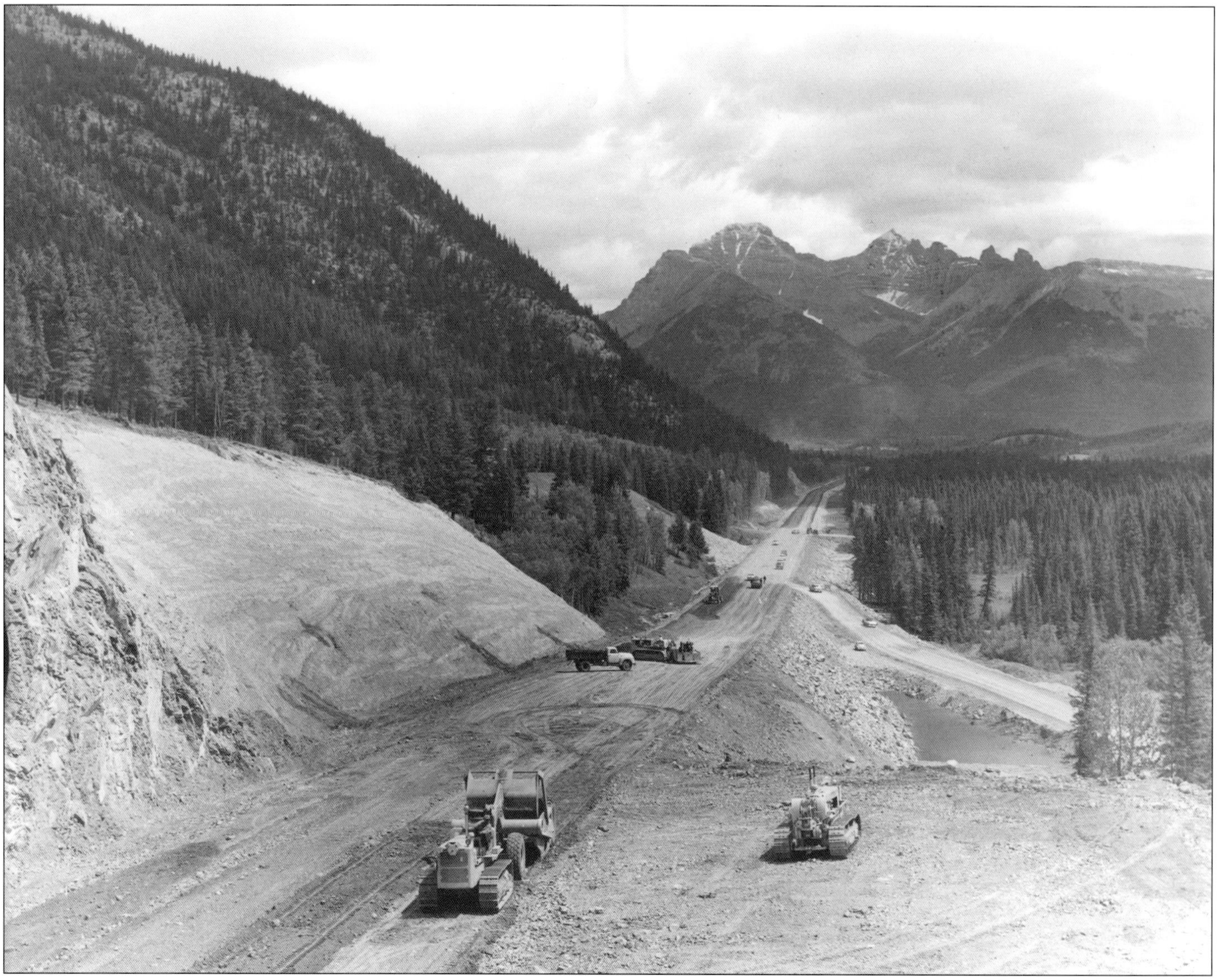

The first tentative steps in upgrading the treacherous road through Banff National Park as part of new Trans-Canada Highway were slow to occur. In 1952 some widening was done at the East Gate and the slashing of the route as far as Mount Norquay was carried out. But it was not until 1955, after the government had confirmed it would be responsible for the entire costs of construction through Banff

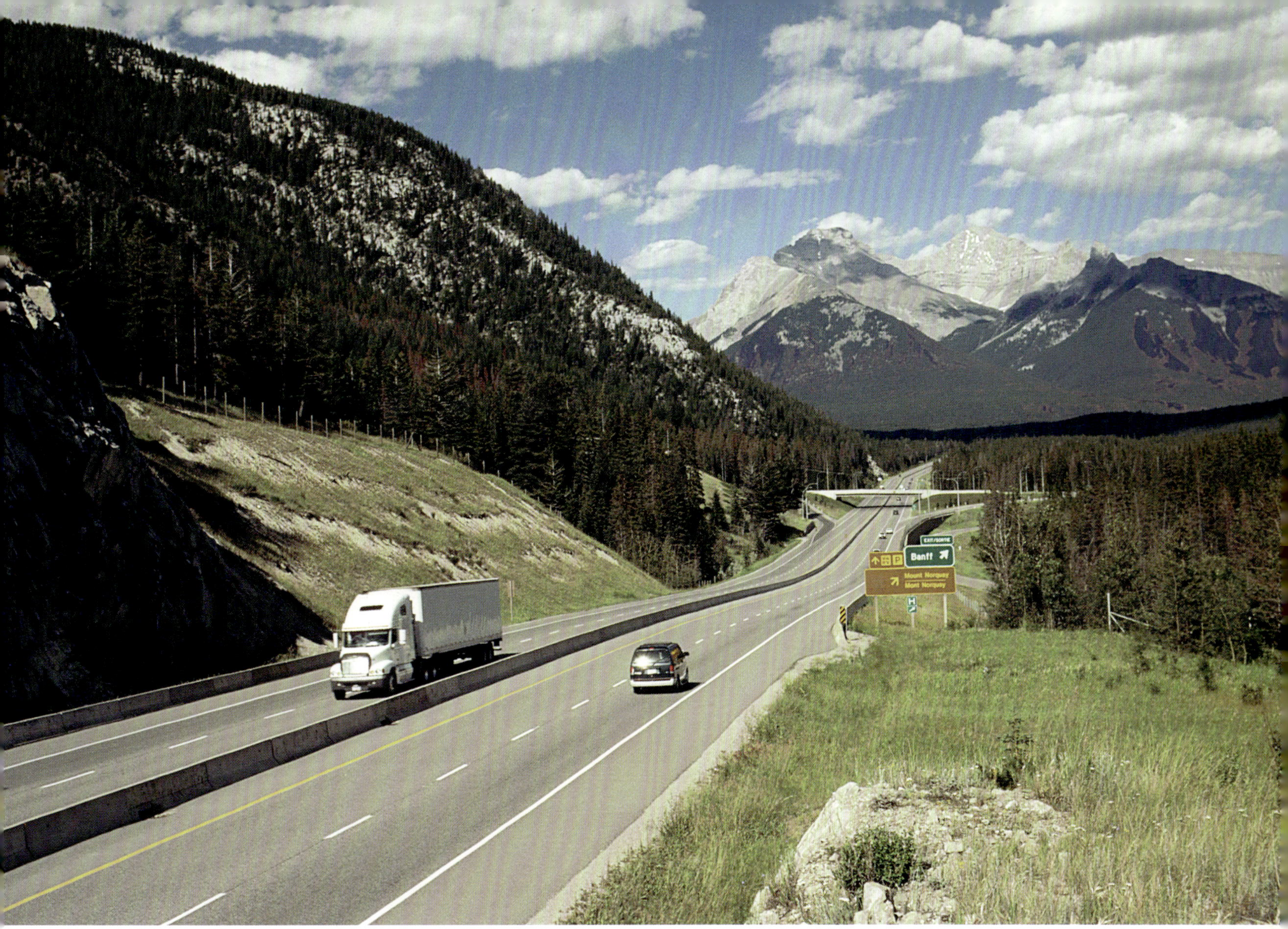

National Park, that the building began along a new route deviating considerably from the original road. As is evident in the Bruno Engler photograph taken near Vermilion Lakes in 1956, work continued that year and the road through the park was not fully completed until 1959. Even before that date its impacts were already apparent, with park visitation already doubling within a decade to 850,000 annually by 1957. By 1962, with the completion of the Trans-Canada through the difficult Rogers Pass section, use had nearly doubled again to 1.5 million. The post-war economic boom, combined with this and other upgraded roads, had unleashed a virtual flood of human use and development in Banff's Bow Valley.[2]

By the mid-1970s safety and traffic flow considerations near Banff required that planning for highway "twinning" begin. Phase 1 of a four-lane divided highway through Banff, from the East Gate to Banff, was completed in 1983; Phase 2, from Banff west to the Sunshine Ski Area turn-off, was finished in 1987. Near Vermilion Lakes the four-lane work included fencing and two wildlife underpasses, specifically designed to protect the bighorn sheep that were once abundant on the lower slopes of Mounts Norquay and Edith. However, an unforeseen consequence of the fencing was that it prevented the sheep from using the roadside cliffs that were important as predator escape terrain. Cougars and coyotes immediately began using the wildlife fence as a trapping device in the hunting of their prey, illustrating the difficulties in adapting human use and wildlife management.[3] In 2003, many mature trees on the lower slopes of Mounts Norquay and Stoney Squaw (centre left) were dying due to colonization by mountain pine beetle and the effects of drought. Effects of the 2003 Fairholme Prescribed Burn are also visible (background right).

6.4A SUNSHINE LODGE, 1939 (BRUNO ENGLER, WHYTE V227)

6.4B BREWSTER BUSES SHUTTLING SKIERS TO SUNSHINE, 1963 (BRUNO ENGLER, WHYTE NA 66-1530)

6.4C SUNSHINE VILLAGE, UPPER TERMINAL OF THE GONDOLA (CW 2002-02C-27)

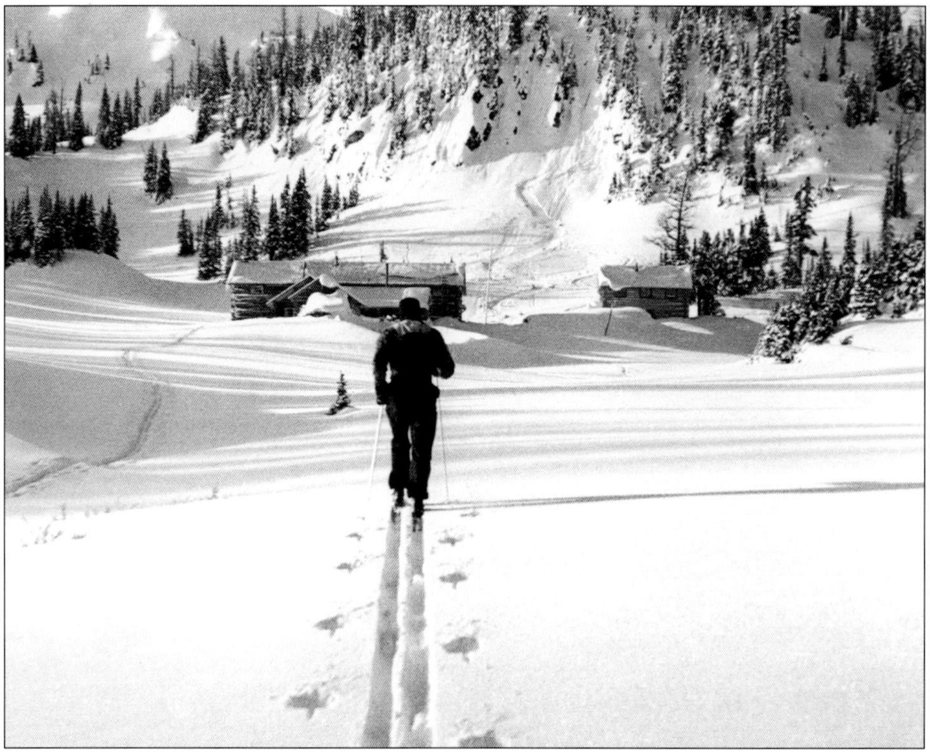

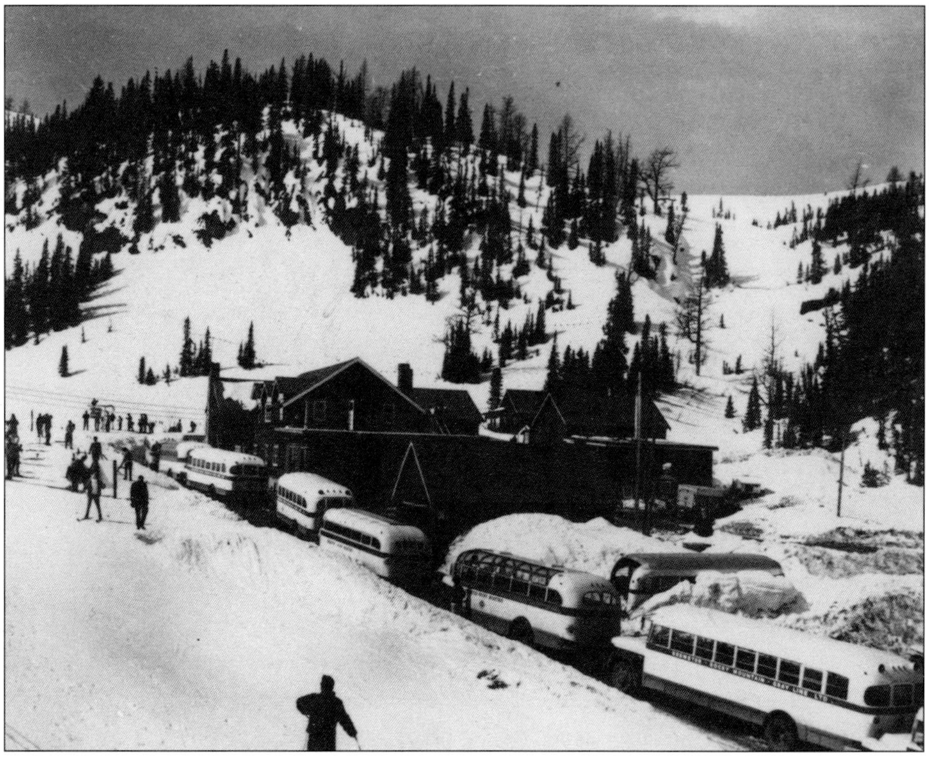

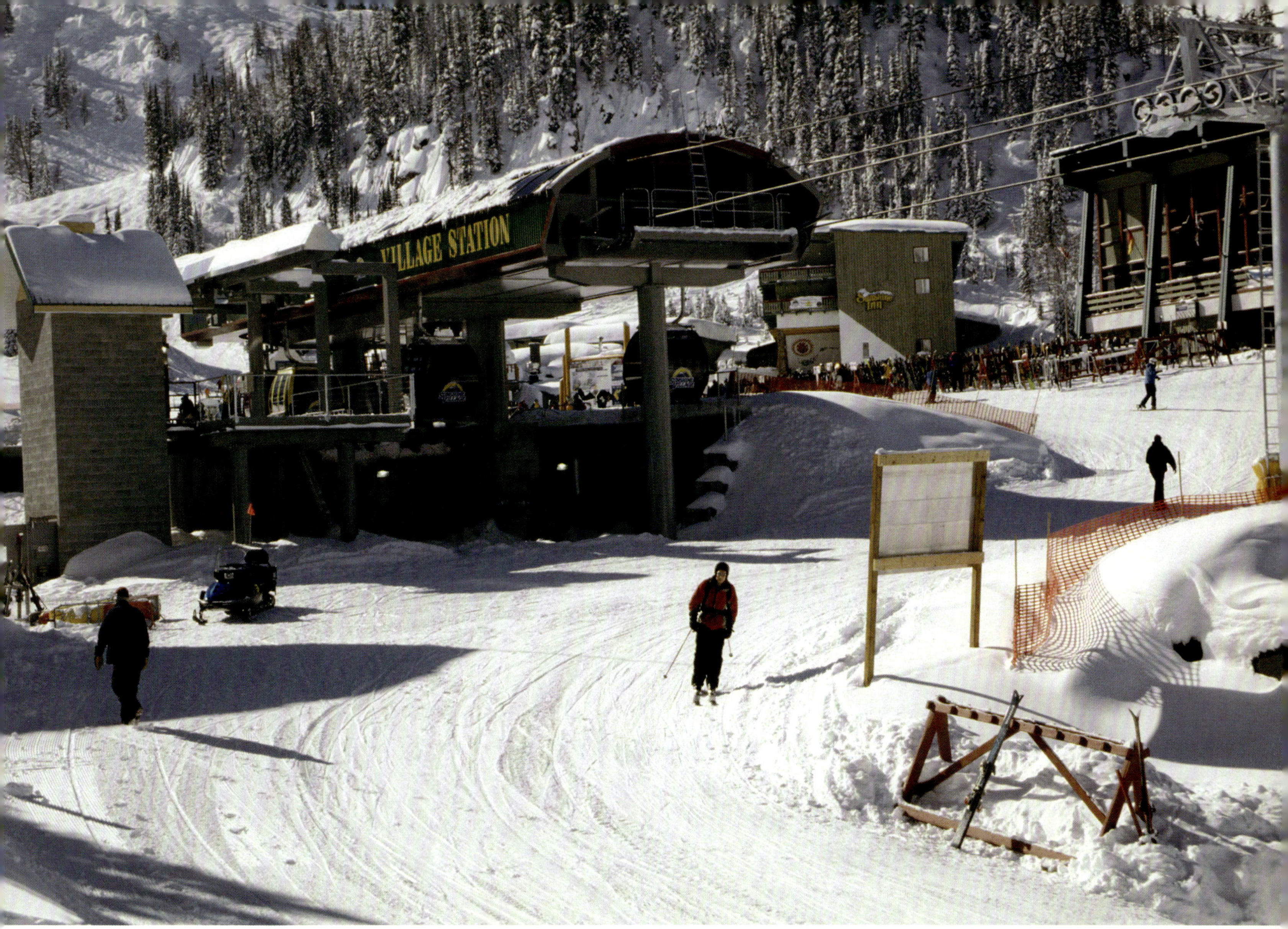

Lying less than twenty kilometres from Banff southwest of the Trans-Canada Highway, Sunshine Village Ski Area sits at the edge of one of the largest alpine areas in the southern Rocky Mountains. Not surprisingly, Sunshine meadows' awesome alpine scenery and close proximity to Banff quickly drew it to the attention of regular summer visitors. Arthur O. Wheeler, founder of the Alpine Club of Canada, established a summer tent-camp near the meadows as a stop on his "Banff to Mount Assiniboine Walking and Riding Tour" in the early 1920s, and in 1928 the Canadian Pacific Railroad built the first cabin at Sunshine for the Trail Riders of the Canadian Rockies. With a warm shelter guaranteed, Banff locals Cyril Paris and Cliff White Sr. made the long ski tour in from Banff the following winter and discovered a powder paradise. In 1934 Jim, Pat, and Dell Brewster leased the lodge and in February hosted the first group of ten paying guests. Bruno Engler, a Swiss guide and photographer, arrived in Canada in 1939 and began working as a winter guide out of the newly completed two-storey log addition to the original lodge. His photograph, taken soon after his arrival, captures the wondrous stillness of a backcountry skier's winter day.

By the end of the Second World War, a four-wheel-drive road reached Sunshine. After a period of ownership by George Encil and Walter Fisher, Cliff White II and his wife Beverly bought the lodge in 1960 and began aggressive marketing to Calgarians who, with the completion of the new Trans-Canada Highway, could now make a day trip for skiing in Banff. Capacity increases included a chairlift on Standish Hill (in the background) and new hotel in 1965, a lift to the top of Lookout Mountain in 1971, and replacement of the infamous bus access system (1963 photograph) with a gondola lift in 1980. Maximum daily skier numbers rose from only four hundred people in 1960 to crowds of over seven thousand by the year 2000. The Ralph Scurfield family, founders of a Calgary-based urban development company, now own the ski area. They have renovated and maintained the 1939 lodge – blocked from view by the gondola lift in the mid-ground of the most recent photograph.[4]

6.5A VIEW FROM SIMPSON SUMMIT, BANFF NATIONAL PARK, 1930S (HOWE STREET BOOKSTORE, GLENBOW NA 735-01)

6.5B SUNSHINE MEADOWS, HOWARD DOUGLAS LAKE AND MT. ASSINIBOINE FROM QUARTZ RIDGE, AUGUST 2001 (CW 2001-08B-20)

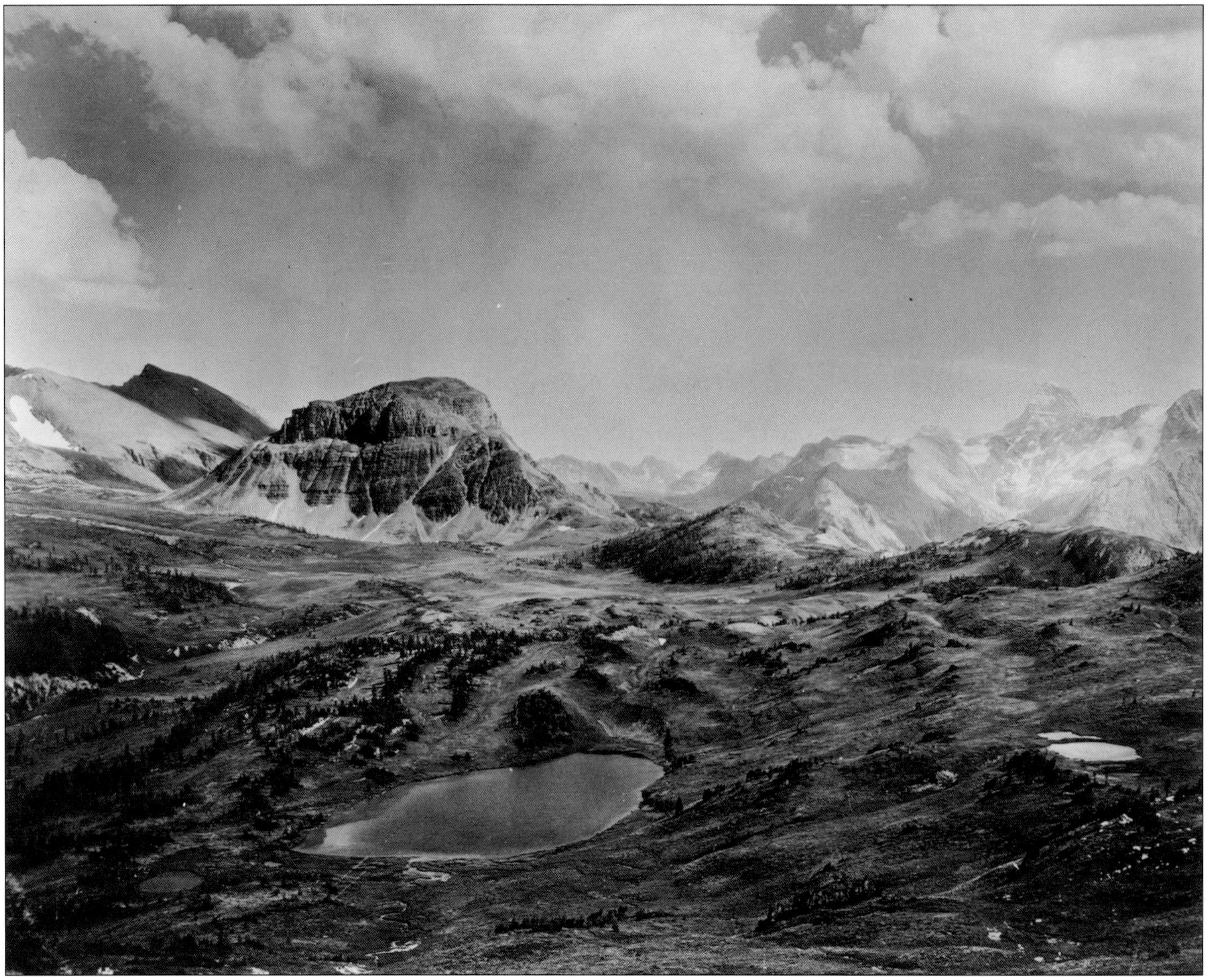

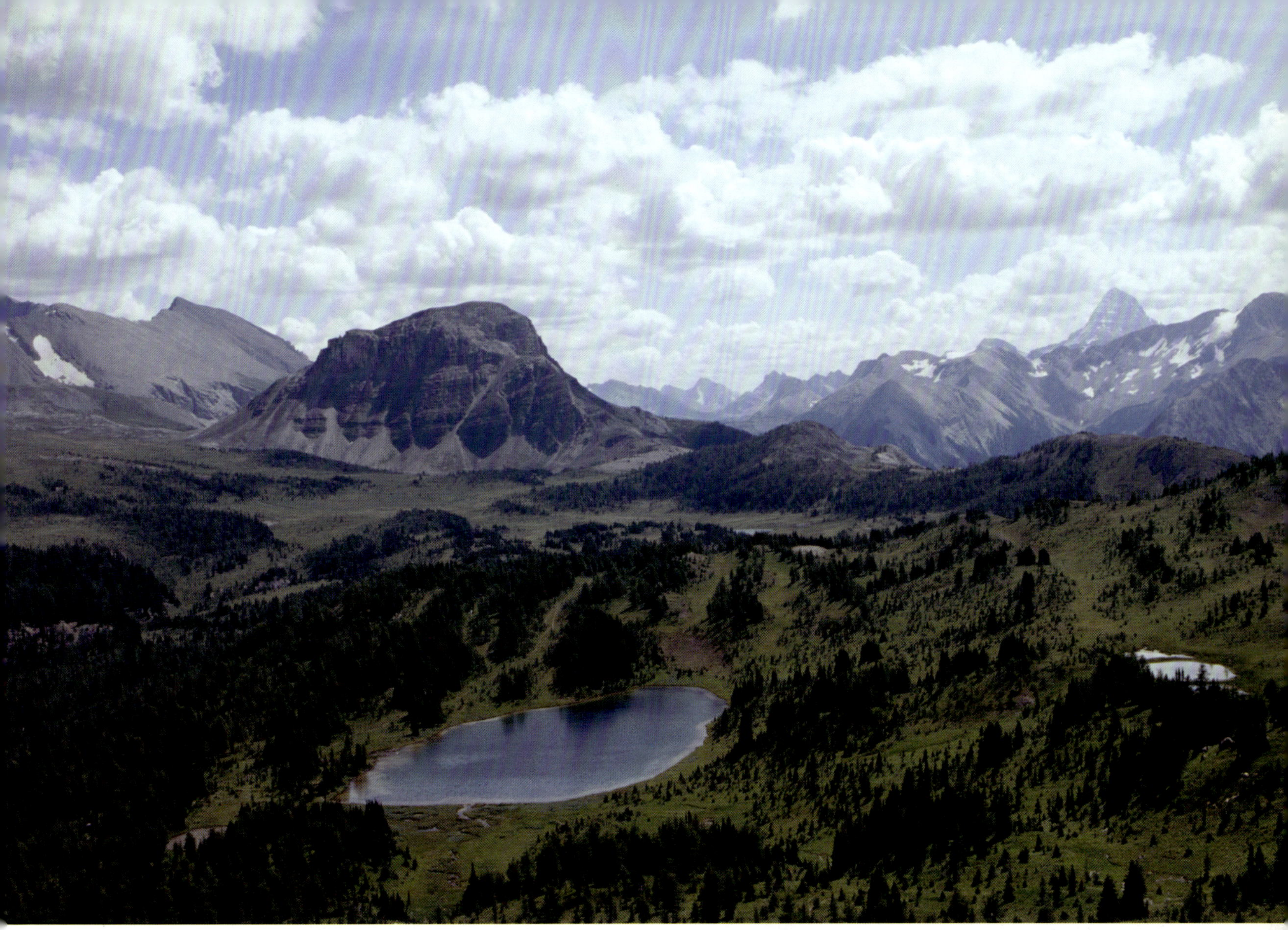

Mount Assiniboine (3618 m), visible in the photographs' right background, is the loftiest peak in the southern Canadian Rockies. Early outfitters discovered that the secret to a rapid trip to the mountain was to avoid the traditional, circuitous access by trail through deep, forested valleys. Instead, a new route was found that directly traversed the beautiful meadows along the Continental Divide near today's Sunshine Ski Area. James Outram, the first to reach the summit of Assiniboine, described it in poetic terms in 1901: "We mount steadily to a breezy, undulating alp, green and flower-strewn, skirting the Continental watershed, and bearing frequent pretty lakelets in the sheltered hollows. Ever and anon a deep gorge dips sharply towards the east or west, giving a glimpse of larger wooded valleys, where Healy Creek and the Simpson River ran to join the Bow and Kootenay, and finally sink to rest in the waters of the rival oceans."[5]

The modern photograph reveals that forests of alpine larch, subalpine fir and Engelmann spruce are rapidly encroaching across the meadows near Citadel Peak (centre left) and Howard Douglas Lake. Is the newly forming forest definitive evidence of a moderating climate? Ancient larch trees and large dead logs barely visible in the historic photograph, but easily found while hiking, show that the advance of forest across the area is a periodic phenomenon. Forest fires occasionally spread into the area from the densely wooded Simpson River valley immediately to the west. For example, in 1920 a fire from the Simpson spotted over the divide and burned out the headwaters of Howard Douglas Creek, including a small area on the far left of the photographs.[6] After burning, forest regeneration was slowed due to strong winds and deep snows at this high elevation. However, the crop of fir saplings visible in the newer picture between the older tree-islands indicates that forest regrowth is accelerating in the last few decades.

6.6A BOW VALLEY AND THE SAWBACK RANGE, 1921 (NATIONAL AIR PHOTOGRAPH LIBRARY CA 114-74)

6.6B HELICOPTER VIEW OF BOW VALLEY AND THE SAWBACK RANGE, SEPTEMBER 1985 (CW 1986-P1-14).

6.6C HELICOPTER VIEW OF BOW VALLEY AND THE SAWBACK RANGE, OCTOBER 2003 (CW 2003-10B-05)

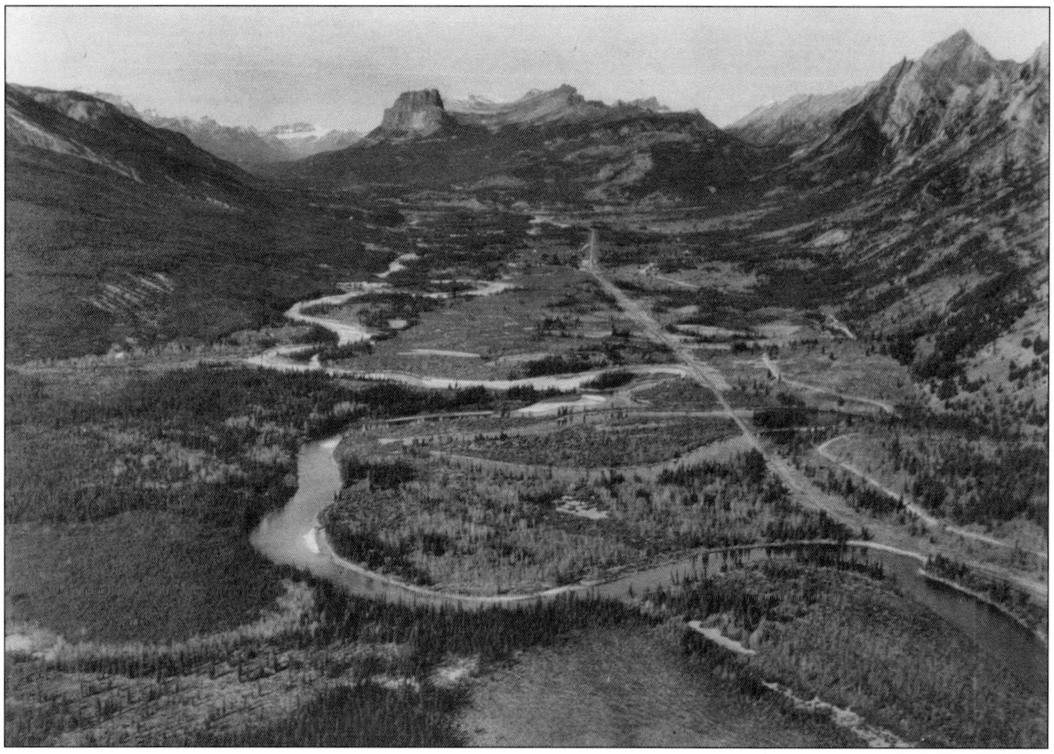

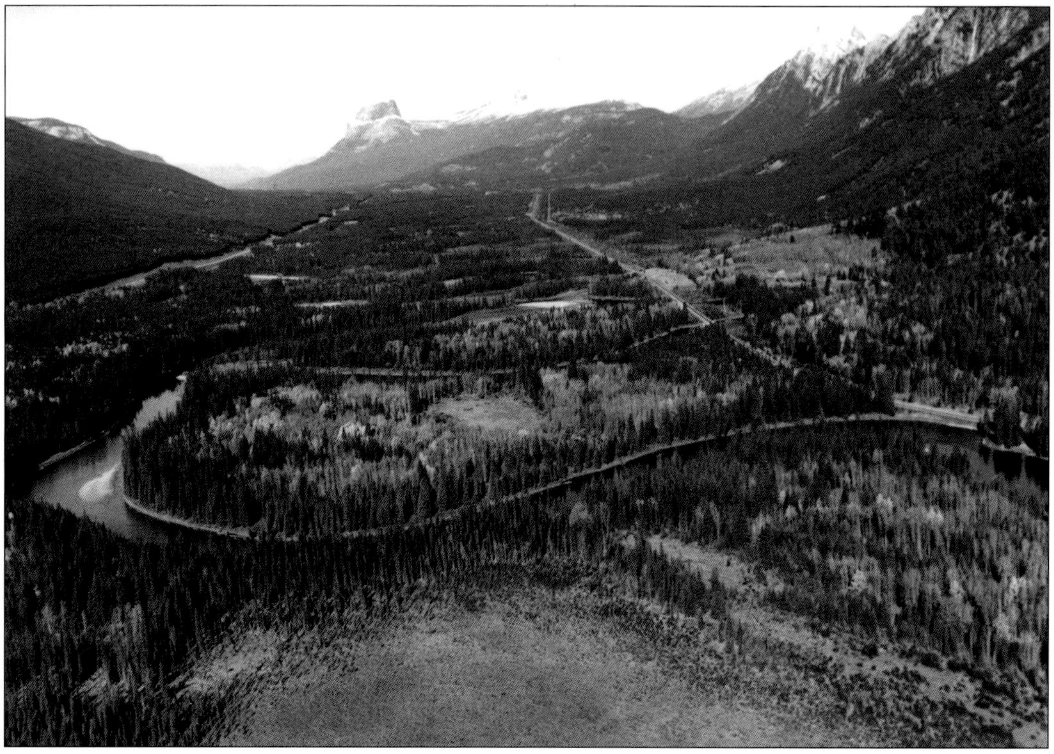

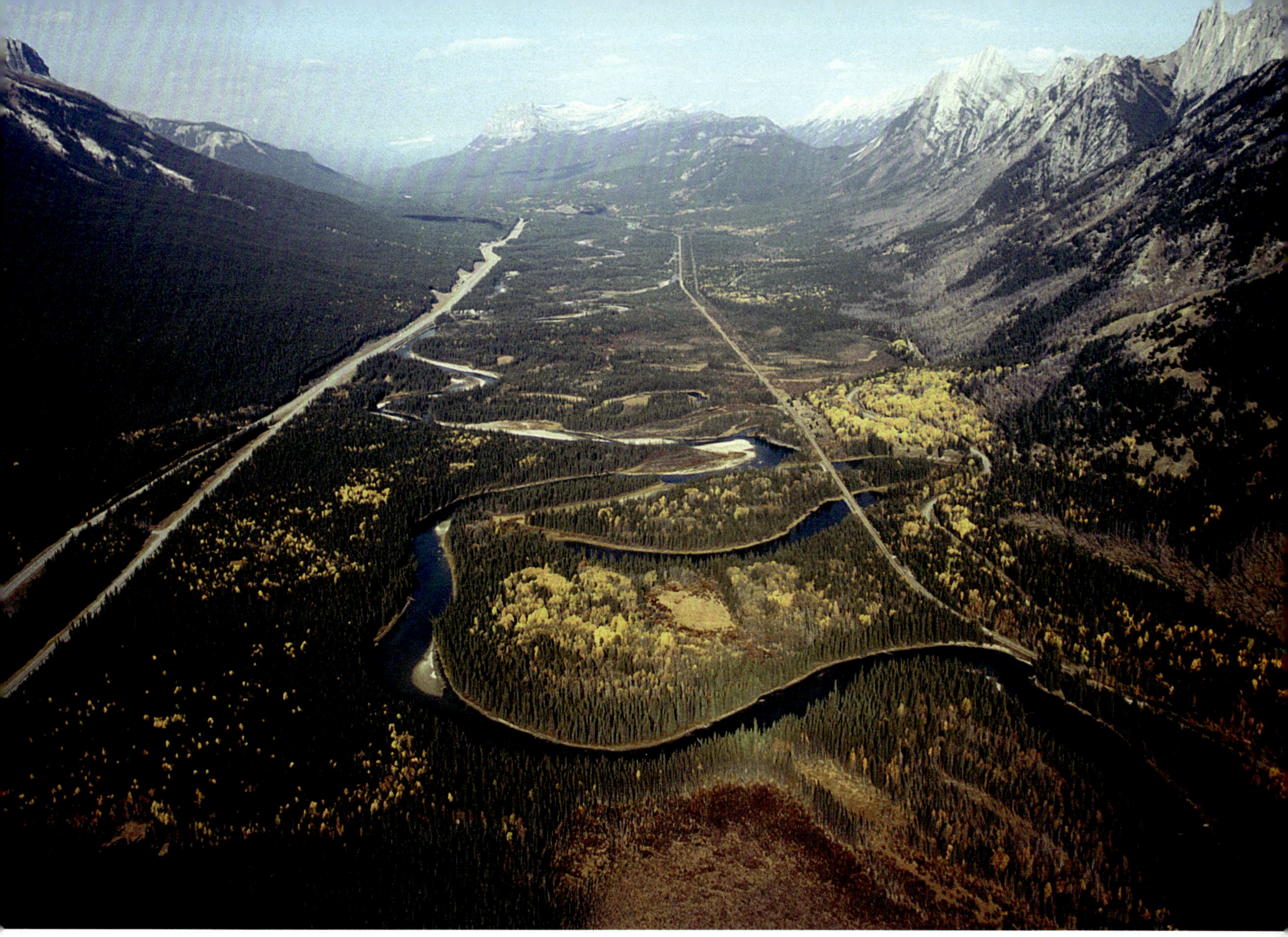

From the Sunshine Village junction to Castle Mountain, the Bow River valley runs along the base of the Sawback Range (on the right) in a northwest to southeast direction following the main trend of the Rocky Mountains. The 1921 photograph, with the railway (straight line right of centre) and the recently built automobile road (curved line right of the railway), still shows the vestiges of a landscape frequently burned by First Nations, and later by the wood and coal-burning locomotives of the CPR. The focus for long-term human burning was probably a corridor of grasslands, willow, and aspen forests along the river, and the dry ungulate winter range slopes rising to the northeast. By the time of the 1985 view, with the passing of generations without fire, the deciduous forests and shrublands were disappearing under dense conifers. Park's staff carried out prescribed burns on large areas of the Sawback Range in 1985, 1994, and 1998, and fired patches are visible in the most recent view.[7] The original 1950s Trans-Canada Highway is visible south (right) of the Bow River in 1985, and the 2003 photo shows the view after the highway was upgraded to four lanes though this portion of the valley in 1997.

6.7A CROSSING WASH AT FIVE MILE CREEK, 1922 (BYRON HARMON, WHYTE NA 71-4493)

6.7B VIEW OF THE MOUNTAINS IN BANFF NATIONAL PARK, CA. 1945 (NATIONAL PARKS, LIBRARY ARCHIVES CANADA PA 145344))

6.7C WEST ENTRANCE, BOW VALLEY PARKWAY, JUNE 2003 (CW 2003-06B-16)

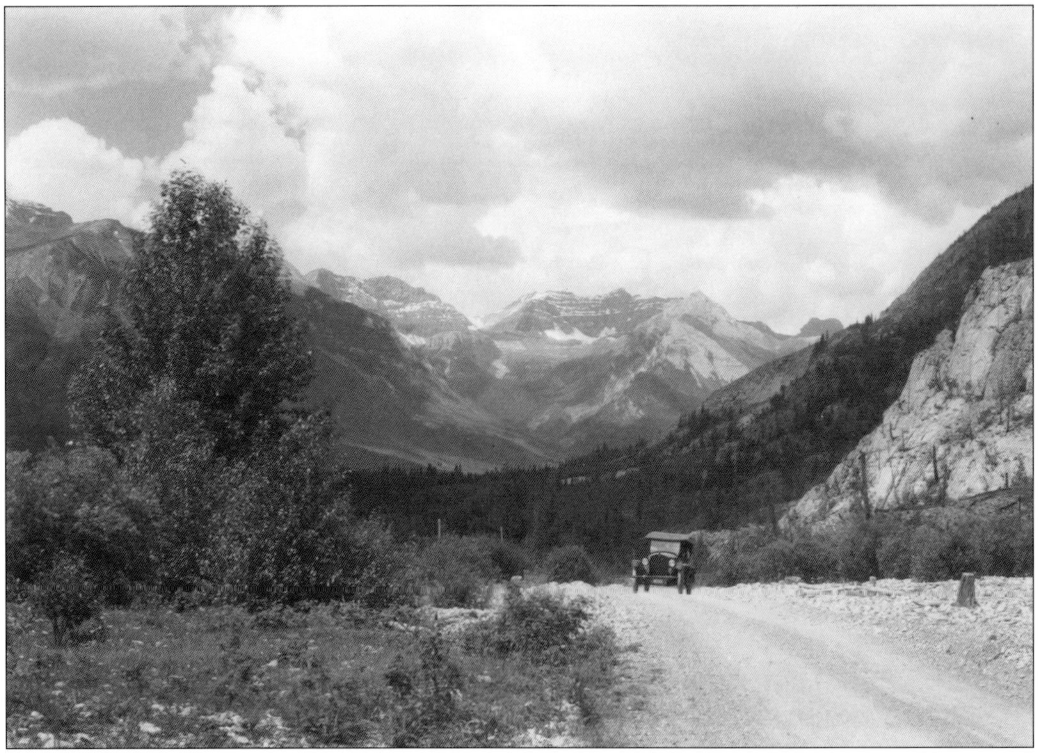

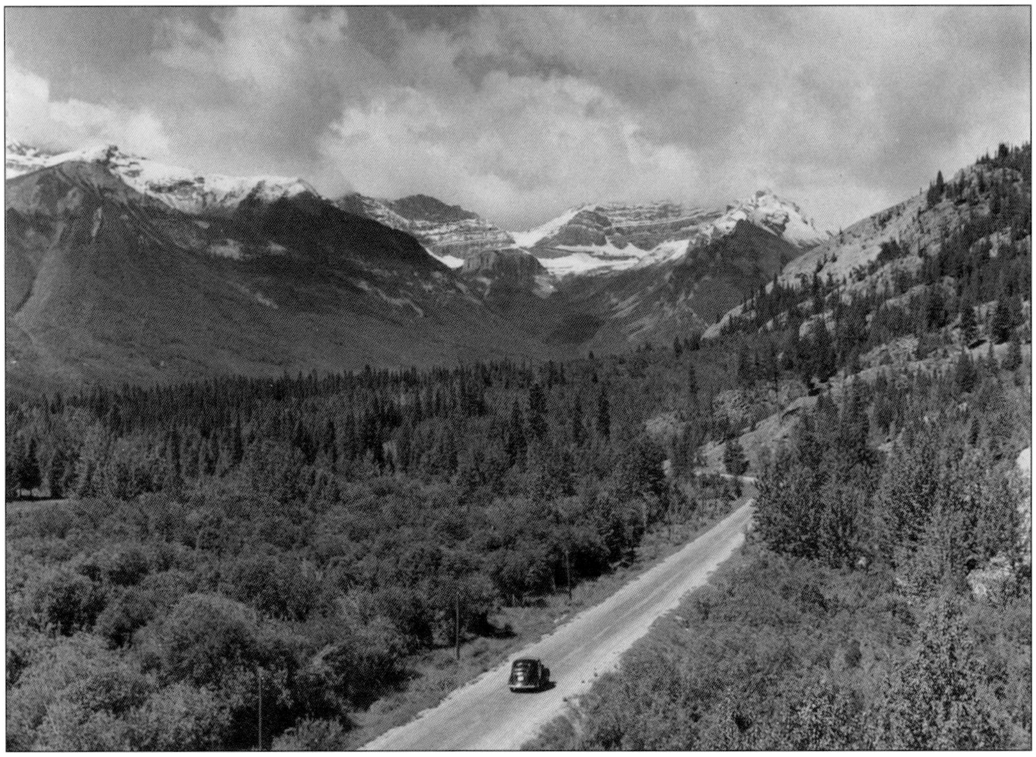

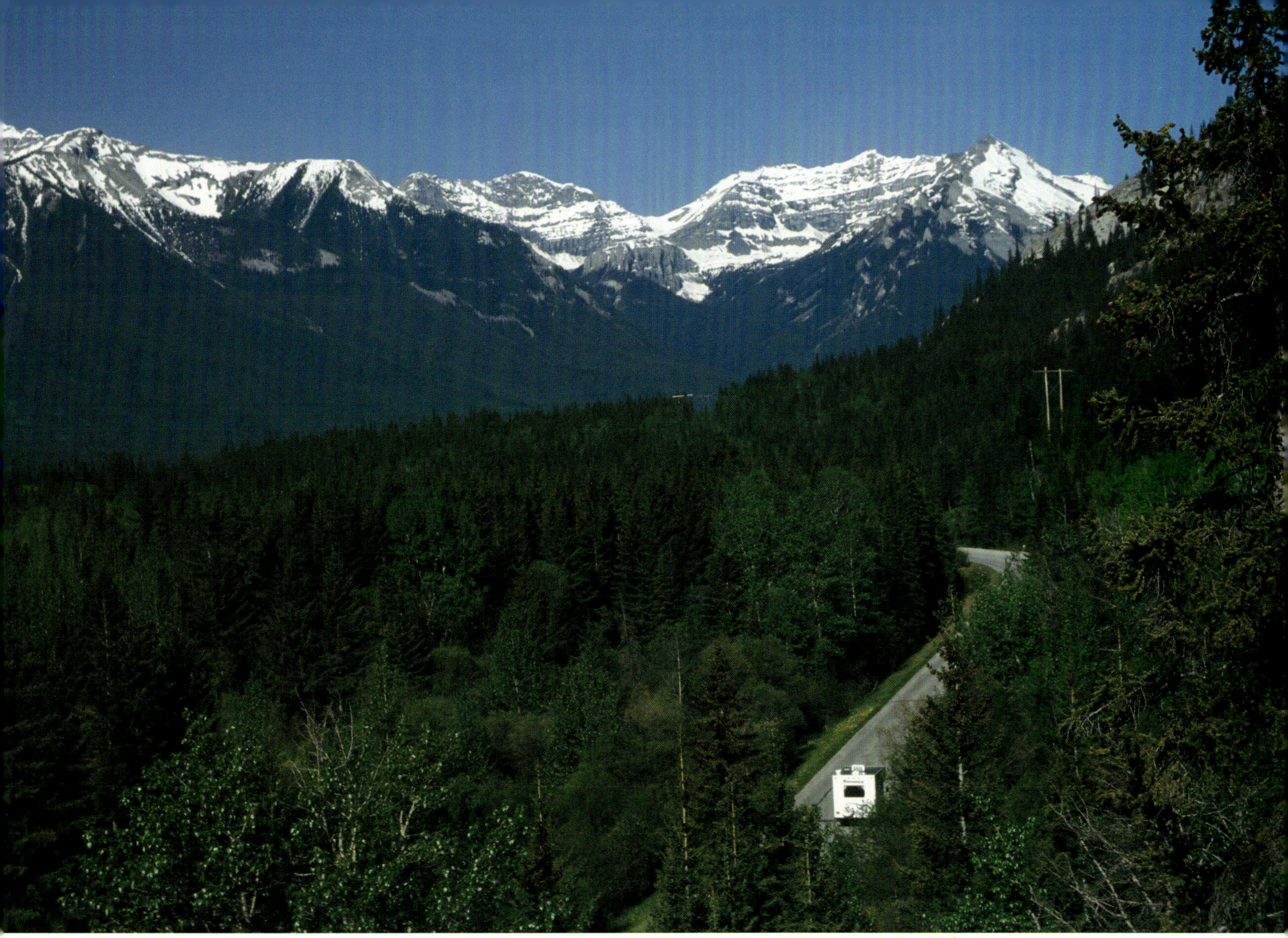

Each year during spring snow melt, or intense summer rainstorms, freshets pour down every main mountain gully, carrying large loads of unstable gravels towards the Bow River and depositing them in fans at the base of steep slopes. These frequently disturbed areas are favoured sites for trembling aspen and balsam poplar. However, while shifting alluvial streams may create good habitat for some plants, they also plug culverts under the railway and highway, and for the last century maintenance crews have waged annual warfare with the fan-building process. Deep ditches are dug to constrain the streams to predefined channels leading to culverts. Alluvial gravel is gathered and piled. But every year, gravity and water bring more deposits down from the slopes, and the mechanical earthmovers repeat their cycle of work. Gradually, with lessening disturbance, alluvial fans are becoming more stable and forests are changing from more open deciduous trees to dense conifers.[8]

Byron Harmon's 1922 photograph shows a recent wash of alluvial materials across the road, and much of the vegetation has been recently disturbed by fire and water flow. Soon after this picture was taken, Five Mile Creek was trenched and diverted eastwards. By the 1940s, willow, balsam poplar and aspen have re-vegetated the roadside, and grown substantially. In 2003, after nearly eighty years without fire or alluvial disturbance, white spruce is increasingly abundant.

6.8A ENGINE ON TRACK NEAR SAWBACK, 1885 (O.B. BUELL, GLENBOW NA 4697-15)

6.8B CONTAINER CARS ON WEST-BOUND FREIGHT TRAIN NEAR SAWBACK, JUNE 2004 (CW 2004-06D-09)

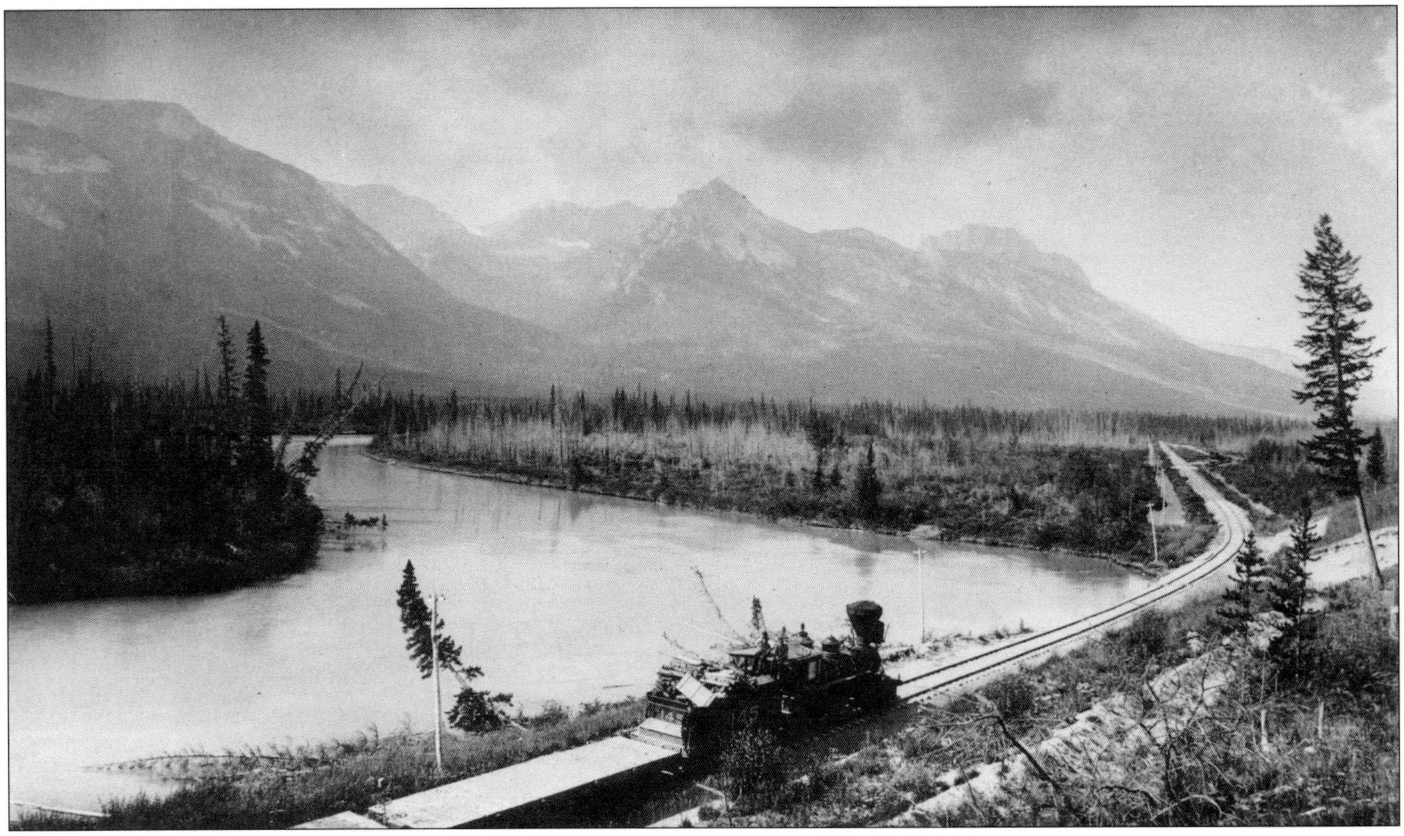

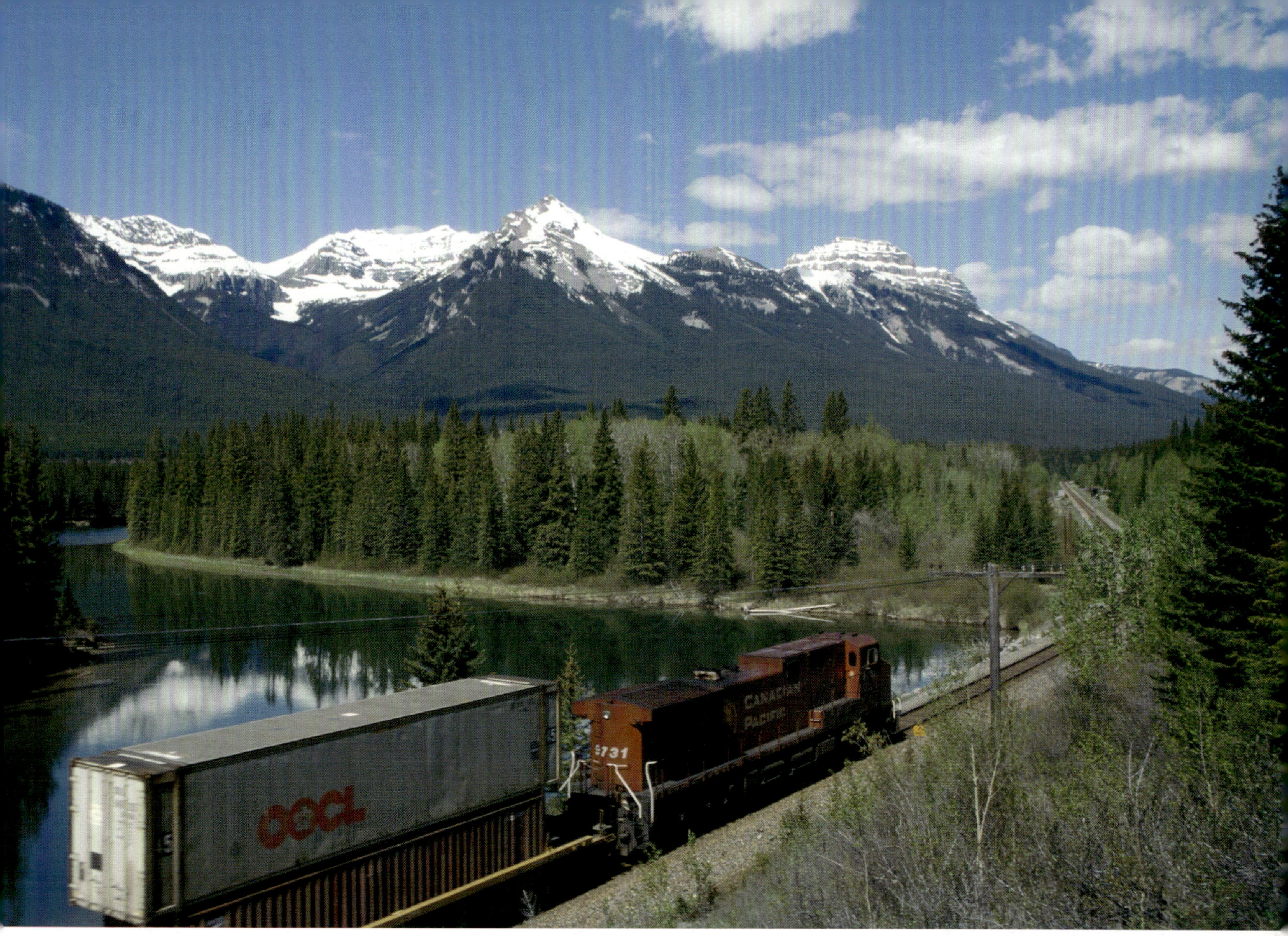

The changing nature of railway freight operations over a period of 120 years is evident in these photographs of the CPR mainline just west of Banff, and they also illustrate changes in vegetation ecology. Wetlands and shrublands along the Bow River are very flammable in early spring, right after the valley-bottom snow has melted but in advance of green-up. First Nations most commonly burned in this season and were likely responsible for the relatively young age of the forests when they were again burned by a new wave of human culture during the period of railroad construction.[9] Sometimes these spring-season human ignitions could smoulder for months, and along with lightning-caused fires, burn up the sides of the valleys later during the summer droughts. For example, Tom Wilson, who later became Banff's first guide and outfitter, recounted that while packing supplies by horse for the first railway surveyors in July 1881, "Excepting for the fact that we encountered a large forest fire near Hole-in-the-Wall Mountain, and had to swim the swollen Bow twice, nothing of importance happened on that trip."[10] Hole-in-the-Wall (Mount Cory) lies just east of the burned scene of the historic photograph. The Douglas fir on the right edge of the old photograph had survived past fires that have pruned away the lower branches. The modern photograph reveals the change in vegetation that has occurred through the elimination of fire for nearly a century.

6.9A HILLSDALE RANCH, 1902 (J. SMITH, GLENBOW NA 4654-11)

6.9B HILLSDALE MEADOWS, SEPTEMBER 1999 (CW 1999-09C-26)

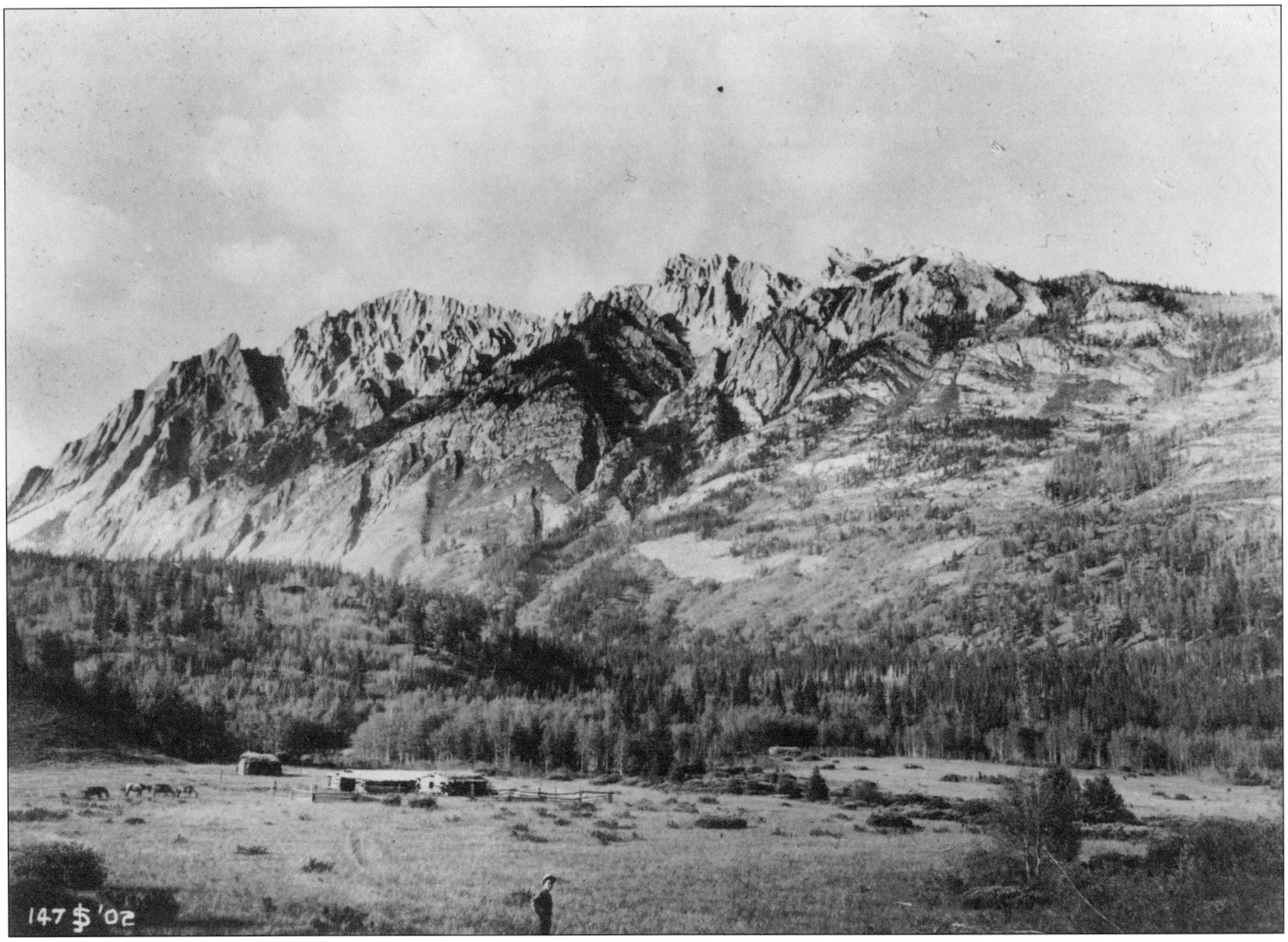

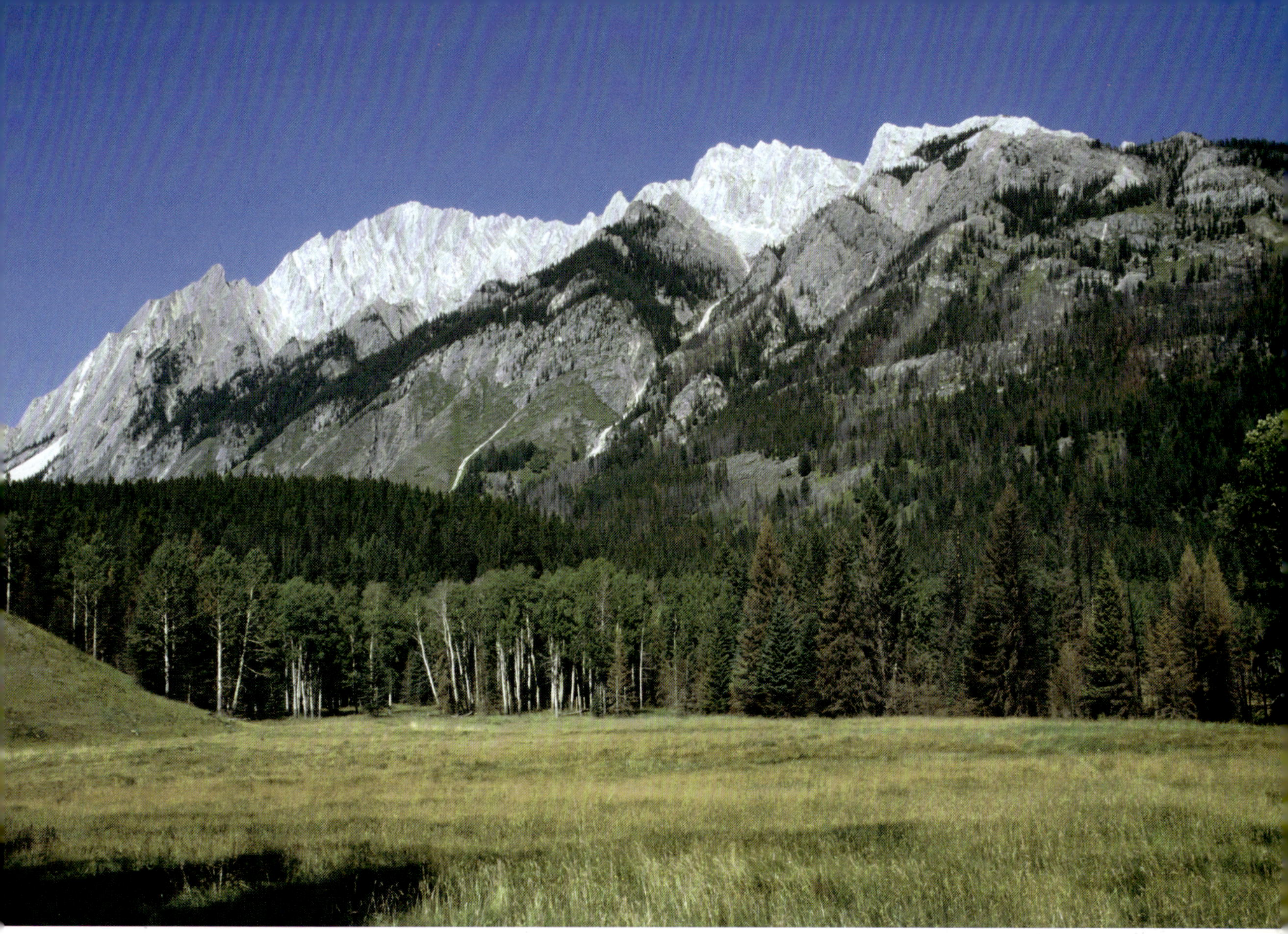

Moving towards the upper reaches of the Bow River, winter snows deepen and the conifer forests thicken. Hillsdale Meadow lies in one of the most westerly areas in the valley where elk and bison could successfully winter in most years. It also became important to First Nations and early settlers because of its ability to sustain year-round horse grazing.[11] In early times the meadows were a favoured camping spot for native peoples travelling back and forth over Vermilion Pass to the Columbia Valley. In 1883 Hillsdale was the location of one of the CPR's main commissary camps for railway construction, during the early 1900s a small ranch operated here, and in the 1930s a park warden and his family lived immediately east at Massive Station. The 1902 photograph shows that frequent fires have run up from the meadow, opening up the forest around Douglas firs in the background and stimulating dense willow and aspen growth. Conifer growth in the recent picture (mostly lodgepole pine and white spruce) has now surrounded the old trees and filled in many of the small grasslands on the background.

Contrast aspen and willow conditions in the two pictures. The older picture shows an almost impenetrable thicket of these species around the meadow perimeter. In the recent picture, taken a few years after a prescribed burn, all regenerating aspen sprouts have been browsed to the ground by elk. Larger, older stems were blackened to a two-metre height by elk debarking during the 1940s, the elk-scarred bark helping the trees survive the burn. Historically, it is likely that elk were hunted to low densities by humans and other predators and did not forage next to the dense, fire-created aspen thickets where their hunters could hide.[12] After the re-introduction of elk from Yellowstone National Park beginning in 1918, they have thrived in the Bow Valley and have had a great impact on aspen and willow growth.[13]

6.10A CASTLE MOUNTAIN AND SILVER CITY, CA. 1887 (BOORNE AND MAY, GLENBOW NA 1753-28)

6.10B SILVER CITY MEADOW, SEPTEMBER 2003 (CW 2003-09A-06)

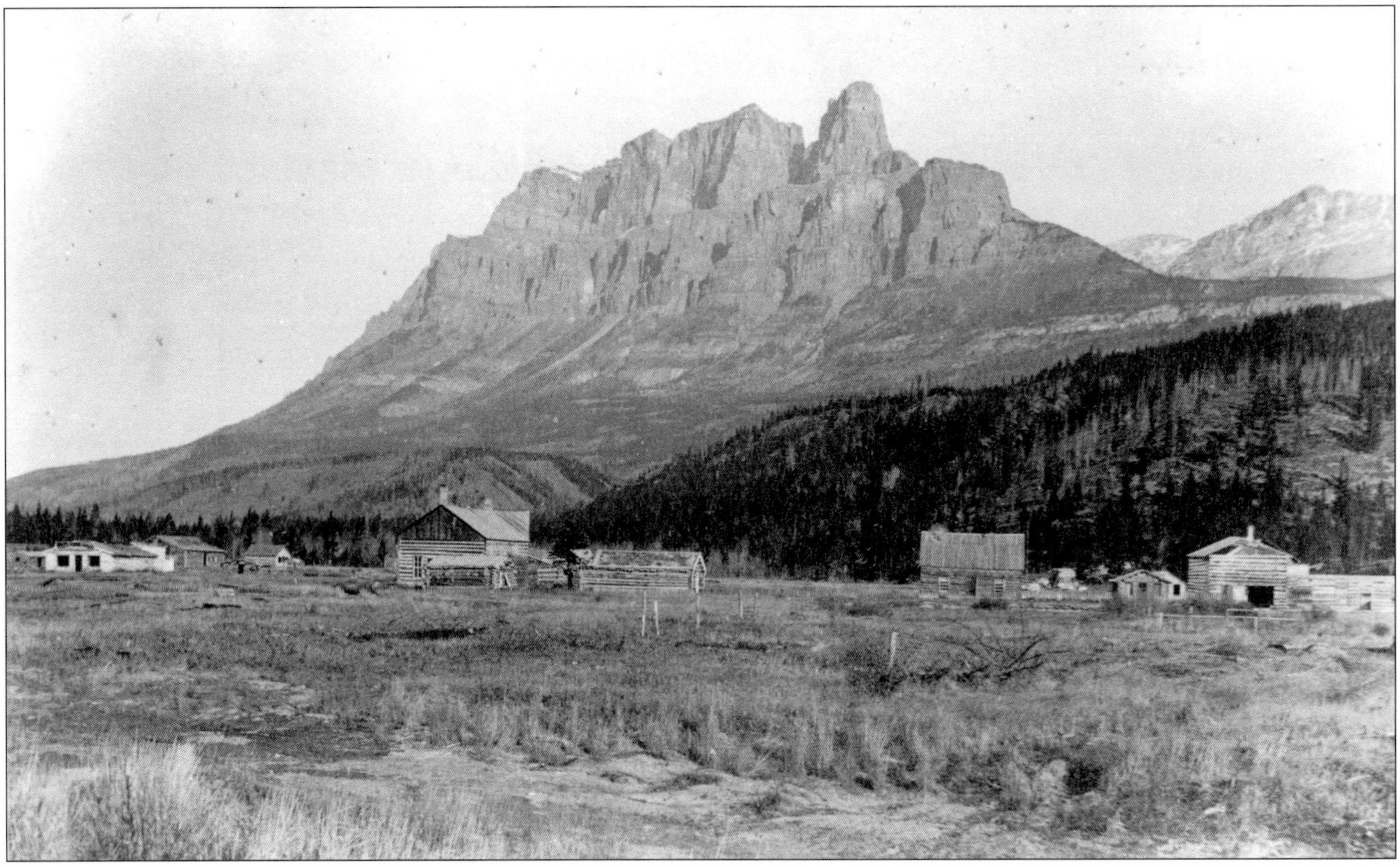

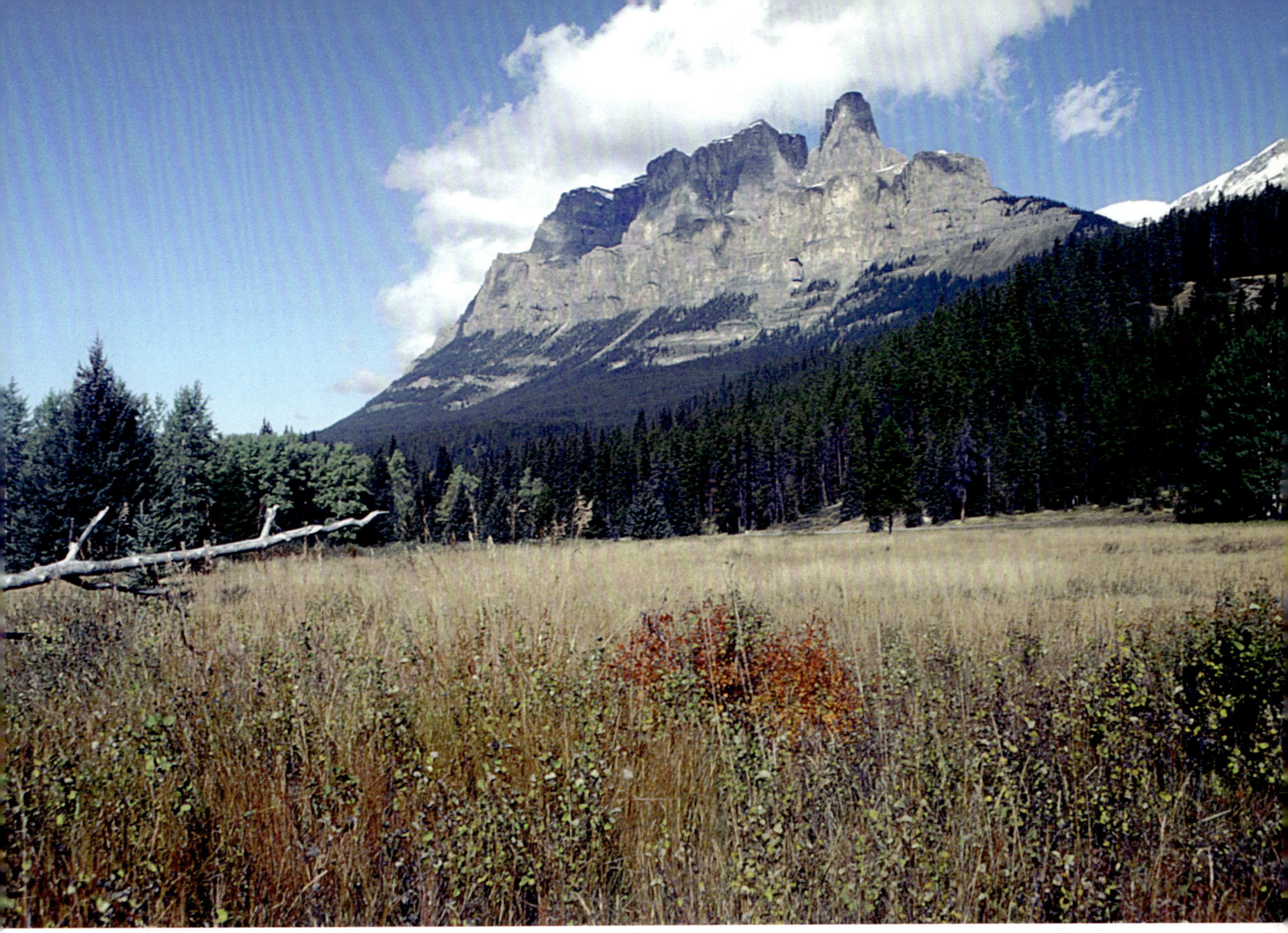

A rough-and-tough bunch of entrepreneurs – prospectors, land speculators, loggers, and saloon keepers – followed the leading end of the railroad as it advanced across the country. In the fall of 1883 this unique human-assemblage reached the Bow Valley and, when word went out about potential rich veins of copper and silver ore in the bedrock around Castle Mountain, Silver City sprang up on Silverton Creek. Historian Eleanor Luxton recounts that it was a bustling little town of some 285 or 300 men, seven married women, and five "girls."[14] Even the government was caught up in the promotion, and the deputy minister of the Interior was pleased to report in 1883, "The prospects of successful mining for the precious metals on the eastern slopes of the Rocky Mountains are exceedingly encouraging." By that time the population had swelled to several thousand as the construction crews of the CPR had appeared on the scene, and although they soon followed the railhead westward, hundreds of would-be miners stayed on over the winter of 1883–84. The town quickly expanded to include at least three hotels, numerous restaurants, and several saloons, often featuring gambling dens at their rear.

Within two years even the most naive new visitors to the area knew that these sedimentary mountains were, in fact, mostly devoid of any mineral-rich deposits. The mining rush was over and the once raucous town in Boorne and May's view has been all but abandoned. Only one man, Joe Smith, continued to believe in the area's hidden riches, and the "Hermit of Castle Mountain" remained Silver City's sole occupant for the next fifty years. One hundred and twenty years after its founding, only some slight depressions scattered over the grassy meadows mark its long-ago existence.[15]

6.11A CASTLE MOUNTAIN INTERNMENT CAMP, CA. 1915 (PARK, CALGARY, GLENBOW NA 1870-2)

6.11B ELDON MEADOW BELOW CASTLE MOUNTAIN, SEPTEMBER 2003 (CW 2003-09A-10)

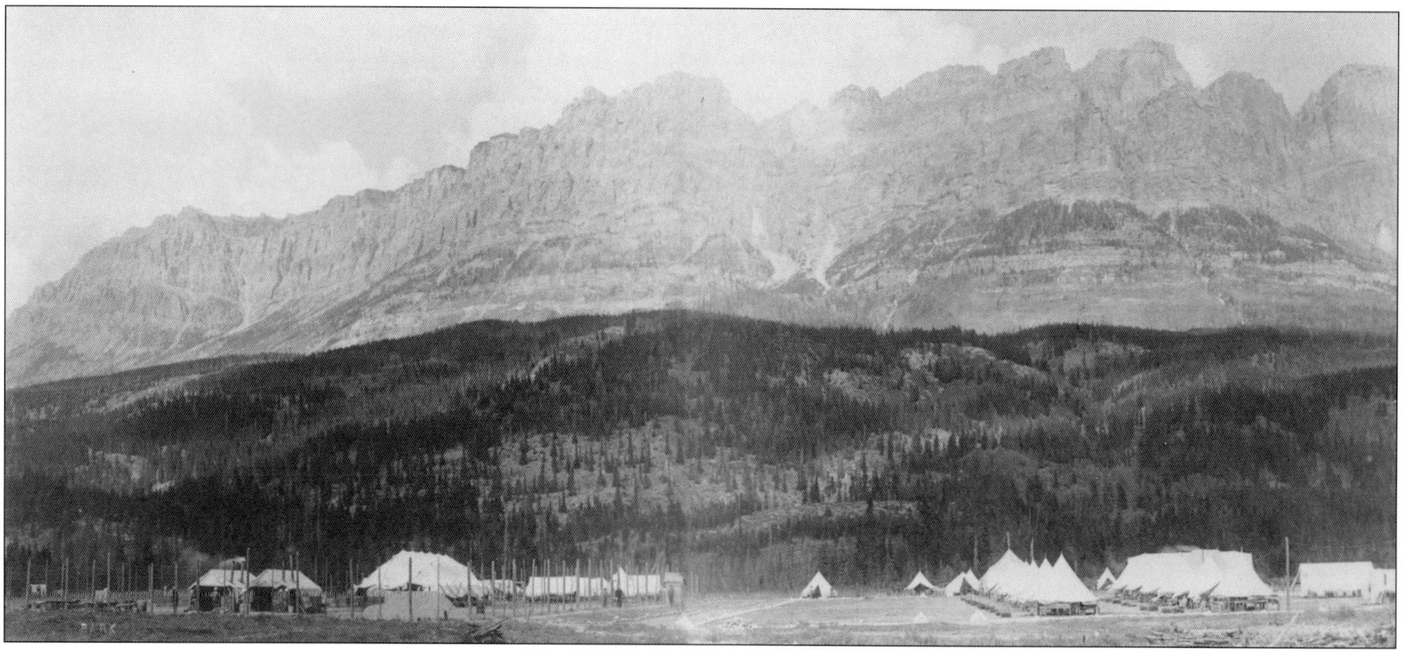

At the start of the First World War, Canada contained thousands of immigrant workers, mainly employed in resource extraction industries and on railroad construction, but not yet full citizens of the country. Parliament promptly listed those from the Austro-Hungarian Empire as "enemy aliens," and if they were unemployed and lived near a city required them to report to a local magistrate. Under regulations in the War Measures Act, any such men who were identified as a security threat could be interned for the duration of the war – but in reality it was an attempt to prevent them from gathering for relief in urban centres. Thousands of men, mostly of Ukrainian origin, were moved to isolated areas of the country to perform useful labour, and in the West many were engaged in work camps set up by the Dominion Parks Branch.

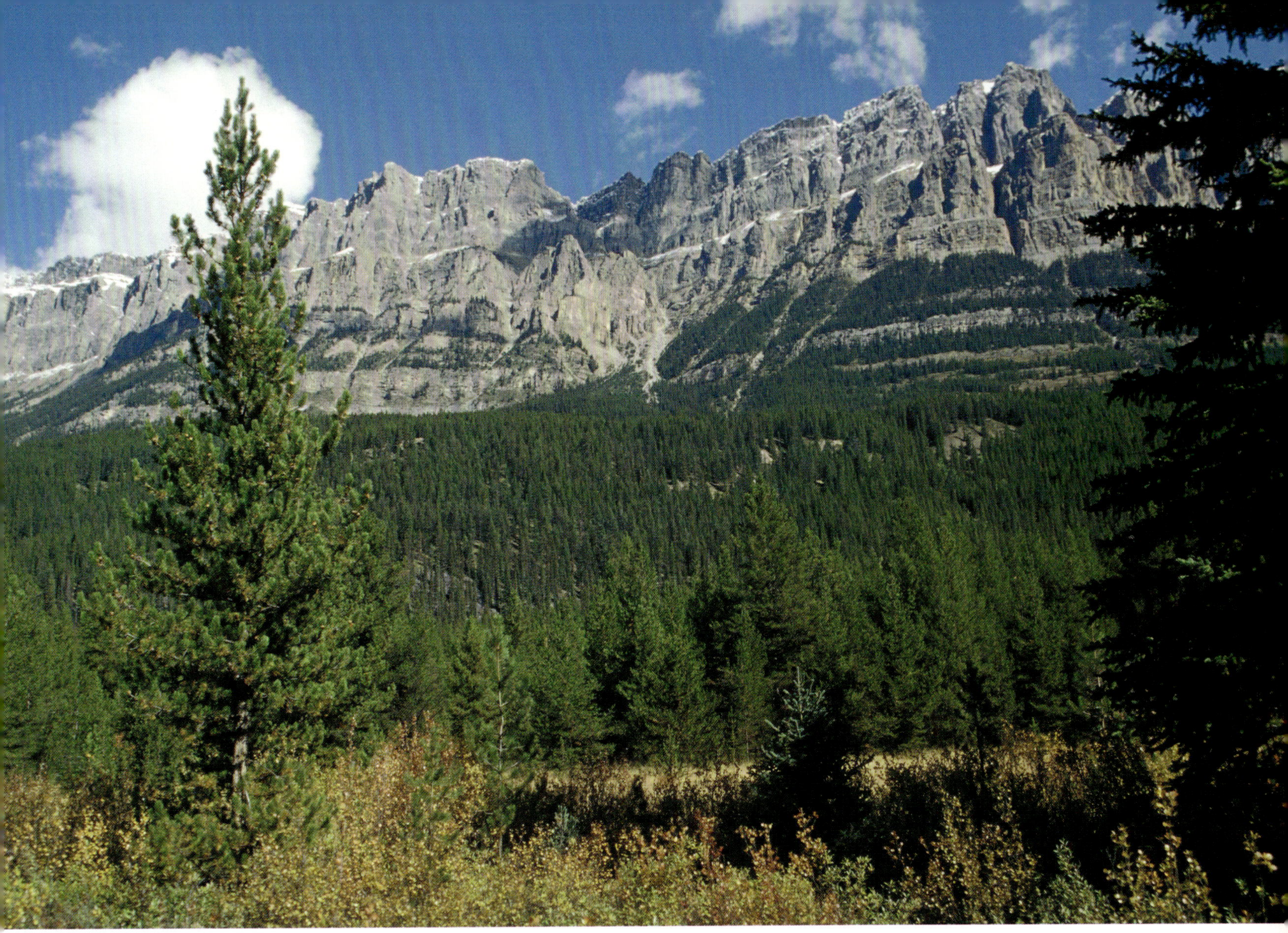

One such camp was created at the foot of Castle Mountain when in July 1915 a workforce of over 150 men began labouring with only pick and shovel to extend the motor-road from Banff to Lake Louise. The prisoners were housed in tents behind a barbed-wire stockade and paid only twenty-five cents per day. In winter they were moved to cramped quarters near the Cave and Basin pool at Banff and did such jobs as building new trails and bridges, widening roads, and clearing timber to expand the Banff Springs Golf Course. Low pay, hard menial labour, and poor living conditions led to low morale for both prisoners and guards in the camps. Because of such problems and a lack of labourers available to Canada's industries due to wartime circumstances, the national park camps closed in 1917, and many workers hired on with the Canadian Pacific Railway or at coal mines in the Crowsnest Pass of British Columbia.

Although the alien internment program appeased a patriotic Canadian public, it is now recognized as unjust treatment to many recent immigrants who posed no real threat to the country. In 1995 the descendants of the workers placed a monument commemorating their forbearers' forced labour along the Bow Valley Parkway near Castle Mountain camp. The meadow once occupied by the site itself is now almost totally overgrown by a forest of lodgepole pine and white spruce.[16]

6.12A BOW RANGE FROM NEAR CASTLE MOUNTAIN, ALBERTA, 1902 (J. SMITH, LIBRARY ARCHIVES CANADA, PA 20462)

6.12B CASTLE MOUNTAIN VILLAGE, JULY 2001 (CW 2001-07D-10)

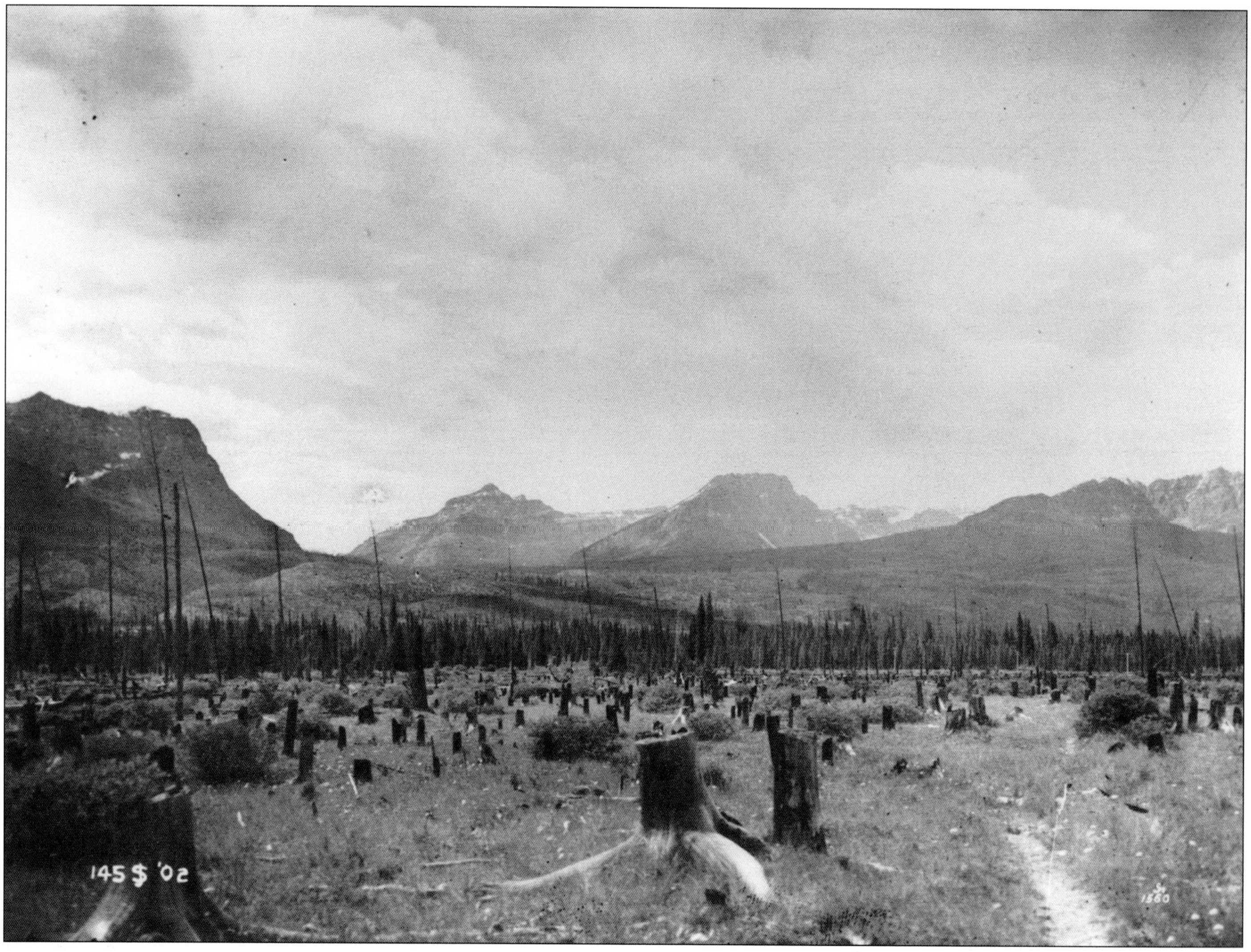

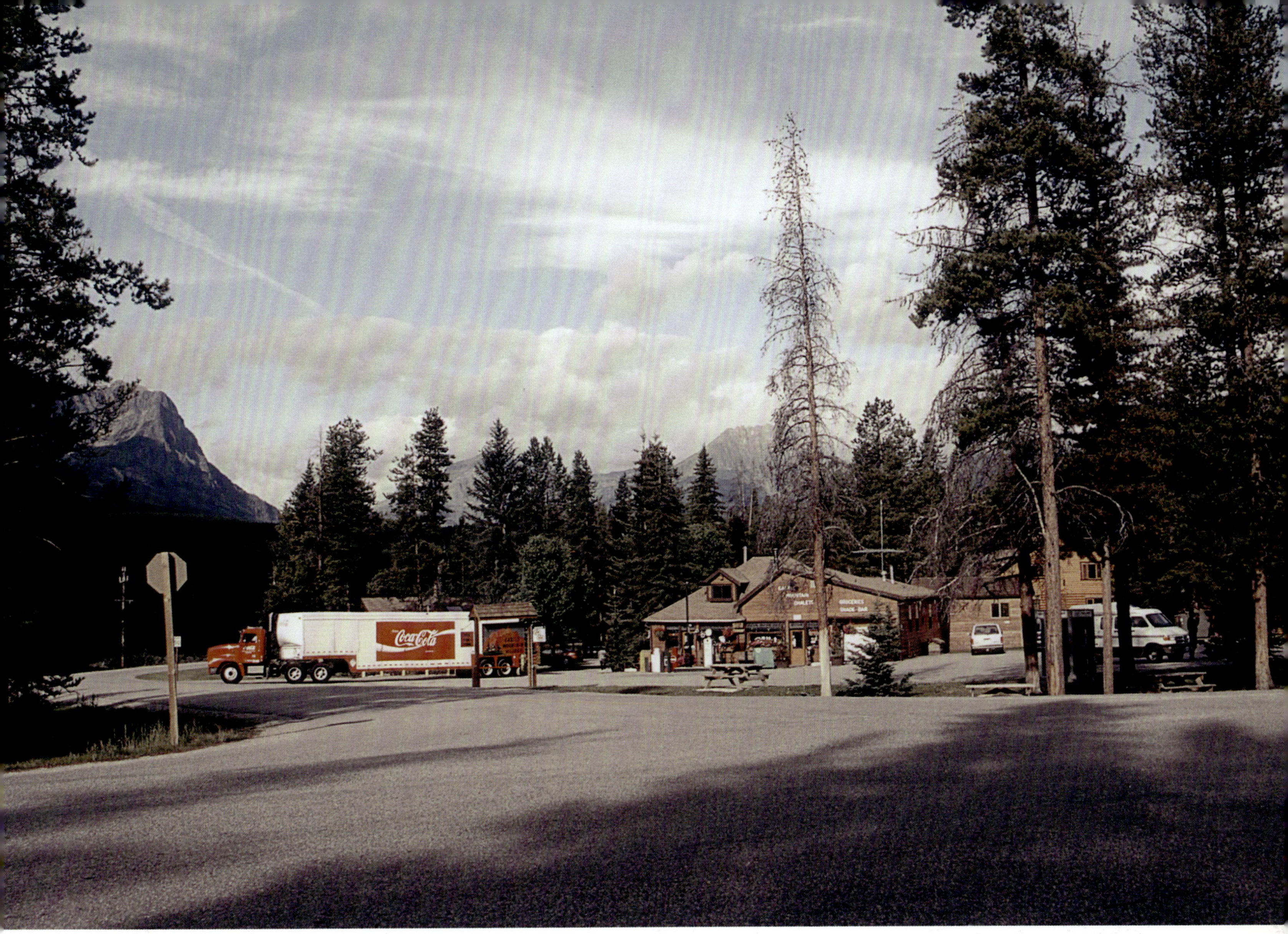

On August 18, 1858, James Hector of the Palliser Expedition camped below Castle Mountain, likely near the junction of the trail visible in the 1902 picture, in preparation for crossing Vermilion Pass. Hector, the Expedition's medical doctor and geologist-naturalist, was exploring passes in this part of the Rockies for possible transportation routes over the divide, while its leader, John Palliser, reconnoitred areas further south. After a day of smoking the meat from a bull moose obtained by "Nimrod," their invaluable Stoney hunter, Hector's party crossed the Bow River and ascended Vermilion Pass, in the centre left of the photographs.[17] In 1923 this would become the route for the Banff-Windermere Highway, the first automobile road across the Rocky Mountains within the mountain national parks. The Canadian Pacific Railroad built a bungalow camp for their "all-expenses paid" automobile tours at the junction of the roads leading west to Lake Louise and south to Radium. The resort, pictured in its rebuilt version, is now open year-round and is called Castle Mountain Village.[18]

The stumps in the historic photograph are close to railroad mainline where trees were often cut to provide ties, bridge timbers, and building materials, but this area was also logged before inclusion in the national park by the Eau Claire and Bow River Lumber Company, which had a timber berth near the base of Castle Mountain. The slash created from logging was very flammable, and fires in 1906 and 1908 fed by this fuel swept through the east side of Vermilion Pass. By the 1920s, except for the logging of fire-killed timber, such commercial activities had ended and the forest had begun to regenerate unimpaired.[19]

6.13A BANFF-WINDERMERE ROAD, KOOTENAY NATIONAL PARK, CA. 1925 (PHOTOGRAPHER UNKNOWN, GLENBOW NA 3884-35)

6.13B KOOTENAY PARKWAY, NEAR KOOTENAY CROSSING WARDEN STATION, SEPTEMBER 2003 (CW 2003-09F-24)

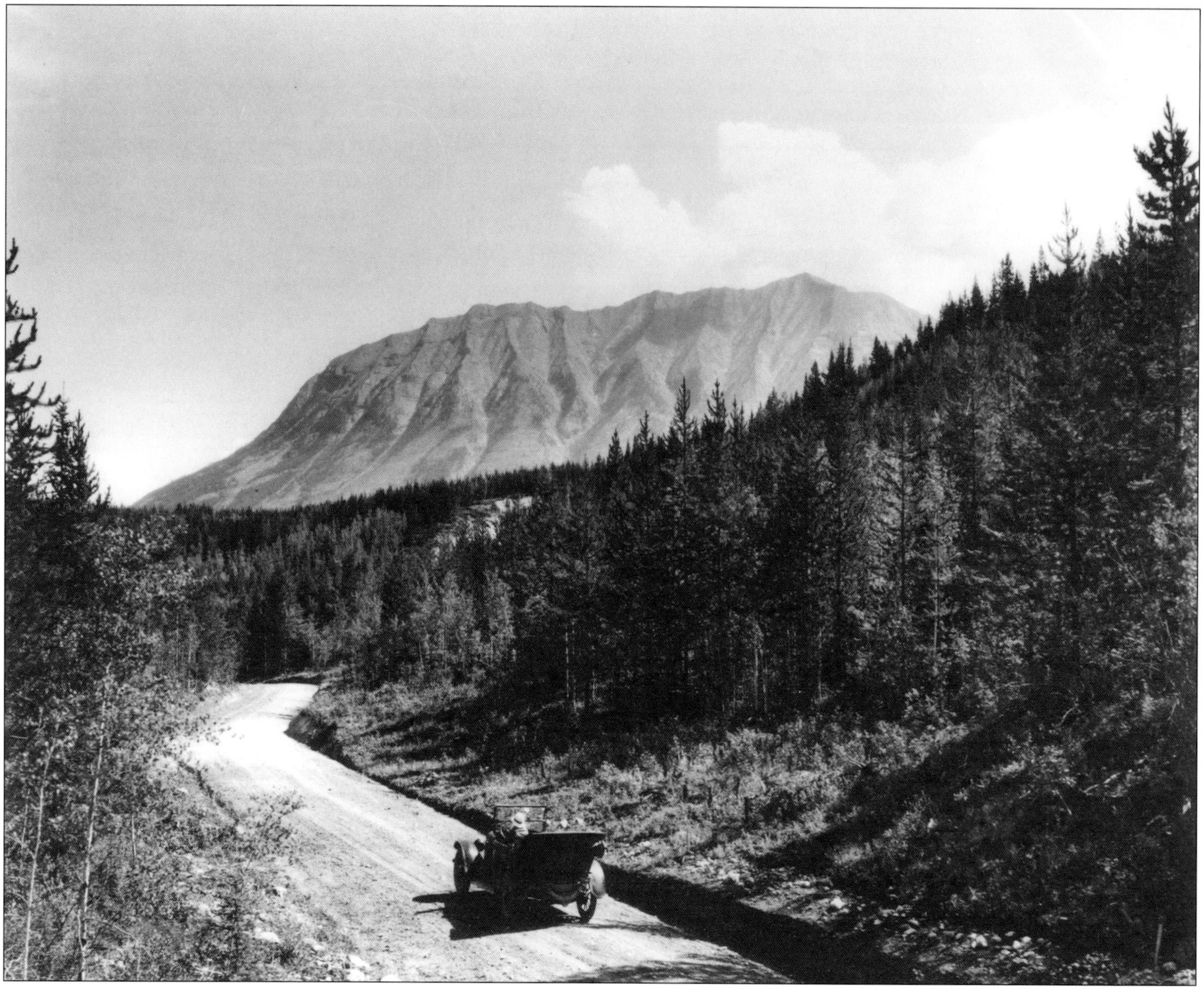

Heading south, Highway 93 through Kootenay National Park climbs over a ridge of land in the centre of the valley to avoid steep terrain in the lower part of Hector's Gorge on the Vermilion River. The road then descends, likely following the route of a long-used trail, to Kootenay Crossing. This parkland of meadows and aspen near the river would have provided an excellent campsite for First Nations, and, after being taken up for private agricultural purposes in the period before the road was built, subsequently became a national parks warden station.

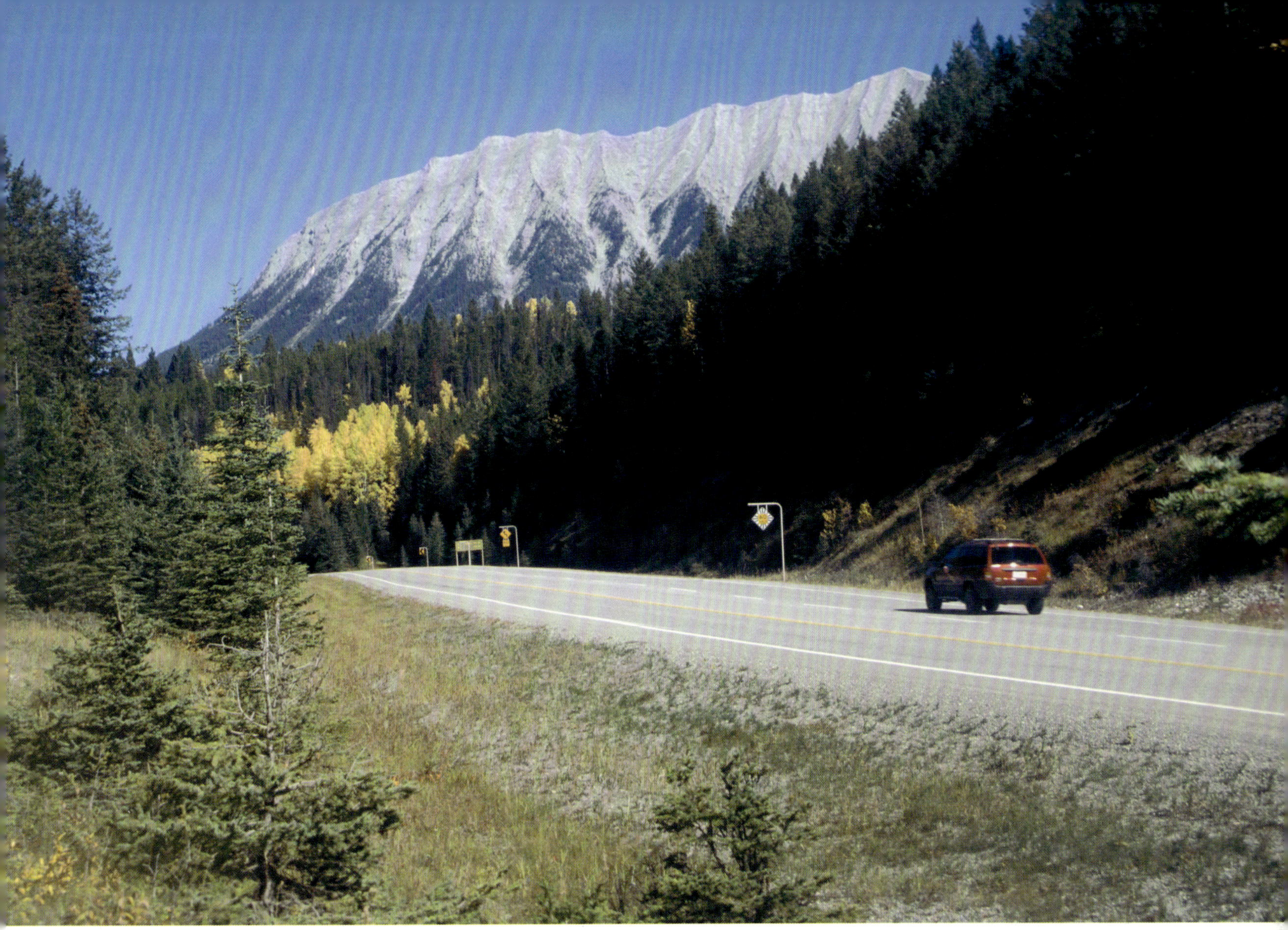

On August 24, 1858, Hector crossed over this hill, but left the main trail to travel northwards up the Kootenay Valley. While travelling from Castle Junction, Hector had observed the campsites and recent horse tracks left by the K'tunaxa (Kootenay) but commented on the generally low human use in the area: "The absence of game, which is very unaccountable, prevents the Indians tenting up this way to trap."[20] The lack of large ungulates was a common problem for almost all travellers through the Rockies, and in this case would soon put Hector's expedition in peril. They nearly starved before reaching the upper Bow Valley, but here "Nimrod" finally killed a moose, and they encountered a campsite of Stoney Nakoda hunters who further assisted the expedition.[21]

By 1960 several hundred elk were using this part of the Kootenay Valley, but today they are almost gone and deer are more abundant. What caused these wide fluctuations in large mammal numbers? Possibly, during prehistoric and early historic times, the combination of First Nations, wolves, bears, and other predators hunted large ungulate populations to very low densities. These "top-down" forces would be particularly important in the upper Kootenay Valley where winter snows made ungulate tracking and killing relatively easy. When Kootenay National Park was established in 1920, the park wardens' first jobs were to eliminate human poaching and to control predators. Combined with habitat resulting from historic forest fires, this created ideal "bottom-up" conditions for a thriving elk population. By 1990 wolves had returned to the area, and natural predators, combined with the road-kill from the increasingly busy highway, had virtually eliminated elk from this part of the valley.[22]

6.14A RADIUM HOT SPRINGS VILLAGE, 1939 (BRUNO ENGLER, WHYTE V227-5239)

6.14B HIGHWAY 93 AND RADIUM LODGE, KOOTENAY NATIONAL PARK, SEPTEMBER 2003 (CW 2003-09E-33)

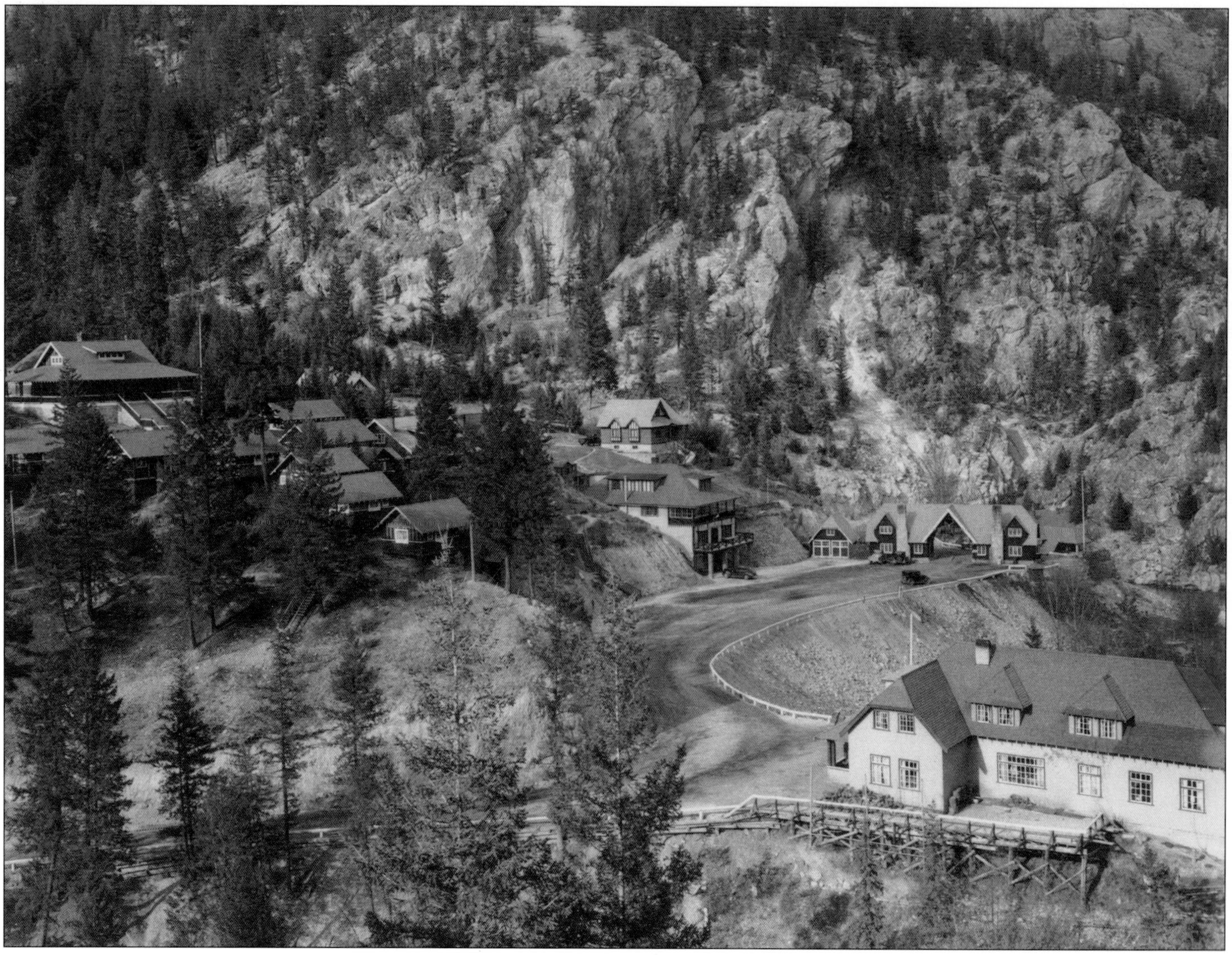

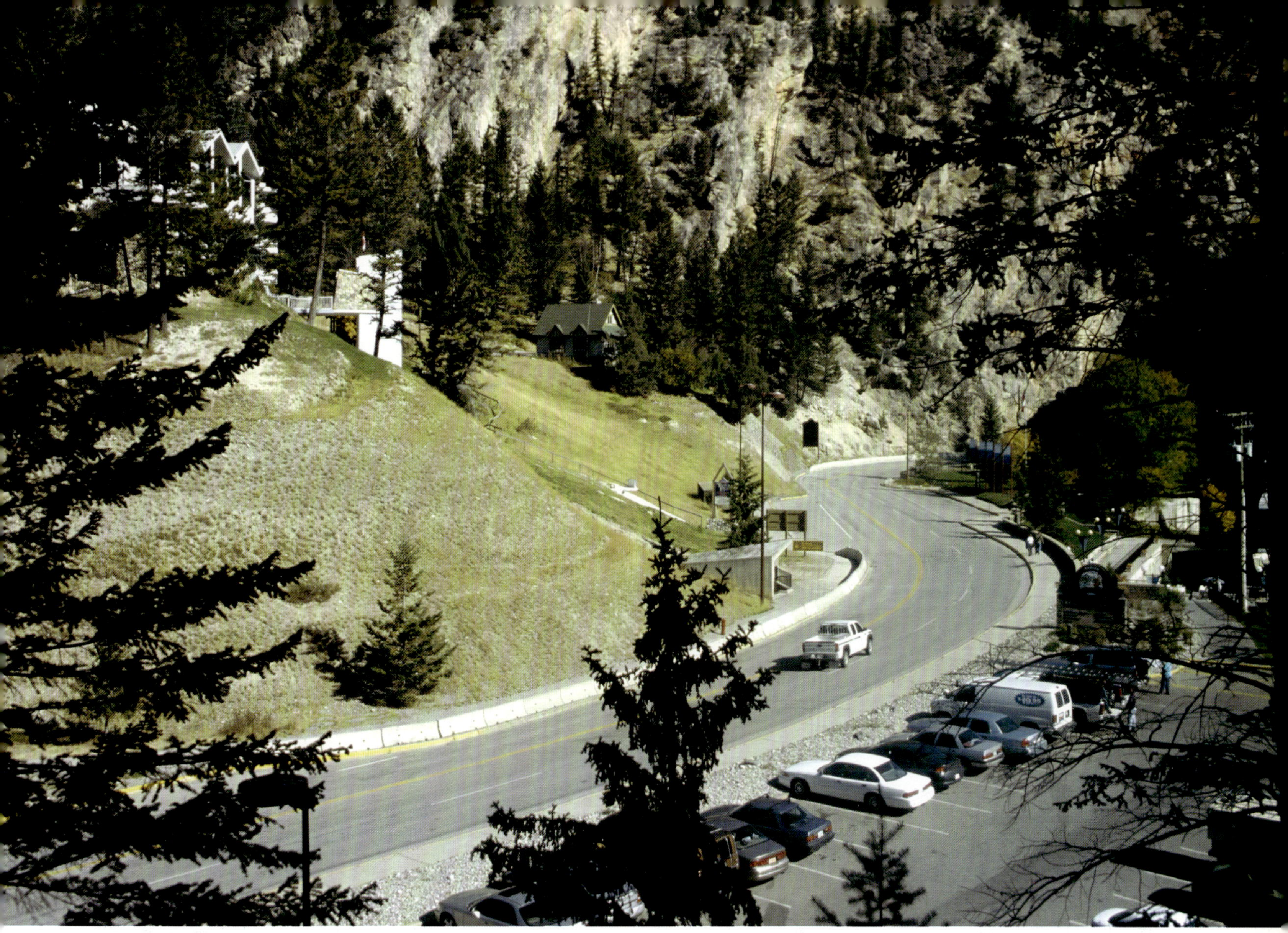

Since the original construction of the Banff-Windermere Highway in 1923, numerous changes have been made to its route and accompanying tourist development. After its completion the Canadian Pacific Railway established a number of automobile bungalow camps along its route, including Storm Mountain, Vermilion Crossing, and, as pictured here, Radium Hot Springs, built in 1926. The site for this camp was on the slopes above the hot springs that had historically been used by First Nations peoples and early miners until 1890, when the provincial government granted it to English developers who eventually built the first concrete bathing pool and associated log dressing rooms and caretaker's residence in 1914. With the planned construction of the Banff-Windermere, the federal government attempted to purchase the springs but eventually was forced to expropriate them in 1922 to secure control over development in the area.[23]

Once in Parks Branch hands, its Town Planning Division laid out a proposed townsite under the direction of noted English planner Thomas Adams. Visible in Bruno Engler's 1939 photograph is part of the resulting development, including the bungalow camp, the original Kootenay Park entrance gates and the park superintendent's residence (the steep-roofed building highest on the slope to the left of the gates). Construction of a widened road in the 1960s as well as the building of new hot pool facilities (the parking area of which is apparent at the bottom of the modern view) changed the area dramatically. The bungalow complex was removed and replaced by the construction of a large motor hotel, the Radium Hot Springs Lodge, visible at the left, and the park gates were moved to a new location three kilometres westward to relieve congestion in the pool area. The only remaining structure from the 1939 scene is the park superintendent's residence.[24]

6.15A LAKE WINDERMERE AND KOOTENAY/SHUSWAP CAMP ON OLD FORT POINT, 1923 (PHOTOGRAPHER UNKNOWN, GLENBOW NA 1135-59)

6.15B INVERMERE, BRITISH COLUMBIA, MAY 2003 (CW 2003-05K-0

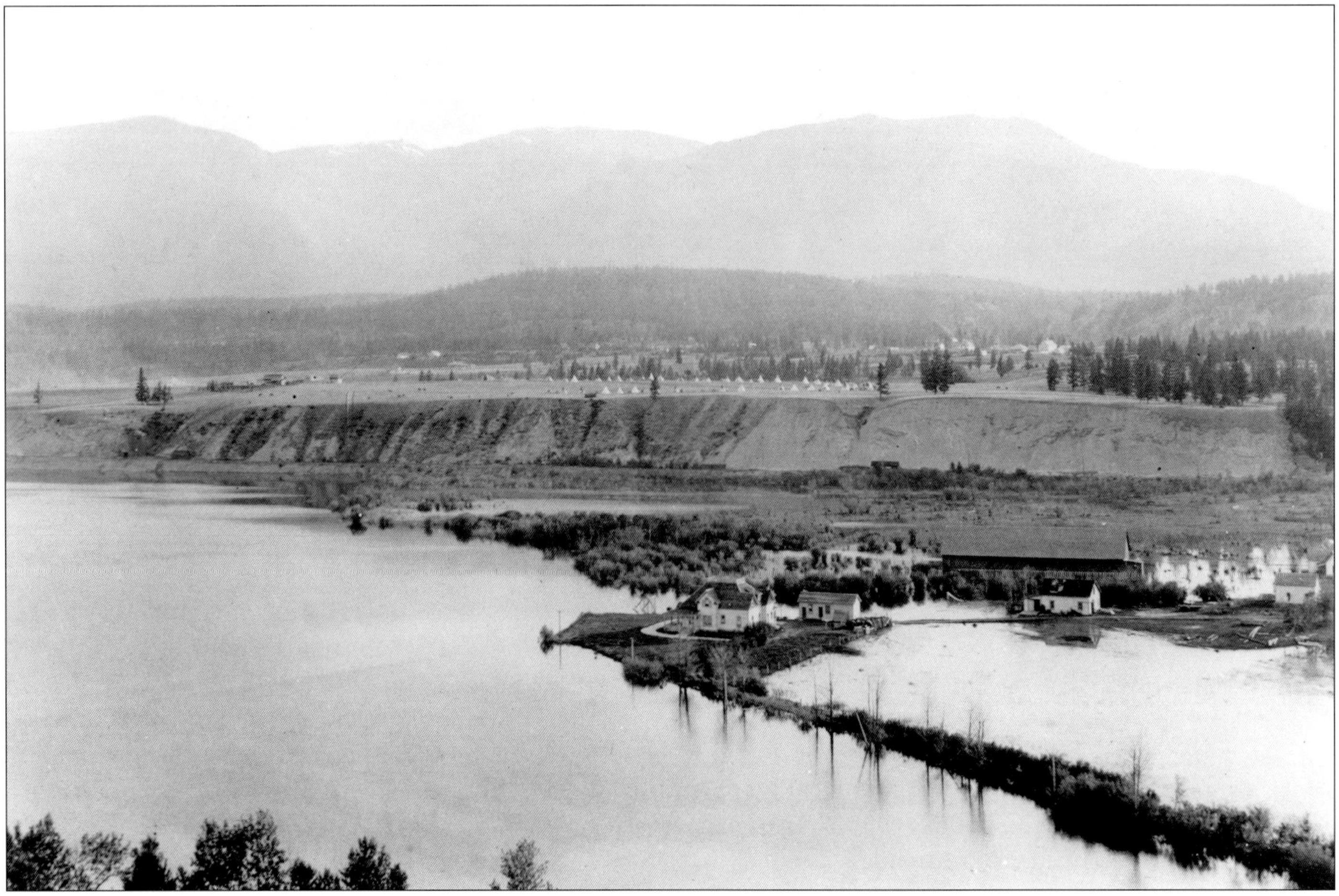

The area of Windermere and Columbia lakes on the headwaters of the Columbia River are populated by First Nations of the K'tunaxa and Shuswap. Prior to the 1780s these peoples routinely visited, and even occupied, the eastern slopes to hunt buffalo. However, this use ended after European diseases decimated native populations and the Peigan, a plains tribe that also hunted the mountain foothills, obtained guns and prevented them from crossing the mountains.[25]

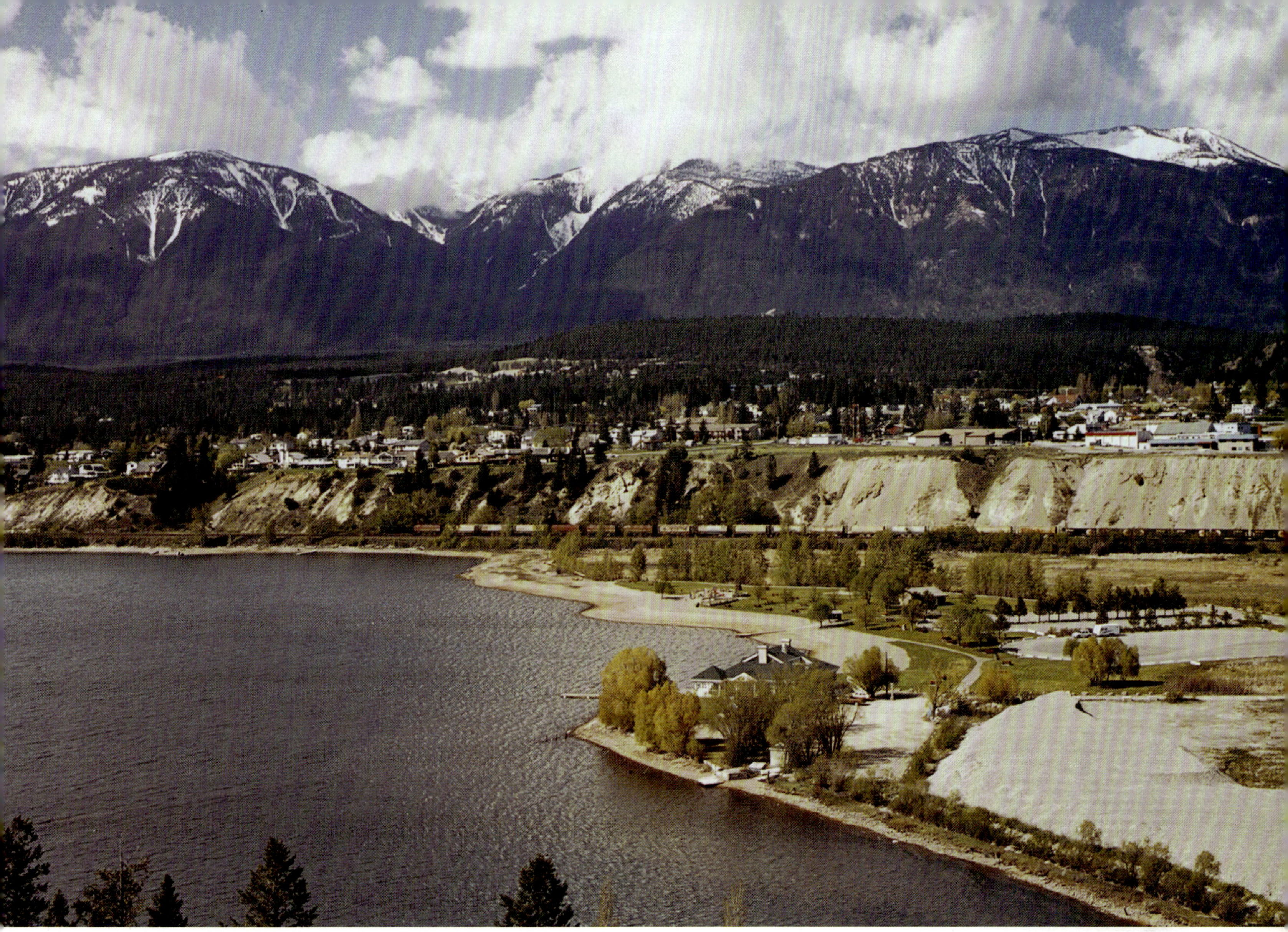

For nearly two decades at the end of the 1700s, Europeans tried to extend their fur-trading enterprises to the west slopes peoples but were hindered by their poor knowledge of trails across the mountain passes and, more importantly, the animosity of the Peigan. Finally, in 1807 David Thompson of the North West Company crossed Howse Pass at the headwaters of the North Saskatchewan River to the Columbia River and ascended it to Lake Windermere on July 12. Thompson and his men began building a warehouse on the Old Fort Point area of today's Invermere townsite, but, concerned about vulnerability to attack, quickly abandoned it for a more secure site about two kilometres north of the lake near where Toby Creek joins the Columbia. Here he built Kootanae House, the first white habitation on the western side of the Rockies, and from this point he expanded trading operations throughout the upper Columbia watershed into today's Montana, Idaho, and Washington.[26]

As is evident in the 1923 view, Old Fort Point was still being used as a First Nations campsite, although perhaps only in conjunction with local celebrations, while the low-lying area around the outlet of the Columbia River from Lake Windermere, known as Athalmere, was already under development. The modern view illustrates the great changes that have taken place in Invermere over the intervening years, largely as a result of its becoming a resort community used heavily by Calgary-based seasonal recreation property owners. The Old Fort Point area is now fully developed with permanent and seasonal residences. The marshlands near the Athalmere have been covered with fill. Part of the area is now a public beach and picnic area, and a major condominium subdivision is under construction in the remaining area.

6.16A DAVID THOMPSON COMMEMORATION FORT, INVERMERE BC, 1923 (PHOTOGRAPHER UNKNOWN, GLENBOW NA 1135-29)

6.16B INVERMERE, BRITISH COLUMBIA, MAY 2003 (CW 2003-05D-10)

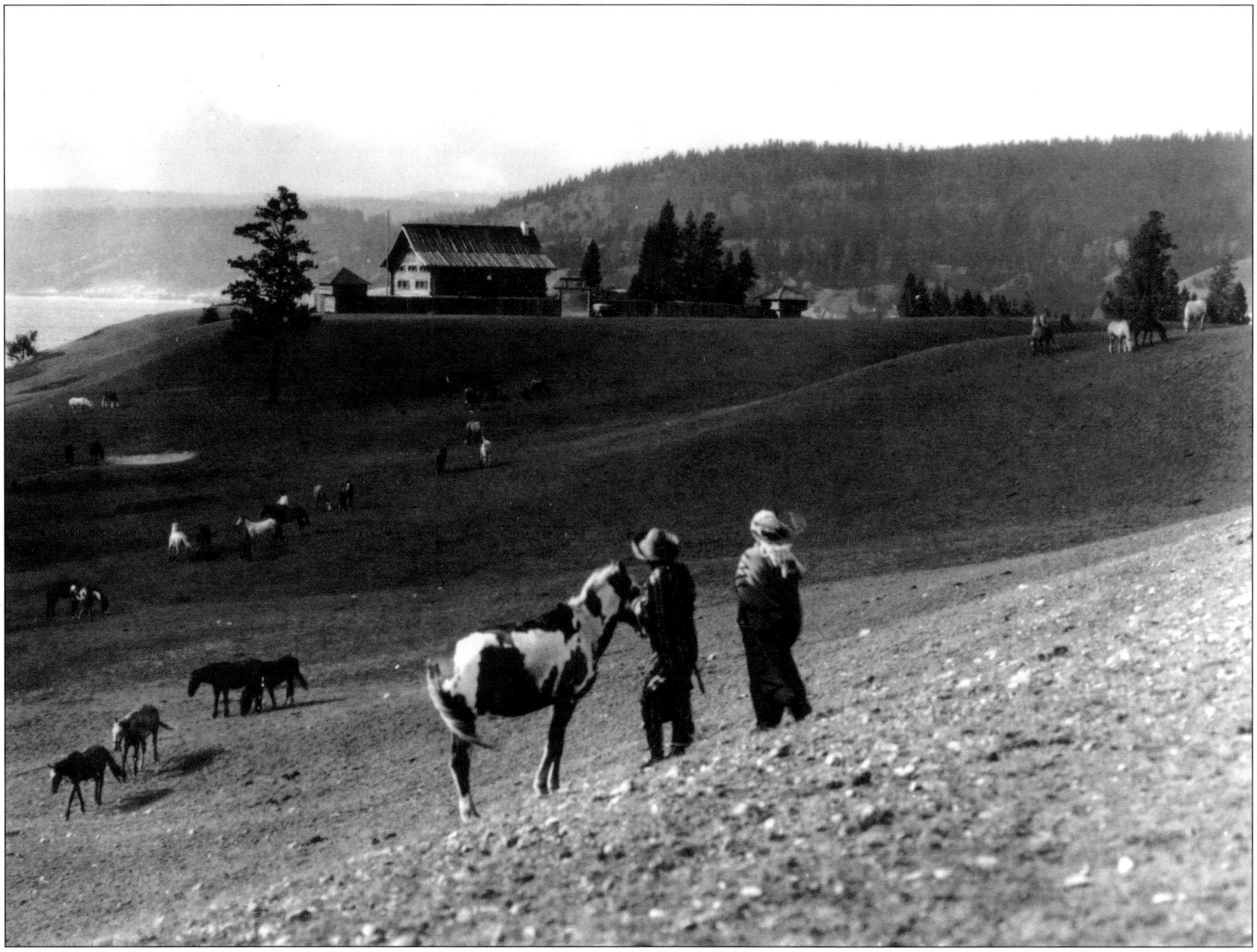

In the early 1920s, tourism promoters built a reconstruction of a fur-trading fort on a point above Lake Windermere in the vicinity of Thompson's abortive attempt to establish his first base in 1807. The building was to serve as an attraction with the opening of the new Banff-Windermere Highway. At the same time the Canadian Pacific Railway built the first of a series of Canadian Rockies auto bungalow camps nearby. While the new fort bore no resemblance to the basic quarters David Thompson constructed at Kootenae House to the north, it did become a landmark of Invermere and served as the location for memorable community celebrations for over fifty years.

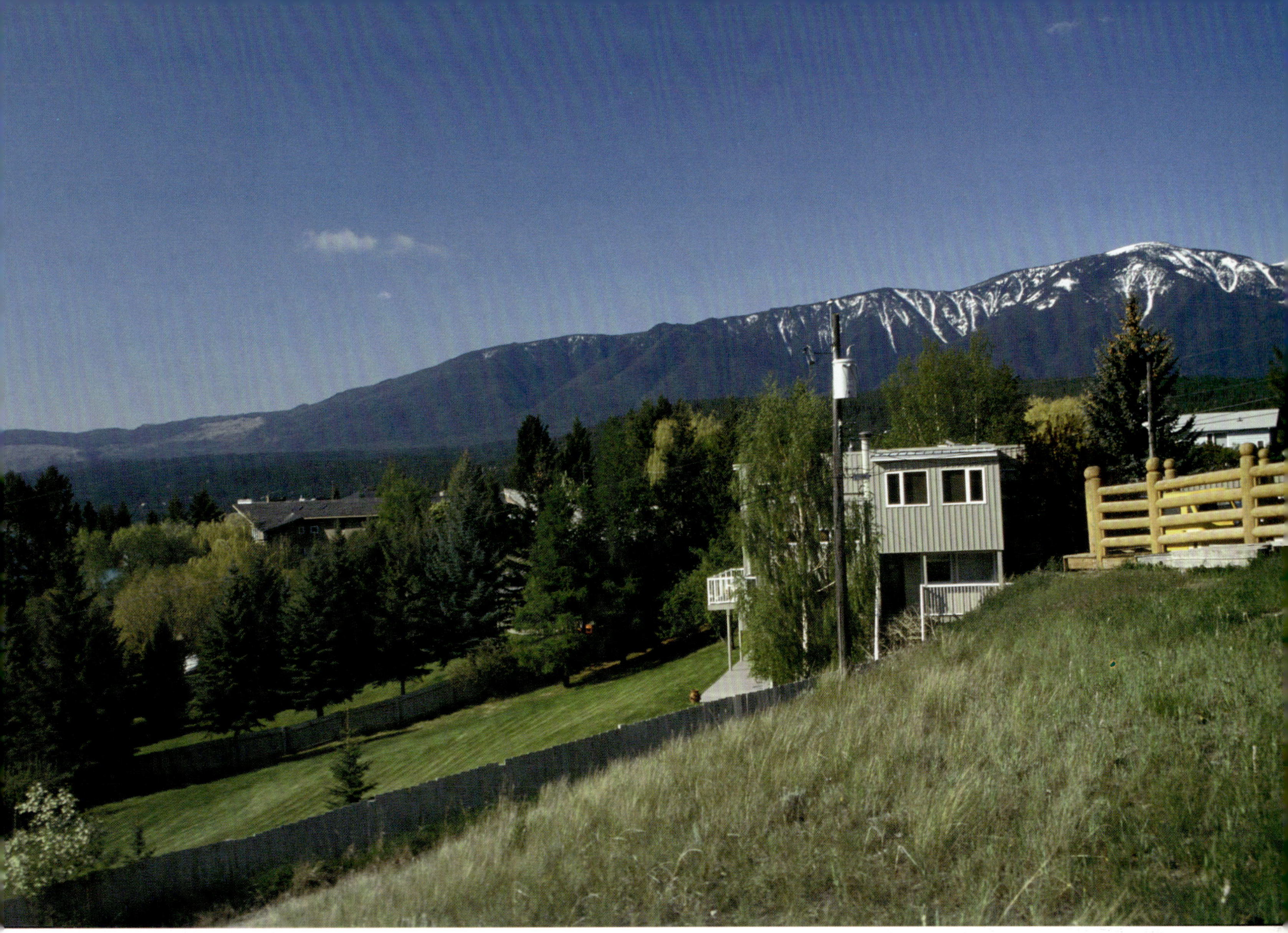

With the completion of the highway in 1923, Invermere and Radium were stops on a ten-thousand-kilometre Grand Circle Tour promoted by the national parks and the CPR. The west half of the circle, the "California to Banff Bee Line," connected Los Angeles, Seattle, and Spokane to Banff, while the return part of the loop, the "Grand Canyon Route," took the traveller south along the east slope of the Rockies to Glacier National Park, Montana, then to Yellowstone, Salt Lake, the Grand Canyon, and back to the west coast. Within Canada, the "Canadian Rockies Circle Tour" linked Banff to Invermere, and returned via Crowsnest Pass, Waterton, and Calgary. In 1928, with completion of a road northwards from Invermere to Golden, motorists could also participate in a shorter circle tour taking them from Banff to Invermere over the Banff-Windermere Highway, on to Golden, and then back to Lake Louise over the "Kicking Horse Trail."[27]

Throughout most of the twentieth century, urban growth around Lake Windermere and the Columbia Valley was slow due to the short tourist season and travel times on rough roads. However, with improvements to the Banff-Windermere Highway in the 1960s, the boom of the petroleum industry in Calgary, and development of nearby Panorama ski area, lakeshore properties were quickly developed, and numerous recreational home and golfing communities now spread across the Columbia Valley. The "Old Fort" was torn down in the 1970s to make room for a housing development in the expanding town of Invermere.

7

"DIVIDENDS IN GOLD AND DIVIDENDS IN HUMAN UNITS"

Government and Private Enterprise Develop the Parks

Apart from the railways, the most fundamental and constant elements of change in Canada's Rocky Mountains have been the Government of Canada and private enterprise, which, hand-in-hand, have changed the face of the mountain landscape over the past 120 years. The fact that the Dominion government very early recognized that much of this great national asset required some form of protection led to the creation of Canada's first national park, Rocky Mountains (Banff) National Park, at the same moment as the railroad arrived. This was followed over the next forty years by the implementation of what eventually became known as the four mountain park block – Banff, Jasper, Yoho, and Kootenay – establishing control over the central Rockies ecosystem. Yet, at the same time, decisions arising with respect to the use of these lands by the government departments responsible meant that they were also developed in certain ways.

During the early park period a symbiotic relationship was formed between the CPR and the government, with the latter developing much of the infrastructure and attractions and the former providing accommodation and services. This was a result of the initial impetus for park creation being an effort to protect mountain lands along the new line for tourism development, effectively eliminating excesses of private control of resorts that were already evident at locales such as Hot Springs, Arkansas, and at numerous European spas. Specifically, it was public interest in the Cave and Basin hot springs, discovered by former railroad workers William and Tom McCardell and Frank McCabe in the flank of Sulphur Mountain in 1883, that led Prime Minister John A. Macdonald to express to Deputy Minister of the Interior A. M. Burgess the hope that "great care had been taken to reserve all the land in or near the Hot Springs of Banff," an action carried out by means of an Order-in-Council to protect the lands "from sale, settlement or squatting." This was just a holding action which allowed the government time to fully examine the lands around the springs, a task carried out by Dominion Land Surveyor George Stewart, who laid out the new Banff townsite across the river and recommended increasing the size of the reservation to take in beauty spots along the Bow River in its vicinity. His suggestions were followed, and on June 23, 1887, the Rocky Mountains Parks Act, creating Canada's first national park inside an oblong block of sixteen kilometres by forty-three kilometres around the springs, received royal assent. In line with Prime Minister Macdonald's belief that it had "all the qualifications necessary to make it a place of great resort" and would bring "not only large pecuniary advantage to the Dominion, but much prestige to the whole country by attracting the population, not only of this continent, but of Europe to this place," the act was quickly followed by government action and private development to make this vision a reality.[1]

Surveyor Stewart had been appointed as the first superintendent of the new park on January 1, 1887, even before the bill creating it was passed, and he quickly set his talents to work. One of his first acts was to have huge consequences for the future of the fledgling town of Banff and how visitors remembered it; he proposed replacing a floating bridge he had constructed at the bend in the river with a more permanent structure to the east so that the main Banff Avenue axis of the townsite, along with a stunning view of Cascade Mountain, could be framed in tourists' viewfinders from the south side of the river. Dr. R. G. Brett, who had been the CPR's surgeon in the area during railroad construction, had already convinced the government to provide him with a lease on this viewpoint and launched a new career as one of the park's foremost entrepreneurs, quickly constructing the Sanitarium, the town's first combined hostelry and hospital, on the site. Meanwhile, Stewart diligently pursued other development work, blasting a tunnel into the Cave spring to improve public access, improving trails to the hot springs to carriage road status to allow larger visitation, improving Banff Avenue to a higher standard and impounding water in a log reservoir near the Upper Hot Springs to distribute to the numerous bathhouses making application for its use.[2]

Once the park had been officially created, much of Stewart's time was taken up in administering the leasing system through which land in the fast-growing village was to be distributed to businessmen and residents.[3] But, at the same time, buoyed by government appropriations to make the area attractive for tourists, he continued making improvements. His own office was moved from a tent at the site of 'Old Banff' at the base of Cascade Mountain to a new log building on the 100 Block of Bear Street, and during the period 1887–88 the first major government facility, an upgraded pool combined with a rustic log bathhouse and caretaker's residence, was erected at the Cave and Basin. Carriage roads for the use of tourists wishing to see the sights by horse and buggy were also developed as rapidly as possible, including the first road to Lake Minnewanka, the famous Loop Drive on the river flats below Mount Rundle and Corkscrew Drive switchbacking its way over the shoulder of Tunnel Mountain. Several private livery companies were soon established to service their needs, and one operated by the ambitious Brewster brothers, Bill and Jim, rapidly began to take on major proportions. Near Cascade Mountain, an animal paddock was created to ensure that visitors had the opportunity to view the park's native animals, whether they were lucky enough to see them in the wild or not, and on Spray Avenue a natural history museum was built to house exhibits for those who did not even venture that far. By 1888 a tourist writing about Banff found it a most agreeable place: "… there are shops selling articles of vertu, posting establishments, several small inns, two churches, a theatre, boats to hire on the river, provision shops, post office; altogether it is a most respectable little town."[4]

Despite the fact that government and private initiatives were mainly aimed at promoting the tourist trade to ensure "large pecuniary advantage to the Dominion," other fiscally beneficial aspects of park lands were not ignored. Macdonald's so-called 'national policy' foresaw the development of all the west's resources in support of ensuring Canada's economic independence from the United States, and this meant that the mountains' timber, mineral, and water resources were to be exploited wherever and whenever possible. Department of the Interior surveyors laid out a number of timber berths along the Bow River and its tributaries in 1883–84, some of which were incorporated into the new park lands, and the newly chartered Eau Claire and Bow River Lumber Company soon obtained cutting rights on several of these. By 1886 it was logging around Kananaskis and Castle Mountain and by the turn of the century it had several major camps in the Spray River valley.[5] Similarly, even before the creation of the park, prospectors imbued with the period's gold rush mentality had spread news of a silver discovery near Castle Mountain, leading to the Rockies' first boomtown, Silver City, established at its base in 1883. Although short-lived, it attracted attention to the area from those with more practical eyes. Dr. George M. Dawson of the Geological Survey of Canada had begun assessing the Rockies' geology in the early 1880s, and in 1886 he produced a map that identified significant coal deposits on the Cascade River. In 1884 the 'Cascade Coal Basin' was laid out, and in 1885 the government began selling mining rights by tender, leading to the establishment of the Canadian Anthracite Coal Company and the beginning of the development of mines and the village of Anthracite at the confluence of the Cascade and the Bow. Initial mining activity soon expanded, with the nearby railroad divisional point of Canmore beginning to receive coal-mining attention by 1887.[6]

Even though the Anthracite mines were inside a national park, and after a major expansion to park boundaries in 1902 Canmore's were too, there was no immediate concern expressed about this seeming incongruity. Indeed, in writing in 1904 of the recent establishment of the CPR's own mines further up the Cascade River at Bankhead, park superintendent Howard Douglas stated, "The new village of Bankhead, instead of being a detriment to the beauties of the park, will, on the contrary, add another to the many and varied attractions of the neighbourhood." Similarly, a survey to identify a source of carbonated lime for the production of cement had in 1905 led to the establishment of a mill by the Western Canada Coal and Cement Company at Exshaw, and Douglas was equally glowing in his assessment, offering, "The erection of these large cement mills within the park will prove an important step in the building up of Western Canada."[7] It was equally taken for granted that supplies of electricity would be needed for these operations, initially provided by steam generation plants at the mines, but the growth of Calgary on the park's eastern flank soon required more and cheaper power. The Calgary Power Company was formed and in 1911 and built its first hydro-electric plant at Horseshoe Falls on the Bow River about fifty kilometres west of the city, leading to the need for water storage capabilities further upstream. In 1912 the Department of the Interior granted the company permission to install a control dam on a tributary of the Cascade River at Lake Minnewanka, and a few years later a second generating plant was added at Kananaskis Falls. By the early 1920s calls were heard to increase the storage capacity of Lake Minnewanka and to create further capacity at Spray Lakes, leading to park waters becoming a hot political issue and giving rise to the creation of the country's first publicly supported conservation organization, the Canadian National Parks Association, opposing further development.[8] Although much of the Spray and Kananaskis watersheds were removed from Banff in the boundary change accompanying the passage of the National Parks Act of 1930, this did not mean that waters in the park were entirely safe from further exploitation, a fact made apparent in 1942 when, under the exigencies of wartime conditions, Calgary Power's Minnewanka project was greatly expanded, including the installation of generating facilities.

The propensity for simultaneous government and private tourism and resource development, first evident at Banff, was emulated in the new Jasper Park, created in 1907 along the upper Athabasca River watershed in preparation for the arrival of the Grand Trunk Pacific and the Canadian Northern. In fact, in this case the initial primacy of resource exploitation was recognized by setting aside the area of thirteen thousand square kilometres as a 'forest park' under the Dominion Lands Act "for the preservation of forest trees on the crests and slopes of the Rocky Mountains and for the proper maintenance throughout the year of the volume of water in the rivers and streams that have their source in the mountains and traverse the Province of Alberta." Grand Trunk Pacific steel reached Fitzhugh station, a divisional point near the confluence of the Athabasca and Miette rivers, in 1911, and in 1913, with a survey of the townsite to encourage the construction of services for the public, it was renamed Jasper and became the new park's administrative headquarters. Superintendent Colonel Maynard Rogers was soon at work creating trail and carriage road connections to area beauty spots, including Pyramid Lake and Maligne Canyon, and providing access to a privately operated tent camp, the forerunner of Jasper Park Lodge, on the shore of Lac Beauvert. As in Banff's case, coal mining had begun simultaneous with the arrival of the railroad, concentrated to the east of Jasper in the area around Roche Miette and leading to the establishment of Jasper Park's own coal-mining community of Pocahontas in 1912. Mining was also carried out further east at Brûlé Lake, but, as in the case of Canmore, these mines would later be eliminated from the park through a boundary change.[9]

Although early government policy allowed, and indeed even encouraged, private natural resource exploitation on park lands, this seeming inconsistency began to change with the closing of the Anthracite, Bankhead, and Pocahontas mines by the early 1920s and the aforementioned changes that left remaining operations outside park boundaries. However, such was not to be the case with respect to tourism development as it continued to be a primary concern of the government and the private sector, a fact made evident by an examination of road and highway development over a fifty-year period. Motor-cars were banned from Banff park in the period after the turn of the century when they first began appearing on Calgary streets. Not only was there no road connecting the city with its mountain playground, but horse livery interests such as the Brewsters used their influence to protect their position from outside competition. This situation began to change when the new Alberta provincial government announced its intention to build a 'coaching road' to Banff's eastern boundary and the Dominion government agreed to upgrade the carriage road connecting it to the townsite. The Calgary-Banff Coach Road was at first seen to be only for horse-drawn vehicles, but in August 1909 Calgarian Norman Lougheed became the first motorist to complete the nine-and-a-half-hour trip over the partially completed route in an automobile. By 1910 the wealthy and influential members of the Calgary Automobile Club were lobbying to be able to bring their cars in the park, and in 1911 they were allowed to do so, albeit under the provision that they park at the police barracks and not use their vehicles during their stay. Over the next few years, restrictions were gradually whittled away, and by 1915 it was even legal for automobiles to be used on the popular sightseeing roads to the Cave and Basin, the Loop Drive, and Lake Minnewanka. As restrictions disappeared, livery interests began to adapt to the change. The newly named Brewster Transport Company sold off twenty-eight head of horses in May 1916 and the same month took delivery of four seven-passenger and one five-passenger Overland touring cars, thereby marking the beginning of the modern internal-combustion age in the valley's tourism industry.[10]

From the First World War onward, the establishment of highways and sightseeing roads in and through the parks went from something that was tolerated to the status of a holy grail. New Dominion Parks Commissioner J. B. Harkin posed the question in 1914, "What motorist will be able to resist the call of the Canadian Rockies when it is known that he can travel through them on first class roads? And what a revenue this country will obtain when thousands of automobiles are traversing the parks."[11] Harkin understood that to get Parliament to provide for appropriations to support the growing park system, he needed to prove their value and made the case that, taking foreign travel receipts into account, they could be self-sufficient. At the same time, Canadians would benefit by being able to access their own parks on the roads built on the backs of foreign tourists and partake of the health-giving aspects of the outdoors by escaping the cities for the salubrious mountains. In 1916 Harkin coined a phrase to describe this dual function of national parks – they provided "dividends in gold and dividends in human units."[12] In seeking these benefits, the government believed its role was to build the roads and some ancillary facilities, such as campgrounds, while other services would be provided by the private sector.

The first major roadway to traverse the Rockies was the result of a 1911 agreement between the Dominion government, the British Columbia government, and the CPR, which would see the Calgary-Banff road extended through Vermilion Pass to link with the Columbia Valley and Cranbrook and from there with existing roads to Vancouver. By the time the war broke out, the road had reached Vermilion Pass from the east, but wartime conditions led the B.C. government to declare itself incapable of fulfilling its commitments, leading to an unforeseen benefit to Canada's park system. After a series of negotiations, the Banff-Windermere Road Agreement was signed in March 1919 wherein the federal government agreed to complete the highway within four years in return for a sixteen-kilometre-wide belt of provincial lands along its right-of-way, which in 1920 would become Kootenay National Park. The Highway was officially opened in June 1923 and Harkin rejoiced in his annual report that it signalled the completion of a ten-thousand-kilometre-long highway system through Canada and the United States providing access to three Canadian and twelve American national parks.

It also marked the government's full commitment to road building as an instrument of policy in continuing to make the parks attractive and accessible to an increasingly motorized public. The basic road system to local sightseeing attractions built in Banff during the First World War and the early 1920s was emulated in Jasper where a former trail to the Miette Hot Springs was upgraded to a passable road, a road was built to Pyramid Lake where a summer cottage subdivision had been surveyed, and a rough track joined the town to Medicine Lake, after which tourists were transferred to boats for a trip down the lake where a second road linked Medicine and Maligne lakes. In the mid-1920s, heavy use by touring cars of the dusty five-kilometre-long gravel road linking the town with Jasper Park Lodge resulted in a paving experiment utilizing natural asphalt taken from the tar sands near Fort McMurray. However, the provincial road system only extended west from Edmonton to Edson, and for many years there was local agitation for a highway, like the Banff-Calgary road, to provide the outside world with access to Jasper. The Dominion and Alberta governments reached agreement on this in 1923, but while the federal portion was completed on old railway grades abandoned with the amalgamation of the two railroads into the Canadian National system, it was 1928 before the provincial leg was finished, and that only suitable for summer use. The completion of this road as an all-weather gravel highway had to await the Depression years, when its upgrading was carried out by unemployed men working on relief projects, and by 1937 connecting roads through Saskatchewan made it possible to drive from Winnipeg to Jasper.[13]

Meanwhile, the decade of the 1930s also saw the building of the most important and scenic road in Canada's mountain parks. The 235-kilometre long Banff-Jasper Highway was one of western Canada's largest Depression-relief projects and when completed in 1940 resulted in the possibility of motorists making a circle tour linking Calgary, Banff, Jasper, and Edmonton. Along this route it was thought desirable that additional tourist amenities be provided, and here private business stepped in with the construction of bungalow camps, such as those at Johnston Canyon and Saskatchewan River Crossing, and even major outlying lodges such as Num-Ti-Jah Lodge at Bow Lake and the Icefields Chalet at the Columbia Icefield.[14]

All these road-building projects, while important for pre-war tourism development, paled in significance to even grander highway projects in the post-war period – the building of transcontinental highways through both Banff and Jasper parks. In 1949 the Canadian government passed the Trans-Canada Highway Act, providing half of the funding for the construction of an all-weather, paved, eight-metre-wide highway across the country. Initial work was tentative, but after 1955 when the government confirmed it would be responsible for the entire costs in Banff National Park, construction proceeded more rapidly along a new route deviating considerably from the original road. Work was completed through the Park by the late 1950s, although the official opening of the Trans-Canada Highway would not occur until 1962 after the difficult Rogers Pass section was completed. Meanwhile, an alternative transcontinental route through Jasper Park was also being promoted and the Yellowhead Highway opened later in the decade.[15]

These superhighways and their associated development helped to unleash a flood of visitors after the pent-up demand of the war years. Again, it was entrepreneurs and capital from the private sector that responded to this changing human use pattern. An interesting chain of events occurred when the new all-weather roads increased public access to the small pioneer ski areas that had begun to spring up at Mount Norquay, Sunshine, and Lake Louise in Banff and at the Whistlers and Marmot Basin in Jasper during the 1930s and 1940s. These facilities grew rapidly during the 1960s and 1970s, fuelled by the development of oil in Alberta and the associated population growth in Calgary and Edmonton as well as changes in technology that introduced mechanical lifts and aerial tramways to virtually pristine mountain slopes. Most importantly, expanding ski areas increased the need for winter accommodations. However, national parks policy limited on-hill hotels, condominiums, and real estate developments. This made it financially viable for the owners of existing accommodations in the communities of Banff, Lake Louise, and Jasper, then usually open only in the summer, to recapitalize aging facilities.[16] After 1970, the private sector invested hundreds of millions of dollars to modernize hotels, restaurants, and other facilities for both summer and winter operation.[17] Moreover, the stability offered by year-round work allowed the tourism industry to hire professional employees dedicated to not just serving visitors, but also to maintaining and interpreting the unique ecological and cultural heritage of the Canadian Rockies. This revitalized private sector attracted regional, national, and international visitors desiring both modern amenities and environmental sensitivity in their development and operation.[18]

Cooperation of the federal government and private enterprise has now been a fact of mountain national park life for 120 years. Today, the private sector operates a full complement of hotels, restaurants, and other services in the Banff, Jasper, and Lake Louise townsites, as well as destination ski resorts and accommodations in remoter areas. These ventures, in combination with rustic campgrounds and modern highways operated by the federal government, continue to influence the geography of the mountain national parks. However, in more recent times there has been a growing appreciation of the need to limit, and even call a halt to, development to maintain stressed mountain ecosystems. Further, changing federal government priorities often limit the funds available to maintain or develop park infrastructure in a timely manner. Therefore, new arrangements to govern and finance the Rocky Mountain national park lands must continue to evolve. For example, since 1990, the towns of Banff and Jasper have established municipal governments with carefully prescribed regulatory and taxing powers and guidance to sustain the national park mandate.[19] In 1998, Parks Canada obtained "agency" status, which allows more flexibility to reinvest gate fees and other income directly back into the park facilities. These innovations, combined with over a century of successful partnership between private and public interests, suggest that by adhering to sound economic and governance principles, the tourism industry, and the mountain ecosystems it depends upon, can flourish into the future.[20]

8.1 BYRON HARMON AND COLUMBIA ICEFIELDS, 1924 (LEWIS FREEMAN, WHYTE NA 71-2159)

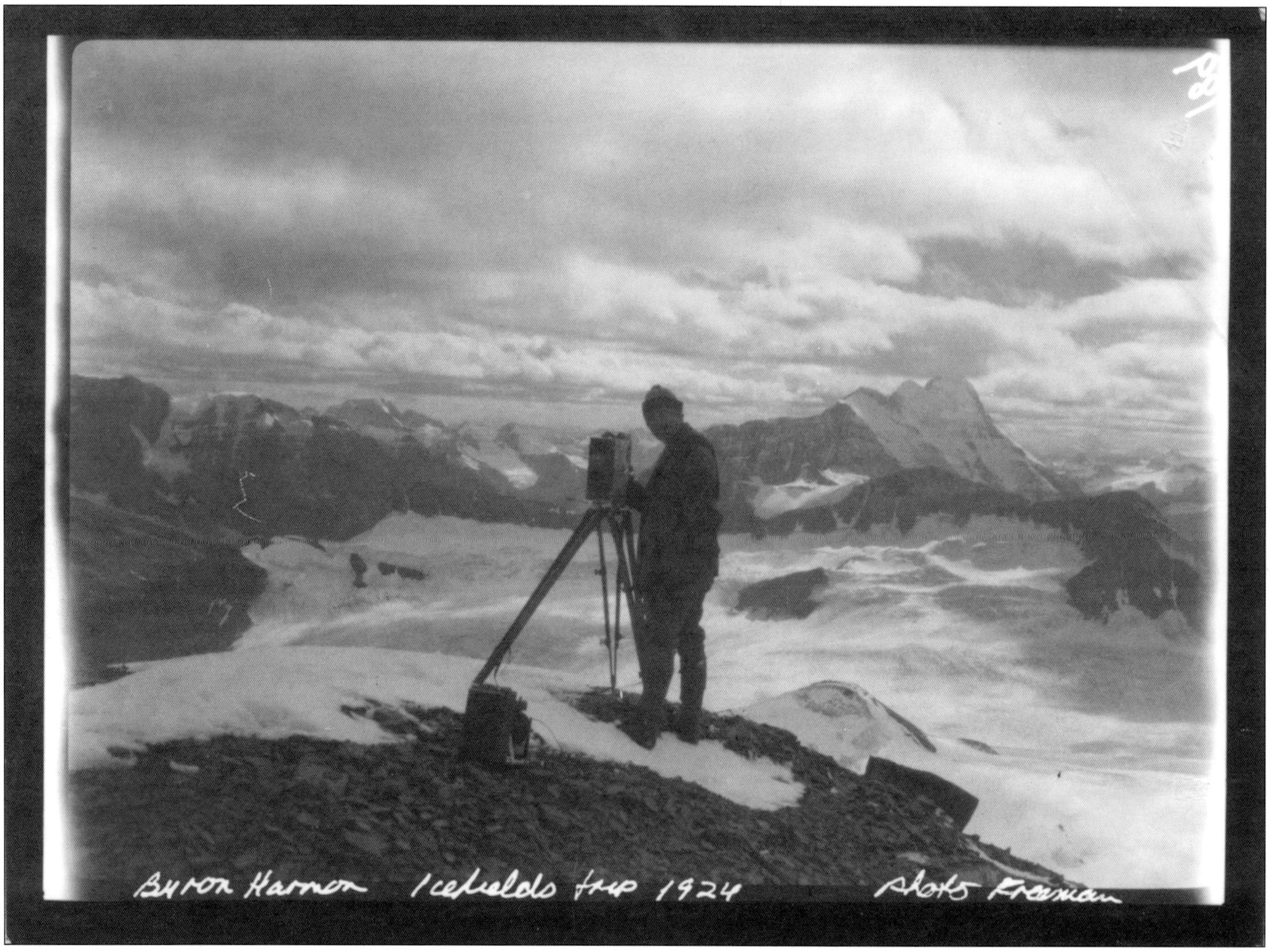

8

HEART OF THE ROCKIES

Lake Louise, Red Deer Valley, Yoho, and the Icefields

West of Banff, the Bow Valley gently ascends to the dense, cool subalpine forests around Lake Louise. This is high mountain country, snowbound six months of the year and draped with icefields and glaciers. First Nations likely used these areas less routinely than lower elevations but certainly came here to hunt moose and bison. After the decline in First Nations' use and the establishment of Rocky Mountains (Banff) National Park, a few hardy visitors would depart Lake Louise each summer for months of pack train travel "off the beaten track" through one of the world's most spectacular landscapes, then almost totally unvisited. Mountaineers, photographers, hunters, anglers, and artists all took their craft into this wildness, leaving the Canadian Rockies with a legacy of aesthetic appreciation and mountain literature. The building of the Banff-Jasper Highway (Icefields Parkway) in the 1930s and 40s pierced through the core of this area, providing an opportunity for millions of people to see what few had seen before.[1]

8.2A LAGGAN AND MT. LEFROY (TEMPLE), CA. 1888 (BOORNE AND MAY, WHYTE NA 66-645)

8.2B LAGGAN STATION, 1895 (CANADIAN PACIFIC RAILROAD, WHYTE NA 66-397)

8.2C LAGGAN STATION, CA. 1910 (CANADIAN PACIFIC RAILROAD, WHYTE NA 66-1238)

8.2D LAKE LOUISE TRAIN STATION, JULY 2001 (CW 2001-07C-01)

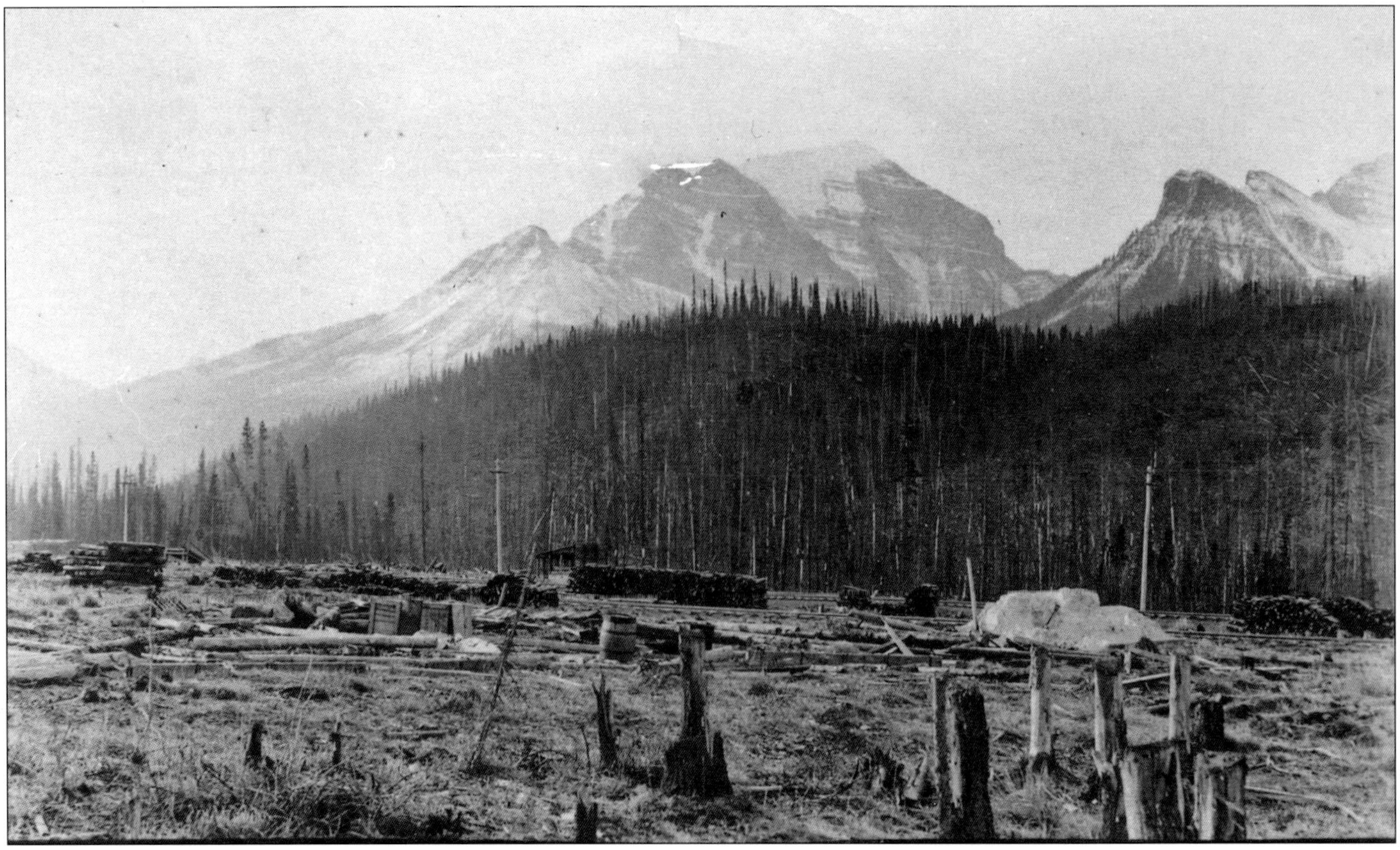

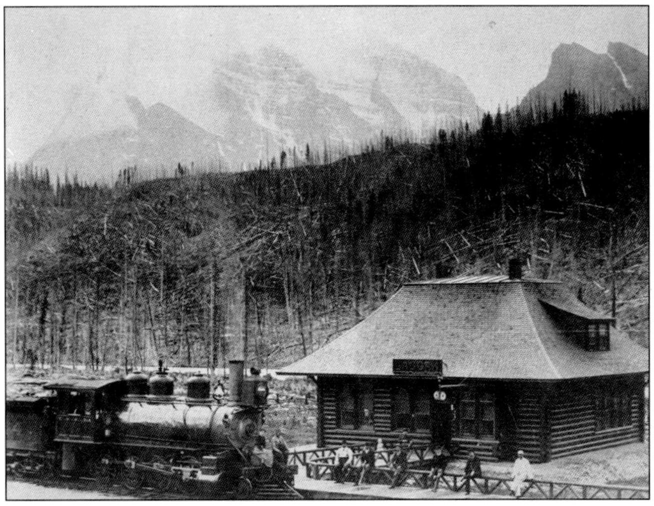

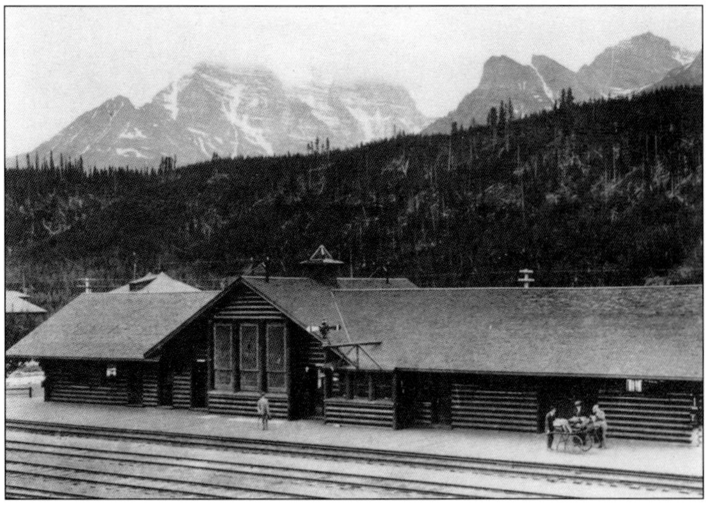

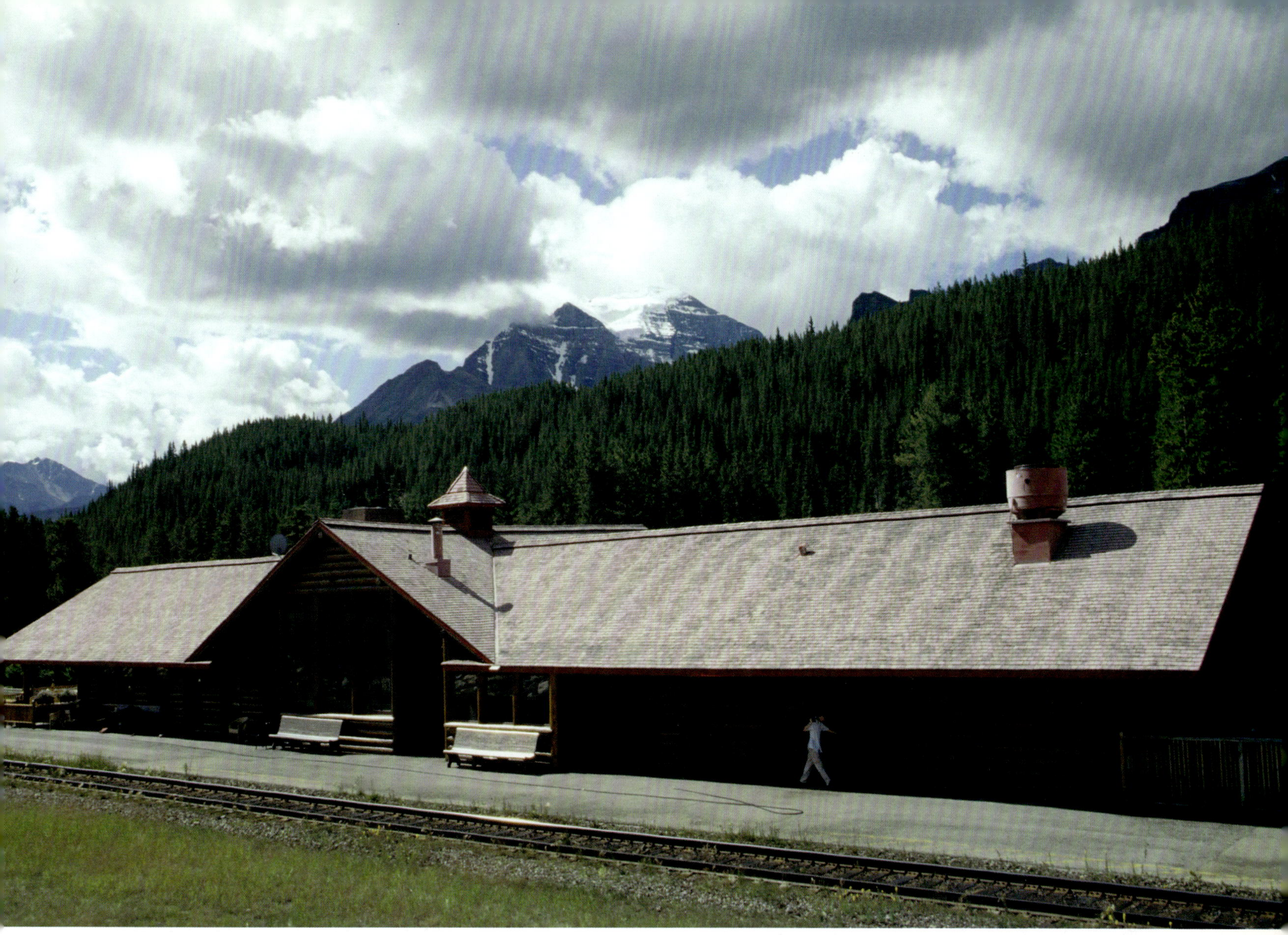

In the early summer of 1884, Arthur P. Coleman, professor of geology at the University of Toronto, took a Canadian Pacific work train to "Holt City" near Lake Louise, where track laying had stopped the previous fall. After a sleepless night sharing a bed with a construction worker, he climbed nearby Mount Whitehorn. Looking back west to Mount Temple (pictured here), Coleman described "nothing but clean air between one and the summits, while down in the valley a trail of smoke from the ' right-of-way' where the timber was burning blurred and sullied the view."[2] Forest fire was a common companion of railroad construction and coal-burning steam engines in the 1880s. In the upper Bow Valley these fires usually occurred in midsummer and were often of high intensity (long flame lengths and rapid rates of spread), and in the vicinity of the railroad line usually burned through 50- to 150-year-old forests that had been repetitively ignited in earlier times by native peoples and lightning.[3]

The views of Lake Louise station site over the past century show both the changing character of the buildings and provide a focus for vegetation changes occurring on the background ridge after the devastation of the construction period. The earliest view shows the site when ties and supplies are still piled awaiting use in building sidings and improvements on the recently completed line. The 1895 view shows the original station bearing the name "Laggan." By 1910 this had been replaced by a larger log building consistent with the company's developing tourism and hotel program at the lake, and the forest had completed some quarter-century of growth. In 1914 the village station was renamed to be consistent with Lake Louise, the world-famous beauty spot it serviced. Some seventy-five years later the station, no longer in use for passenger service, had become a restaurant, while the background forest had reached what would be its expected full maturity if characteristic, long-term fire cycles prevail.

8.3A OUTLET FROM LAKE LOUISE, AUGUST 1900 (VAUX FAMILY, WHYTE NG 4-717)

8.3B OUTLET FROM LAKE LOUISE, SEPTEMBER 2004 (CW 2004-09B-02)

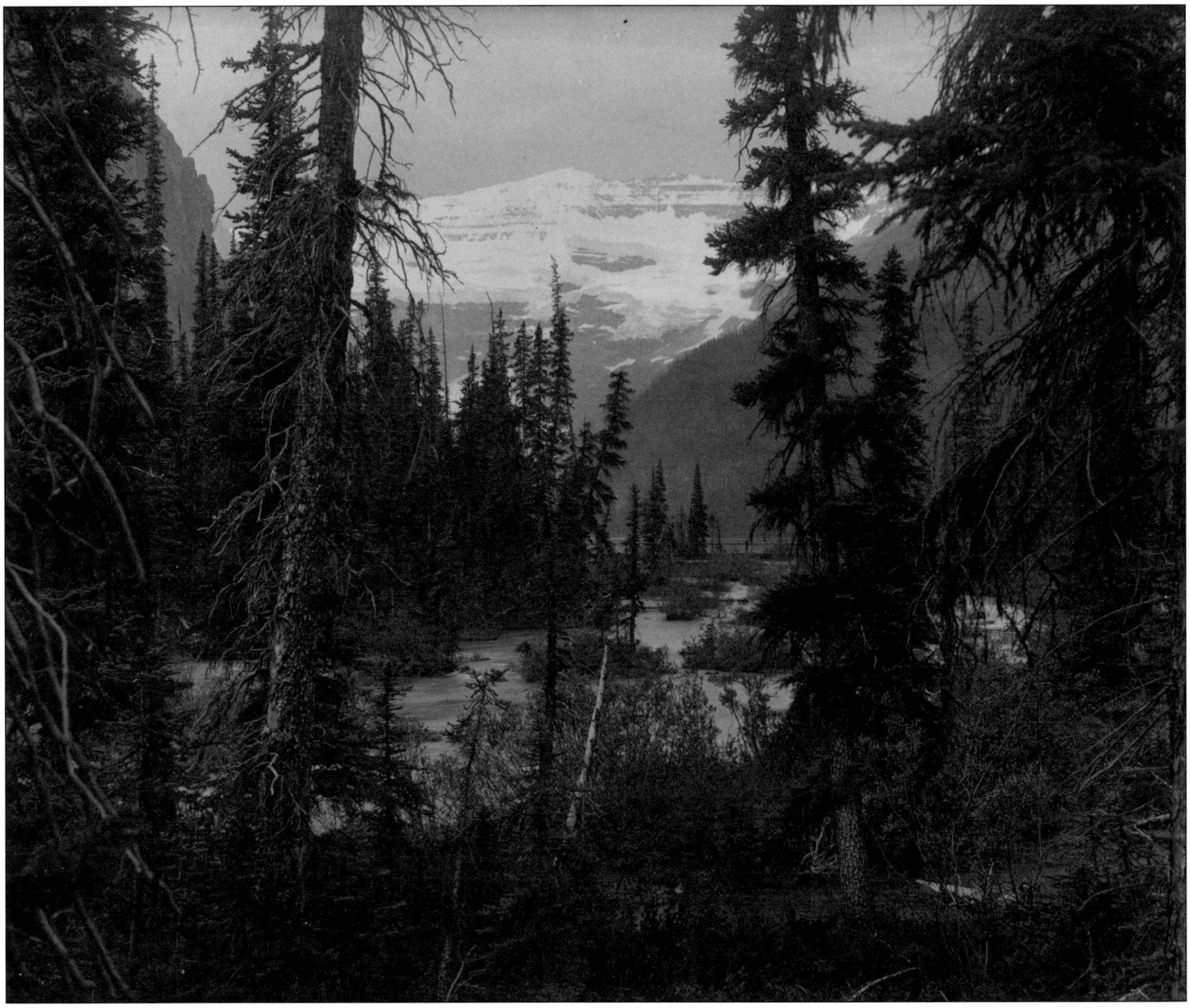

In August 1882, outfitter Tom Wilson made his first visit to the Nakoda's "Lake of the Little Fishes," and recalled, "As God is my judge, I never in all my explorations of these five chains of mountains throughout Western Canada saw such a matchless scene."[4] In the summer of 1888 the Reverends Henry Swanzy and William Spotswood Green, mountaineers with experience in the Alps, took a journey on the CPR to climb at Rogers Pass. Returning eastward, they disembarked at Laggan to see the rumoured wonders of Lake Louise, but, finding no obvious trail, they bushwhacked until

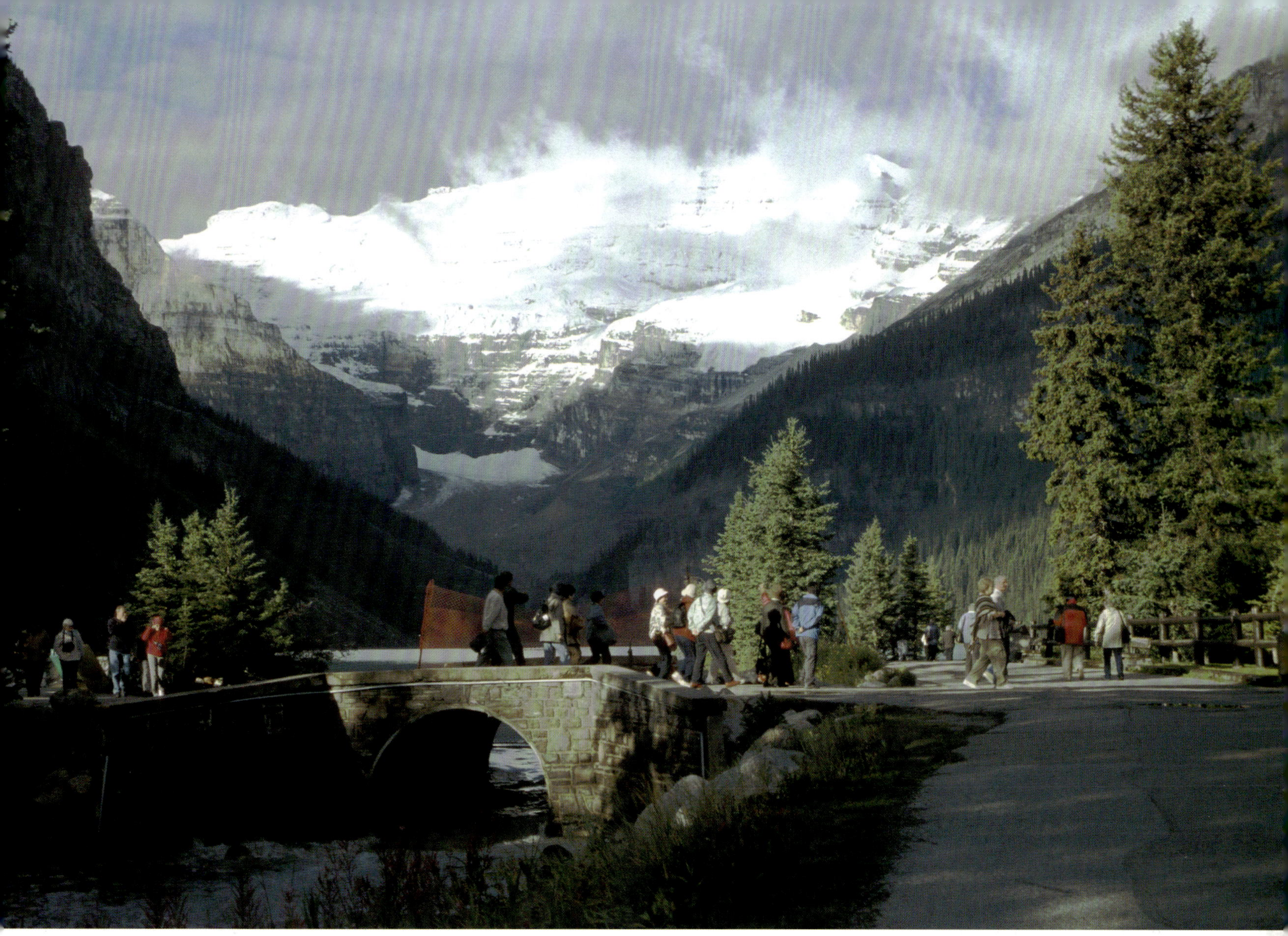

discovering Louise Creek and followed it to the lake. Green's reaction was similar to Wilson's and the millions that have followed them: "I was quite unprepared for the full beauty of the scene. Nothing of the kind could possible surpass it. I was somewhat reminded of the Oeschinen See in Switzerland, but Lake Louise is about twice as long, the forests surrounding it are far richer, and the grouping of mountains is simply perfection."[5]

Upon returning to Montreal, Green and Swanzy stopped to recount their trip to William C. Van Horne, president of the Canadian Pacific Railway. From their descriptions, he recognized Lake Louise as a potential tourism magnet and rapidly focused the company's attention on developing access and accommodation.[6]

On October 30, 1984, UNESCO designated the Rocky Mountain national and provincial parks as a World Heritage Site. The following year, during the national parks centennial celebrations, Prince Philip made the ceremonial announcement and unveiled a commemorative plaque on the shores of Lake Louise: "Beginning in 1885, when part of Banff National Park was removed from public use, the Canadian Rockies have formed the backbone of Canada's protected natural areas system. This extensive area with its large track of wilderness is dedicated as a World Heritage Site for the benefit and enjoyment of all nations."[7]

Today, Parks Canada has difficulty providing parking for the thousands of cars and buses that come to Lake Louise daily during the summer. The sublime forest surrounding the outlet stream has been partially removed to build trails and roads for masses of visitors making their own pilgrimage to its shores.

8.4A CHATEAU LAKE LOUISE, 1920 (BYRON HARMON, WHYTE V263 NA 71-4856)

8.4B CHATEAU LAKE LOUISE, CA. 1940 (BYRON HARMON, WHYTE NA 71-4945)

8.4C CHATEAU LAKE LOUISE, JULY 2003 (CW 2003-07K-09)

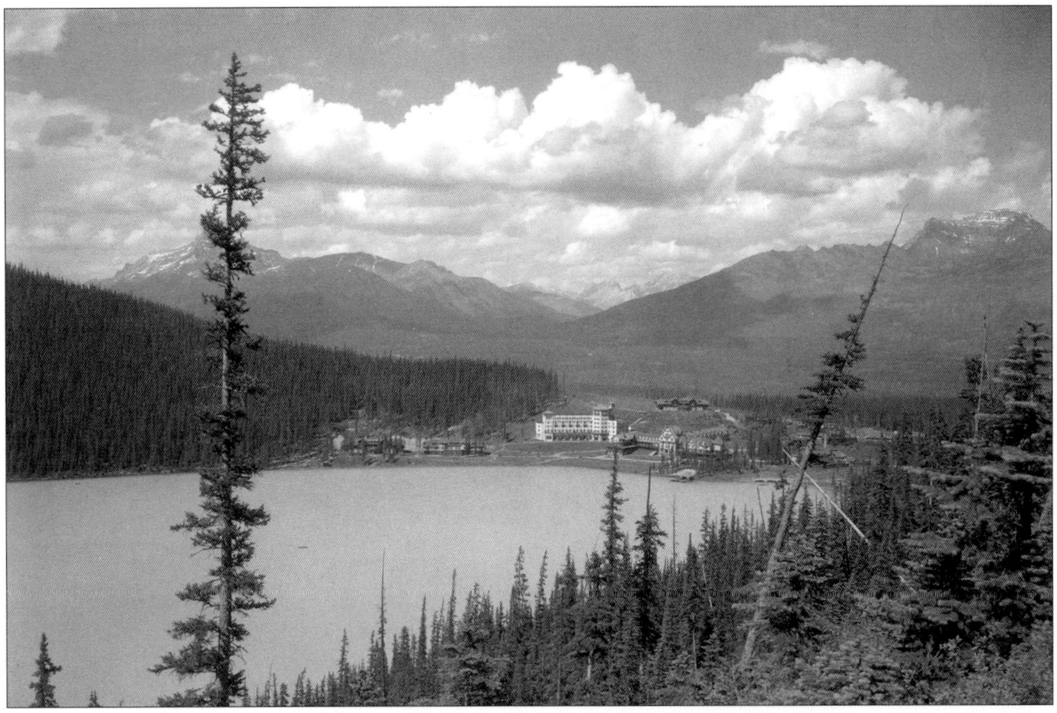

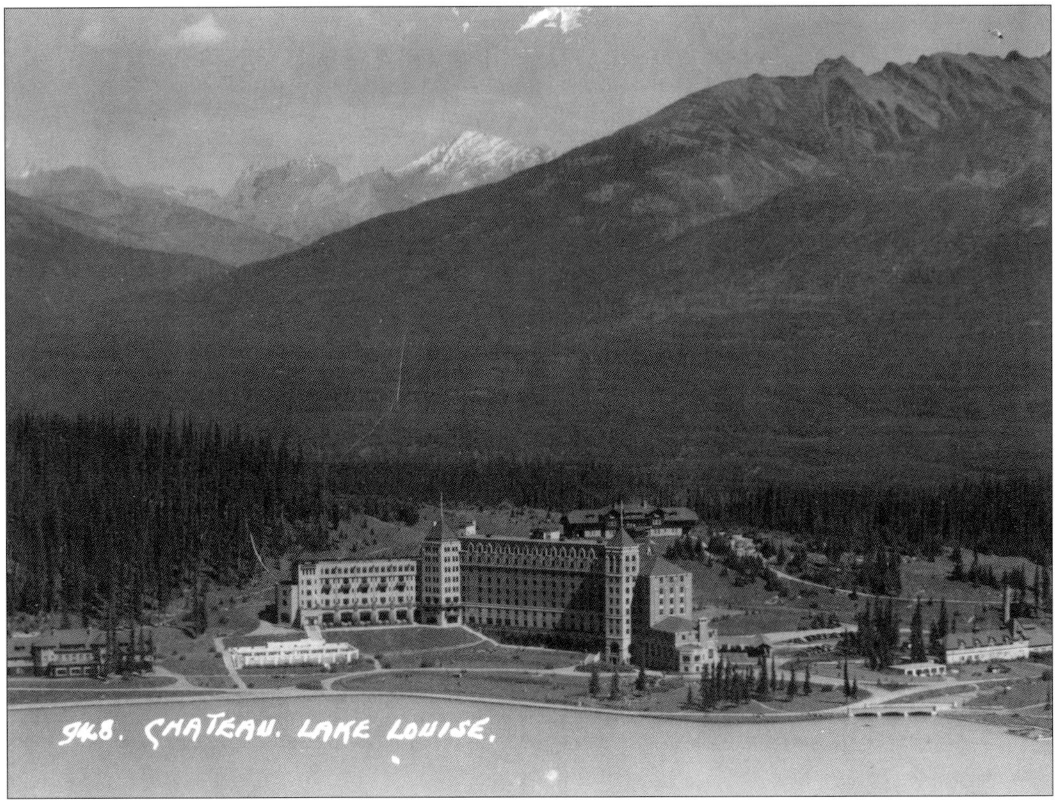

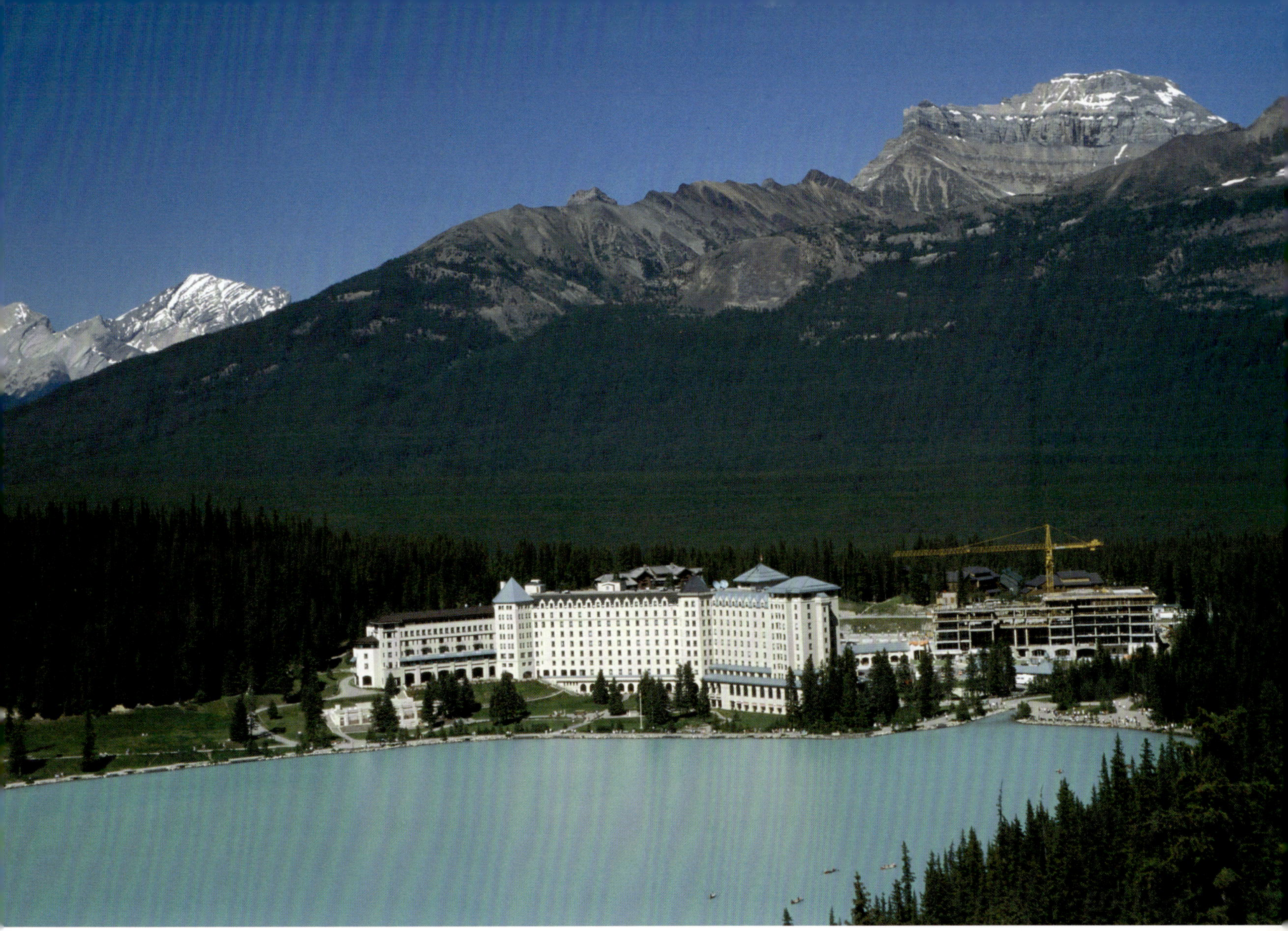

Hotel development on the shore of Lake Louise has perhaps been more diverse and persistent than at any other location in the Canadian Rockies. Originally a one-room log structure built by CPR workers in 1889–90, it burned to the ground in 1891 and was replaced by a simple frame structure in about 1895. Over the next number of years, the "Lake Louise Chalet" was added to as increasing visitation demanded more accommodation, and by 1910 it had become the rather elegant building, part of which was designed by famous British Columbia architect Francis Mawson Rattenbury, visible on the right of Byron Harmon's 1920 view. In the immediate pre-First World War period, the CPR, intent on launching a new Canadian Rockies resort program, determined that what it now referred to as "Chateau Lake Louise" needed a major makeover to support the initiative. Architect Walter Painter, just having completed the Banff Springs Hotel centre tower, designed a new wing, visible in the centre of the 1920 photograph, finished in 1913. It is not clear whether this rather austere concrete structure was intended to be clad with stone, but the war intervened to postpone any further development plans and it was not until 1925, after the Rattenbury wing had burned down the previous year, that Painter's work, shown in the 1940 view, was completed.[8]

After the reinstitution of the CPR's hotel program in the 1970s and 80s, a renovation and new wing featuring increased retail and amenity spaces was built. With growing park winter usage, by 1983 the chateau had begun to stay open year-round. As seen in the 2003 view, and despite the criticisms of environmentalists opposing further development, construction cranes again appeared at the lake as a further addition, a new conference centre and ballroom designed by Robert LeBlond, was commenced.

8.5A PANORAMA FROM MOUNT FAIRVIEW, AUGUST 24, 1904 (VAUX FAMILY, WHYTE NA 80-1283)

8.5B MOUNT VICTORIA FROM FAIRVIEW, CA. 1947 (LLOYD HARMON, WHYTE V108-1014)

8.5C MOUNTS LEFROY AND VICTORIA FROM FAIRVIEW, JULY 2003 (CW 2003-071-35)

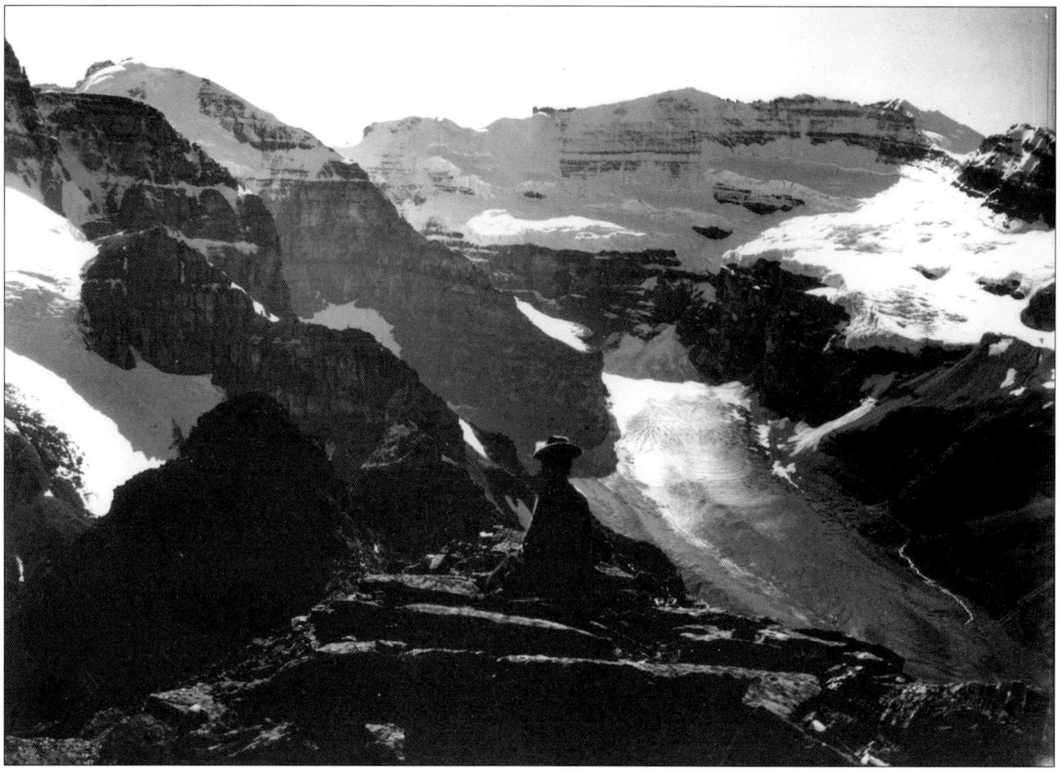

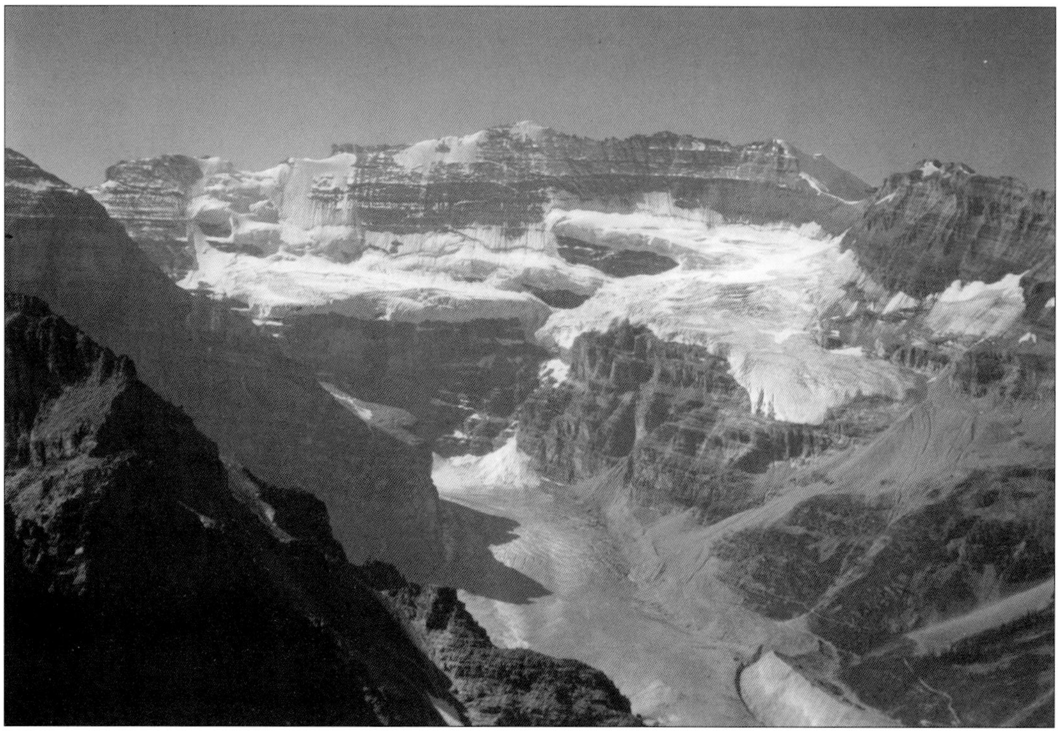

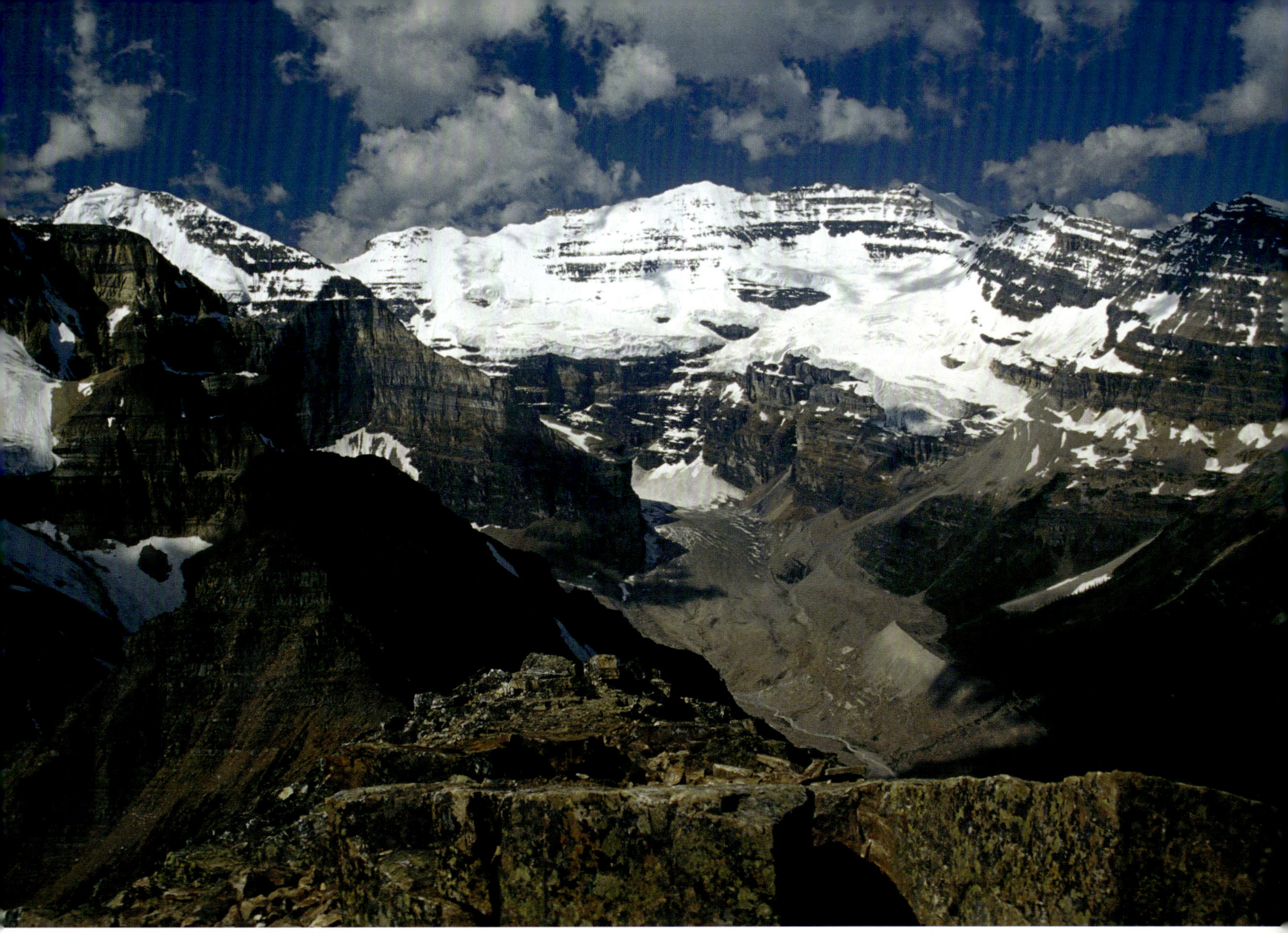

The history of glaciers in the Canadian Rockies has, over the millennia, been one of alternating advance and retreat, but it is only for the last century that scientists have been able to study the phenomenon with any precision. While current techniques include lichen analysis and tree-ring dating, the first method for recording the current phase of glacial recession was by use of the camera and various surveying instruments. Philadelphian George Vaux Sr., and his children, Mary, George Jr., and William Jr., first visited the mountains in 1887 while travelling home from a visit to the American West on the recently completed CPR line. Enamoured by what they saw and possessing the Quakers' keen interest in the natural sciences, family members frequently visited the mountains in the period up to the early 1920s and conducted a decades-long study of glacial recession through repeat photography and more detailed measurements. As members of the Philadelphia Photography Society, the Vauxes became masters in the use of the new "dry-plate" and flexible negatives photography techniques. Their photographs, characteristically showing a well-focused foreground, are among the best for evaluating long-term landscape change in the Selkirks and Rocky Mountains.[9]

The 1904 panorama view from Mount Fairview captured the turn-of-the-century situation at Lake Louise, which is fed by the melt waters of a spectacular set of glaciers. Subsequent views in the late 1940s and in 2003 illustrate that the ice has receded to a lesser degree on the upper glaciers on Mt. Victoria compared to the large-scale retreat of the main glacier in the valley bottom.

8.6A MOUNT TEMPLE FROM SADDLEBACK, AUGUST 1904 (VAUX FAMILY, WHYTE NA 80-1291)

8.6B ALPINE LARCH AND ENGELMANN SPRUCE FOREST ON SADDLEBACK, JULY 2003 (CW 2003-07J-27)

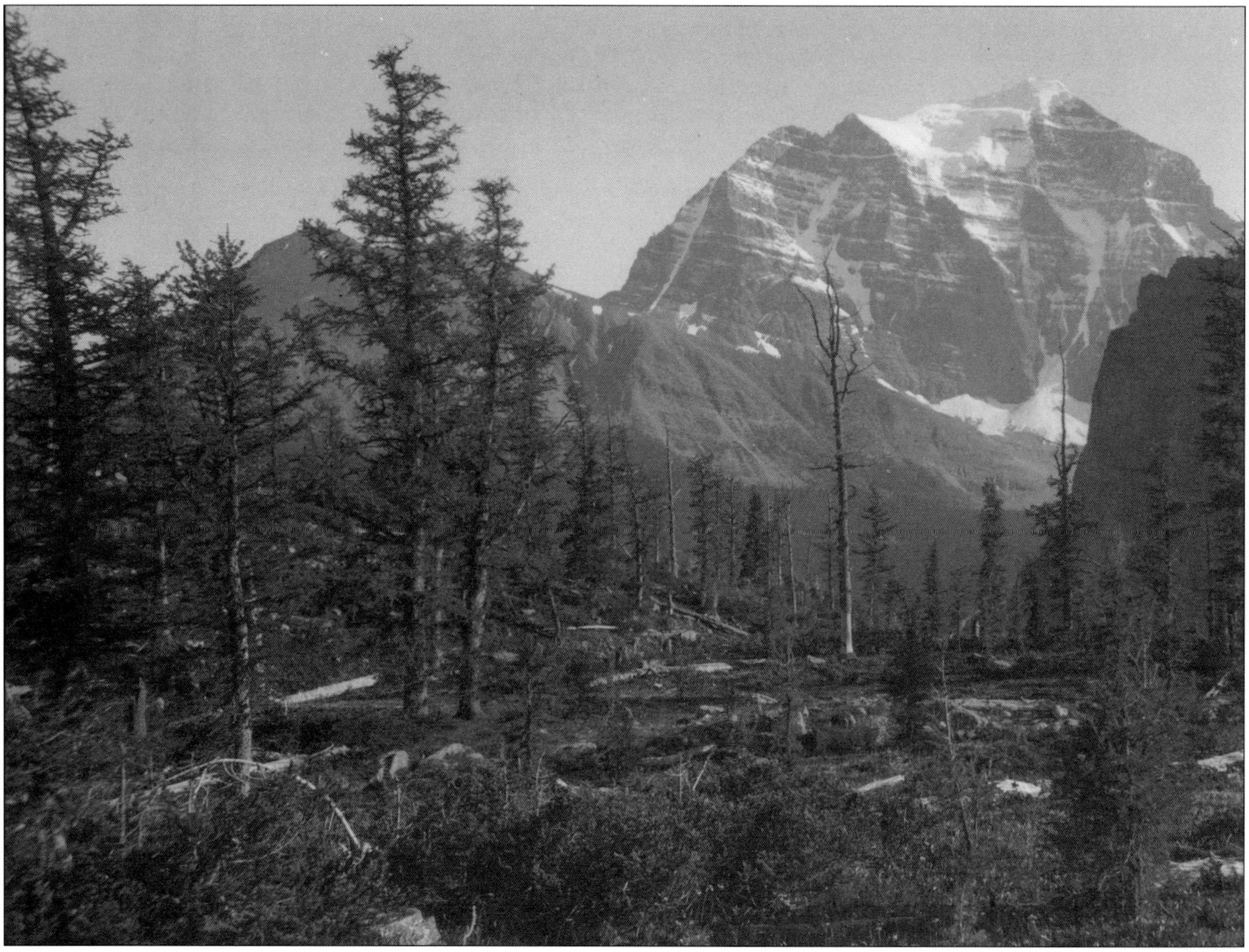

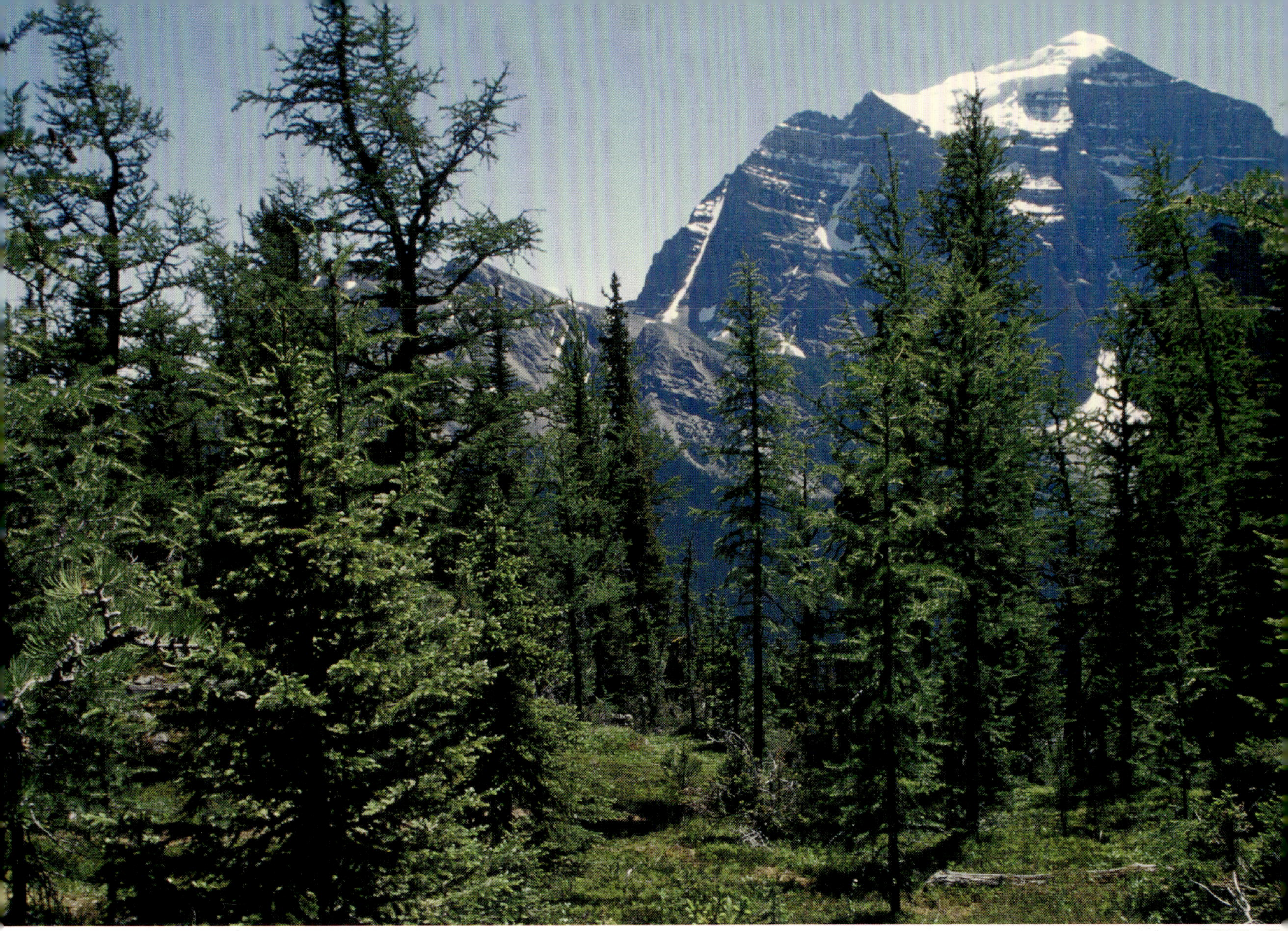

Fires burning in the valley bottoms often climb the nearby slopes. Near treeline, thinner, and often wetter, soils provide less fuel, and fires become less severe. At Saddleback Pass near Lake Louise, the 1904 Vaux family photograph shows that the previous fire (possibly the same burn described in 1884 near the train station) had not killed all the trees but left many old alpine larch surviving to provide a seed-source. The sun-exposed conditions provided by the burn created ideal conditions for regeneration of the young larch seen in the foreground of the old photograph. In 2003 the forest cover is much greater, with shade-loving Engelmann spruce and subalpine fir being more common.[10]

8.7A THE TEN PEAKS, PARADISE VALLEY, 1905 (J. HOWARD CHAPMAN, WHYTE V529-LC-6)

8.7B VALLEY OF TEN PEAKS, CA. 1920 (BYRON HARMON, WHYTE NA 71-5074)

8.7C VALLEY OF TEN PEAKS, 1981 (BRUNO ENGLER, CW-BE-FM-1981-46)

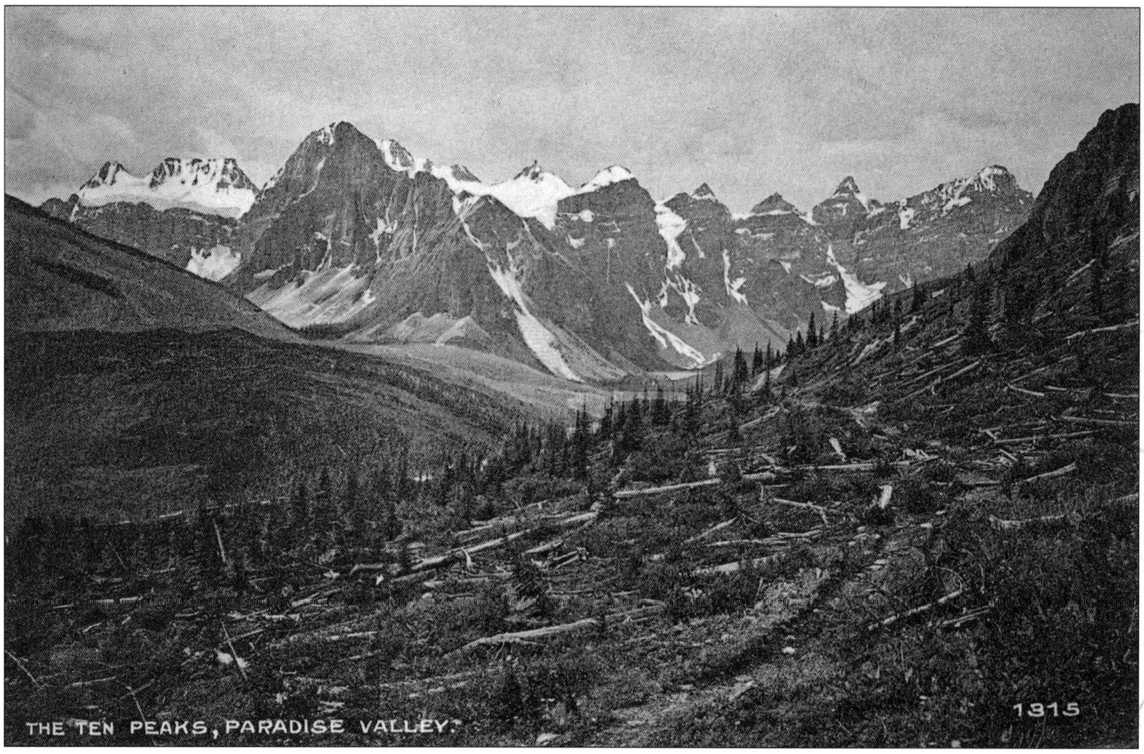

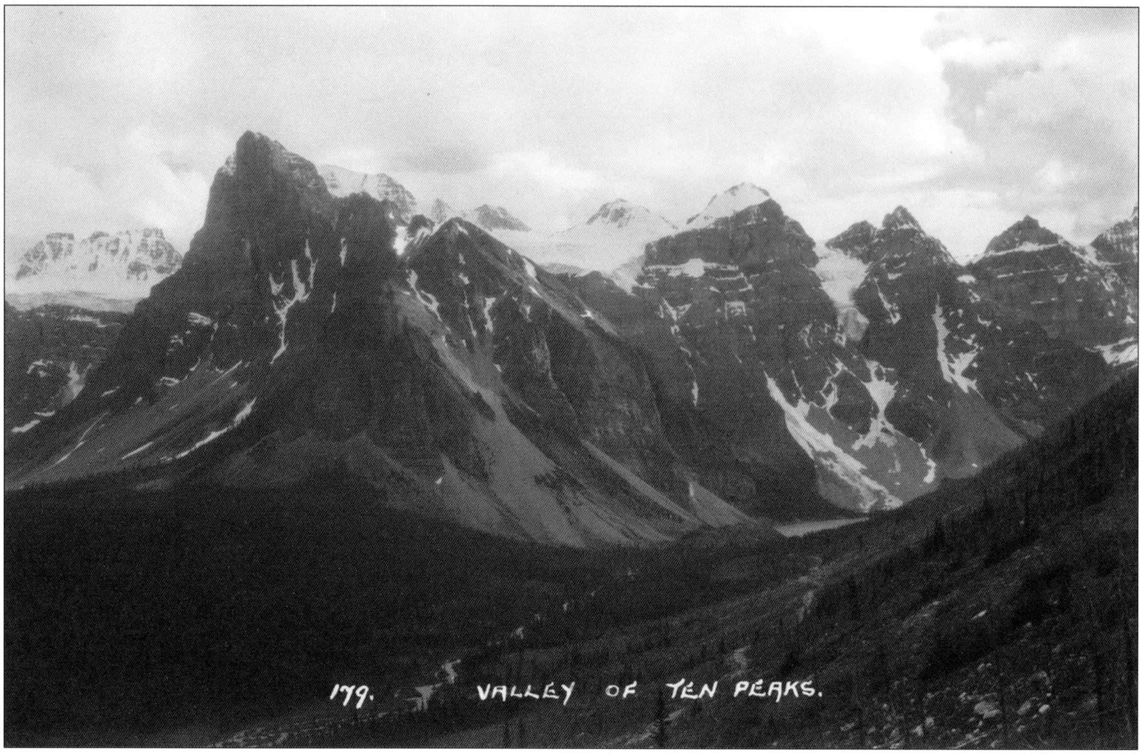

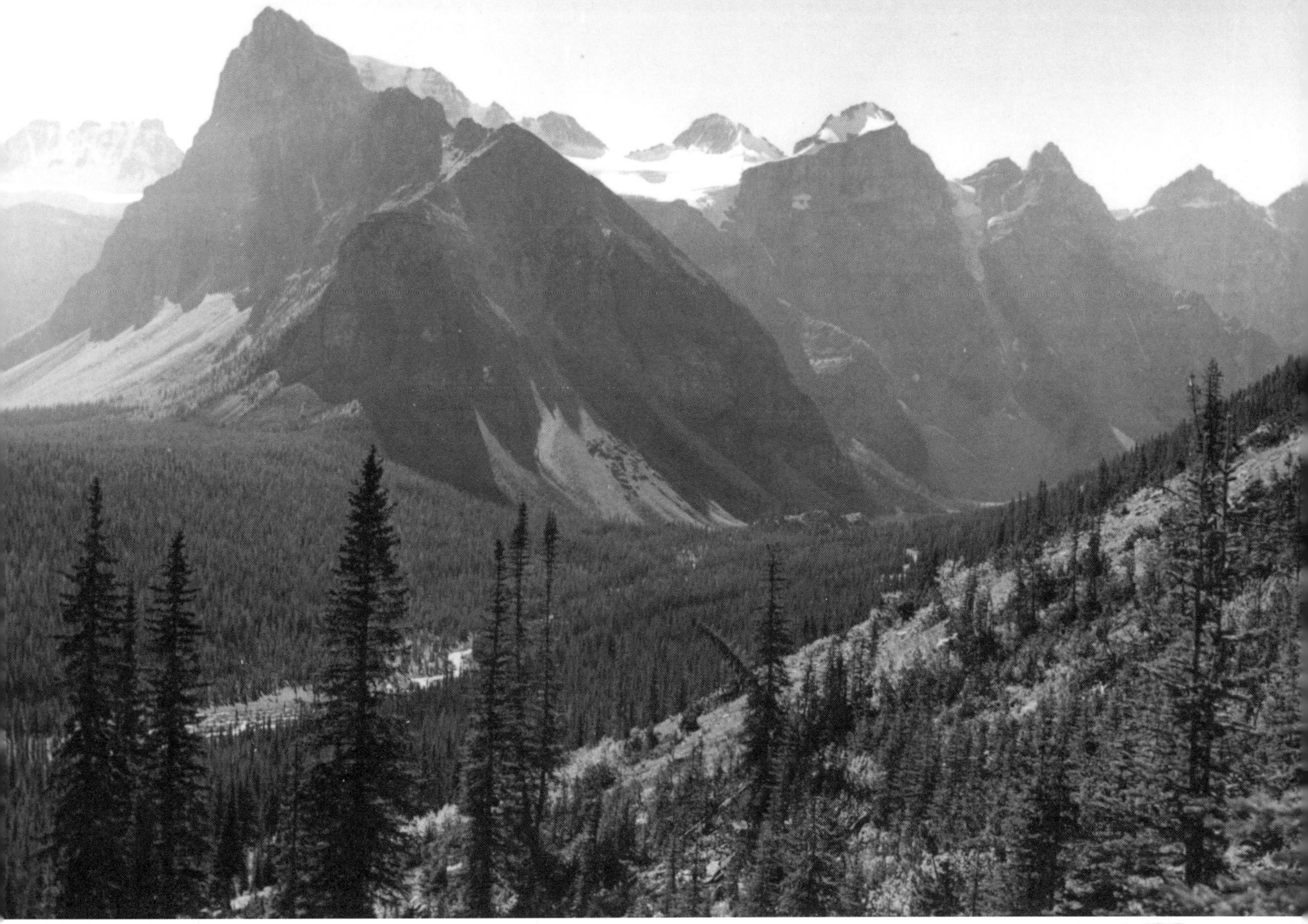

The Valley of Ten Peaks has a relatively unique fire history for a nearly rock-surrounded cirque east of the continental divide. These valleys usually contain ancient forests due to low lightning frequency, and the mountain ridges stop fires from spreading in from the west.[11] However, the valley containing Moraine Lake (visible in the photographs' lower, centre right) appears to have a history of frequent fire. Contrary to Chapman's 1905 depiction, mountaineer Walter Wilcox called it "Desolation Valley" due to the extensive rock moraines and burned forest in its upper reaches. Actually, Wilcox named the next valley to the north "Paradise Valley" because of verdant meadow and forest cover.[12] The Chapman photograph shows many standing snags, fire-killed by burns in about 1835 and partially re-burned by a fire in 1904 that was likely started by campers at Moraine Lake.[13]

The 1920 and 1981 images show regeneration of the forest, although areas of grasses and shrubs remain in large avalanche paths descending the south slopes of Mount Temple. The Dominion Parks Branch began a carriage road from Lake Louise to Moraine Lake in 1902, completing it in 1911. Ongoing improvements made one-way traffic for early sightseeing vehicles possible by 1917, and by 1924 two-way public traffic was permitted. The recently built road is clearly visible in the lower centre of the 1920 Harmon photograph.[14]

8.8A MORAINE LAKE, CA. 1904 (WALTER WILCOX, WHYTE NA 66-581)

8.8B MORAINE LAKE, SEPTEMBER 2004 (CW 2004-09E-13)

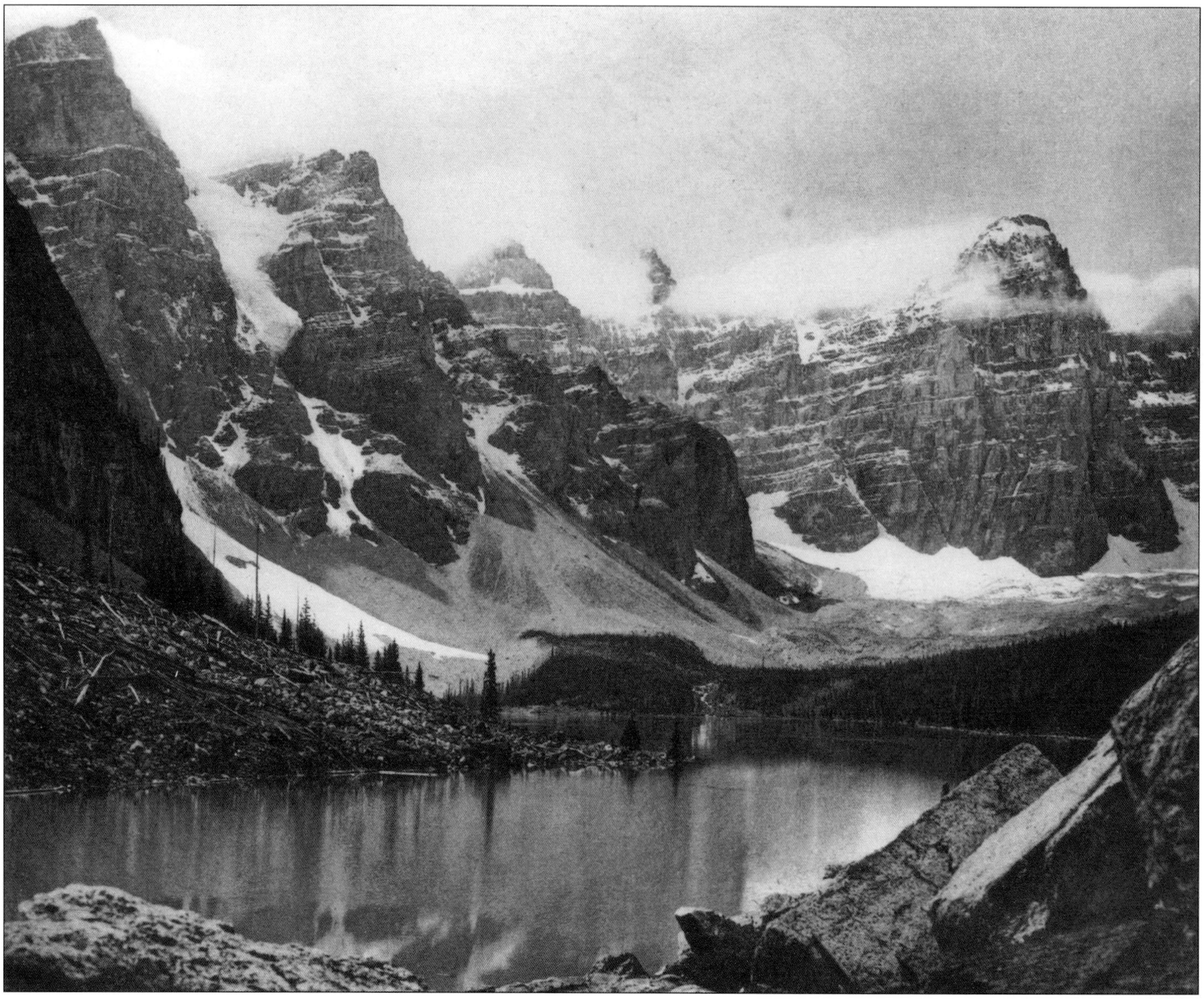

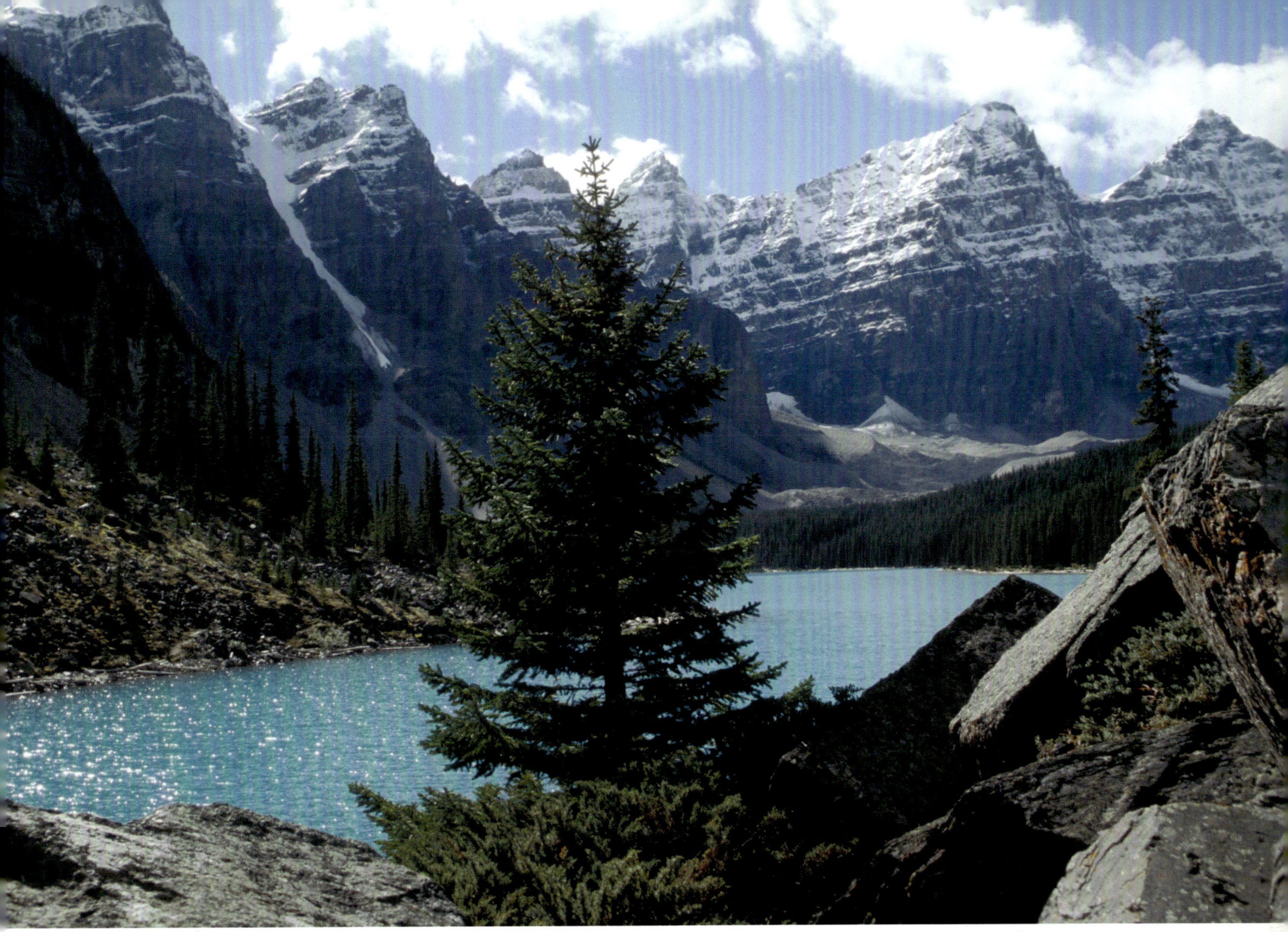

The landscape around Moraine Lake appears little changed in the century between the two photographs. The large angular boulders in the foreground, part of the rockslide that dams the lake, remain in identical positions, but now also occupied with a two-metre-high Engelmann spruce slowly growing in the thin soils. Fallen trees, visible upslope from the lakeshore in the earliest picture, likely date from the ca. 1835 fire and have now rotted away. A new forest is regenerating very slowly here. In the background, the hanging glacier in the upper left of the photograph has changed from a thick ice lobe to a long even slope, mostly made of snow.

8.9A OBLIQUE AIR PHOTOGRAPH OF LAKE LOUISE VILLAGE, 1931 (NATIONAL AIR PHOTOGRAPH LIBRARY A 3414-19)

8.9B LAKE LOUISE VILLAGE FROM HELICOPTER, JUNE 2003 (CW 2003-06H-32)

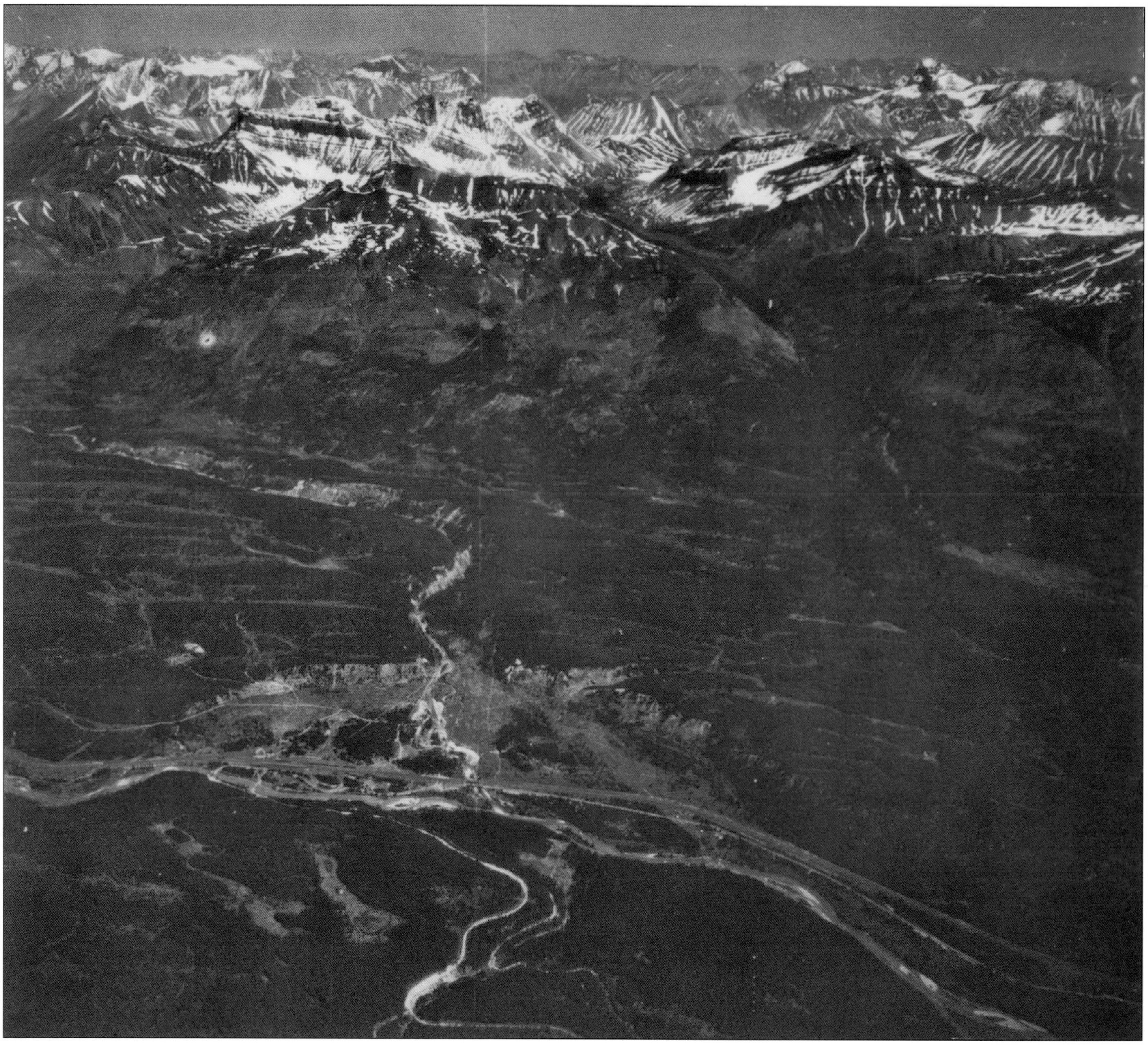

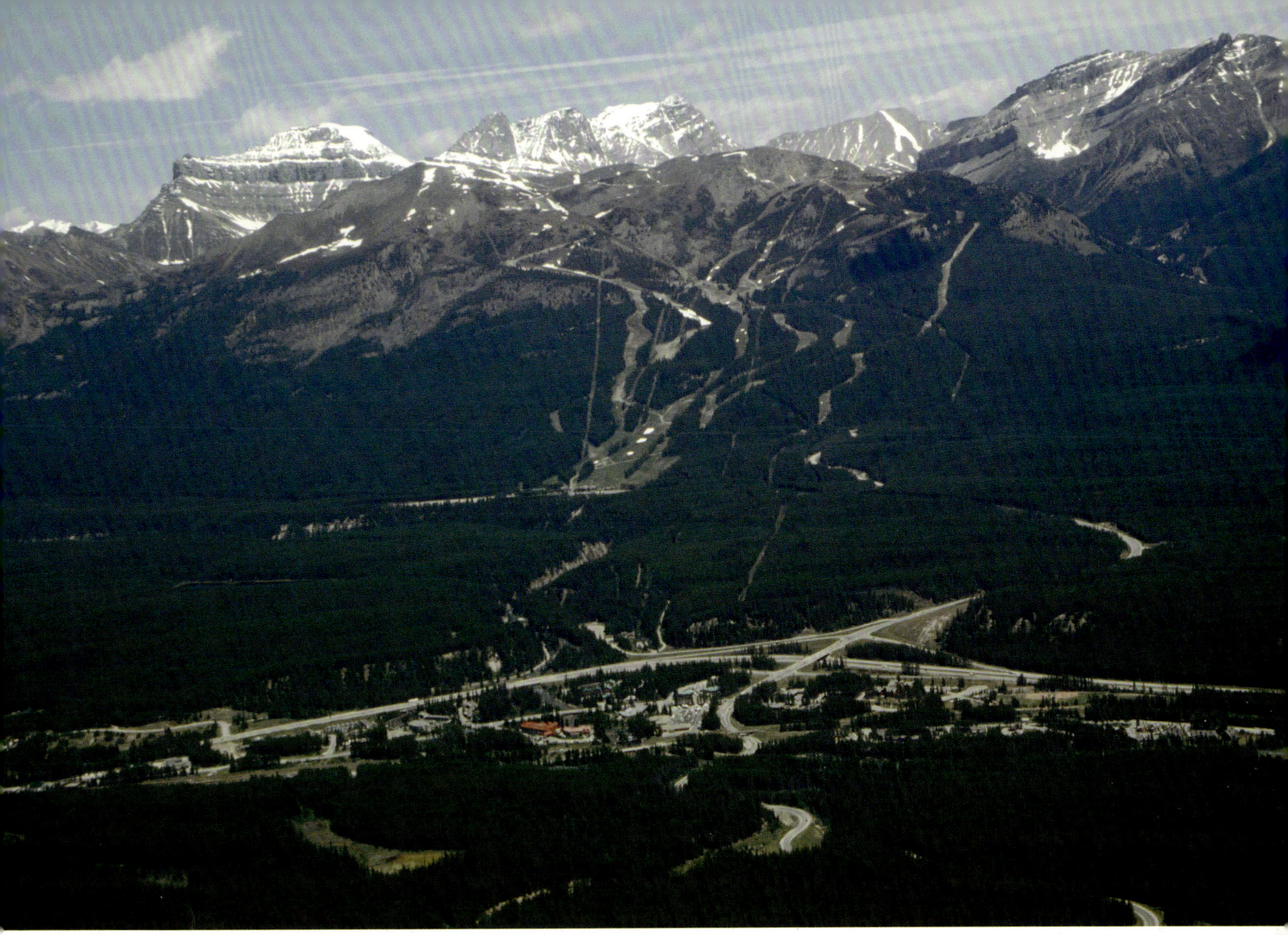

The opening of the Banff-Jasper Highway in late 1939 started a minor building boom at its junction with the road to Field near the Lake Louise train station. In 1940 Jim Boyce built the Lake Louise Ski Lodge, later renamed the Post Hotel, and a motel and a gas station soon followed. In the late 1950s the construction of the Trans-Canada Highway through the area and the establishment of a National Parks Planning Division stimulated a quarter-century of virtually non-stop planning to create a model Visitor Service Centre at Lake Louise. There were several false starts when no public bids were received for the commercial accommodation and shopping centre properties proposed in the plans. Further public debate occurred when Lake Louise Lifts proposed a major resort, to be known as Village Lake Louise, at the bottom of the ski runs on the bench of Mount Whitehorn (background of photographs). In the early 1970s the original village was still a collection of just three small hotels, two gas stations, and a small general store, with the majority of the full-time residents living in a trailer park.[15]

Ministerial direction in 1974 finalized that further development would be mostly adjacent to the highway, not at the ski hill or near the lake, and detailed planning commenced once more. With improving year-round economic conditions due to summer sightseeing and the winter ski industry, the Lake Louise Village Plan was finally successfully implemented in the 1980s. Developments included an information centre, a shopping mall with numerous stores and services, new restaurants, and a wide variety of staff accommodation facilities. In 1988 the Trans-Canada Highway was twinned near Lake Louise, and a modern highway overpass and exits first contemplated more than two decades previously were finally completed.[16]

8.10A LARCH RUN, TEMPLE SKI AREA, 1940S (LLOYD HARMON, WHYTE V108-592)

8.10B LARCH RUN, LAKE LOUISE SKI AREA, MARCH 2004 (CW 2004-03B-35)

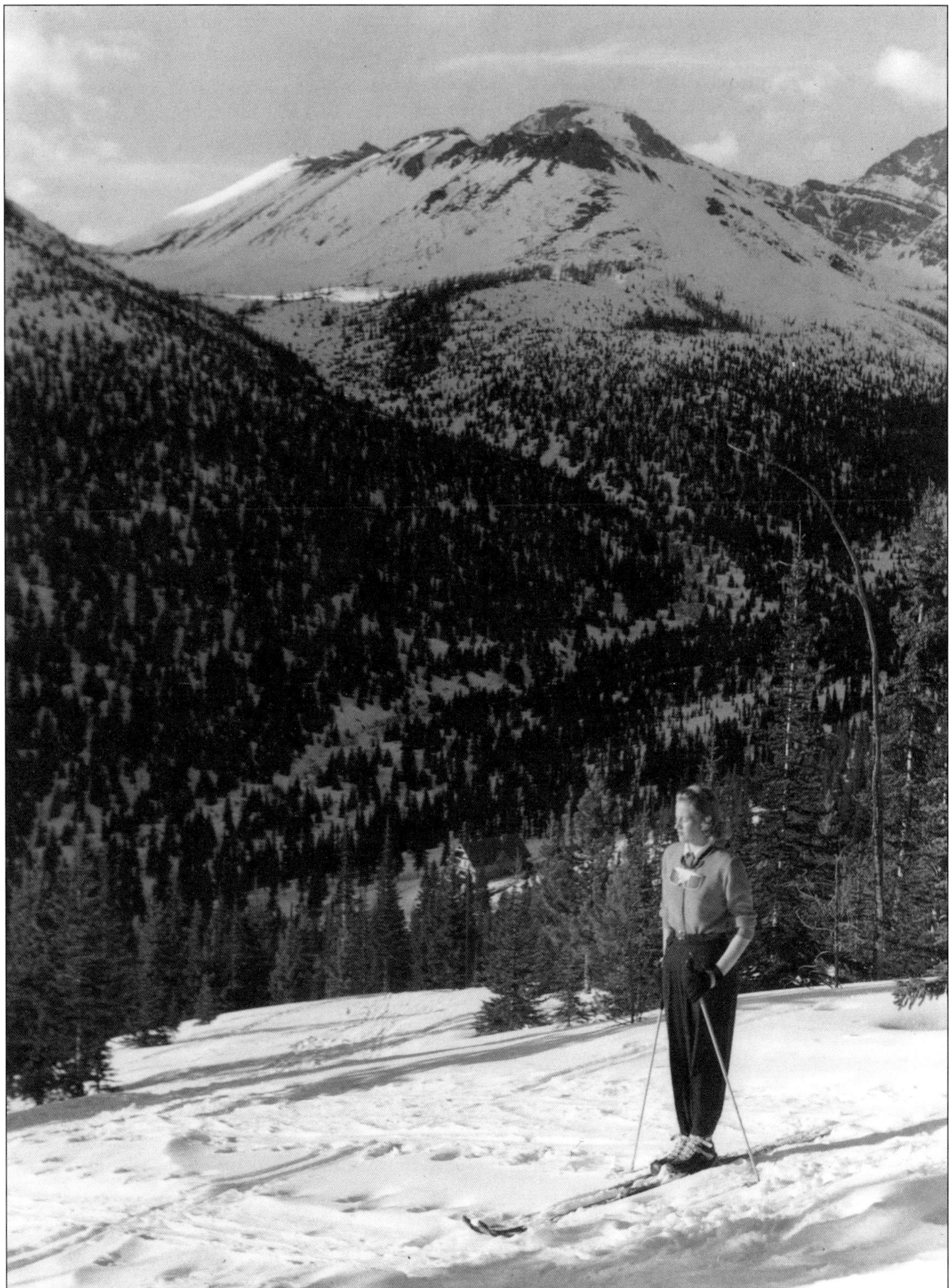

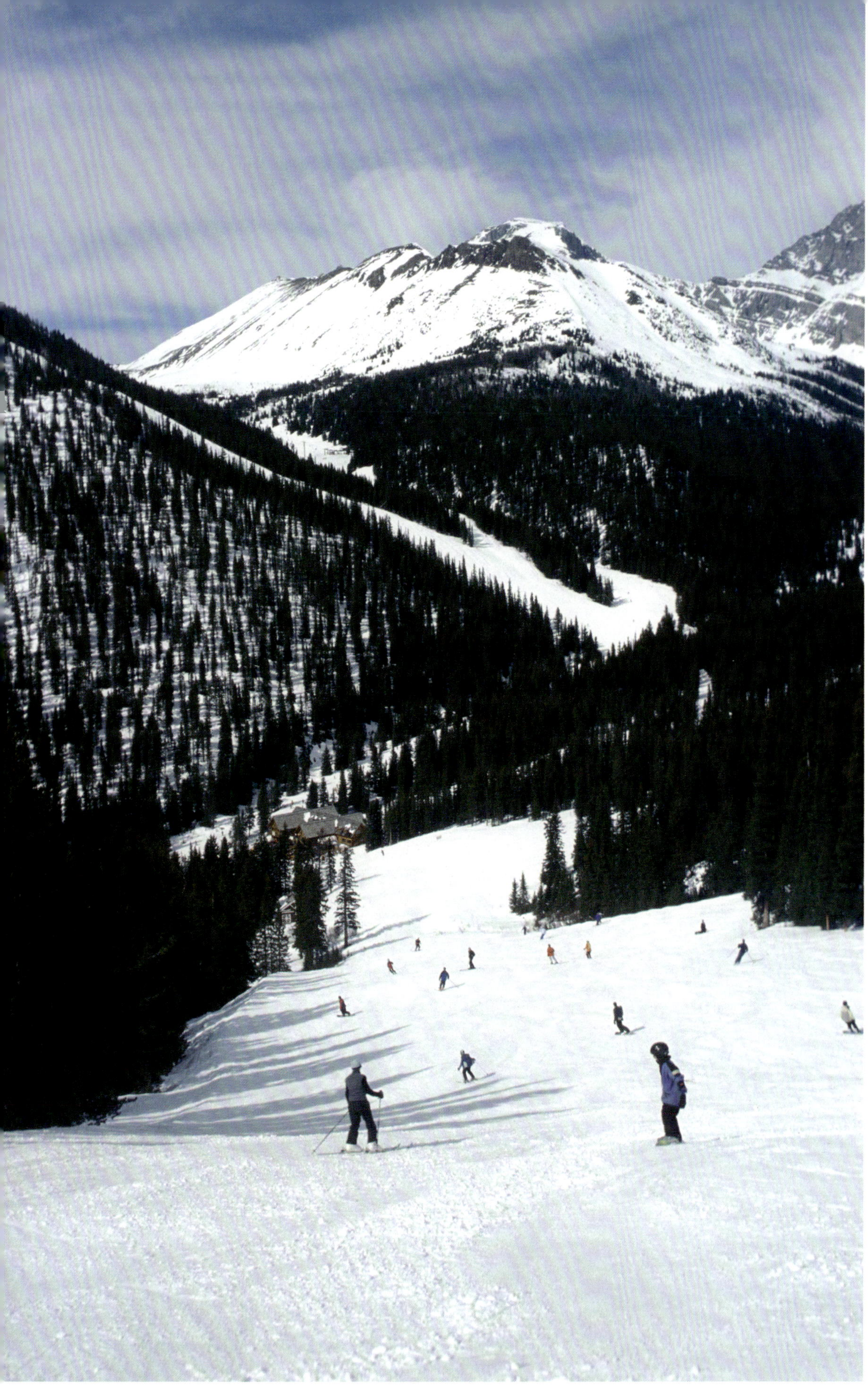

In 1939, the Ski Club of the Canadian Rockies, financed by eccentric British millionaire Sir Norman Watson, built the original Temple Lodge (visible in the mid-ground of the historical photograph). The lodge was part of Watson's dream to create a Swiss Alps type resort, cows and all, in the Ptarmigan Valley. In the 1940s skiers arrived by train at the Lake Louise station and were carried by a sleigh towed with a small tractor up to Temple. During multi-day stays they toured to the nearby slopes of Whitehorn and Purple Bowl. Lake Louise's first ski lift was built near Temple Lodge in 1952, a "Model C Sweden Ski Tow" costing only US$292.50, running two hundred metres from Corral Creek up to an anchor-tree above the lodge. In 1954 a Poma lift was built to the top of Larch Hill, and with the construction of additional lifts on Mount Whitehorn, Temple was linked into the larger Lake Louise ski area. The original Temple Lodge burned down in the summer of 1976 and was replaced by a post and beam structure adjacent to Corral Creek.[17]

A forest fire in the 1880s removed most the trees in the Corral Creek watershed. Until the 1940s skiers could easily pass through the open cover of the slowly regenerating forest. Today, ski run construction here requires cutting dense forests and "glading," and sometimes bulldozing to remove stumps and smooth the terrain. Due to heavy ski traffic, in most years Larch Run must be largely covered with artificial snow.

8.11A POST HOTEL AND MOUNT WHITEHORN, CA. 1963 (BRUNO ENGLER, WHYTE V190-XVIII-3)

8.11B VILLAGE OF LAKE LOUISE AND MOUNT WHITEHORN, MARCH 2004 (CW 2004-03B-08)

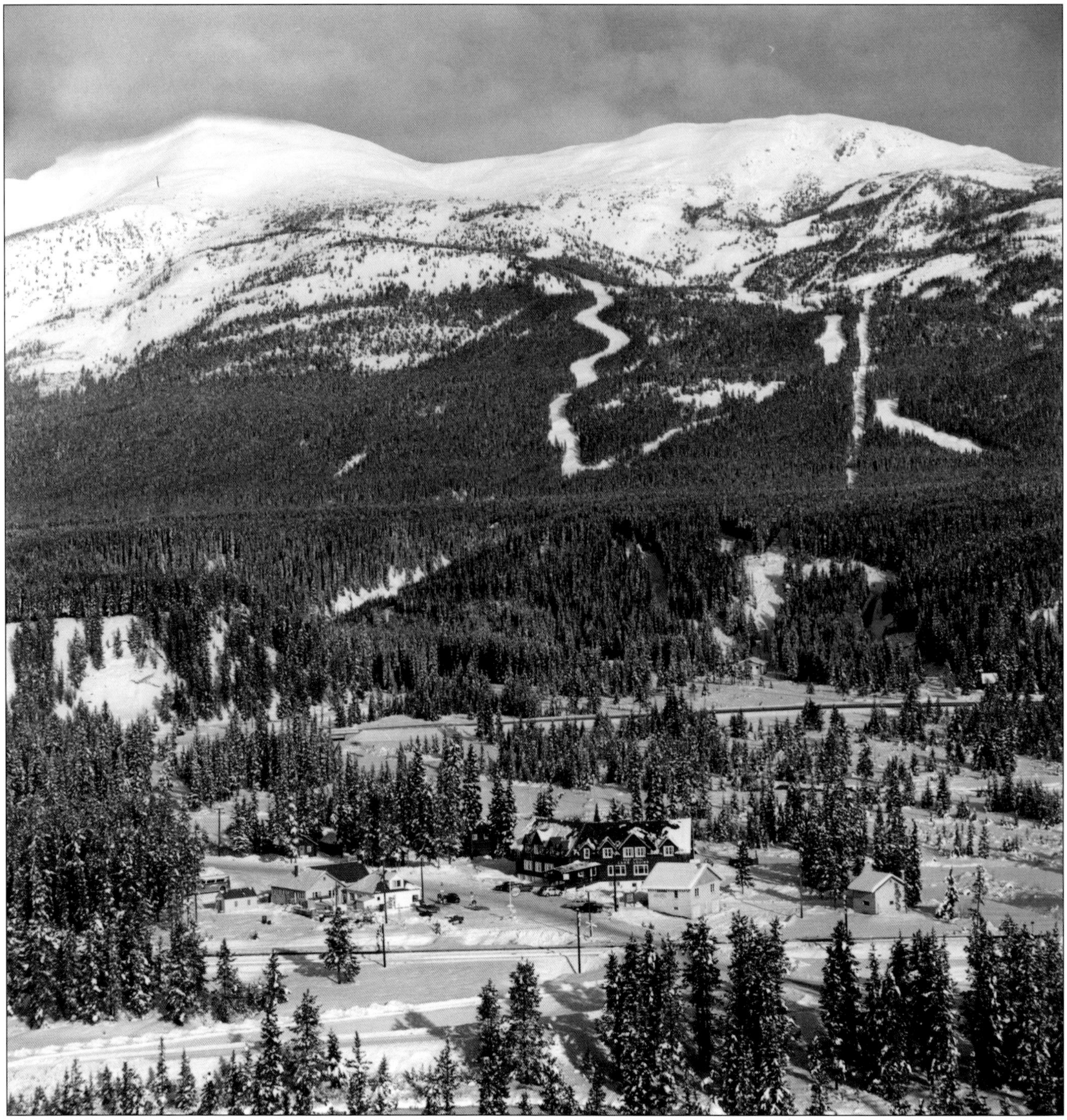

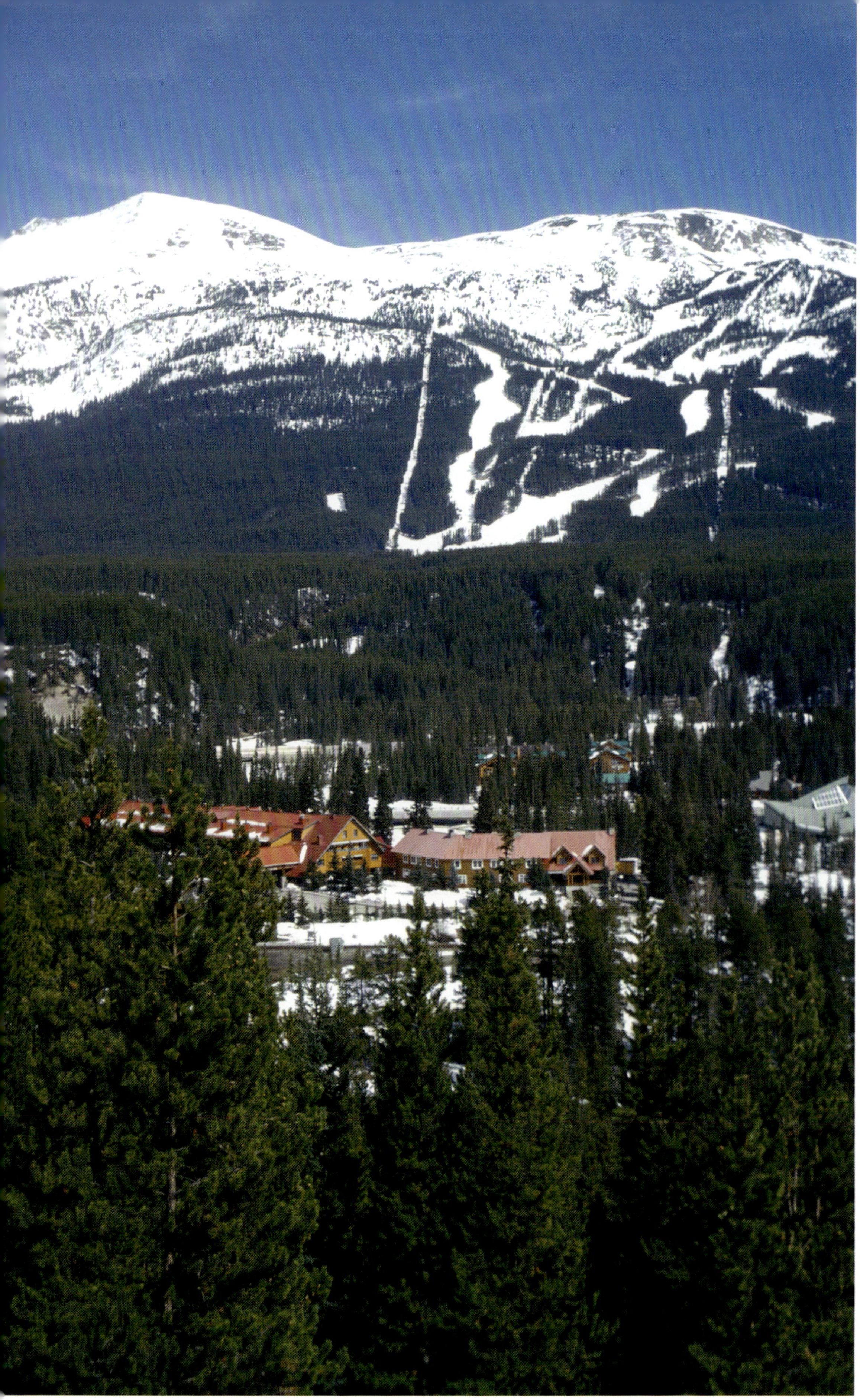

To access his alpine resort, in 1959 Sir Norman Watson built a gondola lift running from near the highway (centre right) to the upper slopes of Mount Whitehorn. In 1960 the Eagle Poma lift was built to take skiers to the top of the ridge where they could descend over the back of the mountain to Temple. The older photograph shows the Men's Downhill ski run, left, and Ladies' Downhill, centre, built by the parks department to support Canada's unsuccessful bid to host the 1968 Olympics in Banff National Park. The recent photograph shows the completed Lake Louise Village in the valley bottom around the expanded Post Hotel. In 1968 Lake Louise Ski Area moved its base lodge to the Fish Creek Bench at the bottom of the downhill runs and since then has built several lifts and numerous runs on the front side of Mount Whitehorn.[18]

8.12A RED DEER VALLEY, OCTOBER 1884 (GEORGE M. DAWSON, GEOLOGICAL SURVEY CANADA ESIC-667)

8.12B RED DEER VALLEY NEAR SANDHILLS, OCTOBER 2002 (CW 2002-10A-03)

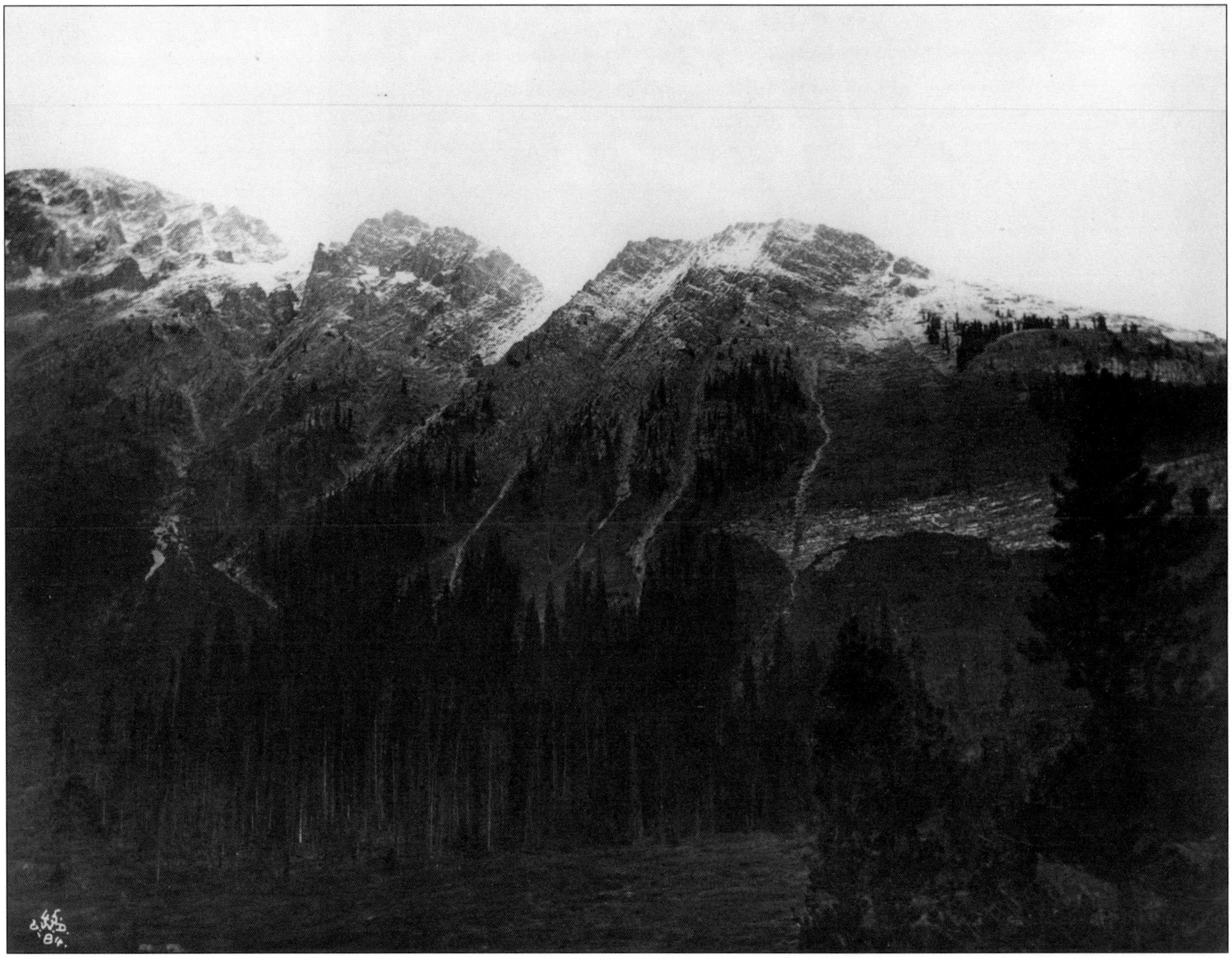

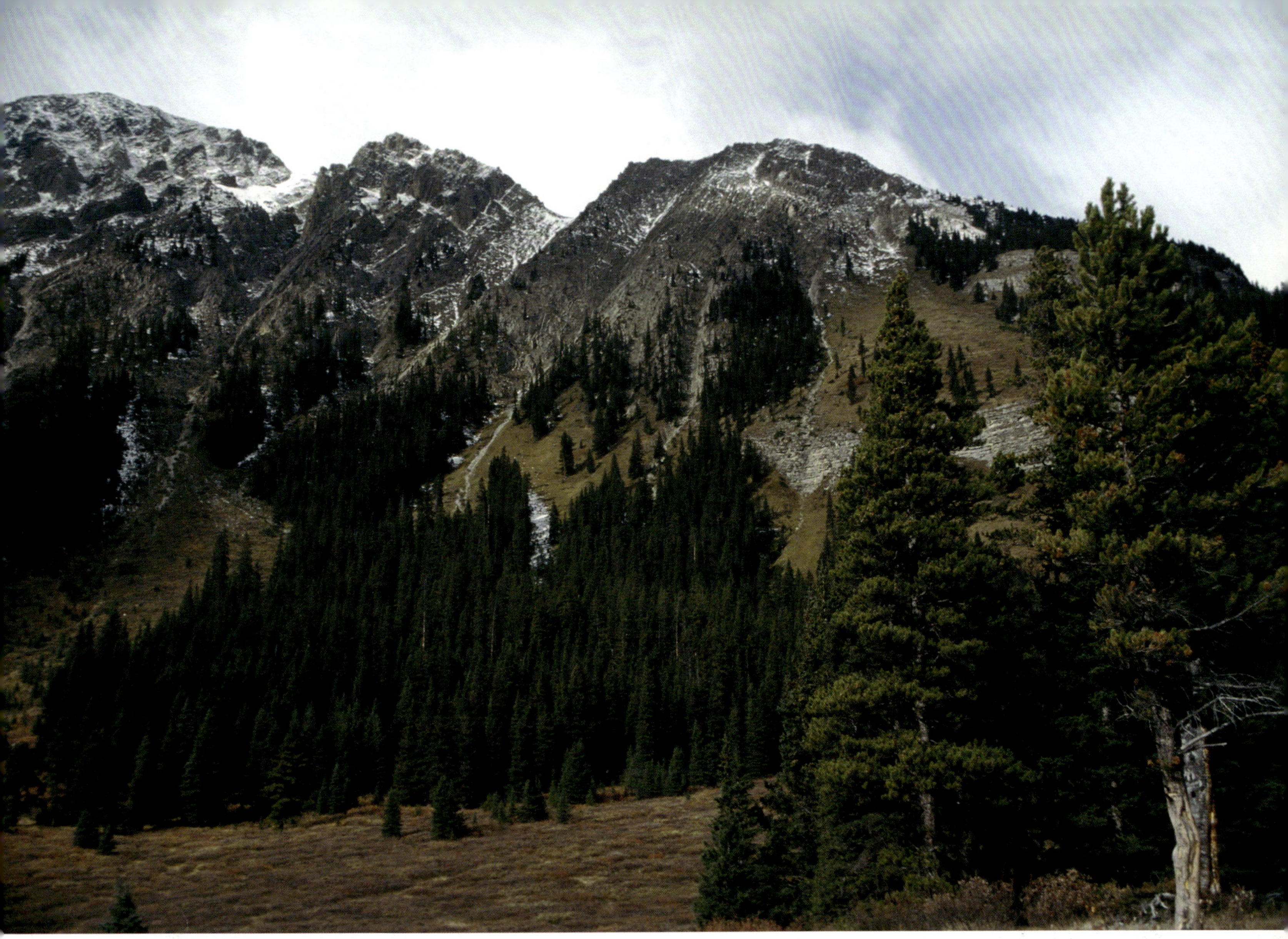

In the fall of 1884 George Mercer Dawson, later the head of the Geological Survey of Canada, made a preliminary reconnaissance of what is now the eastern part of Banff National Park. Ascending the Red Deer River on the route to Lake Louise, he followed the old trail used for many years by K'tunaxa First Nation peoples from the Columbia Valley to the west when they crossed the mountains to hunt bison in the foothills.[19] Dawson's photograph well illustrates the potential effects of long-term native burning patterns. The image shows that the last fire only killed the timber at the base of the mountain. It was likely a low-intensity spring or late fall blaze started by people that burned mostly in the meadows along the trail – not a midsummer, valley-wall to valley-wall holocaust fire.

Why would native peoples only burn carefully in areas along trails? One hypothesis is that they were attempting to use freshly burned corridors to lure bison further west into the mountains. Here, the K'tunaxa could more easily kill them in constrained terrain. In addition, further into the mountains the hunter's families could more fully process the meat and hides with greater safety from attack from Blackfoot Confederacy enemies who dominated the nearby prairies. Archaeological sites showing evidence of bison processing are common in the valley. Today, the Red Deer Valley is a lightly visited part of Banff's backcountry, and few of its infrequent travellers likely consider its long history as a corridor for bison, burning, and First Nations occupants.[20]

8.13A YA-HA-TINDA, AUGUST 1937 (NATIONAL PARKS, WHYTE PC-465-15)

8.13B YA-HA-TINDA, CA. 1956 (NATIONAL PARKS, BNP-43)

8.13C YA-HA-TINDA, 1985 (CW-1986-I-05)

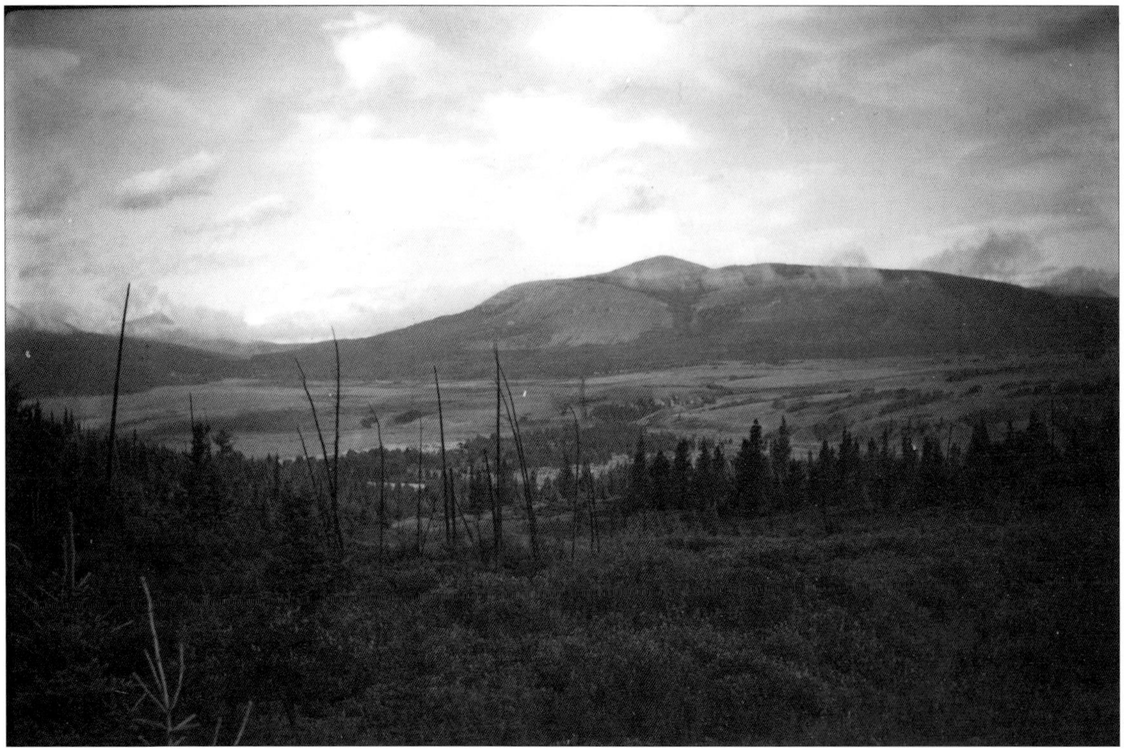

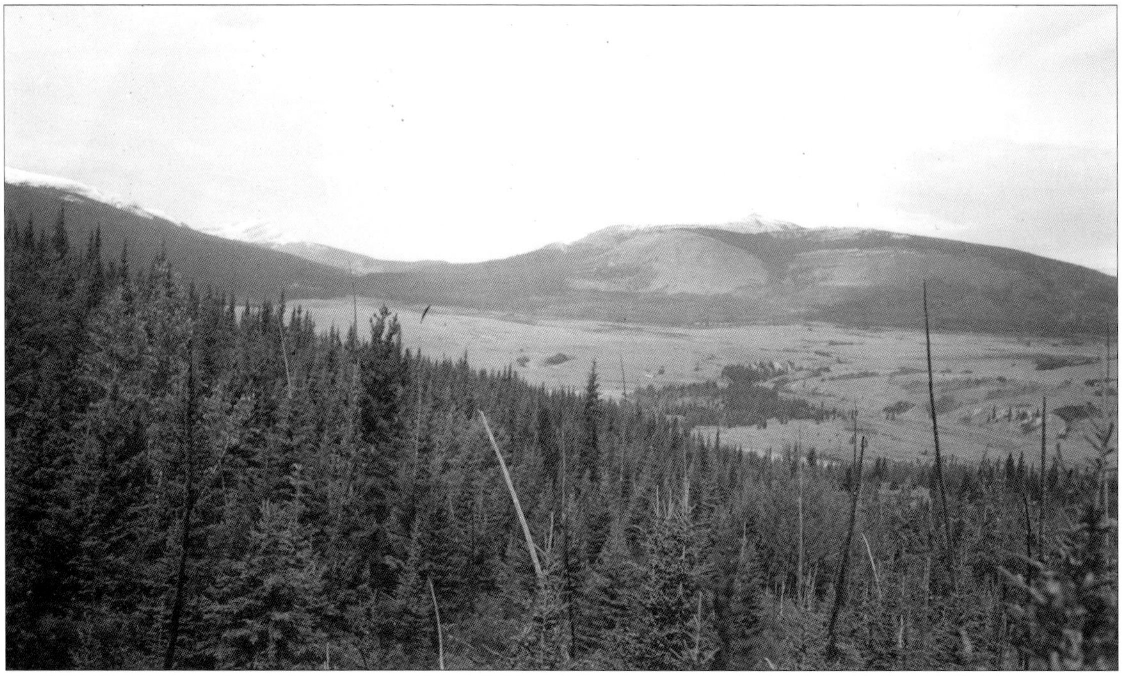

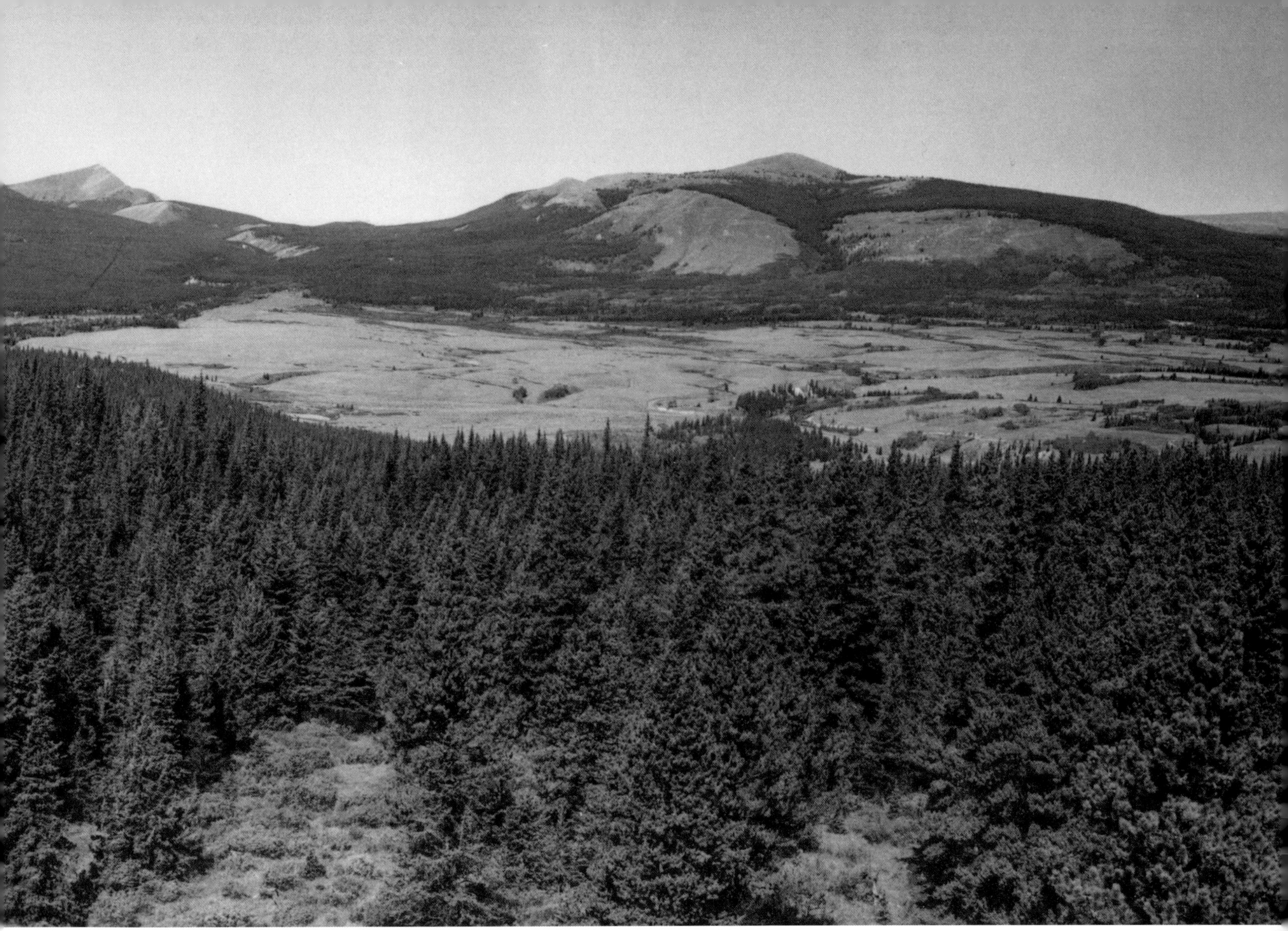

Lying just east of Banff National Park on the Red Deer River, the grasslands of the Ya-Ha-Tinda are a centuries-old refuge for wildlife and First Nations people. The Brewster Brothers leased the land from 1905 to 1917 to winter horses used in their outfitting operation based out of Banff, Lake Louise, and Field. Pat Brewster described how his father, John Brewster, had learned about the area from his Stoney Nakoda friend William Twin and his vision for its use:

> It was just about everything William Twin had described – six or seven miles long and four or five miles wide. The meadow was set among rugged mountains describing a complete circle around the whole location. It had good horsefeed and water. To the Indians it was Ya-Ha-Tinda, Mountain Prairie. To my father, it meant good pasture land for future years. The snowfall was light and the range land was protected by surrounding mountains.[21]

The Parks Branch took over the land in 1917 to winter the warden service's horses. Breeding and horse-breaking operations were established and it became the headquarters for all mountain national park equine operations. The federal and Alberta governments have contended for the Ya-Ha-Tinda's control for generations. Today, while they are not national park lands, the federal government retains surface rights ownership.

The grasslands, snow-free throughout most of the year, are capable of supporting a hundred head of horses over the winter months and are also home to over a thousand elk and several wolf packs. The three views show the stability of the fescue grassland for over seventy years. Although the forest in the foreground continues to become denser after a fire that occurred in 1889, trees and shrubs are only slowly encroaching on the prairie in the middle ground. The Red Deer is one of the last low-elevation Rocky Mountain valleys between Colorado and Jasper that is free of highways, intensive resource exploitation, and tourist developments.[22]

8.14A BREWSTER'S RANCH BUILDINGS ON THE YA-HA-TINDA. CA. 1915 (TEX VERNON-WOOD COLLECTION, WHYTE V192-43-PD)

8.14B PARKS CANADA RANCH BUILDINGS, YA-HA-TINDA, 2004 (CW 2004-04C-12)

8.14C WARDEN COLTS ON THE YA-HA-TINDA RANCH, JULY 2003 (CW 2003-07I-33)

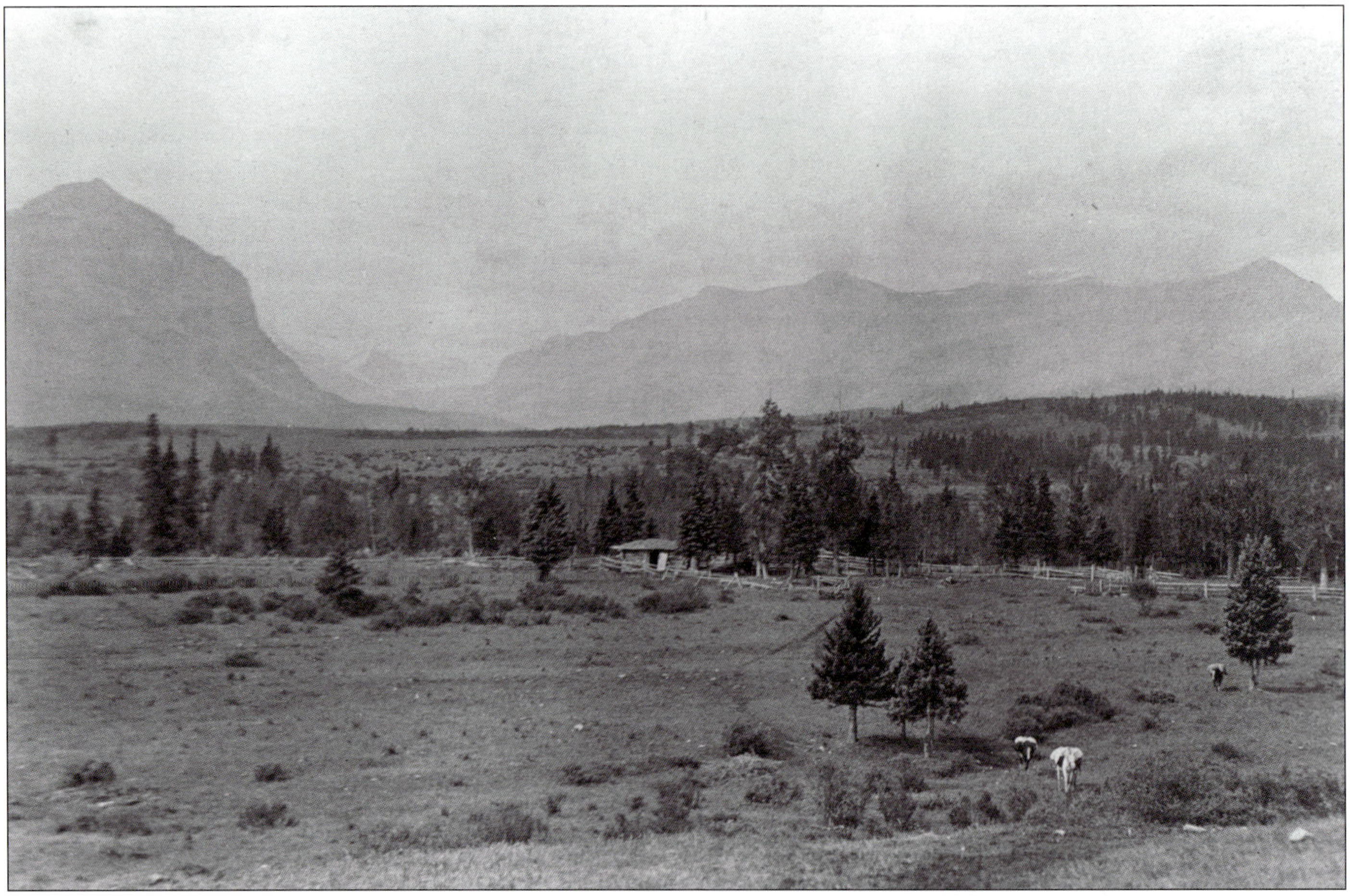

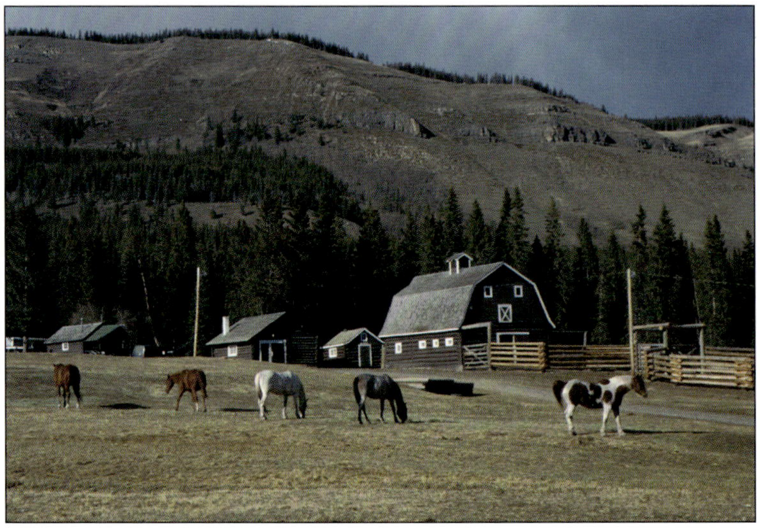

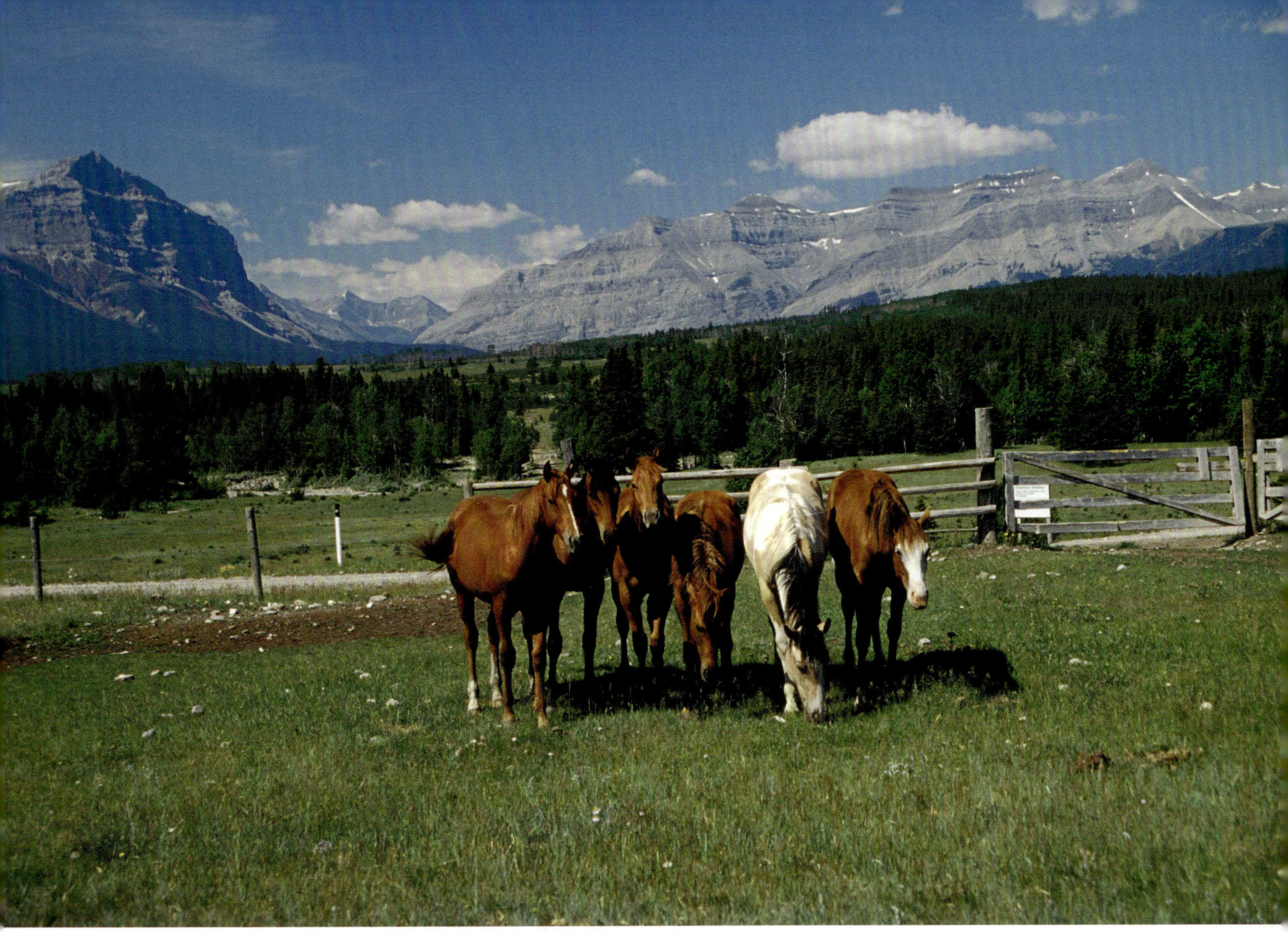

Historically, First Nations likely frequently burned the Ya-Ha-Tinda grasslands and adjacent forests. Fire scars in the growth rings of lodgepole pine on the low ridge behind the Brewster's cabins shown in the old photograph date to approximately 1790, 1839, 1864, 1879, and 1889. Since the 1900s, horses, and more recently elk, graze off over 90 per cent of the grass and litter from the rangelands over the winter, making a spring burn unlikely. By early summer the fescue dominating the grassland is green and lush and will not burn again until the fall. However, it is unlikely that historic First Nations hunters or more recently, the ranch hands, would favour a fall fire that removes forage necessary for over-wintering horses and wildlife.[23]

The Ya-Ha-Tinda ranch houses and barns are now approximately a kilometre up Scalp Creek from the historic location (Fig. 14B). The two-year-old colts in the modern picture of the pasture area are enjoying their last work-free weeks. Soon they will be trained for riding and packing, and after they reach three years old, horses are sent out each summer for backcountry warden patrol duty. Parks Canada is one of only a few park management agencies that continues to maintain a working horse herd.

8.15A POPES PEAK FROM THE RAILROAD ABOVE HECTOR STATION, AUGUST 1901 (VAUX FAMILY, WHYTE NG-4-820)

8.15B SINK LAKE AND POPES PEAK FROM THE RAILROAD NEAR KICKING HORSE PASS, SEPTEMBER 2006 (CW 2006-09C-23)

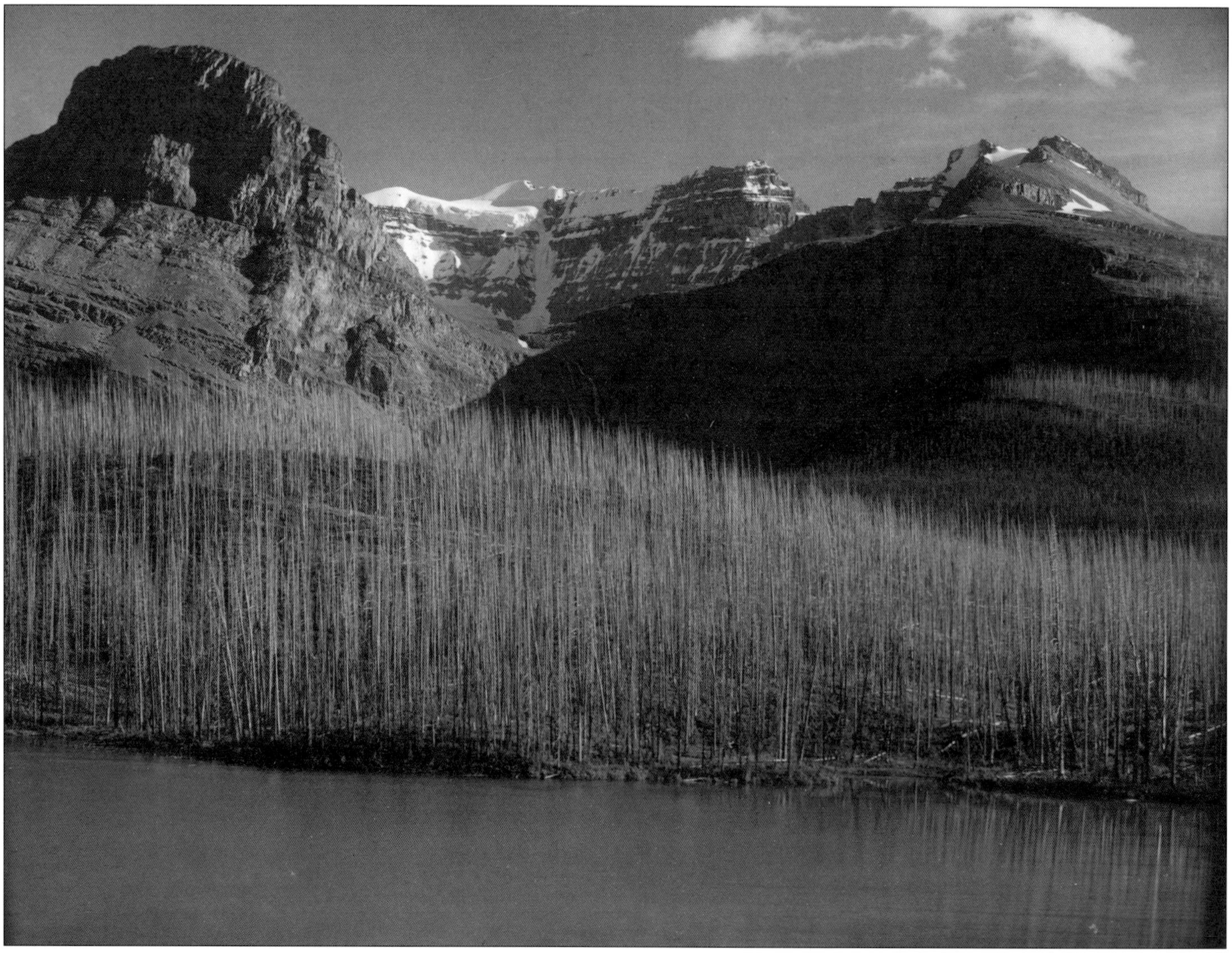

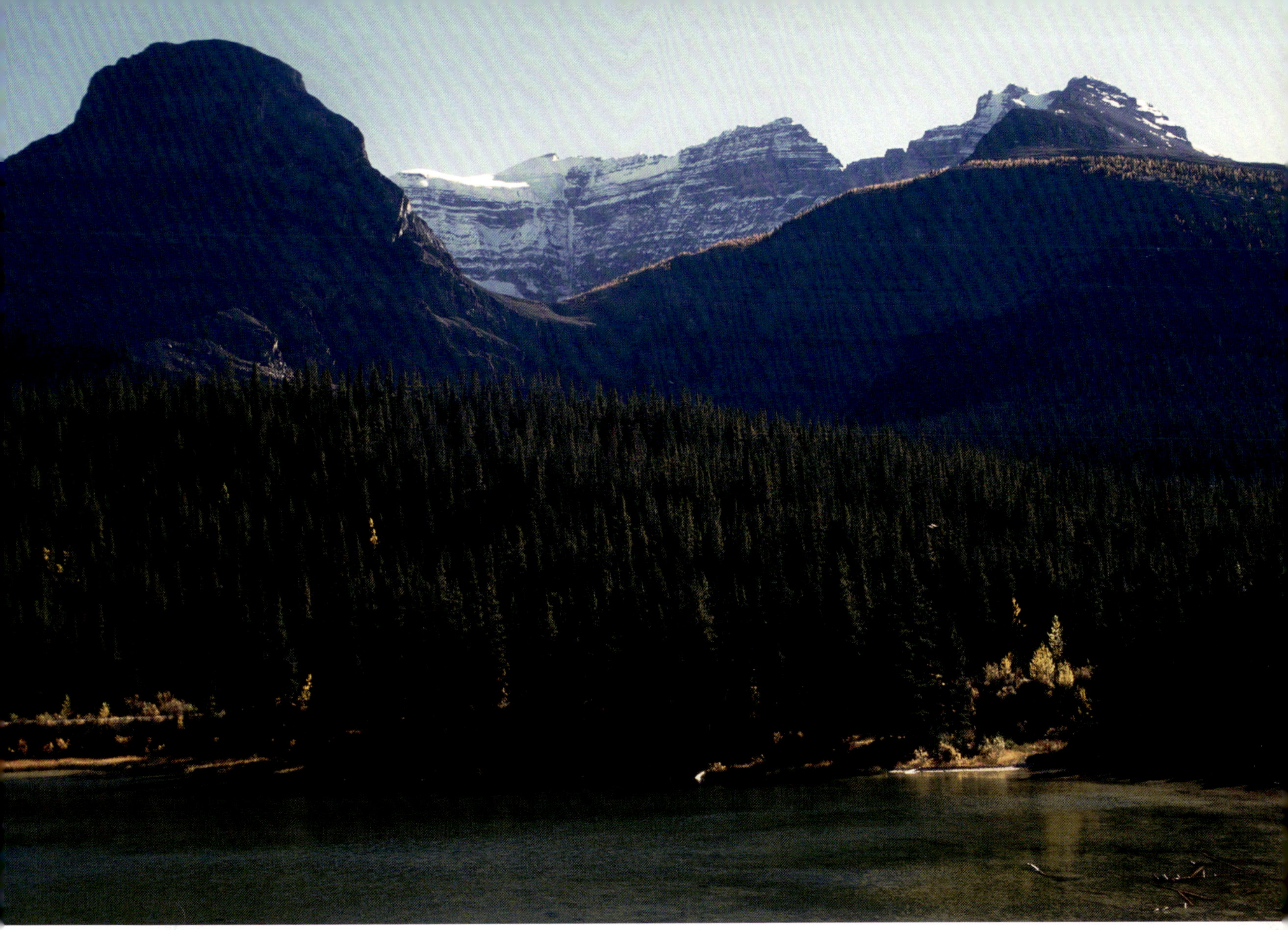

Geographic place names sometimes reflect the exigencies of historic horse travel in the Canadian Rockies. Kicking Horse Pass commemorates explorer Dr. James Hector's painful experience behind an unhappy "cayuse" in 1858. Nearby Bath Creek has a similar equestrian-based name. Tom Wilson recalled that he was riding with Major A. B. Rogers while surveying the railway when they came to the creek swollen with melt water and, despite his warning, the Major attempted to ford it on his horse. Immediately being knocked from his mount, Wilson had to rescue him with a tree branch found close at hand before Rogers was swept away in the bone-chilling water. In his memoirs he recalled that this incident gave the creek its name. Whenever it ran high and muddy with glacial run-off, the men on the survey would say, "Hello, the old man's taking another bath," and hence the name.[24]

The 1901 Vaux family photograph of Popes Peak and Sink Lake near the pass shows evening light on the grey skeleton of a forest nearly totally killed by a fire in the 1880s, a burn that was likely started by activities associated with construction of the railroad. Historically, fires were not frequent at this elevation in the Rocky Mountains, occurring on average every hundred to two hundred years. However, when these forests do burn, it is usually during midsummer in a very dry year, with resulting high fire intensities causing the almost total scorching visible in the photograph. A century later a mature Engelmann spruce and subalpine fir forest has obscured any vestiges of the conflagration.

8.16A MOUNT STEPHEN HOUSE, FIELD, BC, CA. 1905 (TOM JONES BOOK, CW COLLECTION)

8.16B FIELD, BC, SEPTEMBER 2003 (CW 2003-09C-26)

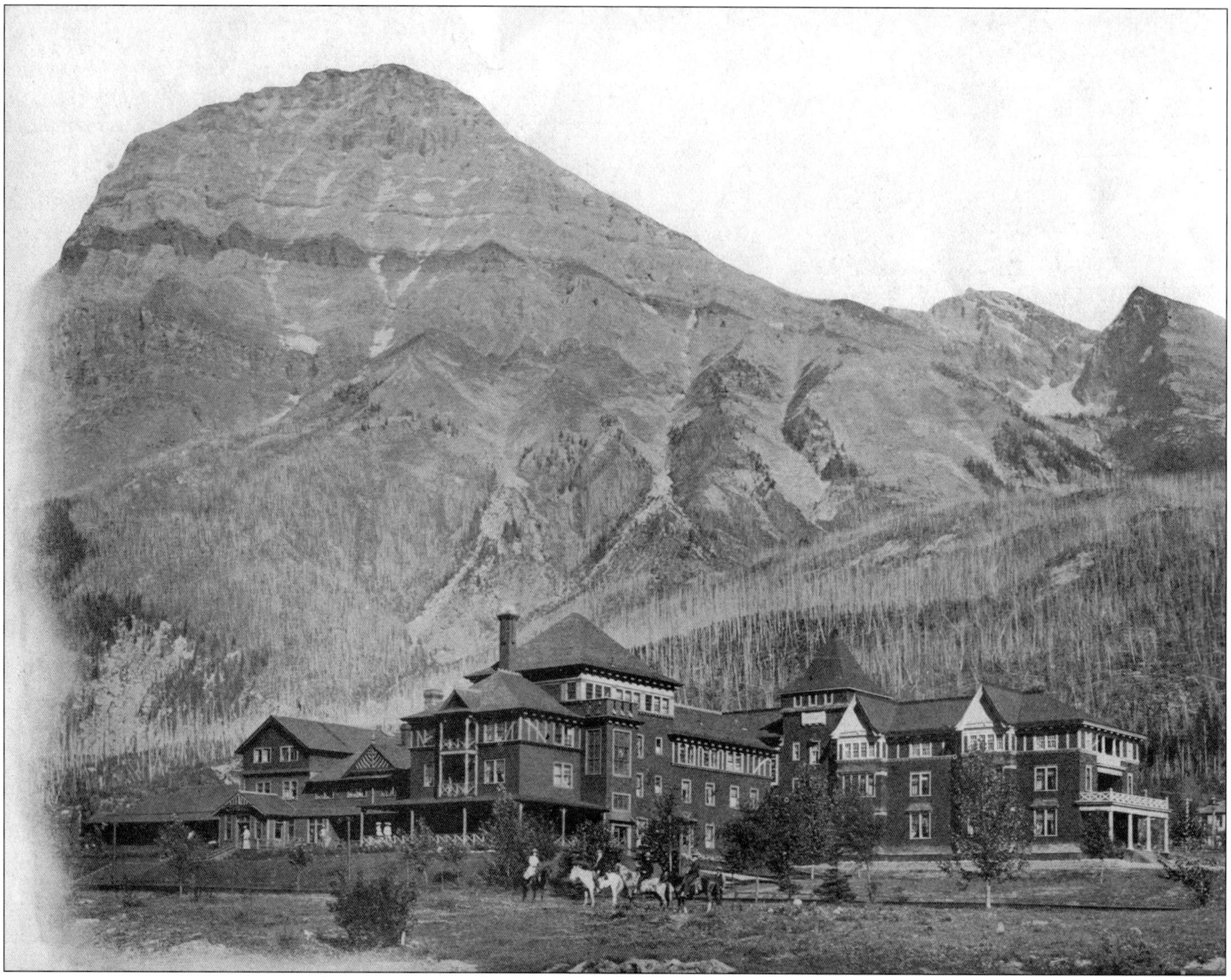

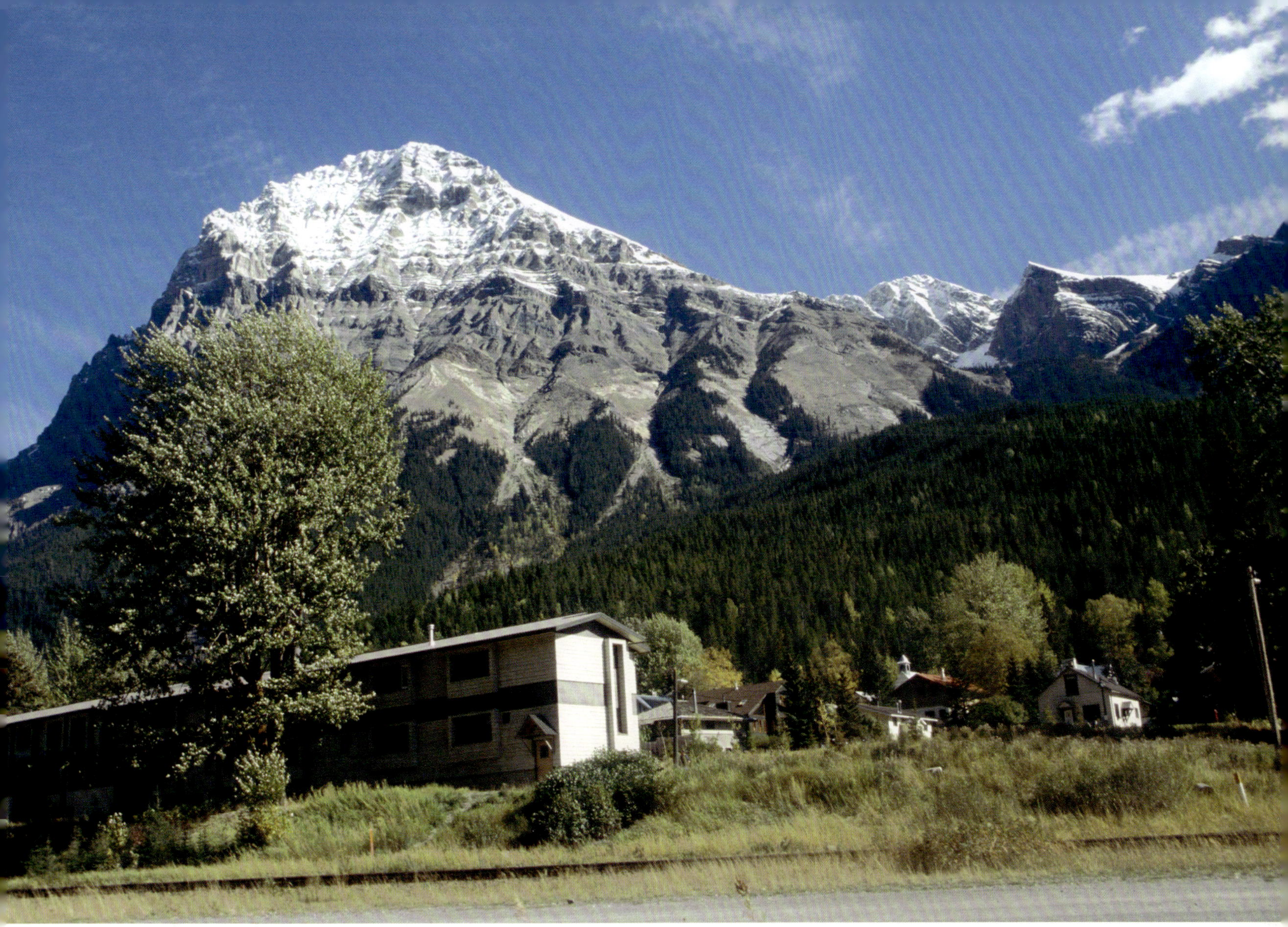

When preparing to begin passenger service on its new line, the CPR realized that its locomotives were not powerful enough to haul heavy dining cars up steep mountain grades. Thus, an immediate priority was to build "hotel dining stops" near Kicking Horse and Rogers passes. CPR General Manager William C. Van Horne took an active part in the design of these buildings, which were also to have a few rooms for tourists wishing to stop over in the midst of the mountains. Selecting a Swiss appearance to fit in with his company's "Canadian Alps" advertising theme, Mount Stephen House at Field, B.C., opened in the fall of 1886 and soon proved so popular that in the years at the end of the century it was undergoing almost continuous expansion.[25]

The village of Field did not grow as rapidly as its sister railroad tourism centres of Banff, Jasper, and Lake Louise. Its location in the shade of Mount Stephen, the Monarch Mine just east of town, the noisy railroad operations associated with being a divisional point, and moving trains up the nearby "Big Hill" to Kicking Horse Pass tended to give the community a more industrial atmosphere. By the end of the 1920s the heyday of the early railroad hotels such as Mount Stephen House and its sister hotel Glacier House at Rogers Pass had come to an end. Mount Stephen House then served as a railway YMCA for many years, but it was demolished in 1954 and replaced with a rather more pedestrian-looking Canadian Pacific staff bunkhouse. With the closing of the Monarch Mine in 1964, Parks Canada began to purchase abandoned houses in the town, but since the 1970s expansion of tourism connected to the Trans-Canada Highway, and particularly the ski hill at Lake Louise, has increased the demand for housing in Field.[26]

8.17A OTTERTAILS MOUNTAINS NEAR LEANCHOIL, CA. 1890 (NOTMAN AND SON, WHYTE NA 66-2310)

8.17B SELKIRK STEAM LOCOMOTIVE AT LEANCHOIL, CA. 1940 (LLOYD HARMON, WHYTE V108-2285)

8.17C LEANCHOIL SIDING, SEPTEMBER 2006 (CW 2006-09C-03)

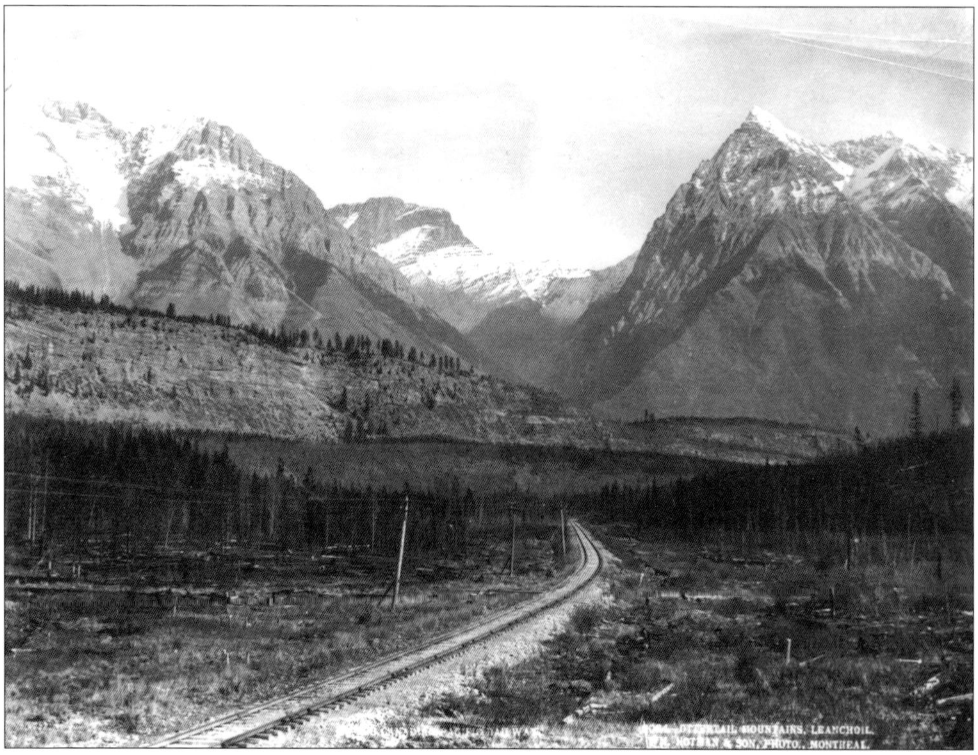

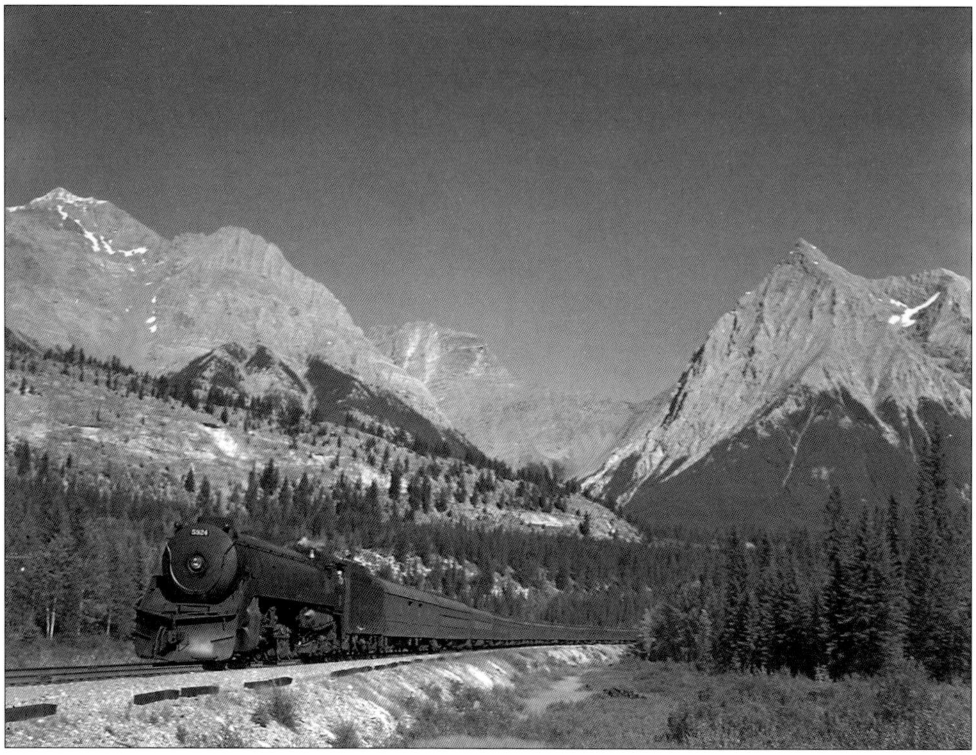

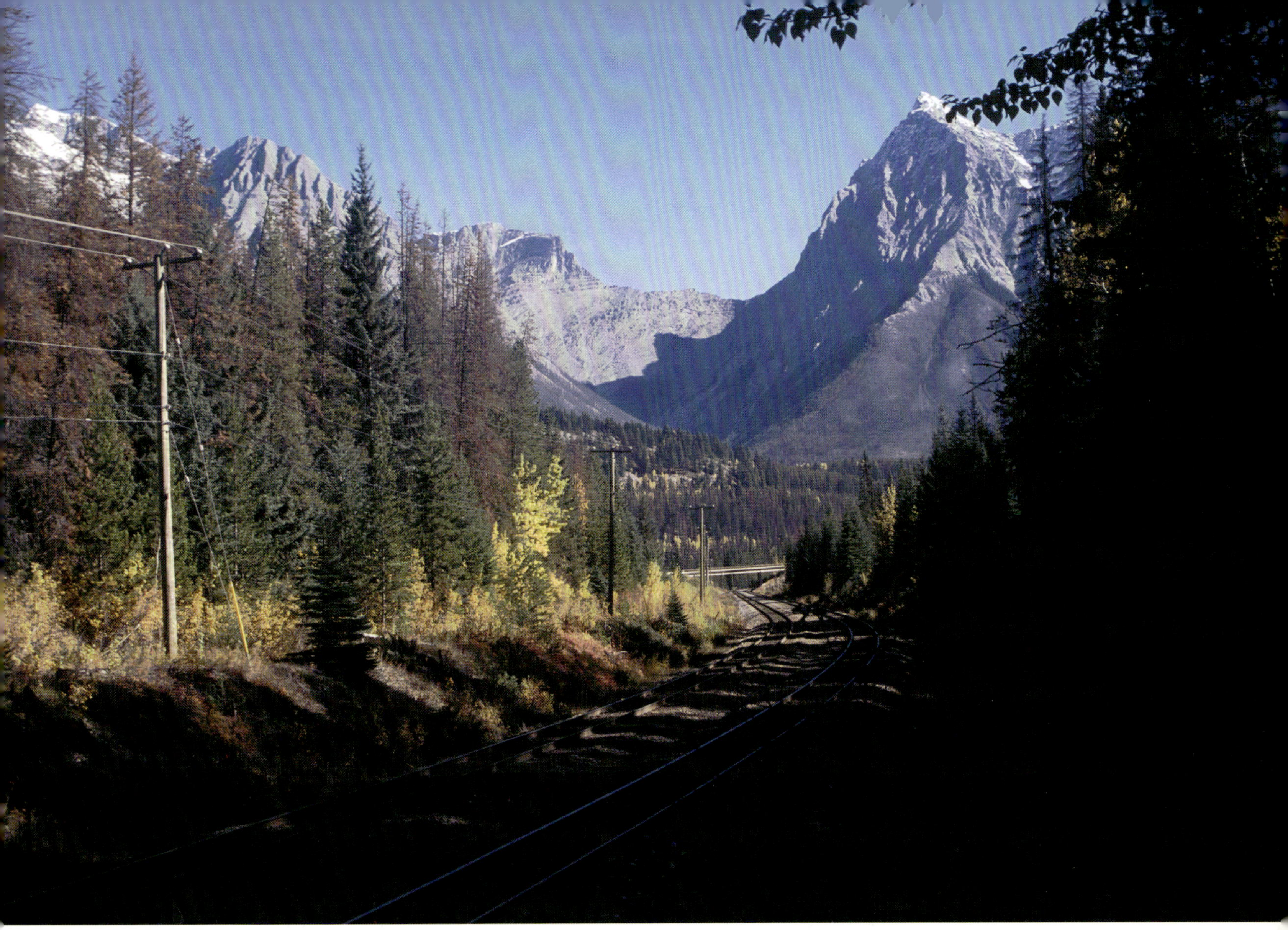

In the early days of CPR passenger operations Van Horne provided travel passes and sometimes a "photographer's car" to those whose images he wished to use in company advertising campaigns. One of them was William McFarlane Notman of the famous Montreal firm of William Notman and Son, who captured the mountain backdrop as the railway descends the Kicking Horse River near Leanchoil about 1890. In 1940 Lloyd Harmon, the son of Banff photographer Byron Harmon, took essentially the same view from a slightly different perspective. Most of lower elevation areas near the railroad were swept by fire during the construction of the line through the region in 1884. However, due to a regime of relatively frequent fires, many Douglas fir visible on the ridge of Mount Hunter (middle left) in the Notman photograph survived this burn. Fifty-odd years later the slopes of the peaks and the right-of-way had become much more eye-appealing for the railway tourist.

By 2006 the forest had matured, and mountain pine beetle had recently killed almost 60 per cent of the lodgepole pine near where the photograph was taken. When these trees fall to the ground, their wood will provide fuel for an extremely severe fire. In May 2005, Parks Canada staff carried out a prescribed burn in a large area at the base of Chancellor Peak (right side of photo) to regenerate a younger forest.[27]

8.18A GOLDEN CITY, COLUMBIA VALLEY, BC, CA. 1884 (CORNELIUS SOULE, WHYTE V425-PA-9)

8.18B TOWN OF GOLDEN, BC, 1911 (J. HOWARD CHAPMAN, BC ARCHIVES A-961)

8.18C GOLDEN, BC, 1947 (BC GOVERNMENT, BC ARCHIVES I-27548)

8.18D GOLDEN, BC, MAY 2004 (DOUG LEIGHTON, CW COLLECTION)

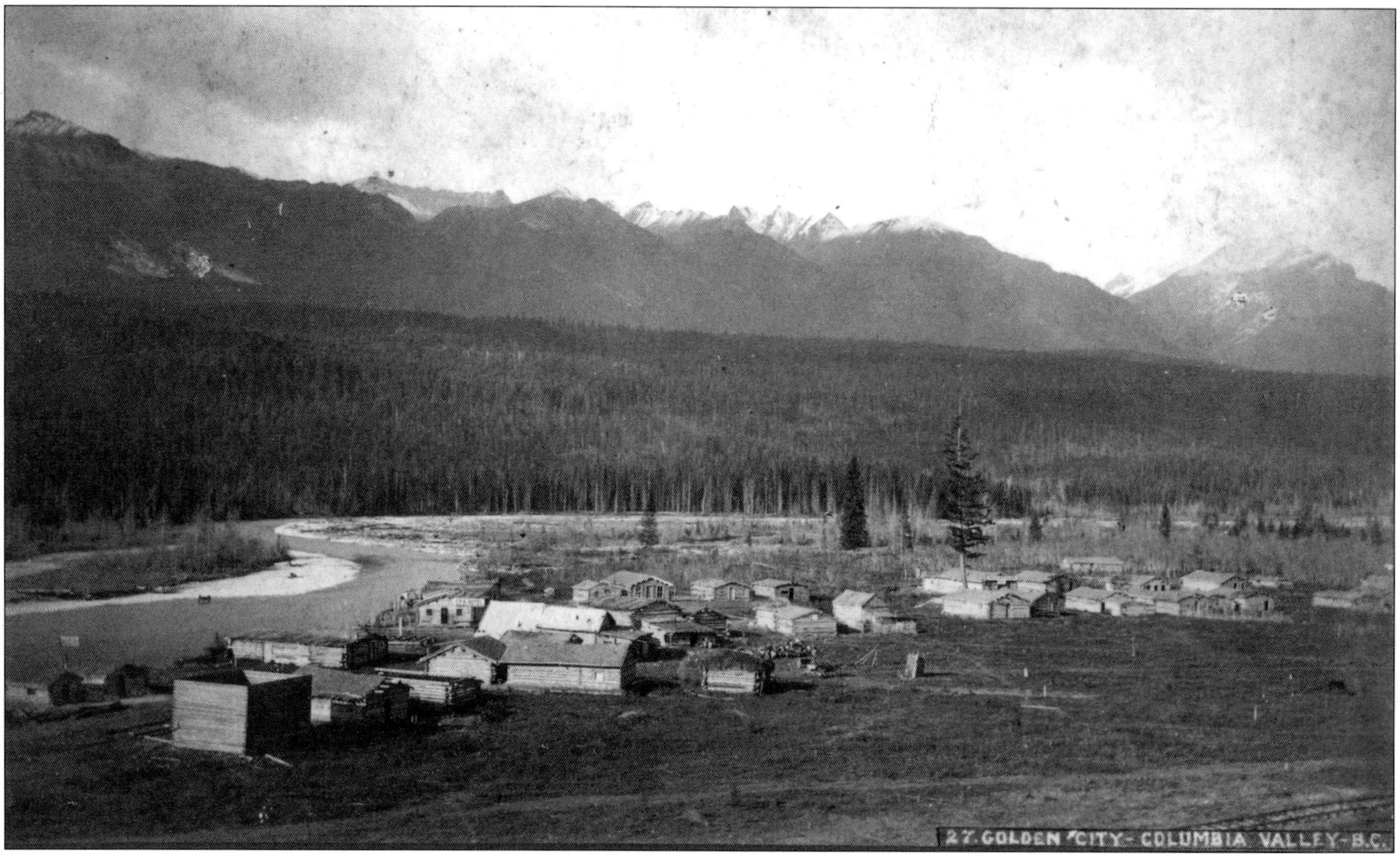

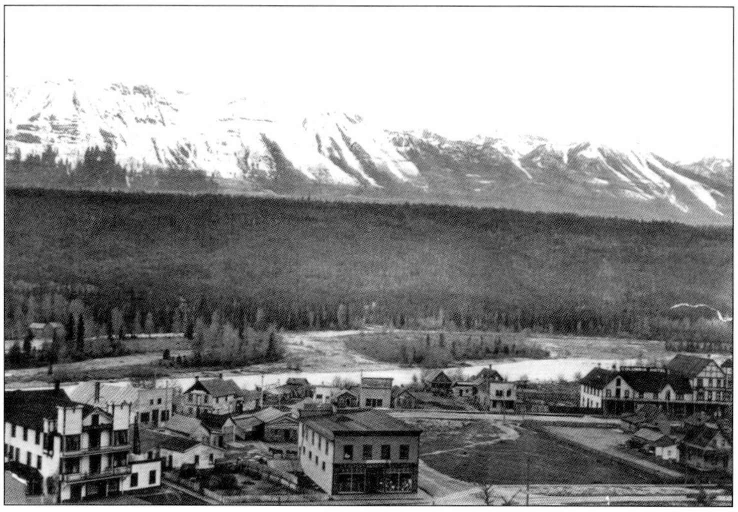

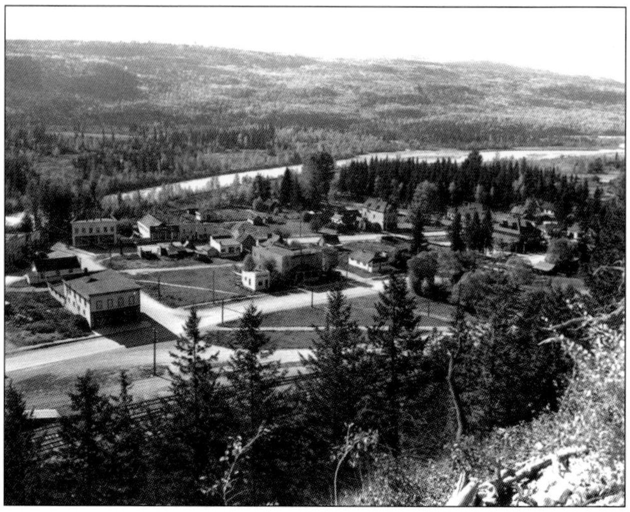

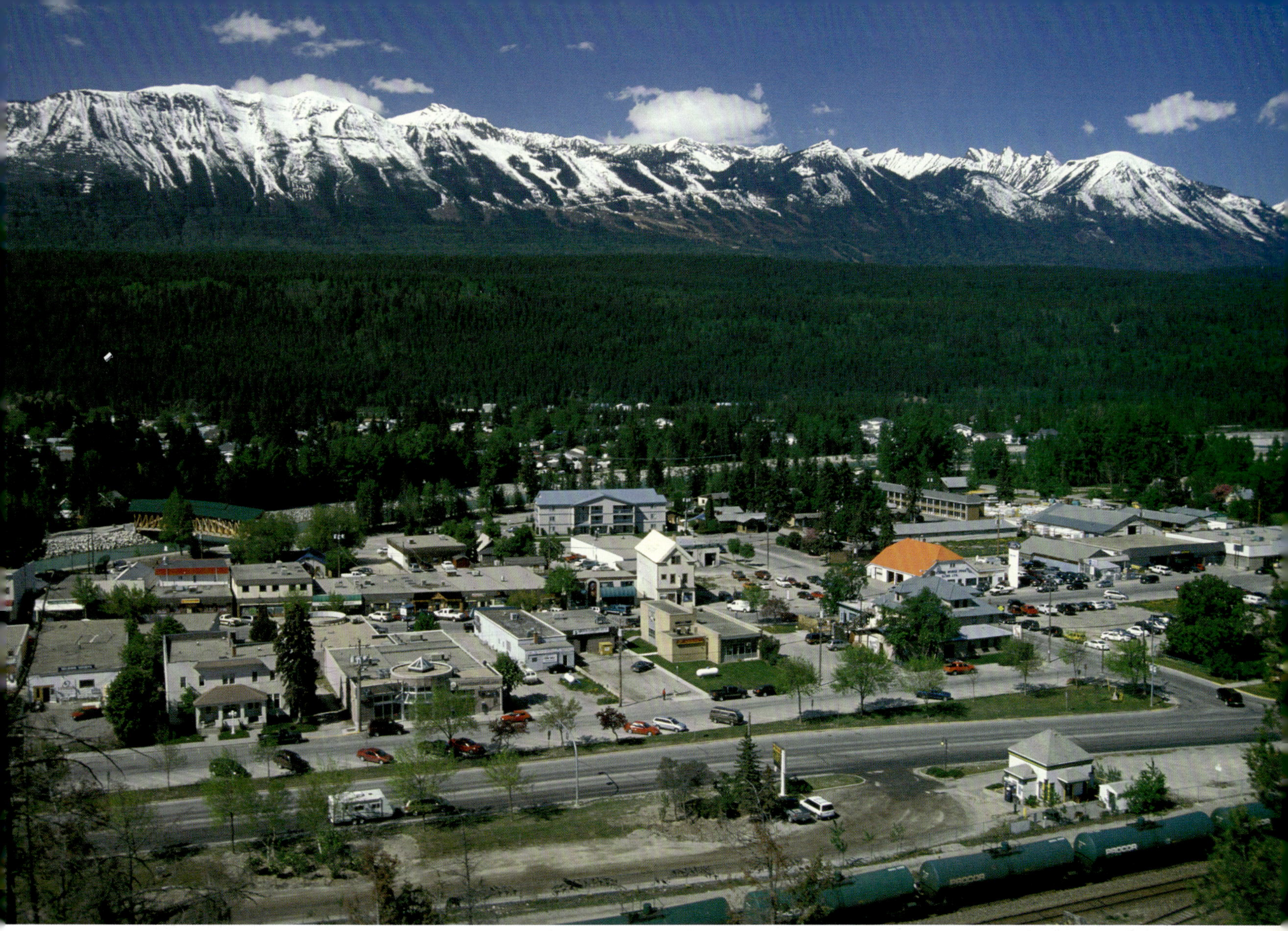

It took the whole construction season of 1884 to push railroad steel from Lake Louise over the continental divide and down through steep grades and unstable tunnels in the canyons of the Kicking Horse to its confluence with the Columbia River. On November 15 the rails reached the end of the canyons, and construction boss James Ross wired Canadian Pacific headquarters, "Track on Columbia Thank God." Here, the over-wintering crews and suppliers hastily built what they called "Golden City," possibly named to upstage "Silver City," the ephemeral town built the year before below Castle Mountain.[28]

In the 1900s the economy of Golden depended on harvesting the dense forests of Douglas fir, red cedar, and mountain hemlock cloaking the Rocky Mountain Trench. By 1990 loggers had felled most of the accessible stands of large, old-growth timber. A major sawmill closed, and the community began to diversify by encouraging tourism. In 2000 entrepreneurs built a gondola lift to the summit of Kicking Horse ski resort, visible in the background of the recent photograph, and the town now attracts skiers from around the world to celebrate its "champagne" powder snow.

8.19A CROWFOOT GLACIER, 1902 (VAUX FAMILY, WHYTE NA 80-1108)

8.19B CROWFOOT GLACIER, 1985 (CW 1985H-6)

8.19C CROWFOOT GLACIER, JULY 2003 (CW 2003-07L-11)

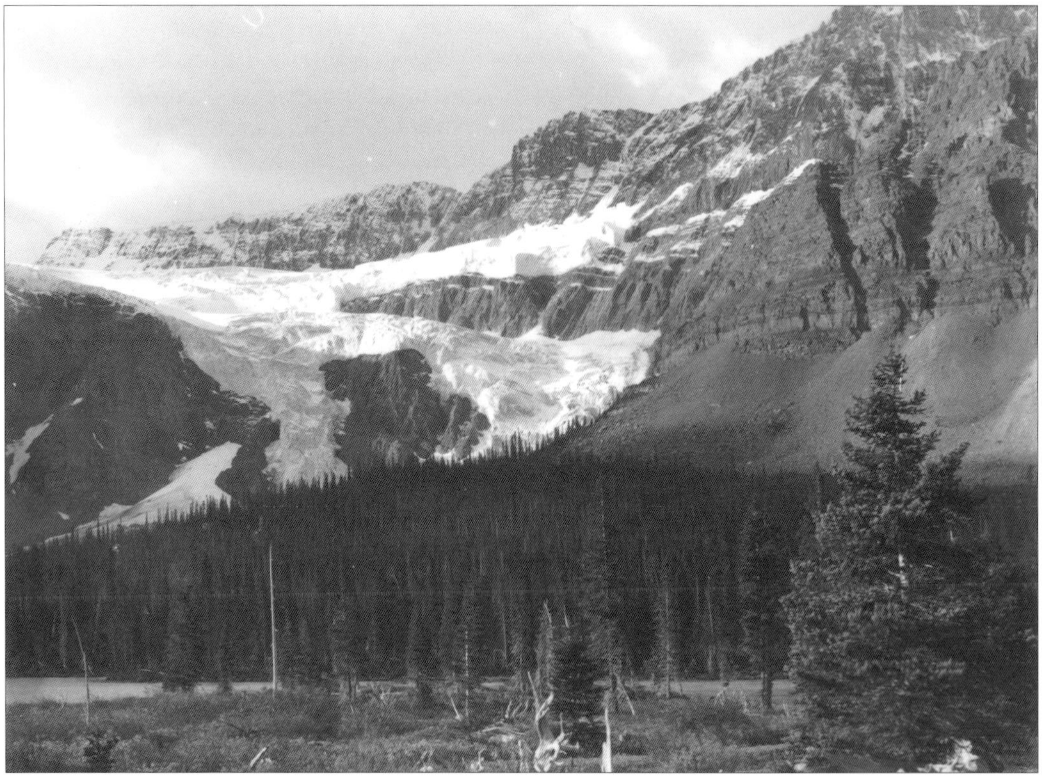

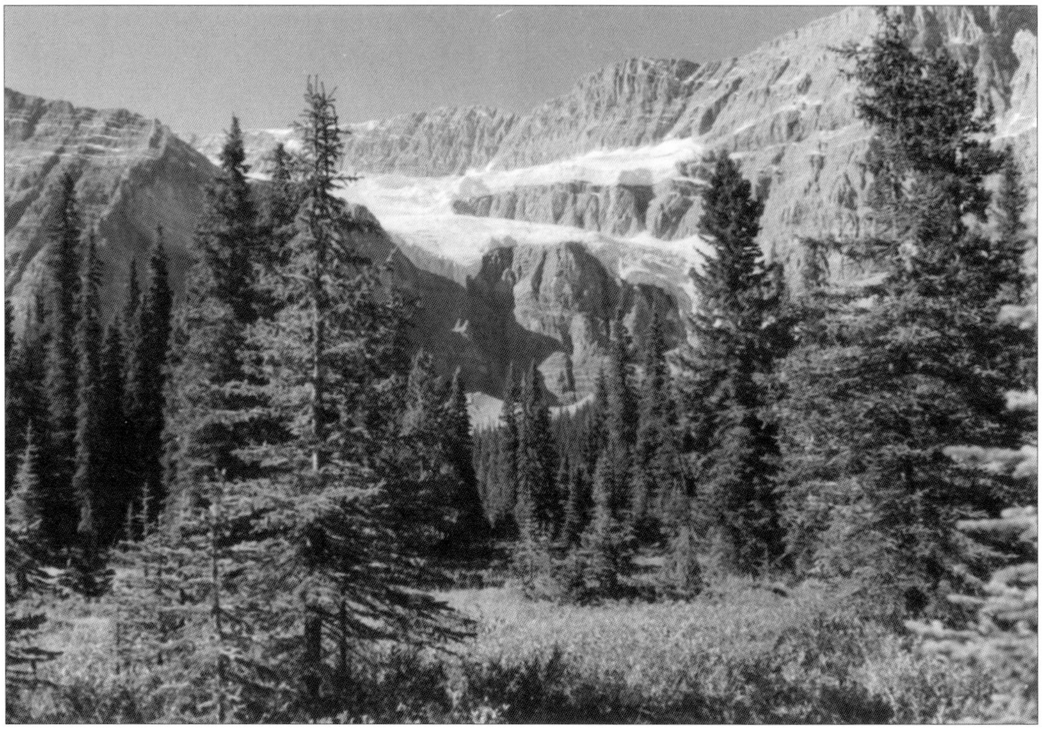

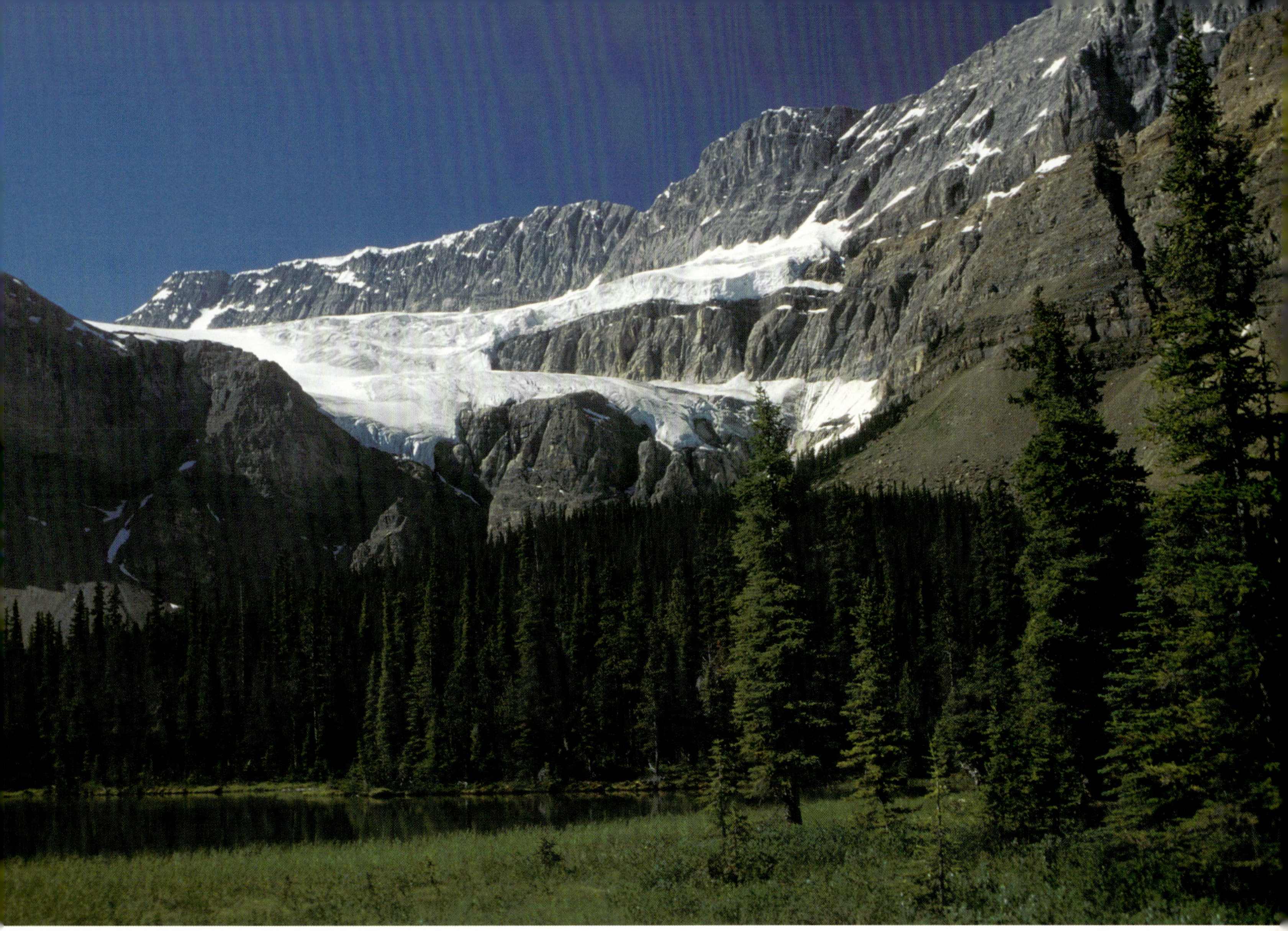

The three-lobed glacier draped over the eastern wall of the Waputik Range north of Lake Louise was named for its resemblance to the talons on a crow's foot. Early horse-outfitted tourists proceeding north of the railway to engage in climbing or exploration rarely saw the sight as the burned-over forests and muskegs along the upper Bow River were notoriously difficult to travel, and instead most parties followed the more direct trail going northeast from Lake Louise up the Pipestone River to the Kootenay Plains.[29] However, those who did occasionally follow the path up the Bow never failed to comment on the unique feature the Crowfoot presented. One of the first was Mary Schäffer, who during her 1907 trip in search of Maligne Lake passed the location in June, and despite the date, like many of those later viewing this high-altitude landmark, found it "still gowned in her winter robes." Nevertheless, she added, "Of peculiar formation, no one can ever fail to recognize her, her name fitting her perfectly."[30]

It was not until the completion of the Banff-Jasper Highway in 1939 that many visitors had the opportunity to lay eyes on the Crowfoot. A roadside pull-out was created to allow tour buses and individual vehicles to stop and admire what is, perhaps, the most obvious and accessible example of glacial recession in the Canadian Rockies. As is apparent by the photographic sequence taken over the last century, within the span of one lifetime the third "toe" of the foot has entirely disappeared and the second one has been greatly decreased in mass.

8.20A BOW LAKE AND GLACIER, AUGUST 1902 (VAUX FAMILY, WHYTE NA 80-1114)

8.20B THE RAMS PASTURE CABIN, NUM-TI-JAH, CA. 1985 (UNKNOWN PHOTOGRAPHER, WHYTE)

8.20C BOW LAKE AND GLACIER, JULY 2003 (CW 2003-07D-14)

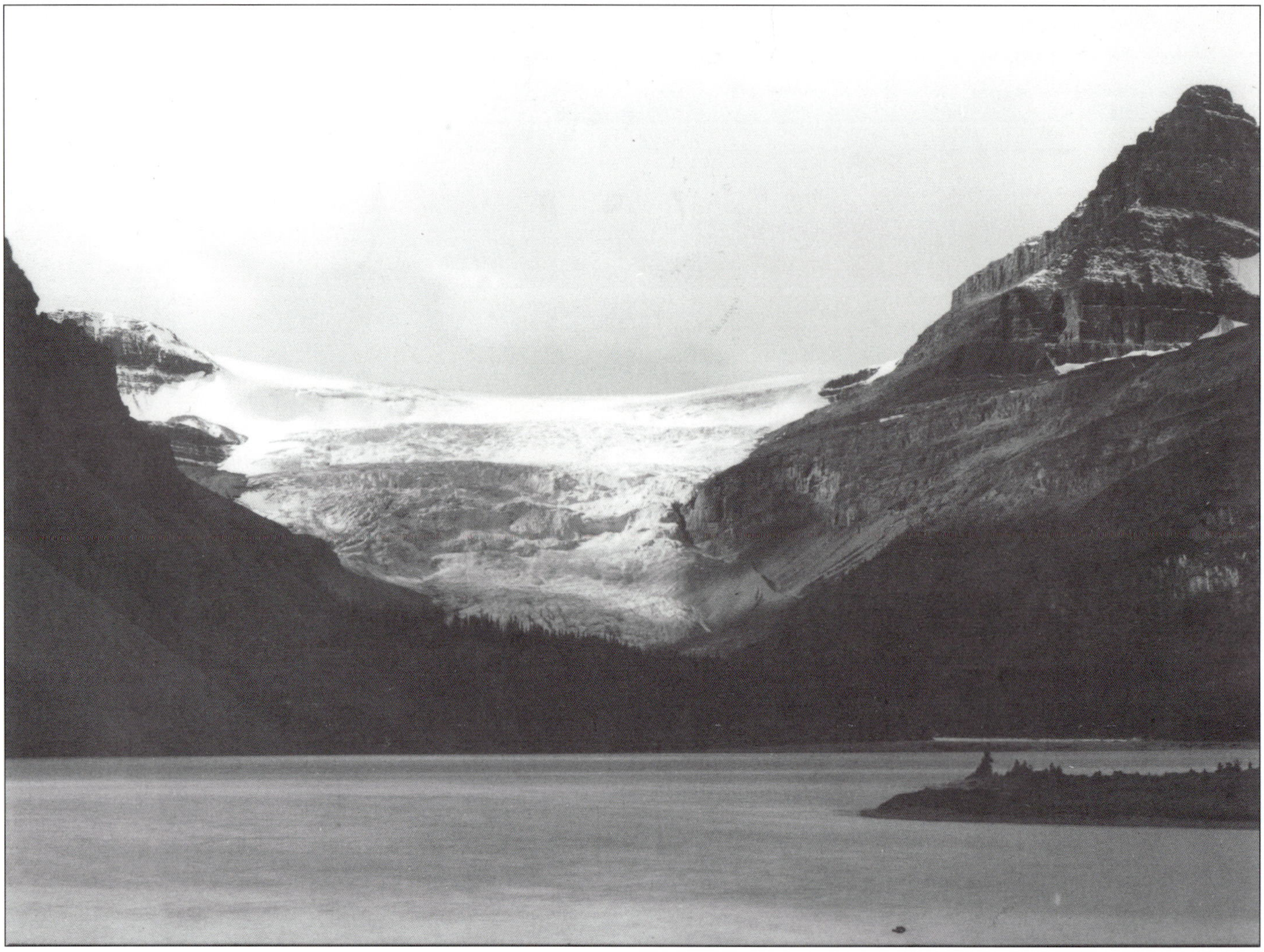

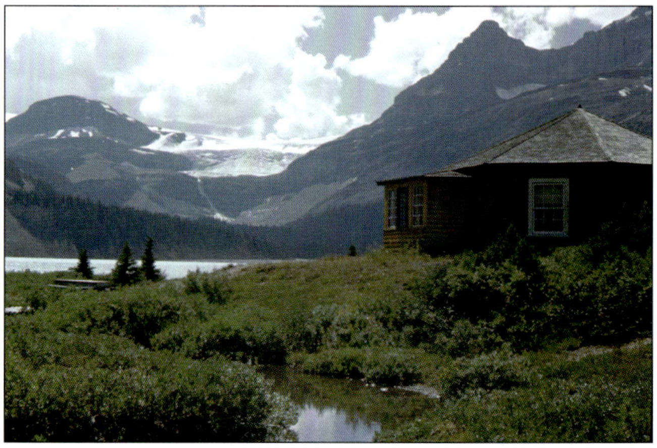

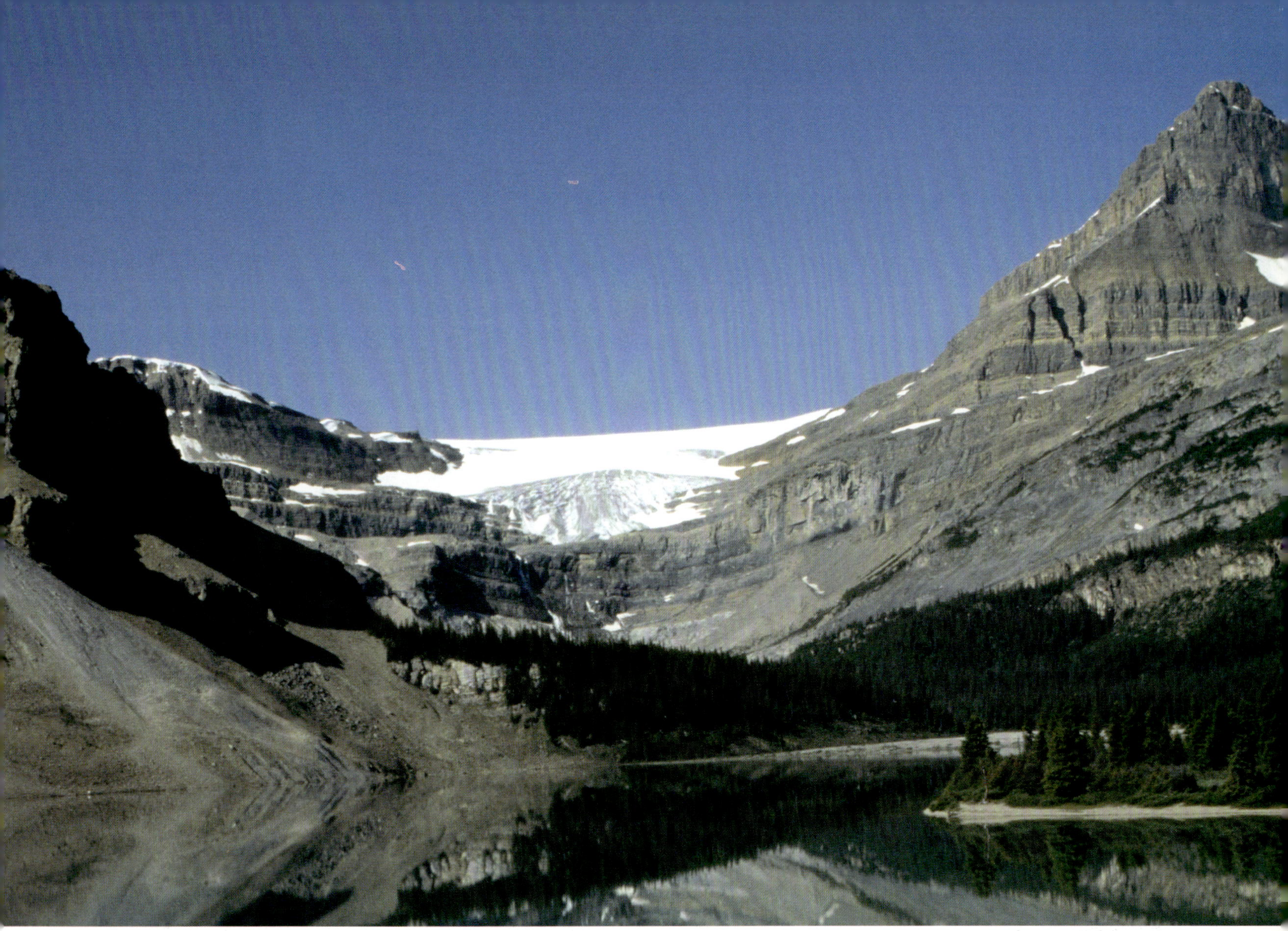

Like Crowfoot Glacier, the icefield that stood at the northwest end of Bow Lake and formed the source of the Bow River system was well known to early travellers. One of those visiting the lake in 1898 was a young English remittance man named Jimmy Simpson, at the time working for outfitter Tom Wilson performing trail clearing for a hunting party. When he first laid eyes on the lake and glacier they were a revelation and he later described them as "the most beautiful thing I'd seen in Canada." Right then and there he fell in love with the party's campsite on the north shore of the lake where a small stream from Bow Pass trickled in and promised himself, "Some day I'll build a shack here."

Simpson was to make good on his pledge, in 1921 gaining a federal government lease on which he constructed a unique octagonal log cabin he called the "Rams Pasture" and a few tent shacks, allowing him to begin a small tourist business. Over the years the operation was expanded when his outfitting business or his figure-skating daughters could provide sufficient investment funds, resulting in the construction of the landmark Num-Ti-Jah Lodge in the 1930s and 40s.

During the years he carried out his lodge and outfitting business at Bow Lake, Simpson was witness to the rapid retreat of the Bow Glacier. When he first arrived, the icefall cascaded over the lower ridge and seemed to come down virtually to the lakeshore, as pictured in the Vaux family's 1902 view. He sometimes used the glacier as a destination for his tourist parties and in the 1930s even created a rink on it so the Simpson Sisters, Margaret and Mary, could practice their professional skating routine in the summertime. He often noted the retreat of the ice over the years in comments to visitors, and by the time he died in 1972 the toe had fully retreated behind the ridge, recession that continued unabated until the time of the modern view some thirty years later. While Num-Ti-Jah remains today as a memorial to Jimmy's ingenuity and persistence, the glacier that accompanied the view of Bow Lake continues to disappear.[31]

8.21A MEADOWS ABOVE BOW LAKE, 1902 (VAUX FAMILY, WHYTE NA 80-1122)

8.21B ICEFIELDS PARKWAY AND MEADOWS ABOVE BOW LAKE, JULY 2001 (CW 2001-07D-02)

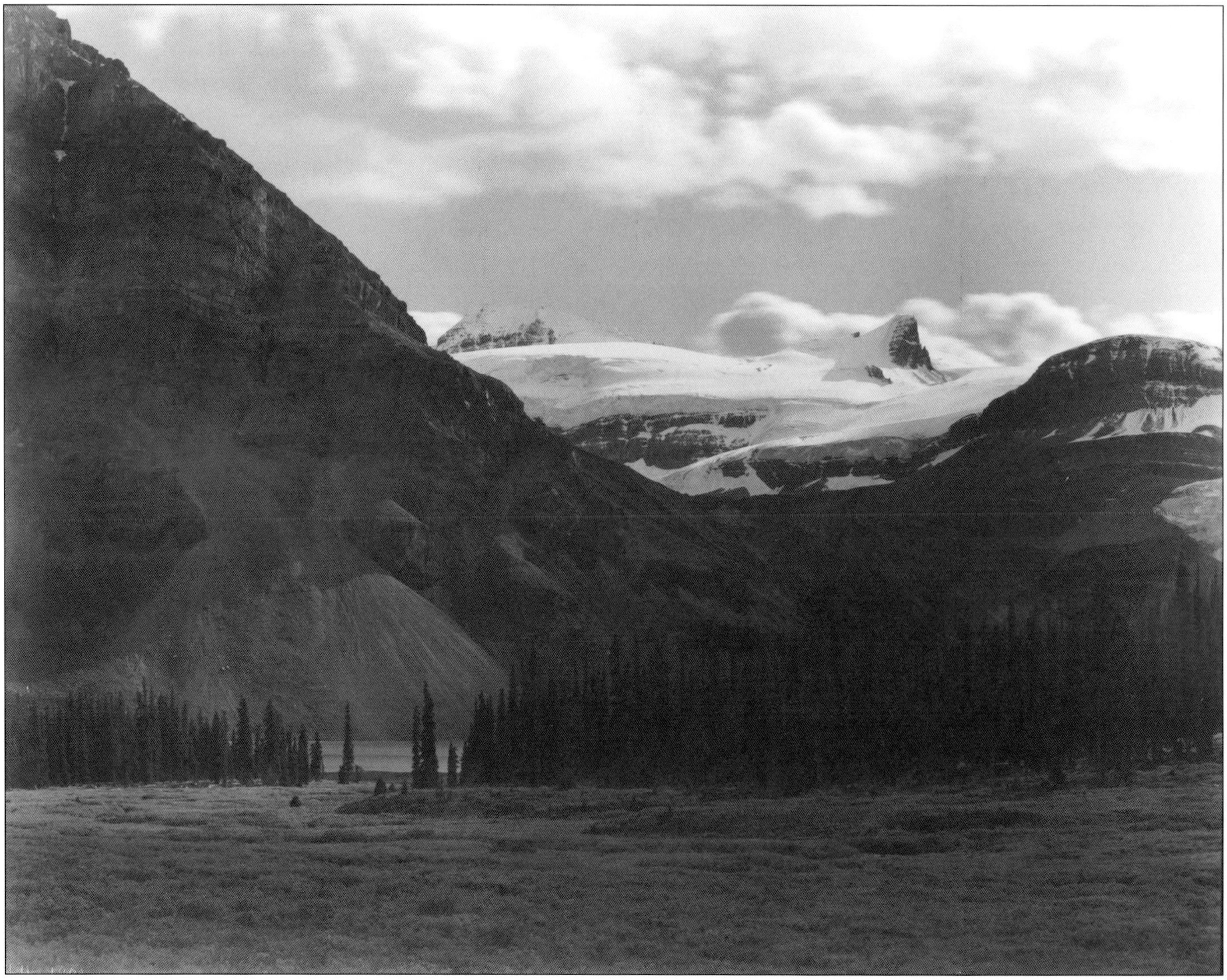

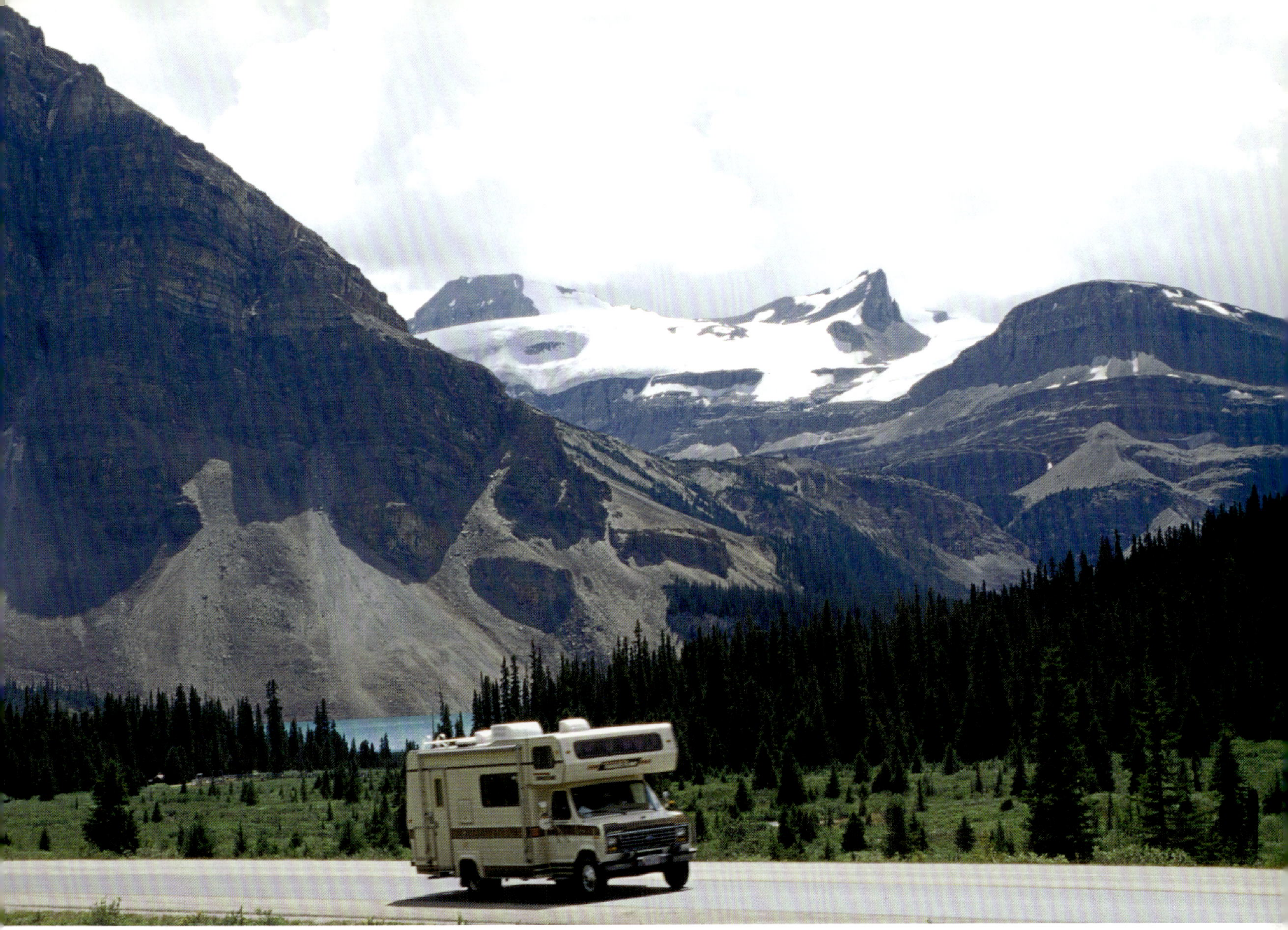

During the Great Depression of the 1930s, the Canadian federal government utilized relief workers to build the Icefields Parkway from Banff to Jasper. At Bow Lake, the road passes Num-Ti-Jah Lodge and ascends into the meadows that extend to the height of Bow Pass. The recent view shows the highway, upgraded in the 1950s, where it crosses a shrubfield of dwarf willow upstream of Bow Lake. Protected from fire by the surrounding glaciers, the lake, wetlands, and bare rock, an ancient forest over four hundred years old rings the meadow. In the century since the first photograph, Engelmann spruce has begun to fill in the meadow, possibly due to slightly drier conditions because the snowfields feeding the wetlands with summer melt-water have shrunk. Bow Glacier, in the background, has retreated dramatically.

8.22A PEYTO GLACIER, 1902 (VAUX FAMILY, WHYTE NA 80-1127)

8.22B PEYTO GLACIER, 1923 (BYRON HARMON, WHYTE NA 71-1799)

8.22C PEYTO GLACIER, SEPTEMBER 1981 (BRUNO ENGLER, CW-BE-FM-1981-48)

8.22D PEYTO GLACIER, JULY 2003 (CW 2003-07D-22)

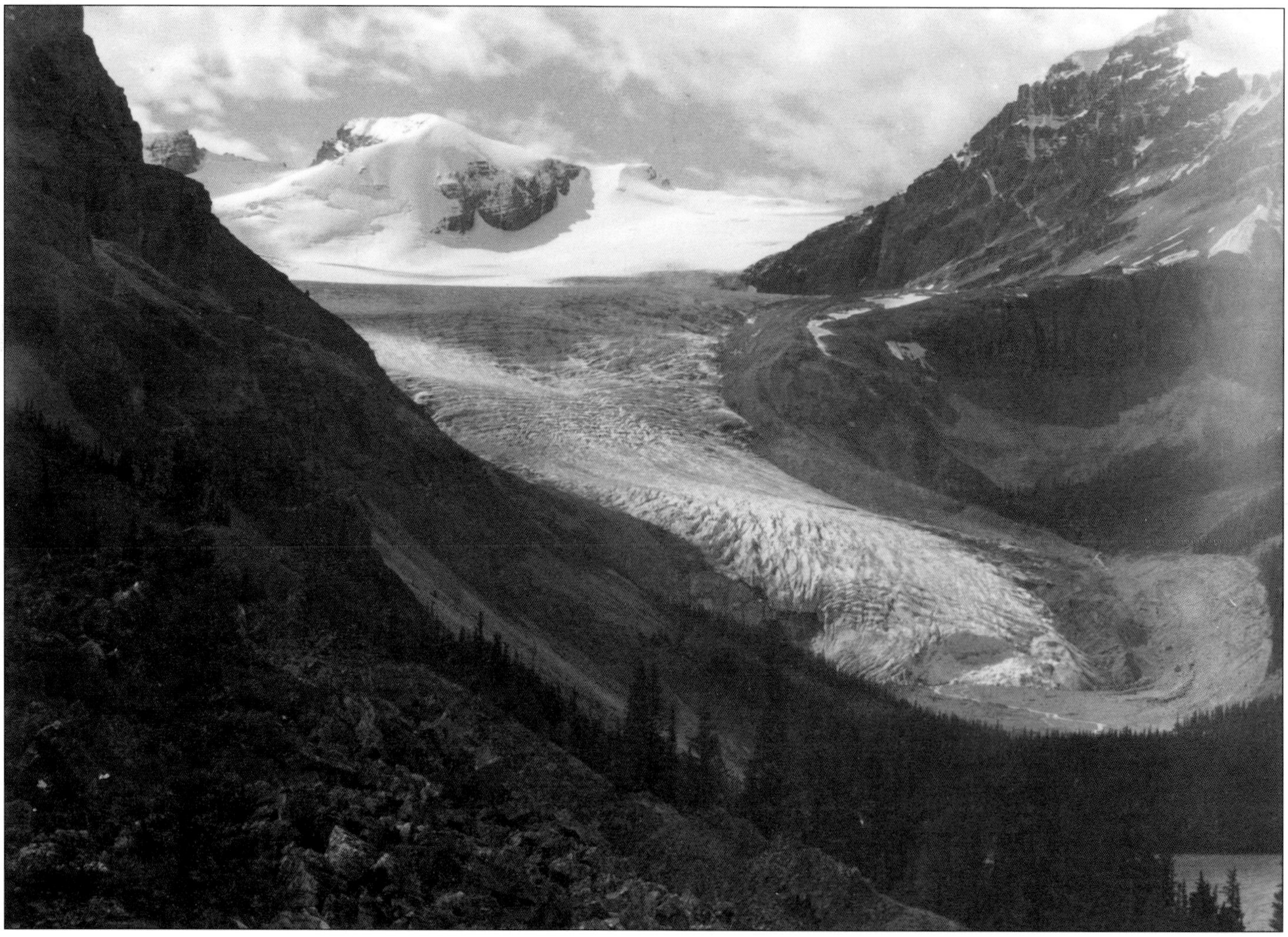

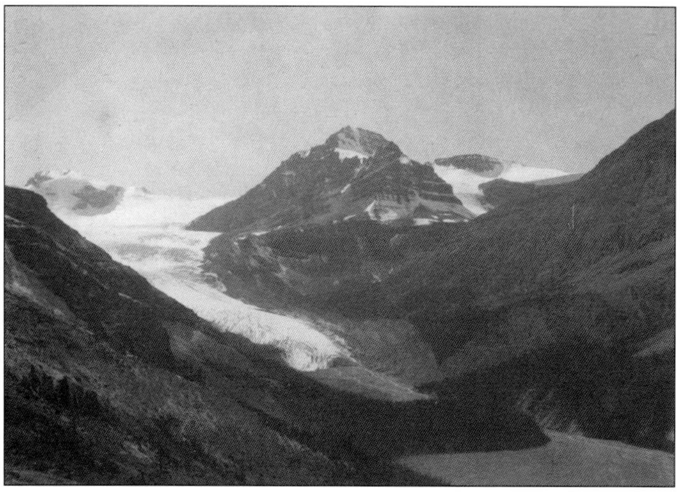

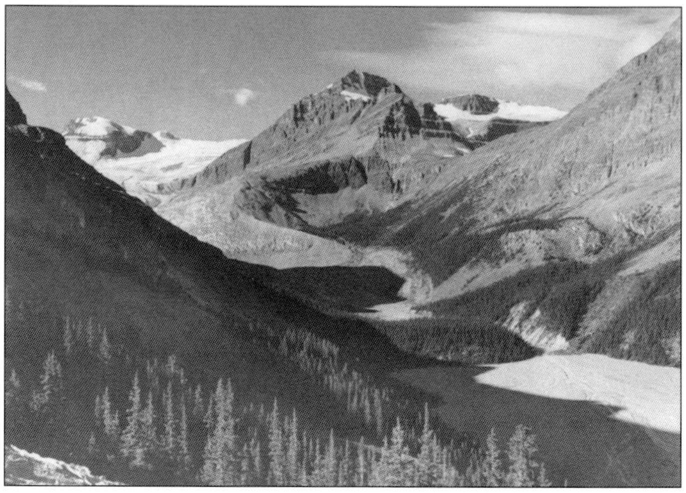

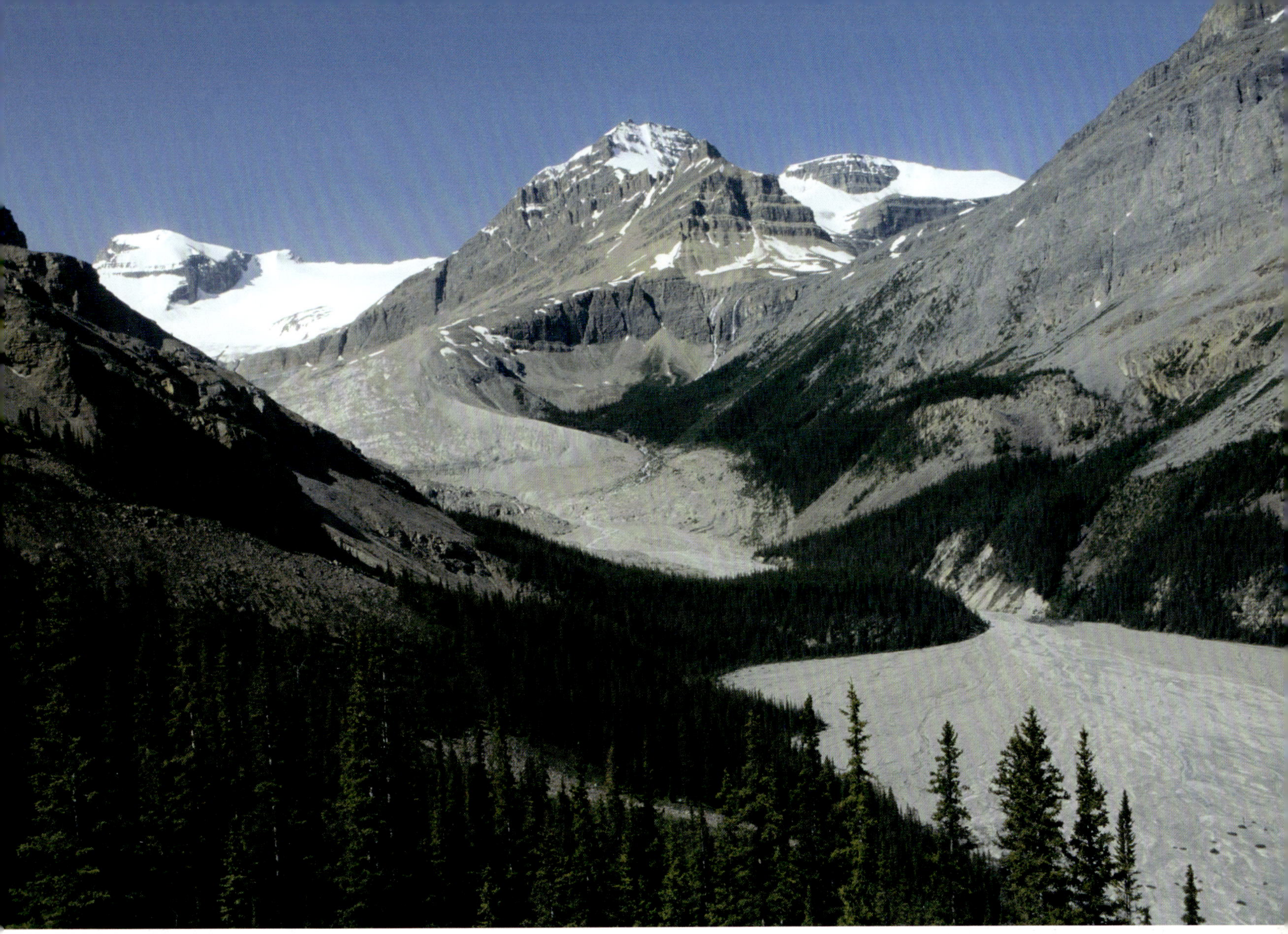

Named after famed mountain guide Bill Peyto, Peyto Lake and Glacier have long been one of the most beautiful and interesting locations for tourists to stop and view on their trips along the Icefields Parkway. Scientists have found them equally fascinating, and the Peyto Glacier, an outlet of the Wapta Icefield, is one of the most extensively studied ice-bodies in North America. Carbon isotope and growth-ring dating of trees shows that the glacier has made several advances since ca. 2,800 years before present, reaching its maximum extent between the years 1836 and 1846 at the end of the "Little Ice Age."[32] By the time of the 1902 photograph, it had already retreated substantially. From about 1940 until 1976, a period of above-average winter snow depth likely slowed glacial recession. However, since then, low snowfall accumulation during winters and a series of warm summers continue to rapidly shrink the glacier. Today, Peyto Glacier has only about 30 per cent of the ice-volume recorded in the earliest photographs.[33]

8.23A INDIAN TEEPEES ON THE SASKATCHEWAN, 1907 (MARY SCHÄFFER, WHYTE V48 NA 65-471)

8.23B KOOTENAY PLAINS NATURAL AREA, OCTOBER, 2003 (CW 2003-10D-29)

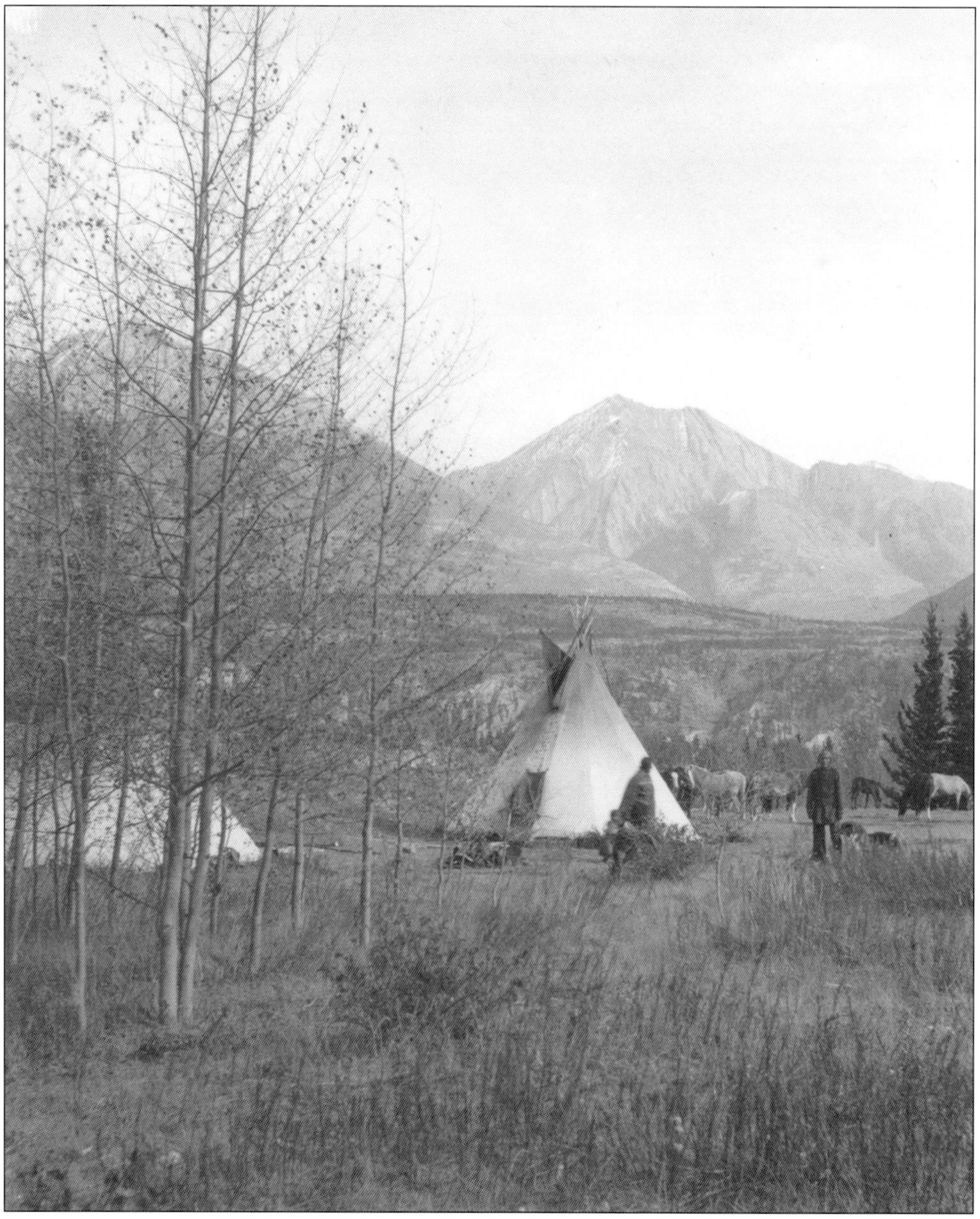

Mary Schäffer took the historic photograph while enjoying an "Indian Summer" on her amazing expedition of 1907 in search of Maligne Lake. After winding through the muskegs of the upper Bow Valley to Bow Pass, her pack train continued northwards along old trails that are today the route of the Icefields Parkway. During July and August her small group ascended to the headwaters of the Alexandra, Sunwapta, and the Chaba rivers. In September the expedition turned southwards, returning to the

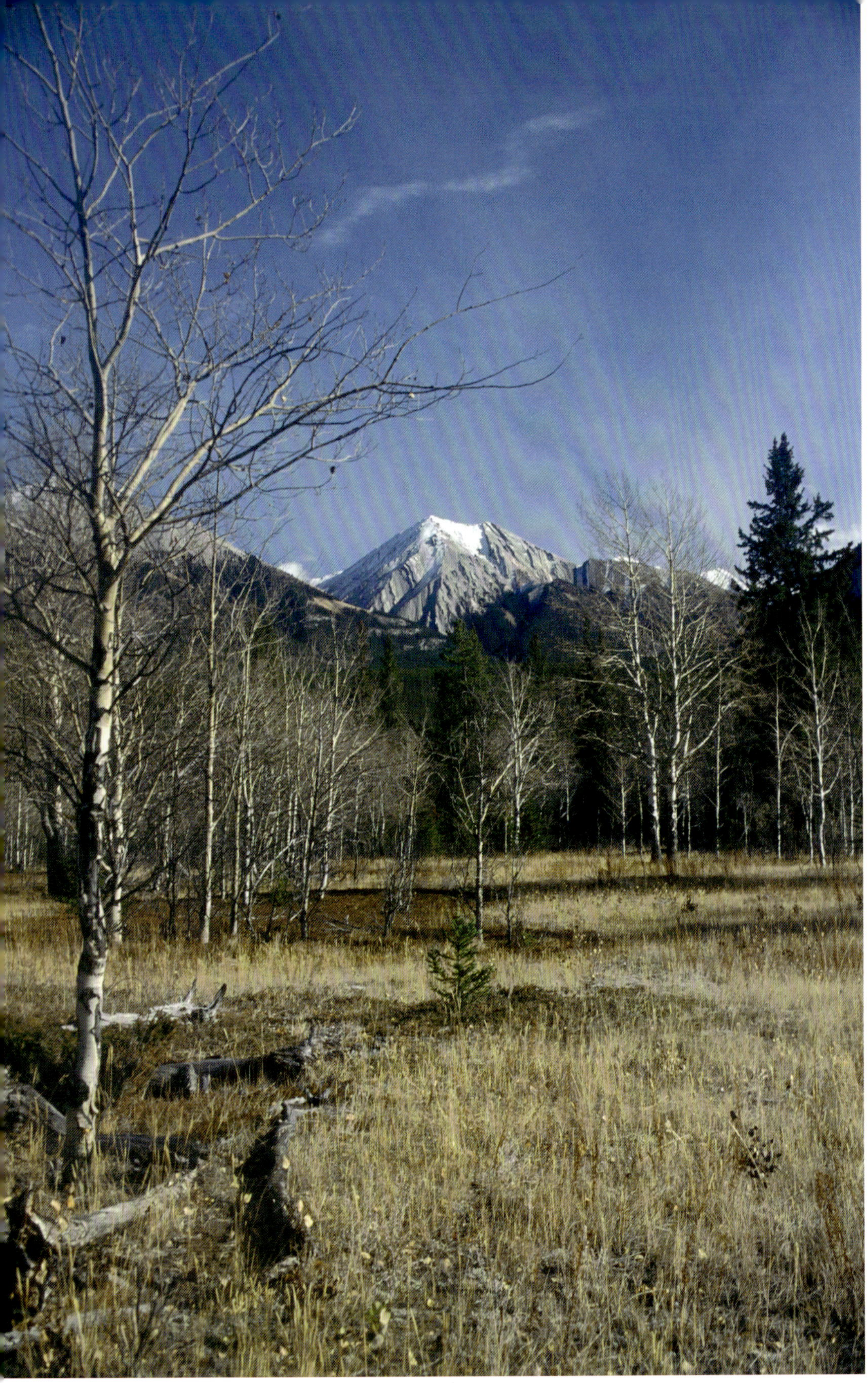

grasslands of the Kootenay Plains along the North Saskatchewan River to rest the horses. Here, Mrs. Schäffer renewed her acquaintance with the families of Silas Abraham and Sampson Beaver of the "Mountain Stoney," whom she had met on a trip a year earlier.[34]

Historically, the Kootenay Plains had some of the most abundant wildlife populations in the Rocky Mountains, a factor related to low human use, and weather patterns which provided good winter grazing and shelter from mountain storms. Fur trader and cartographer David Thompson of the North West Company made several trips through the grasslands while crossing Howse Pass during the years 1807–9. Although Thompson records that game was scarce elsewhere, Kootenay Plains was a reliable place to hunt bighorn sheep, bison, and an occasional elk. In Thompson's time, this area was a buffer zone between the Peigan on the east and the Ktunaxi (Kootenay) peoples to the west.[35] A century later, in 1915, W. N. Millar, Dominion Inspector of Forest Reserves, observed that larger game animals were scarce near the favoured Stoney Nakoda campground on the Kootenay Plains itself. However, for the overall area of the North Saskatchewan, Clearwater, and Brazeau watersheds he stated, "The abundance of wildlife in this region is easily explained by the fact that it has, until the last few years, been the most remote area of the mountains as far as the white hunters are concerned, and that it is sort of a neutral belt between the hunting grounds of the Stonies to the south, and the Crees on the north."[36] Today, much of the original plains area lies under the waters of Abraham Lake reservoir, while the remaining grasslands are a protected natural area appearing little different than they did when Mary Schäffer first visited.

8.24A FORDING THE NORTH SASKATCHEWAN RIVER NEAR KOOTENAY PLAINS, 1907 (D. B. DOWLING, WHYTE NA 66-789)

8.24B LAKE ABRAHAM, 1986 (CW1986-M4-11)

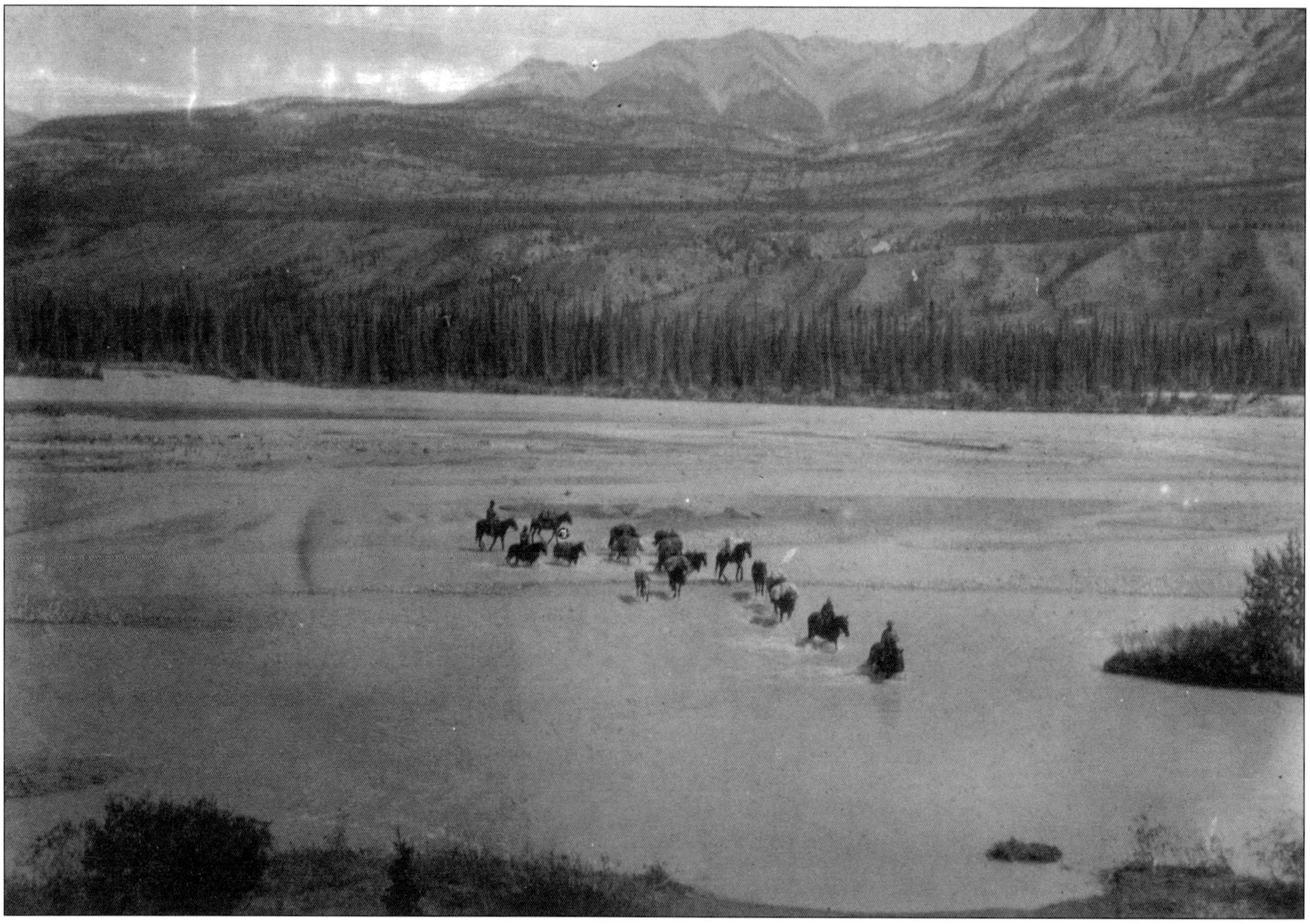

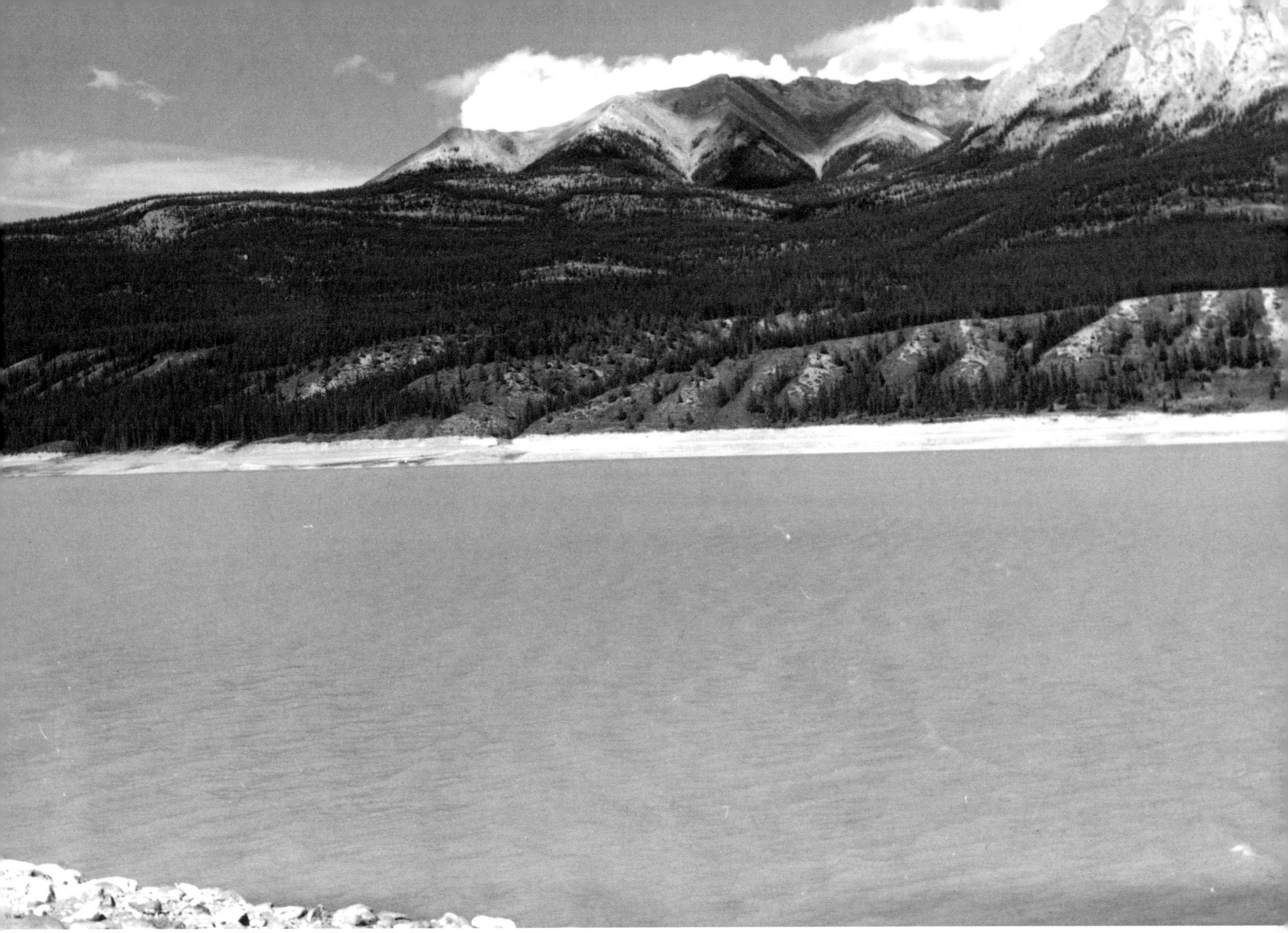

In 1807 David Thompson followed a route used by First Nations up the North Saskatchewan Valley and over what is now Howse Pass to the Columbia River. The fur trade briefly used the pass to reach Kootanae House near Windermere Lake, B.C., until Peigan opposition to the whites' trading with their traditional enemies to the west forced European travellers northwards to the Athabasca Valley.[37] Unlike the Bow and the Athabasca watersheds, the upper North Saskatchewan watershed was not greatly exploited by early Canadian settlers, loggers, and miners, due to the lack of railways or roads. Nonetheless, the historic photograph shows hillsides and mountain slopes south of the river that were frequently burned, likely due to continued First Nations use of the area. By 1986, however, a dense forest covered most of these slopes.

The completion of the Bighorn Dam in 1972 inundated the river under the waters of Lake Abraham. The dam provides "surge power" to serve peak period electricity demands of Albertans, but it unfortunately flooded a large area of prime winter range for elk, moose, and deer.[38]

8.25A SASKATCHEWAN GLACIER, 1924 (LEWIS FREEMAN, WHYTE NA 71-2220)

8.25B SASKATCHEWAN GLACIER FROM THE EDGE OF CASTLEGUARD MEADOWS, JULY 1987 (CW 1987-B6)

8.25B SASKATCHEWAN GLACIER FROM THE EDGE OF CASTLEGUARD MEADOWS, AUGUST 2006 (CW 2006-08B-02)

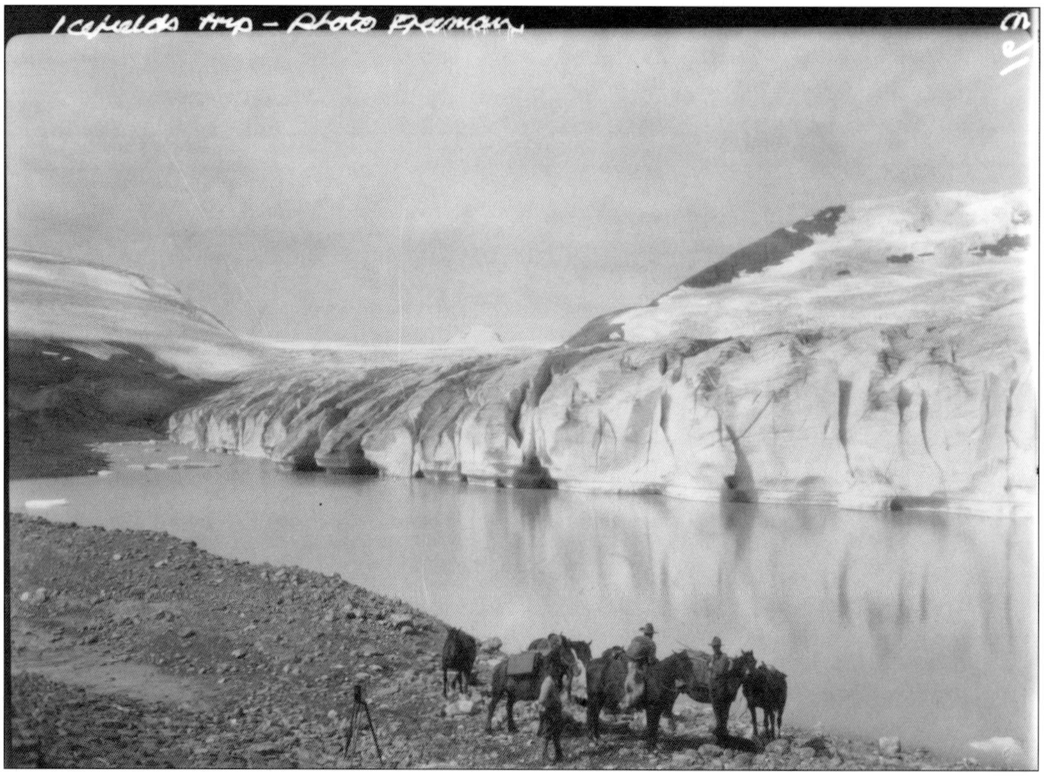

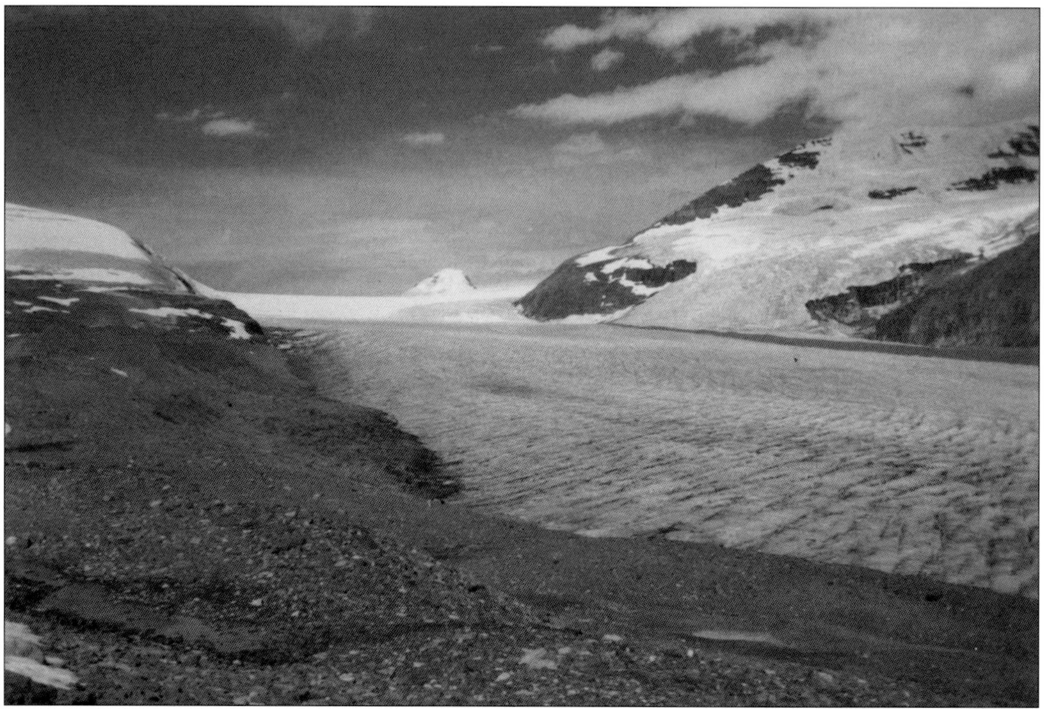

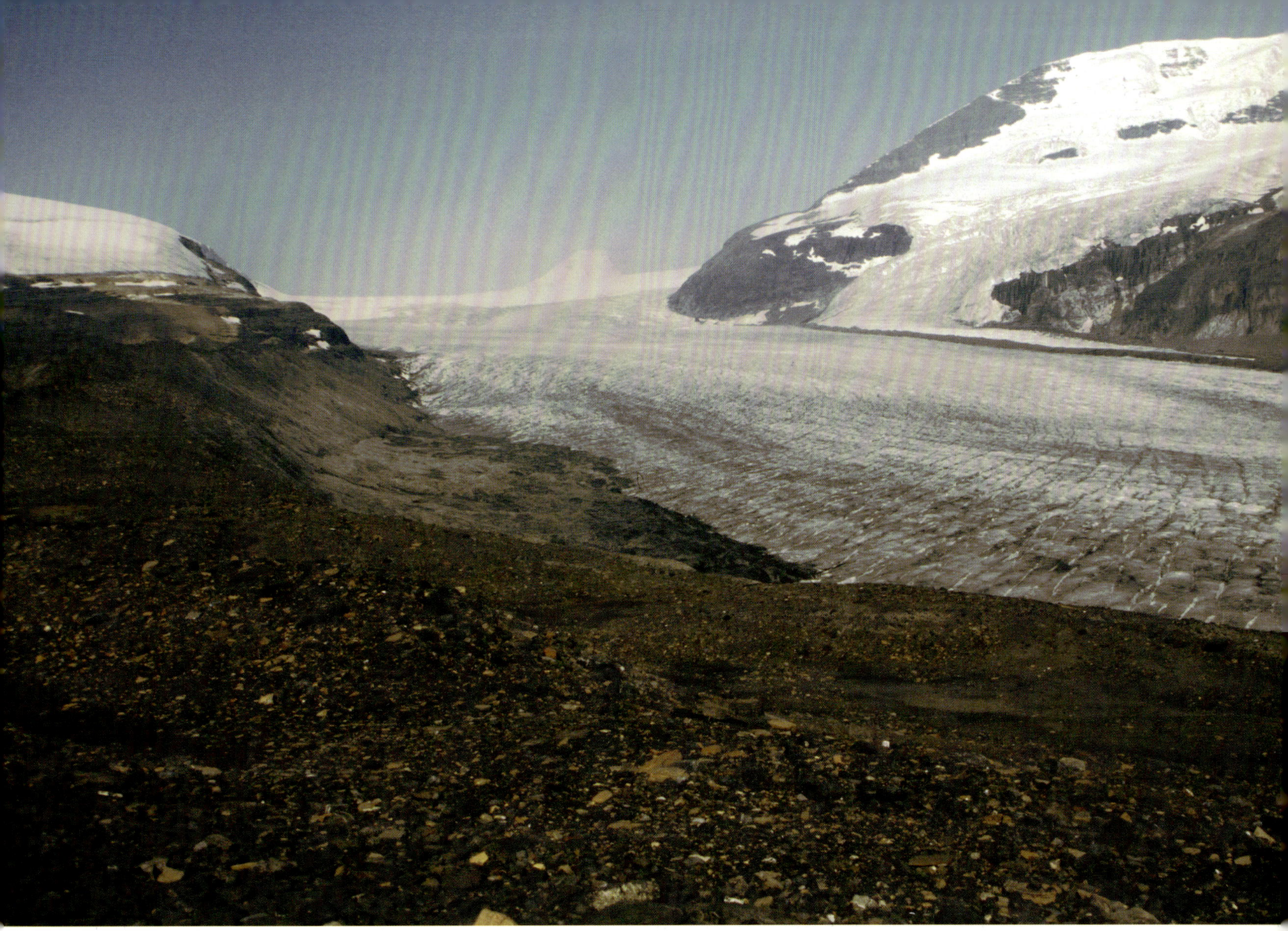

In 1924 renowned Banff photographer Byron Harmon made one of his greatest trips, traversing wilderness trails along the route of today's Icefields Parkway from Lake Louise to near Jasper. Over the course of seventy days and 750 kilometres on the trail, Harmon made four hundred still photographs and over two thousand metres of motion picture film. The party led their horses up the Saskatchewan Glacier, the source of the great North Saskatchewan River, and near Castleguard Meadow, Lewis Freeman took the photograph of Byron Harmon and his outfitters Ulysse Lacasse and Soapy Smith, overlooking a glacier-dammed lake. Mt. Columbia, the highest mountain in Alberta, and the Columbia Icefield lie in the background.[39] By 1987, a massive disappearance of ice had taken place in a period of under seventy years. The only evidence that the glacial lake ever existed here was a level line of water-washed beach sand deposited near where the horses had stood in 1924. Glacial melt continued between 1987 and 2006. Mount Columbia becomes more visible each year from this location as the depth of the Saskatchewan Glacier decreases.

8.26A MOUNT ATHABASCA AND ATHABASCA GLACIER, 1907 FROM A HAND-TINTED LANTERN SLIDE (MARY SCHÄFFER, WHYTE V527-PS-58)

8.26B MOUNT ATHABASCA AND ICEFIELDS PARKWAY, SEPTEMBER 2004 (CW 2004-09C-02)

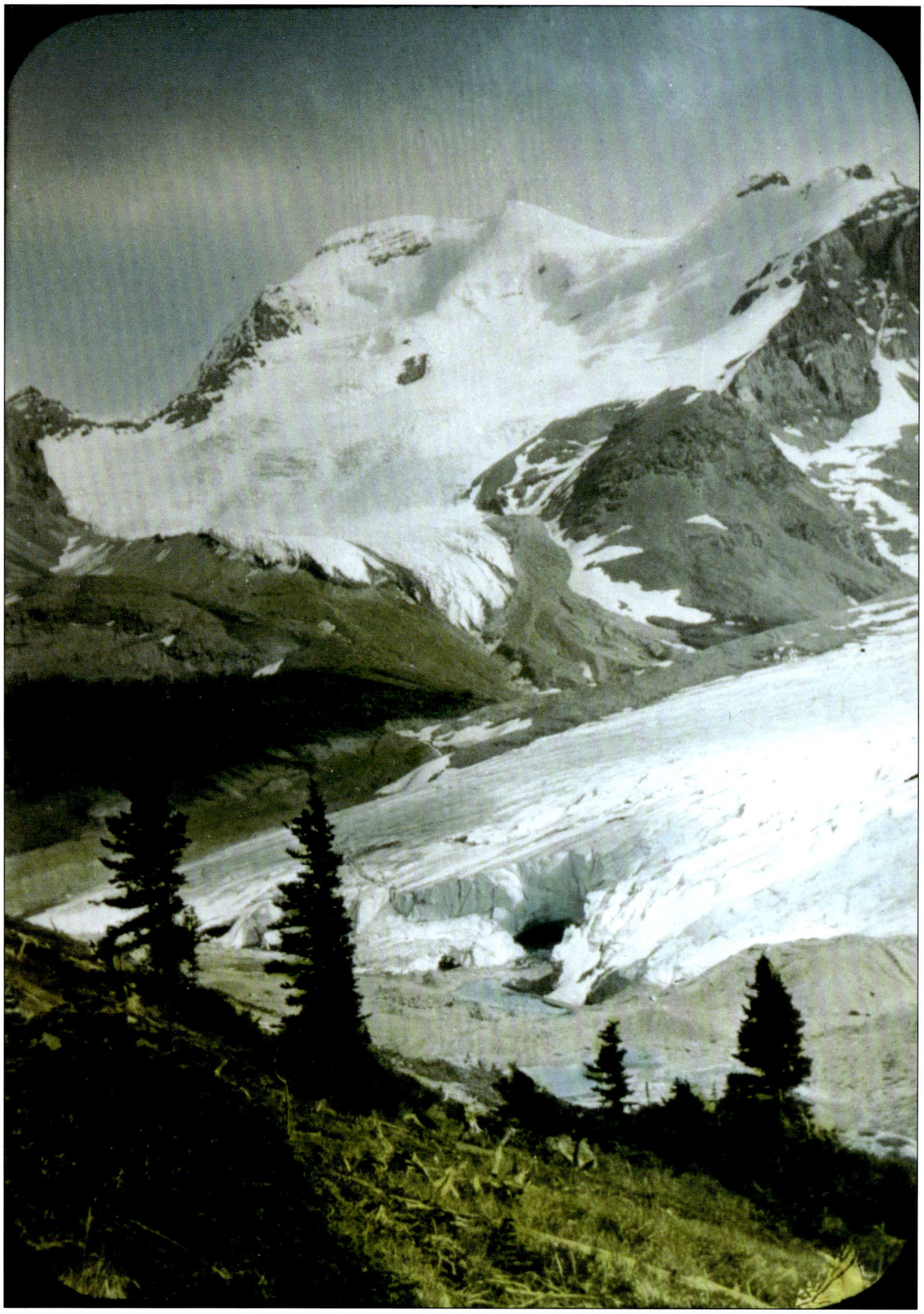

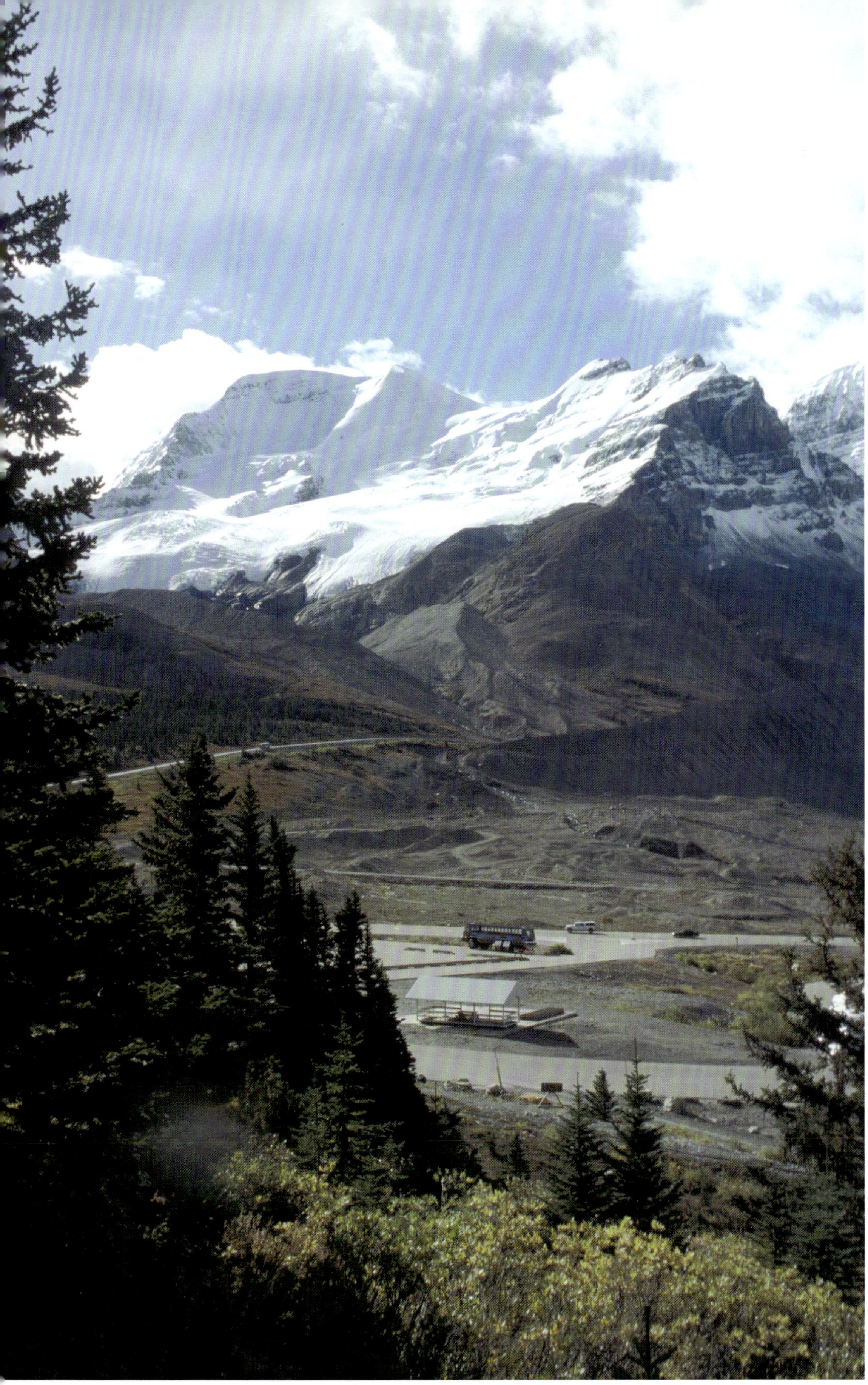

A little more than a century ago much of the area of today's Columbia Icefield Visitors' Centre and the nearby Icefields Parkway was under the ice of the Athabasca Glacier. The usual route of travel was through Nigel Pass to the eastward, but on August 17, 1898, guide Bill Peyto horse-packed mountaineers Norman Collie, Hugh Stutfield, and Hermann Wooley into the meadows below Mt. Athabasca. They had been nineteen days on trail from the railroad at Laggan (Lake Louise) and observed "travelling in the Rockies is far more difficult and tedious now than it was forty years ago, in the days of Hector and Palliser, when game was more abundant, and the passing to and fro of Indians and trappers kept the trails open."[40]

Collie and Wooley made the first ascent of Mt. Athabasca by climbing its northeast ridge (left side of photograph), and Collie described the view of the Columbia Icefield, the hydrological apex of North America:

> To the westward stretched a vast ice-field, probably never before seen by human eye, and surrounded by entirely unknown, unnamed, and unclimbed peaks. From its vast expanse of snows the Saskatchewan glacier takes its rise, and it also supplies the headwaters of the Athabasca; while far away to the west, bending over in those unknown valleys glowing with the evening light, the level snows stretched, to finally melt and flow down more than one channel into the Columbia River, and thence to the Pacific Ocean.[41]

Today, Mount Athabasca, easily accessible from the Icefields Parkway, is one of the most popular ascents in the Canadian Rockies. Thousands have stood on its summit and contemplated the scene, but none are more impressed than Professor Collie in 1898 when he first laid eyes on the "unknown, unnamed, and unclimbed peaks" that lay stretched out before him.

8.27A COLUMBIA ICEFIELD CHALET, CA. 1948 (LLOYD HARMON, WHYTE V108-2132)

8.27B COLUMBIA ICEFIELD VISITOR CENTRE, SEPTEMBER 2004 (CW 2004-09D-18)

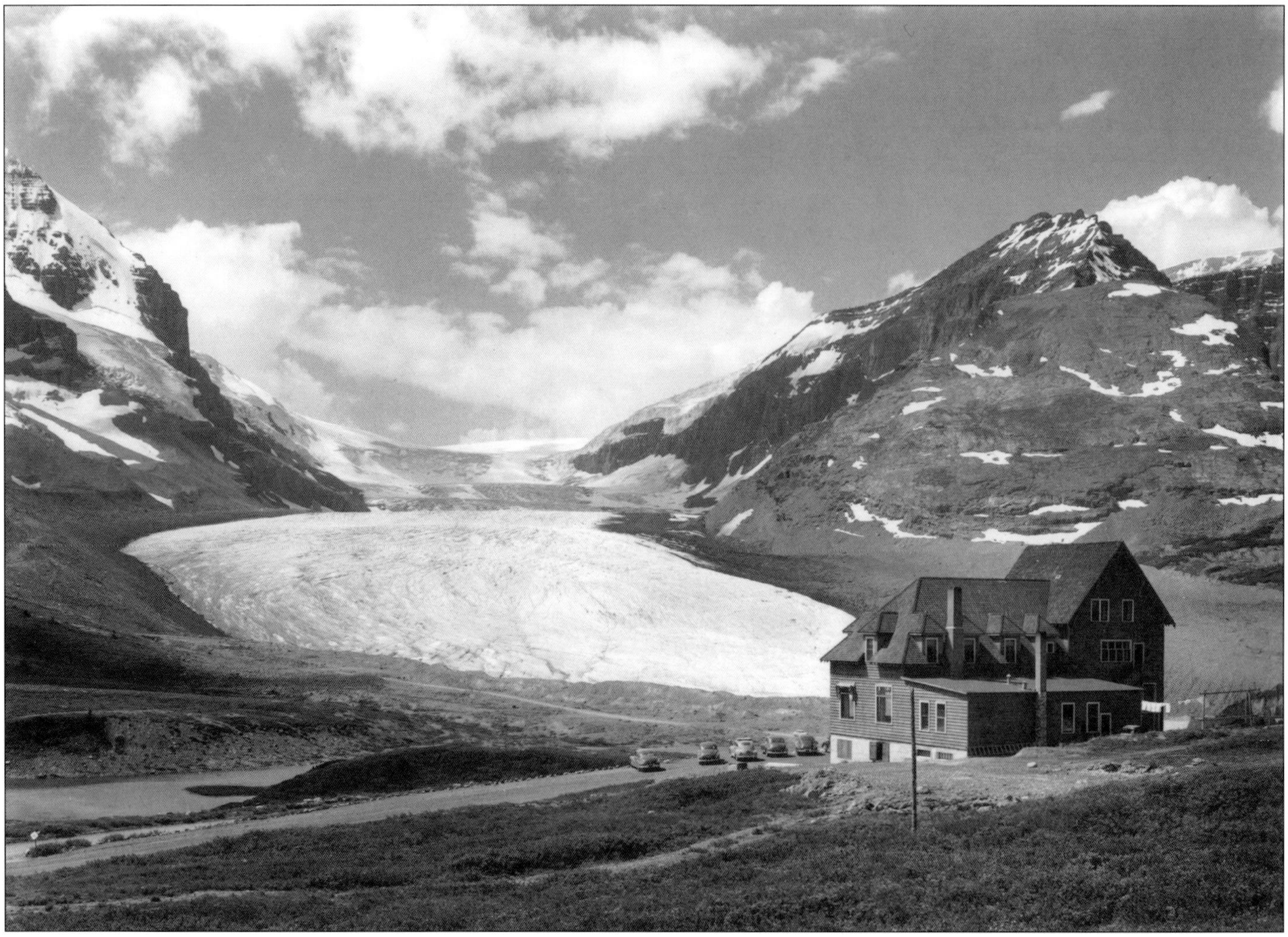

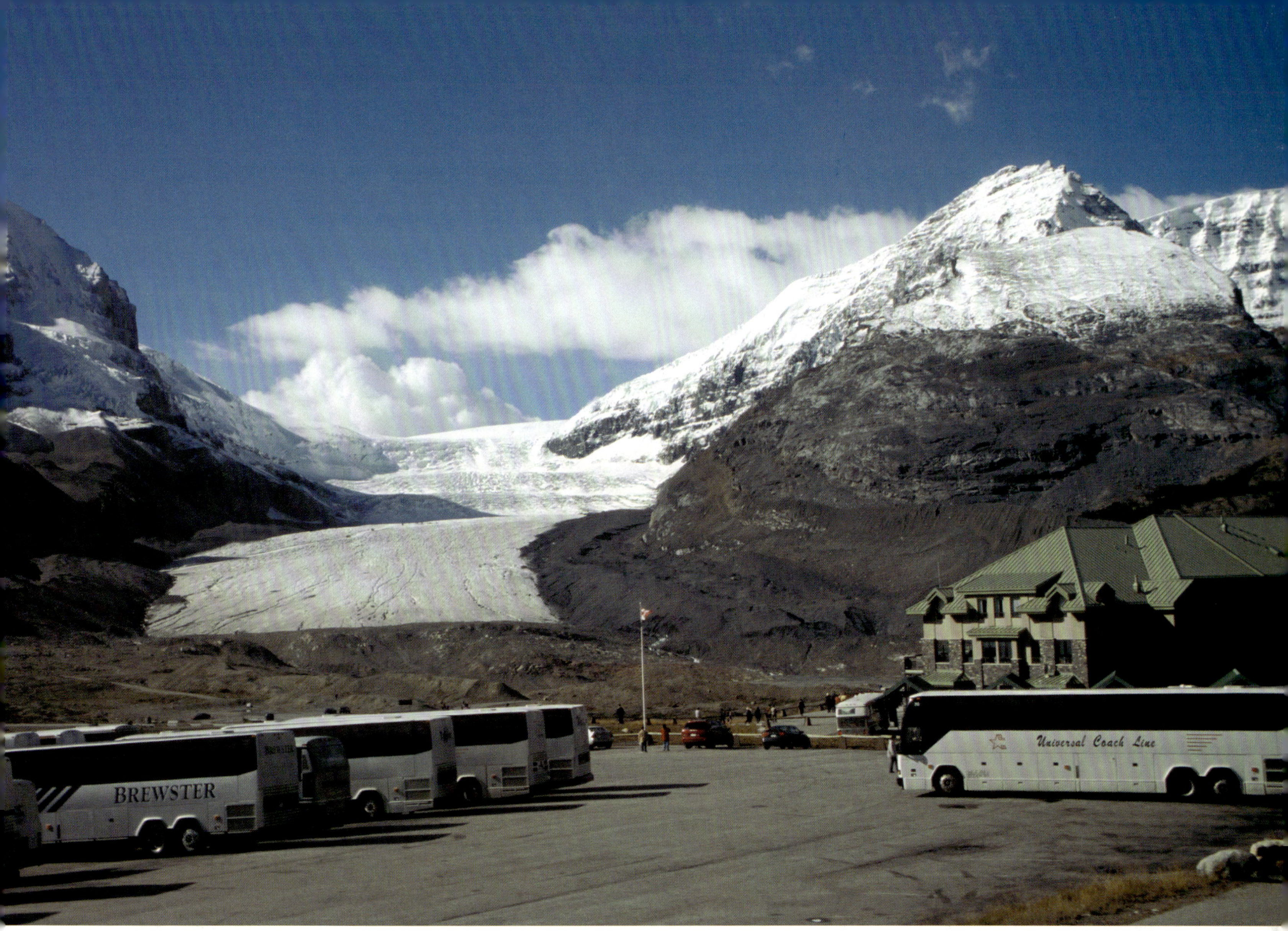

The completion of the Banff-Jasper Highway in 1939 ended an era of long expeditions to visit the remote glaciers and lakes of Banff and Jasper national parks. Banff's and Jasper's original entrepreneurs, the Brewster family, obtained a lease from the federal government for the choicest location for tourism along the entire route. Opened in 1940 on an overlook of the Athabasca Glacier, the Columbia Icefield Chalet was initially profitable but lost money due to gas rationing during most of the Second World War. The early photograph shows the chalet after tourism traffic began to increase again in the post-war period.[42]

In the early 1950s the government licensed snowmobiles to take visitors up on the Athabasca Glacier. By 1960 it had replaced the original narrow and windy Banff-Jasper Highway with a 100 km/hour standard highway, the Icefields Parkway. This made it possible for tour buses from Banff or Jasper to bring masses of tourists each day to ride the "Snow Coaches" up onto the glacier. In 1994 Brewster Transport and Parks Canada partnered to develop the Columbia Icefield Visitors' Centre on the old chalet site to service the multitudes arriving each day from May through September.

Over the last decades, retreat of the Athabasca Glacier has made operation of the over-ice tours increasingly difficult. In the 1950s the snowmobiles simply left the bottom of the glacier. In the 1960s glacial retreat required moving coach access onto the ice two kilometres further up the moraine. By 1990 the continued ice-melt made it impossible for private cars to reach this starting point, and a shuttle bus system to the Snow Coach base was established. Within another half-century, if glacial recession continues at current rates, these unique tours will likely become simply one more vestige of the interesting history of the Canadian Rockies' glaciers.[43]

9

UNIMPAIRED FOR FUTURE GENERATIONS

Balancing Park Use and Preservation

The twin influences of government and private development on mountain parks' landscapes that produced many of the impacts visible in the early photographic record ultimately began to be mitigated by more progressive policies. Beginning in the 1920s some new thinking about the sanctity of national parks started to emerge, and although it would be many years before the concept of parks as fully protected areas took hold, after the passage of the National Parks Act of 1930 the concept of "inviolability,"[1] protection against major development that would impair parks and reduce their ability to be enjoyed by all Canadians in perpetuity, began to inform decision making. The passage of the Act also brought with it changes in park boundaries that eliminated some park lands, in particular those incorporating resource development, so that they could be managed under far less stringent provincial government control. In time, these separate mandates would produce significant differences, both in the way conservation and ecosystem thinking was applied to protected national park mountain lands and the way they would be developed in comparison with increasingly industrialized and urbanized neighbouring landscapes.

Again, it would be Dominion Parks Commissioner J. B. Harkin who would first give voice to the conservation movement, writing in *The Handbook of Canada* in 1924, "The swift onrush of settlement in the last half century has been pushing the wilderness farther and farther back, changing the face of primitive nature, sweeping out of sight much of the virginal beauty that once characterized the whole land. The great forests, the untainted rivers, the rich heritage of wildlife of all kinds – these tend everywhere to disappear. To preserve out of its vast area, for the generations to come, a certain share of primitive nature is the meaning of the national parks movement.... The parks it may be said are the sanctuaries of the original and the wild."[2] In the commissioner's mind there was a difference between development by the government aimed at supporting tourism, so that parks could be made more accessible and be enjoyed by Canadians, and major projects supported by private interests. But because there were already historic commercial enterprises taking place on park lands, including mining and forestry, entrepreneurs felt such activities were fair game. In the 1920s, with the rapid development of western Canada, there was a particular need for water, a resource that could expand the agricultural potential of the semi-arid prairies to the east through irrigation and help to supply the electrical energy that was going to be needed for the Province of Alberta to reach its potential. Irrigation interests were led by the Canadian Pacific Railway, which had acquired a huge block of land in southern Alberta that could be made fertile and saleable with the application of irrigation techniques, a point of view shared by the Dominion Water Power Branch, a sister to the Dominion Parks Branch in the Department of the Interior. Power interests were represented by Calgary Power, controlled by the influential Max Aitken (Lord Beaverbrook) and his Calgary corporate lawyer partner R. B. Bennett, which held a virtual monopoly on electrical generation in southern Alberta. Both activities required mountain waters to be impounded near their source, pitting these interests against Harkin and the Parks Branch, who saw the potential for such development to despoil the beauties of park lands and thereby impair their sanctity and inviolability.[3]

The decade of the 1920s would be marked by the battle for national park lakes – Waterton Lake in Waterton Lakes Park by irrigation interests intent on damming it for use in the irrigation block and Minnewanka and Spray Lakes in Rocky Mountains Park by Calgary Power to supplement the low winter water flow in the Bow River for use in its plants at Horseshoe and Kananaskis falls. Through a masterful manipulation of support by political interests and public organizations, such as the Canadian National Parks Association, which he helped to create, Harkin was able to fend off the powerful interests in both camps. Ultimately, he and his supporters were able to get federal legislation strengthened to protect the inviolability of parks through the mechanism of the National Parks Act of 1930. In its "dedication clause," the Act encompassed some key wording that would henceforth become a springboard from which to launch battles to protect park lands: "These Parks are hereby dedicated to the people of Canada for their benefit, education and enjoyment ... and such Parks shall be maintained and made use of so as to leave them unimpaired for the enjoyment of future generations."[4] However, there was a compromise necessary to gain this protection – in order to appease the strong political and business interests favouring development, the extent of lands to which the new legislation would apply was reduced. Lands that could be developed for their power potential were cut out of Rocky Mountains Park (changed to Banff National Park with the passage of the Act), in particular the Spray Lakes area and the Kananaskis Valley, and, as mentioned, Canmore, Exshaw, and Brûlé with respect to mining and quarrying operations.[5]

History determined that these battles over parks lands would largely be suppressed over the next two decades due to the exigencies of world events. The Great Depression of the 1930s witnessed a step backwards in the Canadian economy, resulting in all private development pressures on mountain lands going into hiatus and the virtual disappearance of the Canadian National Parks Association's role as a public voice for conservation. However, development of public infrastructure, such as buildings and roads, actually flourished in this era as depression relief funds were pumped into the parks by Prime Minister Bennett as a politically acceptable way to help keep the unemployed of the nation off the dole. Just when the Depression was beginning to loosen its grip, Canadians were plunged into the Second World War, and once more attention was focused on wrestling a threatening outside force to the ground. Unfortunately, the pressures of wartime administration had a particularly deleterious effect on the mountain national parks as restrictions on rubber and gasoline resulted in the effective shutting down of the tourist business and also delivered a body blow to the concept of the sanctity of park lands. Despite two decades of keeping the power interests at bay, a simple stroke of a ministerial pen under the auspices of the War Measures Act allowed Calgary Power to construct a major dam and power project at Lake Minnewanka in 1942, ostensibly to support the war effort but clearly illustrating that the National Parks Act could and would be challenged when perceived national interests came into play.

It would be in the 1950s and 1960s that the next chapter in the story of development versus conservation on park lands would be written, one that would provide the seeds for much of what we see in the record today. As mentioned, the rapid expansion of ski resorts in the post-war period was a contributing factor in the flood of new tourism-related facilities appearing in the mountains. Inevitably, there were many who welcomed the new recreational opportunities they provided, but at the same time a few voices began to question whether or not too much recreational and tourism development would begin to impair park lands just as seriously as mining and water powers had threatened to do so in the past. The focus ultimately came to rest on proposals for the Winter Olympics to be held in Banff National Park, an event that would entail major highway, infrastructure, townsite, and ski area expansion. The first efforts in this direction occurred in the lead-up to the 1948 games, but it was not until the 1968 Olympics were on the horizon that serious attempts were organized by a group of Calgary interests, known as the Calgary Olympic Development Association (CODA). Based on a spate of ski area development at Mount Norquay and Lake Louise, they were able to mount a credible bid, including federal government support for a five-thousand-seat arena at Banff, which seemed likely to succeed until the bid committee received some disparaging comments purported to come from the Banff Citizens' Committee referring to it as "the idea of several promoters in Calgary who are looking to make some fast money and do not care what happens to Banff National Park." The bid failed, but an effort to gain the 1972 games was immediately launched, pitting Calgary business and Banff ski interests, on one side, against a new Canadian voice for conservation, the National and Provincial Parks Association of Canada (NPPAC), on the other. Into this debate, Arthur Laing, the minister responsible for parks, inserted a new policy in 1964, intended to direct the development of Canada's national parks, the first real effort to define their future since the 1930 Act. Laing's policy dictated that "urban type" recreational facilities would not be allowed in the parks, but that "recreation facilities in harmony with the purpose and preservation of a park may be introduced as required to meet the recreational needs, but always so as to minimize impairment and not at all if substantial impairment is inevitable."[6] The new voices of conservation again won the day on the 1972 Olympic bid, when Sapporo, Japan, itself in a national park, won out over Banff. CODA president Jack Davis would later attribute this to the fact that "the Sierra Club, the universities, the Audubon Society, fish and game people all lobbied the IOC delegates ... the first appearance of environmentalists."[7]

Despite the failure of the Olympic bids, anticipation of their success had spurred renewed ski area development in Banff and an addendum on winter use accompanying Laing's recreational policy called for "adequate" skiing facilities controlled by "comprehensive long range plans," providing enough certainty for more investment. Pressure for major ski and tourism development continued to build through the 1960s as the regional population began an exponential growth and improvements to jet aircraft, airports, automobiles, and roads brought ever-increasing numbers of recreation-seekers to the mountains. That pressure would result in a proposal for a resort and skiing mega-project at Lake Louise, when Lake Louise Lifts, frustrated at decades of parks department indecision and lack of tourism infrastructure development, joined forces with Imperial Oil in 1970 to promote "Village Lake Louise," a six-thousand-visitor facility at the base of Mount Whitehorn. Although parks authorities agreed to a scaled down version of the village, the concept quickly became the *bête noir* of the NPPAC and other environmental groups, and, in line with the new Trudeau government's call for more open decision making, they were able to force public hearings on the project. These hearings, described by the press as "a three-ring circus," took place in Calgary in March 1972, and, with over ten thousand people ultimately making oral or written presentations, they elicited an outcry against such large-scale development on mountain park lands. Jean Chrétien, the federal minister responsible, had initially favoured the project but was too good a politician to ignore such strong public opinion, and in July 1972 he announced that it would not be approved, offering, "where there is room for doubt priority must be given to park values; and we must err on the side of park protection."[8] It was a statement of which Commissioner Harkin would have been proud, and, indeed, a few months later Chrétien was awarded the NPPAC's first J. B. Harkin Medal for those serving the cause of parks with distinction.[9]

The success of the environmental movement against Village Lake Louise saw the gloves come off in the battle of protection vs. development in the mountain parks. Conservationists, the bit now firmly in their teeth, became more strident in their opposition to recreational and tourism developments; businessmen began to hire their own consultants and specialists to promote their interests, and more often than not took the political route to achieving their goals; parks authorities began to shy away from confrontational public processes and were seized by a lack of ability to produce timely decisions. Continued controversy required that the parks department continually revise and refine its benchmarks in the 1964 policy. Increasingly, policy statements stressed protection of the natural environment from impairment, but this raised the fundamental question: *What is natural?* The 1969 Provisional Management Plans for the mountain national parks recognized that, depending on how this was defined, there could be large differences according to two different management approaches. Under the "evolutionary concept" environments would be allowed to change with minimal human interference. In contrast, under the "era concept" park managers might maintain areas of parks as they appeared during a given time period, and this could include substantial human influences.[10]

Similar issues arose in the United States. In 1963, Starker Leopold and co-authors of the *Report of the Advisory Board on Wildlife Management* recommended an era concept where the goal of managing U.S. parks "should be to preserve, or where necessary, to recreate ecological scene as viewed by the first European visitors." However, due to political influences from the American wilderness movement, and increasing public objection to culling elk, Yellowstone National Park adopted the evolutionary concept for management, and in 1969 began a rigorous "natural regulation" policy of minimal human interference. Recognizing that removing long-term human hunting and burning effects, allowing lightning fires to burn, and letting ungulate populations expand under minimal predation would create unique opportunities for research, the scientific community generally supported what came to be called "Yellowstone's Great Experiment." But the results, including massive wildfires, booming elk populations, and eventually, super-thriving wolf packs, led to further public controversy.[11] In contrast, while initially stressing the minimal-interference, evolutionary approach, Parks Canada's expanded scientific research programs after 1974 attempted to understand the ecology of mountain landscapes and the effects of past and present human use. This research suggested that the Canadian mountain national parks should follow a modified era-approach.[12]

Equally important as these changes in park policy were environmentalists' calls to develop areas outside park boundaries for tourism to relieve the pressure on the mountain parks. The Government of Alberta turned its attention in the 1970s to the recreational development of the eastern slopes in the Kananaskis-Canmore area. Already this area had been utilized for its hydro-electric potential by Calgary Power in the 1950s in the wake of its being cut out of Banff Park in 1930, with power developments at Spray Lakes, Kananaskis, and Three Sisters, and after the completion of the Trans-Canada Highway in 1962, Canmore had begun to take its first tentative steps into the tourism business with the development of a few motels along the new route. The Environmental Conservation Authority's hearings on the eastern slopes took place in 1974, calling for multiple use of the area to continue but recommending "provision of tourist facilities be encouraged outside of the national parks, to support the balanced recreational use of the Eastern Slopes, and to relieve the urban stress on the national parks."[13] This led to the creation of what is now Peter Lougheed Provincial Park and Kananaskis Country in 1977 and provided the basis for the area's final achievement of the Olympic dream when part of the Winter Olympics was held in Canmore in 1988. Already growing in its tourism attributes, the former mining community had even more attention focused on it by the Olympics, and it quickly was transformed into a resort community where a few Calgary weekenders were joined by international pleasure seekers looking for mountain recreation properties, making it into Alberta's fastest growing community.

More sophisticated understanding of the ecological and cultural legacy influencing national park landscapes led to a profound amendment to the National Parks Act in 1988. Parks were required to maintain or restore "ecological integrity" as a first priority in managing national parks: "An ecosystem has integrity when it is deemed characteristic of its natural region including the composition and abundance of native species and biological communities, rates of change, and supporting processes." By evoking tenets from the science of ecology, this definition attempted to put measurable and defensible criteria around the questions of what is natural, and the relative degree of human-caused impairment. It also provided a synthesis between the seemingly mutually exclusive "era" versus "evolutionary" concepts for management direction. The idea of ecological integrity recognized that the long-term influences of humans might be a characteristic and important component of some ecosystems.[14]

The pressures on mountain lands both inside and outside the mountain parks continued to increase throughout the 1980s, and many issues, including the continued warring between environmental and development interests and Parks Canada's perceived inability to take the necessary steps to ensure the ecological integrity of Banff, ultimately led to the federal government's decision to come to grips with the future of the Bow Valley. In March 1994 the federal minister responsible for national parks, Michel Dupuy, announced the Banff–Bow Valley Study, a two-year process tasked with assessing the cumulative environmental effects of development and use in the entire upper Bow Valley watershed, and in particular Banff National Park. Carried out by a six-member expert task force assisted by research staff and the input of a roundtable representing fourteen different interest sectors, its final report would identify what was at stake if action were not taken: "Five million visitors every year, two communities, a transcontinental railway, a four-lane highway, three major ski hills – this growth in visitor numbers and development threatens the mountain environment. If allowed to continue, it will cause serious and irreversible harm to Banff National Park's ecological integrity and its value as a national park. Impairing the ecological integrity and natural beauty of the Park will also weaken its attraction as a tourist destination, and the associated contribution to the local, regional and national economies."[15] To prevent this, the task force called for cooperation to take place locally, regionally, and nationally and provided some five hundred recommendations on everything from managing human use, to applying limits to growth, to undertaking efforts to restore ecological integrity.[16]

The 1997 Banff National Park Management Plan that implemented many of the Banff-Bow Valley Study's recommendations became a benchmark document for Canadian parks. It was a template for new plans across the mountain national parks that limited further tourism development to minimize impairment. Further, on the basis of detailed studies of long-term ecosystem states and processes in the Canadian Rockies, Parks Canada began aggressive programs to restore ecological integrity. In Banff, facilities were moved to increase the movements of wary carnivores through wildlife corridors, thereby increasing predation rates on prey. In addition, Banff and Jasper wardens re-instituted practices of the 1960s by removing elk from areas where predation could not be restored. Engineers installed additional highway fencing and wildlife crossing structures to minimize road-kills and maximize wildlife movement. Banff, Jasper, Yoho, and Kootenay park staff increased prescribed burning in their respective parks to maintain the long-term important role of First Nations' firing of the landscape. The towns of Banff and Jasper installed state-of-the-art sewage treatment systems to reduce nutrient additions to park waterways.[17]

Based on Banff experience, in 1998 Federal Minister Sheila Copps asked an independent panel to assess ecosystem conditions and "provide advice and recommend how best to ensure that ecological integrity is maintained across the system of Canadian National Parks."[18] The "EI Panel Report" provided the basis for the new Canadian National Parks Act in 2001. The report made recommendations for scientific research, ecological restoration, working with aboriginal peoples, and outreach programs to build support from Canadians for the national parks. With relevance to many of the images of change shown in this book, the panel report attached particular importance to understanding the interaction of long-term ecological and cultural processes influencing landscape change. The panel contended, "By managing for the historic ranges of variability, processes that may take the ecosystem into the future are also conserved."[19]

Broadly, we see current changes in management practices in the mountain national parks as the idealistic intention of our recent human culture to conserve the ecological legacy resulting from nearly ten millennia of First Nations use. Today, scientists are increasingly aware that much of the landscape change visible in the photographs in this book, and many of the national parks' most vexing ecological issues, are not simply impairment caused by modern human use and development. More fundamentally, they are due to the dramatically different ways current peoples use the landscape compared to past cultures. For example, the lack of burning shown in recent pictures is not just because modern cultures put out lightning-caused fires, but most importantly, because Native American practices of routinely burning the landscape have ended.[20]

Recognition of this complexity increasingly leads park managers away from choosing simple solutions such as visitor use restrictions, and towards considering the actual root causes of ecosystem change. Consider that historically, grizzly bear numbers may have been low in the Rocky Mountains due to hunting by First Nations. Today low grizzly bear numbers in some park areas is partially due to avoidance of high numbers of people, but often more important are bear-kills from speeding highway and railway traffic, and possibly lack of quality habitat due to forest growth. If Canadians wish to increase grizzly bear numbers in national parks, this cannot be done simply just by widespread restrictions of use on hiking trails. Rather, it will require maintaining relatively large roadless areas with low visitor use where bears are secure from human mortality and habituation, fencing highways and providing wildlife crossing structures wherever possible, reducing traffic speeds on other roads and railways, and using prescribed fire to improve habitat.[21] As another example, the decline in woodland caribou across the mountain parks is, ironically, likely due to the end of First Nations hunting in the Rockies. This has allowed moose, elk, and deer populations to increase. High prey numbers favour increases in numbers of their predators – wolves and grizzly bears. When these carnivores are more abundant, they in turn kill more caribou, which is more vulnerable than other prey. Therefore restoring caribou numbers in national parks will not involve simply more aggressive "natural regulation" policies to remove people from the landscape, but rather will follow the paradigm of ecological integrity and restoring long-term ecosystem states and processes that often include subtle human influences.[22]

Thus, maintaining the mountain parks "unimpaired for the enjoyment of future generations" has proved no simple task. The Banff–Bow Valley Study demonstrated that the greatest gains are made when a range of caring people from many backgrounds work together to solve problems. These citizen groups must be informed not just by the ecological sciences, but by many disciplines, including traditional and community knowledge, archaeology, and history.[23] Moreover, as Commissioner Harkin showed nearly a century ago, solutions will lie in the common ground of what is aesthetically and ecologically valued, what is economically affordable, and what is politically supported.

10.1 CANADIAN PACIFIC SURVEY AT JASPER HOUSE, 1871 (CHARLES HORETZKY, LIBRARY ARCHIVES CANADA PA-9147)

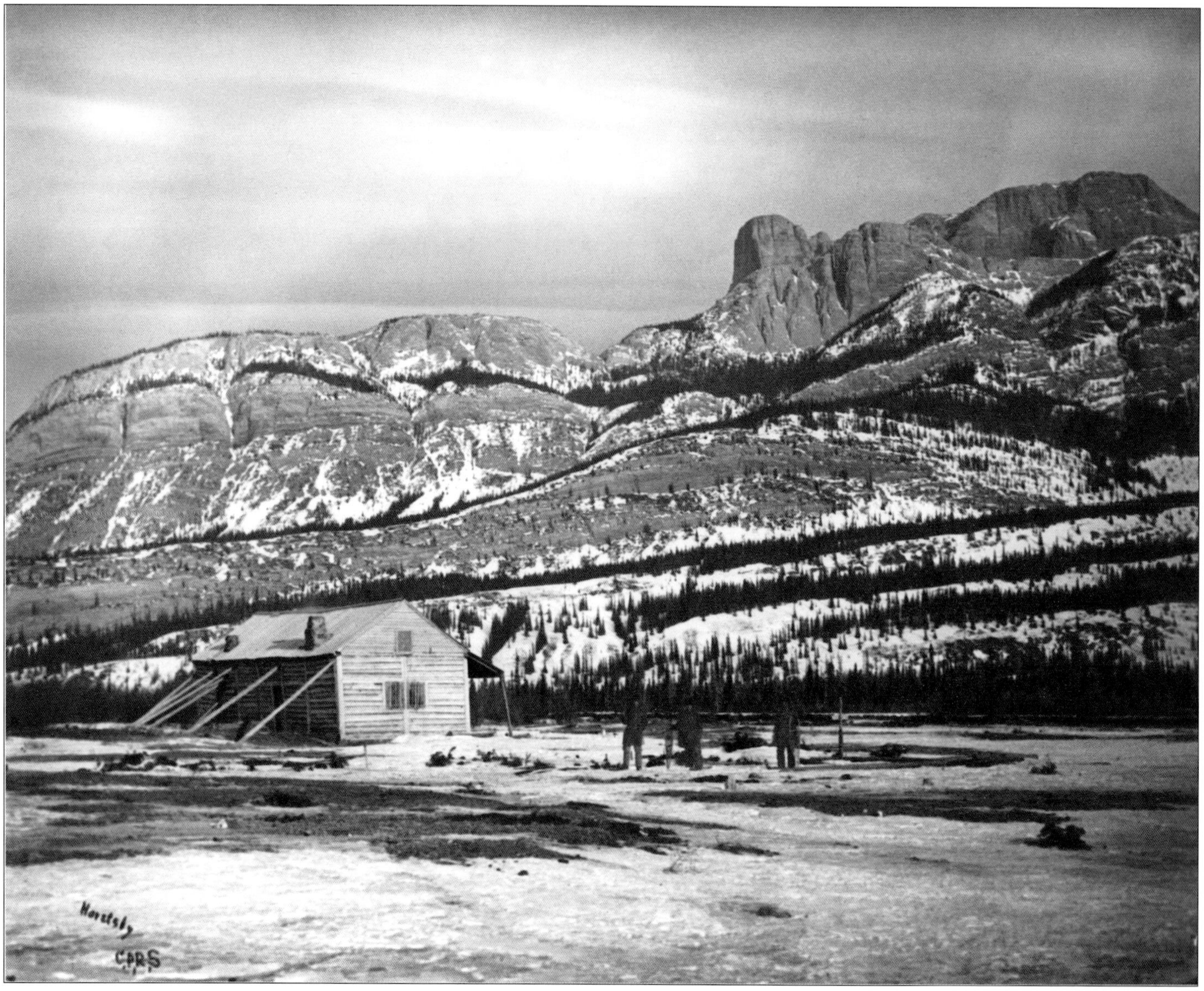

10

THE NORTHWEST PASSAGE BY LAND

Jasper to Edmonton

Whatever Route requires the fewer hands, and has the shortest distance will have the decided advantage. – David Thompson[1]

In early January of 1811 David Thompson led a North West Company fur brigade into the Rocky Mountains through the cold snows of the Athabasca Valley. It was a tough time of year to map a new fur trade transportation route through the Rocky Mountains, but Thompson was in a difficult position.[2] A few weeks earlier a band of Peigan warriors threatened his party when they attempted to use the more southerly route up the North Saskatchewan River and over Howse Pass to resupply the company trading houses in the Columbia River watershed. The Blackfoot Confederacy had successfully blocked most fur-trader access to the peoples west of the Great Divide for nearly two decades. Thompson had resolved to open a fur-traders route further northwards to skirt their territory.[3]

On January 10, 1811, Thompson reached "The Committee's Punchbowl," a small pond at Athabasca Pass, and began his descent to the Columbia River at Boat Encampment. The following summer he made a brief trip downstream, and, after reaching the Pacific Ocean at the mouth of Columbia on July 18, he returned over the mountains and never ventured west again. However, the trading route and network he created between the prairies and the Pacific ensured that the Columbia River watershed would remain under British control into the 1840s. The Athabasca Pass route from Fort Edmonton across the Rockies to trading posts such Spokane House and Fort Astoria proved to be not only safe, but also cost-efficient, and it remained the transcontinental route for European trade for almost five decades.[4] In the process, the area now incorporated in Jasper National Park witnessed the earliest white-European history in the Canadian Rockies.

10.2A JASPER, ALBERTA, CA. 1915 (L. M. PETERSEN, GLENBOW NA 2067-1)

10.2B EVENING LIGHT ON THE TOWN OF JASPER, MAY 2006 (CW 2006-05A-27)

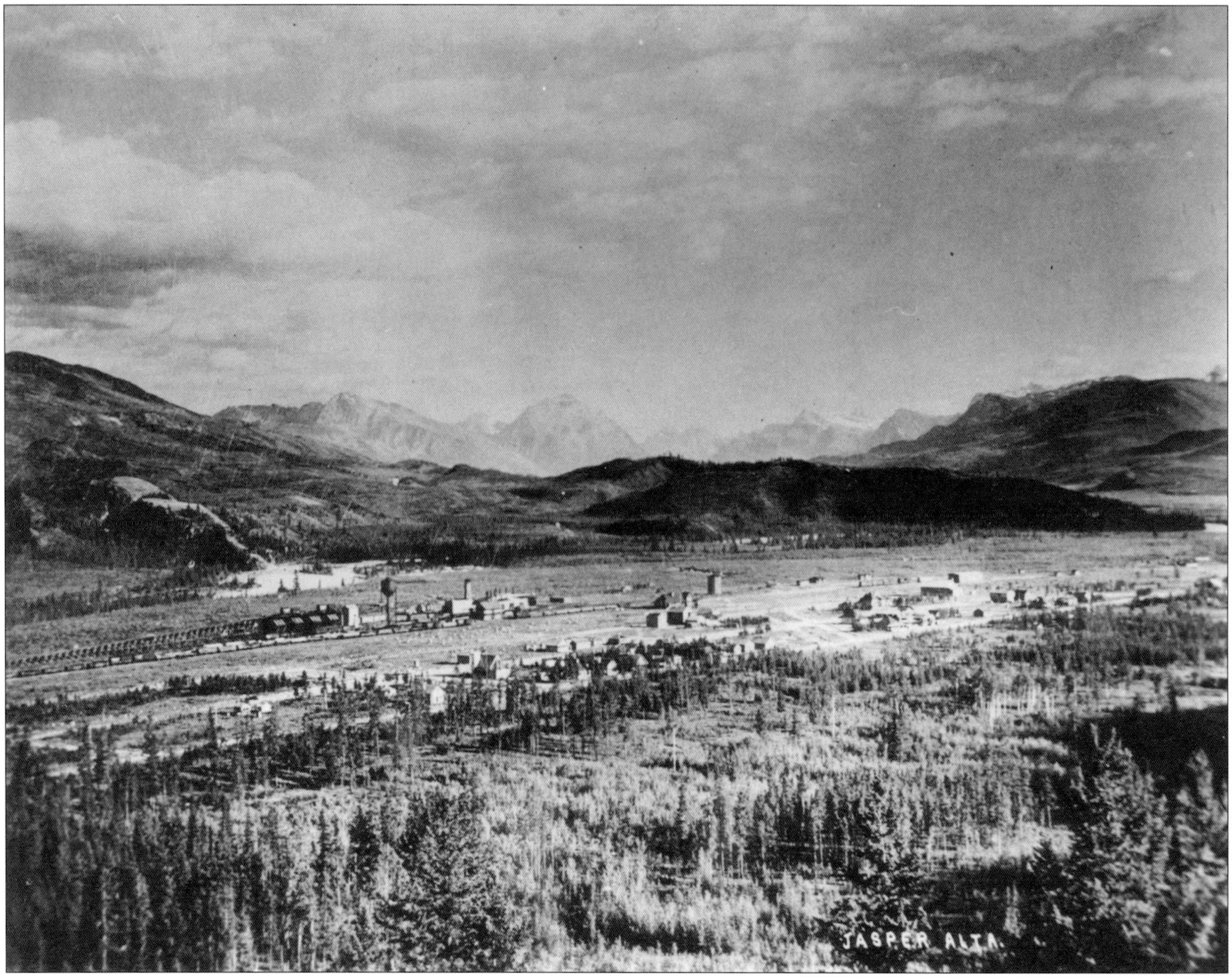

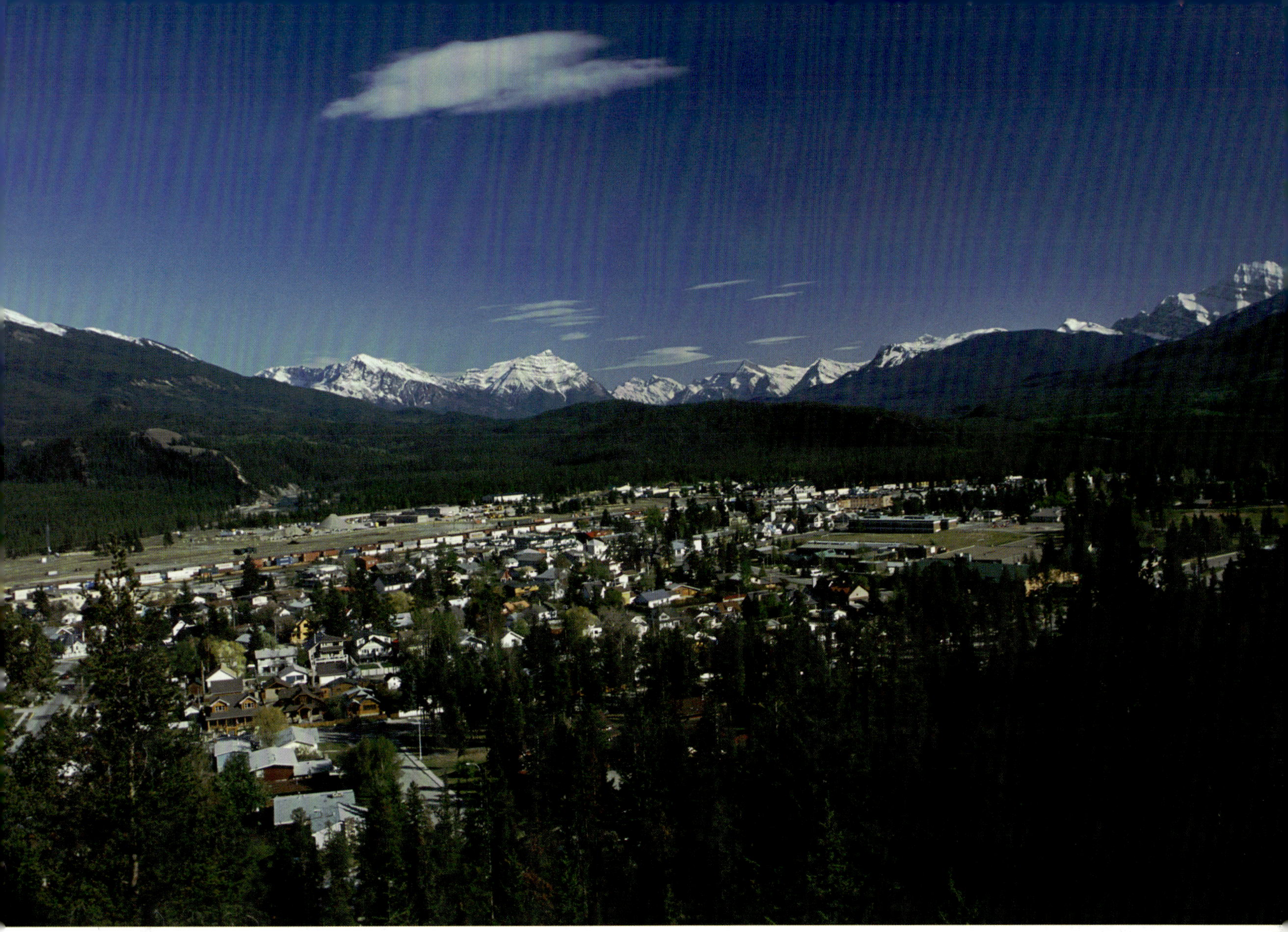

The historic trail to Athabasca Pass likely skirted Old Fort Point, jutting into the Athasbasca River (left side of the photograph) across from the present-day town of Jasper. From here the trail wound through hills east of the river to reach Prairie de la Vache (Buffalo Prairie), the last campsite with good horse feed. The route then crossed the Athabasca River and ascended westward into the Whirlpool River valley behind "La Montagne de la Grande Traverse" (Mt. Edith Cavell, right side of photograph), leading to the famed pass to the Columbia River.[5]

Jasper National Park was first established as a "forest park" in 1907, and in 1911 the Grand Trunk Pacific Railroad, one of the two new transcontinental railways being built through Yellowhead Pass, established a divisional point at what was initially known as "Fitzhugh." By the time the early view of the townsite was taken, the park administration was headquartered in the village and both the Grand Trunk and Canadian Northern railways passed through it, quickly adding to its population. Jasper began to be developed as a tourist centre to rival Banff in the 1920s but was never developed to the same extent and still today maintains its flavour as a Canadian National Railways divisional point combined with a year-round national parks tourism centre.[6]

10.3A TRAIN LEAVING JASPER, GOING EAST, CA. 1940 (DORIS KENSIT COLLECTION, JASPER-YELLOWHEAD 994-45-88)

10.3B CANADIAN NATIONAL RAILWAY FREIGHT TRAIN EAST OF JASPER, JUNE 2004 (CW 2004-06B-08)

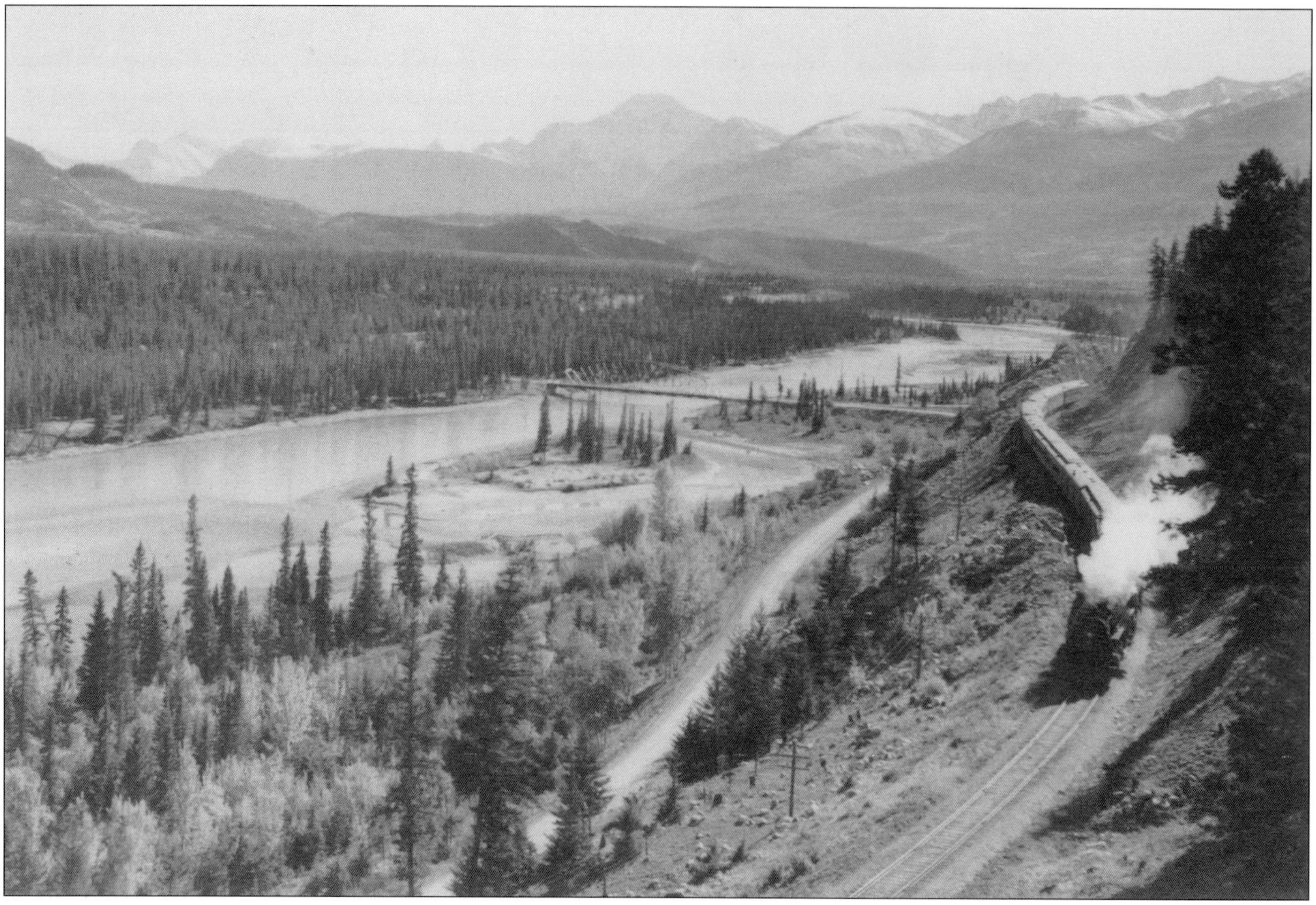

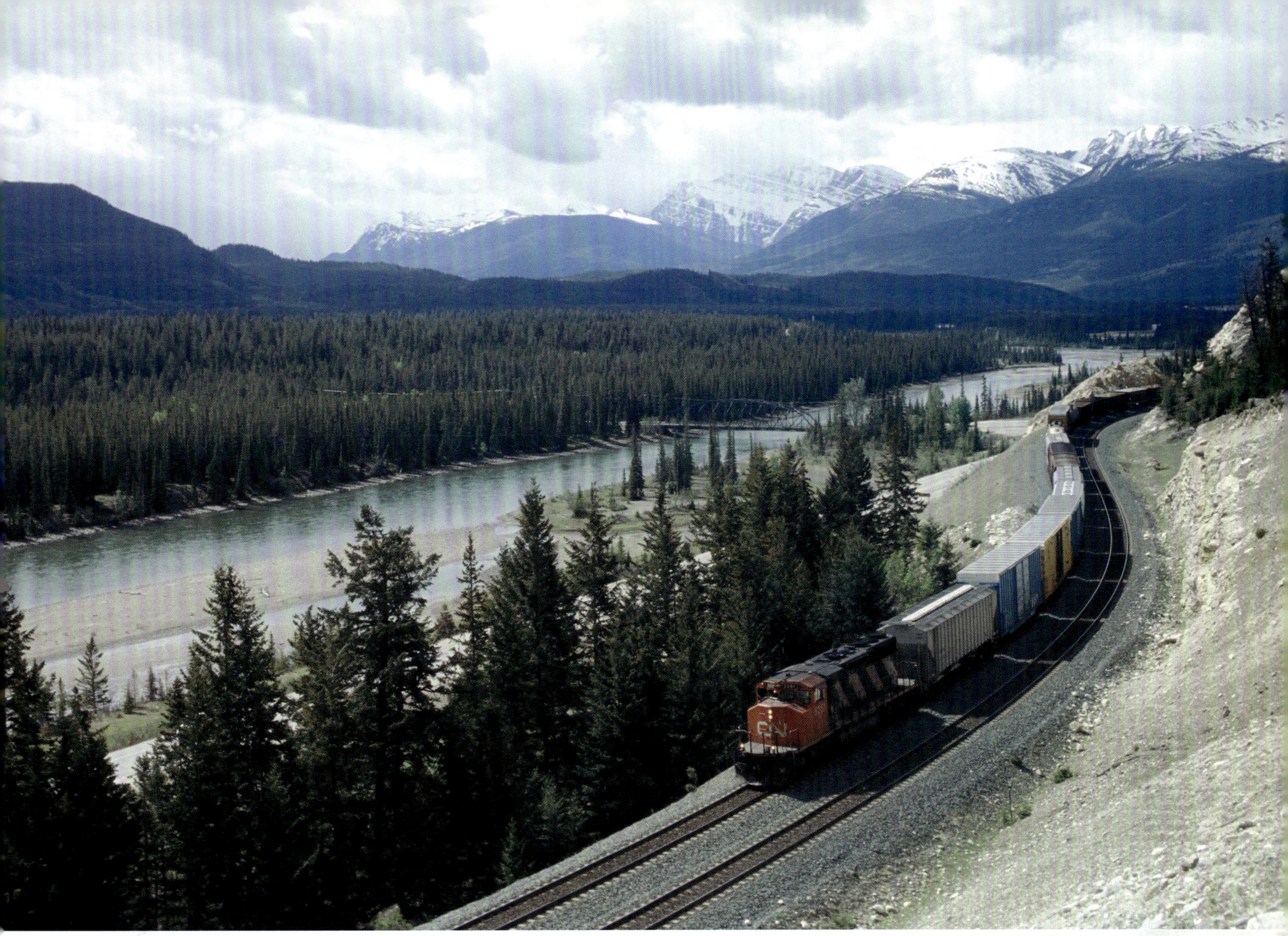

For a short period during the First World War, Jasper was served by two railroads. The steel of the Grand Trunk Pacific Railroad connecting Edmonton to the port of Prince Rupert reached the village in August 1911, and the final connection to the Pacific Ocean was completed in 1914. The Canadian Northern Railway connection to Port Mann near Vancouver was opened through the park in October 1915. The two lines ran side by side through much of the Athabasca Valley, and both used the relatively low Yellowhead Pass to cross the Rockies to the Fraser River drainage. The economic stress of the war led to consolidation of the lines starting in 1916, and rails from the surplus sections were sent to Britain for wartime manufacturing. In 1923 the two companies were merged under federal ownership to form Canadian National Railways, and many sections of the abandoned railway grade were used to build a road from Jasper to the east park boundary between 1923 and 1928. Tourists travelling by automobile could finally reach the park in 1931 when the Alberta government completed the road to the boundary from Edmonton.[7]

The photographs show Canadian National trains on the alignment originally used by the Grand Trunk Pacific. In the earlier view a section of the Canadian Northern Railway's abandoned line is still visible near the Athabasca River, with the newly constructed road in the centre. In the late 1970s Canadian National twinned the line through the Canadian Rockies.

10.4A CONSTRUCTION CAMP NEAR JASPER, ALBERTA, 1914 (MTS LEGAL SURVEYS, LIBRARY ARCHIVES CANADA PA-20847)

10.4B EAST ENTRANCE ROAD TO THE TOWN OF JASPER FROM THE CANADIAN NATIONAL RAILWAY BRIDGE, JULY 2003 (CW 2003-07N-16)

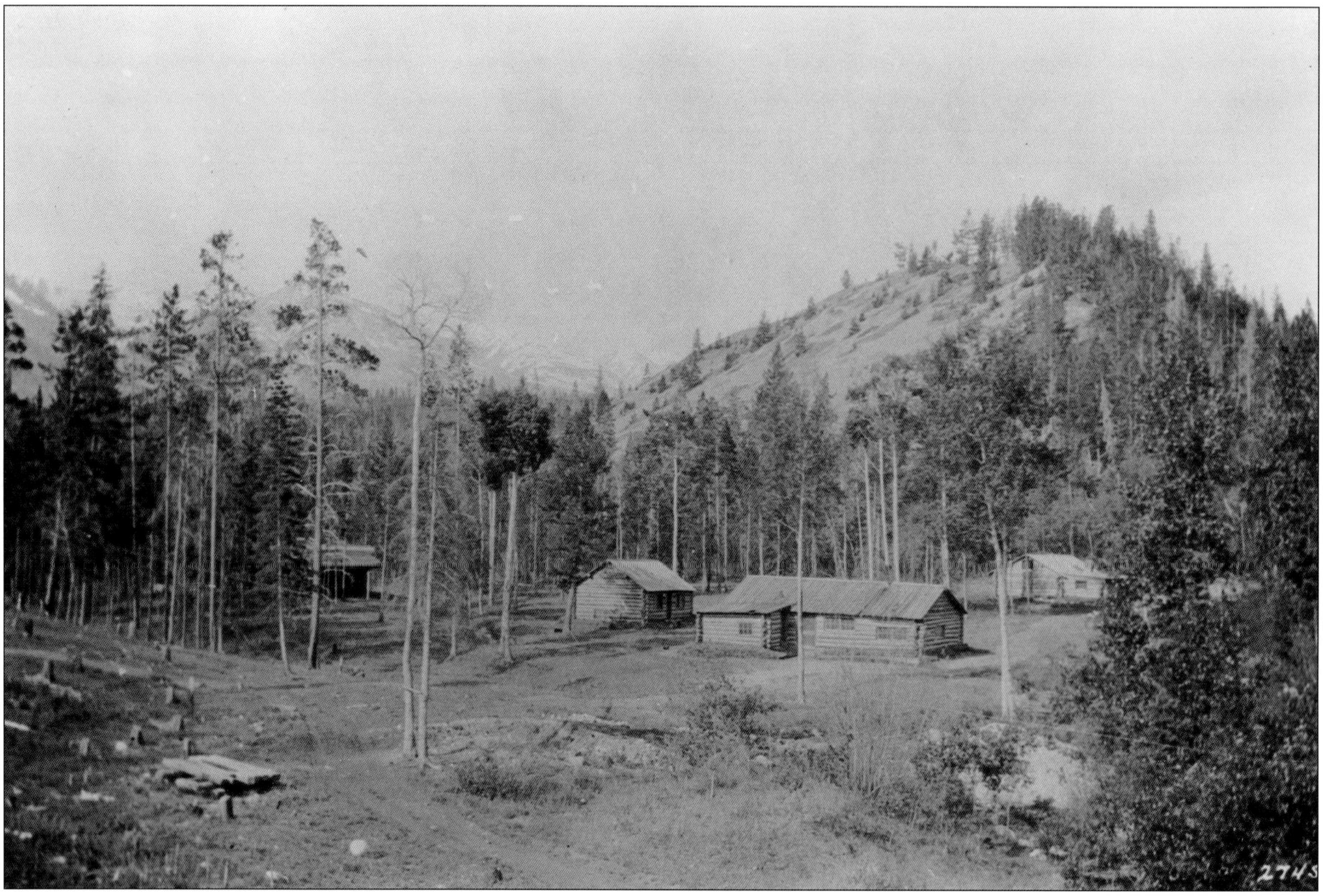

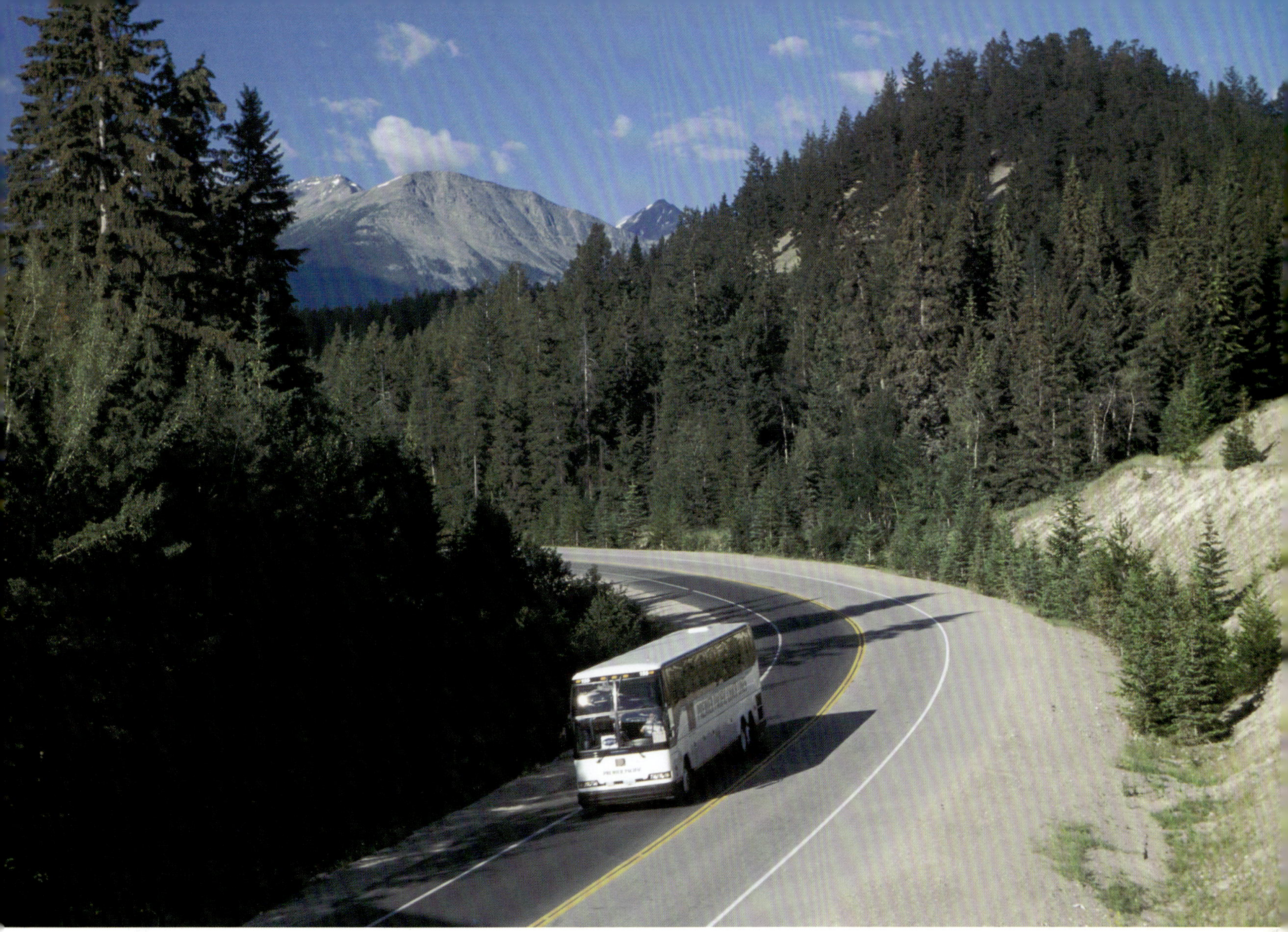

The sheltered forest of trembling aspen and balsam poplar along Cottonwood Creek at the edge of the town of Jasper was likely a long-used First Nations campsite and was likewise utilized during the Athabasca Valley's early fur trade period. In 1824 Hudson's Bay trader Joseph Laroque built what fellow trader Ross Cox described as a "neat little group of wood huts" on the bank of the creek, and it was henceforth a potential campsite for the fur brigades going through Athabasca and Yellowhead passes.[8] With the waning of the trade by the 1860s, the site had been abandoned, but it was taken up anew around 1911 for use as a construction camp in the building of one of the two transcontinental railway lines running through the park. Today the cabins are gone, the creek is held by a ditch, and a busy two-lane road bisects the scene.

10.5A RANGERS PACK TRAIN LEAVING JASPER, 1915 (W. N. MILLAR, DOMINION FOREST COLLECTION 6207)

10.5B SUMMER TRAFFIC, CONNAUGHT DRIVE, JASPER, JULY 2003 (CW 2003-07G-25)

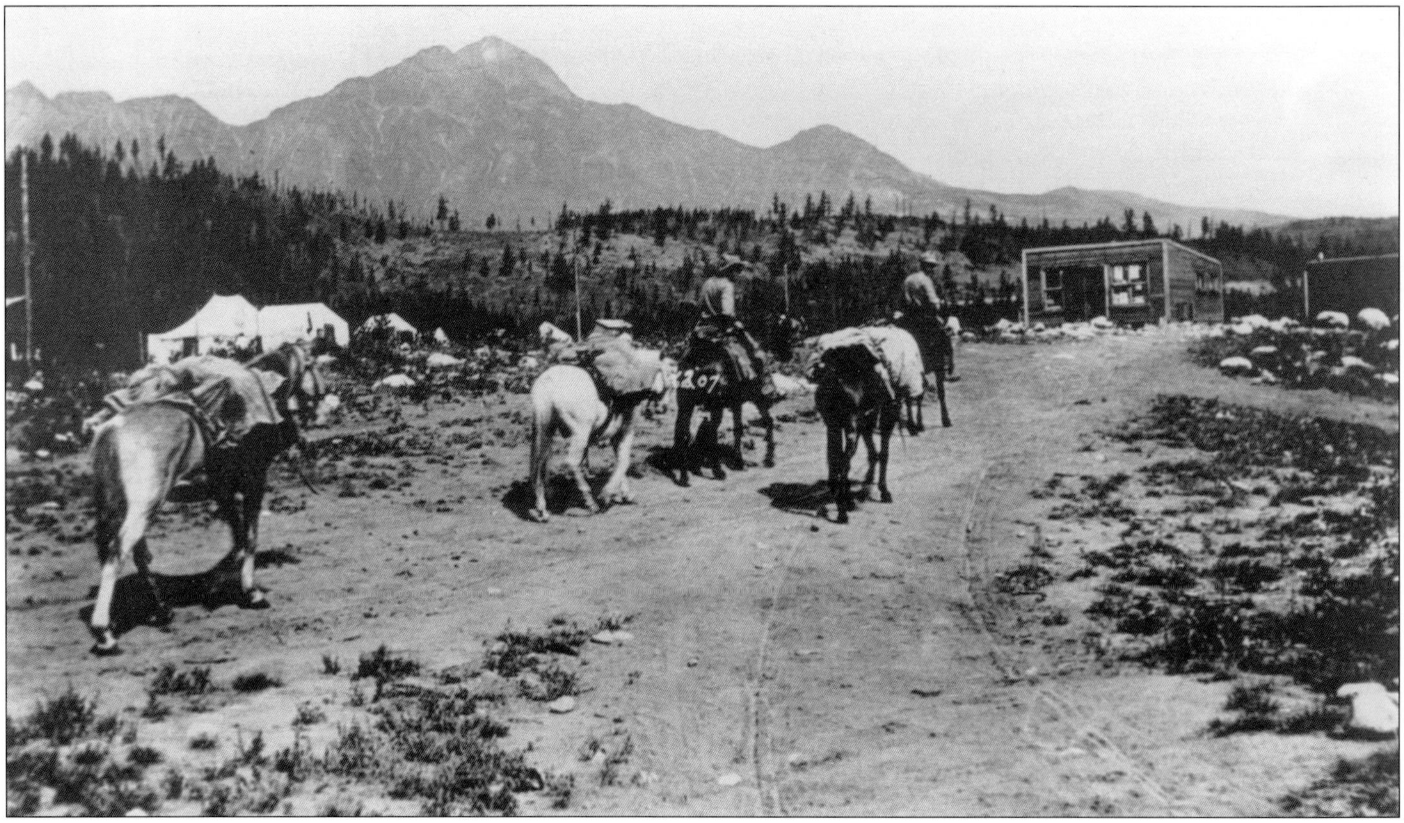

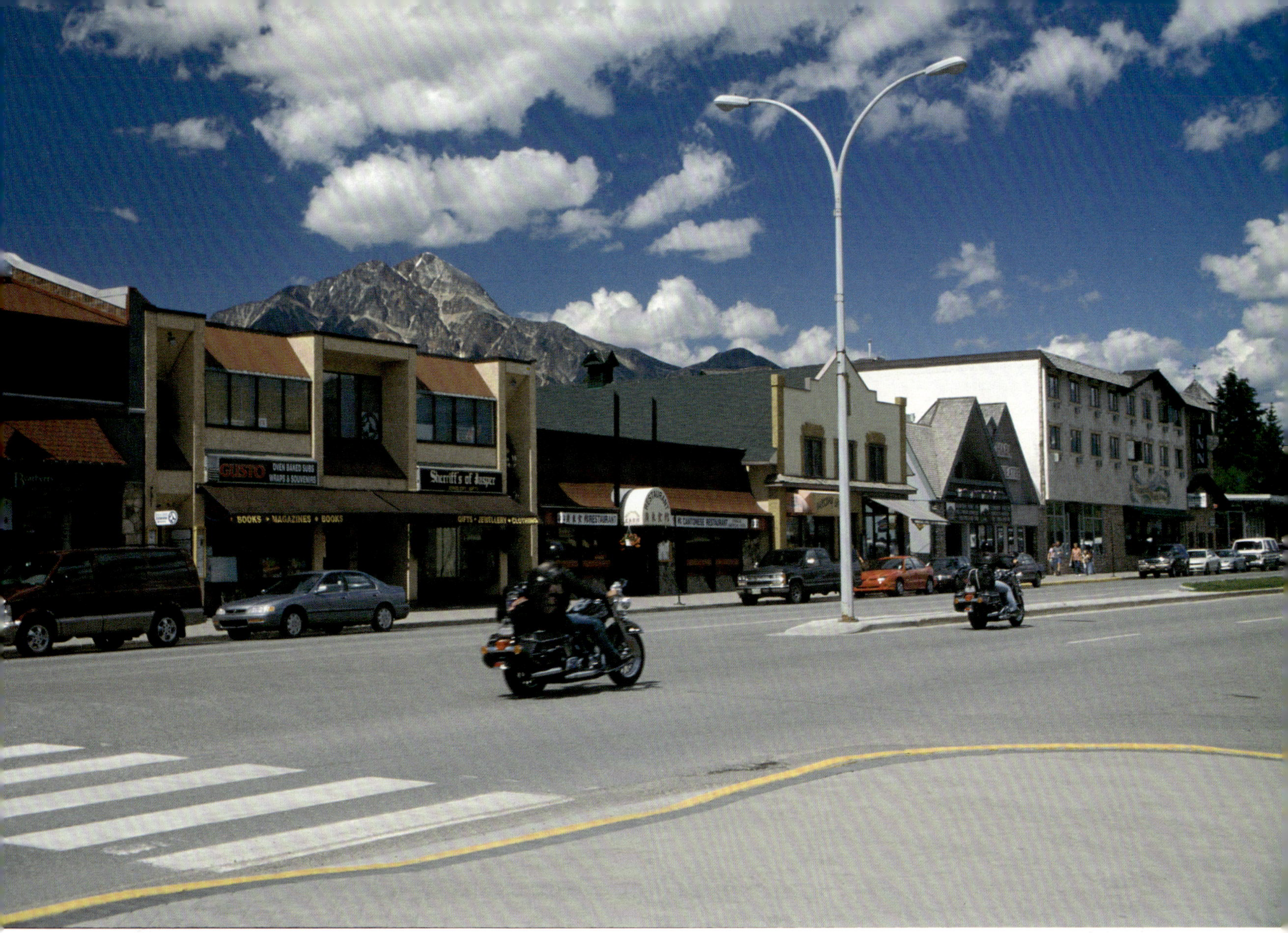

In Forestry Inspector W. N. Millar's 1915 image, a pack train approaches Jasper's main street, Connaught Drive, where it makes a long sweeping turn running from the south to the west as it parallels the Grand Trunk Railroad running through the village. Dominion Land Surveyor H. Matheson made the first street survey in 1913, and the same year the Dominion Parks Branch built its distinctive "boulder bungalow" administration building, providing a model for many other rustic building features in Canada's national parks. The development of the newly surveyed townsite was set back due to the First World War, and until the 1930s, the absence of a road-link to Edmonton also proved an impediment. Although gas rationing in the Second World War initially limited road use, visits to Jasper began to increase dramatically after the completion of the Banff-Jasper Highway in 1939. The current Yellowhead Highway, linking Edmonton, Jasper, and the West Coast and providing a northern alternative to the Trans-Canada, was completed in 1968, ensuring year-round tourist access.[9]

10.6A ROAD TO THE CHURCH FROM JASPER PARK, ALBERTA, 1925 (JOHN BOYD, LIBRARY ARCHIVES CANADA PA 87189)

10.6B PYRAMID AVENUE, TOWN OF JASPER, JULY 1999 (CW 1999-07A-26)

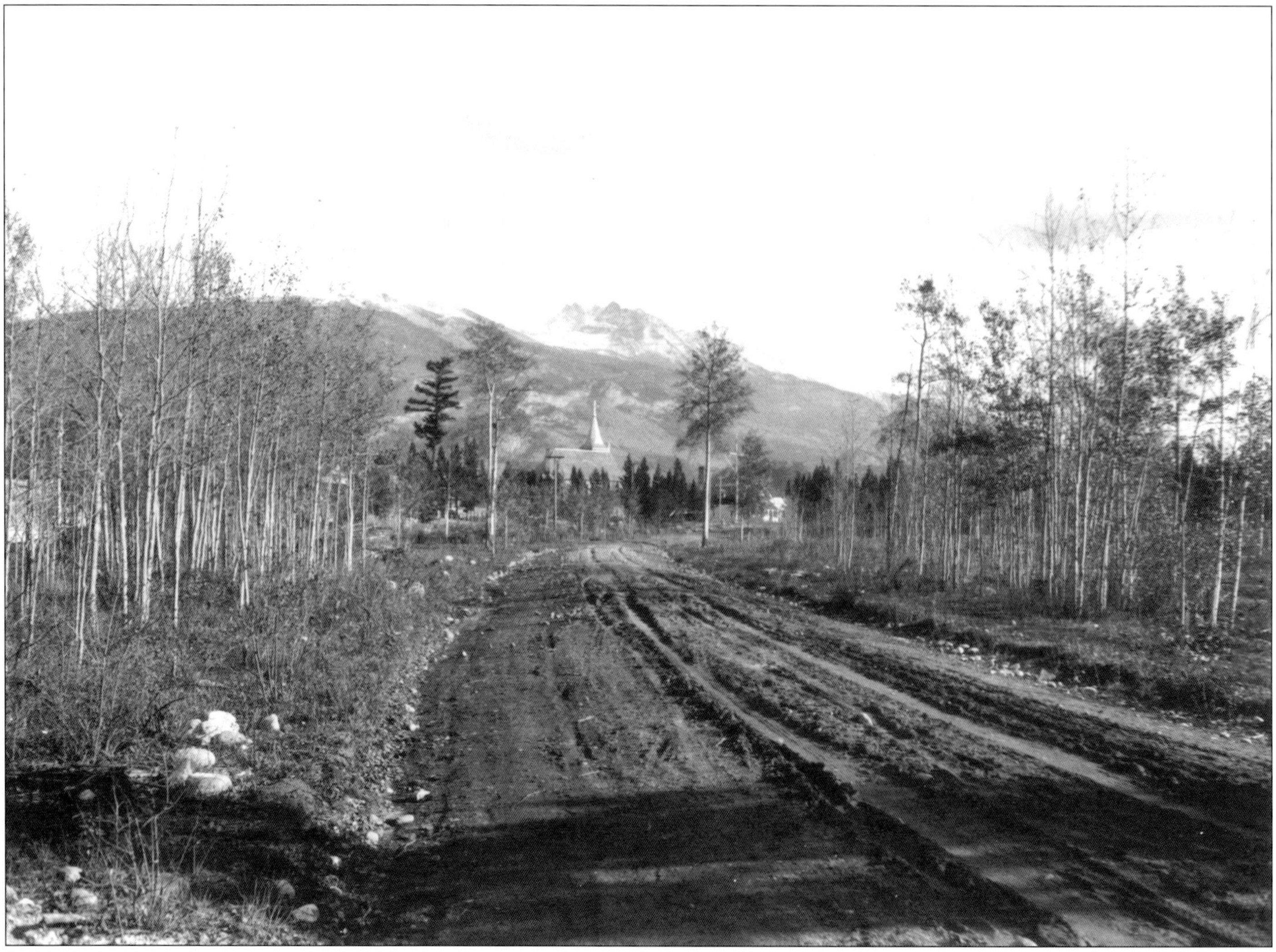

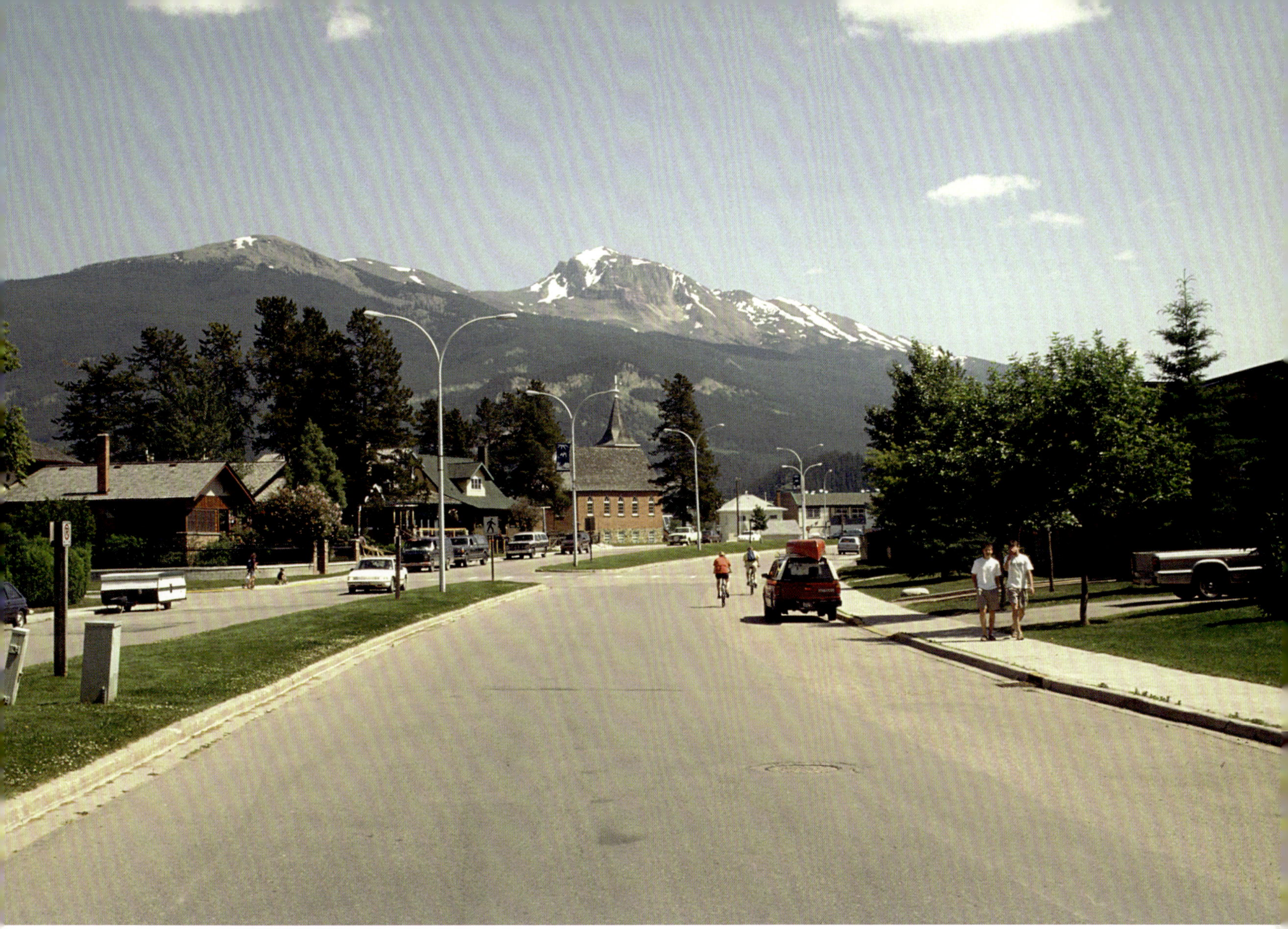

Given its later establishment and more remote location, Jasper's development history was very different from that of its southern neighbour, Banff. In the years before the First World War, Superintendent Colonel Maynard Rogers attempted to provide an infrastructure of services and roads with scant government appropriations, work that almost entirely ground to a halt with the declaration of war in 1914. In the post-war reconstruction period funds were equally scarce so that by the mid-1920s Jasper still remained underdeveloped. However, its late blooming did allow for the Park Branch's new Town Planning Division to carry out work that would make the final result very pleasing. In the 1925 view Pyramid Avenue, framing the 1924 Our Lady of Lourdes Roman Catholic Church (but now owned by the Lutheran congregation) was still a mud road, but its broad character, contributing to the more open feeling of the community compared to Banff, is already evident.[10]

10.7A RETURNING FROM MALIGNE CANYON, SIR ARTHUR CONAN DOYLE PARTY, 1914
(W. J. TOPLEY STUDIO, LIBRARY ARCHIVES CANADA PA 11159)

10.7B ENTRANCE TO JASPER PARK LODGE AND MT. EDITH CAVELL, JULY 2003 (CW 2003-07N-11)

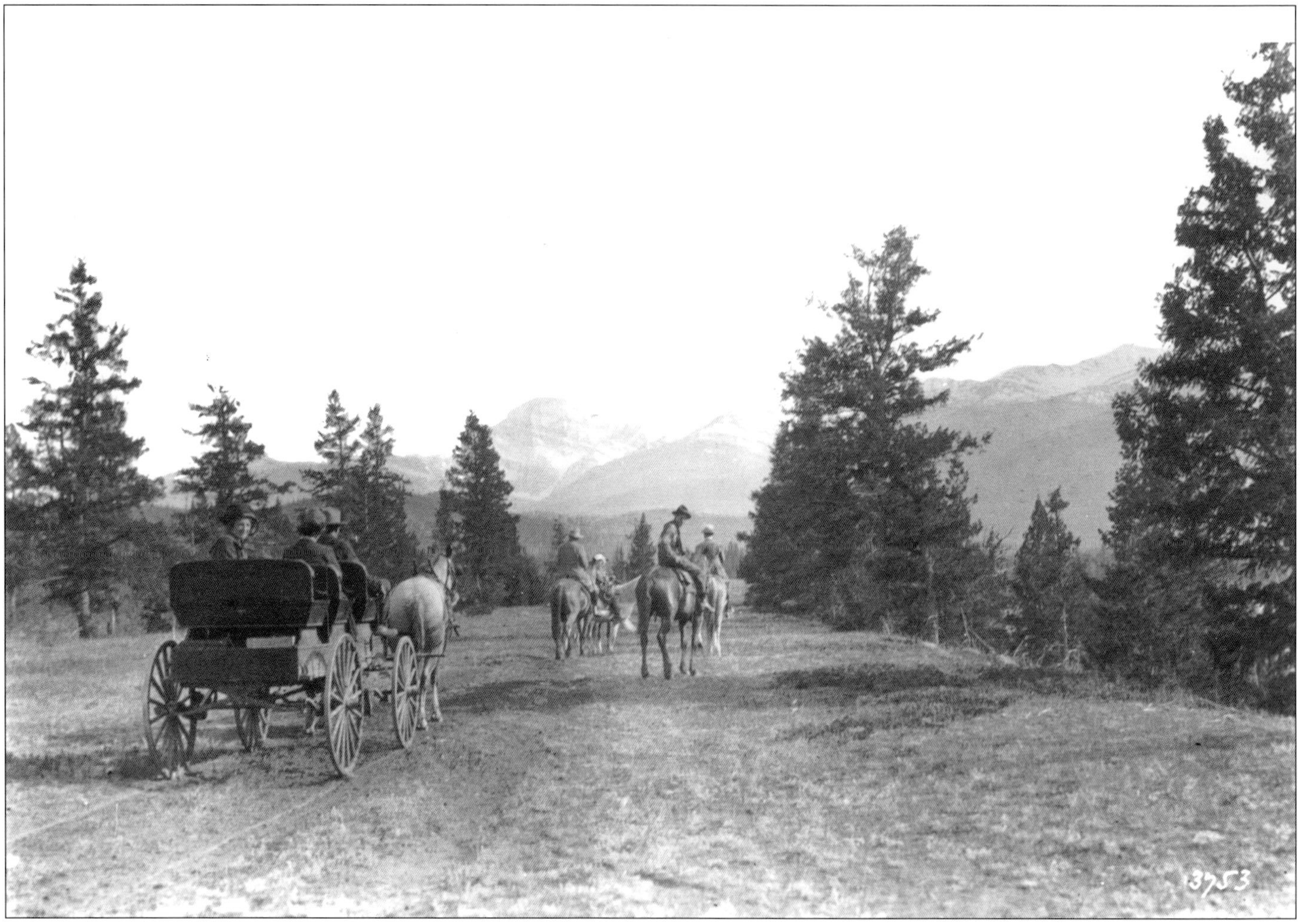

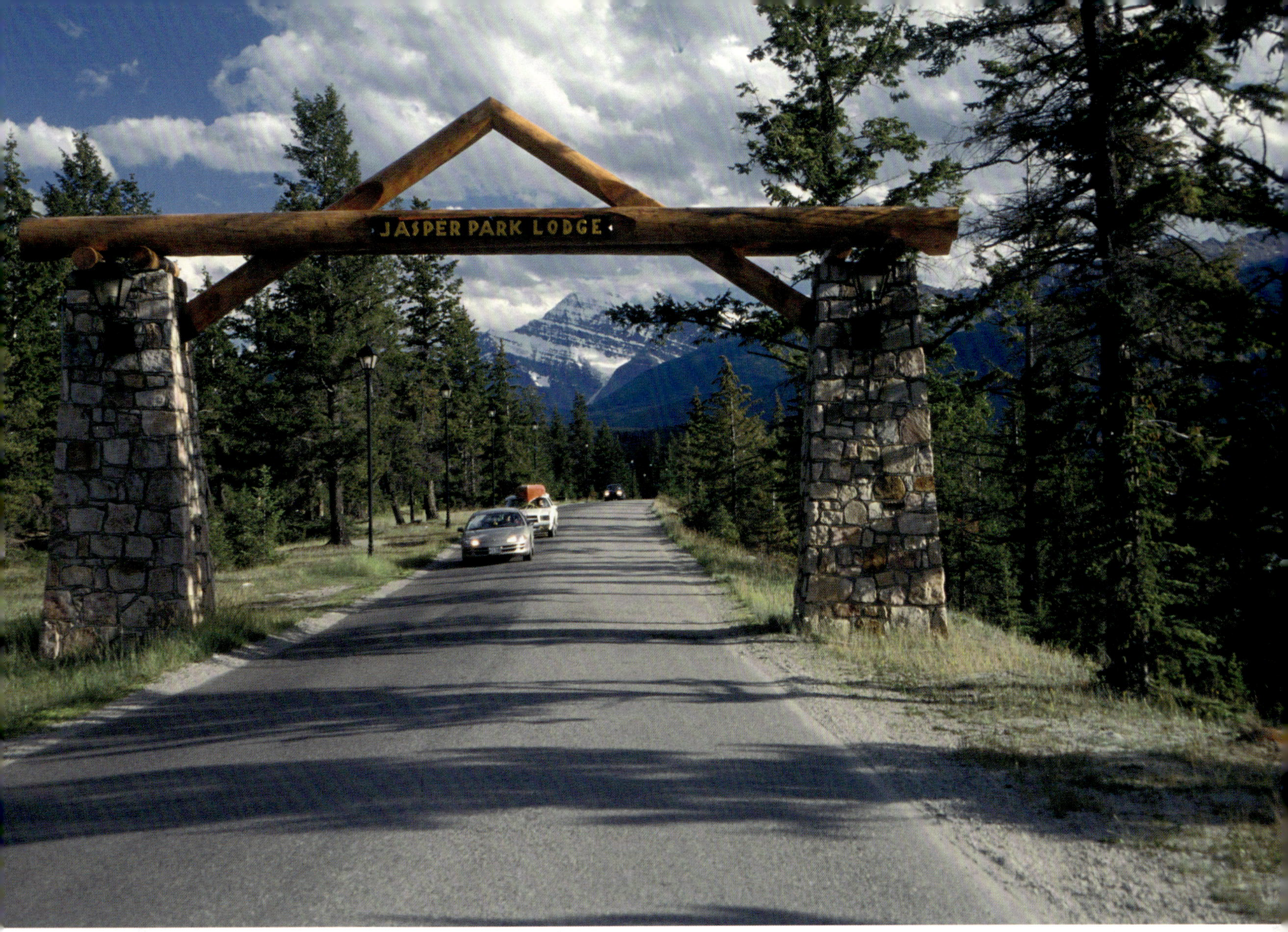

An early task for Jasper's administrators was to build trails to nearby attractions, requiring a bridge across the Athabasca. A wooden bridge at Old Fort Point was completed by 1913, and a section of the historic trail connecting to Athabasca Pass was improved to take visitors to view the wonders of Maligne Canyon, five kilometres to the east. With some scenic trails built, the next major task of the Parks Branch and the railroad companies was to entice visitors to the park. To advertise its wonders, in 1914 the Government of Canada invited Sir Arthur Conan Doyle, author of the popular *Sherlock Holmes* detective series, to visit the area. It also contracted W. J. Topley, a professional photographer from Ottawa, to document the promotional group's forays to Jasper's attractions of the day. Doyle later wrote a poem to "the packer and the packhorse on the Athabasca Trail," commemorating his experiences on these outings, and while in Jasper he laid the cornerstone for its Anglican Church and scouted out a location for a golf course.[11]

Today, the road to Jasper Park Lodge follows the old Athabasca Pass Trail. Mount Edith Cavell is framed in the entrance archway to the hotel's grounds. The mountain, an important landmark for the fur brigades, was originally known as "La Montagne de la Grande Traverse." It loomed over the point where the trail left the Athabasca Valley to ascend the Whirlpool River to cross the continental divide. In 1916 the mountain was officially named to commemorate Edith Cavell, the British nurse shot for helping prisoners of war escape German-occupied Belgium.[12]

10.8A TENT CITY NEAR JASPER, CA. 1915 (JASPER PARK LODGE COLLECTION, JASPER YELLOWHEAD PA 21-2)

10.8B OLD MAN MOUNTAIN AND JASPER PARK LODGE, 1920s (CANADIAN NATIONAL RAILWAYS, JASPER YELLOWHEAD PA 21-35)

10.8C JASPER PARK LODGE AND LAC BEAUVERT, JUNE 2004 (CW 2004-06C-17)

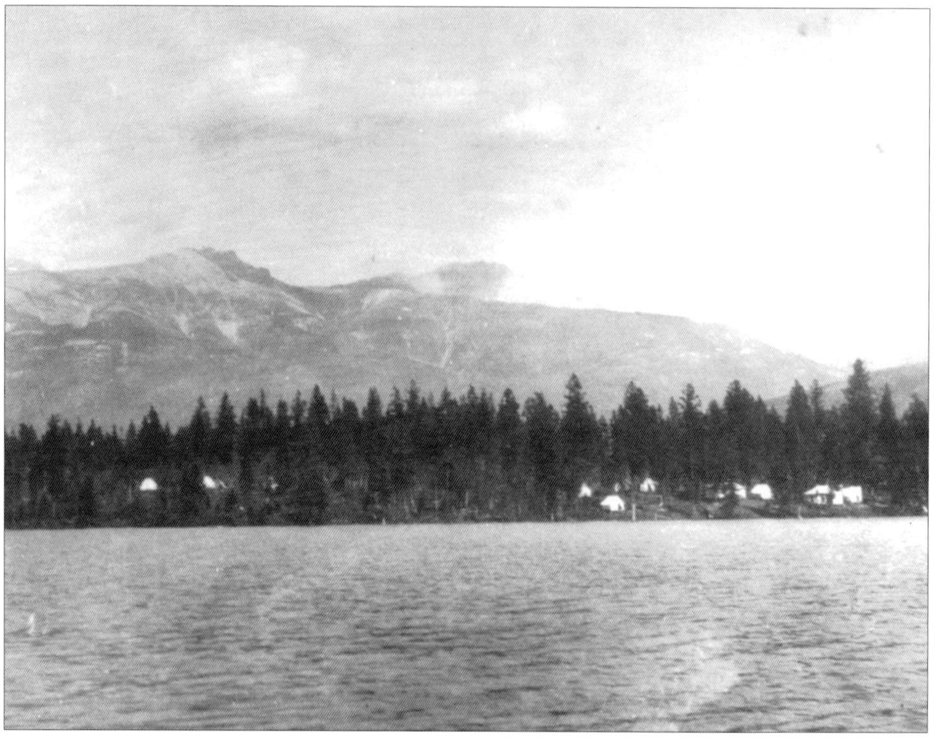

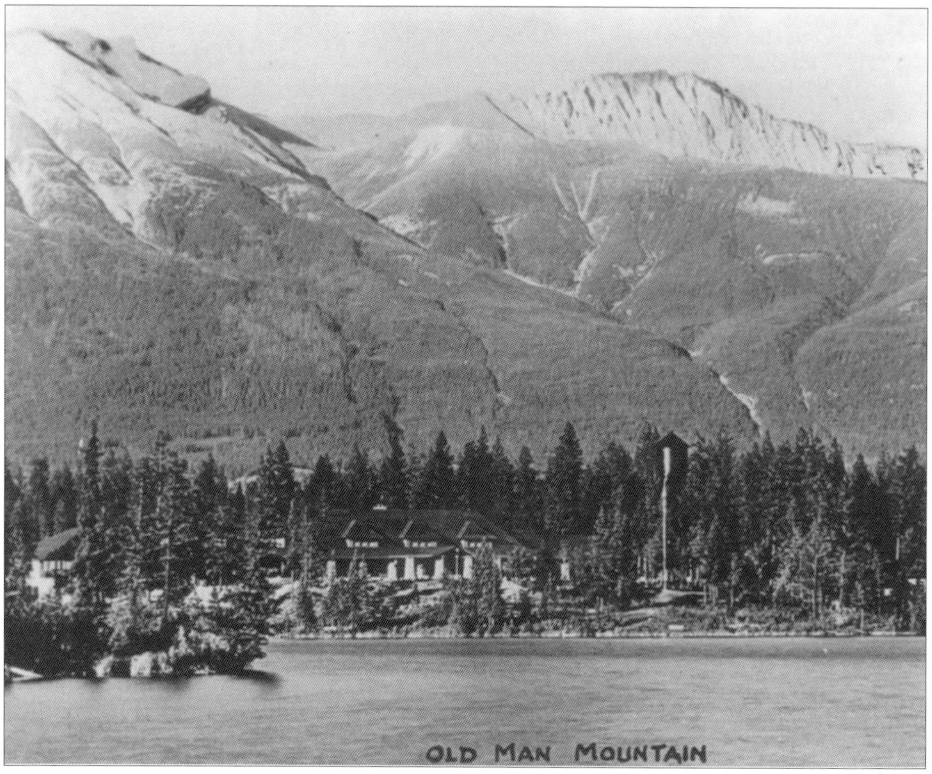

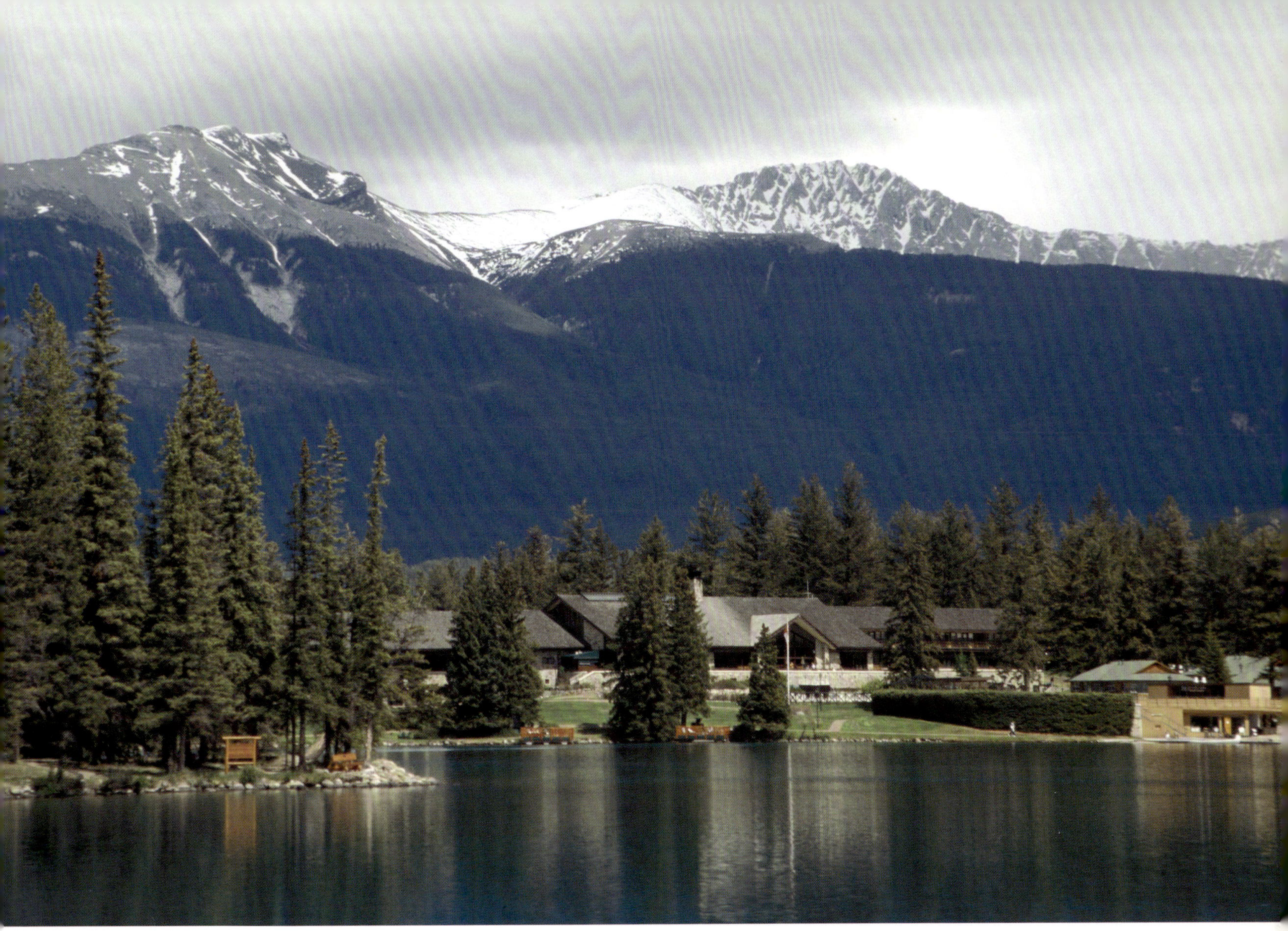

As in Banff, the railroads through Jasper recognized the importance of tourism as a source of revenue. In 1911, Charles M. Hays, president of the Grand Trunk Pacific Railway, applied to the Department of the Interior for "the exclusive privileges of constructing and operating hotels and supplying transportation facilities for passengers through and over roads and trails in the Jasper Park Government Reserve."[13]

Foremost in the company's plans was the construction of the luxury "Chateau Miette," rivalling the Banff Springs Hotel, to be located on the railway near the trail accessing the Miette Hot Springs. With the failure of these plans and the onset of war, less grandiose schemes had to be pursued, and in 1915 Fred and Jack Brewster worked with Robert Kenneth, president of the Alberta Tent and Mattress Company, to build a temporary tent-camp on the shore of Lake Beauvert on the trail from Jasper to Maligne Canyon. In 1915 the company advertised, "During the coming summer, Jasper Alta. is expected to become the central and popular resort in the wonderful Jasper Park, on the line of the Grand Trunk Pacific Railroad in the Canadian Rockies.... Preparatory to the building of the proposed Grand Trunk Pacific hotels in the Mountain territory, accommodation this year will be provided by the erection of a tent city. The sleeping tents will contain floorboards and will be equipped and furnished with comfortable beds and all the accessories that go to make up a modern bedroom."[14]

10.9A THE BUNGALOWS, JASPER PARK LODGE, CA. 1927 (F. H. SLARK, WHYTE NA 66-2418)

10.9B JASPER PARK LODGE, JULY 2003 (CW 2003-07G-10)

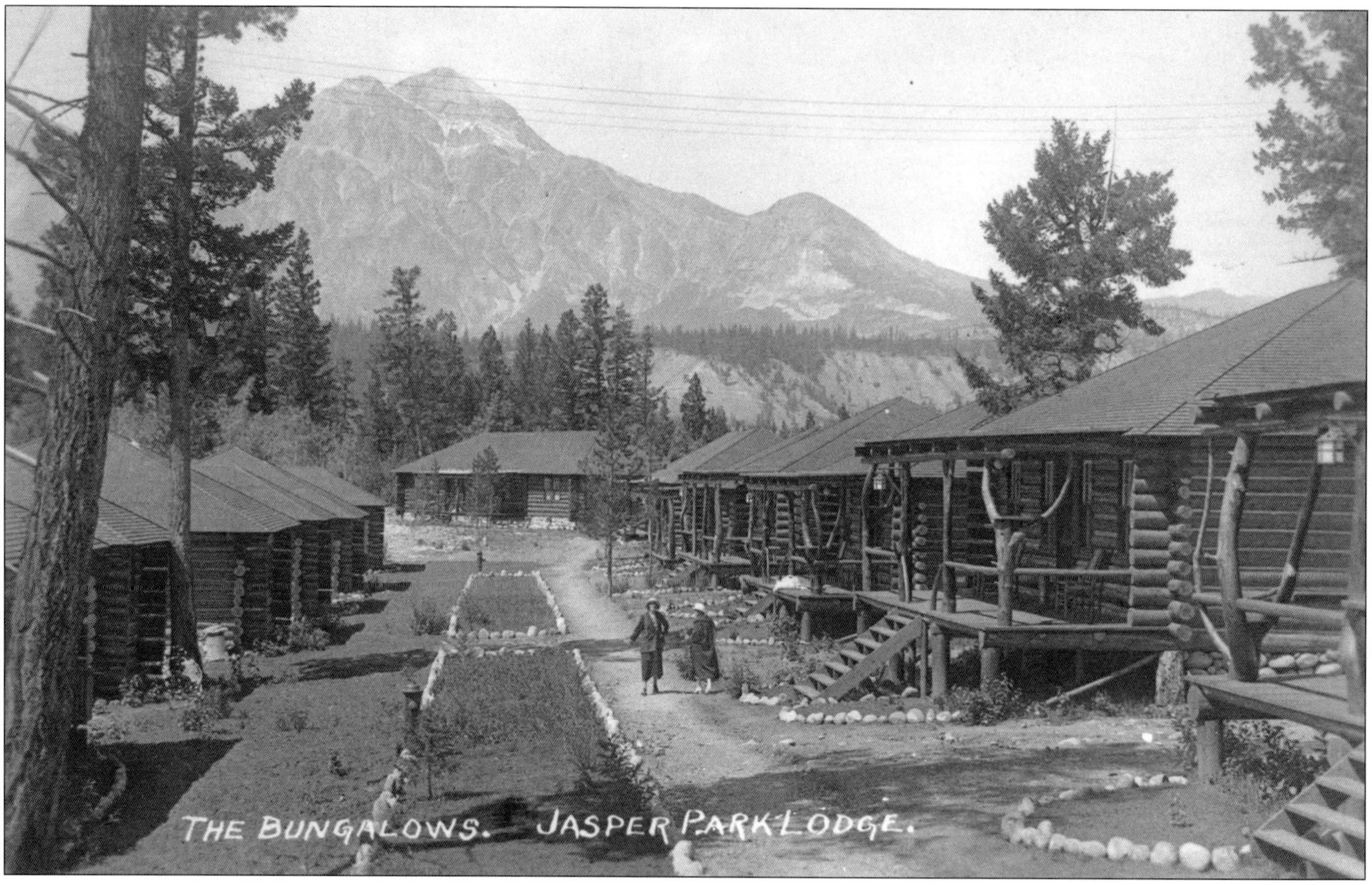

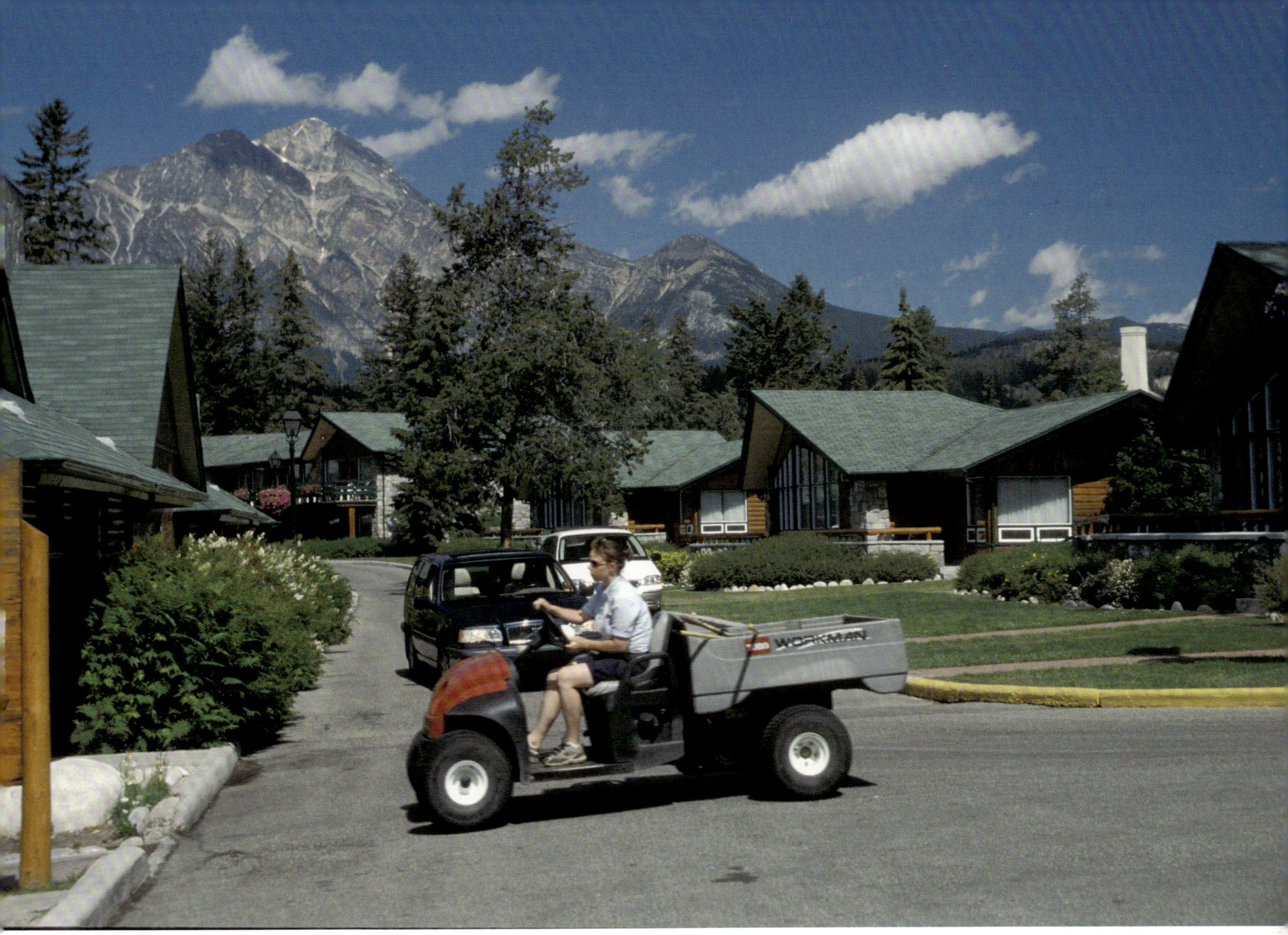

In the winter of 1922–23, Sir Henry Thornton, president of the newly established Canadian National Railways, headed the development of the Jasper Park Lodge on the site of "Tent City." From the beginning the motif of the hotel was rustic, more integrated with its natural setting than the castle and chateau designs of Canadian Pacific's hotels in Banff and Lake Louise. When completed, the main structure of the Lodge was touted as the largest single-floor log building in the world. In July 1952 a fire destroyed the original central log building, but remaining true to the design tradition, Canadian National Hotels replaced the lodge with a large, single-storey building blending in well with the attractions of nearby Lake Beauvert. In the tradition of the rustic atmosphere of "Tent City," Jasper Park Lodge also provided accommodations in individual log bungalows, laid out like a long village street curving around the lakeshore, complete with lamps and gardens. One of the unique features in the operation of this design was the use of bicycles, and uniformed waiters balancing a room service tray while they pedalled to their assignment made for an interesting experience.

The rebuilding program after the 1952 fire left the cabin motif intact. With constant upgrading it has continued to add a special historic flavour to a stay at Jasper Park Lodge, now owned and operated by Fairmont Hotels & Resorts. Today, instead of using bicycles, staff use golf carts to provide room service to the cabins, and to maintain the hotel's extensive grounds.[15]

10.10A SKI JUMPING ON THE WHISTLERS SKI HILL, JASPER, CA. 1960
(HARRY ROWED, DORIS KENSIT COLLECTION, JASPER YELLOWHEAD 994.45.135)

10.10B FOREST COVER ON ABANDONED SKI RUNS ABOVE WHISTLERS HOSTEL, JASPER, FEBRUARY 2004 (CW 2004-02D-21)

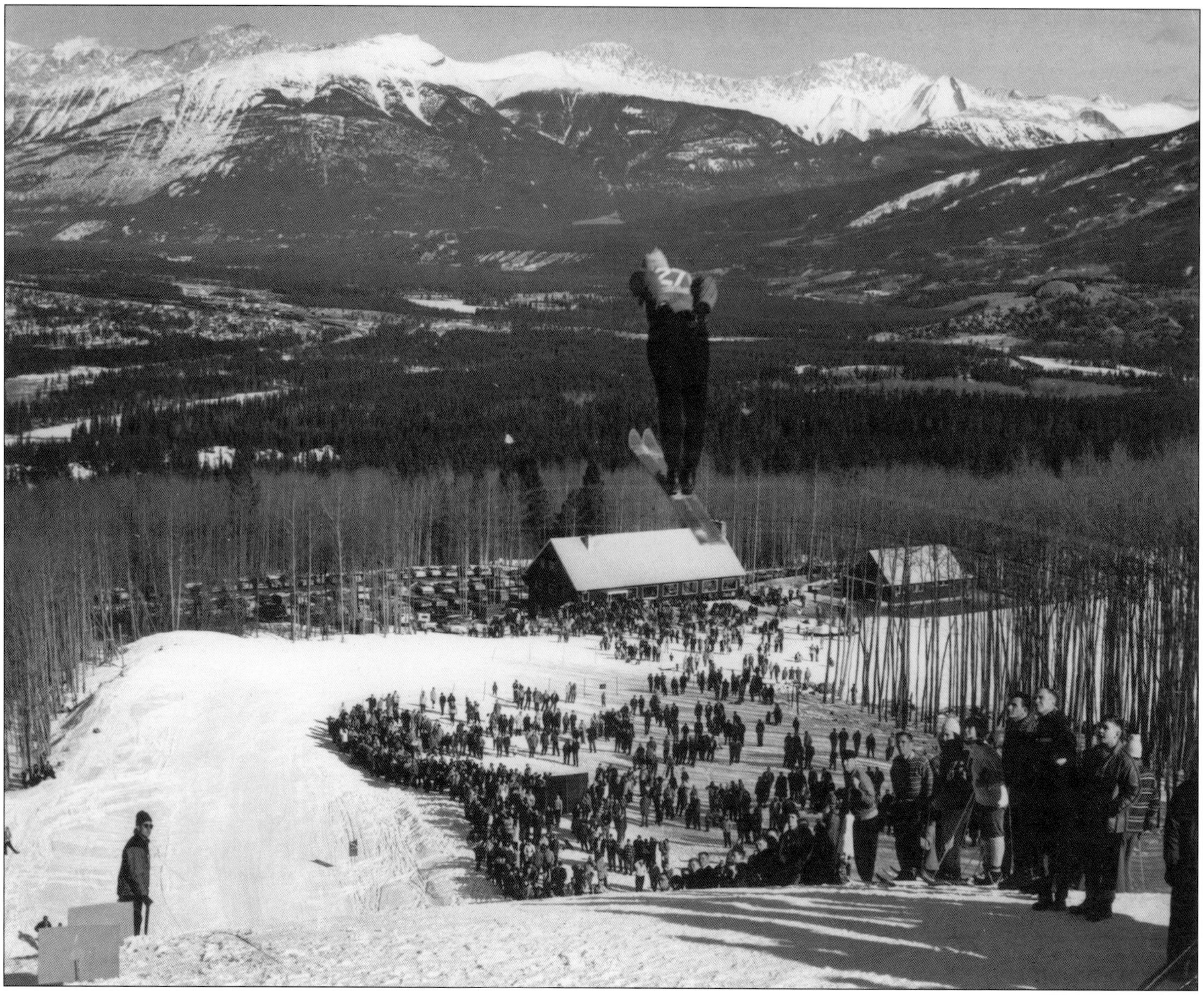

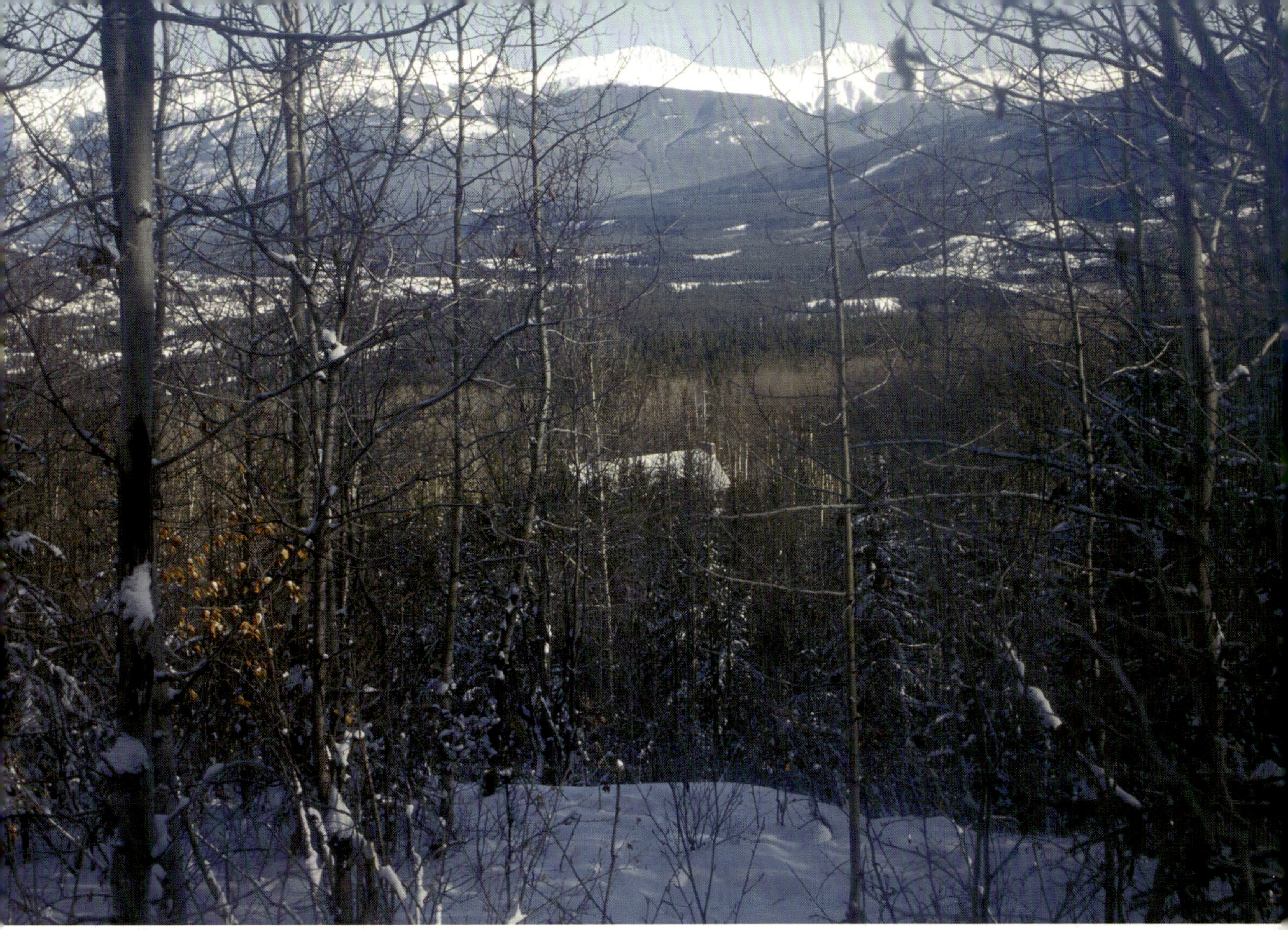

The first ski area to be developed at Jasper beginning in the mid-1930s was at The Whistlers, southwest of the town, although permanent facilities and a lodge were not constructed until after the Second World War. Beginning in the 1950s the development of the nearby Marmot Basin began to overshadow the area, and although it was used for competitions into the early 1960s, such as the ski jumping seen in the earlier view, Whistlers Hill was soon abandoned. The original lodge was transformed into a hostel and the ski slopes quickly began to return to their more natural condition, as pictured in 2004. After only some forty years of forest growth, the hostel roofline is barely visible through the heavy vegetation[16]

10.11A ON ROAD TO PYRAMID LAKE, JASPER NATIONAL PARK, 1914 (W. J. TOPLEY STUDIO, LIBRARY ARCHIVES CANADA PA 11068)

10.11B PYRAMID LAKE ROAD LOOKING EAST, JULY 1999 (CW 1999-07A-17)

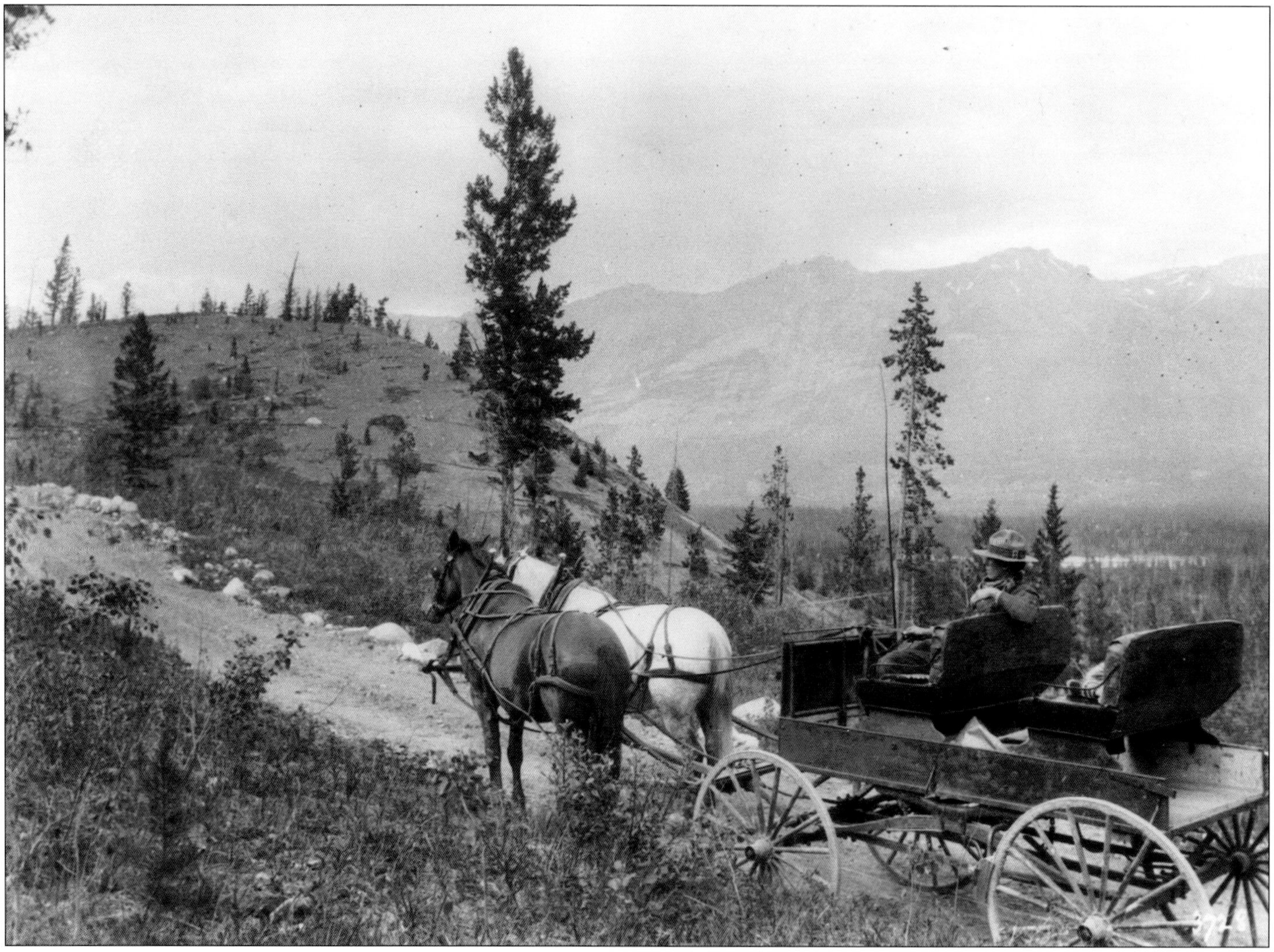

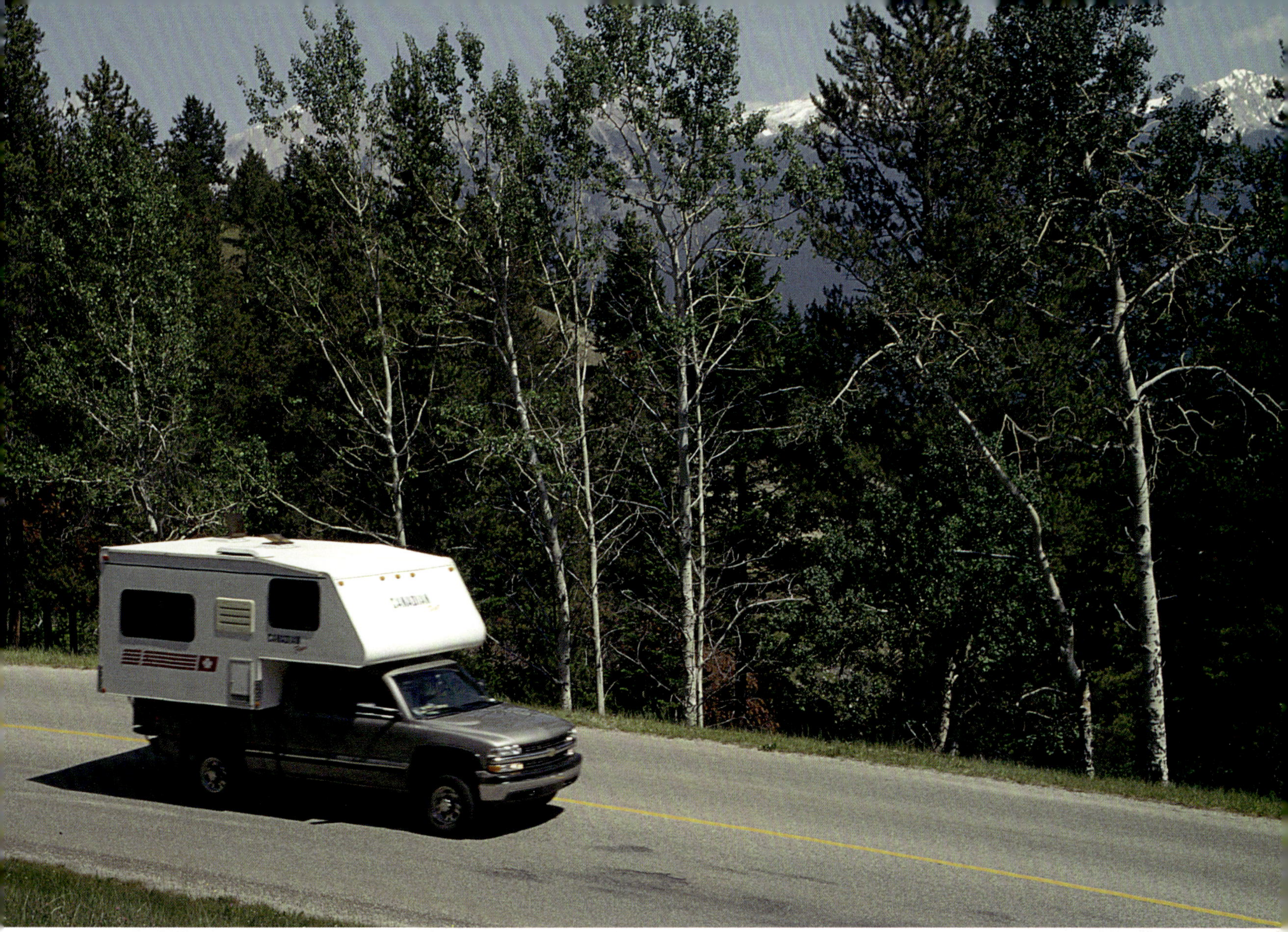

Forest fire researcher Gerald Tande used fire-scarred tree growth-rings to develop a chronology of fires for the last four hundred years in the Athabasca Valley near Jasper. Along this section of the Pyramid Lake Road he produced a history that speaks to the frequency and intensity of fires, dating them to 1678, 1714, 1727, 1758*, 1780, 1797, 1807, 1834, 1837, 1847*, 1858, 1861, 1869, 1878, 1889*, and 1905. The dates identified with an asterisk were large fires that swept across most of the valley, probably high-intensity burns that occurred during hot, dry summers. The other fires covered much smaller areas and likely occurred in the spring with lower flame lengths.[17]

The 1914 view shows the pattern of vegetation resulting from this mixture of frequent low-intensity fires interspersed with periodic hot burns. A few large, thick-barked Douglas fir, veterans of many fires, dot the landscape. Lodgepole pine and trembling aspen remain in shrubby form due to frequent burns. Since the last fire in 1905 a dense forest has grown here, but if a future wildfire occurs in the summer, likely all trees will be killed due to the abundant fuels.[18]

10.12A YELLOWSTONE ELK RELEASED NEAR THE TOWN OF JASPER, 1920 (PHOTOGRAPHER UNKNOWN, JASPER YELLOWHEAD 84.32.280)

10.12B COTTONWOOD SLOUGH AND PYRAMID MOUNTAIN, 2004 (CW 2004-02B-11)

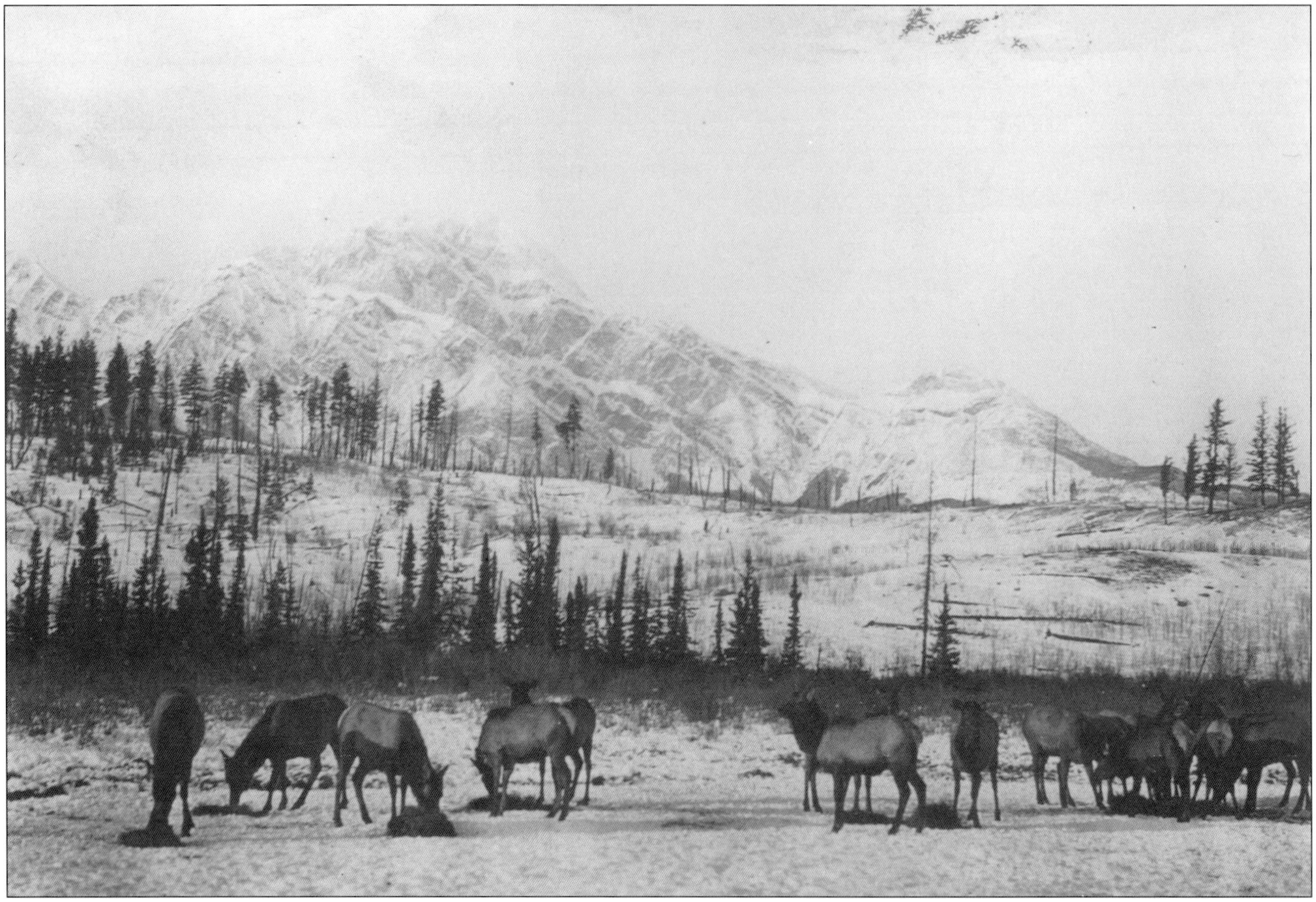

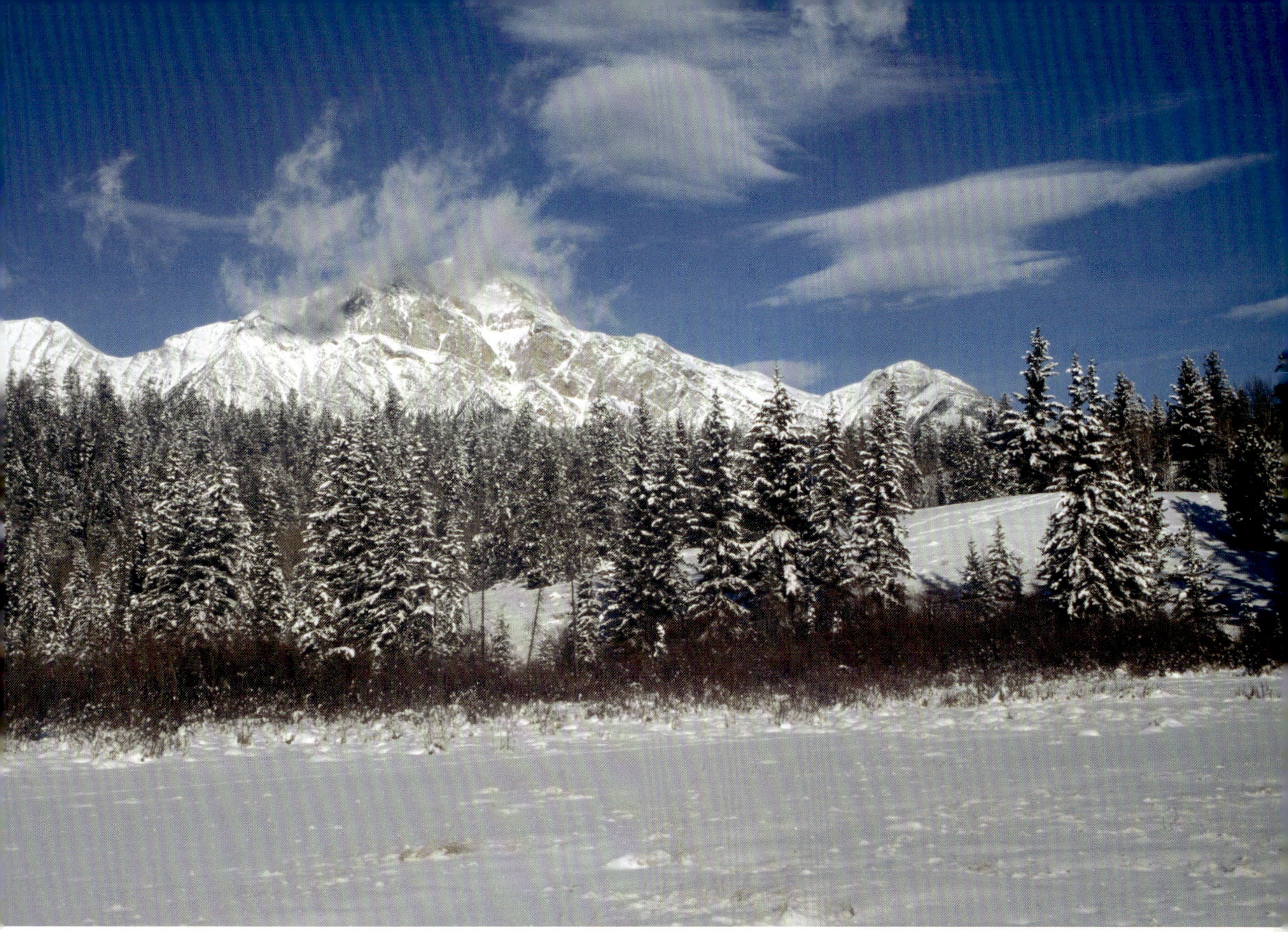

First Nations often burned montane areas in the valley bottoms, such as those near the towns of Jasper and Banff. Although frequent burning created ideal habitat, elk numbers were historically low due to the effects of hunting by humans, wolves, and other predators. In fact, with additional hunting pressure from early white settlers, elk had nearly disappeared from the Canadian Rockies by 1900.[19] Between 1917 and 1920 surplus elk from Yellowstone National Park were made available to Canada by the U.S. National Parks Service and were brought by rail to Banff and Jasper. The first animals delivered to Banff were kept in the animal enclosure over the winter, but they fared so well that subsequent releases were carried out at several locations in the park near the railway line. The 1920 photograph shows the first animals brought to Jasper feeding on hay immediately after their arrival.[20]

With the removal of First Nations from the parks, and predator control programs that continued until the 1960s, elk soon became overly abundant. The warden service culled elk herds from the 1940s until the late 1960s, but thereafter began to restore the roles of non-human predators, such as wolves and cougars, in reducing elk numbers. However, due to modern human effects on predators, and the removal of First Nations hunting, elk numbers are currently higher than long-term conditions in many areas, and the abundance of highly palatable shrubs is declining. Young aspen stems and willow were abundant in the historic photograph of Cottonwood Slough, but the 2004 photograph shows that aspen and willow cover is now low due to intense browsing combined with fire suppression.[21]

10.13A ARTHUR CONAN DOYLE PARTY AT MALIGNE CANYON, ALBERTA, 1914 (W. J. TOPLEY STUDIO, LIBRARY ARCHIVES CANADA PA 11183)

10.13B MALIGNE CANYON INTERPRETIVE TRAIL, JULY 2003 (CW 2003-07N-20)

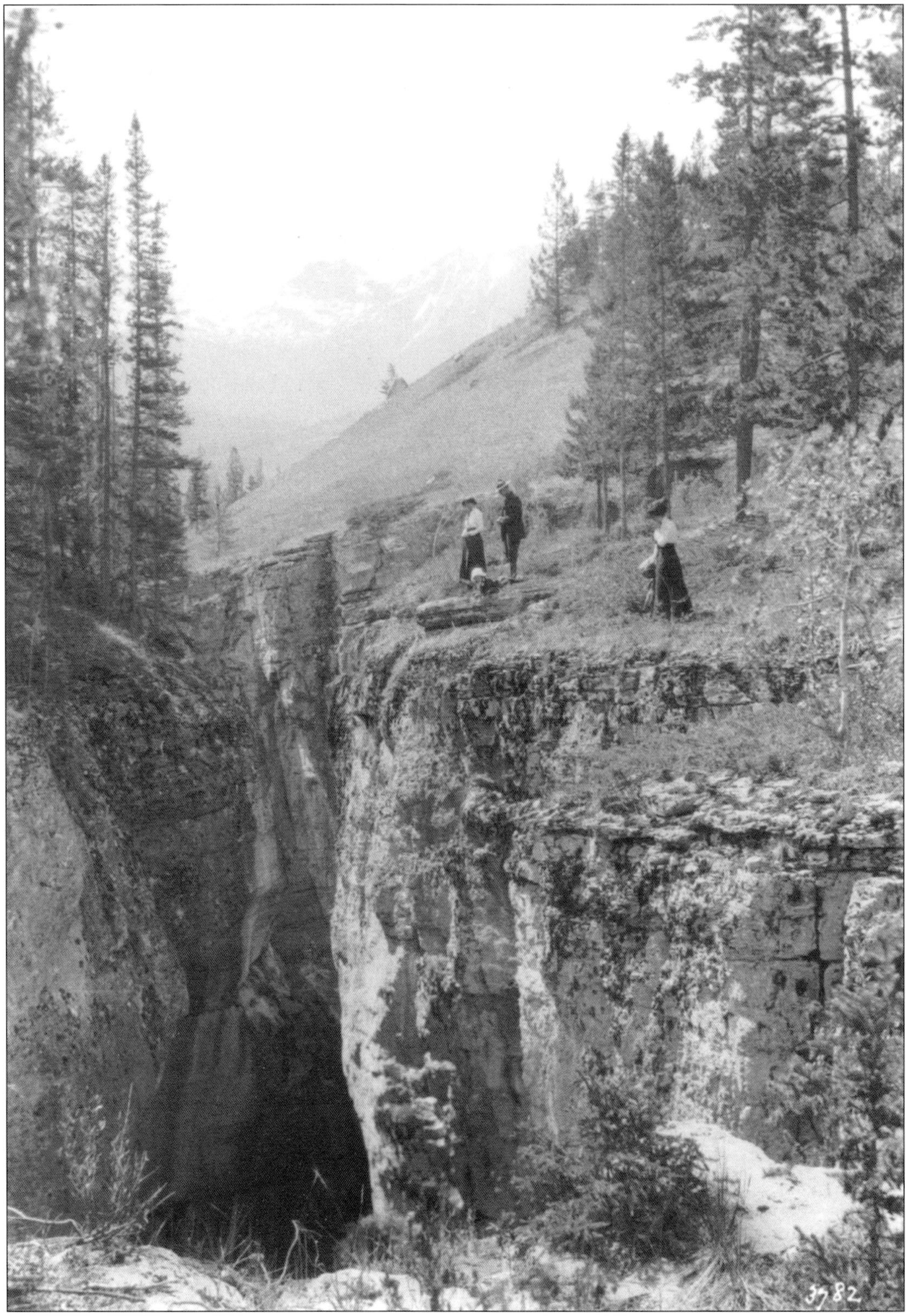

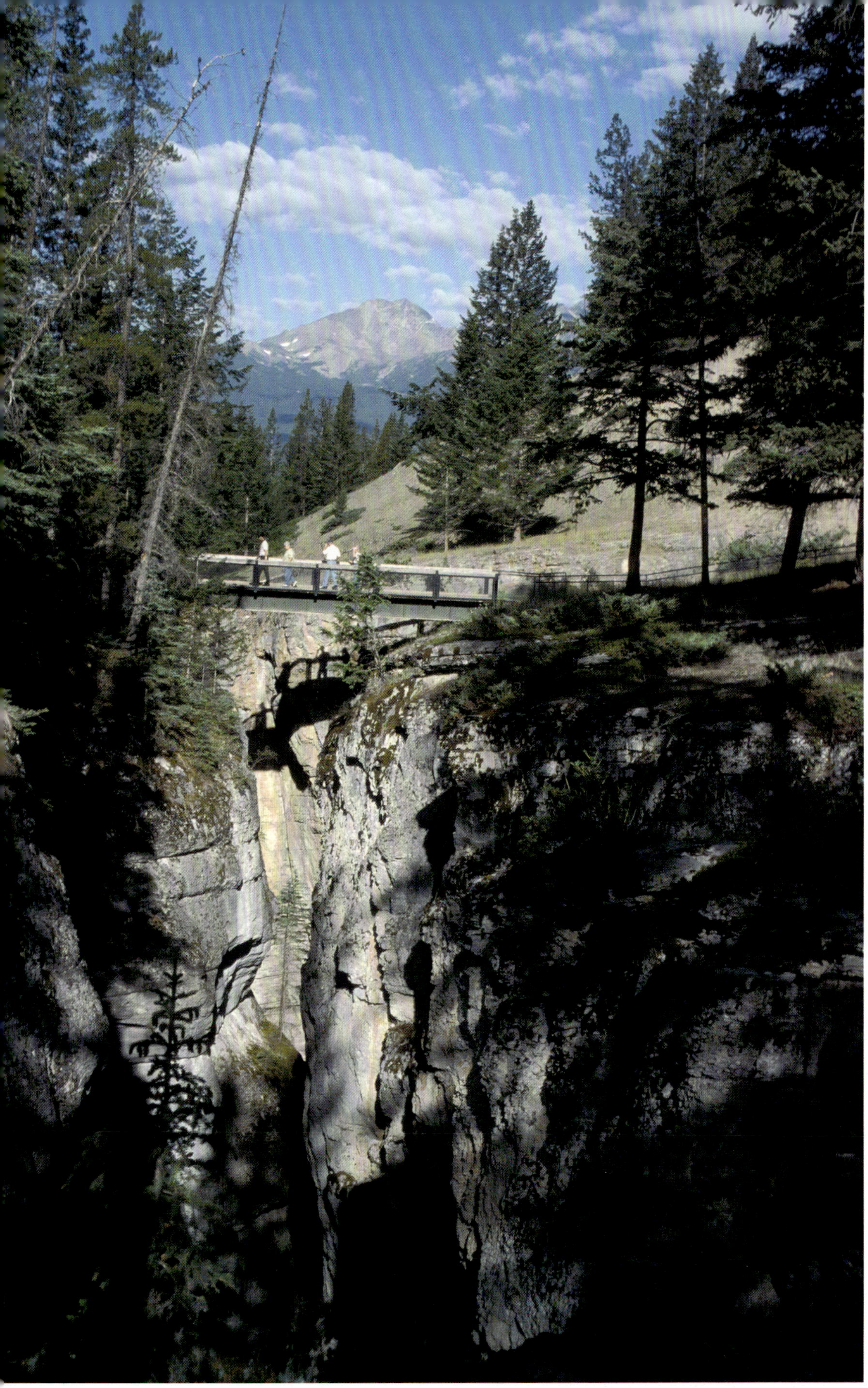

"Any other canyon is like a crack in a teapot." (Visitor to Maligne Canyon)[22]

Pleistocene glaciers carved the Athabasca Valley deep, leaving the Maligne River drainage perched some 150 metres higher than the main valley. When the last glacier retreated, it left morainal deposits that blocked an older valley to the southwest. The Maligne River found a new route through narrow limestone fissures, cutting a canyon over fifty metres deep.

Historically, visitors to the canyon would reach it in a two-hour trip by horse-drawn carriage from Jasper. Today, thousands visit the canyon by means of a paved highway extending to Maligne Lake. However, the scene that greets them remains little changed from the days when the redoubtable author of *Sherlock Holmes* first visited in 1914.

10.14A MALIGNE LAKE AT THE NARROWS, CA. 1930 (BYRON HARMON, WHYTE V263 NA-1326)

10.14B SPIRIT ISLAND AND MALIGNE LAKE, 1996 (DOUGLAS LEIGHTON, LEIGHTON COLLECTION)

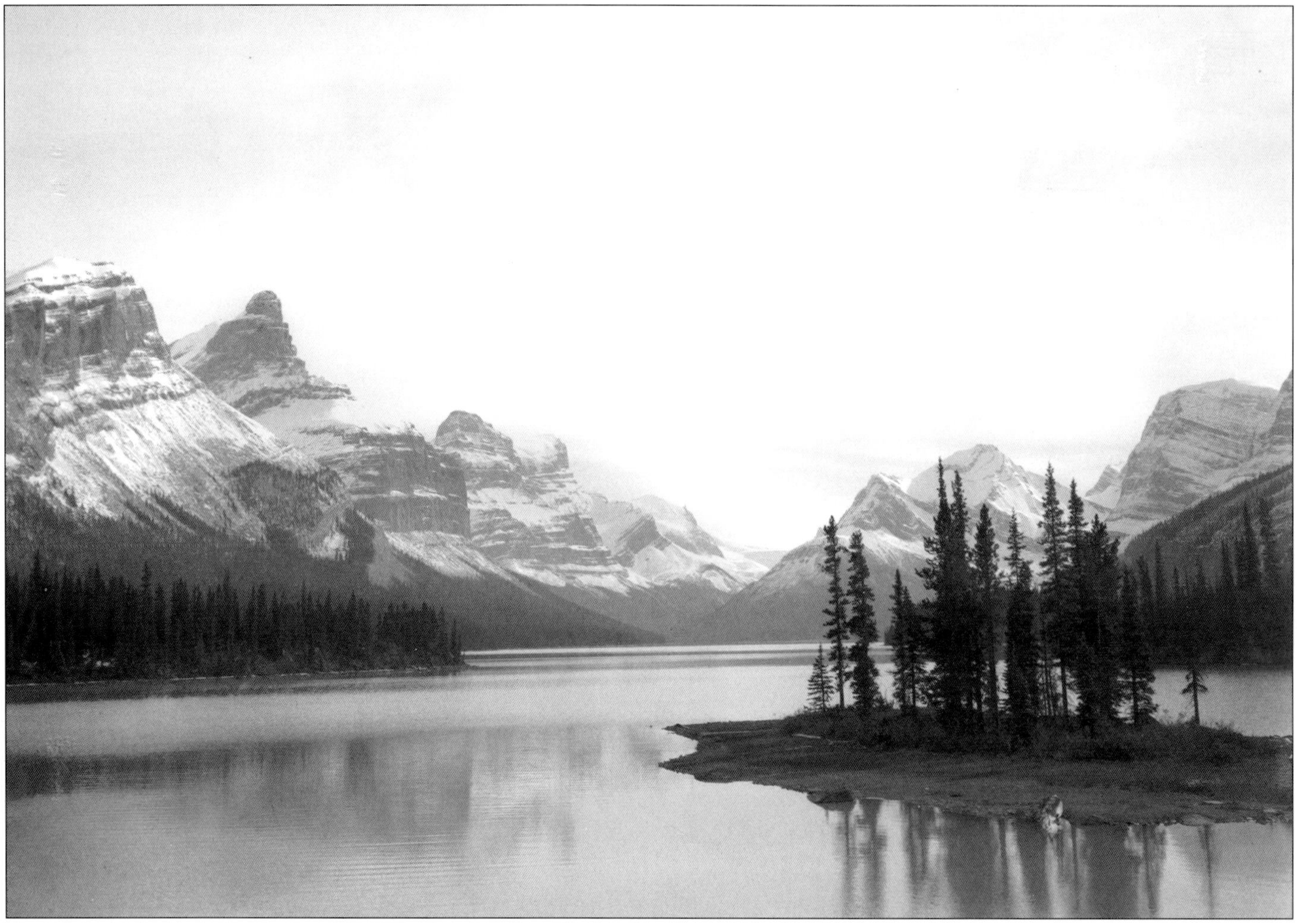

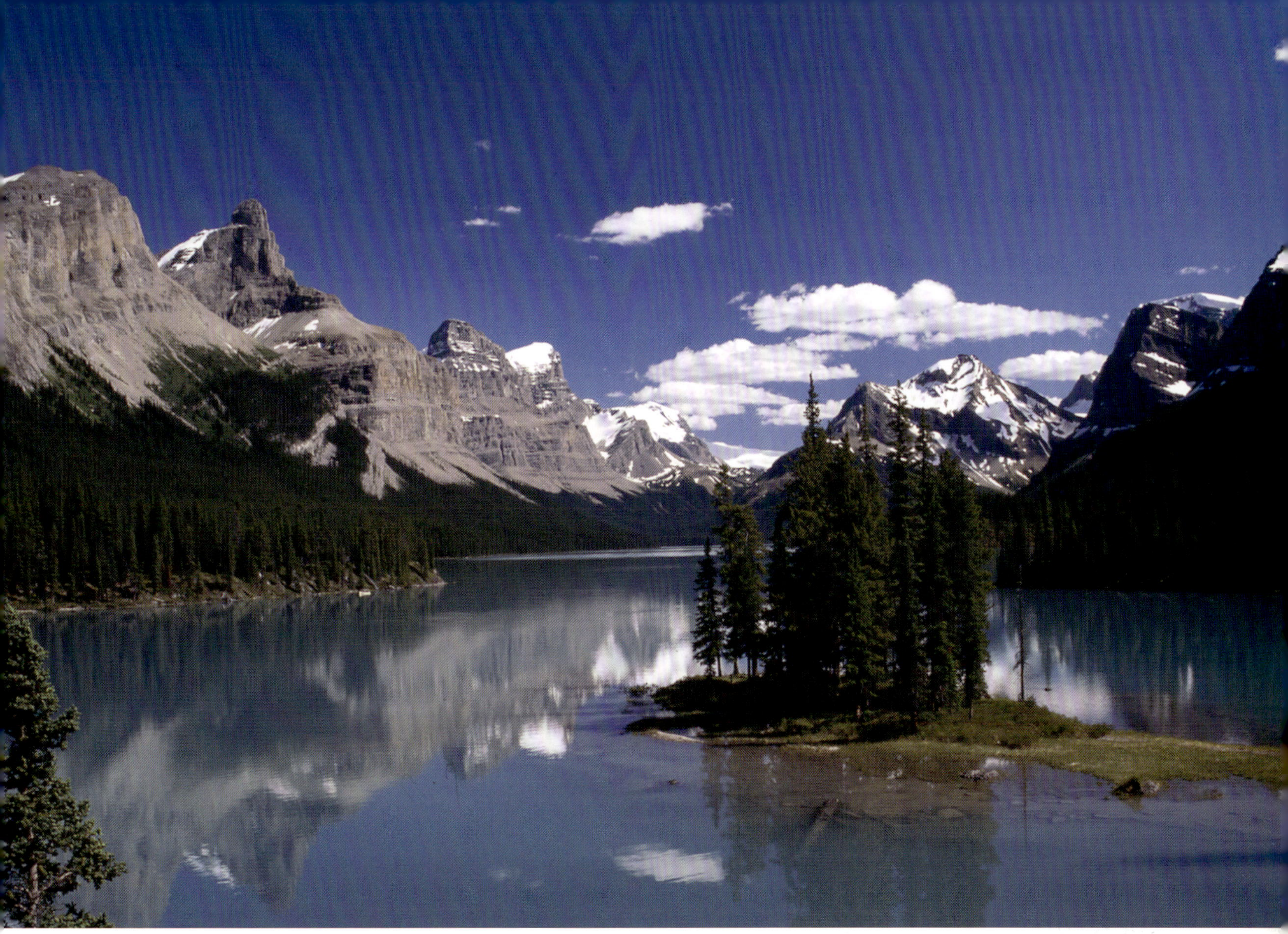

A high point of Mary Schäffer's summer-long expeditions north from Banff to visit the Athabasca Valley was her party's "discovery" of Maligne Lake. While at Kootenay Plains in the fall of 1907, she had spoken with Sampson Beaver, a well-travelled Nakoda hunter, who drew her a map showing the way to what he called "Chaba Imne," a beautiful lake to the northward that he had visited as a boy. Mrs. Schäffer decided that this lake would become her quest, and after a winter of planning and nearly a month on the trail, her expedition reached the mysterious lake on July 7, 1908. Building a rough log raft, the party voyaged up the lake until they reached the "Narrows," and "there burst upon us that which, all our company agreed, was the finest view any of us had ever beheld in the Rockies."[23] Although railway surveyor Henry McLeod had previously reached the lake, many of the geographic names in its vicinity, such as Mounts Unwin and Warren, bear witness to the 1907 trip. Long-time Jasper outfitter Curly Phillips began a tour boat service on the lake in the 1930s, and the site of the Narrows became one of the most famous locations for Canadian Rockies photographs.

Although in 1996 professional photographer Doug Leighton took his photograph from a slightly different viewpoint from Byron Harmon's classic view (probably due to increased forest cover), the rock and glacier-walled south end of Maligne Lake is little changed from Schäffer's time. This area has low lightning ignition occurrence. Further, because the upper reaches of the valley surrounding the lake do not provide a through travel route, and are too high in elevation to provide good habitat for many wildlife species, early Europeans, and likely First Nations, did not frequently travel or hunt here. Thus, the forests surrounding the lake had a low frequency of fires caused either by people or lightning. It appears unburned in both photographs.[24]

10.15A CANADIAN PACIFIC SURVEY AT JASPER HOUSE, 1871 (CHARLES HORETZKY, LIBRARY ARCHIVES CANADA PA 9173)

10.15B JASPER HOUSE NATIONAL HISTORIC SITE, FEBRUARY 2004 (CW 2004-02B-23)

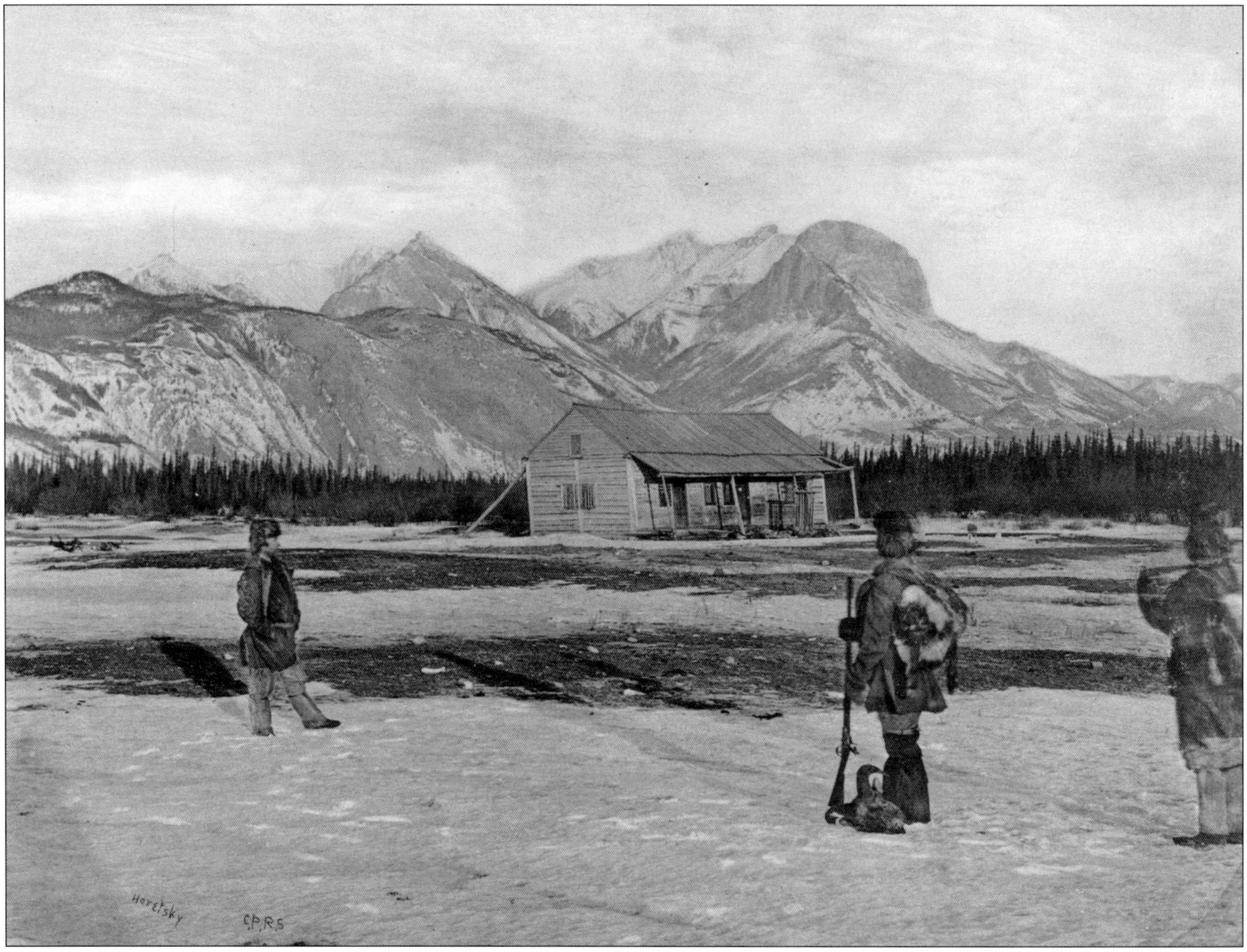

The location of Jasper on the historic fur trade route over Athabasca Pass made it the site for some of the earliest non-native structures in the Canadian Rockies. Horses to assist in carrying fur trade goods were initially kept at a "campment" or "house" at Henry House in the vicinity of the mouth of the Miette River, the farthest that boats could be taken up the Athabasca River. As well, a supply depot for the Columbia brigades was constructed on the northwestern shore of Brûlé Lake about 1813, and a decade later it was being referred to as "Jasper's House" in Governor Simpson's correspondence, a

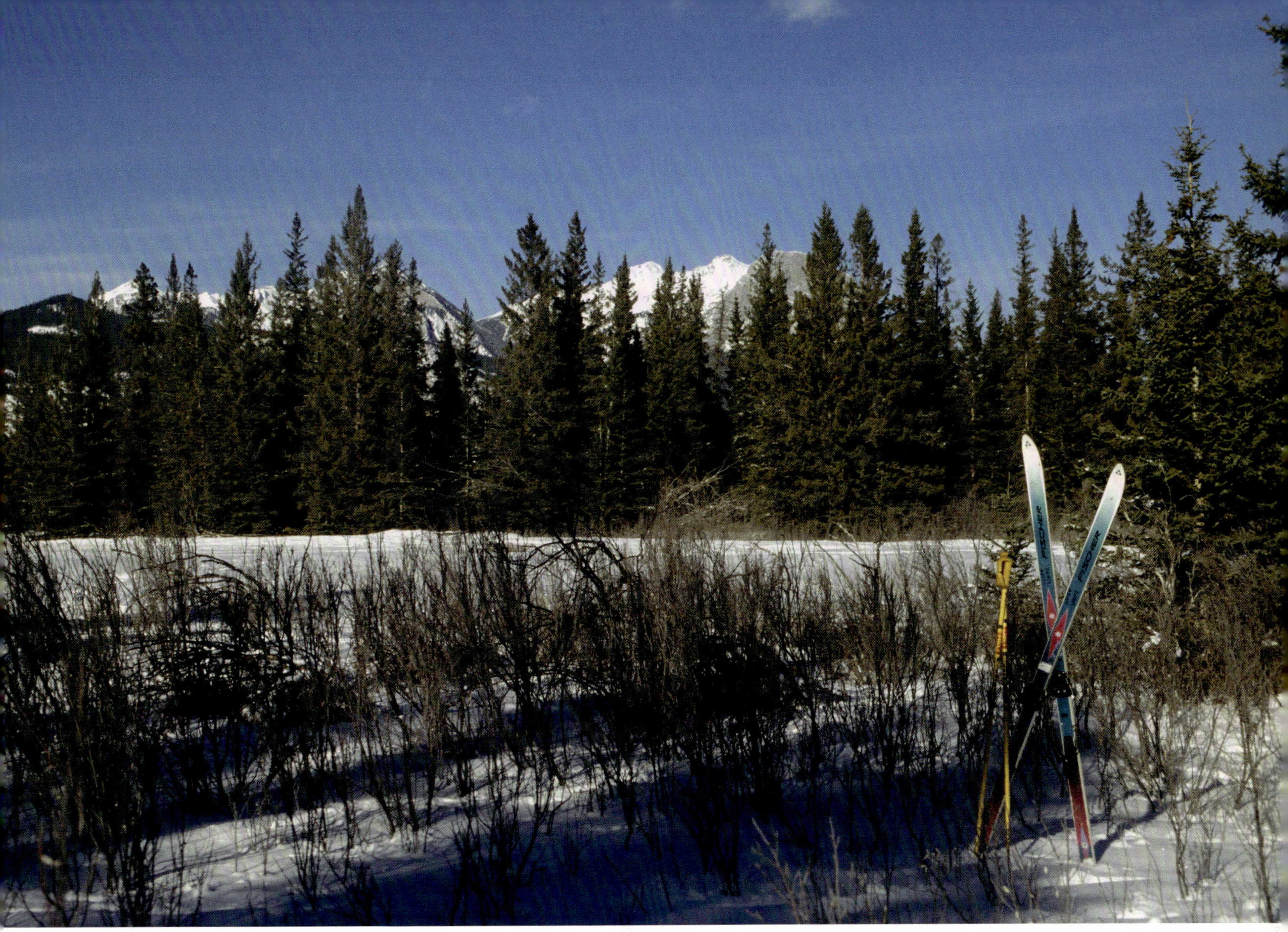

reference to Jasper Hawse, the "old clerk" who had been placed in charge in 1817. About 1830 the original post was replaced by a more substantial development, apparently consisting of up to three buildings, located at the north end of Jasper Lake on the west side of the Athabasca.[25] The "new" Jasper House subsequently was placed under the command of numerous fur trade worthies, including Michael Klyne, Colin Fraser, and Henry Moberly. Moberly first visited the post in 1854 as part of a summer hunting party, approaching it by the usual route from Fort Edmonton northwest to Fort Assiniboine on the Athabasca River and then upstream by boat to the house. However, when he returned to rebuild the now abandoned post in 1858, he blazed a pack trail directly west from Edmonton to Jasper House, the route that would eventually be followed by both transcontinental railway lines after 1910, and the road from Edmonton to Jasper in the late 1930s.[26]

In 1871 photographer Charles Horetzky visited the post as a member of the party of surveyor Walter Moberly, Henry Moberly's brother, sent out as part of the first CPR surveys to determine the possibility of a route through Yellowhead Pass.[27] Horetzky's images of the now-abandoned Jasper House are the earliest known photographs taken in the Canadian Rockies; photography was in its infancy, requiring that the photographer carry his darkroom with him as the glass plate, after being coated, sensitized, and exposed, had to be developed on the spot, a process that could take from three to six hours to complete.[28] The trading post's buildings gradually deteriorated due to neglect, although they were occupied by Jasper pioneer Lewis Swift and his family in the 1890s and were apparently torn down by a Grand Trunk survey party in 1910. Today, vestiges of Jasper House are nearly invisible, and the location is a national historic site.[29]

10.16A MINE BUILDINGS AT POCAHONTAS, JASPER NATIONAL PARK, 1915 (PHOTOGRAPHER UNKNOWN, JASPER YELLOWHEAD PA 39-20)

10.16B POCAHONTAS, JASPER NATIONAL PARK, FEBRUARY 2004 (CW 2004-02E-07)

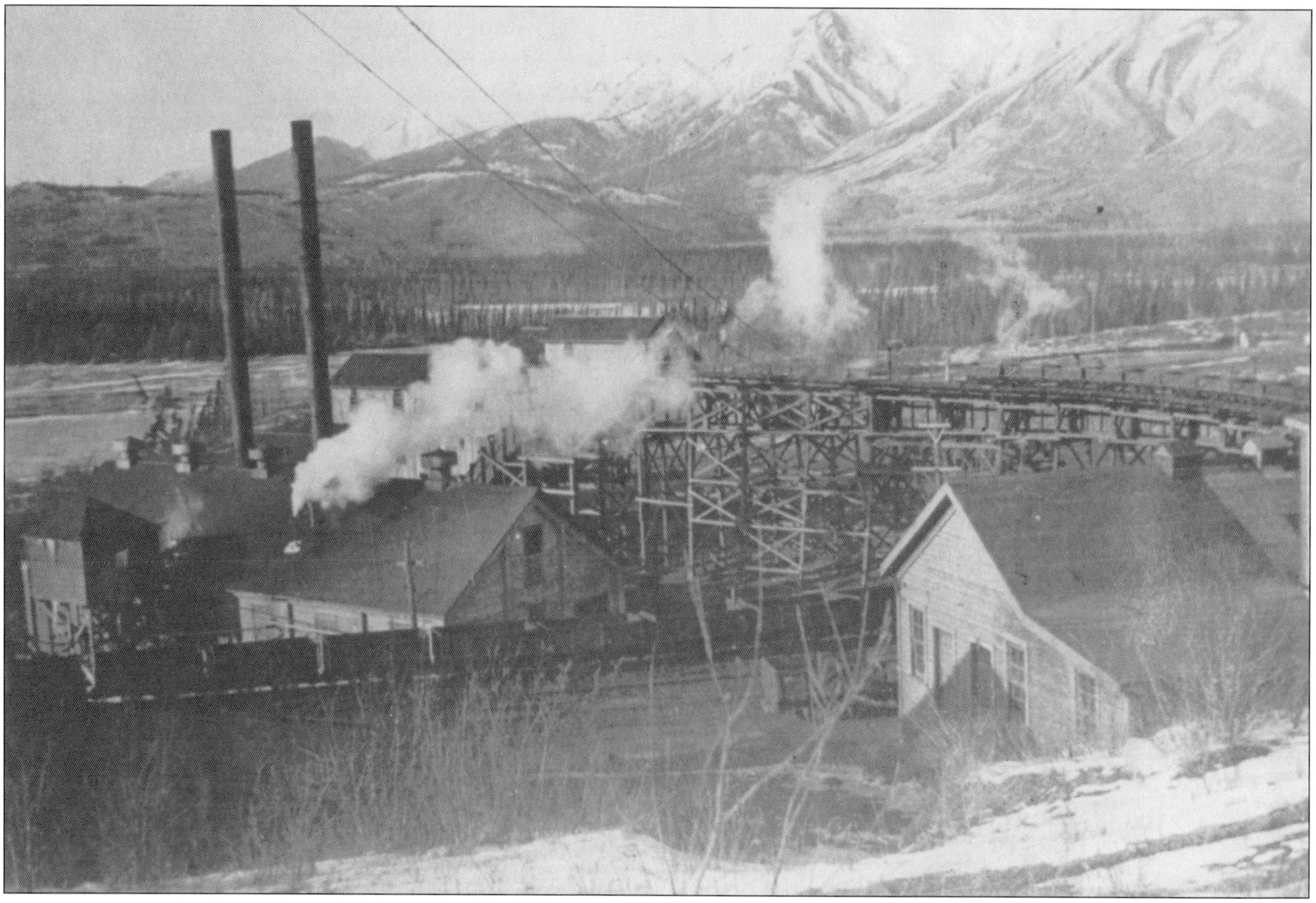

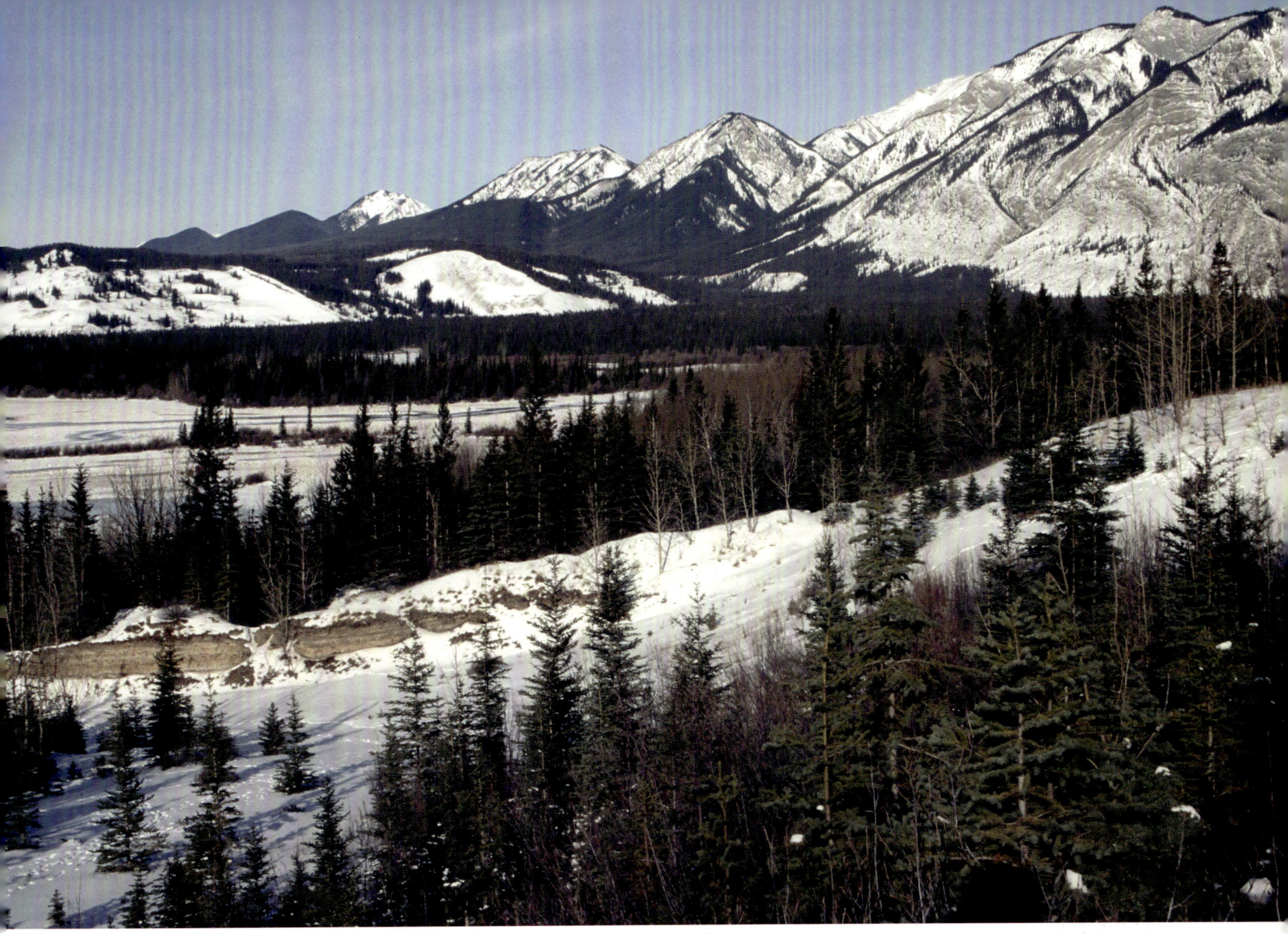

Jasper's experiment with industrial development occurred where coal seams outcropped about eight kilometres inside the national park boundary. Prospector's staked claims here in 1908 in preparation for the coming of the Grand Trunk Pacific Railway, and within two years Jasper Park Collieries was in production. Over two hundred men worked the seam by 1913, removing three to five hundred tons of coal per day. Miners named their village "Pocohontas" after a successful coal town in Virginia. Coal mining here became unprofitable after 1916 when the Grand Trunk Railway line east of the mine was shut down. For a few years, the coal was sent west to Jasper for redistribution, but the mine eventually closed in August 1921.[30]

In 1937, a service station and gas station opened just east of the photograph's view at the junction of the recently constructed Edmonton-Jasper Highway and the road to Miette Hot Springs. The operator added bungalow cabins in 1957 to accommodate increasing numbers of tourists. These facilities are rather spartan compared to the Grand Trunk Pacific's 1912 grandiose plan to compete with the Banff Springs Hotel by building the elaborate "Chateau Miette" near here. The chateau was proposed to accommodate railway passengers visiting the hot springs. As with coal mining, the proposal proved financially impossible when the railway line south of the Athabasca River ceased operations.[31]

10.17A FROM THE POCOHONTAS HIGHWAY, JASPER NATIONAL PARK, 1927 (MCDERMID STUDIO, GLENBOW ND 3-3930)

10.17B HIGHWAY 16 NEAR THE JASPER EAST GATE, JULY 2003 (CW 2003-07M-15)

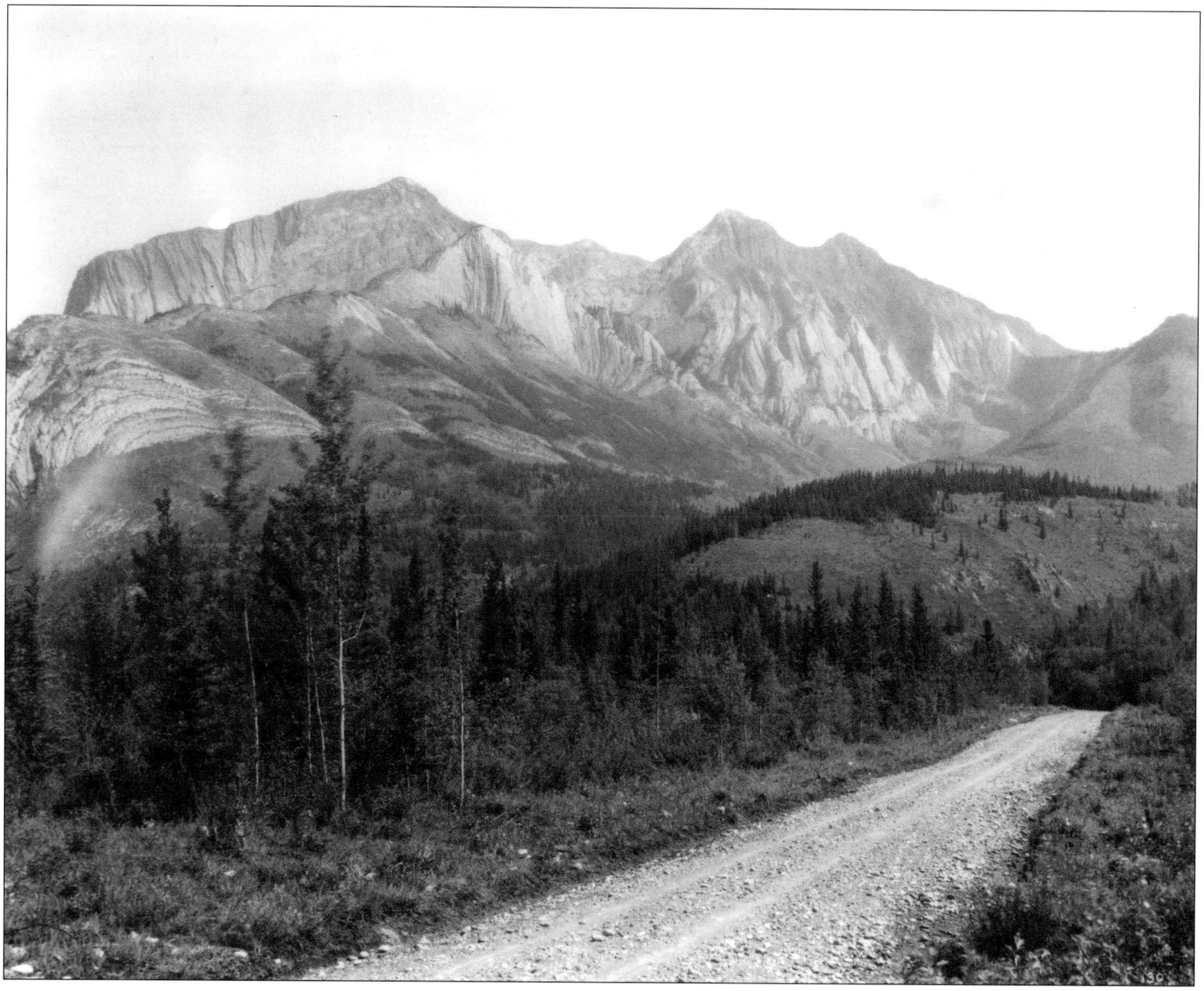

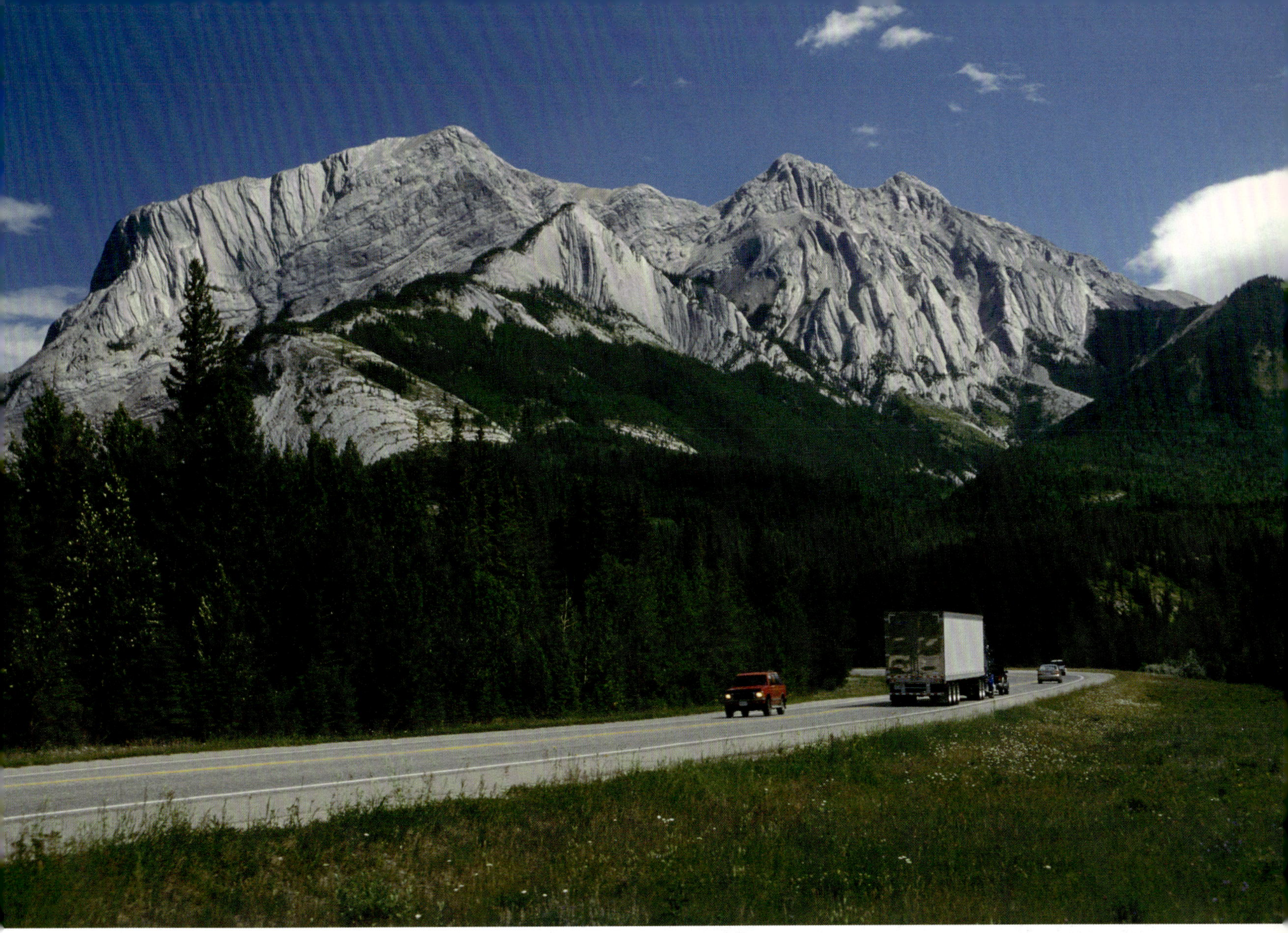

When the Grand Trunk and Canadian Northern railways were completely amalgamated, this left many sections of abandoned railway grade between Edmonton and Jasper. In June 1922, Charles Neimeyer used the grade for the first car-trip between Edmonton and Jasper. It took six days.[32] In 1923, Jasper National Park began building a formal road east from the town of Jasper that was completed through to the east boundary of the park by 1928. However, routine motor travel from Edmonton had to wait until 1931 when the province of Alberta completed its section of the road. By 1967, under a major park trunk highway program, Highway 16 from Jasper to the boundary had been reconstructed and paved to today's condition. The historic photograph was actually taken about three hundred metres to the southeast on a section of old road, now grown over, which was bypassed by the new highway.[33]

10.18A AIR PHOTOGRAPH, ATHABASCA RIVER NORTH OF EDSON, 1950 (ALBERTA SUSTAINABLE RESOURCE DEVELOPMENT, AIR PHOTO DIVISION)

10.18B AIR PHOTOGRAPH, ATHABASCA RIVER NORTH OF EDSON, 1985 (ALBERTA SUSTAINABLE RESOURCE DEVELOPMENT, AIR PHOTO DIVISION)

10.18C AIR PHOTOGRAPH, ATHABASCA RIVER NORTH OF EDSON, 1993 (ALBERTA SUSTAINABLE RESOURCE DEVELOPMENT, AIR PHOTO DIVISION)

10.18D SATELLITE IMAGE, ATHABASCA RIVER NORTH OF EDSON, 2000 (LANDSAT 7 IMAGE, BANFF NATIONAL PARK COLLECTION).

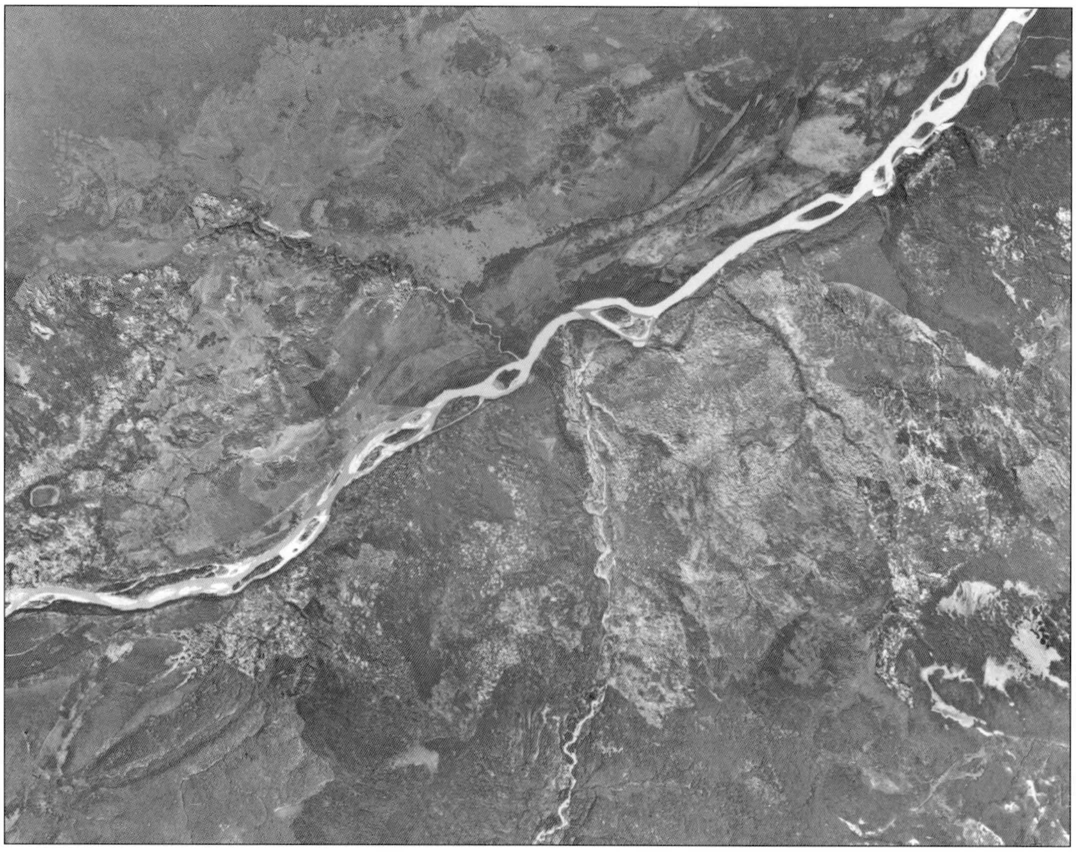

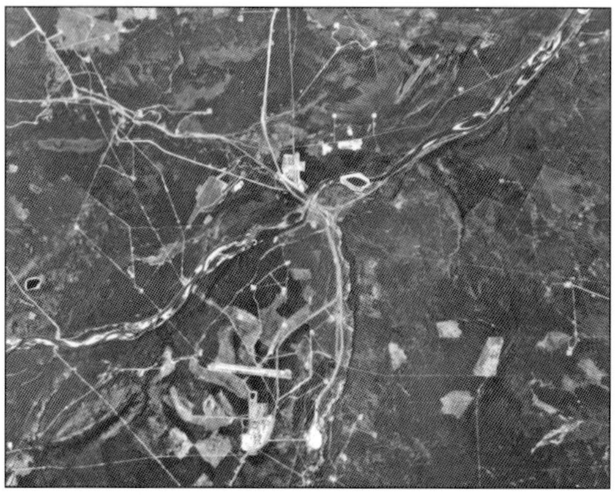

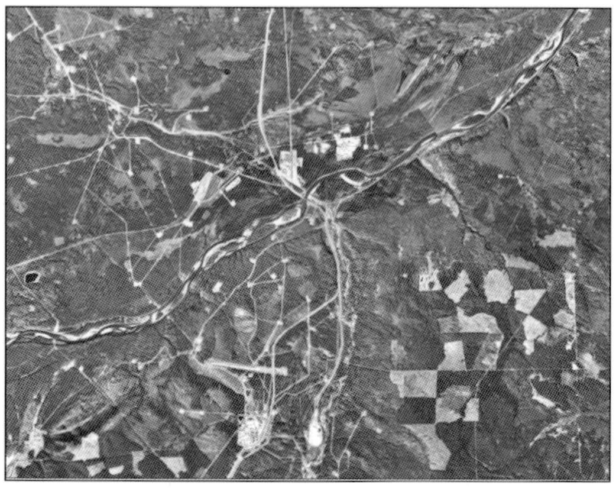

Boreal forest guards the eastern slopes of the Canadian Rockies in central Alberta. Early travellers making the trip from the parklands near Edmonton to Jasper House in the Athabasca Valley cursed this forest, often a brûlé of recently burned snags, interspersed with boggy "muskegs." The fur brigades partially avoided the woods by making a direct portage by horse from the North Saskatchewan to Fort Assiniboine, and hence up the Athabasca River by boat to Jasper House. Later, travellers to the

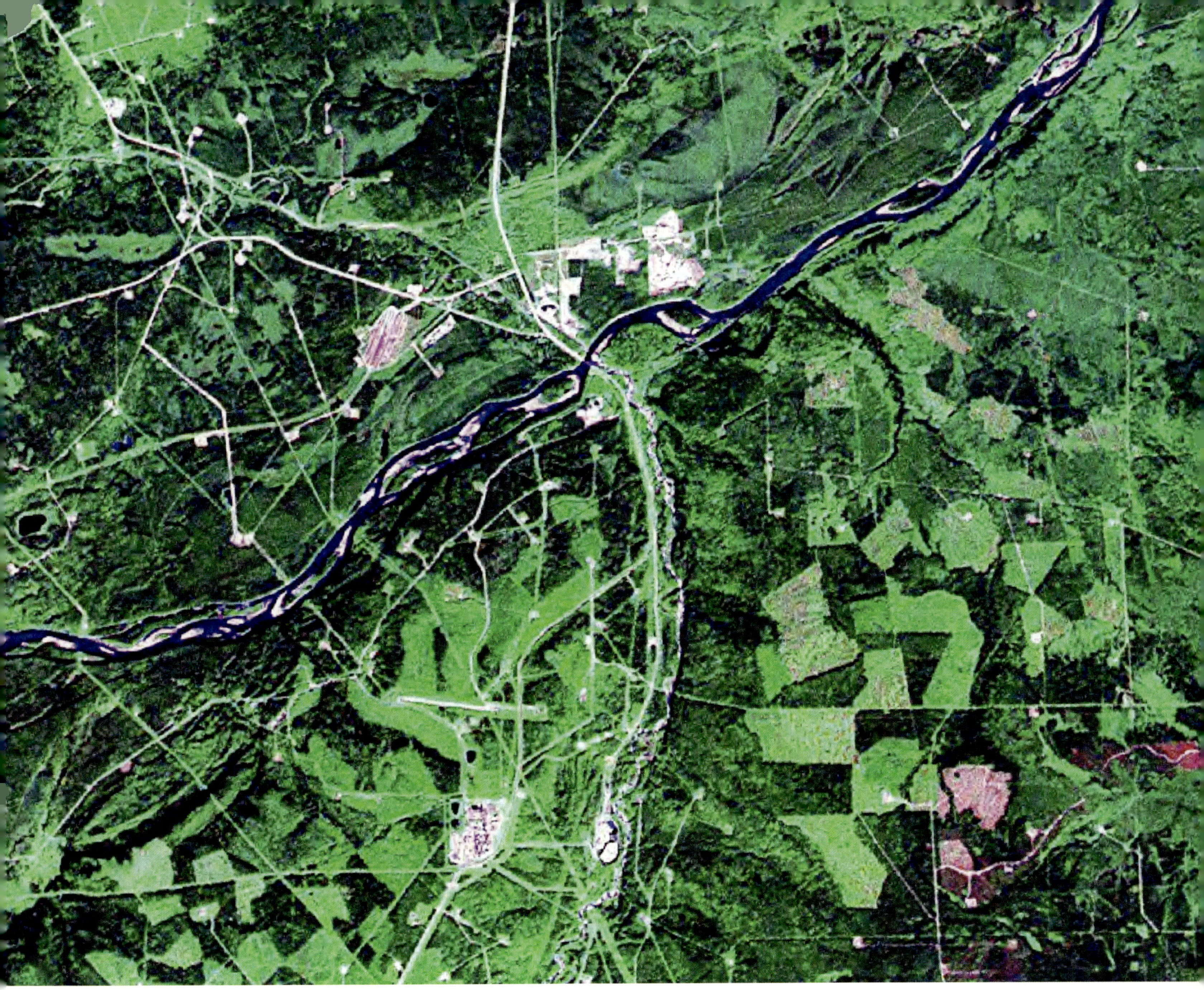

Athabasca valley in what is now Jasper National Park followed the overland trail cleared by Henry John Moberly in 1858, which is today roughly the route of Highway 16.[34] After construction of the railroad, several small saw mills operated in the Hinton and Edson areas. In 1955, the Alberta government signed a prototype "Forest Management Agreement" with the St. Regis Paper Co. of New York for 770,000 hectares lying on both sides of the Athabasca River east of the Jasper park boundary. By 2005, the logging and wood processing industry, along with petroleum, agriculture, and tourism, were the primary economic drivers of Alberta's strong economy.[35]

The four images in this series show the cumulative effects of industry on an area along the Athabasca River north of Edson. The earliest air photograph shows an immature forest regenerating after fire suppression began to reduce the long-term forest disturbance frequency in the 1940s. By the 1980s the forest had matured enough to allow timber harvesting (square cut blocks), and the petroleum industry's mosaic of well-sites, pipelines, gas processing plants, and roads was intensifying. The most recent image is from a satellite, the most cost-effective way to track this rapid rate of massive development across the huge area of Alberta. These levels of land use are becoming more common across much of Alberta's boreal forest, and this is implicated in rapid declines in populations of species such as grizzly bear and woodland caribou.[36]

10.19A FORT EDMONTON, OCTOBER 22, 1879 (GEORGE MERCER DAWSON, LIBRARY ARCHIVES CANADA PA 38033)

10.19B NORTH SASKATCHEWAN RIVER VALLEY AND EDMONTON, APRIL 2004 (CW 2004-04G-17)

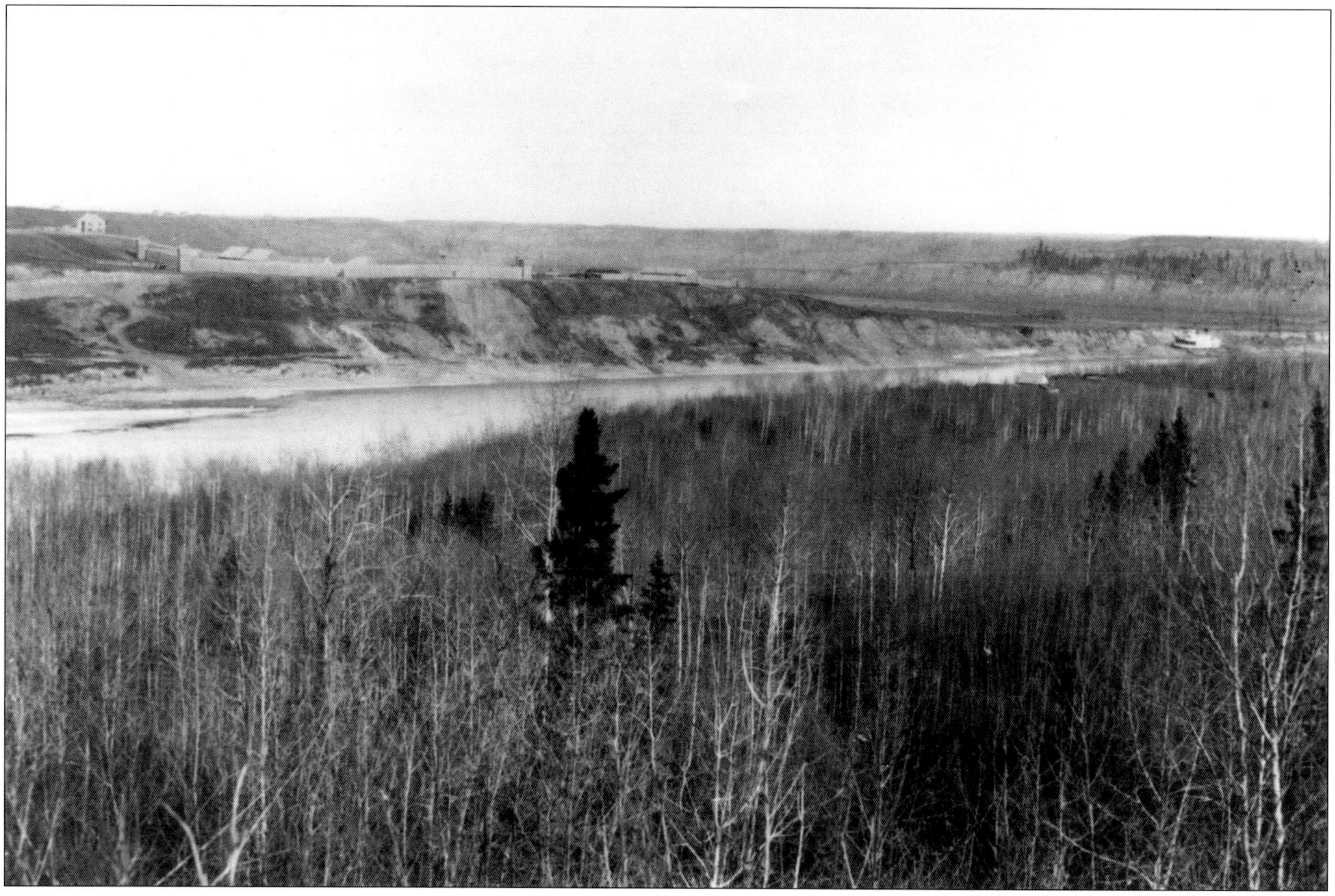

For nearly a hundred years after 1795, Fort Edmonton was the bastion of European civilization in western Rupert's Land, the Hudson's Bay Company's fur-trading territory that eventually became Canada. The fort and its predecessors lay on the North Saskatchewan River, the main highway for the southern fur trade from Hudson Bay to the Pacific. From here, short portages linked to the Athabasca and Battle rivers, and main overland trails led east to Fort Garry (Winnipeg), southwards towards the South Saskatchewan watershed and Rocky Mountain House, and northwards to Athabasca Landing. Most importantly, it lay in the land occupied by the Cree, a large and powerful First Nation long affiliated with the fur-trading industry. Thus, Fort Edmonton was relatively secure for British

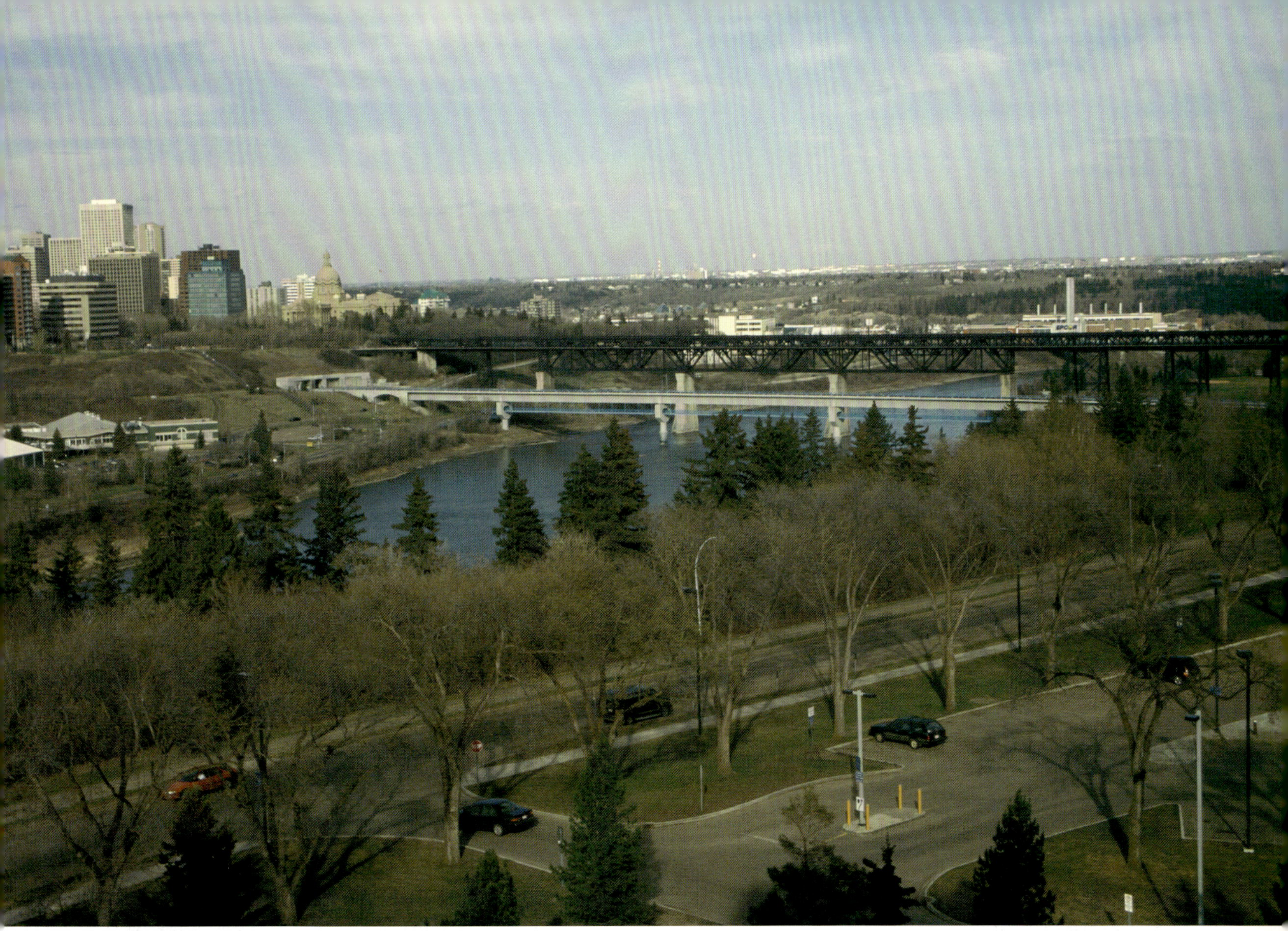

and Canadian trappers, unlike areas further south where First Nations sustained by bison were more independent of, and often hostile to, European trade. However, recognizing that the nations of the Blackfoot Confederacy lay immediately to the south, the Hudson's Bay Company followed its usual policy of building the fort on the north shore of the river. This provided some delay and protection from attack coming from the south.[37]

With the completion of the Calgary and Edmonton Railway in 1891, fur trading was eclipsed by numerous other industries. The stockades around the old fort were torn down as the three-centuries-old Hudson's Bay Company rapidly changed to serve new customers. In 1905, Alberta became a province, and Edmonton, then a city of nine thousand residents, was chosen as its capital. One of the province's first expenditures was to purchase the prominent lands above the river as the location for the legislature building. Construction of the great dome, visible in the current photograph, began in 1908. Over the last century, Edmonton has evolved as Canada's "Gateway to the North." Oil production and refining provide a large component of the city's employment as it services the massive industrial development on the Athabasca tar sands in northern Alberta. By 2005, Edmonton's population, in combination with satellite muncipalities, had risen to over one million.[38]

10.20 FORT EDMONTON IN WINTER, LOOKING WEST FROM THE FLATS, 1871 (CHARLES HORETZKY, GLENBOW NA 1408-4)

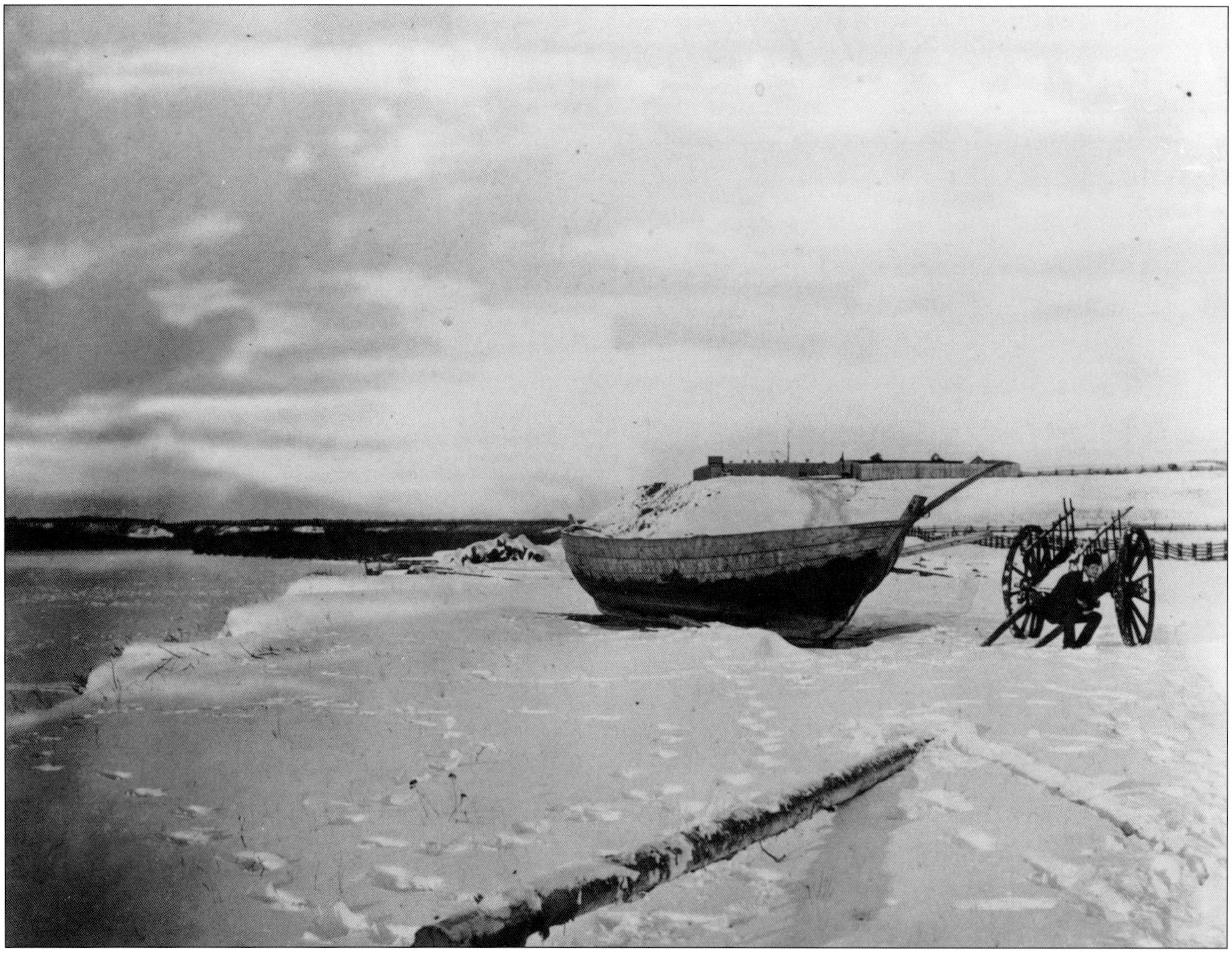

11

SYNTHESIS

The Processes of Landscape Change

As the photographs in this book clearly show, the landscape of the Canadian Rockies can change greatly over time. Compared to the late 1800s, the landscape of today is one of less ice and snow, more evergreen trees, less grasslands, and of course, a much more visible presence of humans. What are the environmental drivers causing these changes? Has the last century been one of unusual rates of change? Or have many of the conditions we see occurred periodically in the past? In this final chapter, we provide a more detailed discussion of the main processes of change, and our current understanding of their long-term role.

GEOLOGY AND ICE AGES

The Rockies are a wonderful place to contemplate time – lots of time. It took over 500 million years of erosion and deposition to form the mostly ocean-bottom strata that constitute these mountains, and another 100 or so million years to uplift and erode them to their current forms.[1] In that time there have been two complete ice ages (each lasting about around 10 million years), and we are now in the beginnings of a third. Within each ice age, there is a cycle of glaciations, each of 60,000 to 80,000 years, separated by brief inter-glacials of less than 20,000 years. Glaciation cycles seem to be controlled by a 100,000-year oscillation in the earth's annual orbit around the sun, known as the Milankovitch Cycle to honour its discoverer.[2]

In the most recent ice age, the Pleistocene Epoch, there have already been nearly twenty cold periods, with the last one – the Wisconsin Glaciation – beginning to melt about 18,000 years ago. Although each ice advance has helped obscure evidence of its predecessors, it is likely that all have nearly completely ice-inundated the Rockies. Only steep and high peaks, called *nunataks*, jutted above each wave of the ice. And with every glaciation, the moving ice carved and ground the ridges and valleys into the landscapes we so admire today. The Rocky Mountain peaks seem deceptively permanent, but from a geologic perspective they are simply a "work in progress" that has been repetitively shaped by ice and water in the past and will be reshaped many times again. At the Columbia Icefields we can see remnants of these large-scale forces at work.[3]

We are currently in the Holocene, a relatively short time of planetary warmth that has melted away most of the ice. This has allowed another cycle of an important ecological process– the return of life, at a regional scale, to the previously glaciated areas of the Rockies and much of Canada. This ebb and flow of plants and wildlife, forced by the repetitive glaciations, may be the most significant general cause of biodiversity patterns at northern latitudes and high elevations. Species adapted to shifting their ranges thousands of kilometres, or lower in elevation, during glaciations were favoured most at this broad scale of time and space. They could rapidly disperse across distance and elevation as the climate changed.[4] For example, paleoecologists can, from pollen found in lake bottoms, discern that white spruce has spread northwards quickly, with its light, wind-disseminated seeds finding fertile ground on the bare soils left by melting ice. However, over time, spruce is often replaced by lodgepole pine, which has migrated northwards more slowly due to heavier seeds but is better adapted to some site conditions. Perhaps this pattern, evident in the early Holocene, has occurred many times before in the Pleistocene.[5]

RECENT CLIMATE CHANGE AND CURRENT GLACIAL FLUCTUATIONS

The great ice sheets of the Wisconsin glaciation melted rapidly. The Rocky Mountain Trench (the great valley now holding the headwaters of the Columbia River and Lake Windermere, Fig. 6.15) was likely ice-free in its southern area by about 13,000 years ago. The foothills near Calgary had also been released from the ice blanket by this time.[6] Amazingly, less than a thousand years later, the ice had retreated to an extent less than we see today. Paleoecologists date this melting pattern by counting the annual layers of sediment deposition, called *varves*, in the bottom of lakes found immediately downstream of glaciers. Varves from Crowfoot Lake, at the base of the Crowfoot Glacier (Fig. 8.19) show the near disappearance of the glacier by 11,500 years ago. This occurred during a few hundred years of relatively warm, dry climate. Then, at 10,800 years ago, there was a sharp re-cooling in the climate, and a quick re-advance of ice to just above the lake. Glaciers across the Northern Hemisphere, especially in Europe, also advanced rapidly at exactly the same time. This rapid onslaught of cold, wet weather, called the Younger Dryas event, was likely caused by a major change in the Atlantic Ocean's Gulf Stream current, which occurred with the ongoing glacial melting. However, by 10,000 years ago, the varve-record shows the return to a much warmer and dryer climate, and suggests that many glaciers may have disappeared.[7]

Paleoecologists can also infer prehistoric vegetation patterns by identifying the species of plant pollen imbedded in the lake bottom sediments. Immediately after the continental glaciation, subalpine vegetation in the Rockies appears to have been dry, open shrublands dominated by sagebrush and grasses. The first forests at upper elevations were of five-needled pines. Today, white-bark pine stands, likely remnants of this early revegetation, are commonly found on warm, dry slopes near the lower tongues of glaciers.[8] During the Holocene inter-glacial, there have been periods of minor glacial advances from about 5,000 to 4,000 years and from about 3,000 to 1,800 years before the present. The most recent advance, called the Little Ice Age, began nearly eight hundred years ago and lasted until about 1850. This fluctuating climate caused broad, long-term changes in vegetation cover. For example, lake-bed pollen ratios from the Kootenay Valley (Fig. 6.13) show that a dry, parkland vegetation dominated by Douglas fir and western larch was predominant prior to about 4,700 years ago, followed by a shift toward more dense forests of spruce and lodgepole pine, likely coincident with glacial advances.[9]

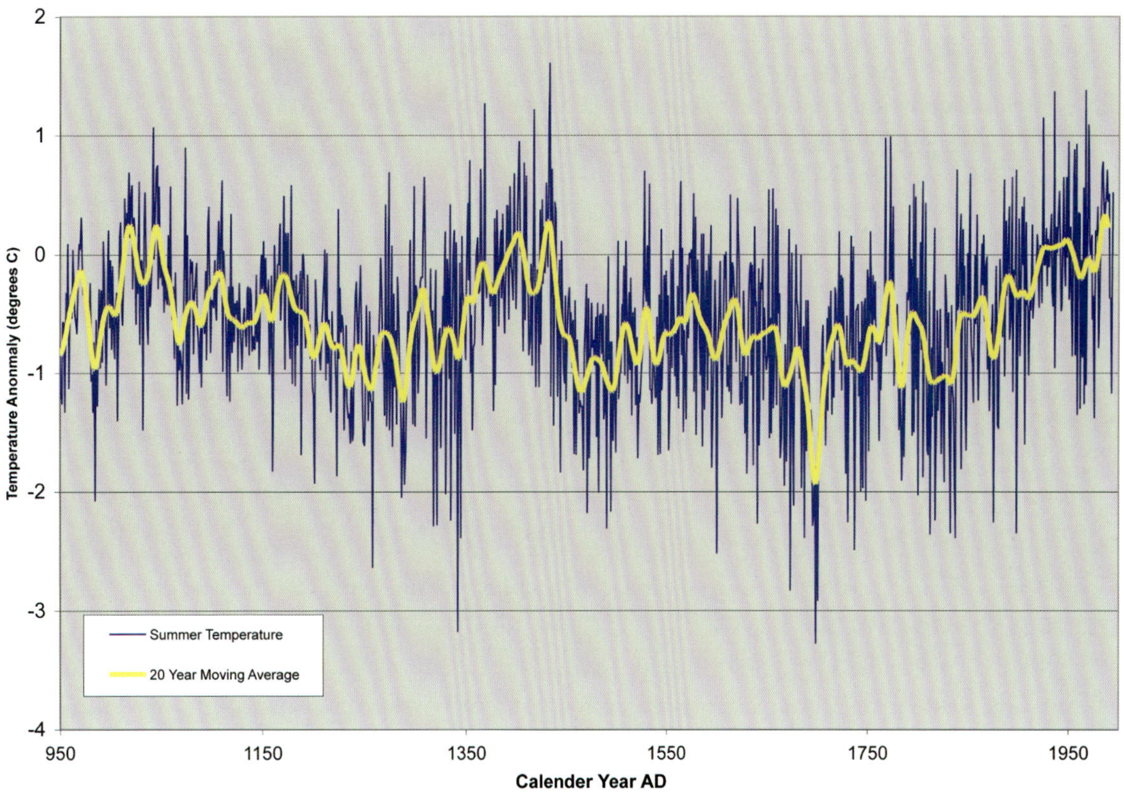

FIGURE 11.1. SUMMER (APRIL TO AUGUST) TEMPERATURE ANOMALIES (°C) FOR THE COLUMBIA ICEFIELDS AREA (AD 950 TO 1994) FOR THE CANADIAN ROCKIES RECONSTRUCTED FROM WEATHER CORRELATIONS TO TREE-RING GROWTH PATTERNS. SOURCE: DATA FROM B. H. LUCKMAN AND R.J.S. WILSON, "SUMMER TEMPERATURES IN THE CANADIAN ROCKIES DURING THE LAST MILLENNIUM: A REVISED RECORD," *CLIMATE DYNAMICS* (2005): 138.

The climate for the last millennium is becoming more clearly known through tree-ring studies. The pattern of ring growth under recent known weather conditions (for example, summer temperature) can be extended back in time as far as we can date living and dead trees (Fig. 11.1).[10] It appears that the Rockies had relatively warm summers until 1200. After the onset of the Little Ice Age about this time, summers were cold through 1350, again from the 1450s to about 1510, and extremely cold around 1700. Ongoing cool temperatures continued until the mid-1800s, with a run of cold summers around 1810. The resulting minor reglaciation (called the Peyto Advance, after Peyto Glacier, Fig. 8.22) reached a maximum in the 1860s and is visible in our earliest photographs of many glaciers.[11]

Since the time of the first photographs, the tree-ring and weather station record indicates vigorous climatic warming. By the time of the 1902 photograph, the Peyto Glacier had already retreated significantly from its maximum extent, and this rapid rate of ice-disappearance continued, as is visible in the 1923 photograph (Fig. 8.22). Although climatic warming may have decreased somewhat in the 1940s and 1950s, 1961 to 2000 was the warmest period in the past eight hundred years. Glaciers such as the Bow (Fig. 8.20), Peyto (Fig. 8.22), Saskatchewan (Fig. 8.25), and Athabasca (Fig. 8.27) have receded to upper elevations that have likely not been ice-free for over a thousand years. Most scientists believe that this warming trend is counter to the predicted pattern of cooling that would be occurring as the planet enters the next expected glaciation. Human burning of fossil fuels is releasing a massive amount of potentially climate-warming "greenhouse" gases into the atmosphere. Within the next hundred years, carbon dioxide concentrations in the atmosphere will exceed levels of any time in the past several hundred thousand years, and possibly much longer. This could trigger chain reactions of worldwide biophysical events including continued melting of glaciers and ice-caps, rising sea levels, increased burning of forests, expanding deserts, and, inevitably, the need for great changes in human economic and social systems.[12]

WEATHER EVENTS

Although climate, or the long-term pattern of weather, tends to control general glacial and vegetation cover patterns, it is often extreme weather events such as intense rains, drought, or snowfalls that shape many landscapes.

Floods, Fans, and Dams – Every year, in the months of May and June, highway, railway, and municipal maintenance crews play a million-dollar-a-hand poker game with Nature. The deck is shuffled earlier in the winter with the pattern of snowfalls and snow melting. The interplay of warm western chinooks and Arctic high-pressure systems determines the depth of the spring snowpack in the high country. The game is then played out in the spring as the temperature warms. If the snow begins to melt early and consistently, the risk of flooding declines. But if the days of May and early June are cool, and the snow keeps falling at high elevations, the odds of flooding begin to climb. When June's inevitable hot spell comes after a late spring, there remains one last card to play. If Nature draws in a warm, low-pressure system to end the hot spell, and rain falls to the top of the peaks on a saturated snow-pack, a flood is nearly certain. Millions of rivulets, swollen with rain and snowmelt, and sometimes laden with rock debris, cascade down from the high country, merging into flooding creeks and rivers that can wash away bridges and inundate low-lying communities. The largest recorded flooding event over much of the area probably occurred in June 1923 when both the Bow and Columbia rivers flooded large valley bottom areas (Fig. 4.18).[13] Recently, heavy rains in June 2005 caused heavy flooding in the foothills of the east slopes, but fortunately little rain fell near the continental divide.

Although floods are costly to many current land users, they make and maintain some of the Rockies' most ecologically valuable landscapes. Where rivulets and creeks slow when reaching the valley bottoms, they deposit much of the eroded material they carry into *alluvial fans*. Finer materials, deposited by water, create the larger and flatter fans at the bottom of large drainage basins. Coarse materials, deposited by debris flows, or slurries of mud and gravel, form the steeper fans at the bottom of small, steep basins. Although fans were created most rapidly at the end of the last glaciation, they are reactivated during floods. Surging water and debris flows shift position across the fans, creating a diverse landscape favoured by species such as aspen and grasslands used in winter by wildlife.[14] Larger fans provided a source of water, forage, and wildlife, and so were favoured campsites for early peoples, and later these became today's townsites and visitor service centres. To protect facilities and roads, meandering streams across the fans have often been straightened and channelled. Materials hauled down and deposited by water and debris flows no longer contribute to building the fan or to river sediments but are instead mechanically moved out of stream channels (Fig. 11.2). The process of natural fan renewal and maintenance is thus halted.[15]

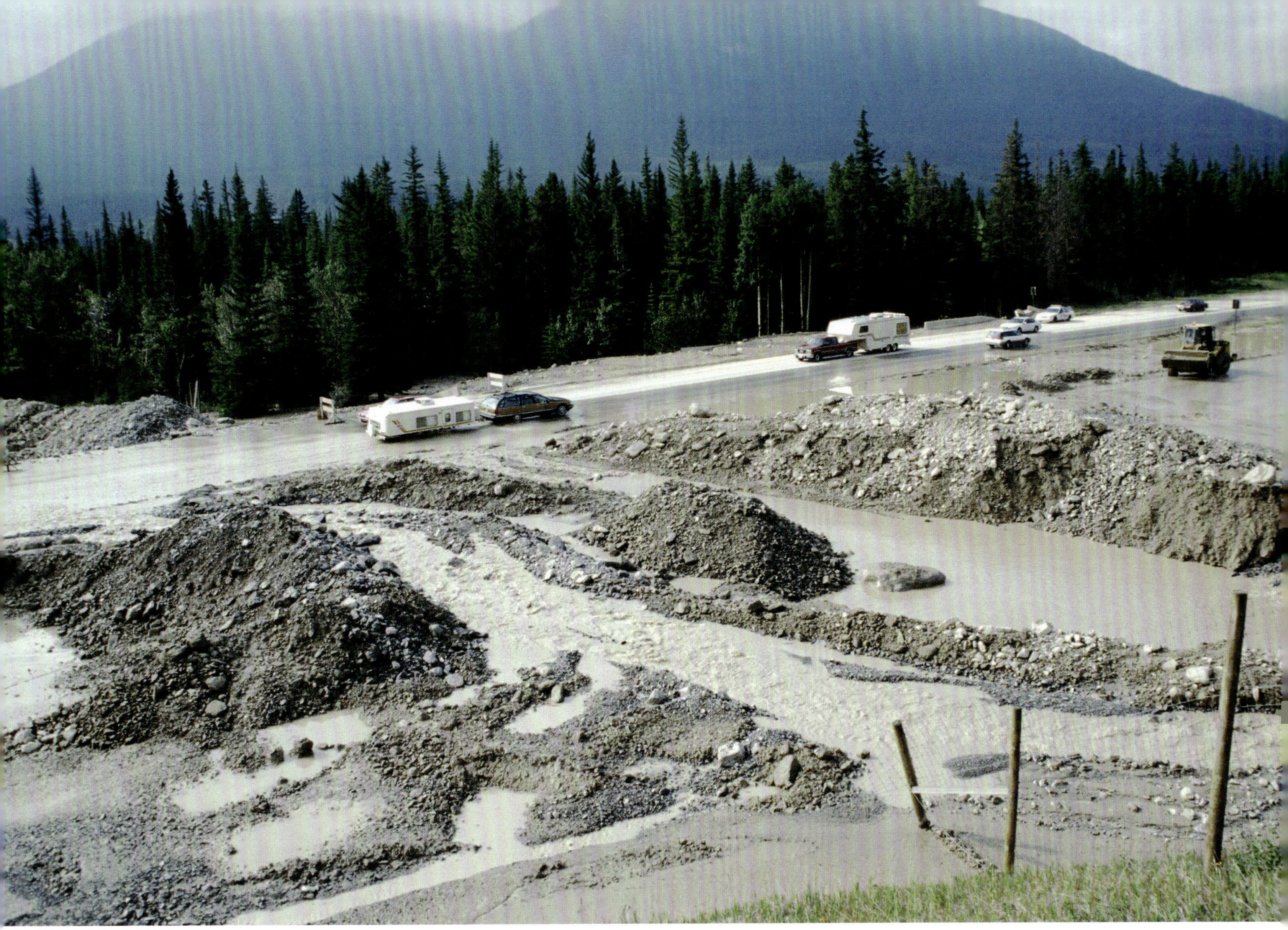

FIGURE 11.2. MACHINERY REMOVING GRAVEL FROM THE FIVE MILE CREEK ALLUVIAL FAN NEAR BANFF AFTER IT FLOODED OVER THE TRANS-CANADA HIGHWAY DURING A THUNDERSTORM IN AUGUST 1999 (CW 1999-08B-07).

Most rivers in the mountain parks are not dammed, so periodic flooding still renews streamside wetlands and riparian zones. However, two main tributaries to the Bow River immediately downstream of Banff, the Spray and the Cascade, are both impounded (see Fig. 4.14). Effects on landscape near the Bow River have been dramatic. First of all, from a human perspective, partially controlling the spring floods of the river, in combination with a series of dikes, has made the town of Canmore a much safer place for its residents.[16] From an ecological viewpoint, damming has reduced the area of flood-created gravel flats, side channels, and recently disturbed vegetation. The abundance of species such as balsam poplar and willow that historically thrived near the river is declining (Fig. 2.16).

Avalanches – "It wasn't just the amount of snow that fell that caused so many avalanches, but the manner in which it fell" is the old adage of the professional avalanche forecaster. Almost any photograph of the Rockies shows the long, narrow alleyways that are bowled through the forests when winter snows slip from the steep slopes above (for good examples, see Figs. 2.13, 4.8, 4.16, 8.12). The largest avalanche cycles are obviously related to major storms. However, early winter cold snaps, so common in the area, can be important in shaping conditions later in the season. Cold temperatures create unconsolidated, large snow crystals that can become buried in the snowpack. When overloaded by later snowfalls, this weak layer can result in "climax avalanches" that slide right to the ground.

These massive avalanches may blast down slide paths only every decade or so but easily can snap off nearby large trees. In many years a rapid spring warming causes the snowpack to suddenly turn into a flowing mass of destruction. Many steep, south-facing grassy slopes of the mountains are kept treeless by these spring avalanches (see Figs. 2.12, 4.15).[17]

Drought and Tree Die-off – The Rockies near Banff and Jasper lie inland of several moisture-catching mountain ranges to the west and are adjacent to the dry, southern prairies of Canada. In fact, the montane valley bottoms and adjacent southwest facing slopes have a semi-arid climate. Valley-bottom areas of coarse well-drained soils, such as near the bottom of Cascade Mountain (Fig. 4.4) or the Ya-Ha-Tinda (Fig. 8.13), are so droughty that trees sometimes cannot survive periods of dry weather.[18] Furthermore, once mature, dense forests have formed due to fire suppression, droughts have accelerated tree mortality. For example, since 1999, mountain pine beetle has killed many mature drought-stressed lodgepole pine on sun-exposed slopes in the Bow Valley, such as on Mt. Stoney Squaw (Fig. 6.3b). In both Banff and Jasper, many old Douglas firs that survived numerous past droughts due to more open conditions caused by fires are now dying due to competition for moisture in increasingly dense stands of trees.

FIRE CAUSED BY HUMANS AND LIGHTNING

Almost all historic photographs taken at lower elevations in the Rockies show landscapes created by prolific fire – young forests, burnt snags whitened by weathering, open grass and shrublands. Today these views are predominantly of mature evergreen forest. How much fire occurred historically? What caused all these fires? Why don't these landscapes burn today?

Historic Fire Frequency over Space – The evidence of how often past fires occurred is most easily interpreted by the study of tree rings, called *dendrochronology.* In some locations, tree species such as lodgepole pine grow back in even-aged stands after an intense fire. By collecting disks or cores from the base of these trees, and counting back through the annual growth rings to the core, the approximate date of burning, and subsequent forest stand origin (plus or minus a few years) can be determined. Furthermore, fires sometimes scar, but do not kill, species such as lodgepole pine, larch, or Douglas fir. A dendrochronologist can often determine the exact year of these fire scars by careful cross-dating of samples from several trees.[19] The patterns that emerge from sampling numerous trees in an area are maps showing a kaleidoscope of historic fires, overlaid one over another through time, each having a unique burning pattern, size, and direction of burn, depending on the interaction of weather, fuel, and topography conditions.

Several dendrochronological studies from the Canadian Rockies show similar fire frequency variability by elevation and aspect prior to the 1900s (Fig. 11.3). Valley-bottom montane areas of meadow, aspen, and Douglas fir, such as near the towns of Banff and Jasper, burned at average intervals of about twenty to fifty years prior to 1900. Moving up in elevation, dense subalpine forests of lodgepole pine, such as those surrounding the village of Lake Louise, burned less frequently, usually about every fifty to a hundred years on south- and west-facing slopes, and a hundred to 150 years on north and east aspects. Upper subalpine forests of Engelmann spruce, subalpine fir, and alpine larch usually had long intervals of greater than 150 years.[20] Furthermore, fire frequency appears to vary with

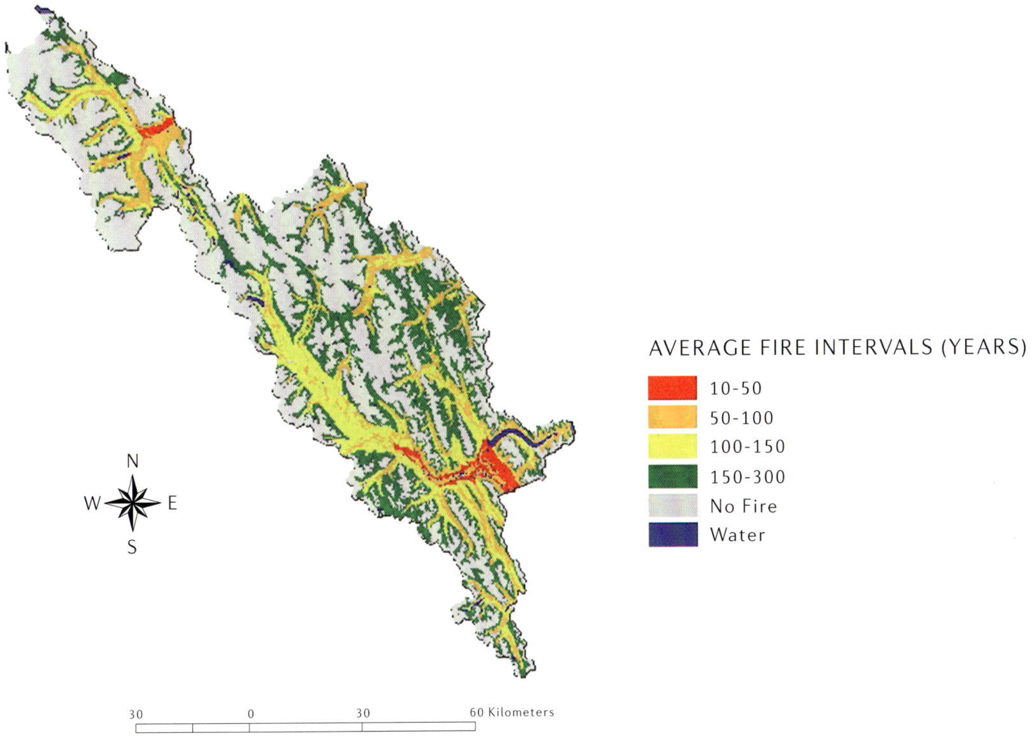

FIGURE 11.3. AVERAGE FIRE INTERVALS FOR THE BANFF NATIONAL PARK LANDSCAPE PRIOR TO THE YEAR 1900. SOURCE: C. A. WHITE, I. R. PENGELLY, D. ZELL, AND M. P. ROGEAU, *LANDSCAPE FIRE REGIMES AND VEGETATION RESTORATION IN BANFF NATIONAL PARK, ALBERTA*, OCCASIONAL PAPER BNP-2003-1 (BANFF, AB: PARKS CANADA, 2003), 36.

the size and orientation of mountain valleys.[21] For example, because most fires are driven by southwest winds, the headwaters of valleys running in a north and east direction, and ringed with rock in their headwaters often have old, infrequently burned forests. These old-growth forests are visible near Upper Kananaskis Lake (Fig. 2.13a), Lake Louise (Fig. 8.3a), Bow Lake (Fig. 8.21a), Peyto Glacier (Fig. 8.22a), and on the south end of Maligne Lake (Fig. 10.14a).[22]

Fire Ignition – Lightning and lightning-caused fires are ten to a hundred times more frequent on the west slopes of the Rockies compared to the east slopes. This appears to occur because the prevailing western winds create an area of relatively stable air and thus thunderstorm-free conditions as they flow downslope into Alberta.[23] Yet despite this inequality of natural ignition, consider an interesting phenomenom: the historic frequency of fire is relatively similar on both sides of the mountain range. This is strong evidence that past fire frequency was not limited by the amount of ignition. On the west slopes, ignition by lightning was common, and on the east slopes, ignition by humans was likely highly important. However, prior to reduced burning by First Nations and recent fire-suppression efforts, the relatively equal fire frequencies on east and west slopes indicate that regional factors such as similar climate and drought frequency were the primary determinants of burned area.[24]

Fire Frequency Changes over Time – East of the continental divide, fire intervals (averaged over elevation and aspect) appear to have been relatively short (60 to 70 years) from the 1300s to the 1700s. After the year 1760, the average fire interval increased to about 175 years, and for the period 1940 until 1990, burning nearly ceased.[25] Likely the reduction in the populations of native peoples due to European diseases caused the first reduction of burning prior to 1800.[26] After this, even a pulse of burning caused by early white settlers and railroad construction in the Bow and Kicking Horse valleys (see Figs. 8.2a, 8.15a, 8.17a) did not change the general trend of less fire over time. Today, due to effective prevention of human-caused fires on the east slopes, fire intervals would be expected to be in the thousands of years due to low lightning-ignition rates. West of the continental divide, where heli-attack crews aggressively suppress lightning-ignited fires, intervals between fires are also expected to be very long.[27] However, in both east and west slope national and provincial parks, managers are allowing some lightning fires to burn and are also doing prescribed burning. Fire is returning to the landscape.

VEGETATION CHANGE

Then and now photographs for the Rockies vividly show plant cover changes at all elevations and site moisture levels. Figure 11.4 is a stylized model of the pattern of change evident over the last hundred years for different elevations and site moisture levels. In general, dense forests of Engelmann and white spruce, subalpine fir, and lodgepole pine are increasing, while the coverage of more open vegetation types such as aspen, grasslands, and alpine meadows is declining.

Vegetation change over time is called *succession*. Plant regeneration by wind, water, or animal-borne seed on bare mineral soil after extreme disturbances such as glaciation, landslides, or water erosion is *primary succession*. After less extreme disturbances such as fire, intense animal grazing, or avalanches, living portions of plants and a buried seed bank in the soil result in more rapid recovery of vegetation called *secondary succession*. As is visible in most pictures, succession usually leads to more vegetation cover. Over time, trees and shrubs grow to greater heights. Less visible is a general trend towards complexity, with more species of plants filling the various niches created as vegetation structure and cover increases.[28]

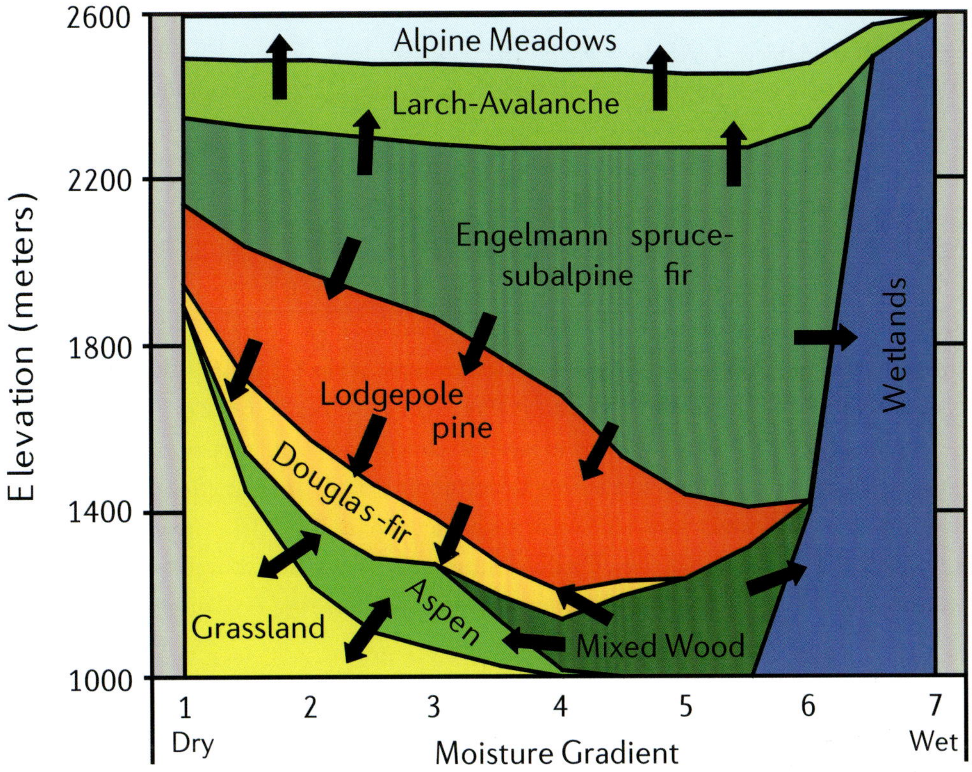

FIGURE 11.4. PATTERNS OF VEGETATION CHANGE IN BANFF AND JASPER NATIONAL PARKS. IN GENERAL, CONIFER FORESTS OF SPRUCE AND SUBALPINE FIR ARE INCREASING IN COVER. OPEN FORESTS OF DOUGLAS FIR, ASPEN, AND LARCH ARE GRADUALLY DECLINING IN COVER.

What causes succession? The mechanisms reflect the great trade-offs for plant survival. First is the method of plant arrival or regeneration on a site. Some plants such as fireweed have evolved light wind-blown seeds to rapidly invade disturbed areas. Birds carry seeds from limber and white-bark pines. The roots of buffalo berry, willow, or saskatoon survive disturbance and rapidly resprout to dominate an area. Secondly, succession is driven by competition between plant species. Increasing plant density often decreases availability of light, soil nutrients, and water. Plants that are most competitive under these conditions have higher survival rates as succession proceeds. For example, trembling aspen is relatively intolerant to shade and is thus seldom found in older dense forests of more shade-tolerant conifers such as white spruce or Douglas fir. Furthermore, vegetation change is influenced by tolerance of plant species to ongoing weather extremes, animal use, or disturbance events.[29]

Primary Succession after Glaciation – The best location for observing primary succession is at the toes of retreating glaciers such as Peyto (Fig. 8.22) or the Athabasca (Fig. 8.26). During the four hundred years prior to the 1890s, glaciers advanced into the upper subalpine forest, and as they recede with a warming climate, the forest reclaims the bare mineral soil left from the churning ice. The first plant recolonizers, seeding within a few years of deglaciation, are hardy dwarf shrubs such as yellow mountain avens and legume (nitrogen-fixing) species, including purple hedysarum. By twenty-five to fifty years, shrubs such as willow and dwarf birch are more common. Gradually, trees including Engelmann spruce, whitebark pine, and lodgepole pine increase in cover, until a hundred to two hundred years after icemelt, a new forest occupies the area.[30]

The Rise and Fall of Alpine Treeline – At the *ecotone* or ecological boundary zone between alpine meadows and subalpine forest, trees are growing at their physiological limit. Thus succession at treeline is very susceptible to climate change and extreme weather events. For example, near the Columbia Icefields, a series of cold summers in the 1690s likely killed larger Engelmann spruce and subalpine fir in forests near treeline and thus caused a general retreat of the tall forest downslope by the mid-1700s. A remnant shrub, or *krummholz*, forest remained (Fig. 8.26a).[31] Similarly, during droughts, forest fires can occur at upper elevations and cause a long-term removal of these forests if regeneration conditions are not favourable after fire.[32] During warm periods, in contrast, secondary succession advances treeline upslope. This is currently occurring throughout the Canadian Rockies (Fig. 11.4), as is evident in photographs from Sunshine Meadows (Fig. 6.5). Treelines increase their elevation in three ways. First, layering, or the vertical growth of ground-touching spruce and subalpine fir branches, causes relatively continual expansion of existing krummholz islands at their edges. Secondly, periods of favourable spring and summer weather (warm with adequate moisture) can result in a major pulse of seedlings between krummholz patches. Finally, year-round periods of favourable weather are needed to maintain the warm temperature in the deeper soils necessary for root system growth that supports taller trees.[33]

Subalpine Forests after Fire – Coniferous forests of lodgepole pine, subalpine fir, and Engelmann spruce, found at middle elevations in the Rockies, usually follow a classic secondary succession pattern of regeneration. Hot fires burn these dense forests on average every hundred years or so. Immediately after fire, the burnt forest seems like an ecological wasteland – most of the trees are dead, and the soil is often deeply blackened and charred. But life remains everywhere, and secondary succession can be rapid. First, there are the sprouters. Shrubs such buffalo berry and menziesia may be top-killed by the burn, but the root crown survives below the soil and can send up sprouts within days. The roots of herbs such as showy aster, arnica, and strawberry also are frequently insulated in the soil and regrow green shoots rapidly. Within a year come the seedling plants. The windblown seeds of fireweed are the most obvious example. The purple flowers of this nitrogen-fixer can blanket an area the year after fire. Found under these prolific herbs and shrubs, and nearly invisible for a few years, are the seedlings of trees. If lodgepole pine dominated the previous forest, the fire will have opened wax-sealed cones in the tree-canopy, spilling millions of seeds onto the recently burned soil. Spruce and subalpine fir seedlings may also be common and are blown in on the wind from nearby survivors. By twenty years after fire, a dense new forest has regrown. The repeat photographs show many examples of this successional pattern such as in the Cascade valley (Fig. 4.15), near Castle Junction (Fig. 6.12), above Lake Louise train station (Fig. 8.2), and near Kicking Horse Pass (Fig. 8.15).[34]

Successional Pathways in the Montane – Low-elevation forests, found near the towns of Banff, Jasper, and Windermere, have experienced a wide variety of fire behaviour. Fire suppression has changed forest structure from shrublands and open savannah-type environments maintained by frequent understory or tree-thinning fires to dense forests likely to burn with high intensities, killing all trees (Figs. 11.5 and 11.6). In areas heavily used by First Nations, such as near Canmore (Fig. 2.14), Cascade Falls (Fig. 4.4), Hillsdale Meadows (Fig. 6.9), the Kootenay Plains (Fig. 8.23), or Jasper (Fig. 10.2), the average length of time between fires may have been very short (less than twenty years). Frequent human-caused fires, in combination with relatively low wildlife densities near hunter camps, often created grasslands ringed by dense thickets of unbrowsed trembling aspen (Fig. 10.6a). Fire intervals

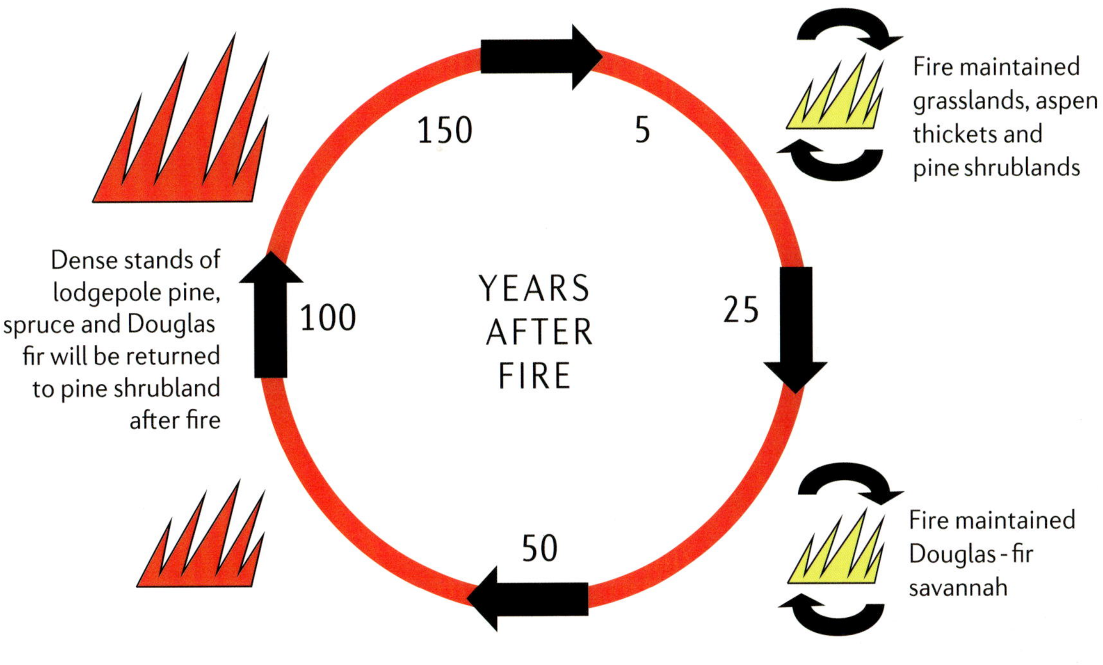

FIGURE 11.5. VEGETATION SUCCESSIONAL PATTERNS AND FIRE INTENSITY IN THE MONTANE ECOREGION.

were slightly longer, say from thirty to fifty years, on dry, south-facing montane hillsides. These were only moderately severe burns that killed younger trees but only scorched mature thick-barked Douglas fir. The result was a savannah-like forest of shrubs and short conifers surrounding sentinel Douglas firs (Figs. 4.10a, 6.9, 10.11, 11.6). In cooler and moister montane areas, fires were less frequent, allowing tree-density and organic matter to increase. When fires did occur, perhaps during mid-summer drought periods every fifty to a hundred years, flame lengths were long and killed almost all the trees, such as occurred in the 1880s near Sundance Canyon (Fig. 4.20a).[35]

Fire Suppression and Prescribed Burning – The farmers, loggers, miners, and tourism entrepreneurs that replaced First Nations in the mountains needed to protect their fences and buildings from the scourge of fire. Similarly, early tourists desired green rather than frequently burnt mountainsides. Removal of native peoples likely did much to reduce fire frequency in more remote valleys, but steam locomotives along the railways continued to spark numerous fires until engine design changes and railway fire patrols occurred after 1900. Increasing law enforcement and fire suppression efforts by national park wardens, Dominion Forestry Rangers, and eventually the provincial Forest Services had, by 1950, drastically limited the area burned in the Canadian Rockies.[36] Many photographs in this book show the success of these programs in turning young frequently burned shrublands into dense continuous carpets of conifer. The effects of reduced fire activity cascaded through all components of Rocky Mountain ecosystems, affecting plants, wildlife, and humans alike.[37] By 1990, national parks had begun prescribed burning programs to partially restore fire (Figs. 4.7d, 11.7). Today, plans require that national park managers maintain a minimum of 50 per cent of the long-term fire regime.[38]

1934 (BYRON HARMON, GLENBOW NA 841-418)

1981(BRUNO ENGLER, CW-BE-FM-1981-31)

2003 (CW 2003-09B-07)

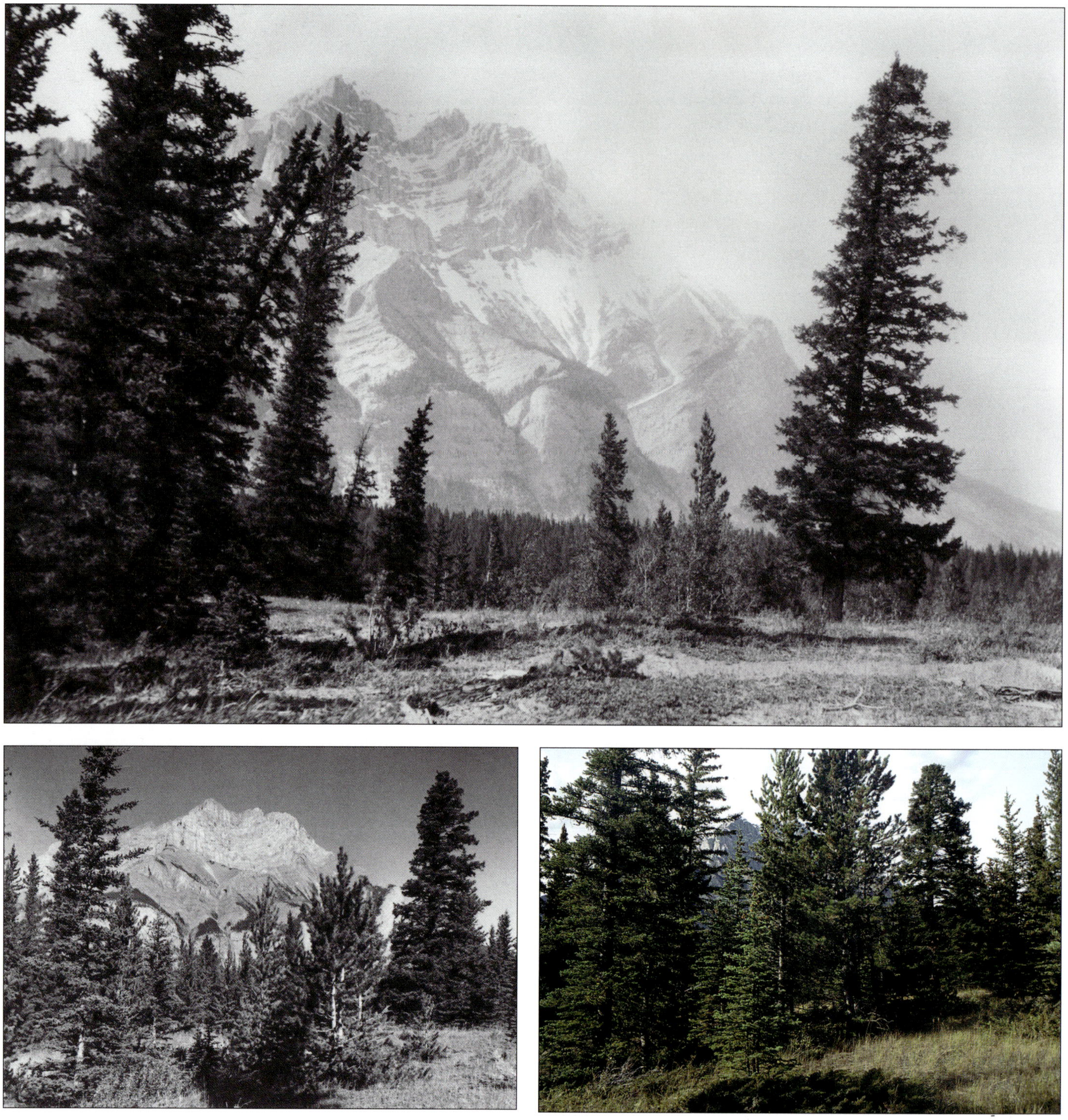

FIGURE 11.6. CHANGING MONTANE VEGETATION NEAR THE HOODOOS, BANFF NATIONAL PARK. THE 1934 PHOTO SHOWS A LARGE, THICK-BARKED DOUGLAS FIR, A VETERAN OF MANY UNDERSTORY FIRES, SURROUNDED BY A FEW WHITE SPRUCE IN A SHRUBLAND OF YOUNG LIMBER PINE, LODGEPOLE PINE, AND JUNIPER. BY 1981, ONGOING FIRE SUPPRESSION HAS ALLOWED SPRUCE AND PINE TO INCREASE IN HEIGHT AND DENSITY. THE 2003 VIEW SHOWS A DENSE FOREST THAT COULD BURN WITH A HIGH-INTENSITY FIRE, KILLING THE OLD TREE.

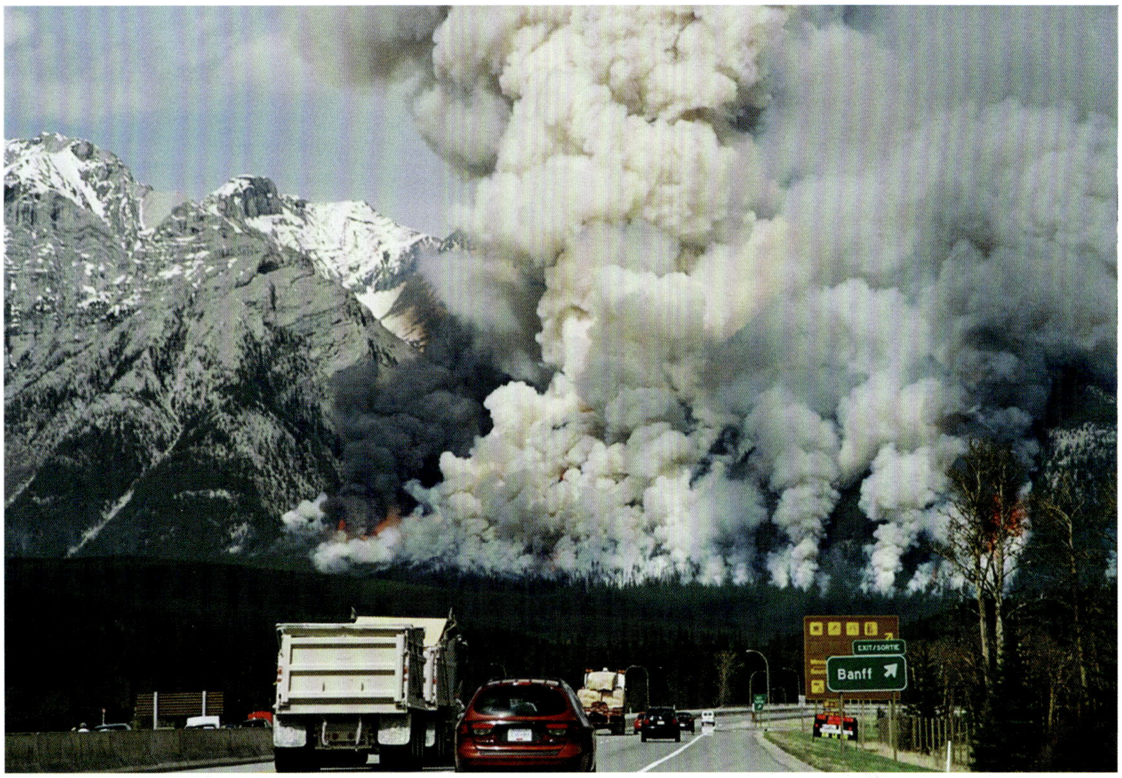

FIGURE 11.7. PRESCRIBED BURNING IN BANFF NATIONAL PARK, 2003 (RANDY KOMAR)

Aging Pine and Mountain Pine Beetle – The reduction of burning so visible across almost the whole landscape today has been a boon for some species – especially a little insect that thrives on mature lodgepole pine trees. Mountain pine beetles likely always exist in small, local populations across the landscape. However, when large areas of forest reach about sixty to eighty years of age, and a period of warm summers and winters occurs, beetle populations can explode. Under the right climatic conditions, millions of the insect's larvae will successfully over-winter under a pine tree's bark, growing to adults by midsummer, and then flying up to several kilometres to burrow under the bark of another group of large susceptible pine trees. Mountain pine beetles are carriers of the blue stain fungus, which, in combination with the girdling effect of the insect, kill the trees within a few days. By the following spring, the dead trees' foliage will fade to a reddish colour. The dead trees are hosts for large numbers of secondary insects, and the woodpeckers that forage on them. In the 1940s and the 1970s, and again in the latter 1990s, the beetle killed large areas of Kootenay and Yoho national parks lodgepole pine forests (Fig. 8.17c). In 1997, the forests of the lower Bow Valley in Banff National Park were also attacked (Fig. 6.3b). Parks Canada accelerated prescribed burning programs to remove mature lodgepole pine that could provide habitat for mountain pine beetle to spread into commercial timber-producing lands further to the east.[39]

HUMANS, WILDLIFE, AND LANDSCAPE CHANGE

As the ice sheets of Wisconsin Glaciation melted, a group of giant land mammals, the "Pleistocene megafauna," began to recolonize the Rocky Mountains and foothills – likely in the same ways they had after the twenty or so previous glaciations of the Ice Age. These species likely included dire wolves, sabre tooth tigers, woolly mammoths, camels, and horses. For example, near Calgary, bones of the Mexican ass, a member of the horse family, and giant bison have been found in gravels where they were deposited by the Bow River about eleven thousand years ago.[40]

However, the Holocene would be much different from previous Pleistocene interglacials for these ice-age veterans. Dispersing out of Eurasia was a new and very deadly predator species – *Homo sapiens*. For thousands of years, humans have had the capability to hunt or capture most of the large animals on the planet. The archaeological record of human dispersal out of Africa, from continent to continent, and island and island, shows a wave of extinction of those species that could not adapt to human hunting, and survival of those that could. In North America, within a few hundred years, most of the long-evolved Pleistocene giant species would be extinct – victims of human hunting, influenced in some areas by climate and vegetation change.[41] However, migrating from Asia along with people came a suite of new, smaller mammals, well-adapted to human hunting and burning. These species included grizzly bear, wolf, a more compact species of bison, moose, and elk. In modern times, the tradition of human hunting continues throughout much of the Rocky Mountains. Although over-hunting eliminated bison, and nearly elk, from the Canadian Rockies by 1900, today's hunter selects from relatively abundant populations of elk, deer, bighorn sheep, and moose. Although hunting is restricted in national parks, other human mortality sources include highways, railways, and removal of problem wildlife.[42]

Although scientists have some understanding of climate and fire effects on landscape change over time, changes in Rocky Mountain wildlife populations remain poorly understood. A good way to understand this complexity of wildlife, vegetation, and landscape change is with a *food web*. For the Rocky Mountain ecosystem, Figure 11.8 shows how physical factors such as availability of sunlight, moisture, and soil nutrients influence the productivity of plant species. The plants provide food for herbivores (plant-eaters), represented here by animals such as beaver, moose, and mountain pine beetle. Energy and nutrients then move up from herbivores to carnivores (meat-eaters), such as wolves and woodpeckers, or omnivores (species that eat both meat and plants) such as humans and bears. The remains of dead animals feed scavengers such as ravens and magpies.[43]

Lines show potential interactions between species, and heavy lines indicate where some of these interactions tied to humans, past and present, may be very strong. What is immediately apparent is that there are many linkages, and when we recognize that this diagram only shows a small percentage of the species and potential links, we can appreciate that there are many processes influencing wildlife and landscape change. Furthermore, the diagram accentuates the pervasive links between people and almost all other ecosystem components. Unlike other species that may have evolved specifically to use, or be used by, a few other select species, humans are the paramount generalists. We are adapted to use many other species for food, shelter, tools, medicine, and ceremony. Interdisciplinary studies of traditional knowledge, history, and archaeology show that the life ways of past human cultures in the Rocky Mountains and adjacent areas were complex and intricately linked to many species and processes.[44]

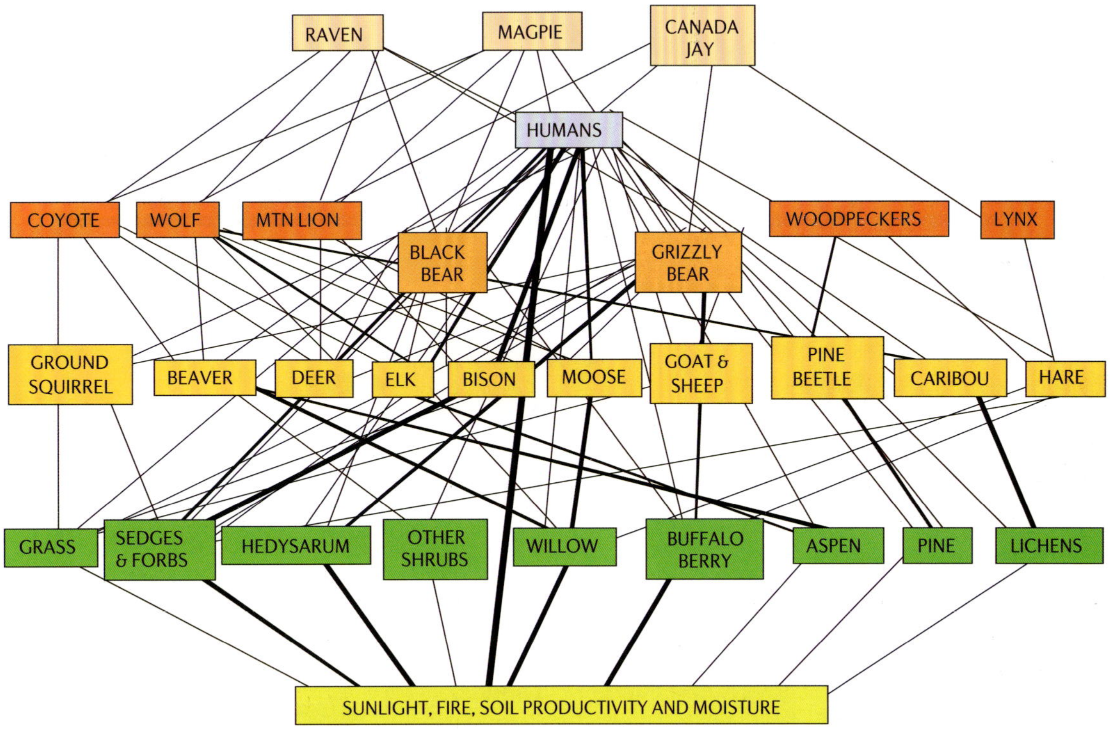

FIGURE 11.8. FOOD WEB DIAGRAM FOR THE CANADIAN ROCKIES TERRESTRIAL ECOSYSTEM. DARKER LINES SHOW POTENTIAL STRONG INTERACTIONS BETWEEN SPECIES.

Human Effects on Wildlife – The food web diagram shows potential linkages between species but does not tell us much about the processes making these links. A key theme of this book is that humans, past and present, have great significance in ecological and landscape change. Accordingly, Figure 11.9 shows more specifics of how humans may influence several indicator wildlife and plant species for Rocky Mountain ecosystems.

This flow chart is known as a *trophic model* because it relates plants (autotrophs) that directly pick up energy from the environment to animals (heterotrophs) that must eat other living matter. The model shows three ways people affect wildlife. First, people directly kill species by hunting or high-speed driving on roads. Furthermore, many animals become a risk or pest to humans and must be killed by wildlife control officers. Secondly, wildlife has a behavioural response to humans. Today, in many areas of the Canadian Rockies, large mammal species are greatly outnumbered by human residents or visitors. Thus, long-term "wild" behaviour to avoid hunting by First Nations can change to habituation when animals are not hunted. Finally, people have significant effects on wildlife habitat by activities such as burning, fire suppression, logging, or road construction. In the following sections, we discuss examples of these interactions.[45]

Top-down or Bottom Up? How do ecosystems work? One of the great ongoing debates between ecologists is whether "top-down" or "bottom-up" processes prevail between trophic levels. In other words, are the basic physical processes (fire, sunlight, moisture, etc.) most important in ecosystem function by bottom-up influences on plant productivity, which in turn alters abundance of herbivores

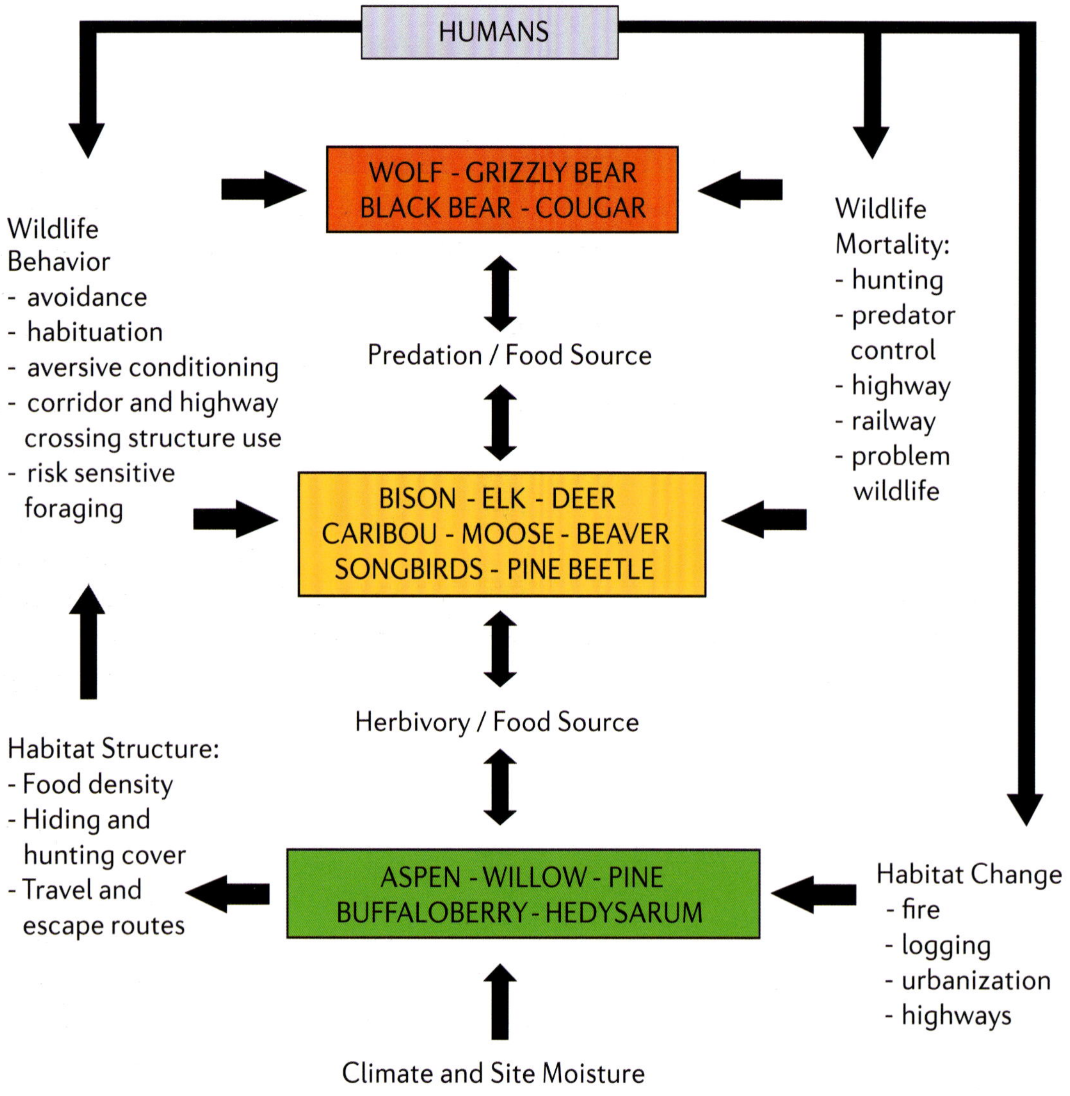

FIGURE 11.9. TROPHIC MODEL FOR ROCKY MOUNTAIN ECOSYSTEM INDICATOR SPECIES SHOWING KEY ECOLOGICAL PROCESSES.

and carnivores? Or, is it possible that the top-down effects of predation and herbivory are dominant processes influencing wildlife and plant productivity? For many years, ecologists leaned towards the "bottom-up" perspective, arguing that carnivores were "a non-essential adjunct" in the functioning of Rocky Mountain ecosystems. From this viewpoint, the relative abundance of prey such as elk, and plant species such as aspen, would be most dependent on physical processes such as climate.[46] However, more recently, research suggests that top-down processes, often including the effects of the ecosystem's top predator, humans, can be surprisingly important in how landscapes change over time.[47]

Traditionally, many ecologists believed that prey species such as bison, elk, or deer were abundant and were held at a high-density "carrying capacity" by food availability and climatic factors.[48] Under this viewpoint, predators would only kill the "doomed surplus," or weak and infirm animals that would certainly die each winter. However, research is showing that the assemblage of Rocky Mountain predators – humans, wolves, cougars, grizzly bears, and black bears – routinely reduced ungulate populations substantially below carrying capacity. The journals of David Thompson and other early European travellers repeatedly report little game in mountain valleys.[49] Recently, when wolves recolonized the Bow Valley in the 1980s, their effects, in combination with killing of elk by other predators, reduced elk numbers from nearly a thousand to less than four hundred. But although this seems strong evidence for the "top-down" hypothesis, there are also important "bottom-up" influences. First, climate interacts strongly to determine predator kill rates. During deep-snow winters, ungulates are relatively immobile, but wolves hunt more successfully.[50] Secondly, in recently burned landscapes, or areas with a long history of low ungulate density and resulting higher abundance of palatable shrubs, ungulates have more food and can possibly space themselves to reduce predation. Historic photographs (e.g., the Bow Valley, Fig. 6.9a) show a recently burned, lightly browsed landscape with abundant habitat for bison, elk, bighorn sheep, and other prey species. The modern landscape, largely overgrown with forest, has fewer areas of high quality habitat, and shrubs are often highly browsed.

Demise of the Eastslope Human-Bison Ecosystem – In the 1800s, white settlers, Metis, and First Nations conducted one of the greatest mass wildlife killings ever documented by historians. Plains bison, once numbering in the millions on the plains, and occupying the east slopes of the Rocky Mountains, were nearly extinct by 1883.[51] In 1877, Treaty 7 (Fig. 2.1) made provisions to resettle Stoney Nakoda, Siksika, and other First Nations in the South Saskatchewan watershed on a limited area of reserve land. With the end of bison hunting, the Canadian government intended for native peoples to avoid starvation by rapidly becoming farmers or ranchers. In addition, by 1910, most of the prairies were fenced, farmed, and ranched, and no return to past conditions was possible.

However, in the more inaccessible mountains and foothills, a millennium-old cultural life cycle of hunting and gathering could not be ended instantaneously. Until the 1920s, family bands of First Nations followed their traditional pattern of hunting in mountain valleys in summer and fall (see Fig. 8.23a) and returning to reserves in winter. But the combined hunting pressure of native hunters and the newly arrived tourists and settlers drove many wildlife populations, already at relatively low density in the Rocky Mountains, towards extirpation. After the disappearance of bison, elk numbers were next to decline to nearly zero. Bighorn sheep and goats were also eliminated from many areas in the late 1800s and early 1900s.[52] Thus, the first assignment for newly established parks' superintendents in Banff and Jasper was to rebuild populations of featured species such as elk, deer, bighorn sheep, and mountain goats for the benefit of tourists within the parks and outfitters guiding big game hunters around their boundaries. Banff staff even began keeping a herd of captive bison in a paddock near the bottom of Cascade Mountain starting in 1898 (Figs. 4.16, 11.10).[53] Killing of this wildlife by

FIGURE 11.10. CAPTIVE WOOD BISON IN THE BANFF PADDOCK, 1986 (DOUGLAS LEIGHTON).

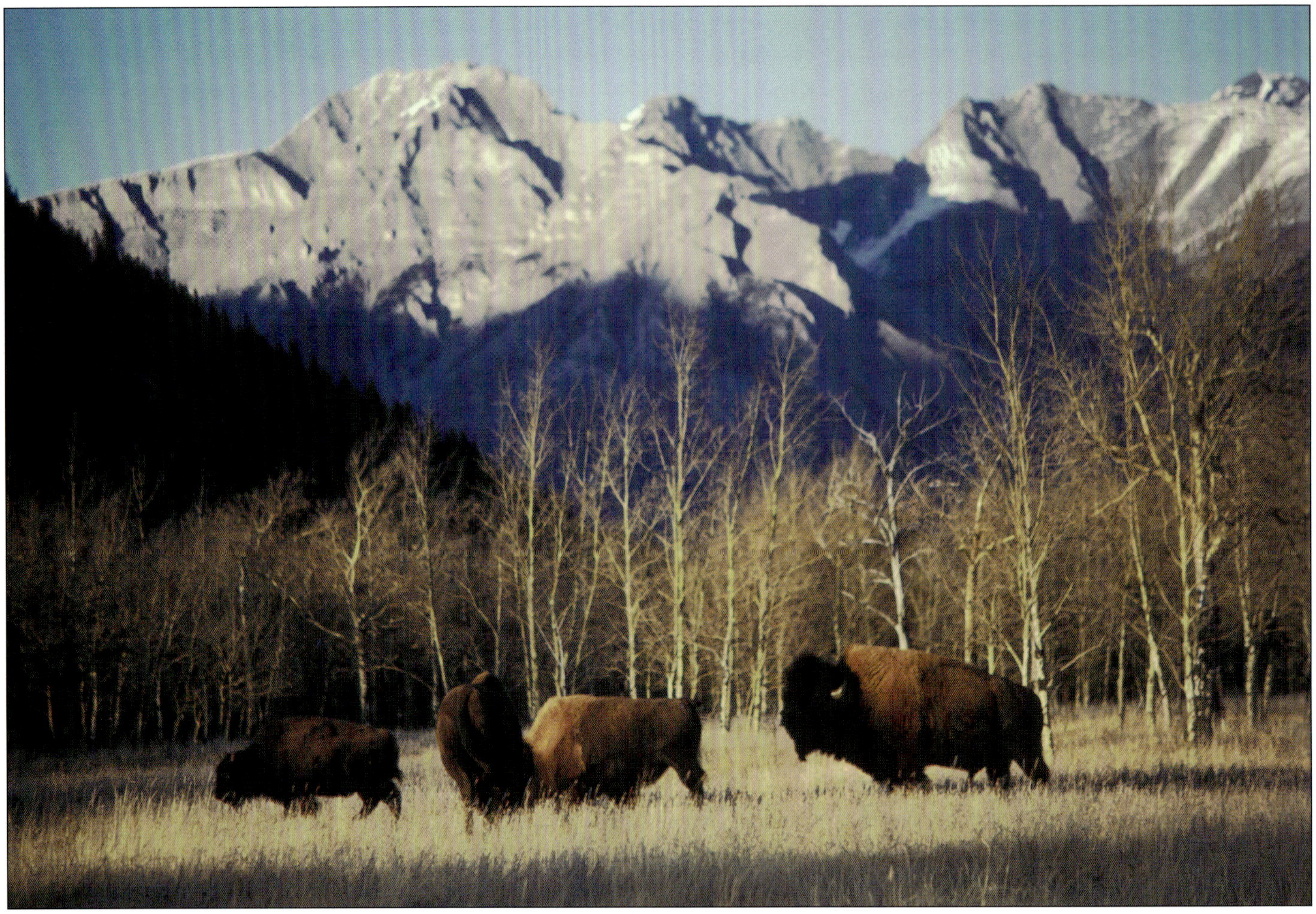

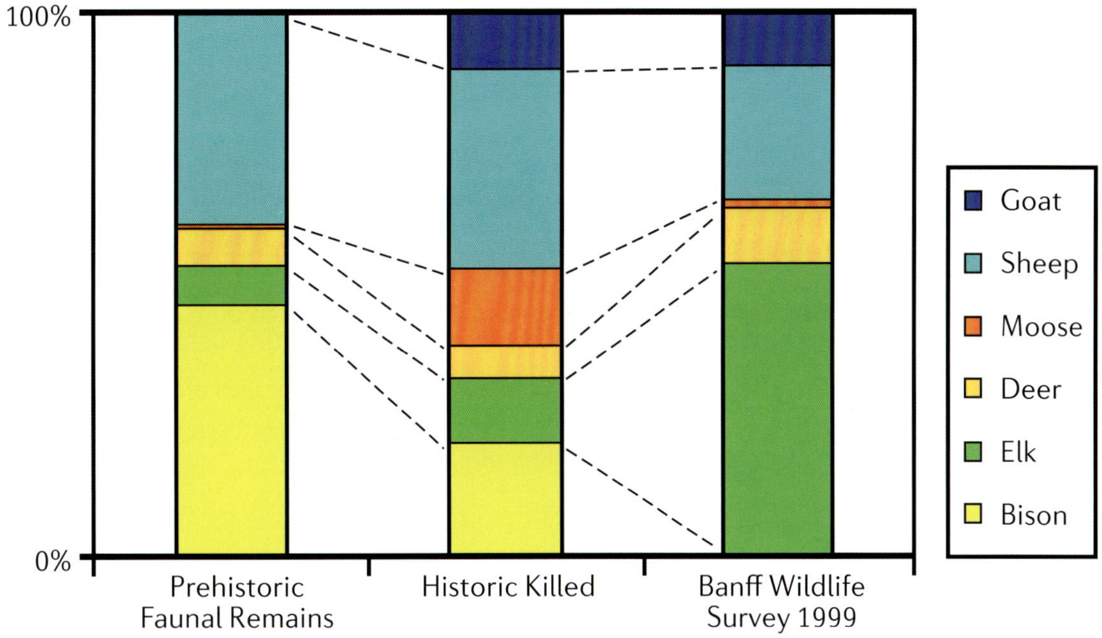

FIGURE 11.11. CHANGING RELATIVE ABUNDANCES OF NATIVE LARGE HERBIVORES ALONG THE EASTERN SLOPES OF BANFF NATIONAL PARK FROM ARCHAEOLOGICAL AND HISTORICAL STUDIES, AND RECENT WILDLIFE SURVEYS.

any means was discouraged. Native carnivores were controlled. And, of course, any hunting by First Nations was stopped. In addition, over time, park officials were increasingly stringent in requiring that permits be obtained for use of plants (no flower-picking!), lighting fires, and grazing horses. This in effect ended ten thousand years of subsistence human use of Rocky Mountain ecosystems.[54]

With the demise of bison and First Nations traditional land use, so ended a long-evolved ecosystem linking plains, foothills, and mountains. Figure 11.11 shows the relative change in large herbivore abundance (east of the continental divide) from prehistoric through historic to the present time periods as approximated from bones in archaeological sites, first-person explorer journal accounts of hunting, and recent wildlife surveys.[55] This major shift in the large mammal assemblage was caused by the chain-reaction of losing the long-term patterns of predation by wolves, people, and other predators. Competition interactions between bison, elk, and other herbivores, bison grazing effects on native bunch grasses, and human travel, hunting, and burning habits tied to bison also completely changed. The landscape as viewed in early photographs was often created by these processes, and many of the changes visible since then may be due to their cessation. Today, it takes meticulous scientific research to reconstruct how this historic ecosystem may have worked. In many ways, we may never know.[56]

Bison Wallows and Aspen Seedlings – In the past, bison were the dominant large herbivore on valley-bottom ecosystems of the eastern slope of the Rocky Mountains. Although humans and predators may have limited the abundance of other large prey such as elk, the vast migrating bison herds on the plains were less susceptible to over-hunting. Periodically, some herds followed trails off of the plains into mountains. These bison replenished the abundance of mountain-dwelling bison whose movements were constrained by the rugged terrain and thus were likely periodically hunted to low densities.[57] Herds of cows and bull bison would rendezvous each year in midsummer to mate. The peak of the "rut" in the northwest plains and foothills was early August, and in the mountains, it is likely that the valley-bottom grasslands were favoured locations. Here bulls would demonstrate their prowess by horn-gouging and pawing out deep dusty wallows, spewing soil in all directions. Explorers on the prairies reported the bellowing of the bulls "so as to form an almost continued roar."[58]

Wallowing may help explain how aspen colonized and persisted in some dryer valley-bottom areas. Today in the Rockies, aspen stems created from seed are uncommon, likely due to competition from grasses and shrubs. Aspen stands are most commonly clones regenerated from suckering of pre-existing root systems. However, in past times, bison wallows in moister areas on the edge of meadows could have formed perfect habitats for germination of aspen seeds. Stands of aspen often ringed valley-bottom meadows (Figs. 2.12, 2.14, 4.4, 10.12). Where the grasslands have not been greatly disturbed by recent human activity, such as on the Ya-Ha-Tinda Ranch (Figs. 8.13, 8.14), wallows dating back prior to the decline of bison in the 1800s are still clearly visible. Aspen, gooseberry, and other moisture-loving shrubs are often found in these depressions.[59]

The Predator Control and Elk-Culling Experiment – Early Government of Canada land managers wanted to increase big game numbers in the Rocky Mountains for tourism and sport hunting. Until the 1960s park wardens were routinely ordered to kill predators, including coyotes, wolves, cougars, and grizzly bears.[60] Even today, outside of parks, control of wolf populations is often required to protect cattle herds. Elk from Yellowstone National Park were transplanted to Banff and Jasper areas between 1917 and 1920 (Fig. 10.12a) to replenish resident herds depleted by over-hunting. A not entirely unexpected consequence of predator control was an exponential increase in these elk numbers, to over three thousand by 1945, for example, in the Bow Valley of Banff National Park. In the absence of predators, elk numbers are regulated by food. By the 1940s, biologists feared that starving elk could cause long-term damage to plant species important for grazing and browsing food. Ironically, concurrent with predator control, park wardens were then ordered to also cull elk. Wardens shot or trucked out several thousand elk from Banff and Jasper national parks from 1940 to 1969.[61] Since the 1960s, park administrators have increasingly recognized the importance of the predator's role in Rocky Mountain ecosystems. Today, the health of predator populations is used as an indicator of "ecological integrity" as required by Parks Canada legislation.

Restoring Landscapes of Fear – Human and carnivore influences on prey behaviour patterns interacted with the direct effects of killing and reducing numbers. Historically, Rocky Mountain valley bottoms were the favoured travel routes for wolves, bears, and human hunters. Accordingly, to avoid these predators, elk, deer, and other prey made spring season migrations to the alpine and spent more time on the rugged terrain on the steep valley sides.[62] However, when predators are rare, elk, deer, bighorn sheep and other prey will forage on the lower slopes where food is most abundant and the effort to obtain it is minimized. An extreme example of predator effects on prey behaviour occurred after the 1985 recolonization of wolves of the Bow Valley in Banff National Park. By 1997, most the remaining elk in the valley had concentrated near the Town of Banff where high human use repelled wolves and cougars. These elk used the fertilized lawns, playing fields, and golfing grounds in and around the town year round. Traditional spring through fall elk migrations to the high country nearly ceased as elk minimized their exposure to carnivores by staying in the town. After several generations

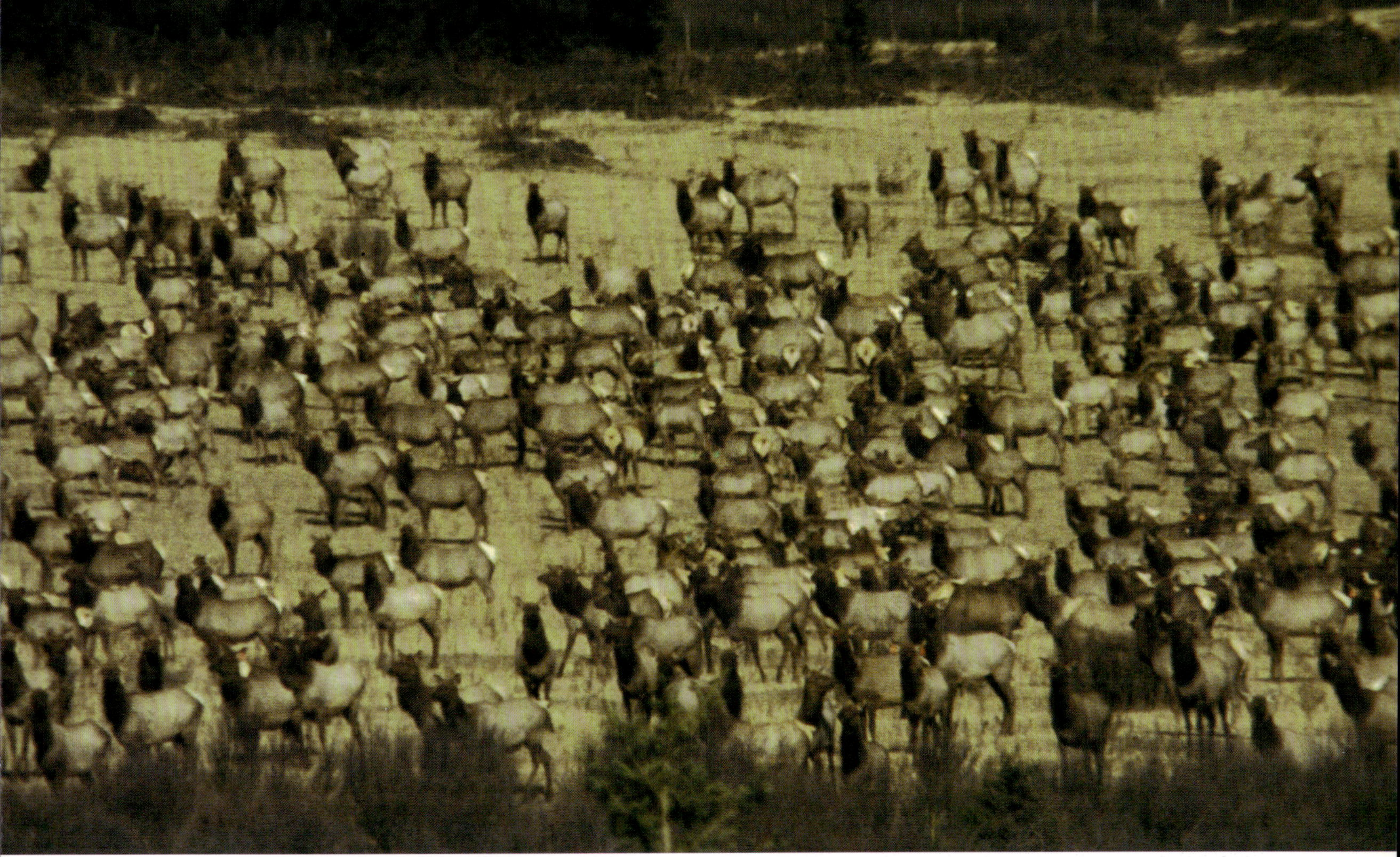

FIGURE 11.12. PARTIALLY HUMAN-HABITUATED HERD OF COW ELK ON THE YA-HA-TINDA RANCH (CW 1995-04A-13)

of calves were born and raised in the townsite, elk aggression to humans and browsing impacts on plants reached intolerable levels in 1999. Park managers alleviated the problem by reducing human use levels in wildlife movement corridors around the town (see Figs. 4.16, 4.24) to allow routine use by carnivores, and by capturing and trucking highly habituated elk back to the wildlands.[63]

Similarly, between 1980 and 2000, wildlife biologists observed a change in movement patterns of elk using the Ya-Ha-Tinda Ranch east of Banff National Park (Fig. 8.13). Prior to the 1990s, elk cows wintered on the ranch, but each spring migrated westwards, dispersing widely across Banff National Park. By 2000, nearly half the herd no longer migrated in summer. The cow elk recognized that they were protected from human hunting, and increasing numbers of recreational equestrians visiting the ranch in spring and summer were displacing wary wolves during the day, thus providing the elk with a relatively safe location to birth and nurse their calves. In turn, the relatively persistent and high population of elk now using the ranch year-round (Fig. 11.12) provided ideal conditions for a stable "halo" of wolf packs to form in the region around the ranch. These predators in turn further decimated the number of elk that used the halo areas or migrated out of the core zone, in addition to reducing numbers of other secondary prey such as moose, goats, bighorn sheep, and caribou. Starting in 2003, managers began to reinvigorate the migratory patterns of ranch-dwelling elk by herding them westward by horseback in June. Historically, First Nations hunters would have stimulated these movements.[64]

A. LOW ELK DENSITY (CW 1999-06B-16)

B. MODERATE TO HIGH ELK DENSITY (CW 1998-05D-29)

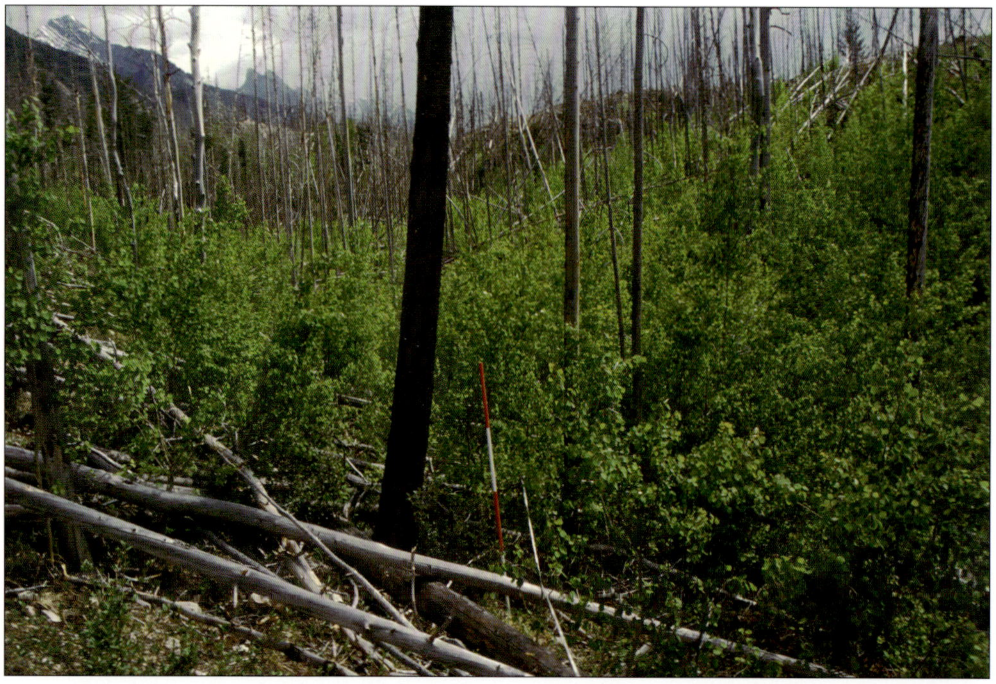

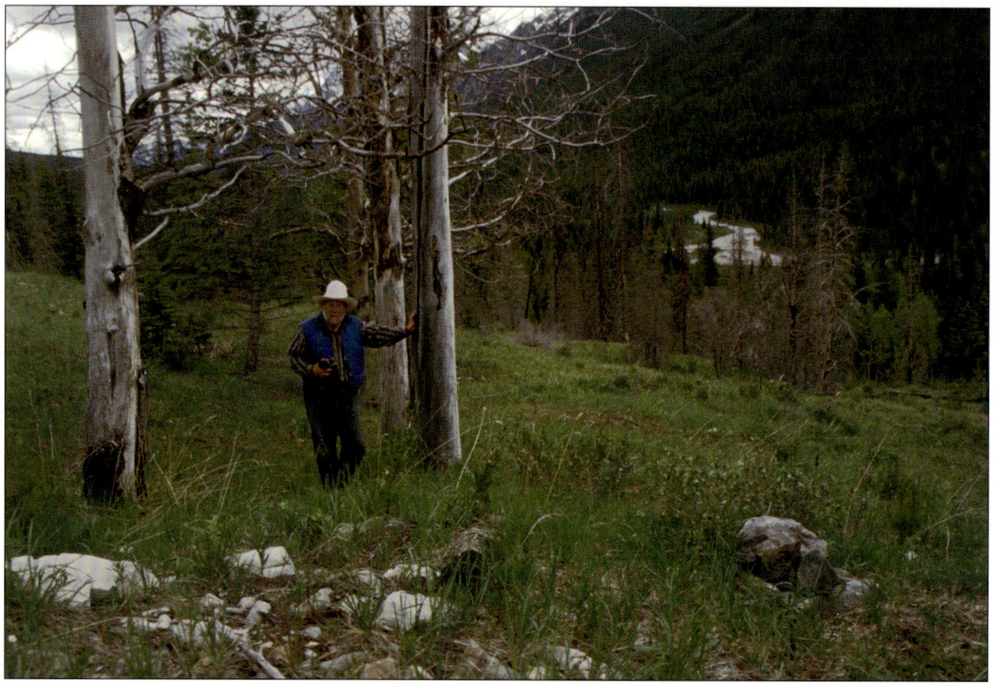

FIGURE 11.13. TREMBLING ASPEN STANDS ABOUT TEN YEARS AFTER BEING BURNED WITH PRESCRIBED FIRES. THE BURN IN AN AREA OF LOW ELK DENSITY (< 1 ELK/KM^2) REGENERATED OVER 10,000 SAPLINGS PER HECTARE TO HEIGHTS GREATER THAN TWO METRES. IN THE AREA OF MODERATE ELK DENSITY (2 TO 4 ELK/KM^2) THE FIRE KILLED MATURE ASPEN, AND STIMULATED SPROUTING OF NUMEROUS ROOT SHOOTS, BUT NO STEMS GREW TO GREATER THAN 0.5 METRES BEFORE BEING BROWSED BY ELK.

People, Browsing Wildlife, and the Decline of Aspen and Other Plants – Historically, frequent fires killed conifers and the above-ground portions of aspen and other species such as willow, balsam poplar, saskatoon, and red osier dogwood. When they are lightly browsed, these plants then sprout back prolifically from surviving roots (Fig. 11.13a). However, as described above, removal of predators increases the density of elk and other herbivores on valley-bottom ranges through direct (increased abundance) and indirect (reduced wildlife movement) effects. Moreover, as shown in Figure 11.11, the relative abundance of herbivores has shifted from bison (a grazer) to elk (a browsing generalist). In the Canadian Rocky Mountain national parks, where bison were eliminated by the 1870s, and predators were controlled for most of the 1900s, this has caused dramatic effects on ungulate winter ranges. The abundance of palatable trees and shrubs has been sharply decreased due to browsing by numerous elk (Figs. 4.19, 6.9, 10.12).

In the past, many foresters and wildlife biologists believed that fire might be a cure-all for the effects of heavy elk feeding. They believed that fire could cause prolific sprouting of tree and shrub shoots that could "swamp" ongoing browsing. For example, across western North America, managers have lit prescribed fires across thousands of hectares with the objective of regenerating trembling aspen. Unfortunately, in areas of high elk density, this practice has accelerated aspen's demise. Older aspen trees and willows, too tall to be consumed by herbivores, are top-killed by fire, and the resprouting shoots are browsed intensively. After several years, even the long-lived root systems of these plants may die, and the age-old cycle of fire and regeneration is broken (Fig. 11.13b).[65]

Beaver, Willow, and Elk – Beavers are nature's dam builders and can have a dramatic effect on valley-bottom stream and vegetation conditions. High elk densities cause an interesting process of landscape change when they interact with beaver and willow. In montane wetlands such as near Vermilion Lakes near Banff, and in the Athabasca Valley around Jasper, beaver historically would occupy an area once willows and aspens reached approximately the two metres in height necessary to build strong dams and lodges. Once the stems near a lodge were utilized, the beavers would move on, leaving the immediate area for the necessary ten to thirty years it took for aspen and willow to regrow. However, in parks, recent high densities of elk often remove much of this regeneration before it reaches even a metre in height, precluding the reoccupation cycle by beaver (Fig. 11.14). For example, the number of beaver lodges in the Vermilion Lakes declined from over ten in the early 1980s to one by 1999, and water levels in the lakes dropped accordingly. Reductions in elk densities by restoring predators and relocating or aversively conditioning human-habituated elk can allow a return of the long-term beaver-willow cycle to wetlands.[66]

Bears, Burning and Shrubs – Biologists studying bears in the Canadian Rockies notice an obvious pattern. Bears, especially grizzly bears, love recently burned areas. Fires create ideal grizzly habitat. Dead trees falling after the fire are quickly filled with ants – a bear delicacy. Hedysarum, a legume species, thrives on recently burned and open habitats. Its nutritious root-tuber is a staple food for bears in early spring and fall. Buffalo berry quickly resprouts after burning, and in open young forests, produces prolific berry crops that may totally sustain the bear population in August. But the relationship between bears and plant regrowth after burning may be even more complex. Bears are opportunistic omnivores and will switch from eating plants to hunting animals whenever possible. In spring, bears are often specialists at finding and eating elk and moose calves. By reducing densities of these herbivores, bears can enhance the post-fire regeneration of heavily browsed species such as red osier dogwood, saskatoon, aspen, and willow. Historic photographs show prolific regeneration of these browse species in burns, possibly partially due to the role of bears hunting browsing animals.[67]

FIGURE 11.14. WILLOW PROTECTED FROM ELK BROWSING BY A FENCE ERECTED BY RESEARCHERS AT THE OUTLET OF FIRST VERMILION LAKE NEAR BANFF (CW 2000-08A-19).

FIGURE 11.15. SMALL HERD OF CARIBOU IN THE UPPER PIPESTONE RIVER VALLEY OF BANFF NATIONAL PARK, CA. 1992 (PARKS CANADA-BANFF NATIONAL PARK).

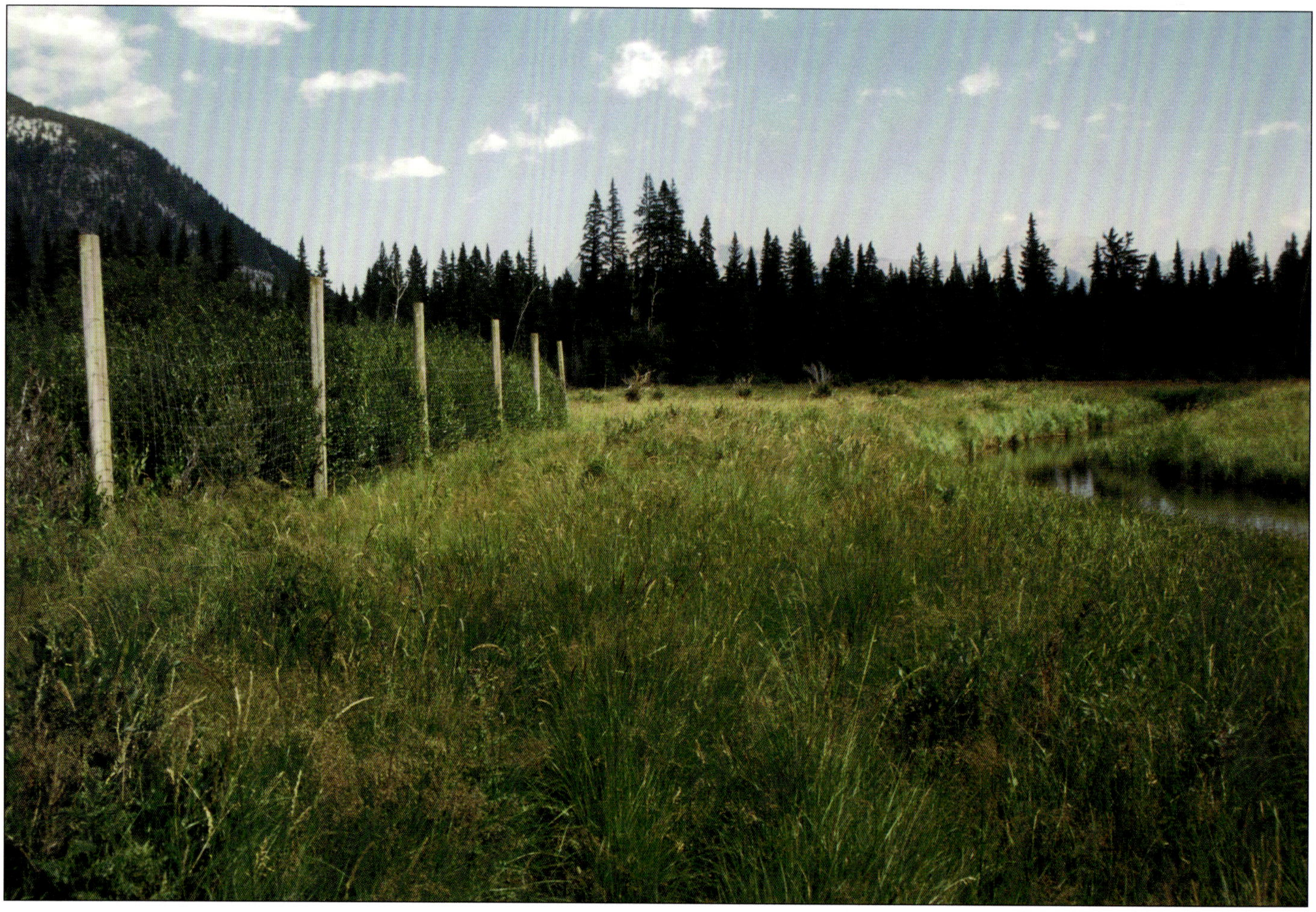

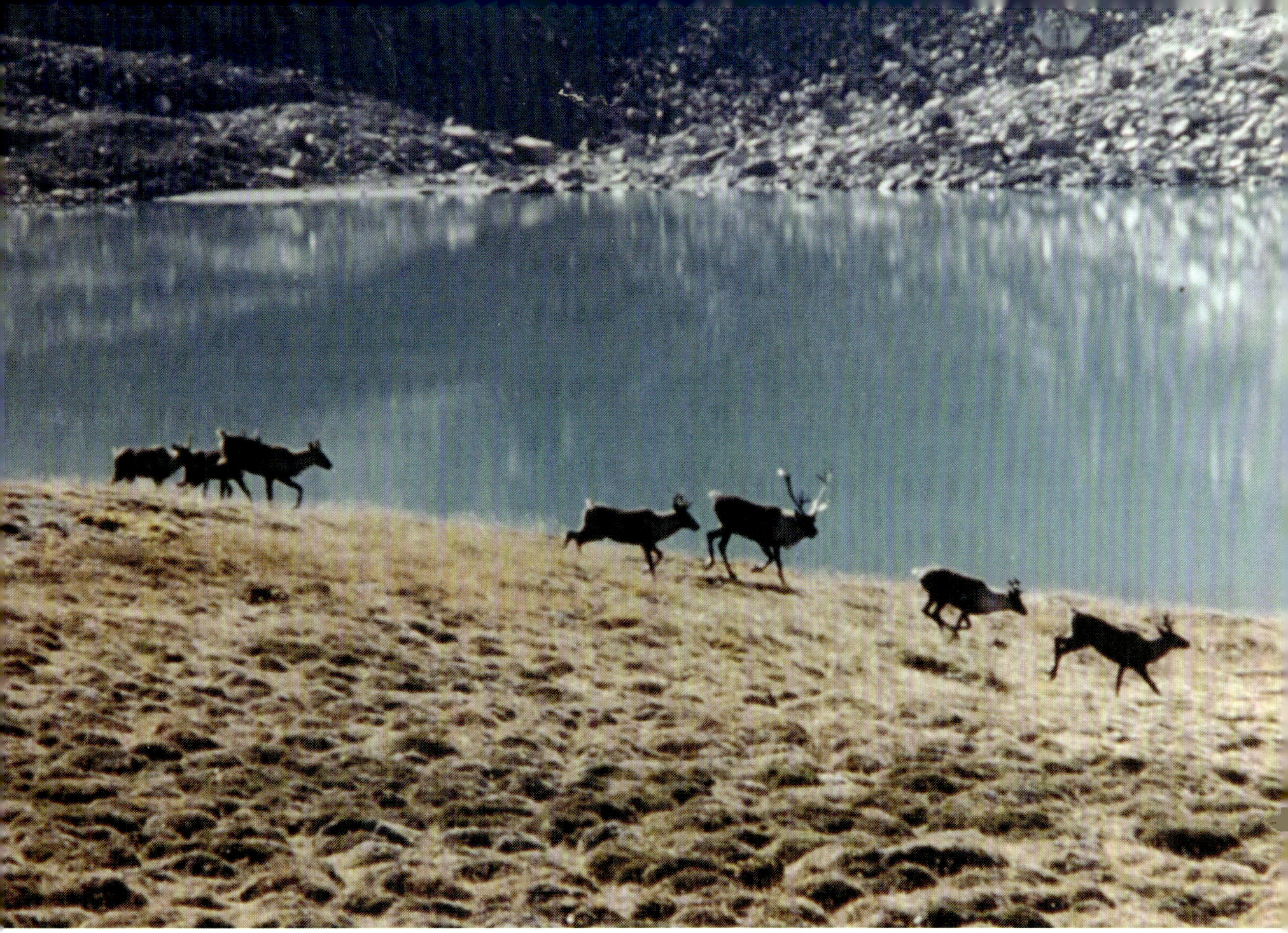

Losing Caribou: A Lesson in Regional-level Landscape Change – Two of the woodland caribou herds in most rapid decline lie not in Alberta's industrialized boreal forest (Fig. 10.18), but rather in the remotest wildernesses of Banff and Jasper national parks (Fig. 11.15). What's going on here? Well, first, it's not likely lack of habitat or food. Caribou prefer feeding on the lichens found in older forests at higher elevations. Due to fewer fires, and as the photographs in this book clearly show, there is an increasing amount of old forest in the Canadian Rockies – perhaps providing at least a five-hundred-year high in the amount of food available.[68] Rather, the answer may lie in the abundance of the caribou's primary enemy – the wolf. During the period of intensive predator control, from the 1920s until about 1960, populations of elk, deer, or moose, the primary prey for wolves, all grew. However, once predator control eased on national parks and adjacent lands after 1960, the abundance of prey boosted wolf numbers, possibly to all-time highs. As described above, some human developments, such as townsites in national parks, allow elk and deer to partially avoid wolf predation. This, in combination with modern hunting restrictions, causes an abnormal stable situation of ongoing high prey and resulting high wolf densities. Wolves, being wide-ranging, do not stay only at low elevations near primary prey. They search out caribou in the remote, high-country valleys, and have systematically reduced the numbers of what was already a rare species. So one can simply look at the low-elevation winter ranges to ascertain the population trend of caribou at higher elevations up to a hundred kilometres away. If the browsed condition of aspen and willow indicates that deer, elk, or moose densities are high and stable, it is likely that caribou in the region will be at risk. Two current examples of this situation are

FIGURE 11.16. WILDLIFE CROSSING OVERPASS ON THE TRANS-CANADA HIGHWAY, BANFF NATIONAL PARK, 2005 (ANTHONY CLEVENGER, PARKS CANADA).

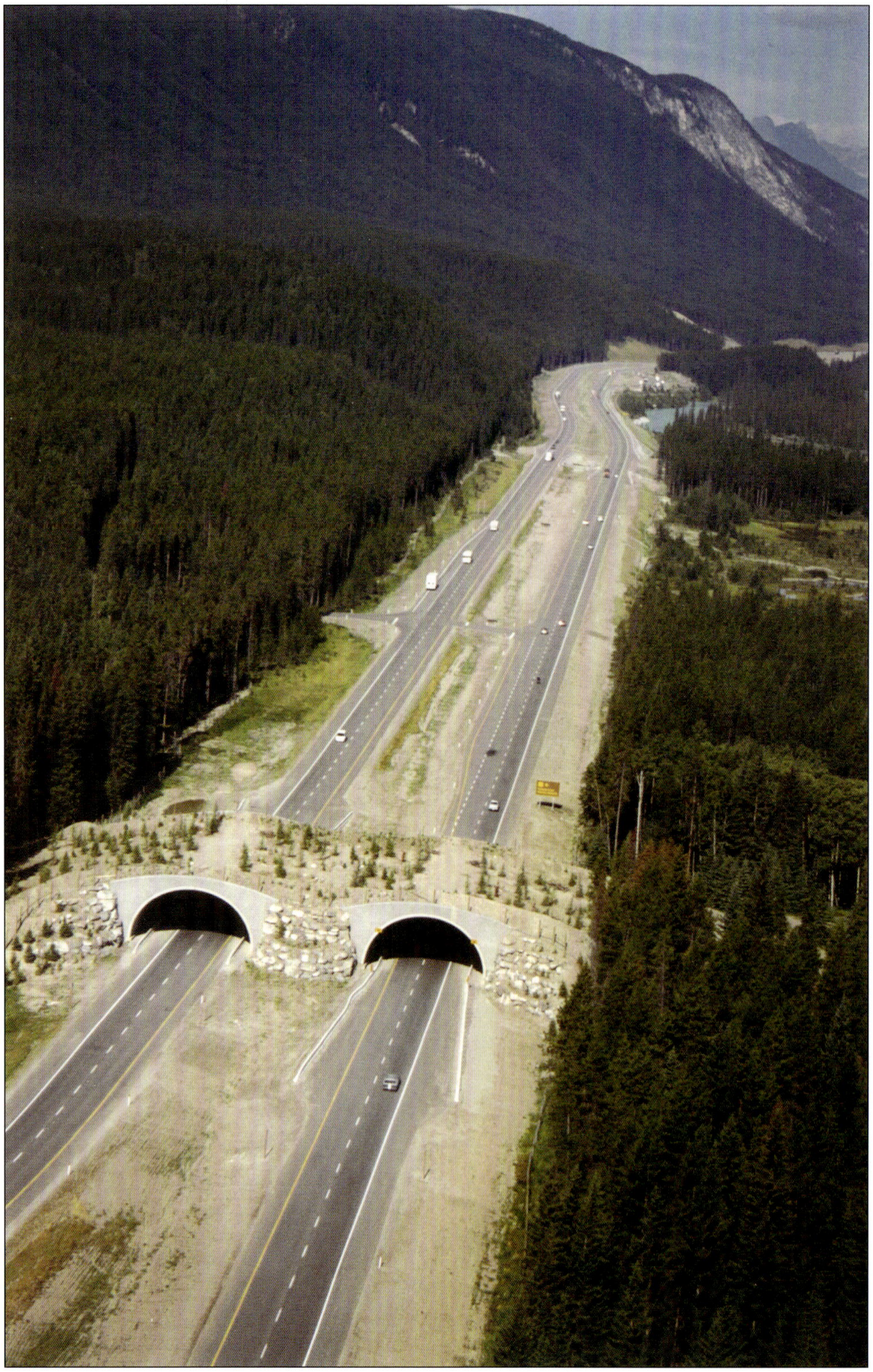

the effects of high elk densities on the Ya-Ha-Tinda Ranch (Fig. 11.12) and the Athabasca Valley on remote bands of caribou in the Red Deer and Maligne valleys, respectively.[69]

How can declining caribou herds in the mountain national parks be restored? Although the "quick fix" of aggressive predator control may be appropriate in some situations, probably the most important task is to reduce the abnormally high populations of elk and other species that are the primary prey for wolves. One option is to improve wildlife movement corridors around high-human-use areas to increase predator access that will eventually reduce elk numbers. Where necessary, direct prey reduction by human hunting or relocation is also required. Less prey will result in reduced wolf numbers, and less predation on caribou. Another option may be to restore bison, a less favourable prey for wolves (thus resulting in fewer wolves for a given number of bison versus elk). Furthermore, bison historically may have utilized alpine areas less frequently than today's migrating elk, thus attracting fewer wolves in caribou habitat. Finally, by limiting human activities in winter that pack snow trails into caribou habitat that are in turn used by wolves, land managers may also reduce caribou predation rates.[70]

THE MODERN URBAN-INDUSTRIAL FOOTPRINT

Above we discussed the often subtle landscape changes resulting from the interaction of changing human cultures with wildlife and vegetation. We conclude with a brief discussion of much more obvious landscape change resulting from direct physical and mechanical landscape change by humans of the industrial age.

Railways and Highways – Historic trails are relatively invisible in old photographs, but the routes for modern mechanized transportation dominate many of today's scenes. These human-made vectors do not just visually impair the modern landscape, but fundamentally alter ecosystem processes. Streams must be diverted and ditched to flow through culverts or bridges. In some cases, poorly placed culverts completely block fish migration. Busy highways may restrict the movements of wary carnivores such as grizzly bears or wolves, or if animals are naive to the dangers of speeding vehicles, they may perish while crossing unfenced roadways or railways. For example, moose numbers often decline rapidly in areas with highways. The Trans-Canada Highway in the lower Bow Valley of Banff National Park (Figs. 4.12c, 4.16b, 6.3b, 6.6c) is a world-renowned prototype for reducing highway impacts on wildlife. Fences stop most animals from being hit by vehicles, and specially designed wildlife crossing structures allow most species to cross under or over the road (Fig. 11.16). However, even with expensive engineering solutions, wildlife movement patterns are often clearly altered. For example, for several years in the 1990s, wolves using the area east of Banff townsite had not yet learned to use the highway crossing underpasses and usually stayed north of the highway (right side of Fig. 4.12c). To avoid predation by wolves, elk simply stayed on the south side of the highway closer to Banff townsite.[71]

Dams – Agriculture, industry, and urbanization need water for irrigation, power, or other needs. Calgary Power Limited (now TransAlta Corporation) had built dams on the Bow River (Fig. 2.9), and most its main tributaries, including the Kananaskis (Fig. 2.13), Spray, and Cascade (Fig. 4.14) by 1955. In 1971, the company completed its largest hydro-power project, the Bighorn Dam on the North Saskatchewan, which created Lake Abraham (Fig. 8.24).[72] West of the Rockies, BC Hydro's massive

FIGURE 11.17. TIMBER HARVESTING (CW 2003-03C-03).

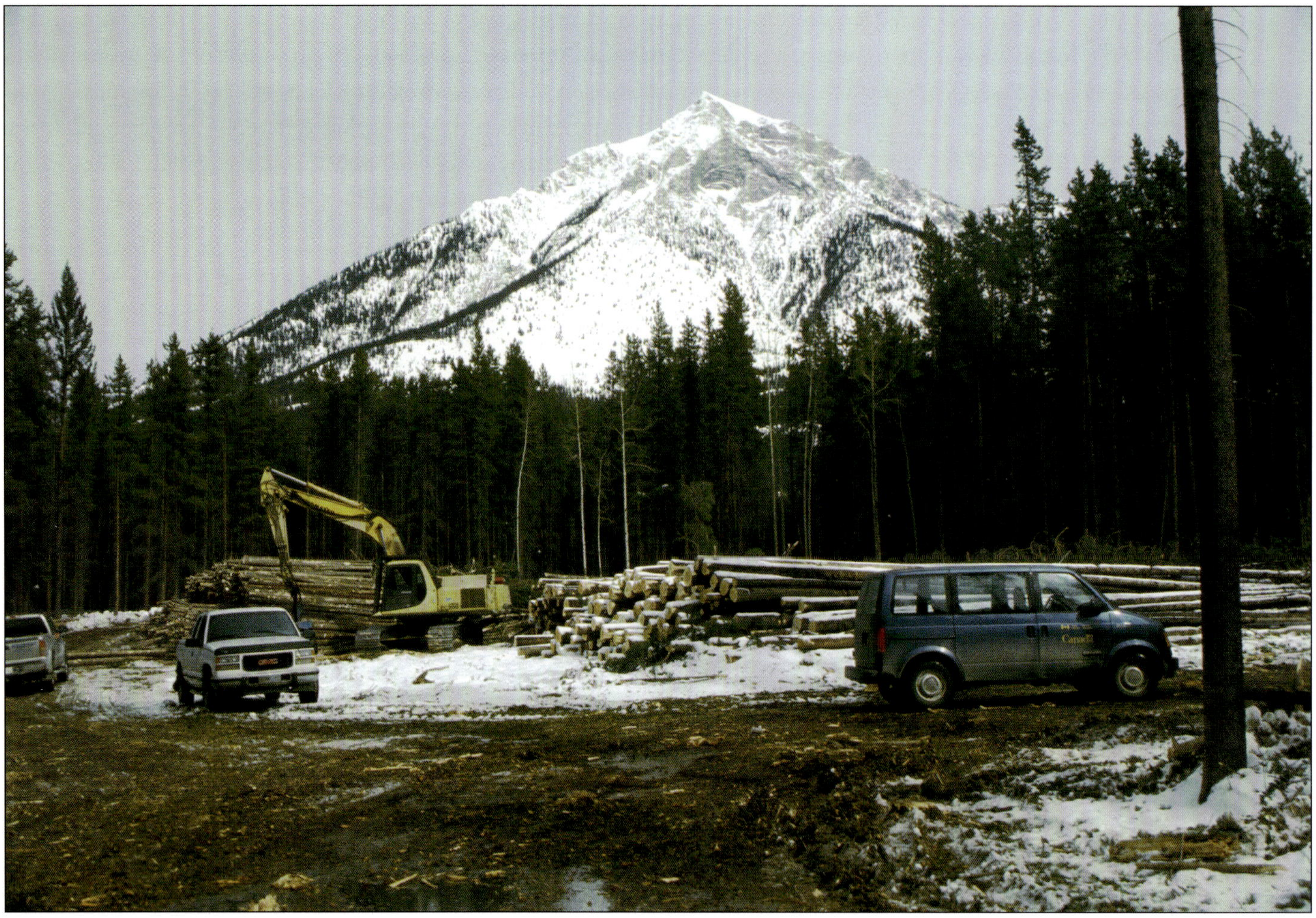

Mica Dam inundated much of the Rocky Mountain Trench north of Golden under the deep waters of Lake McNaughton.[73] These reservoirs have obviously completely eliminated many areas of ecologically rich valley bottoms. Further, the dams completely block upstream fish movement and dramatically reduce the level of peak flooding in downstream areas. This may be beneficial to urban development on floodplains such as much of downtown Canmore, Alberta (Fig. 2.16), but the dampening of the spring flood greatly changes the character of stream-side vegetation and wildlife habitat.[74]

Industrial Use of Public Lands – Several industries have altered the Rocky Mountains and foothills. Ranching began in the 1880s, which, as noted above, required predator control and eventually fencing. Timber harvesting has for over a hundred years been an important industry (Fig. 11.17). Although commercial logging was removed from national parks (not until 1970 in Yoho National Park), most of the area outside parks is under commercial licence for harvesting to provide wood for mills in communities such as Radium, Golden, Hinton, Edson, Sundre, and Cochrane. Mining of coal and limestone remain important in several areas. And along the east slopes, a dominant industry continues to be oil and natural gas exploration and extraction. The combination of mining, logging, and oil and gas industries cumulatively causes major changes in the landscape (Fig. 10.18). Increased human access on roads built for industrial development can particularly impact wildlife populations due to hunting and other interactions.[75]

Tourism and Recreation – Although there have been ephemeral booms tied to coal, minerals, timber, and petroleum, the long-term engines of economic growth in many Rocky Mountain communities are increasingly tourism and recreation. As other resources are depleted, town after town has turned to exploiting the clear blue skies, spectacular mountain scenery, large areas of wildlands, and deep winter powder snow to attract visitors from around the globe. The railway companies were the first to capitalize on this natural wealth – building world-famed hotels at Banff (Figs. 4.6, 4.7), Lake Louise (Fig. 8.4), Field (Fig. 8.16), and Jasper (Figs. 10.8, 10.9) to attract train passengers.[76] However, it was the building of roads and the North American embrace of the automobile that made the Canadian Rockies a paradise for all. By the 1950s, each summer, millions of people simply loaded their kids in the car and drove to the mountains for a day, a week, even a month. These travellers were accommodated in park campgrounds and bungalow camps such as at Castle Junction (Fig. 6.12b), Radium Hot Springs (Fig. 6.14), Num-Ti-Jah (Fig. 8.20c), and the Icefields Chalet (Fig. 8.27), and in expanding campgrounds.[77] Easy road access to the mountains also fuelled the great expansion into winter recreation. After 1960, skiers from Calgary could speed west down the new Trans-Canada to reach mountain ski areas within two hours (Figs. 4.22, 6.4, 8.11). The age of rapid jet-aircraft travel to nearby international airports and an excellent highway system for use by rental cars and tour buses completed the list of ingredients that would bring boom times to the Rockies. Year-round visitation stimulated large-scale replacement of Banff, Lake Louise, and Jasper commercial facilities after 1970. Quaint seasonal bungalows and motels were transformed to modern fully winterized hotels (Fig. 4.23). Today, millions of visitors, coming year-round, stay in numerous hotels and motels that line the streets of Rocky Mountain towns.[78]

FIGURE 11.18. CONSTRUCTION OF NEW MOUNTAIN HOMES IN CANMORE, ALBERTA (CW 2006-03A-22)

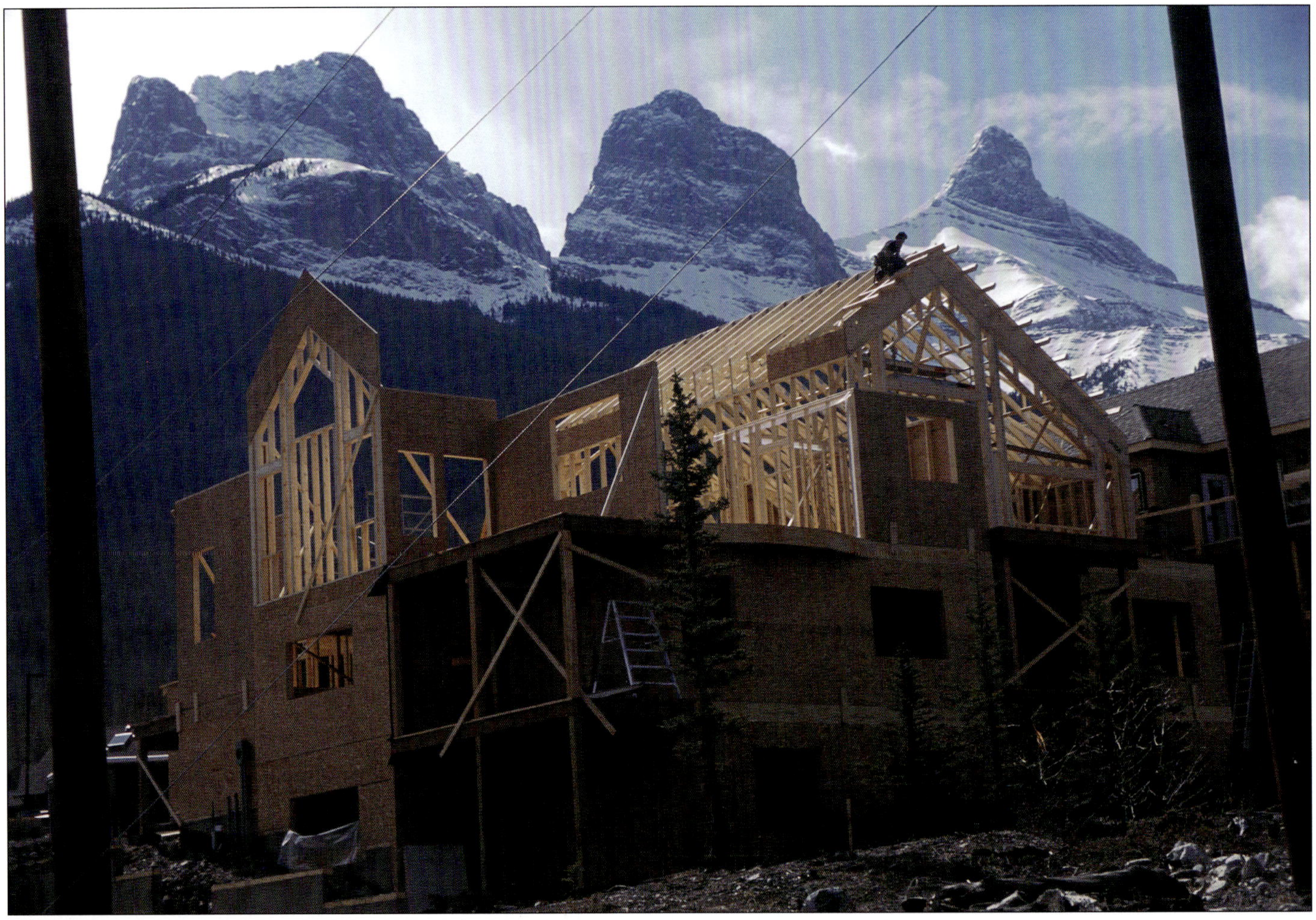

Cities, Towns, and Country Homes – In the last two decades, urban growth has become the new driver of landscape change in the Canadian Rockies and foothills. Thousands of North Americans, Europeans, and people of other nationalities are not just visiting the mountains; they are moving here. The modern economy depends on a highly mobile workforce dependent on the Internet and quick access to international airports. These workers are attracted to a scenic environment, world-class recreational facilities, and the amenities provided by small cities and well-developed towns.[79] Unlike the American Rocky Mountains, most of the Canadian Rockies is publicly owned, so more urban growth has been concentrated in the lower foothills in towns such as Cochrane (Fig. 2.4) or Turner Valley (Fig. 2.8), in the Columbia Valley in towns such as Invermere (Fig. 6.16) and Golden (Fig. 8.18), or the inner Rocky Mountain towns themselves, including Canmore (Fig. 2.14), Banff (Fig. 4.18), and Jasper (Fig. 10.2), that have limited development potential due to surrounding park lands. The Calgary-Edmonton-Banff-Jasper-Invermere regional population increased from under five hundred thousand people in 1950 to over two million by the year 2000. These people need housing, schools, hospitals, shopping centres, roads, and recreational opportunities. Increasingly, people are moving away from towns and cities and are building homes on ranches or farms subdivided into *acreages* next to the public forest lands and parks. This urban growth, fuelled by Alberta's and British Columbia's booming economies, will bring about some of the greatest landscape management challenges of the future.[80]

12

APPENDICES

APPENDIX A: SELECTED BIOGRAPHIES FOR PHOTOGRAPHERS

BOORNE AND MAY

William Hanson Boorne (1859–1945) and his cousin Ernest Gundry May operated the firm of Boorne and May in Edmonton and Calgary between 1886 and 1893, specializing in portrait, landscape, and architectural photography. During its short time in business, it was one of the most active and prestigious photographic firms in western Canada, commencing business just at the time when the CPR was building its line through western Canada and opening new and unseen vistas for photographic arts. The photographs used in *The Lens of Time* largely originated from an album entitled "Landscapes" consisting of a hundred views along the line of the CPR through the Rockies and Selkirks and presented to "William Whyte, General Superintendent, Western Division C. P. R., Winnipeg. With Boorne and May's Compliments. Calgary. January 1889."

OLIVER B. BUELL

Oliver B. Buell (1844–1910) was an American photographer who earned much of his livelihood as a lecturer and lantern-slide show entertainer travelling around the United States, Canada, and perhaps even Europe as "Professor" O. B. Buell. Prior to 1882 he was already photographing in the vicinity of Ottawa, Montreal, and Quebec City to acquire images for his shows, and in 1884 was one of the first photographers to go west over the partially completed CPR line to capture its construction. His early presence on the western scene allowed him to take a number of famous views, including the trial of Louis Riel and portraits of noted individuals, such as chiefs Crowfoot and Poundmaker. Because of his stature, in 1886 Van Horne provided him with a private photographer's car to travel the line between Calgary and Vancouver, and the resulting work, some of which was used for CPR advertising material, is the source of the views used in this work.

BRUNO ENGLER

Bruno Engler (1915–2001) was a mountain guide and photographer when he arrived in Canada from his native Switzerland in 1939. Initially, he worked as a mountain guide for the Canadian Pacific

Railway in the summer and as a ski instructor for Sunshine Ski Area in the winter. During the Second World War he served as a mountain warfare instructor of the Canadian Army and then went into business as a freelance photographer working for the National Film Board and other organizations. He was a technical advisor, cameraman, and actor for many movies made in the Banff area. Later in his career he established his business, Alpine Films, at Banff and continued to carry out numerous photography contracts for government agencies, including many with the Banff National Park Warden Service.

BYRON HARMON

Byron Hill Harmon (1876–1942) was born in Tacoma, Washington, and operated a photographic portrait business there before setting out in 1903 as an itinerant photographer travelling around the United States and Canada. He arrived in Banff in 1903 and before long made it his goal to photograph every mountain in the Canadian Rockies. Between 1906 and 1913, he was official photographer of the Alpine Club of Canada, making many expeditions to remote mountain areas as part of his assignment, while at the same time building up a business of post cards, viewbooks, and framing prints sold out of his shop in Banff. Eventually, he became one of Banff's leading businessmen, building the Harmon Block to incorporate his drug store, fountain lunch, bookstore and photographic shop. During the 1920s he financed some of his own alpine expeditions and then for the remainder of his career focused on photographing scenery and activities along the CPR line through the mountains.

DOUGLAS LEIGHTON

Douglas Leighton, one of the Canadian Rockies' finest contemporary colour photographers, grew up in Banff and the Okanagan Valley. Prior to starting his career as a freelance photographer in 1985, he worked as a park naturalist in British Columbia, developing his photography, writing, and interpretive skills. His photographs have been published by the National Geographic Society, Audubon Society Books, and Time-Life, and in 1989 a portfolio of his work was selected for the National Museum of Natural Science's "The Nature of Photography" exhibition, celebrating 150 years of photography in Canada. He has produced many best-selling books of photography, including *The Canadian Rockies* (1993) and *The Canadian West – Alberta* (1995). He now lives and works in the Columbia Valley north of Golden, B.C.

VAUX FAMILY

Mary (1860–1940), George Jr. (1863–1927), and William Jr. (1872–1908) were Philadelphia-born Quakers who first visited the Canadian mountains during an 1887 summer trip on the CPR to Glacier House in Rogers Pass. They were already involved with photography at this time as members of the Photographic Society of Philadelphia and took their first views of the Illecillewaet and other Selkirk glaciers that summer. Thereafter, they returned frequently over the next two decades, with George and Mary's photography focusing on mountain landscapes while William's concentrated on the movement and physical features of glaciers, becoming the first scientific work carried out with photography in Canada's mountains. Due to the size of their large-format cameras and the bulky nature of their glass plate negatives, the two brothers took most of the photographs during their trips, while their sister was responsible for developing them in the darkroom. William Vaux died in 1908 and George did not return after 1911; however, Mary married Dr. Charles Walcott, director of the Smithsonian Institution, and came back to the region virtually every summer for forty years.

APPENDIX B: PHOTOGRAPH INFORMATION

Collection Code: Alberta Sustainable Resource Development, Air Photograph Distribution (AB-APD); British Columbia Archives (BCAR); Cliff White Collection (CW); Dominion Forestry Collection (DFOR); Douglas Leighton Collection (DL); Glenbow Museum Archives (GBOW), Jasper Yellowhead Museum Archives (JYMA); National Archives of Canada (NAC); National Air Photograph Library (NAPL); Parks Canada, Banff (PC-BA); Whyte Museum of the Canadian Rockies (WMCR).

Figure	Collection	File Number	Description	Photographer	Year	Latitude	Longitude	Elev
2.1	GBOW	NA-0040-01	Crowfoot speaks at Treat 7	Stapleton, A.B.	1877			
2.2a	GBOW	NA-0843-03	Blackfoot Crossing, Indians with Governor General	Marquess of Lorne	1881			
2.2b	GBOW	NA-1698-2	Blackfoot Crossing	Oliver, W. J.	1930s	50°47′07″	112°53′03″	820
2.2c	CW	2003-09C-11	Blackfoot Crossing	White, Cliff	2003			
2.3a	GBOW	NA-0615-01	Calgary	Lowndes, J.M.	1885	51°02′17″	114°02′45″	1070
2.3b	GBOW	NA-0670-053	Calgary from south of Elbow River	Higinbothom, P.	1895			
2.3c	CW	2003-09B-35	Calgary from Scotchman's Hill	White, Cliff	2003			
2.4a	GBOW	NA-2864-205-28-16	Cochrane from east	Cioni, Terry	1972	51°11′27″	114°27′13″	1189
2.4b	CW	2004-01A-2	Cochrane from east	White, Cliff	2004			
2.5a	GBOW	NA-4697-59	Stoney Indians, Morley	Buell, O.B.	1885	51°11′27″	114°49′21″	1206
2.5b	CW	2001-07D-17	Nakoda First Nation	White, Cliff	2001			
2.6a	GBOW	NA-0067-08	Gathering horses on the Bar U Ranch	Lane Studio	1930s	50°25′44″	114°26′51″	1397
2.6b	CW	2003-05B-24	House on the Eden Valley Reserve (photopoint 100 m N of historic view)	White, Cliff	2003			
2.7a	GBOW	NA-2084-04	Northwest Cattle Company Ranch, Pekisko	Smyth, S.A.	ca. 1896	50°25′11″	114°14′41″	1260
2.7b	GBOW	NA-0026-360	George Lane's Bar U Ranch	Bird, R.A.	ca. 1935			
2.7c	CW	20071013-228	Bar U Ranch (photopoint approximate to originals)	White, Cliff	2003			
2.8a	GBOW	NA-0067-67	View of Turner Valley	Lane Studio	1930s	50°40′02″	114°16′08″	1224
2.8b	CW	2003-06A-25	Turner Valley	White, Cliff	2003			
2.9a	GBOW	NA-4697-62	Rapids, Kananaskis Falls	Buell, O.B.	1885	51°05′48″	115°03′38″	1279
2.9b	CW	1997-07C-14	Seebee Dam (photopoint moved 50 m upstream due to bridge location)	White, Cliff	1997			
2.10a	WMCR	NA-0071-3436	East Gate Rocky Mountains Park	Harmon, Byron	1921	51°04′34″	115°07′48″	1284
2.10b	CW	2001-08A-23	Old location of East Gate of Rocky Mountains NP	White, Cliff	2001			
2.11a	WMCR	NA-0066-1761	Trail to Kananaskis Lakes, Rocky Mountains Park	Harmon, Byron	1914	51°00′59″	115°04′06″	1449
2.11b	CW	2003-07C-17	Highway 40 and Barrier Lake (photopoint approximate to original due to highway location)	White, Cliff	2003			
2.12a	GBOW	NA-0695-52	Whiteman Flat	Pocaterra, George	1911	50°42′42″	115°07′08″	1603
2.12b	CW	2001-06C-1	Helipad, Peter Lougheed Provincial Park (photopoint moved back 50 m to include helipad)	White, Cliff	2001			
2.13a	WMCR	NA-0071-571	Upper Kananaskis Lake	Harmon, Byron	1910s	50°38′03″	115°09′12″	1747
2.13b	CW	2003-07B-19	Upper Kananaskis Lake, after the dam	White, Cliff	2003			
2.14a	GBOW	NA-3740-5	Canmore, Northwest Territory	W. Notman and Son	1889	51°05′35″	115°20′23″	1345
2.14b	CW	BE-FM-1981-13	Canmore, 1981	Engler, Bruno	1981			
2.14c	CW	1996-08A-33	Canmore, 1996	White, Cliff	1996			
2.15a	NAC	PA-038305	Canmore, Alberta	Geologic Survey	1903	51°04′44″	115°22′23″	1367
2.15b	CW	2001-08C-16	Canmore Creek	White, Cliff	2001			
2.16a	NAPL	CA-114-84	Air Photograph, Canmore, Rocky Mountain Parks	National Air Photo	1921	51°04′41″	115°22′22″	2200
2.16b	CW	2001-10A-10	Canmore from helicopter	White, Cliff	2001			
4.1	N/A	N/A	Painting: "H. J. Warre's 'Camp in the Mountains'"	Warre, H. J.	1845			
4.2a	WMCR	V428-PD1-33	Oiled road along Rundle Range	MacKinnon, J.S.	1920	51°07′41″	115°23′41″	1327
4.2b	CW	2003-07A-11	Approaching the East Gate, Banff National Park (photopoint approximate to original)	White, Cliff	2003			
4.3a	GBOW	NA-4967-30	Engine 146, Siding 29	Buell, O.B.	1885	51°11′32″	115°33′07″	1398
4.3b	CW	1999-09B-23	Canadian Pacific tracks east of the Town of Banff (photopoint 50 m NE from historic view)	White, Cliff	1999			
4.4a	WMCR	NA-0071-3530	Woodworth Ranch, Cascade Falls	Fulmer, Alice	1886	51°12′26″	115°32′12″	1395
4.4b	CW	2001-07C-6	Minnewanka Interchange, Trans-Canada Highway (photopoint moved 200 m back from historic view to include highway)	White, Cliff	2001			
4.5a	GBOW	NA-4697-22	Hot Springs near Siding 29	Buell, O.B.	1885	51°10′08″	115°35′32″	1441

4.5b	GBOW	NA-0529-09	Cave and Basin	Unknown	1892			
4.5c	CW	2006-06B-35	Cave and Basin National Historic Site (photopoint moved 50 m north due to trees)	White, Cliff	1996			
4.6a	WMCR	NA-0066-1942	Canadian Pacific Railroad Hotel at Banff	Unknown	ca. 1890	51°09'59"	115°33'54"	1395
4.6b	CW	2005-11B-15	Banff Springs Hotel	White, Cliff	2005			
4.7a	WMCR	V263-NG-0011-07	Banff Springs Hotel and Bow Valley	Harmon, Byron	ca. 1905	51°09'36"	115°34'04"	1539
4.7b	WMCR	V469-1701	Banff Springs Hotel and Bow Valley	Noble, George	ca. 1920			
4.7c	WMCR	V263-NA71-3737	Banff Springs Hotel and Bow Valley	Harmon, Byron	ca. 1930			
4.7d	CW	2003-06E-13	Fairmont Banff Springs Hotel and prescribed burn	White, Cliff	2003			
4.8a	WMCR	NA-0673-0027	Cascade Mountain from Main Street, Banff	Thom, A.B.	1886	51°10'27"	115°34'16"	1383
4.8b	WMCR	NA-0071-3392	Banff Avenue	Harmon, Byron	ca. 1928			
4.8c	CW	2003-05L-36	Banff Avenue	White, Cliff	2003			
4.9a	WMCR	NG-0004-626	Cascade Mountain from below Tunnel Mountain	Vaux family	1900	51°10'26"	115°32'15"	1368
4.9b	CW	2004-06D-03	Banff Springs Golf Course Club House (photopoint probably 100 m NE from original)	White, Cliff	2004			
4.10a	GBOW	NA-0714-236	Stoney Indian camp	McCowan, Dan	1920s	51°10'14"	115°32'43"	1363
4.10b	CW	2003-05L-33	17th Hole, Fairmont Banff Springs Golf Course	White, Cliff	2003			
4.11a	GBOW	NA-0637-16	Bow Falls, Banff	Fulmer, A.	1889	51°09'56"	115°33'31"	1368
4.11b	WMCR	NA-0066-1348	Log run on the Bow River at Bow Falls	Woodruff, John	ca. 1890			
4.11c	CW	2001-08D-11	Bow Falls, Banff	White, Cliff	2001			
4.12a	WMCR	NA-0066-0713	Anthracite and Cascade Mountain from Hoodoos	Photographer unknown	ca. 1895	51°11'37"	115°29'19"	1400
4.12b	CW	BE-FM-1981-14b	Anthracite	Engler, Bruno	1981			
4.12c	CW	2003-06A-8	Anthracite	White, Cliff	2003			
4.13a	WMCR	NA-0066-2446	Bankhead Townsite, higher view	Photographer unknown	ca. 1908	51°14'11"	115°31'50"	1607
4.13b	CW	2003-02A-8	Bankhead and the Fairholme Range (photopoint approximate due to increased tree cover)	White, Cliff	2003			
4.14a	WMCR	NA-0066-0634	Lake Minnewanka west end, Rocky Mountains Park	Boorne and May	1888	51°14'54"	115°29'46"	1473
4.14b	CW	BE-FM-1981-48	Lake Minnewanka Reservoir (photopoint moved due to higher water levels)	Engler, Bruno	1981			
4.15a	NAPL	A 3412 38	Cascade Valley at Stoney Ck, oblique air photograph	National Air Photo	1931	51°19'36"	115°34'20"	2700
4.15b	CW	2003-06C-18	Cascade Valley at Stoney Ck, view from helicopter	White, Cliff	2003			
4.16a	WMCR	NA-0071-3711	Tally-ho in Buffalo Paddock	Harmon, Byron	1910	51°11'44"	115°33'00"	1394
4.16b	CW	2004-04F-01	Trans-Canada Highway and elk (photopoint approximate to original)	White, Cliff	2004			
4.17a	WMCR	NG-0005-022	Hoodoos near Banff	Paris, George	1890	51°11'19"	115°31'20"	1368
4.17b	CW	BE-FM-1981-18	Hoodoos near Banff	Engler, Bruno	1981			
4.17c	CW	1996-07H-30	Hoodoos near Banff	White, Cliff	1996			
4.18a	WMCR	NA-0066-0624	Banff townsite from Tunnel	Boorne and May	ca. 1899	51°10'27"	115°33'06"	1584
4.18b	WMCR	NA-0066-1280	Bow Valley from Tunnel at height of 1923 flood	Photographer unknown	1923			
4.18c	CW	2004-05A-14	Town of Banff and Vermilion Lakes Wetlands	White, Cliff	2004			
4.19a	WMCR	NA-0071-6244	Mount Rundle and Echo Creek	Harmon, Byron	1918	51°10'56"	115°35'16"	1384
4.19b	CW	BE-FM-1981-35	Mount Rundle and Echo Creek	Engler, Bruno	1981			
4.19c	CW	1996-05A-29	Mount Rundle and Echo Creek	White, Cliff	1996			
4.19d	CW	2005-09B-05	Mount Rundle and Echo Creek	White, Cliff	2005			
4.20a	GBOW	NA-4654-02	Democrat at Sundance Canyon	Smith, J.	1902	51°09'17"	115°36'58"	1481
4.20b	CW	2003-05I-15	Sundance Canyon Bike Trail	White, Cliff	2003			
4.21a	WMCR	NA-0071-3967	Ivand Nelson, Champion Amateur Ski Jumper	Harmon, Byron	1921	51°11'28"	115°32'47"	1442
4.21b	CW	2004-02A-12	Powerline 0.5 km east of Banff	White, Cliff	2004			
4.22a	WMCR	NA-0071-3614	On the slopes of Mt. Norquay	Harmon, Byron	ca. 1932	51°12'10"	115°36'19"	1810
4.22b	CW	2003-02A-13	Snow terrain park at Mt. Norquay (photopoint moved back 200 m to include terrain park and view of new day lodge)	White, Cliff	2003			
4.23a	GBOW	NA-2126-15	Grand View Hotel, Banff, Alberta	Photographer unknown	1905	51°09'07"	115°33'31"	1549
4.23b	CW	2003-02A-21	Rimrock Hotel (photopoint moved 200 m NW from original to include modern hotel)	White, Cliff	2003			
4.24a	WMCR	NG-0005-97	View from Sulphur Mountain towards Lake Minnewanka	Paris, George	1898	51°08'41"	115°34'29"	2231
4.24b	CW	2005-09C-29	View from the top of the Sulphur Mountain Gondola	White, Cliff	2005			
6.1	NAC	PA-123211	Banff to Windermere Highway	National Parks	1923			
6.2a	WMCR	V263-NA-3472	Rocky Mountain Tours and Transport cars at 1st Vermilion Lake	Harmon, Byron	1924	51°11'02"	115°35'51"	1382
6.2b	CW	2003-09B-18	Evening stroll on the Vermilion Lakes Road	White, Cliff	2003			
6.3a	PC-BA	Not numbered	Constructing the Trans-Canada Highway above Vermilion Lake	Engler, Bruno	1956	51°11'05"	115°35'38"	1398
6.3b	CW	2003-07D-05	Trans-Canada Highway and Mt. Norquay Intersection	White, Cliff	2003			
6.4a	WMCR	Not numbered	Sunshine Ski Lodge	Engler, Bruno	ca. 1939	51°04'48"	115°46'52"	2168
6.4b	WMCR	NA-0066-1530	Brewster Rocky Mountain Grayline Buses at Sunshine	Engler, Bruno	1963			
6.4c	CW	2002-02C-27	Sunshine Village, upper terminal of gondola (photopoint 100 m N from original due to gondola terminal)	White, Cliff	2002			

6.5a	GBOW	NA-0735-01	View from Simpson Summit, Banff National Park	Howe St. Book Shop	1930s	51°02'27"	115°45'04"	2355
6.5b	CW	2001-08B-20	Howard Douglas Lake and Mt. Assiniboine from Quartz Ridge	White, Cliff	2001			
6.6a	NAPL	CA-114-074	Air photograph of Bow Valley and the Sawback Range	National Air Photo	1921	51°09'60"	115°42'03"	2000
6.6b	CW	1986-P1-14	Helicopter view of Bow Valley and the Sawback Range	White, Cliff	1986			
6.6c	CW	2003-10B-05	Helicopter view of Bow Valley and the Sawback Range	White, Cliff	2003			
6.7a	WMCR	NA-0071-4493	Crossing wash at Five-mile Creek	Harmon, Byron	1922	51°10'18"	115°39'37"	1410
6.7b	NAC	PA-145344	View of the mountains in Banff National Park	National Parks	1945			
6.7c	CW	2003-06B-16	West entrance, Bow Valley Parkway	White, Cliff	2003			
6.8a	GBOW	NA-4967-15	Engine on track near Sawback	Buell, O.B.	1885	51°10'09"	115°41'53"	1399
6.8b	CW	2004-06D-9	Container cars on westbound freight train near Sawback	White, Cliff	2004			
6.9a	GBOW	NA-4654-11	Hillsdale Ranch	Smith, J.	1902	51°13'34"	115°47'07"	1410
6.9b	CW	1999-09C-26	Hillsdale	White, Cliff	1999			
6.10a	GBOW	NA-1753-28	Castle Mountain and Silver City	Boorne and May	ca. 1887	51°15'42"	115°54'08"	1424
6.10b	CW	2003-09A-06	Silver City Meadows	White, Cliff	2003			
6.11a	GBOW	NA-1870-2	Castle Mountain Internment Camp	Park, Calgary	ca. 1915	51°17'24"	115°58'12"	1450
6.11b	CW	2003-09A-10	Small meadow near Eldon (photopoint approximate to historic view due to denser tree cover)	White, Cliff	2003			
6.12a	NAC	PA-020462	The Bow Range from near Castle Mountain, Alta.	Smith, J.	1902	51°16'09"	115°55'03"	1440
6.12b	CW	2001-07D-10	Castle Mountain Village (photopoint approximate to original due to denser tree cover)	White, Cliff	2001			
6.13a	GBOW	NA-3884-35	Banff-Windermere Road, Kootenay National Park	Photographer unknown	1920s	50°53'20"	116°02'41"	1188
6.13b	CW	2003-09F-24	Kootenay Parkway, 1 km east of Kootenay Crossing	White, Cliff	2003			
6.14a	WMCR	V227-5239	Radium Hot Springs, BC, village view	Engler, Bruno	1939	50°37'60"	116°03'13"	1034
6.14b	CW	2003-09E-33	Radium Hot Pools	White, Cliff	2003			
6.15a	GBOW	NA-1135-59	Lake Windermere and Ktunaxa and Shuswap camp on Fort Point	Photographer unknown	1923	50°30'54"	116°01'00"	847
6.15b	CW	2003-05K-2	Athalmere and Invermere, BC	White, Cliff	2003			
6.16a	GBOW	NA-1135-0029	David Thompson Commemoration Fort, Lake Windermere, BC	Photographer unknown	1923	50°29'54"	116°01'12"	810
6.16b	CW	2003-05D-10	Invermere, BC	White, Cliff	2003			
8.1	WMCR	NA-0071-2159	Byron Harmon and Columbia Icefields	Freeman, Lewis	1923			
8.2a	WMCR	NA-0066-0645	Mt. Lefroy (Temple), Laggan	Boorne and May	ca. 1888	51°25'43"	116°11'08"	1539
8.2b	WMCR	NA-0066-0397	Laggan Train Station	Canadian Pacific	ca. 1895			
8.2c	WMCR	NA-0066-1238	Laggan Train Station	Canadian Pacific	ca. 1910			
8.2d	CW	2001-07C-01	Lake Louise Train Station	White, Cliff	2001			
8,3a	WMCR	NG-0004-0717	Outlet from Lake Louise	Vaux family	July, 1900	51°25'01"	116°12'57"	1739
8.3b	CW	2004-09B-2	Outlet from Lake Louise	White, Cliff	Sept, 2004			
8.4a	WMCR	V263-NA-0071-4856	Chateau Lake Louise from lake overlook	Harmon, Byron	1920	51°24'48"	116°13'04"	1813
8.4b	WMCR	NA-0071-4945	Chateau Lake Louise from lake overlook	Harmon, Byron	ca. 1940			
8.4c	CW	2003-07K-9	Chateau Lake Louise from lake overlook	White, Cliff	2003			
8.5a	WMCR	NA-0080-1283	Panorama from Mount Fairview (no. 64)	Vaux family	1904	51°23'57"	116°13'27"	2656
8.5b	WMCR	V108-1014	Mount Victoria from Fairview	Harmon, Lloyd	ca. 1947			
8.5c	CW	2003-07I-35	Mount Victoria from Fairview	White, Cliff	2003			
8.6a	WMCR	NA-0080-1291	Mt. Temple from Saddleback	Vaux family	1904	51°23'32"	116°12'54"	2187
8.6b	CW	2003-07J-27	Mt. Temple from Saddleback (photopoint approximate to original due to increased tree cover)	White, Cliff	2003			
8.7a	WMCR	V529-LC-006	The Ten Peaks and Paradise Valley	Chapman, J. Howard	1905	51°21'39"	116°09'46"	1911
8.7b	WMCR	NA-0071-5074	Valley of Ten Peaks	Harmon, Byron	ca. 1920			
8.7c	CW	BE-FM-1981-46	Valley of Ten Peaks (photopoint approximate to original due to increased tree cover)	Engler, Bruno	1981			
8.8a	WMCR	NA-0066-0581	Moraine Lake	Wilcox, Walter	ca. 1900	51°19'40"	116°10'40"	1876
8.8b	CW	2004-09E-13	Moraine Lake	White, Cliff	2004			
8.9a	NAPL	A3414-19	Lake Louise Village and Whitehorn from airplane	National Air photo	1931	51°24'06"	116°12'47"	2650
8.9b	CW	2003-06H-32	Lake Louise Village and Whitehorn from helicopter	White, Cliff	2003			
8.10a	WMCR	V108-592	Larch Run, Temple Ski Area	Harmon, Lloyd	1940s	51°26'40"	116°06'38"	2168
8.10b	CW	2004-03B-35	Larch Run, Lake Louise Ski Area	White, Cliff	2004			
8.11a	WMCR	V190-XVIII-3	Post Hotel and Mt. Whitehorn	Engler, Bruno	1960	51°25'27"	116.11'04"	1603
8.11b	CW	2004-03B-8	Hamlet of Lake Louise and Mt. Whitehorn	White, Cliff	2004			
8.12a	NAC	GSC-ESIC-667	Mountain on Red Deer River	Dawson, G.M.	1884	51°35'22"	115°57'06"	1861
8.12b	CW	2002-10A-03	Sandhills Meadow	White, Cliff	2002			
8.13a	WMCR	PC-465-15	Looking north to Ya-Ha-Tinda Ranch	National Parks	Aug, 1937	51°42'30"	115°30'51"	1735
8.13b	WMCR	BNP-43	Looking north to Ya-Ha-Tinda Ranch	National Parks	ca. 1955			
8.13c	CW	1986-I-05	Looking north to Ya-Ha-Tinda Ranch (photographed from helicopter due to increased forest cover)	White, Cliff	1986			

8.14a	WMCR	V192-43 (PD)	Brewster Buildings on Ya-Ha-Tinda Ranch	Vernon-Wood, Tex coll.	1910s	51°44'30"	115°33'56"	1604
8.14b	CW	2003-07I-33	Warden colts on Ya-Ha-Tinda Ranch (photopoint moved 100 m east from historic view to include horses)	White, Cliff	2003			
8.14c	CW	2004-04C-12	Parks Canada ranch buildings on Ya-Ha-Tinda	White, Cliff	2004			
8.15a	WMCR	NG-0004-0820	Popes Peak from the railroad above Hector Station	Vaux family	1901	51°27'05"	116°18'30"	1621
8.15b	CW	2006-09C-23	Sink Lake and Popes Peak	White, Cliff	2003			
8.16a	WMCR	Not numbered	Mt. Stephen House, Field	Jones, Tom	ca. 1905	51°23'41"	116°29'32"	1242
8.16b	CW	2003-09C-26	Field, BC	White, Cliff	2003			
8.17a	WMCR	NA-0066-2310	Ottertail Mountains, Leanchoil	Notman, WM and son	1889	51°13'14"	116°36'52"	1170
8.17b	WMCR	V108-2285	Selkirk steam locomotive at Leanchoil	Harmon, Lloyd				
8.17c	CW	2006-09C-03	Leanchoil Siding	White, Cliff	2004			
8.18a	WMCR	V425-PA-0009	Golden City, Columbia Valley, BC	Soule, Cornelius	ca. 1884	51°18'04"	116°57'51"	794
8.18b	BCAR	A-00961	Town of Golden	Chapman, J. Howard A.	c.1911			
8.18c	BCAR	I-27458	Golden	BC Government	1947			
8.18d	DL	Not numbered	Golden, BC, 2004	Leighton, Doug	2004			
8.19a	WMCR	NA-0080-1108	Crowfoot Glacier	Vaux family	1902	51°39'29"	116°25'44"	1940
8.19b	CW	1985-H6	Crowfoot Glacier	White, Cliff	1985			
8.19c	CW	2003-07L-11	Crowfoot Glacier (photopoint moved about 100 m NW due to increased forest cover)	White, Cliff	2003			
8.20a	WMCR	NA-0080-1114	Bow Glacier and Bow Lake	Vaux family	1902	51°40'48"	116°27'34"	1938
8.20b	CW	2003-07D-14	Bow Glacier and Bow Lake	White, Cliff	2003			
8.20c	WMCR	Not numbered	The Rams Pasture, Num-Ti-Jah,	Photographer unknown	ca. 1985			
8.21a	WMCR	NA-0080-1122	Meadows above Bow Lake	Vaux family	1902	51°41'04"	116°27'56"	1975
8.21b	CW	2001-7D-02	Icefields Parkway and Bow Lake (photopoint moved about 100 m NE to include Icefields Parkway)	White, Cliff	2001			
8.22a	WMCR	NA-0080-1127	Peyto Glacier, no. 149	Vaux family	1902	51°42'50"	116°30'28"	2090
8.22b	WMCR	NA-0071-1799	Peyto Glacier, 1923	Harmon, Byron	1923			
8.22c	CW	BE-FM-1981-48	Peyto Glacier	Engler, Bruno	1981			
8.22d	CW	2003-07D-22	Peyto Glacier	White, Cliff	2003			
8.23a	WMCR	V48-NA-0065-471	Tipi on the Kootenay Plains	Schäffer, Mary	ca. 1907	52°04'03"	116°24'52"	1354
8.23b	CW	2003-10D-29	Kootenay Plains (difficult to exactly relocate historic photopoint)	White, Cliff	2003			
8.24a	WMCR	NA-0066-789	Fording the North Saskatchewan River at Kootenay Plains	Dowling, D.B.	1906	52°07'20"	116°25'39"	1330
8.24b	CW	1986-M4-11	Lake Abraham (photopoint moved due to reservoir)	White, Cliff	1986			
8.25a	WMCR	NA-0071-2220	Ice-dam lake on edge of North Saskatchewan Glacier	Freeman, Lewis	1924	52°07'55"	117°11'19"	2230
8.25b	CW	1987-B6	Saskatchewan Glacier from edge of Castleguard Meadows	White, Cliff	1987			
8.25c	CW	2006-08B-02	Saskatchewan Glacier from edge of Castleguard Meadows	White, Cliff	2006			
8.26a	WMCR	V527-PS-58	Mount Athabasca	Schäffer, Mary	ca. 1906	52°13'20"	117°14'01"	1957
8.26b	CW	2004-09C-2	Mount Athabasca and Icefields Parkway (photopoint approximate due to increased forest cover)	White, Cliff	2004			
8.27a	WMCR	V108-2132	Icefields Chalet	Harmon, Lloyd	ca. 1950	52°13'17"	117°13'45"	1973
8.27b	CW	2004-09D-18	Icefields Interpretive Centre and Athabasca Glacier (repeat photopoint approximate due to redevelopment)	White, Cliff	2004			
10.1	NAC	PA-009147	Canadian Pacific Survey at Jasper House	Horetzky, Charles	1871			
10.2a	GBOW	NA-2067-01	Jasper, Alta.	Peterson, L.M.	ca. 1915	52°53'13"	118°05'08"	1112
10.2b	CW	2006-05A-27	Jasper, evening light (photopoint approximate to historic view due to increased tree cover)	White, Cliff	2006			
10.3a	JYMA	994-45-88	Train leaving Jasper going east	Doris Kensit fonds	ca. 1940	52°55'58"	118°03'31"	1060
10.3b	CW	2004-06B-8	Canadian National freight train east of Jasper	White, Cliff	2004			
10.4a	NAC	PA-020487	Old construction camp near Jasper, Alta.	MTS Legal Surveys	1914	52°53'41"	118°04'25"	1053
10.4b	CW	2003-07N-16	East entrance to Jasper from Canadian National Railway bridge (repeat photopoint approximate to historic view due to highway and railway construction)	White, Cliff	2003			
10.5a	DFOR	06207	Rangers pack train leaving Jasper	Millar, W. N.	ca.1915	52°52'32"	118°04'49"	1057
10.5b	CW	2003-07G-25	Connaught Street, Jasper, Alberta (position approximate to historic view)	White, Cliff	2003			
10.6a	NAC	PA-087189	Road to the church from Jasper Park, Alberta, October	Boyd, John	1925	52°52'50"	118°05'05"	1065
10.6b	CW	1999-07A-26	Pyramid Avenue, Jasper	White, Cliff	1999			
10.7a	NAC	PA-011159	Road to Maligne Canyon, Sir A. Conan Doyle party, Jasper Park	Topley, W. J.	1914	52°53'51"	118°03'30"	1031
10.7b	CW	2003-07N-11	Entrance gate to Jasper Park Lodge and Mount Edith Cavell (position approximated to historic view)	White, Cliff	2003			
10.8a	JYMA	PA-000021-02	Tent City near Jasper, now site of JPL Lodge	JPL Collection	ca.1915	52°52'58"	118°03'49"	1028
10.8b	JYMA	PA-000021-35	Old Man Mountain and Jasper Park Lodge	Canadian National Railway	ca. 1920s			
10.8c	CW	2004-06C-17	Lac Beauvert and Jasper Park Lodge	White, Cliff	2004			
10.9a	WMCR	NA-0066-2418	The Bungalows at Jasper Park Lodge, ca. 1925	Slark, F. H.	ca. 1925	52°53'13"	118°03'30"	1030
10.9b	CW	2003-07G-10	Bungalows at Jasper Park Lodge	White, Cliff	2003			
10.10a	JYMA	994.45.135	Ski jumping on Whistler's Ski Hill	Rowed, Harry	1961	52°51'04"	118°06'51"	1284
10.10b	CW	2004-02D-21	Forest cover on old ski runs above Whistler Hostel, Jasper	White, Cliff	2004			

10.11a	NAC	PA-011068	On road to Pyramid Lake	Topley, W.J.	1914	52°53'24"	118°04'54"	1122
10.11b	CW	1999-07A-17	On road to Pyramid Lake	White, Cliff	1999			
10.12a	JYMA	84.32.280	Elk in snow, Pyramid Mountain	Unknown	1920s	52°53'38"	118°05'30"	1120
10.12b	CW	2004-02B-11	Cottonwood Slough	White, Cliff	2004			
10.13a	NAC	PA-011183	At Maligne Canyon, Alta.	Topley, W. J.	1914	52°55'13"	118°00'06"	1157
10.13b	CW	2003-07N-20	Maligne Canyon Interpretive Trail	White, Cliff	2003			
10.14a	WMCR	V263-NA-1326	Maligne Lake and Spirit Island	Harmon, Byron	1924	52°38'38"	117°29'33"	1672
10.14b	DL	Not numbered	Maligne Lake and Spirit Island	Leighton, Doug	19xx			
10.15a	NAC	PA-009173	Canadian Pacific Survey at Jasper House	Horetzky, Charles	1871	53°08'49"	117°59'01"	999
10.15b	CW	2004-02B-23	Jasper House National Historic Site	White, Cliff	2004			
10.16a	JYMA	PA-39-20	Pochohontas Coal Mine	Pochohontas Collection	1911	53°12'02"	117°55'48"	1010
10.16b	CW	2004-02E-7	Pochohontas, Jasper National Park (repeat photograph approximate to historic view due to highway construction impacts)	White, Cliff	2004			
10.17a	GBOW	ND-0003-3930	From the Pochohontas Highway, Jasper National Park	McDermid Studio	1927	53°12'38"	117°51'28"	1025
10.17b	CW	2003-07M-15	Highway 16, near Fiddle River (moved 300 m NW to include modern highway)	White, Cliff	2003			
10.18a	AB-APD	Mosaic	Athabasca River near Benbow Crossing	AB Air photographs	1950	54°08'16"	116°35'28"	862
10.18b	AB-APD	Mosaic	Athabasca River near Benbow Crossing	AB Air photographs	1980			
10.18c	AB-APD	Mosaic	Athabasca River near Benbow Crossing	AB Air photographs	1990			
10.18d	PC-BA	Not numbered	Athabasca River near Benbow Crossing	Processed Landsat 5 image	2003			
10.19a	NAC	PA-038033	Fort Edmonton Alberta, October 22	Dawson, G. M.	1879	53°31'45"	113°31'31"	678
10.19b	CW	2004-04G-17	North Saskatchewan River Valley, Edmonton (photographed from 3rd floor, Biological Sciences Building , University of Alberta)	White, Cliff	2004			
10.20	GBOW	NA-1408-04	View of Fort Edmonton in winter, looking west from the flats	Horetzky, C.	1871			
11.2	CW	2005-06D-21	Removing gravel from alluvial fan channel, June 2005	White, Cliff	2005			
11.6a	GBOW	NA-0841-418	Douglas- fir above Hoodoos, 1934	Harmon, Byron	1934			
11.6b	CW	BE-FM-1981-31	Douglas- fir above Hoodoos, 1981	Engler, Bruno	1981			
11.6c	CW	2003-09B-7	Douglas- fir above Hoodoos, 2003	White, Cliff	2003			
11.7	Komar	Not numbered	Prescribed burning in Banff National Park	Komar, Randy	2003			
11.10	DL	Not numbered	Captive bison in Banff Paddock, ca. 1995	Leighton, Doug	ca. 1995			
11.12	CW	1995-04A-13	Large herd of elk on Ya-Ha-Tinda Ranch in 1993	White, Cliff	1993			
11.13a	CW	1999-06B-16	Trembling aspen stand after being burned: low elk density	White, Cliff				
11.13b	CW	1998-05D-29	Trembling aspen stand after being burned: moderate elk density	White, Cliff				
11.14	CW	2000-08A-19	Willow protected from elk browsing by a fence					
11.15	PC-BA	Not numbered	Woodland caribou in Banff National Park	Parks Canada	ca. 1990			
11.16	PC-BA	Not numbered	Wildlife crossing structure, Trans-Canada Highway	Parks Canada	2005			
11.17	CW	2003-03C-03	Timber harvesting in the Canadian Rockies	White, Cliff	2004			
11.18	CW	2006-03A-22	Building mountain homes, Canmore	White, Cliff	2006			

APPENDIX C: MAPS OF PHOTOGRAPH LOCATIONS

MAP 1: PHOTOGRAPH LOCATIONS FOR CHAPTER 2: BLACKFOOT CROSSING TO CANMORE AREA.

MAP 2: PHOTOGRAPH LOCATIONS FOR CHAPTER 4: BANFF AREA.

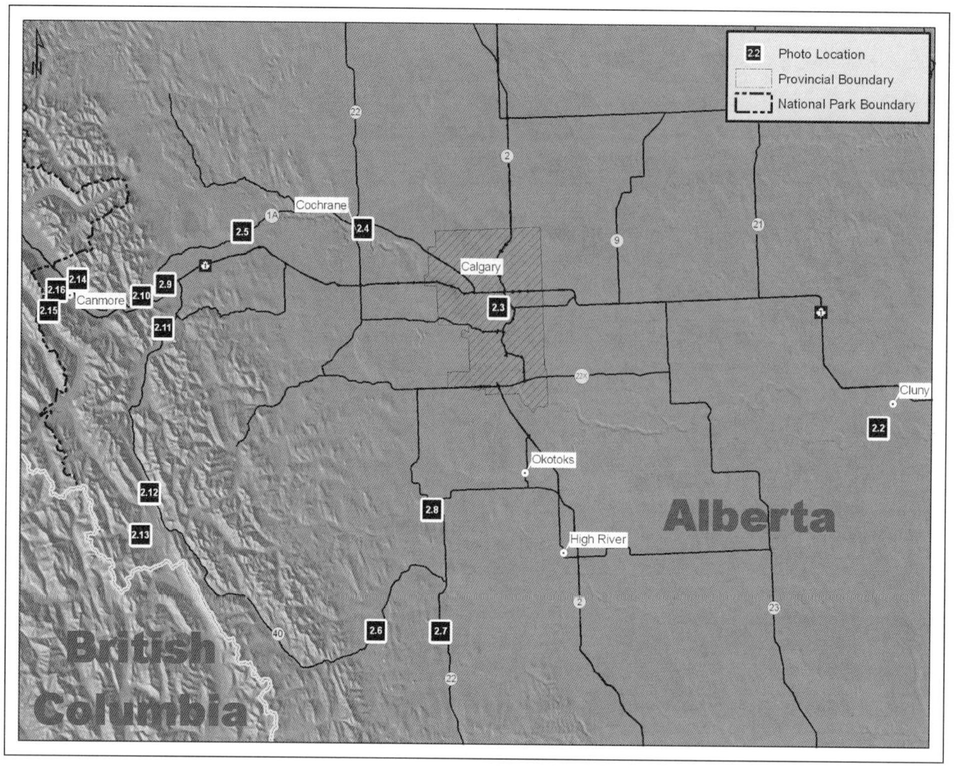

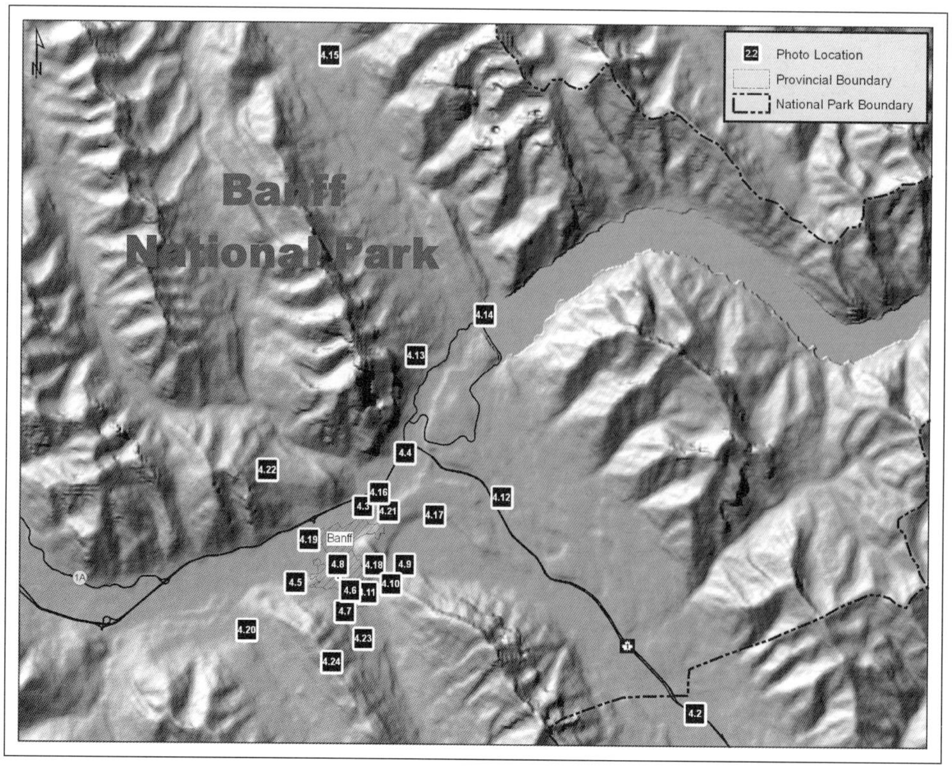

MAP 3: PHOTOGRAPH LOCATIONS FOR CHAPTER 6: BANFF TO RADIUM AREA.

MAP 4: PHOTOGRAPH LOCATIONS FOR CHAPTER 8:
LAKE LOUISE, RED DEER RIVER, YOHO, AND ICEFIELDS PARKWAY AREA.

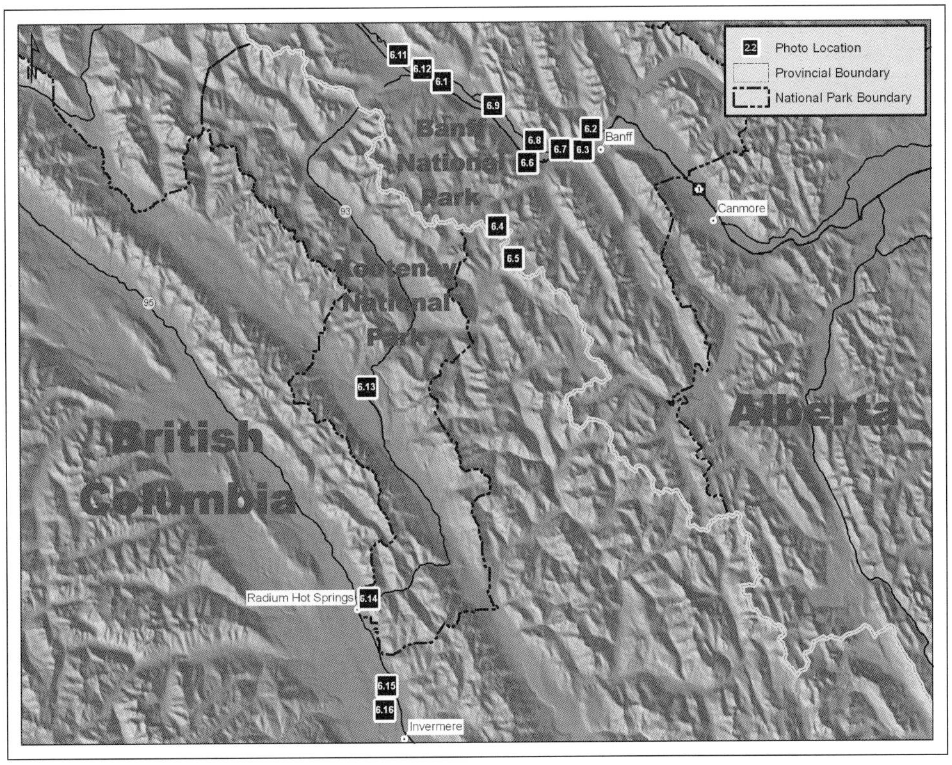

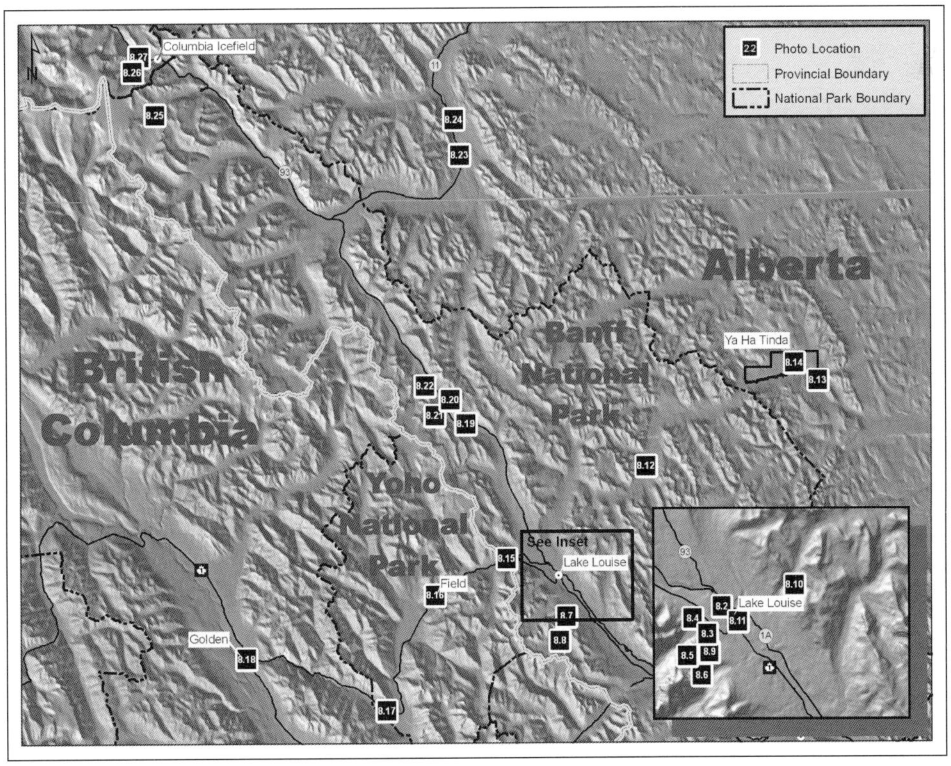

MAP 5: PHOTOGRAPH LOCATIONS FOR CHAPTER 10: JASPER TO EDMONTON AREA.

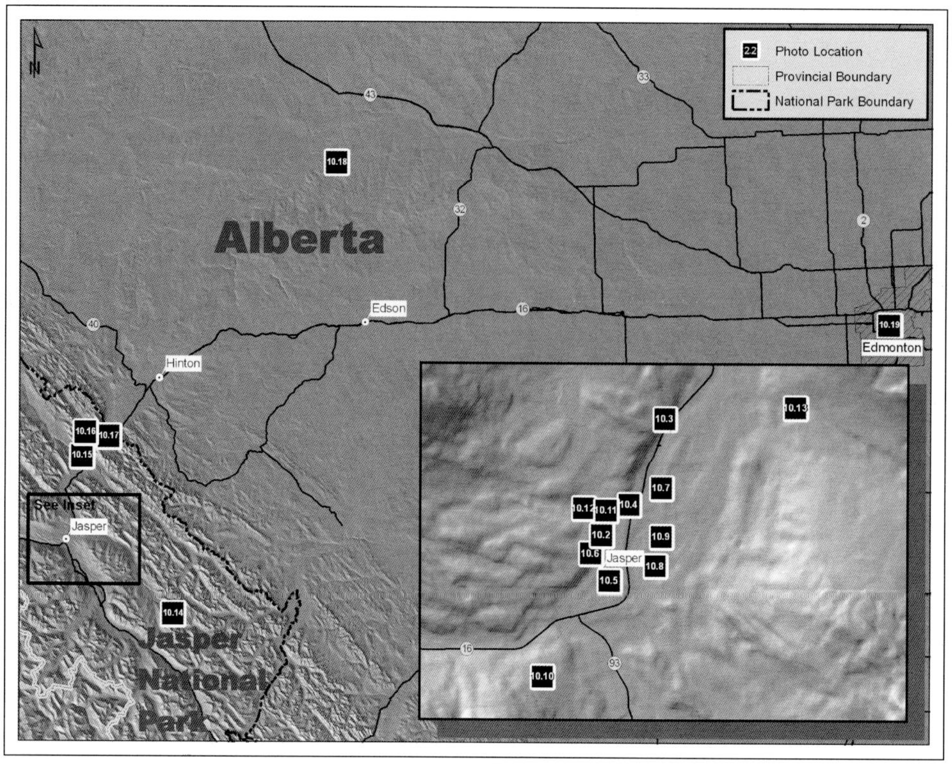

APPENDIX D: SPECIES NAMES

FUNGI	
fungi, blue stain	Ophiostoma spp.
FLORA	
avens, yellow mountain	Dryas drummondii
aspen, trembling	Populus tremuloides
arnica, yellow	Arnica cordifolia
aster, showy	Aster conspicuous
birch, dwarf	Betula pumila
buffaloberry	Shepherdia canadensis
cedar, western red	Thuja plicata
cottonwood, plains	Populus trichocarpa
dogwood, red-osier	Cornus stolonifera
Douglas fir	Pseudotsuga menziesii
fescue, rough	Festuca campestris
fireweed	Epilobium angustifolium
fir, subalpine	Abies lasiocarpa
gooseberry	Ribes lacustre
hedysarum, purple	Hedysarum mackenzii
hedysarum, yellow	Hedysarum sulphurescens
hemlock, western	Tsuga heterophylla
larch, alpine	Larix lyalli
larch, western	Larix occidentalis
menziesia	Menziesia glabella
pine, limber	Pinus flexilis
pine, lodgepole	Pinus contorta
pine, white-bark	Pinus albicaulis
poplar, balsam	Populus balsamifera
saskatoon	Amelanchier alnifolia
spruce, Engelmann	Picea engelmannii
spruce, white	Picea glauca
strawberry	Fragaria Virginia
willow	Salix spp.
willow, dwarf	Salix glauca
FAUNA	
bear, black	Ursus americanus
bear, grizzly	Ursus arctos
beaver	Castor canadensis
beetle, mountain pine	Dendroctonus ponderosae
bison, plains	Bison bison bison
bison, wood	Bison bison athabascae
caribou, woodland	Rangifer tarandus caribou
cougar	Felis concolor
coyote	Canis latrans
deer, mule	Odocoileus hemionus
deer, whitetail	Odocoileus virginianus
elk	Cervus elaphus
goat, mountain	Oreamnos americanus
ground squirrel, Columbian	Spermophilus columbianus
hare, snowshoe	Lepus americanus
jay, gray	Perisoreus canadensis
lynx, Canada	Lynx canadensis
magpie, black-billed	Pica pica
moose	Alces alces
raven, common	Corvus corax
sheep, bighorn	Ovis canadensis
wolf, gray	Canis lupus

BIBLIOGRAPHY

Achuff, P. L., and I. G. W. Corns. "Vegetation." In *Ecological (Biophysical) Land Classification of Banff and Jasper National Parks. Volume 2: Soil and Vegetation Resources*, edited by W.D. Holland and G.M. Coen, 71–156. Edmonton: Alberta Institute of Pedology, 1982.

Achuff, P. L., I. R. Pengelly, and C. A. White. *Special Resources of Banff National Park*. Banff: Parks Canada, 1986.

Alberta Environmental Conservation Authority. "Land Use and Resource Development in the Eastern Slopes." *Proceedings of the Public Hearings*, Part 3. Edmonton: Alberta Environment, 1974.

Alberta Woodland Caribou Recovery Team. *Alberta Woodland Caribou Recovery Plan 2004/05–2013/14*. Alberta Species at Risk Recovery Plan No. 4. Edmonton: Alberta Sustainable Resource Development, 2005.

Appleby, E. *Canmore: Story of an Era*. Calgary: Friesen, 1975.

Arcese, P., and A.R.E. Sinclair. "The Role of Protected Areas as Ecological Baselines." *Journal of Wildlife Management* 61 (1997): 587–602.

Armstrong, C., and H. V. Nelles, "Competition vs. Convenience: Federal Administration of Bow River Waterpowers, 1906–1913." In *The Canadian West: Social Change and Economic Development*, edited by H. C. Klassen, 163–80. Calgary: University of Calgary, Comprint, 1977.

Arno, S. F. "Forest Fire History in the Northern Rockies." *Journal of Forestry* 78 (1980): 460–65.

Arno, S. F., and J. R. Habeck. "Ecology of Alpine Larch (*Larix lyalli* Parl.) in the Pacific Northwest." *Ecological Monograph* 42 (1972): 417–50.

Banff-Bow Valley Study. *Banff-Bow Valley at the Crossroads: Summary Report of the Banff-Bow Valley Task Force*, edited by R. Page, S. Bayley, J. D. Cook, J. E. Green, and J.R.B. Ritchie. Ottawa: Department of Canadian Heritage, 1996.

Banff-Bow Valley Study. *Banff-Bow Valley at the Crossroads: Technical Report of the Banff-Bow Valley Task Force*, edited by R. Page, S. Bayley, J. D. Cook, J. E. Green, and J.R.B. Ritchie. Ottawa: Department of Canadian Heritage, 1996.

Baker, W. M. *The Mounted Police and Prairie Society 1873–1919*. Regina: Canadian Plains Research Centre, University of Regina, 1998.

Barrett, S. W., and S. F. Arno. "Indian Fires as an Ecological Influence in the Northern Rockies." *Journal of Forestry* 80 (1982): 647–51.

Barringer, M. D. *Selling Yellowstone: Capitalism and the Construction of Nature*. Lawrence: University of Kansas Press, 2002.

Beckstead, G.R.E. *Banff Floodplain Study*. Edmonton: Alberta Environment, 1980.

Bella, L. *Parks for Profit*. Montreal: Harvest House, 1987.

Belyea, B., ed. *Columbia Journals: David Thompson*. Montreal and Kingston: McGill-Queen's University Press, 1994.

Binnema, T. *Common and Contested Ground: A Human and Environmental History of the Northwestern Plains*. Norman: University of Oklahoma Press, 2001.

Binnema, T., and M. Niemi. "'Let the Line be Drawn Now:' Wilderness, Conservation, and the Exclusion of Aboriginal People from Banff National Park in Canada." *Environmental History* 11 (2006): 724–50.

Birrell, A. "Fortunes of a Misfit: Charles Horetzki." *Alberta Historical Review* 19 (1971): 9–25.

Bott, R., P. Murphy, and R. Udell. *Learning from the Forest*. Calgary: Fifth House, 2003.

Bow Corridor Ecosystem Advisory Group. *Wildlife Corridor and Habitat Patch Guidelines for the Bow Valley. Town of Canmore, MD. Bighorn, Banff National Park and the Alberta Government*. Canmore, AB: Alberta Provincial Parks, 1998.

Bow River Basin Council. *Nurture, Renew, Protect: A Report on the State of the Bow River Basin*. Calgary: Bow River Basin Council, 2005.

Boyce, M. S. "Natural Regulation or Control of Nature?" In *The Greater Yellowstone Ecosystem: Redefining America's Wilderness Heritage*, edited by R. B. Keiter and M. S. Boyce, 183–207. New Haven, CT: Yale University Press, 1991.

Brewster, F. O. *Weathered Wood: Anecdotes and History of the Banff-Sunshine Area*. Banff: Altitude Publishing, 1977.

Brown, J. K., and J. K. Smith, and L. J. Lyon, eds. *Wildland Fires in Ecosystems: Effects of Fire on Flora*. Fort Collins, CO: Rocky Mountain Forest and Range Experiment Station, 2000.

Budiansky, S. 1995. *Nature's Keepers: The New Science of Nature Management*. New York: Free Press, 1995.

Burns, R. J., and M. Schintz. *Guardians of the Wild: A History of the Warden Service of Canada's National Parks*. Calgary: University of Calgary Press, 2000.

Burpee, L. J., ed. "York Factory to the Blackfeet Country: The Journal of Anthony Henday, 1754–1755." *Transactions of the Royal Society of Canada*, Series 3, Vol. 1, Sec. 2 (1907): 307–61.

Byrne, A. R. *Man and Landscape Change in Banff National Park before 1911*. Studies in Land Use History and Landscape Changes No. 1. Calgary: Department of Geography, University of Calgary, 1968.

Canada. "Report of the Superintendent of Rocky Mountains Park," *Department of the Interior Report: 1905–06*, 11.

Canada. "Report of the Superintendent of Rocky Mountains Park," *Department of the Interior Report: 1907*, 14–15.

Canada. "Report of the Commissioner of Dominion Parks," *Department of the Interior Report: 1914*, 5.

Canada. "Report of the Commissioner of Dominion Parks," *Department of the Interior Report: 1916*, 15.

Canadian Parks Service. *Banff National Park Management Plan*. Ottawa: Environment Canada, 1988.

Cautley, R. W., and A. O. Wheeler. *Report of the Commission Appointed to Delimit the Boundary between the Provinces of Alberta and British Columbia. Part II. Kicking Horse to Yellowhead Pass*. Ottawa: Office of the Surveyor General, 1924.

Cavell, E. *Legacy in Ice: The Vaux Family and the Canadian Alps*. Banff: Whyte Foundation, 1983.

Chase, A. *Playing God in Yellowstone: The Destruction of America's First National Park*. San Diego: Harcourt Brace, 1986.

Choquette, W. "Early Post Glacial Habitation of the Upper Columbia Region." In *Early Human Occupation in British Columbia*, edited by R.L. Carlson and L. Dalla Bonna, 45–50. Vancouver: UBC Press, 1996.

Churcher, C. S. "Pleistocene Ungulates from the Bow River Gravels at Cochrane Alberta." *Canadian Journal of Earth Sciences* 5 (1968): 1467–1488.

Clevenger, A. P., and N. Waltho. "Factors Influencing the Effectiveness of Wildlife Underpasses in Banff National Park, Alberta, Canada." *Conservation Biology* 14 (2000): 47–56.

Cochrane and Area Historical Society. *Big Hill Country: Cochrane and Area*. Cochrane, AB: Cochrane and Area Historical Society, 1977.

Cole, G. F. "An Ecological Rationale for the Natural or Artificial Regulation of Native Ungulates in Parks." *Transactions of the North American Wildlife Conference* 36 (1971): 417–25.

Coleman, A. P. *The Canadian Rockies, New and Old Trails*. Toronto: Henry Frowde, 1911.

Cowan, I. McT. "Some Vital Statistics of Big Game on Overstocked Mountain Range." *Transactions of the North American Wildlife Conference* 15 (1950): 581–88.

Cronan, W. "The Trouble with Wilderness; or Getting Back to the Wrong Nature." *Environmental History* 1 (1995): 7–28.

———. *Uncommon Ground: Toward Reinventing Nature*. New York: Norton, 1995.

Daubenmire, R. "The Western Limits of the Range of the American Bison." *Ecology* 66 (1985): 622–24.

Dawson, G. M. *Preliminary Report on the Physical and Geological Features of that Portion of the Rocky Mountains between Latitudes 49º and 51º30.'* Montreal: Dawson Brothers, 1886.

Day, R.J. "Stand Structure, Succession, and Use of Southern Alberta Rocky Mountain Forests." *Ecology* 53 (1972): 472–77.

DeByle, N. V., and R. P. Winokur, eds. *Aspen: Ecology and Management in the Western United States*. USDA Forest Service General Technical Report RM-119. Fort Collins, CO: Rocky Mountain Forest and Range Experiment Station, 1985.

Dempsey, H. A. *The Golden Age of the Canadian Cowboy*. Calgary: Fifth House, 1995. Calgary. 169pp.

Demuth, M. N., and R. Keller. "An Assessment of the Mass Balance of the Peyto Glacier (1966–1995) and Its Relation to Recent and Past Century Climate Variability." In *Peyto Glacier: One Century of Science*, edited by M. N. Demuth, D. S. Munro, and G. L. Young, 83–133. Saskatoon: National Water Research Institute, 2006.

de Scally, F. A. *Alteration and Restoration of Alluvial Fan Processes in Banff National Park*. Consultant Report. Banff: Parks Canada, 1999.

Dickenson, W. R. "Changing Times: The Holocene Legacy." *Environmental History* 5 (2000): 503–30.

Draper, D. "Towards Sustainable Mountain Communities: Balancing Tourism Development and Environmental Protection in Banff and Banff National Park," *Ambio* 29 (2000): 408–15.

Duke, D., M. Hebblewhite, P. C. Paquet, C. Callaghan, and M. Percy. "Restoration of a Large Carnivore Corridor in Banff National Park." In *Large Mammal Restoration: Ecological and Social Challenges in the 21st Century*, edited by D. Maehr, R.F. Noss, and J.L. Lavlin, 261–75. Covelo, CA: Island Press. 2001.

Eagles, P.F.J. "International Trends in Park Tourism: The Emerging Role of Finance" *George Wright Forum* 20 (2003): 25–57.

Engler, B. *Bruno Engler Photography*. Calgary: Rocky Mountain Books, 2001.

Evans, S. M. *The Bar U and Canadian Ranching History*. Calgary: University of Calgary Press, 2004.

Fedge, D. W., J. W. White, M. C. Wilson, D. E. Nelson, J. S. Vogel, and J. R. Southon. "Vermilion Lakes Site: Adaptions and Environments in the Canadian Rockies during the Late Pleistocene and Early Holocene." *American Antiquity* 60 (1995): 81–108.

Feick, J., and D. Draper. "Valid Threat or 'Tempest in a Teapot?' An Historical Account of Tourism Development and Canadian Rocky Mountain World Heritage Site Designation." *Tourism Recreation Research* 26 (2001): 35–46.

Finch, D. A. *Hell's Half Acre: Early Days in the Great Alberta Oil Patch.* Surrey: Heritage House, 2005.

Fischer, W. C., and B. D. Clayton. *Fire Ecology of Montana Forest Habitat Types East of the Continental Divide.* USDA Forest Service General Technical Report INT-141. Ogden, UT: Intermountain Forest and Range Experiment Station, 1983.

Flannery, T. *The Eternal Frontier: An Ecological History of North America.* New York: Atlantic Monthly Press, 2001.

Flook, D. R. *Causes and Implications of Observed Sex Differential in the Survival of Wapiti.* Canadian Wildlife Service Report Series No. 11. Ottawa: Queen's Printer, 1970.

Foran, M., and E. Cavell. *Calgary: An Illustrated History.* Toronto: James Lorimer, 1978.

Forman, R.T.T., J. Bissonnette, A. Clevenger, C. Cutshall, V. Dale, L. Fahrig, C. Goldman, K. Heanue, J. Jones, D. Sperling, F. Swanson, T. Turrentine, and T. Winter. *Road Ecology: Science and Solutions.* Washington, DC: Island Press, 2002.

Fraser, E. *The Canadian Rockies: Early Travels and Explorations.* Edmonton: Hurtig, 1969.

Gadd, B. *Bankhead: The Twenty Year Town.* Calgary: Coal Association of Canada, 1989.

———. *Handbook of the Canadian Rockies.* Jasper, AB: Corax Press, 1995.

Gainer, B. *The Human History of Jasper National Park.* Report No. 441. Jasper, AB: Parks Canada, 1981.

Geist, V. Mountain Sheep: A Study in Behaviour and Evolution. Chicago: University of Chicago Press, 1971.

———. *Buffalo Nation: History and Legend of the North American Bison.* Saskatoon: Fifth House, 1996.

Gibbon, J. M. *Steel of Empire.* Toronto: McClelland and Stewart, 1935.

Gibeau, M. L., A. P. Clevenger, S. Herrero, and J. Wierzchowski. "Grizzly Bear Response to Human Development and Activities in the Bow River Watershed, Alberta, Canada." *Biological Conservation* 103 (2002): 227–36.

Gilpin, J. F. *Edmonton, Gateway to the North: An Illustrated History.* Burlington, ON: Windsor Publications, 1984.

Goble, D. D. "Salmon in the Columbia Basin. From Abundance to Extinction." In *Northwest Lands, Northwest Peoples: Readings in Environmental History*, edited by D. D. Goble and P. W. Hirt, 229–63. Seattle: University of Washington Press, 1999.

Great Plains Research Consultants, *Jasper National Park: A Social and Economic History.* Microfiche Report 198. Ottawa: Parks Canada, 1985.

Green, W. S. *Among the Selkirk Glaciers, being the Account of a Rough Survey in the Rocky Mountain Regions of British Columbia.* London: MacMillan, 1890.

Gruell, G. E. *Fire's Influence on Wildlife Habitat on the Bridger-Teton National Forest, Wyoming: Volume 1 Photographic Record and Analysis.* USDA Forest Service Research Paper INT-235. Ogden, UT: Intermountain Forest and Range Experiment Station, 1980.

Gruell, G. E. *Fire and Vegetative Trends in the Northern Rockies: Interpretations from 1871–1982 Photographs.* USDA Forest Service General Technical Report INT-158. Ogden, UT: Intermountain Forest and Range Experiment Station, 1983.

Habeck, J. R., and R. W. Mutch. "Fire Dependent Forests in the Northern Rocky Mountains." *Quaternary Research* 3 (1973): 408–24.

Haines, F. "The Western Limits of the Bison Range." *Pacific Northwest Quarterly* 31 (1940): 389–98.

Hallett, R. C., and R. C. Walker. "Paleoecology and its Application to Fire and Vegetation Management in Kootenay National Park, British Columbia." *Journal of Paleolimnology* 24 (2000): 401–14.

Hamer, D. "Buffaloberry (*Shepherdia canadensis* [L.] Nutt.) Fruit Production in Fire Successional Bear Feeding Sites." *Journal of Range Management* 49 (1996): 520–29.

———. "Forest Fires Influence on Yellow Hedysarum Habitat and its Use by Grizzly Bears in Banff National Park, Alberta." *Canadian Journal of Zoology* 77 (1999): 1513–1520.

———, and S. Herrero. *Ecological Studies of the Grizzly Bear in Banff National Park.* Final Report for Parks Canada Contract WR4-80. Calgary: University of Calgary, 1983.

Harkin, J. B. "Canada's National Parks." In *The Handbook of Canada*, edited by W. A. Parks, 98–112. Toronto: University of Toronto Press, 1924.

Harmon, A. *Park History: Banff National Park.* Internal Report. Banff: Banff National Park, 1959.

Harmon, C. *Great Days in the Rockies: the Photographs of Byron Harmon.* Toronto: Oxford University Press, 1978.

Hart, E. J. *The Battle for Banff: Exploring the Heritage of the Banff-Bow Valley, Part II, 1930 to 1985.* Banff: EJH Literary Enterprises, 2003.

———. *The Brewster Story: From Pack Train to Tour Bus.* Banff: EJH Literary Enterprises, 1981.

———. *Diamond Hitch: The Early Outfitters and Guides of Banff and Jasper.* Banff: Summerthought, 1979.

———. *Golf on the Roof of the World: A History of the Banff Springs Golf Club.* Banff: EJH Literary Enterprises, 1999.

———. *Jimmy Simpson, Legend of the Rockies.* Banff: Altitude Publishing, 1993.

———. *The Place of Bows: Exploring the Heritage of the Banff-Bow Valley, Part I, to 1930.* Banff: EJH Literary Enterprises, 1999.

———. *The Selling of Canada: The CPR and the Beginnings of Canadian Tourism.* Banff: Altitude Publishing, 1983.

———. *Trains, Peaks & Tourists: The Golden Age of Canadian Travel.* Banff: EJH Literary Enterprises, 2000.

Hattersly-Smith, G. "The Symposium on Glacier Mapping." *Canadian Journal of Earth Sciences* 3 (1966): 737–43.

Hawkes, B. C. "Fire History and Fuel Appraisal of Kananaskis Provincial Park, Alberta." Master's thesis, University of Alberta, 1979.

———. "Fire History of Kananaskis Provincial Park: Mean Fire Return Intervals." In *Proceedings of the Fire History Workshop*, edited by W. H. Romme, 42–45. USDA Forest Service General Technical Report RM-81. Fort Collins, CO: Rocky Mountain Forest and Range Experiment Station, 1980.

Hebblewhite, M. "Linking Predation Risk and Forage to Ungulate Population Dynamics." Ph.D. diss., University of Alberta, 2006.

———. *Ya Ha Tinda Elk and Wolf Project: Third Quarter Progress Report, 30 September 2004 to 31 December 2004.* Edmonton: University of Alberta, 2004.

———, E. H. Merrill, L. E. Morgantini, C. A. White, J. R. Allen, E. Bruns, L. Thurston, and T. E. Hurd. "Is the Migratory Behavior of Montane Elk Herds in Peril? The Case of Alberta's Ya Ha Tinda Elk Herd." *Wildlife Society Bulletin* 34 (2006): 1280–94.

———, D. H. Pletscher, and P. C. Paquet. "Elk Population Dynamics in Areas With and Without Wolves in Banff National Park." *Canadian Journal of Zoology* 80 (2002): 789–99.

———, C. A. White, C. G. Nietvelt, J. A. McKenzie, T. E. Hurd, J. M. Fryxell, S. E. Bayley, and P. C. Paquet. "Human Activity Mediates a Trophic Cascade Caused by Wolves." *Ecology* 86 (2005): 2135–2144.

———, J. Whittington, M. Bradley, G. Skinner, A. Dibb, and C. A. White, "Conditions for Caribou Persistence in the Wolf-Elk-Caribou Systems of the Canadian Rockies." *Rangifer* 17 (2007): forthcoming.

Herrero, S., ed. *Biology, Demography, Ecology, and Management of Grizzly Bears In and Around Banff National Park and Kananaskis Country.* Eastern Slopes Grizzly Bear Project. Calgary: University of Calgary Faculty of Environmental Design, 2005.

Heusser, C. J. "Postglacial Environments in the Canadian Rocky Mountains." *Ecological Monographs* 26 (1956): 263–302.

Higgs, E. *Nature by Design: People, Natural Processes, and Ecological Restoration.* Cambridge, MA: MIT Press, 2003.

Hodgins, D. W., J. E. Green, G. Harrison, and J. Roulet. "From Confrontation to Conservation: The Banff National Park Experience." In *Wilderness Science in a Time of Change Conference*, edited by S. F. McCool, D. N. Cole, W. T. Borrie, and J. O'Loughlin. USDA Forest Service Proceedings RMRS-P-15-Vol-2, 281–89. Ogden, UT: Rocky Mountain Forest and Range Experiment Station, 2000.

Holland, W. D., and G. M. Coen, eds. *The Ecological (Biophysical) Land Classification of Banff and Jasper National Parks.* Publication SS-82-44. Edmonton: Alberta Institute of Pedology, 1982.

Holmgren, E. J., and P. M. Holmgren. *Over 2000 Place Names of Alberta.* Saskatoon: Western Producer Prairie Books, 1976.

Holroyd, G. L., and K. J. Van Tighem. *Ecological (Biophysical) Land Classification of Banff and Jasper National Parks: Volume 3. The Wildlife Inventory.* Canadian Wildlife Service Report. Calgary: Parks Canada, 1983.

Huck, B., and D. Whiteway. *In Search of Ancient Alberta.* Winnipeg: Heartland Associates, 1998.

Hudson, S., B. Ritchie, and S. Timur. "Measuring Destination Competitiveness: An Empirical Study of Canadian Ski Resorts." *Tourism and Hospitality Planning & Development* 1 (2004): 79–94.

Hunter, E. *The Spirit of Mount Norquay: A History of Skiing Banff National Park's Mount Norquay.* Banff: Banff Mount Norquay, 2000.

Hurd, T. E. "Factors Limiting Moose Numbers and Their Interactions with Elk and Wolves in the Central Rocky Mountains, Canada." Master's thesis, University of British Columbia, 1999.

Innes, H. A. *A History of the Canadian Pacific Railway.* Toronto: McClelland and Stewart, 1923.

Intergovernmental Panel on Climate Change. *Climate Change 2001: The Scientific Basis.* Cambridge: Cambridge University Press, 2001.

Jackson, C. S. *Picture Maker of the Old West: William H. Jackson.* New York: Charles Scribner, 1947.

Jackson, L. E., R. A. Kostachuk, and G. M. Macdonald. "Identification of Debris Flows Hazard on Alluvial Fans in the Canadian Rocky Mountains." *Reviews in Engineering Geology* 7 (1987): 115–24.

Johansen, D. *Empire of the Columbia: A History of the Pacific Northwest.* New York: Harper and Row, 1967.

Johnson, E. A., and G. I. Fryer. "Historical Vegetation Change in the Kananaskis Valley, Canadian Rockies." *Canadian Journal of Botany* 65 (1987): 853–58.

———, and G. I. Fryer. "Population Dynamics in Lodgepole Pine- Engelmann Spruce Forests." *Ecology* 70 (1989): 1335–45.

———, and C. P. S. Larsen. "Climatically Induced Change in Fire Frequency in the Southern Canadian Rockies." *Ecology* 72 (1991): 194–201.

———, and D. R. Wowchuk. "Wildfires in the Canadian Rocky Mountains and the Relationship to Mid-Tropospheric Anomalies." *Canadian Journal of Forest Research* 23 (1993): 1213–22.

Jones, K. R. *Wolf Mountains. A History of Wolves along the Great Divide.* Calgary: University of Calgary Press, 2002.

Kariel, H. G. "Land Use Alberta's Foothill Country." *Western Geography* 7 (1997): 20–46.

Kay, C. E. "Aboriginal Overkill: The Role of Native Americans in Structuring Western Ecosystems." *Human Nature* 5 (1994): 359–98.

———. "Aboriginal Overkill and the Biogeography of Moose in Western North America." *Alces* 32 (1996): 1–24.

———. "Are Ecosystems Structured from Top-Down, or Bottom-Up: A New Look at an Old Debate." *Wildlife Society Bulletin* 26 (1998): 484–98.

———, and R. T. Simmons, eds. *Wilderness and Political Ecology: Aboriginal Influences and the Original State of Nature*. Salt Lake City: University of Utah Press, 2002.

———, and C. A. White. "Long-Term Ecosystem States and Processes in the Central Canadian Rockies: A New Perspective on Ecological Integrity and Ecosystem Management." *George Wright Society Annual Conference on Research and Resources in Parks and on Protected Lands* 8 (1995): 119–32.

———, B. Patton, and C. A. White. "Historical Wildlife Observations in the Canadian Rockies: Implications for Ecological Integrity." *Canadian Field Naturalist* 114 (2000): 561–83.

———, C. A. White, I. R. Pengelly, and B. Patton. *Long-term Ecosystem States and Processes in Banff National Park and the Central Canadian Rockies*. Occasional Report 9. National Parks Branch. Ottawa: Parks Canada, 1999.

Keane, R. E., K. C. Ryan, T. T. Veblen, C. D. Allen, J. A. Logan, and B. Hawkes. "The Cascading Effects of Fire Exclusion in Rocky Mountain Ecosystems." In *Rocky Mountain Futures: An Ecological Perspective*, edited by J. Baron, 133–52. Washington, DC: Island Press, 2002.

Keigley, R. B., and F. H. Wagner. "What is 'Natural': Yellowstone Elk Population- A Case Study." *Integrative Biology* 4 (1999): 133–48.

Kessell, S. R., and W. C. Fischer. *Predicting Post-Fire Plant Succession for Fire Management Planning*. USDA Forest Service General Technical Report INT-94. Ogden, UT: Intermountain Forest and Range Experiment Station, 1981.

Kostaschuk, R. A., G. M. MacDonald, and P. E. Putman. "Depositional Processes and Alluvial Fan Drainage Basin Morphometric Relationships near Banff, Alberta, Canada." *Earth Surface Processes and Landforms* 11 (1986): 471–84.

Krebs, C. J. *Ecology*. New York: Harper Collins, 1996.

———, S. Boutin, and R. Boonstra, eds. *Ecosystem Dynamics in the Boreal Forest: The Kluane Project*. Oxford: Oxford University Press, 2001.

Kucera, R. E. *Exploring the Columbia Icefield*. Calgary: High Country Colour, 1999.

Kurten, B., and E. Anderson. *Pleistocene Mammals of North Ame*rica. New York: Columbia University Press, 1983.

Langemann, E. G. "Zooarchaeological Research in Support of a Reintroduction of Bison to Banff National Park Canada." *Conference of the International Council of Archaeolzoology* 9 (2002): 79–89.

———, and W. Perry. *Banff National Park of Canada: Archaeological Resource Description and Analysis*. Calgary: Parks Canada, 2002.

Lavallée, O. *Van Horne's Road*. Toronto: Railfare Enterprises, 1974.

Leopold, A. S., S. A. Cain, C. Cottam, I. N. Gabrielson, and T. L. Kimball. "Report of the Advisory Board on Wildlife Management (The Leopold Report)." Insert 4-63. *National Park Magazine*. April, 1963.

Lewis, H. T. "Indian Fires of Spring." *Natural History* 89 (1980): 76–83.

Lothian, W. F. *A Brief History of Canada's National Parks*. Ottawa: Environment Canada–Parks, 1987.

———. *A History of Canada's National Parks*. Vol. 1. Government of Canada Publication QS-7034-010-EE-A1. Ottawa: Parks Canada, 1976.

———. *A History of Canada's National Parks*. Vol. 3. Government of Canada Publication QS-7034-010-EE-A1. Ottawa: Parks Canada, 1979.

———. *A History of Canada's National Parks*. Vol. 4. Government of Canada Publication QS-7034-010-EE-A1. Ottawa: Parks Canada, 1981.

Luckman, B. H. "Landscape and Climate Change in the Central Canadian Rockies during the 20th Century." *The Canadian Geographer* 42 (1998): 319–36.

———. "The Little Ice Age and the Canadian Rockies." *Geomorphology* 32 (2000): 357–84.

———. "The Neoglacial History of the Peyto Glacier." In *Peyto Glacier: One Century of Science*, edited by M. N. Demuth, D. S. Munro, and G. L. Young, 25–57. Saskatoon: National Water Research Institute, 2006.

———. and T. Kavanagh. "Impact of Climate Fluctuations on Mountain Environments in the Canadian Rockies." *Ambio* 29 (2000): 371–80.

———. and R. J. S. Wilson. " Summer Temperatures in the Canadian Rockies During the Last Millennium: A Revised Record." *Climate Dynamics* (2005): 131–44.

Luxton, E. G. *Banff: Canada's First National Park*. Banff: Summerthought, 1975.

Lyman, R. L. "Aboriginal Overkill in the Intermountain West of North America: Zooarchaelogical Tests and Implications." *Human Nature* 15 (2004): 169–208.

MacDonald, G. M. "Late Quaternary Paleoenvironments of the Morley Flats and Kananaskis Valley of Southwestern Alberta." *Canadian Journal of Earth Sciences* 19 (1982): 23–35.

———. and L. C. Cwynar. "A Fossil Pollen Based Reconstruction of the Late Quarternary History of Lodgepole Pine (*Pinus contorta* spp. Latifolia) in the Western Interior of Canada." *Canadian Journal of Forest Research* 15 (1985): 1039–44.

MacGregor, J. G. *Edmonton: A History*. Edmonton: Hurtig, 1975.

MacLaren, I. "Cultured Wilderness in Jasper National Park." *Journal of Canadian Studies* 34 (1999): 7–28.

———, with E. Higgs and G. Zezulka-Mailloux. *Mapper of Mountains: M.P. Bridgland in the Canadian Rockies 1902–1930*. Edmonton: University of Alberta Press, 2005.

Mann, C. C. 1491: New Revelations of the Americas before Columbus. New York: Alfred Knopf, 2005.

Martin, P. S., and R. G. Klein, eds. *Quaternary Extinctions: A Prehistoric Revolution*. Tucson: University of Arizona Press, 1989.

Marty, S. *A Grand and Fabulous Notion: The First Century of Canada's Parks*. Ottawa: Canadian Government Publication Centre, 1984.

Masters, A. M. "Changes in Fire Frequency in Kootenay National Park." *Canadian Journal of Botany* 68 (1990): 1763–67.

McCart, J., and P. McCart. *On the Road with David Thompson*. Calgary: Fifth House, 2000.

McDonald, P. *Where the River Brought Them: 200 Years at Rocky Mountain House and Area*. Rocky Mountain House, AB: Creative Office Design and Publishing, 2001.

McDougall, J. *Opening the Great West*. Occasional Paper 6. Calgary: Glenbow-Alberta Institute, 1970.

McGuire, T. M., and J. F. Morrall. "Strategic Highway Improvements to Minimize Environmental Impacts Within The Canadian Rocky Mountain National Parks." *Canadian Journal of Civil Engineering* 27 (2000): 523–32.

Meagher, M., and D. B. Houston. *Yellowstone and the Biology of Time*. Norman: University of Oklahoma Press, 1998.

Millar, W. N. *Game Preservation in the Rocky Mountain Forest Reserve*. Forestry Branch Bulletin 51. Ottawa: Department of the Interior, 1915.

Milton, V., and W. B. Cheadle. *The Northwest Passage by Land*. 1865. Reprint. Toronto: Coles, 1970.

Moberly, H. J., and W. B. Cameron. *When Fur Was King*. Toronto: J. M. Dent, 1929.

Morgantini, L. E. *The Ya Ha Tinda: An Ecological Overview*. Calgary: Parks Canada, 1995.

———, and R. J. Hudson. "Migratory Patterns of the Wapiti, *Cervus elaphus*, in Banff National Park, Alberta." *Canadian Field Naturalist* 102 (1988): 12–19.

Morris, A. *The Treaties of Canada with the Indians*, 1880. Reprint. Calgary: Fifth House, 1991.

Murphy, P. J. *A History of Forest and Prairie Fire Control Policy in Alberta*. Edmonton: Alberta Energy and Natural Resources, 1985.

———, and T. W. Peterson. "Athabasca Pass: Portal on the Trans Canada Road 1811–1860." Paper presented at the *Rupert's Land Colloquium*. May 25–29, 2004. Kenora.

Nadeau, L. B., and I. G. W. Corns. "Post-fire Vegetation of the Montane Natural Region of Jasper National Park." *Forest Ecology and Management* 163 (2002): 165–83.

Nash, R. M. *Wilderness and the American Mind*. New Haven, CT: Yale University Press, 1967.

National and Historic Parks Branch. *Banff National Park Provisional Master Plan*. Ottawa: Queen's Printer, 1969.

Nelson, J. G. "Some Observations on Animals, Landscape and Man in the Bow Valley Area: c. 1750–1885." In *Vegetation, Soils and Wildlife*, edited by J.G. Nelson and M.J. Chambers, 63–96. Toronto: Methuen, 1969.

———, and A. R. Byrne. "Man as an Instrument of Landscape Change: Fires Floods, and National Parks in the Bow Valley, Alberta." *Geographical Review* 26 (1966): 226–38.

Netting, R. M. *Balancing on an Alp: Ecological Change and Continuity in a Swiss Mountain Community*. Cambridge: Cambridge University Press, 1981.

Nielsen, S. E., S. Herrero, M. S. Boyce, R. D. Mace, B. Benn, M. L. Gibeau, and S. Jevons. "Modelling the Spatial Distribution of Human-Caused Grizzly Bear Mortalities in the Central Rockies Ecosystem of Canada." *Biological Conservation* 120 (2004): 101–13.

Nietvelt, C. G. "Herbivory Interactions between Beaver (*Castor canadensis*) and Elk (*Cervus elaphus*) on Willow (*Salix* spp.) in Banff National Park, Alberta." Master's thesis, University of Alberta, 2001.

Oltmann, R. *My Valley, The Kananaskis*. Calgary: Rocky Mountain Books, 1997.

Ommaney, C.S.I. *Glacier Surveys by District Personnel of the Water Survey of Canada. 2. The Peyto Glacier*. Inland Waters Directorate, Glacier Inventory Note 7. Ottawa: Department of the Environment, 1972.

Outram, J. *In the Heart of the Canadian Rockies*. New York: MacMillan, 1906.

Pacas, C., D. Bernard, N. Marshal, and J. Green. *State of the Banff-Bow Valley Report*. Banff: Banff-Bow Valley Study, 1996.

Parks Canada. *Banff National Park Management Plan*. Ottawa: Department of Canadian Heritage, 1997.

———. *Elk Management Strategy in the Bow Valley, Banff National Park*. Environmental Screening Report. Banff: Banff National Park, 1999.

———. *Public Hearing Report: Mountain Parks and Lake Louise Area*. Ottawa: Department of Indian and Northern Affairs, 1974.

———. *Regional Forest Management Strategy*: Environmental Screening Report. Banff: Banff National Park, 2002.

———. *Ya Ha Tinda Ranch: Fuel Break-Prescribed Fire-Elk Conditioning-Elk Proof Fencing*. Environmental Screening Report. Banff: Banff National Park, 2005.

Parks Canada Agency. *"Unimpaired for Future Generations?" Protecting Ecological Integrity with Canada's National Parks. Volume I: A Call to Action*. Report of the Panel on the Ecological Integrity of Canada's National Parks. Ottawa: Public Works and Government Services, 2000.

———. *"Unimpaired for Future Generations?" Protecting Ecological Integrity with Canada's National Parks. Volume II: Setting a New Direction for Canada's National Parks.* Report of the Panel on the Ecological Integrity of Canada's National Parks. Ottawa: Public Works and Government Services, 2000.

Peacock, S. M., and N. J. Turner. " 'Just Like a Garden,' Traditional Resource Management and Biodiversity Conservation on the Interior Plateau of British Columbia." In *Biodiversity and Native America*, edited by P. E. Minnis and W. J. Elisens, 133–79. Norman: University of Oklahoma Press, 2000.

Perla, R. I., and M. Martinelli. *Avalanche Handbook.* USDA Forest Service Agriculture Handbook 489. Fort Collins, CO: Rocky Mountain Forest and Range Research Station, 1978.

Perry, W. "Siding 29, Using Archival Maps in a High-Tech World," *Research Links* 11 (2003): 18.

Pielou, E. C. *After the Ice Age: The Return of Life to Glaciated North America.* Chicago: University of Chicago Press, 1991.

Poll, D. M. *Wildlife Mortality on the Kootenay Parkway, Kootenay National Park.* Radium, BC: Parks Canada, 1989.

Pyne, S. J. "Burning Banff." *Interdisciplinary Studies in Literature and Environment* 11 (2004): 221–47.

———. *Fire in America: A Cultural History of Wildland and Rural Fire.* Princeton: Princeton University Press, 1982.

Reasoner, M. A., and U. M. Huber. "Postglacial Paleoenvironments and Climate History of the Upper Bow Valley, Banff National Park, Canada." *Quaternary Science Review* 18 (1999): 475–92.

———. G. Osborn, and N. W. Rutter. "Age of the Crowfoot Advance in the Canadian Rocky Mountains: A Glacial Event Coeval with the Younger Dryas Oscillation." *Geology* 22 (1994): 439–42.

Rhemtulla, J. M., R. J. Hall, E. S. Higgs, and S. E. Macdonald. "Eighty Years of Change: Vegetation in the Montane Ecoregion of Jasper National Park, Alberta, Canada." *Canadian Journal of Forest Research* 32 (1999): 2010–2021.

Ritchie, J.B.R. "Crafting a Value-driven Vision for a National Tourism Treasure." *Tourism Management* 20 (1999): 273–82.

Ritchie, J. C., and G. M. MacDonald. "The Patterns of Postglacial Spread of White Spruce." *Journal of Biogeography* 13 (1986): 527–40.

Roberts, M. *The Western Avernus.* Toronto: J. M. Dent, 1924.

Robinson, B. *Banff Springs: Story of a Hotel.* Banff: Summerthought, 1973.

Roe, F. G. *The North American Buffalo.* Toronto: University of Toronto Press, 1951.

Rogeau, M. P., and D. Gilbride. *Forest Stand Origin Mapping of Banff National Park.* Banff: Parks Canada, 1994.

———, I. R. Pengelly, and M. J. Fortin. "Using a Topography Model to Predict and Monitor Fire Cycles in Banff National Park." In *Proceedings of the 22nd Tall Timbers Fire Ecology Conference: Fire in Temperate, Boreal, and Montane Ecosystems*, edited by R. T. Engstrom, K. E. M. Galley, and W. J. de Groot, 55–69. Tallahassee, FL: Tall Timbers Research Station, 2004.

Rogers, G. F., H. E. Malde and R. M. Turner. *Bibliography of Repeat Photography for Evaluating Landscape Change.* Salt Lake City: University of Utah Press, 1984.

Rood, S. B., K. Taboulchanas, C. E. Bradley, and A. R. Kalischuk. "Influence of Flow Regulation and Channel Dynamics on Riparian Cottonwoods along the Bow River, Alberta." *Rivers* 7 (2003): 33–48.

Rylatt, R. M. *Surveying the Canadian Pacific: Memoir of a Railway Pioneer.* Salt Lake City: University of Utah Press, 1991.

Sachro, L. L., W. L. Strong, and C. C. Gates. "Prescribed Burning Effects on Summer Elk Forage Availability in the Subalpine Zone, Banff National Park, Canada." *Environmental Management* 77 (2005), 183–93.

Sandford, R. W. *Lake Minnewanka: The Spirit and the Waters.* Banff: Lake Minnewanka Boat Tours, 1999.

———. *Sunshine: Its Human and Natural Heritage.* Banff: Sunshine Village Corporation, 1984.

———, ed. *A Mountain Life: The Stories and Photographs of Bruno Engler.* Canmore, AB: Alpine Club of Canada, 1996.

Scace, R. C. *Banff: A Cultural Historical Study of Land Use and Management in a National Park Community to 1945.* Studies in Land Use and Landscape Change 2. Calgary: Department of Geography, University of Calgary, 1968.

Schäffer, M.T.S. "The 1911 Expedition to Maligne Lake." In *A Hunter of Peace: Mary T. S Schäffer's Old Indian Trails with her heretofore unpublished account 1911 Expedition to Maligne Lake*, edited by E.J. Hart, 79–152. Banff: Whyte Foundation, 1980.

———. "Old Indian Trails." In *A Hunter of Peace: Mary T. S Schäffer's Old Indian Trails with her heretofore unpublished account 1911 Expedition to Maligne Lake*, edited by E.J. Hart, 15–78. Banff: Whyte Foundation, 1980.

Schindler, D. W. "The Eastern Slopes of the Canadian Rockies, Must We Follow the American Blueprint." In *Rocky Mountain Futures: An Ecological Perspective*, edited by J. Baron, 285–89. Washington, DC: Island Press, 2002.

———, and C. Pacas. "Cumulative Effects of Human Activity on Aquatic Ecosystems the Bow Valley of Banff National Park." In *Ecological Outlooks Project: A Cumulative Effects Assessment and Futures Outlook of the Banff Bow Valley*, edited by J. Green, C. Pacas, L. Cornwell, and S. Bayley, chap. 5. Ottawa: Department of Canadian Heritage, 1996.

Scott, C. *Powder Pioneers.* Calgary: Rocky Mountain Books, 2005.

Scott, D., and R. Suffling, eds. *Climate Change and Canada's National Park System.* Adaption and Impacts Research Group. Ottawa: Environment Canada, 2000.

Shepherd. L. K. "Caribou Habitat Selection in Relation to Lichen and Fire in Jasper and Banff National Parks." Master's thesis, University of Alberta, 2006.

Silversides, B. *Fort de Prairies: The Story of Fort Edmonton*. Surrey, BC: Heritage House, 2005.

Simpson, G. *An Overland Journey Round the World in the Years 1841 and 1842*. London: Lea and Blanchard, 1847.

Skjonsberg, T. *Eastern Slopes Wildlife Study: 1984–1987*. Banff: Parks Canada, 1993.

Smith, C. *Jasper Park Lodge: In the Heart of the Canadian Rockies*. Altona, MB: Friesen, 1985.

Smith, D. B. *Centennial City: Calgary, 1894–1994*. Calgary: University of Calgary Press, 1994.

Snow, J. *These Mountains are our Sacred Places: The Story of the Stoney Indians*. Toronto: Samuel Stevens, 1977.

Southesk, Earl of. *Saskatchewan and the Rocky Mountains: A Diary and Narrative of Travel, Sport, and Adventure during a Journey through the Hudson's Bay Company's Territories, in 1859 and 1860*, 1875. Reprint. Edmonton: Hurtig, 1969.

Spry, I. M. *The Palliser Expedition: An Account of John Palliser's British North American Exploration Expedition, 1857–1860*. Toronto: MacMillan, 1963.

———, ed. *The Papers of the Palliser Expedition, 1857–1860*. Toronto: Champlain Society, 1968.

Stewart, O. C. *Forgotten Fires: Native Americans and the Transient Wilderness*, edited with introductions by H.T. Lewis and M. K. Anderson. Norman: University of Oklahoma Press, 2002.

Stelfox, B., S. Herrero, and D. Ryerson. "Implications of Historical, Current, and Likely Future Trajectories of Human Landuses and Population Growth to Grizzly Bears in the Alberta Portion of the CRE." In *Biology, Demography, Ecology and Management of Grizzly Bears in and around Banff National Park and Kananaskis Country*, edited by S. Herrero, 202–22. Calgary: Faculty of Environmental Design, University of Calgary, 2005.

Stokes, M. A., and T. L. Smiley. *An Introduction to Tree-Ring Dating*. Chicago: University of Chicago Press, 1968.

Stringer, P. W. "An Ecological Study of Grasslands in Banff, Jasper, and Waterton Lakes National Parks." *Canadian Journal of Botany* 51 (1973): 383–411.

Stutfield, H. E. M., and J. N. Collie. 1903. *Climbs and Explorations in the Canadian Rockies*. 1903. Reprinted, Calgary: Aquila Books, 1998.

Sveinbjörnsson, B. "North American and European Treelines: External Forces and Internal Processes Controlling Position." *Ambio* 29 (2000): 389–95.

Tande, G. F. "Fire History and Vegetation Pattern of Coniferous Forests in Jasper National Park, Alberta." *Canadian Journal of Botany* 57 (1979): 1912–1931.

Tilden, F. *Following the Frontier with F. Jay Haynes: Pioneer Photographer of the Old West*. New York: Alfred Knopf, 1964.

———. *The National Parks: What They Mean to You and Me*. New York: Alfred Knopf, 1955.

Timoney, K., and P. Lee. "Environmental Management in Resource-rich Alberta, Canada: First World Jurisdiction, Third World Analogue?" *Journal of Environmental Management* 63 (2001): 387–405.

Touche, R. *Brown Cows, Sacred Cows: A True Story of Lake Louise*. Hanna, AB: Gorman Publishers, 1990.

Tough, G. W. "A Study of Coal Mining: Cascade Coal Basin." Master's thesis, University of Calgary, 1969.

Travis, W. R., D. M. Theobald, and D. B. Fagre. "Transforming the Rockies: Human Forces, Settlement Patterns and Ecosystem Effects." In *Rocky Mountain Futures: An Ecological Perspective*, edited by J. Baron, 1–24. Washington, DC: Island Press, 2002.

Treaty 7 Elders and Tribal Council, W. Hildebrandt, S. Carter, and D. First Rider. *The True Spirit and Original Intent of Treaty 7*. Montreal and Kingston: McGill-Queen's University Press, 1996.

Turner, R. D., and W. E. Rees. "A Comparative Study of Parks Policy in Canada and the United States." *Nature Canada* 2 (1973): 31–36.

Urquhart, I., ed. *Assault on the Rockies: Environmental Controversies in Alberta*. Edmonton: Rowan Books, 1998.

Van Wagner, C. E., M. A. Finney, and M. Heathcott. "Historical Fire Cycles in the Canadian Rocky Mountain National Parks." *Forest Science* 52 (2006): 704–17.

Wagner, F. H., R. Foresta, R. B. Gill, D. R. McCullough, M. R. Pelton, W. F. Porter, and H. Salwasser, eds. *Wildlife Policies in the U.S. National Parks*. Washington, DC: Island Press, 1995.

Waiser, W. A. *Park Prisoners: The Untold History of Western Canada's National Parks, 1915–1946*. Calgary: Fifth House, 1995.

Warre, H. J. *Sketches in North America and the Oregon Territory*, 1848. Reprint. New York: Imprint Society, 1970.

White, C. A. "Fire and Biomass in Banff National Park Closed Forests." Master's thesis, Colorado State University, 1985.

———. *Wildland Fires in Banff National Park, 1880–1980*. National Parks Branch. Occasional Paper 3. Ottawa: Parks Canada, 1985.

———, and M. C. Feller. "Repeat Photography of Trembling Aspen in the Canadian Rocky Mountains." In *Proceedings of the 22nd Tall Timbers Fire Ecology Conference: Fire in Temperate, Boreal, and Montane Ecosystems*, edited by R. T. Engstrom, K. E. M. Galley, and W. J. de Groot, 2–22. Tallahassee, FL: Tall Timbers Research Station, 2004.

———, and W. Fisher. "Consilience and Ecological Restoration in Banff National Park." In *Interdisciplinary Research and Management in Mountain Areas*, edited by L. Taylor and A. Ryall, 113–32. Mountain Community Conference Series No. 4. Banff: Mountain Culture at the Banff Centre, 2004.

———, M. C. Feller, and S. Bayley. "Predation Risk and the Functional Response of Elk-Aspen Herbivory." *Forest Ecology and Management* 181 (2003): 77–97.

———, M. C. Feller, and P. Vera. "New Approaches for Testing Fire History Hypotheses." *Proceedings of the International Conference on Science and Management of Protected Areas* 4 (2001): 398–411.

———, T. E. Hurd, M. Hebblewhite, and I. R. Pengelly. "Mitigating Fire Suppression, Highway, and Habitat Fragmentation Effects in the Banff Bow Valley Ecosystem, Banff National Park: Preliminary Evolution of a Before-After-Control-Impact (BACI) Design with Path Analysis." In *Monitoring the Effectiveness of Biological Conservation*, edited by J. Innes and J. Timko. Vancouver: Forrex, 2007.

———, E. G. Langemann, C. C. Gates, C. E. Kay, T. Shury, and T. E. Hurd. "Plains Bison Restoration in the Canadian Rocky Mountains: Ecological and Management Considerations." *Proceedings of the George Wright Biannual Conference on Research and Resource Management in National Parks and on Public Lands* 11 (2001): 152–60.

———, C. E. Olmsted, and C. E. Kay. "Aspen, Elk, and Fire in the Rocky Mountain National Parks of North America." *Wildlife Society Bulletin* 26 (1998): 449–62.

———, I. R. Pengelly, D. Zell, and M. P. Rogeau. *Landscape Fire Regimes and Vegetation Restoration in Banff National Park, Alberta.* Occasional Paper BNP-2003-1. Banff, AB: Parks Canada, 2003.

———, I. R. Pengelly, D. Zell, and M. P. Rogeau. "Restoring Heterogeneous Fire Regimes in Banff National Park." In *Mixed Severity Fire Regimes: Ecology and Management*, edited by L. Taylor, J. Zelnik, S. Cadwallader, and B. Hughes, 255–66. Association of Fire Ecology. Pullman: Washington State University Extension, 2005.

Whittington, J., C. Cassady St. Clair, and G. Mercer. "Spatial Responses of Wolves to Roads and Trails in Mountain Valleys." Ecological Applications 15 (2005): 543–53.

Whyte, J. *Indians in the Canadian Rockies.* Banff: Altitude Publishing, 1985.

Wierzchowski, J., M. Heathcott, and M.D. Flannigan. "Lightning and Lightning Fire, Central Cordillera, Canada." *International Journal of Wildland Fire* 11 (2002): 41–51.

Wikeem B. M., and T. J. Ross. 2002. "Plant Succession in the Rocky Mountain Trench: Influence of Historic Factors." *Rangelands* 24 (2002): 17–20.

Wilcox, W. D. 1909. *The Rockies of Canada.* New York: Putnam, 1909.

Wilson, T. E. *Trail Blazer of the Canadian Rockies.* Calgary: Glenbow-Alberta Institute, 1972.

Woodley, S. J., J. Kay, and G. Francis, eds. *Ecological Integrity and the Management of Ecosystems.* Delray Beach, FL: St. Lucie Press, 1993.

Woods, J. "Ecology of a Partially Migratory Elk Population." Ph.D. diss., University of British Columbia, 1991.

Young, G. J., and A. D. Stanley. *Canadian Glaciers in the International Hydrological Decade Program, 1965–1974. No. 4 Peyto Glacier, Alberta.* Inland Waters Directorate Scientific Series 71: Ottawa: Fisheries and Environment Canada, 1976.

Zinkan C., and I. Syme. "Changing Dimensions of Park Management." *Forum for Applied Research and Public Policy* 12 (1997): 39–42.

NOTES

Chapter 1 INTRODUCTION

1 See R. M. Netting, *Balancing on an Alp: Ecological Change and Continuity in a Swiss Mountain Community* (Cambridge: Cambridge University Press, 1981), for an anthropological study of human population and development growth in a space-constrained alpine valley.

2 The perception that western North America lands evolved with minimal human influences led to the first wilderness areas being legislated in the western United States, defined as "an area where the earth and its community of life are untrammelled by man." See R. M. Nash, *Wilderness and the American Mind* (New Haven, CT: Yale University Press, 1967); S. J. Pyne, *Fire in America: A Cultural History of Wildland and Urban Fire* (Princeton, NJ: Princeton University Press, 1982), 15–19.

3 M. Foran and E. Cavell, *Calgary: An Illustrated History* (Toronto: James Lorimer, 1978).

4 S. Marty, *A Grand and Fabulous Notion: The First Century of Canada's Parks* (Ottawa: Canadian Government Publication Centre, 1984).

5 E. Cavell, *Legacy in Ice: The Vaux Family and the Canadian Alps* (Banff: Whyte Foundation, 1983), 16–17 describes evolving photographic technology of the period.

6 For more details on photography and the Canadian Pacific Railroad, see E. J. Hart, *The Selling of Canada: The CPR and the Beginnings of Canadian Tourism* (Banff: Altitude Publishing, 1983), 32–39.

7 Byron Harmon was the most productive of the early commercial photographers; see C. Harmon, *Great Days in the Rockies: The Photographs of Byron Harmon* (Toronto: Oxford University Press, 1978).

8 F. Tilden, *The National Parks: What They Mean to You and Me* (New York: Alfred Knopf, 1955), 111–12.

9 Biographies of these famous American photographers include C. S. Jackson, *Picture Maker of the Old West: William H. Jackson* (New York: Charles Scribner, 1947); F. Tilden, *Following the Frontier with F. Jay Haynes: Pioneer Photographer of the Old West* (New York: Alfred Knopf, 1964).

10 The CPR's early advertising campaigns are described by Hart, *Selling of Canada*, 21–53.

11 A. R. Byrne, *Man and Landscape Change in Banff National Park before 1911*, Studies in Land Use History and Landscape Changes No. 1 (Calgary: Department of Geography, University of Calgary, 1968), 53–71.

12 Horetzky entered the Rocky Mountains via the Athabasca Valley, used as the main trans-Canada route for the Northwest and Hudson Bay Company's fur brigades after 1811. See E. Fraser, *The Canadian Rockies Early Travels and Explorations* (Edmonton: Hurtig, 1969), 20–25.

13 The repeat photography technique to analyze landscape change has been widely used in Western North America and elsewhere. For example, see: G. F. Rogers, H. E. Malde, and R. M. Turner, *Bibliography of Repeat Photography for Evaluating Landscape Change* (Salt Lake City: University of Utah Press, 1984); G. Hattersly-Smith, "The Symposium on Glacier Mapping," *Canadian Journal of Earth Sciences* 3 (1966): 737–43; G. E. Gruell, *Fire's Influence on Wildlife Habitat on the Bridger-Teton National Forest, Wyoming. Volume 1: Photographic Record and Analysis*, USDA Forest Service Research Paper INT-235 (Ogden, UT: Intermountain Forest and Range Experiment Station, 1980); G. E. Gruell, *Fire and Vegetative Trends in the Northern Rockies: Interpretations from 1871–1982 Photographs*, USDA Forest Service General Technical Report INT-158 (Ogden, UT: Intermountain Forest and Range Experiment Station, 1983); M. Meagher and D. B. Houston, *Yellowstone and the Biology of Time: Photographs Across a Century* (Norman: University of Oklahoma Press, 1998).

14 For more details on historic photographers and repeat photography in the Canadian Rocky Mountains, see Cavell, *Legacy in Ice*; C. Harmon, *Great Days*; Byrne, *Man and Landscape Change*: 82–85; C. E. Kay, C. A. White, I. R. Pengelly, and B. Patton, *Long-term Ecosystem States and Processes in Banff National Park and the Central Canadian Rockies*, Occasional Report 9, National Parks Branch (Ottawa: Parks Canada, 1999), 4.1–4.26; R. W. Sandford, ed., *A Mountain Life: The Stories and Photographs of Bruno Engler* (Canmore, AB: Alpine Club of Canada, 1996); J. M. Rhemtulla, R. J. Hall, E. S. Higgs, and S. E. Macdonald, "Eighty Years of Change: Vegetation in the Montane Ecoregion of Jasper National Park, Alberta, Canada," *Canadian Journal of Forest Research* 32 (1999): 2010–2021; E. Higgs, *Nature by Design: People, Natural Processes, and Ecological Restoration* (Cambridge, MA: MIT Press, 2003), 131–42; C. A. White and M. C. Feller, "Repeat Photography of Trembling Aspen in the Canadian Rocky Mountains," in *Proceedings of the 22nd Tall Timbers Fire Ecology Conference: Fire in Temperate, Boreal, and Montane Ecosystems*, ed. R. T. Engstrom, K.E.M. Galley, and W. J. de Groot, 2–22; I. MacLaren with E. Higgs and G. Zezulka-Mailloux, *Mapper of Mountains: M. P. Bridgland in the Canadian Rockies 1902–1930* (Edmonton: University of Alberta Press, 2005), 243–63.

Chapter 2 INTO THE MOUNTAINS

1 L. J. Burpee, ed., "York Factory to the Blackfeet Country: The Journal of Anthony Henday, 1754–1755," *Transactions of the Royal Society of Canada*, Ser. 3, Vol. 1, Sec. 2 (1907): 307–61.

2 For examples of maps drawn by First Nations sources, see B. Belyea, ed., *Columbia Journals: David Thompson* (Montreal and Kingston: McGill-Queen's University Press, 1994), 293–99; T. Binnema, *Common and Contested Ground: A Human and Environmental History of the Northwestern Plains* (Norman: University of Oklahoma Press, 2001), 145–52.

3 The major fur-trading route across the Rocky Mountains was moved north to the Athabasca Valley in 1810 due to ongoing conflicts with the Blackfoot Confederacy. See Belyea, *Columbia Journals*, 248–59; Binnema, *Common and Contested Ground*, 135–39.

4 See A. Morris, *The Treaties of Canada with the Indians*, rev. ed. (1880; repr. Calgary: Fifth House, 1991), 245–75; Treaty 7 Elders and Tribal Council, W. Hildebrandt, S. Carter, and D. First Rider, eds., *The True Spirit and Original Intent of Treaty 7* (Montreal and Kingston: McGill-Queen's University Press, 1996).

5 As a result of over-hunting by Metis, early white settlers and traders, and First Nations, bison were essentially extirpated from Canadian plains by 1879. See F. G. Roe, *The North American Bison* (Toronto: University of Toronto Press, 1951), 467–88; V. Geist, *Buffalo Nation: History and Legend of the North American Bison* (Saskatoon: Fifth House, 1996), 69–99.

6 In 1879, the Canadian government contracted to Andrew Onderdonk of New York to start construction up the Fraser Canyon in British Columbia. Railway construction west of Winnipeg began in 1880. See H. A. Innes, *A History of the Canadian Pacific Railway* (Toronto: McClelland and Stewart, 1923); O. Lavallée, *Van Horne's Road* (Toronto: Railfare Enterprises, 1974).

7 Bow River Basin Council, *Nurture, Renew, Protect: A Report on the State of the Bow River Basin* (Calgary: Bow River Basin Council, 2005), 142–56; S. B. Rood, K. Taboulchanas, C. E. Bradley, and A. R. Kalischuk, "Influence of Flow Regulation and Channel Dynamics on Riparian Cottonwoods along the Bow River, Alberta," *Rivers* 7 (2003): 33–48.

8 The North West Mounted Police had a evolving and complex role in Alberta and Saskatchewan, see W. M. Baker, *The Mounted Police and Prairie Society 1873–1819* (Regina: Canadian Plains Research Centre, University of Regina, 1998).

9 Lavallée, *Van Horne's Road*, 95–104.

10 References for the history of Calgary include Foran and Cavell, *Calgary*; D. B. Smith, *Centennial City, Calgary 1894–1994* (Calgary: University of Calgary Press, 1994).

11 For a history of the town and surrounding region, see Cochrane and Area Historical Society, *Big Hill Country: Cochrane and Area* (Cochrane, AB: Cochrane and Area Historical Society, 1977).

12 J. McDougall, *Opening the Great West* (Calgary: Glenbow-Alberta Institute, 1970), Occasional Paper 6.

13 The history of the Stoney First Nation and its interaction with Banff National Park is described by: J. Snow, *These Mountains Are Our Sacred Places: The Story of the Stoney Indians* (Toronto: Samuel Stevens, 1977); Hart, *Place of Bows*, 71–73; T. Binnema and M. Niemi, "'Let the Line be Drawn Now': Wilderness, Conservation, and the Exclusion of Aboriginal People from Banff National Park in Canada," *Environmental History* 11 (2006): 724–50.

14 See Binnema, *Common and Contested Ground*, for a detailed history of First Nations in the northern Great Plains area from ca. AD 200 to 1806.

15 The Department of Indian Affairs purchased the Eden Valley Ranch in the 1940s to provide a permanent land base for a group of Stoney (Nakoda) living in the Highwood Valley. See S. M. Evans, *The Bar U and Canadian Ranching History* (Calgary: University of Calgary Press, 2004), 290–91.

16 H. A. Dempsey, *The Golden Age of the Canadian Cowboy* (Calgary: Fifth House, 1995), provides a referenced and illustrated history of this period of Alberta's history.

17 See Evans, *The Bar U*, for a detailed history of the ranch.

18 Foran and Cavell, *Calgary*, 123–28; D. A. Finch, *Hell's Half Acre: Early Days in the Great Alberta Oil Patch* (Surrey: Heritage House, 2005).

19 The supply of cheap electricity was critical to the growth of Calgary industry. See Foran and Cavell, *Calgary*, 79–82.

20 See C. Armstrong and H. V. Nelles, "Competition vs. Convenience: Federal Administration of Bow River Waterpowers, 1906–1913," in *The Canadian West: Social Change and Economic Development*, ed. H. C. Klassen, 163–80 (Calgary: University of Calgary, Comprint, 1977).

21 See Byrne, *Man and Landscape Change*, 141, for a detailed map of park boundary changes.

22 P. Parker, "Annie Staple … Keeper of the Gate," *Banff Crag and Canyon*, Feb. 7, 1973, 7.

23 The rationale for park boundary changes is described by W. F. Lothian, *A History of Canada's National Parks*, Vol. 1. Government of Canada Publication QS-7034-010-EE-A1S-7034 (Ottawa: Parks Canada, 1976), 36–38.

24 I. M. Spry, ed., *The Papers of the Palliser Expedition 1857–1860* (Toronto: Champlain Society), 265; Hart, *Place of Bows*, 54–60.

25 Byrne, *Man and Landscape Change*, 118–20; 122–37.

26 R. Oltmann, *My Valley: The Kananaskis* (Calgary: Rocky Mountain Books, 1997), 171–73; E. J. Hart, *The Battle for Banff: Exploring the Heritage of the Banff Bow Valley, Volume 2* (Banff: EJH Literary Enterprises, 2003), 83–90, 334.

27 C. A. White, *Wildland Fires in Banff National Park*, National Parks Branch. Occasional Paper 3 (Ottawa: Parks Canada, 1985), 24; C. A. White, M. C. Feller, and P. Vera, "New Approaches for Testing Fire History Hypotheses," *Proceedings of the International Conference on Science and Management of Protected Areas* 4 (2001): 398–411.

28 W. N. Millar, *Game Preservation in the Rocky Mountain Forest Reserve*, Forestry Branch Bulletin 51 (Ottawa: Department of the Interior, 1915); Byrne, *Man and Landscape Change*, 117–18; Lothian, *History of Canada's National Parks*, 4:16–17.

29 B. C. Hawkes, "Fire History and Fuel Appraisal of Kananaskis Provincial Park" (master's thesis, University of Alberta, 1979), 56–65.

30 Spry, *Papers of the Palliser Expedition*, 266–73; I. M. Spry, *The Palliser Expedition: An Account of John Palliser's British North American Exploration Expedition 1857–1860* (Toronto: MacMillan, 1963), 133–36.

31 Oltmann, *My Valley*, 48–63.

32 E. Appleby, *Canmore, The Story of an Era* (Calgary: Friesen, 1975), 26–34; Hart, *Place of Bows*, 99–102.

33 Appleby, *Canmore*, 140–49.

34 Hart, *Battle for Banff*, 327–29.

35 The linked wildlife corridors established around the communities of Banff, Harvey Heights, Canmore, and Deadmans Flats make the Bow Valley a unique example of cooperation between federal, provincial, and municipal governments towards regional conservation. See Bow Corridor Ecosystem Advisory Group, *Wildlife Corridor and Habitat Patch Guidelines for the Bow Valley: Town of Canmore, M.D. Bighorn, Banff National Park and the Alberta Government* (Canmore, AB: Alberta Provincial Parks, 1998).

36 Appleby, *Canmore*, 150–53.

Chapter 3 A KEYSTONE SPECIES?

1 W. R. Dickenson, "Changing Times: The Holocene Legacy," *Environmental History* 5 (2000): 528.

2 M.T.S. Schäffer, "Old Indian Trails of the Canadian Rockies," in *A Hunter of Peace: Mary T. S. Schäffer's Old Indian Trails with her heretofore unpublished account 1911 Expedition to Maligne Lake*, ed. E. J. Hart, 68 (Banff: Whyte Foundation, 1980).

3 Fraser, *Canadian Rockies*, 8.

4 The North American wilderness myth is considered by W. Cronan, "The Trouble with Wilderness; or, Getting Back to the Wrong Nature," *Environmental History* 1 (1995): 7–28; W. Cronan, *Uncommon Ground: Toward Reinventing Nature* (New York: Norton, 1995); S. Budiansky, *Natures' Keepers: The New Science of Nature Management* (New York: Free Press, 1995), 3–26; O. C. Stewart, *Forgotten Fires: Native Americans and the Transient Wilderness*, ed. H. T. Lewis and M. K. Anderson (Norman: University of Oklahoma Press, 2002); C. E. Kay and R. T. Simmons, eds., *Wilderness and Political Ecology: Aboriginal Influences on the Original State of Nature* (Salt Lake City: University of Utah Press, 2002); C. C. Mann, *1491: New Revelations of the Americas before Columbus* (New York: Alfred Knopf, 2005). For recent cultural perceptions of wilderness in the Canadian Rockies, see I. MacLaren, "Cultured Wilderness in Jasper National Park," *Journal of Canadian Studies* 34 (1999): 7–28; Higgs, *Nature by Design*, 27–46.

5 Kay et al., *Long-term Ecosystem States*, 7.9–7.11.

6 B. Huck and D. Whiteway, *In Search of Ancient Alberta* (Winnipeg: Heartland Associates, 1998).

7 D. W. Fedge, J. W. White, M. C. Wilson, D. E. Nelson, J. S. Vogel, and J. R. Southon, "Vermilion Lakes Site: Adaptions and Environments in the Canadian Rockies during the Late Pleistocene and Early Holocene," *American Antiquity* 60 (1995): 81–108.

8 For an interpretation of interactions between eastern and western slope cultures in archaeological sites of the Banff area, see E. G. Langemann and W. Perry, *Banff National Park of Canada: Archaeological Resource Description and Analysis* (Calgary: Parks Canada, 2002), 13–44.

9 C. E. Kay, B. Patton, and C. A. White, "Historical Wildlife Observations in the Canadian Rockies: Implications for Ecological Integrity," *Canadian Field Naturalist* 114 (2000): 561–83.

10 Kay et al., *Long-term Ecosystem States*; Belyea, *Columbia Journals*; Spry, *Palliser Expedition*; C. E. Kay, "Aboriginal Overkill: The Role of Native Americans in Structuring Western Ecosystems," *Human Nature* 5 (1994): 359–98.

11 Potential theories for moose population expansion are described by C. E. Kay, "Aboriginal Overkill and the Biogeography of Moose in Western North America," *Alces* 32 (1996): 1–24. Bison distribution theories are reviewed by: F. Haines, "The Western Limits of the Bison Range," *Pacific Northwest Quarterly* 31 (1940): 389–98; R. Daubenmire, "The Western Limits of the Range of American Bison," *Ecology* 66 (1985): 622–24; Geist, *Buffalo Nation*, 38–41; C. A. White, E. G. Langemann, C. C. Gates, C. E. Kay, T. Shury and T. E. Hurd, "Plains Bison Restoration in the Canadian Rocky Mountains: Ecological and Management Considerations," *Proceedings of the George Wright Biannual Conference on Research and Resource Management in National Parks and on Public Lands* 11 (2001): 152–60.

12 For use of fire by First Nations in the Rocky Mountains, see: H. T. Lewis, "Indian Fires of Spring," *Natural History* 89 (1980): 76–83; S. W. Barrett and S. F. Arno, "Indian Fires as an Ecological Influence in the Northern Rockies," *Journal of Forestry* 80 (1982): 647–51; White, Feller, and Vera, "New Approaches for Testing Fire History Hypotheses," 398–411; S. M. Peacock and N. J. Turner, "'Just Like a Garden', Traditional Resource Management and Biodiversity Conservation on the Interior Plateau of British Columbia," in *Biodiversity and Native America*, ed. P. E. Minnis and W. J. Elisens, 133–79 (Norman: University of Oklahoma Press, 2000).

13 J. Wierzchowski, M. Heathcott, and M. D. Flannigan, "Lightning and Lightning Fire, Central Cordillera, Canada," *International Journal of Wildland Fire* 11 (2002): 41–55.

14 Lewis, "Indian Fires."

15 C. E. Van Wagner, M. A. Finney, and M. Heathcott, "Historical Fire Cycles in the Canadian Rocky Mountain National Parks," *Forest Science* 52 (2006): 704–17. The cause of declining fire occurrence in the Rockies is controversial and has been attributed to climate change by A. M. Masters, "Changes in Fire Frequency in Kootenay National Park," *Canadian Journal of Botany* 68 (1990): 1763–1767; E. A. Johnson and C.P.S. Larsen, "Climatically Induced Change in Fire Frequency in the Southern Canadian Rockies," *Ecology* 72 (1991): 194–201. However, B. H. Luckman and T. Kavanagh, "Impact of Climate Fluctuations on Mountain Environments in the Canadian Rockies," *Ambio* 29 (2000): 371–80, could detect no evidence that climatic changes caused recent declines in fire occurrence. The alteration of First Nations land use patterns due to disease (Binnema, *Common and Contested Ground*, 120–28) and settlement on reserves are better correlated with periods of reduced fire. Also see White, *Wildland Fires*; White and Feller, "Repeat Photography of Trembling Aspen."

Chapter 4 BIRTHPLACE OF PARKS

1 H. J. Warre, *Sketches in North America and the Oregon Territory*, rev. ed. (1848; repr. New York: Imprint Society, 1970); Hart, *Place of Bows*, 52–54.

2 Lothian, *History of Canada's National Parks*, 1:38; Hart, *Place of Bows*, 257–62.

3 Hart, *Battle for Banff*, 153–58.

4 T. M. McGuire and J. F Morrall, "Strategic Highway Improvements to Minimize Environmental Impacts within the Canadian Rocky Mountain National Parks," *Canadian Journal of Civil Engineering* 27 (2000): 523–32; A. P. Clevenger and N. Waltho, "Factors Influencing the Effectiveness of Wildlife Underpasses in Banff National Park, Alberta, Canada," *Conservation Biology* 14 (2000): 47–56.

5 "How Banff Got Its Name," *Banff Crag and Canyon*, October 27, 1939.

6 W. Perry, "Siding 29, Using Archival Maps in a High-Tech World," *Research Links* 11 (2003): 18.

7 G. Simpson, *An Overland Journey Round the World in the Years 1841 and 1842* (London: Lea and Blanchard, 1847); Spry, *Palliser Expedition*, 143–44; Earl of Southesk, *Saskatchewan and the Rocky Mountains*, rev. ed. (1875; repr. Edmonton: Hurtig, 1969), 250–51.

8 Lothian, *History of Canada's National Parks*, 1:23–24; Hart, *Place of Bows*, 90–91.

9 Hart, *Battle for Banff*, 142–43.

10 Hart, *Place of Bows*, 110, 123.

11 Hart, *Battle for Banff*, 332–33, 348–49.

12 B. Robinson, *The Banff Springs Hotel* (Banff: Summerthought, 1973), 9–18, 45–48.

13 See R. D. Turner and W. E. Rees, "A Comparative Study of Parks Policy in Canada and the United States," *Nature Canada* 2 (1973): 31–36.

14 R. C. Scace, *Banff: A Cultural Historical Study of Land Use and Management in a National Park Community to 1945*, Studies in Landuse and Landscape 2 (Calgary: Department of Geography, University of Calgary, 1968) describes evolution of the Banff leasehold system.

15 The protracted process followed by Banffites to obtain community-level government is described by Hart, *Battle for Banff*, 307–16.

16 E. J. Hart, *Golf on the Roof of the World: A History of the Banff Springs Golf Club* (Banff: EJH Literary Enterprises, 1999), 10, 24–25, 44–48, 124.

17 Low elevation areas in Banff National Park have limited area, are significant for numerous species and ecological processes, and also are important for human development. See P. L. Achuff, I. R. Pengelly, and C. A. White, *Special Resources of Banff National Park* (Banff: Parks Canada, 1986), 105–15.

18 Langemann and Perry, *Banff National Park of Canada*, 97.

19 Byrne, *Man and Landscape Change*, 92–96; Hart, *Place of Bows*, 102–4.

20 Byrne, *Man and Landscape Change*, 102–3.

21 Appleby, *Canmore*, 51.

22 Lothian, *History of Canada's National Parks*, 4:100; Hart, *Battle for Banff*, 156.

23 B. Gadd, *Bankhead, The Twenty-Year Town* (Calgary: Coal Association of Canada, 1989) provides an illustrated history of the short-lived mining town.

24 J. Whyte, *Indians in the Canadian Rockies* (Banff: Altitude Publishing, 1985), 41–44; Hart, *Place of Bows*, 25–26; Simpson, *Overland Journey*, 75; Fraser, *Canadian Rockies*, 1–9; R. W. Sandford, *Lake Minnewanka: The Spirit and the Waters* (Banff: Lake Minnewanka Boat Tours, 1999) provides an illustrated natural and cultural history of the area.

25 E. G. Luxton, *Banff: Canada's First National Park* (Banff: Summerthought, 1975), 98; Hart, *Place of Bows*, 225–29.

26 Hart, *Battle for Banff*, 78–81.

27 Biological and fire history studies done all or partially in the ecologically rich Cascade Valley include: V. Geist, *Mountain Sheep: A Study in Behaviour and Evolution* (Chicago: University of Chicago Press, 1971); D. Hamer and S. Herrero, *Ecological Studies of the Grizzly Bear in Banff National Park*, Final Report for Parks Canada Contract WR4-80 (Calgary: University of Calgary, 1983); White, *Wildland Fires*; Achuff, Pengelly, and White, *Special Resources*, 105–6; T. Skjonsberg, *Eastern Slopes Wildlife Study: 1984–1987* (Banff: Parks Canada, 1993); M. P. Rogeau and D. Gilbride, *Forest Stand Origin Mapping of Banff National Park* (Banff: Parks Canada, 1994).

28 National and Historic Parks Branch, *Banff National Park Provisional Master Plan* (Ottawa: Queen's Printer, 1969), 10.

29 Parks Canada, *Public Hearing Report: Mountain Parks and Lake Louise Area* (Ottawa: Department of Indian and Northern Affairs, 1974); Hart, *Battle for Banff*, 236–39.

30 Canadian Parks Service, *Banff National Parks Management Plan* (Ottawa: Environment Canada), 130.

31 Lothian, *History of Canada's National Parks*, 4:17–18.

32 The 1997 Banff National Park Management Plan required the removal of facilities from the area, including the bison paddock, community and warden horse corrals, the airport, and the Department of National Defence Cadet Camp. A dramatic increase in carnivore use occurred in the area within three years, partially due to high elk densities near the town of Banff. See D. Duke, M. Hebblewhite, P. C. Paquet, C. Callaghan, and M. Percy, "Restoration of a Large Carnivore Corridor in Banff National Park," in *Large Mammal Restoration: Ecological and Social Challenges in the 21st Century*, ed. D. Maehr, R. F. Noss, and J. L. Lavlin, 261–75 (Covelo, CA: Island Press, 2001).

33 B. Gadd, *Handbook of the Canadian Rockies* (Jasper, AB: Corax Press, 1995), 148–49.

34 Historical fire years estimated from tree-ring counts from fire-scarred lodgepole pine and written accounts. See Rogeau and Gilbride, *Forest Stand Origin*, 18; White, *Wildland Fires*, 35–36.

35 J. G. Nelson and A. R. Byrne, "Man as an Instrument of Landscape Change: Fires, Floods, and National Parks in the Bow Valley, Alberta," *Geographical Review* 56 (1966): 226–38; G.R.E. Beckstead, *Banff Floodplain Study* (Edmonton: Alberta Environment, 1980).

36 T. E. Hurd, "Factors Limiting Moose Numbers and their Interactions with Elk and Wolves in the Central Rocky Mountains, Canada" (master's thesis, University of British Columbia, 1999); C. G. Nietvelt, "Herbivory Interactions between Beaver (*Castor canadensis*) and Elk (*Cervus elaphus*) on Willow (*Salix* spp.) in Banff National Park, Alberta" (master's thesis, University of Alberta, 2001); M. Hebblewhite, C. A. White, C. G. Nietvelt, J. A. McKenzie, T. E. Hurd, J. M. Fryxell, S. E. Bayley, and P. C. Paquet, "Human Activity Mediates a Trophic Cascade Caused by Wolves," *Ecology* 86 (2005): 2135–2144.

37 Parks Canada, *Elk Management Strategy in the Bow Valley, Banff National Park*, Environmental Screening Report (Banff: Banff National Park, 1999). Increased use of the area by predators and relocation of human-habituated elk reduced the population near Banff townsite from over four hundred animals in 1997 to less than a hundred by 2003.

38 *Banff Crag and Canyon*, January 6, 1917.

39 Hart, *Place of Bows*, 297–98.

40 Hart, *Battle for Banff*, 48–51; C. Scott, *Powder Pioneers* (Calgary: Rocky Mountain Books, 2005), 102–4; E. Hunter, *The Spirit of Mount Norquay: A History of Skiing Banff National Park's Mount Norquay* (Banff: Banff Mount Norquay, 2000).

41 Robinson, *Banff Springs Hotel*, 103; Hart, *Battle for Banff*, 257–61.

42 Hunter, *Mount Norquay*, 13–17, 42–47.

43 *Banff Crag and Canyon*, January 27, 1993; Hart, *Place of Bows*, 124.

44 "Sentimenal Journey," by L. Trono, *Banff Crag and Canyon*, May 26, 1993.

45 Banff-Bow Valley Study, *Banff-Bow Valley at the Crossroads: Technical Report of the Banff-Bow Valley Task Force*, ed. R. Page, S. Bayley, J. D. Cook, J. E. Green, and J. R. B. Ritchie (Ottawa: Department of Canadian Heritage, 1996), 196–97.

46 Hart, *Battle for Banff*, 188–90.

47 Banff-Bow Valley Study, *Banff-Bow Valley at the Crossroads: Technical Report*, 193–98; Parks Canada, *Banff National Park Management Plan* (Ottawa: Department of Canadian Heritage, 1997), 21–23.

Chapter 5 "IF WE CAN'T EXPORT THE SCENERY"

1 L. Bella, *Parks for Profit* (Montreal: Harvest House, 1987), 5–24, describes the early economic importance of mountain tourism to the Canadian Pacific Railroad and Government of Canada.

2 G. M. Grant, "The C.P.R. by the Kicking Horse Pass and the Selkirks," *The Week*, January 10, 1884, 86.

3 M. Roberts, *The Western Avernus* (Toronto: J. M. Dent, 1924), 48–49.

4 M.T.S. Schäffer, "The 1911 Expedition to Maligne Lake," in *A Hunter of Peace: Mary T. S. Schäffer's Old Indian Trails with her heretofore unpublished account 1911 Expedition to Maligne Lake*, ed. E. J. Hart, 138–39 (Banff: Whyte Foundation, 1980).

5 The problem of fires along the railways is described by R. J. Burns and M. Schintz, *Guardians of the Wild: A History of the Warden Service of Canada's National Parks* (Calgary: University of Calgary Press, 2000), 27–31; White, *Wildland Fires*, 28–46.

6 J. M. Gibbon, *Steel of Empire* (Toronto: McClelland and Stewart, 1935), 325–26; Hart, *Selling of Canada*, 21–67.

7 See Robinson, *Banff Springs*, 5, 11–18.

8 Hart, *Selling of Canada*, 60–62, 73–75, 90–91.

9 Robinson, *Banff Springs*, 50–52.

10 C. Smith, *Jasper Park Lodge: In the Heart of the Canadian Rockies* (Altona, MB: Friesen, 1985), 6–26.

11 Hart, *Banff Springs Golf Club*, 44–49.

Chapter 6 THE CALIFORNIA–BANFF BEELINE

1 E. J. Hart, *The Brewster Story: From Packtrain to Tour Bus* (Banff: EJH Literary Enterprises, 1981), 55–56, 72–73.

2 Hart, *Battle for Banff*, 154–58.

3 McGuire and Morrall, "Strategic Highway Improvements"; C. Pacas, D. Bernard, N. Marshal, and J. Green, *State of the Banff-Bow Valley Report* (Banff, AB: Banff-Bow Valley Study, 1996), 3–22.

4 R. W. Sandford, *Sunshine: Its Human and Natural Heritage* (Banff: Sunshine Village Corporation, 1984) 21–28; Hart, *Battle for Banff*, 45–48, 198; Scott, *Powder Pioneers*, 104–5, 176–77.

5 J. Outram, *In the Heart of the Canadian Rockies* (New York: MacMillan, 1906), 50.

6 White, *Wildland Fires*, 54–55.

7 C. A. White, I. R. Pengelly, D. Zell, and M. P. Rogeau, *Landscape Fire Regimes and Vegetation Restoration in Banff National Park, Alberta*, Occasional Paper BNP-2003-1 (Banff, AB: Parks Canada, 2003), 32.

8 F. A. de Scally, *Alteration and Restoration of Alluvial Fan Processes in Banff National Park*, Consultant Report (Banff: Parks Canada, 1999), 10–17.

9 White, Feller, and Vera, "New Approaches for Testing Fire History Hypotheses."

10 T. E. Wilson, *Trail Blazer of the Canadian Rockies* (Calgary: Glenbow-Alberta Institute, 1972), 21.

11 James Hector of the Palliser Expedition camped here on August 17, 1858, calling it "a spot of very rich pasture." See Spry, *Papers of the Palliser Expedition*, 297; Hart, *Place of Bows*, 72.

12 White and Feller, "Repeat Photography of Trembling Aspen."

13 I. McT. Cowan, "Some Vital Statistics of Big Game on Overstocked Mountain Range," *Transactions of the North American Wildlife Conference* 15 (1950): 581–88.

14 Luxton, *Banff*, 52–53.

15 Lothian, *History of Canada's National Parks*, 1:16–17; Hart, *Place of Bows*, 95–98.

16 W. A. Waiser, *Park Prisoners: The Untold History of Western Canada's National Parks, 1915–1946* (Calgary: Fifth House, 1995), 6–47.

17 Spry, *Papers of the Palliser Expedition*, 296–99.

18 Hart, *Place of Bows*, 272–74.

19 White, *Wildland Fires*, 36–47.

20 Spry, *Papers of the Palliser Expedition*, 305.

21 Kay, Patton, and White, "Historical Wildlife Observations in the Canadian Rockies," 561–83; Spry, *Papers of the Palliser Expedition*, 147–53.

22 Kay, Patton, and White, "Historical Wildlife"; Burns and Schintz, *Guardians of the Wild* (Calgary: University of Calgary Press, 2000), 87–98; D. M. Poll, *Wildlife Mortality on the Kootenay Parkway, Kootenay National Park* (Radium, BC: Parks Canada, 1989); C. E. Kay, "Are Ecosystems Structured from Top-Down, or Bottom-Up: A New Look at and Old Debate," *Wildlife Society Bulletin* 26 (1998): 484–98.

23 W. F. Lothian, *A Brief History of Canada's National Parks* (Ottawa: Environment Canada-Parks, 1987), 61.

24 Lothian, *History of Canada's National Parks*, 1:58–61; Hart, *Place of Bows*, 260–76.

25 Binnema, *Common and Contested Ground*, 128–35.

26 Belyea, *Columbia Journals*, 54–74.

27 Hart, *Brewster Story*, 74–75.

Chapter 7 DIVIDENDS IN GOLD

1 Lothian, *History of Canada's National Parks*, 1:26; Hart, *Place of Bows*, 109–10, 119–20.

2 Bella, *Parks for Profit*, provides a description of early park development in Banff, and national parks' overall development program for tourism and other industries.

3 Scace, *Banff: A Cultural Historical Study*, 26–45; Lothian, *History of Canada's National Parks*, 1:26–29; Lothian, *History of Canada's National Parks*, 2:56–58, describe the development of the leasing system which gave private land tenure in Banff National Park for business or residential purposes.

4 W. S. Green, *Among the Selkirk Glaciers being the Account of a Rough Survey in the Rocky Mountains Region of British Columbia* (London: MacMillan, 1890), 236; Hart, *Place of Bows*, 120–25.

5 Byrne, *Man and Landscape Change*, 119–21; Bella, *Parks for Profit*, 35–37.

6 G. W. Tough, "A Study of Coal Mining: Cascade Coal Basin" (master's thesis, University of Calgary, 1969), 34–50; Lothian, *History of Canada's National Parks*, 4:96–98; Bella, *Parks for Profit*, 25–32.

7 Canada, "Report of the Superintendent of Rocky Mountains Park," *Department of the Interior Report: 1905–06*, 11; Canada, "Report of the Superintendent of Rocky Mountains Park," *Department of the Interior Report: 1907*, 14–15.

8 Hart, *Place of Bows*, 225–29.

9 See Great Plains Research Consultants, *Jasper National Park: A Social and Economic History*, Microfiche Report 198 (Ottawa: Parks Canada, 1985).

10 Hart, *Brewster Story*, 51–54.

11 Canada, "Report of the Commissioner of Dominion Parks," *Department of the Interior Report: 1914*, 5.

12 Canada, "Report of the Commissioner of Dominion Parks," *Department of the Interior Report: 1916*, 15.

13 Lothian, *History of Canada's National Parks*, 1:38, 44, 54.

14 Hart, *Battle for Banff*, 23–28.

15 Lothian, *History of Canada's National Parks*, 1:54.

16 Ski resorts are significant tourism and recreational developments in the Banff and Jasper national parks. Histories of ski area development are provided by Sandford, *Sunshine*; R. Touche, *Brown Cows, Sacred Cows: A True Story of Lake Louise* (Hanna, AB: Gorman Publishers, 1990); Hunter, *Norquay*; Scott, *Powder Pioneers*. Although parks policy on ski area development may have stimulated reinvestment in existing communities, lack of on-hill accommodations made the resorts themselves less competitive with other destination ski areas such as Whistler, BC. See S. Hudson, B. Ritchie, and S. Timur, "Measuring Destination Competitiveness: An Empirical Study of Canadian Ski Resorts," *Tourism and Hospitality Planning & Development* 1 (2004): 79–94.

17 The postwar success of the joint investments of many private developers and the federal government in the Canadian mountain national parks contrasts sharply with the ongoing financial difficulties in Yellowstone National Park, as described by M. D. Barringer, *Selling Yellowstone: Capitalism and the Construction of Nature* (Lawrence: University of Kansas Press, 2002), 118–20, 179–82.

18 The process to develop a deeper commitment to national park values within the private sector is described by J.R.B. Ritchie, "Crafting a Value-Driven Vision for National Tourism Treasure," *Tourism Management* 20 (1999): 273–82. Today, the Banff Heritage Tourism Corporation provides both government and private participants with a framework and training to maintain high quality heritage tourism in the Rocky Mountain World Heritage Site parks.

19 D. Draper, "Towards Sustainable Mountain Communities: Balancing Tourism Development and Environmental Protection in Banff and Banff National Park," *Ambio* 29 (2000): 408–15.

20 P.F.J. Eagles, "International Trends in Park Tourism: The Emerging Role of Finance," *George Wright Forum* 20 (2003): 25–57, evaluates potential governance and financing models being developed for national parks in Canada, Australia, South Africa, and other countries.

Chapter 8 HEART OF THE ROCKIES

1 For a history of backcountry travel in this area, see E. J. Hart, *Diamond Hitch: The Early Outfitters and Guides of Banff and Jasper* (Banff, AB: Summerthought, 1979).

2 A. P. Coleman, *The Canadian Rockies: New and Old Trails* (Toronto: Henry Frowde, 1911), 20–23.

3 White, *Wildland Fires*, 25–34; M. P. Rogeau, I. R. Pengelly, and M. J. Fortin, "Using a Topography Model to Predict and Monitor Fire Cycles in Banff National Park," in *Proceedings of the 22nd Tall Timbers Fire Ecology Conference: Fire in Temperate, Boreal, and Montane Ecosystems*, ed. R. T. Engstrom, K.E.M. Galley, and W. J. de Groot, 55–69 (Tallahassee, FL: Tall Timbers Research Station, 2004).

4 Hart, *Place of Bows*, 81.

5 Green, *Selkirk Glaciers*, 244.

6 Hart, *Selling of Canada*, 60–62.

7 J. Feick and D. Draper, "Valid Threat or 'Tempest in a Teapot?' An Historical Account of Tourism Development and Canadian Rocky Mountain World Heritage Site Designation," *Tourism Recreation Research* 26 (2001): 35–46, describes the international designation and unsuccessful attempts by environmental groups in the 1990s to have it removed.

8 Hart, *Selling of Canada*, 87–89.

9 Cavell, *Legacy in Ice*, 6–18.

10 S. F. Arno and J. R. Habeck, "Ecology of Alpine Larch (*Larix lyalli* Parl.) in the Pacific Northwest," *Ecological Monographs* 42 (1972): 417–50.

11 Rogeau, Pengelly, and Fortin, "Fire Cycles in Banff."

12 W. D. Wilcox, *The Rockies of Canada* (New York: Putnam, 1909), 111–18.

13 Rogeau and Gilbride, *Forest Stand Origin*, Map Sheet 6; White, *Wildland Fires*, 41–42.

14 A. Harmon, *Park History: Banff National Park*, Internal Report (Banff, AB: Banff National Park, 1959), 20, 30.

15 Lothian, *History of Canada's National Parks*, 3:29–35; Touche, *Brown Cows*, 134–47; Hart, *Battle for Banff*, 229–46.

16 Parks Canada, *Public Hearing Report*, 1; Hart, *Battle for Banff*, 342–46.

17 Touche, *Brown Cows*, 81–87; Scott, *Powder Pioneers*, 106–9.

18 Touche, *Brown Cows*, 100–119; Lothian, *History of Canada's National Parks*, 3:29–30.

19 G. M. Dawson, *Preliminary Report on the Physical and Geological Features of that Portion of the Rocky Mountains* (Montreal: Dawson Brothers, 1886), 146–48.

20 White et al., "Plains Bison Restoration."

21 F. O. Brewster, *Weathered Wood: Anecdotes and History of the Banff-Sunshine Area* (Banff, AB: Altitude Publishing, 1977), 11.

22 For the history of Ya Ha Tinda, see Lothian, *History of Canada's National Parks*, 4:77–80; Burns and Schintz, *Guardians of the Wild*, 132–34.

23 See L. E. Morgantini, *The Ya Ha Tinda: An Ecological Overview* (Calgary: Parks Canada, 1995), for a description of this unique ecosystem. Fire history of the grassland is described by White, Feller, and Vera, "New Approaches for Testing Fire History Hypotheses"; Parks Canada, *Ya Ha Tinda Ranch, Fuel Break-Prescribed Fire-Elk Conditioning-Elk Proof Fencing*, Environmental Screening Report (Banff, AB: Banff National Park, 2005).

24 Wilson, *Trail Blazer*, 18–19.

25 Hart, *Selling of Canada*, 14, 87.

26 Lothian, *History of Canada's National Parks*, 3:35–42.

27 See C. A. White, "Fire and Biomass in Banff National Park Closed Forests" (master's thesis, Colorado State University, 1985).

28 Lavallée, *Van Horne's Road*, 182.

29 See H.E.M. Stutfield and J. N. Collie, *Climbs and Explorations in the Canadian Rockies*, rev. ed. (1903; repr. Calgary: Aquila Books, 1998), 24–28, for a description of the horse trail through the upper Bow Valley.

30 Schäffer, "Old Indian Trails," 24.

31 See E. J. Hart, *Jimmy Simpson, Legend of the Rockies* (Banff, AB: Altitude Publishing, 1993), for a history of Simpson's activities at Bow Lake.

32 B. H. Luckman, "The Neoglacial History of Peyto Glacier," in *Peyto Glacier: One Century of Science*, ed. M. N. Demuth, D. S. Munro, and G. J. Young, 25–57 (Saskatoon: National Water Research Institute, 2006).

33 M. N. Demuth and R. Keller, "An Assessment of the Mass Balance of Peyto Glacier (1966–1995) and its Relation to Recent and Past-Century Climatic Variability," in *Peyto Glacier: One Century of Science*, ed. M. N. Demuth, D. S. Munro, and G. J. Young, 83–133 (Saskatoon: National Water Research Institute, 2006). Other research on this well-studied glacier includes C.S.I. Ommaney, *Glacier Surveys by District Personnel of the Water Survey of Canada 2: The Peyto Glacier*, Inland Waters Directorate Glacier Inventory 7 (Ottawa: Department of the Environment, 1972); G. J. Young and A. D. Stanley, *Canadian Glaciers in the International Hydrological Decade Program 1965–1974: No. 4 Peyto Glacier*, Inland Waters Directorate Scientific Series 71 (Ottawa: Fisheries and Environment Canada, 1976).

34 Schäffer, "Old Indian Trails," 68–73.

35 Belyea, *Columbia Journals*, 98–100; Kay, Patton, and White, "Historical Wildlife Observations."

36 Millar, *Game Preservation*, 35.

37 Belyea, *Columbia Journals*.

38 For a history of the Bighorn Dam, see P. McDonald, *Where the River Brought Them: 200 Years at Rocky Mountain House and Area* (Rocky Mountain House, AB: Creative Office Design and Publishing, 2001), 490–94.

39 Harmon, *Great Days*, 18–19.

40 Stutfield and Collie, *Climbs and Explorations*, 81.

41 Stutfield and Collie, *Climbs and Explorations*, 107.

42 Hart, *Brewster Story*, 113–14; Hart, *Battle for Banff*, 69–70.

43 R. E. Kucera, *Exploring the Columbia Icefield* (Calgary: High Country Colour, 1999), provides a history of the recession of the Athabasca Glacier.

Chapter 9 UNIMPAIRED FOR FUTURE GENERATIONS

1 J. B. Harkin, "Canada's National Parks," in *Handbook of Canada*, ed. W. A. Parks, 98 (Toronto: University of Toronto Press, 1924).

2 Hart, *Place of Bows*, 226–27; Harkin, "Canada's National Parks," 98.

3 Hart, *Battle for Banff*, 79–81.

4 National Parks Act (1930), 2021 George V Chapter 33.

5 Lothian, *History of Canada's National Parks*, 1:37–38.

6 *Banff Crag and Canyon*, March 17, 1965.

7 Touche, *Brown Cows*, 107.

8 *Park News*, Vol. 8, No. 4, July 1972.

9 For a complete description of the Olympic Games and Village Lake Louise episodes, see Hart, *Battle for Banff*, 194–206, 238–45.

10 See National and Historic Parks Branch, *Banff National Park Provisional Master Plan*, 6–7, for a description of the "era" versus "evolutionary" approaches to managing national park ecosystems.

11 See A. S. Leopold, S. A. Cain, C. Cottam, I. N. Gabrielson, and T. L. Kimball, "Report of the Advisory Board on Wildlife Management," Insert 4-63, *National Parks Magazine* (April, 1963). See also G. F. Cole, "An Ecological Rationale for the Natural or Artificial Regulation of Native Ungulates in Parks," *Transactions of the North American Wildlife Conference* 36 (1971): 417–25; A. Chase, *Playing God in Yellowstone: The Destruction of America's First National Park* (San Diego: Harcourt Brace, 1986); F. H. Wagner, R. Foresta, R. B. Gill, D. R. McCullough, M. R. Pelton, W. F. Porter, and H. Salwasser, eds., *Wildlife Policies in U.S. National Parks* (Washington, DC: Island Press, 1995), 131–34, 168–69. The scientific research opportunities provided by the natural regulation policy in Yellowstone are discussed by M. S. Boyce, "Natural Regulation or Control of Nature," in *The Greater Yellowstone Ecosystem: Redefining America's Wilderness Heritage*, ed. R. B. Keiter and M. S. Boyce, 183–207 (New Haven, CT: Yale University Press, 1991); P. Arcese and A.R.E. Sinclair, "The Role of Protected Areas as Ecological Baselines," *Journal of Wildlife Management* 61 (1997): 587–602.

12 Parks Canada, *Public Hearing Report*, 8–9, recognized that future land use planning would require more detailed scientific information. In the 1970s, Parks Canada began numerous detailed ecological studies. See W. D. Holland and G. M. Coen, eds., *The Ecological (Biophysical) Land Classification of Banff and Jasper National Parks*, Publication SS-82-44 (Edmonton: Alberta Institute of Pedology, 1982); G. L. Holroyd and K. J. Van Tighem, *Ecological (Biophysical) Land Classification of Banff and Jasper National Parks. Volume 3: The Wildlife Inventory*, Canadian Wildlife Service Report (Calgary: Parks Canada, 1983). Research on archaeological and historical resources is summarized by Langemann and Perry, *Banff National Park of Canada*. In addition, research was conducted on the long-term role of influences of humans on ecosystems. See White, *Wildland Fires*; Kay et al., *Long-term Ecosystem States*.

13 Alberta Conservation Authority, "Land Use and Resource Development in the Eastern Slopes," *Proceedings of the Public Hearings*, Part 3 (Edmonton: Alberta Environment, 1974), 75.

14 S. J. Woodley, J. Kay, and G. Francis, eds., *Ecological Integrity and the Management of Ecosystems* (Delray Beach, FL: St. Lucie Press, 1993), provides a series of papers on the ecological integrity paradigm. The concept evolved from the 1988 to 2001 amendments to the National Parks Act. The quoted definition for ecological integrity was recommended by Parks Canada Agency, *"Unimpaired for Future Generations?"* Vol. 2. Setting a New Direction for Canada's National Parks. Report on the Panel of Ecological Integrity (Ottawa: Public Works and Government Services, 2000), 1.8–1.17.

15 Banff-Bow Valley Study, *Banff-Bow Valley at the Crossroads: Summary Report of the Banff-Bow Valley Task Force*, ed. R. Page, S. Bayley, J. D. Cook, J. E. Green, and J.R.B. Ritchie (Ottawa: Department of Canadian Heritage, 1996), 4.

16 Banff-Bow Valley Study, *Banff-Bow Valley at the Crossroads: Technical Report*, 155–318; D. W. Hodgins, J. E. Green, G. Harrison, and J. Roulet, "From Confrontation to Conservation: The Banff National Park Experience," in *Wilderness Science in a Time of Change Conference*, ed. S. F. McCool, D. N. Cole, W. T. Borrie, and J. O'Loughlin, USDA Forest Service Proceedings RMRS-P-15-Vol-2, 281–89 (Ogden, UT: Rocky Mountain Forest and Range Experiment Station, 2000).

17 Parks Canada, *Banff National Park Management Plan*, 11–26; C. A. White and W. Fisher, "Consilience and Ecological Restoration in Banff National Park," in *Interdisciplinary Research and Management in Mountain Areas*, Mountain Community Conference Series No. 4, ed. L. Taylor and A. Ryall, 113–32 (Banff, AB: Mountain Culture at the Banff Centre, 2004). Ecosystem changes resulting from these restoration actions, as of 2004, were significant and are reviewed by C. A. White, T. E. Hurd, M. Hebblewhite, and I. R. Pengelly, "Mitigating Fire Suppression, Highway, and Habitat Fragmentation Effects in the Banff Bow Valley Ecosystem," in *Monitoring the Effectiveness of Biological Conservation*, ed. J. Innes and J. Timko, (Vancouver: Forrex, 2007).

18 Parks Canada Agency, *"Unimpaired for Future Generations?" Protecting Ecological Integrity with Canada's National Parks. Volume 1: A Call to Action*. Report of the Panel on the Ecology Integrity of Canada's National Parks (Ottawa: Public Works and Government Services, 2000), 1–2.

19 Parks Canada Agency, *"Unimpaired for Future Generations?" Protecting Ecological Integrity with Canada's National Parks. Volume 2: Setting a New Direction for National Parks*, 1–17.

20 For the management implications of long-term human influences on fire, see White, *Wildland Fires*, 97–98; Kay et al., *Long-term Ecosystem States*, 5.1–5.27; S. J. Pyne, "Burning Banff," *Interdisciplinary Studies in Literature and Environment* 11 (2004): 221–47.

21 Kay, Patton, and White, "Historical Wildlife Observations," indicates relatively few grizzly bears during the early historical period. For recommendations on grizzly bear management, see: M. L. Gibeau, A. P. Clevenger, S. Herrero, and J. Wierzchowski, "Grizzly Bear Response to Human Development and Activities in the Bow River Watershed, Alberta, Canada," *Biological Conservation* 103 (2002): 227–36; S. Herrero, ed., *Biology, Demography, Ecology, and Management of Grizzly Bears in and around Banff National Park*

and Kananaskis Country, Eastern Slopes Grizzly Bear Project (Calgary: University of Calgary, Faculty of Environmental Design, 2005), 38–56, 231–32.

22 Recommendations for caribou conservation are described by Alberta Woodland Caribou Recovery Team, *Alberta Woodland Caribou Recovery Plan 2004/05–2013/14*, Alberta Species at Risk Recovery Plan No. 4 (Edmonton: Alberta Sustainable Resource Development, 2005). Links between high elk and wolf density and resulting declining caribou numbers in Banff are described by Parks Canada, *Ya Ha Tinda Ranch*, 82–94; M. Hebblewhite, J. Whittington, M. Bradley, G. Skinner, A. Dibb, and C. A. White, "Conditions for Caribou Persistence in the Wolf-Elk-Caribou Systems of the Canadian Rockies," *Rangifer* 17 (2007): forthcoming.

23 Several papers review the progress of the Banff Bow Valley Study in using interdisciplinary research to inform stakeholders. See C. Zinkan and I. Syme, "Changing Dimensions of Park Management," *Forum for Applied Research and Public Policy* 12 (1997): 39–42; Ritchie, "National Tourism Treasure"; Hodgins et al., "Confrontation to Conservation"; White and Fisher, "Consilience and Ecological Restoration."

Chapter 10 THE NORTHWEST PASSAGE BY LAND

1 Belyea, *Columbia Journals*, 258.

2 A winter crossing of the Rockies was unusual; however, fur brigades routinely travelled through the Rockies in the late fall and early spring when the rivers had low water levels, but were not ice-covered, and before deep snow accumulated on the passes.

3 See Binnema, *Common and Contested Ground*, 129–94, for a detailed description of the fur trade's extended conflict with the Blackfoot over access to the First Nations west of the Rocky Mountains. David Thompson's near-violent skirmish with the Peigan in October 1810 along the North Saskatchewan is described by numerous authors. For a recent interpretation of these events, see J. McCart and P. McCart, *On the Road with David Thompson* (Calgary: Fifth House, 2000), 183–92.

4 See Belyea, *Columbia Journals*, 117–56, for Thompson's trip to the Pacific. The history of the Columbia District of the fur trade industry is described by D. Johansen, *Empire of the Columbia: A History of the Pacific Northwest* (New York: Harper and Row, 1967), 91–135.

5 Dr. James Hector provides a description of the Athabasca Pass trail in the vicinity of the town of Jasper. See Spry, *Papers of the Palliser Expedition*, 378–80. A summary of other accounts of trips over the pass is provided by R. W. Cautley and A. O. Wheeler, *Report of the Commission Appointed to Delimit the Boundary between the Provinces of Alberta and British Columbia: Part II. Kicking Horse to Yellowhead Pass* (Ottawa: Office of the Surveyor General, 1924), 93–96.

6 Lothian, *History of Canada's National Parks*, 1:52–54.

7 Lothian, *History of Canada's National Parks*, 1:52–54.

8 B. Gainer, *The Human History of Jasper National Park*, Report No. 441 (Jasper, AB: Parks Canada, 1981), 48.

9 Lothian, *History of Canada's National Parks*, 1:52–54.

10 Lothian, *History of Canada's National Parks*, 1:52–54.

11 C. Smith, *Jasper Park Lodge*, 34; MacLaren, Higgs and Zezulka-Mailloux, *Mapper of the Mountains*, 103–5.

12 E. J. Holmgren and P. M. Holmgren, *Place Names of Alberta* (Saskatoon: Western Producer Prairie Books, 1976), 85–86.

13 C. Smith, *Jasper Park Lodge*, 1.

14 C. Smith, *Jasper Park Lodge*, 7.

15 C. Smith, *Jasper Park Lodge*, 27–33.

16 Scott, *Powder Pioneers*, 109–10.

17 G. F. Tande, "Fire History and Vegetation Pattern of Coniferous Forests in Jasper National Park, Alberta," *Canadian Journal of Botany* 57 (1979): 1912–1931.

18 Rhemtulla et al., "Eighty Years of Change"; White et al., *Landscape Fire Regimes*.

19 Kay, Patton, and White, "Historical Wildlife."

20 Holroyd and Van Tighem, *Wildlife Inventory*, 405, describe elk reintroductions to Banff and Jasper national parks.

21 J. Whittington, C. Cassady St. Clair, and G. Mercer, "Spatial Responses of Wolves to Roads and Trails in Mountain Valleys," *Ecological Applications* 15 (2005): 543–53, describes wolf displacement by humans near the town of Jasper. The interacting effects of high human use on predators, elk and aspen are described by C. A. White, C. E. Olmsted, and C. E. Kay, "Aspen, Elk, and Fire in the Rocky Mountain National Parks of North America," *Wildlife Society Bulletin* 26 (1998): 449–62; Hebblewhite et al., "Human Activity."

22 C. Smith, *Jasper Park Lodge*, 7.

23 Schäffer, "Hunter of Peace," 96.

24 Frequency of lightning strikes in the Canadian Rockies is analyzed by Wierzchowski, Heathcott, and Flannigan, "Lightning and Lightning Fire, Central Cordillera, Canada," 41–51.

25 Gainer, *Human History*, 47–48, 52–53; P. J. Murphy and T. W. Peterson, "Athabasca Pass: Portal on the Trans Canada Road 1811–1860," Paper presented at *Rupert's Land Colloquium*, May 25–29, 2004, Kenora.

26 H. J. Moberly and W. B. Cameron, *When Fur Was King* (Toronto: J. M. Dent, 1929), 51–52, 94–95.

27 Activities of the Canadian Pacific Railway Survey in the Athabasca Valley are described by R. M. Rylatt, *Surveying the Canadian Pacific: Memoir of a Railway Pioneer* (Salt Lake City: University of Utah Press, 1991), 112–87; MacLaren, Higgs, and Zezulka-Mailloux, *Mapper of Mountains*, 16–22.

28 A. Birrell, "Fortunes of a Misfit: Charles Horetzki," *Alberta Historical Review* 19 (1971): 9–25.

29 Gainer, *Human History*, 54.

30 Lothian, *History of Canada's National Parks*, 3:73–74; MacLaren, Higgs, and Zezulka-Mailloux, *Mapper of Mountains*, 30–34.

31 C. Smith, *Jasper Park Lodge*, 2–5.

32 R. Bott, P. J. Murphy, and R. Udell, *Learning from the Forest* (Calgary: Fifth House, 2003), 22–23.

33 Lothian, *History of Canada's National Parks*, 1:54.

34 Bott, Murphy, and Udell, *Learning from the Forest*, 22–23. The most acclaimed description of this horrible trail is provided by V. Milton and W. B. Cheadle, *The Northwest Passage by Land*, rev. ed. (1865; repr. Toronto: Coles, 1970), 203–33.

35 The history of the Hinton Forest Management Agreement is described by Bott, Murphy, and Udell, *Learning from the Forest*, 32–40. Current information on Forest Management Agreements is available on the Alberta Government website: http://www3.gov.ab.ca/srd/forest/managing/fma/index.html.

36 K. Timoney and P. Lee, "Environmental Management in Resource-rich Alberta, Canada: First World Jurisdiction, Third World Analogue," *Journal of Environmental Management* 63 (2001): 387–405.

37 B. Silversides, *Fort de Prairies: The Story of Fort Edmonton* (Surrey, BC: Heritage House, 2005), 1–6.

38 Standard references for the history of the City of Edmonton include: J. G. MacGregor, *Edmonton: A History* (Edmonton: Hurtig, 1975); and J. F. Gilpin, *Edmonton, Gateway to the North: An Illustrated History* (Burlington, ON: Windsor Publications, 1984).

Chapter 11 SYNTHESIS

1 See Gadd, *Canadian Rockies*, 45–142, for an excellent synthesis of mountain-building processes.

2 E. C. Pielou, *After the Ice Age: The Return of Life to Glaciated North America* (Chicago: University of Chicago Press, 1991), 5–18.

3 Gadd, *Canadian Rockies*, 145–60, describes glaciation effects on the Rockies.

4 Pielou, *After the Ice Age*, 81–103; T. Flannery, *The Eternal Frontier: An Ecological History of North America* (New York: Atlantic Monthly Press, 2001), 146–69.

5 J. C. Ritchie and G. M. Macdonald, "The Patterns of Post-Glacial Spread of White Spruce," *Journal of Biogeography* 13 (1986): 527–40; G. M. MacDonald and L. C. Cwynar, "A Fossil Pollen Based Reconstruction of the Late Quaternary History of Lodgepole Pine (*Pinus contorta* spp. Latifolia) in the Western Interior of Canada," *Canadian Journal of Forest Research* 15 (1985): 1039–1044.

6 W. Choquette, "Early Post-Glacial Habitation of the Upper Columbia Region," in *Early Human Occupation in British Columbia*, ed. R. L. Carlson and L. Dalla Bonna, 45–50 (Vancouver: UBC Press, 1996); G. M. MacDonald, "Late Quaternary Paleoenvironments of the Morley Flats and Kananaskis Valley of Southwestern Alberta," *Canadian Journal of Earth Sciences* 19 (1982): 23–35.

7 M. A. Reasoner and U. M. Huber, "Postglacial Paleoenvironments and Climate History of the Upper Bow Valley, Banff National Park, Canada," *Quaternary Science Review* 18 (1999): 475–92; M. A. Reasoner, G. Osborn, and N. W. Rutter, "Age of the Crowfoot Advance in the Canadian Rocky Mountains: A Glacial Event Coeval with the Younger Dryas Oscillation," *Geology* 22 (1994): 439–42.

8 Reasoner and Huber, "Postglacial Paleoenvironments."

9 R. C. Hallett and R. C. Walker, "Paleoecology and its Application to Fire and Vegetation Management in Kootenay National Park, British Columbia," *Journal of Paleolimnology* 24 (2000): 401–14.

10 B. H. Luckman, "The Little Ice Age and the Canadian Rockies," *Geomorphology* 32 (2000): 357–84.

11 B. H. Luckman, "Landscape and Climate Change in the Central Canadian Rockies during the 20th Century," *Canadian Geographer* 42 (1998): 319–36; Luckman and Kavanagh, "Impact of Climate Fluctuations."

12 Intergovernmental Panel on Climate Change, *Climate Change 2001, The Scientific Basis* (Cambridge: Cambridge University Press, 2001); see D. Scott and R. Suffling, eds., *Climate Change and Canada's National Park System* (Ottawa: Environment Canada, 2000), 78–96, for predicted effects from climate change specific to the Canadian Rockies.

13 Beckstead, *Banff Floodplain Study.*

14 Holland and Coen, *Land Classification*, 299–307; Holroyd and Van Tighem, *Wildlife Inventory*, 559–62.

15 R. A. Kostaschuk, G. M. MacDonald, and P. E. Putman, "Depositional Processes and Alluvial Fan Drainage Basin Morphometric Relationships near Banff," *Earth Surface Processes and Landforms* 11 (1986): 471–84; L. E. Jackson, R. A. Kostachuk, and G. M. Macdonald, "Identification of Debris Flow Hazard on Alluvial Fans in the Canadian Rocky Mountains," *Reviews in Engineering Geology* 7 (1987): 115–24; de Scally, *Alluvial Fan Processes*, 10–17.

16 For details of floods, see Appleby, *Canmore*, 80–81, 106, 150–53.

17 See R. I. Perla and M. Martinelli, *Avalanche Handbook*, USDA Forest Service Agriculture Handbook 489 (Fort Collins, CO: Rocky Mountain Forest and Range Research Station, 1978), for types of avalanches. Avalanche effects on Rocky Mountain plant communities are described in Holland and Coen, *Land Classification*, 23–32, 504–5.

18 P. W. Stringer, "An Ecological Study of Grasslands in Banff, Jasper and Waterton Lakes National Parks," *Canadian Journal of Botany* 51 (1973): 383–411; Holland and Coen, *Land Classification*, 179–80, 305–7.

19 M. A. Stokes and T. L. Smiley, *An Introduction to Tree-Ring Dating* (Chicago: University of Chicago Press, 1968).

20 See S. F. Arno, "Forest Fire History in the Northern Rockies," *Journal of Forestry* 78 (1980): 460–65. Fire history studies in the Canadian Rockies include Tande, "Fire History"; B. C. Hawkes, "Fire History of Kananaskis Provincial Park: Mean Fire Return Intervals," in *Proceedings of the Fire History Workshop*, ed. W. H. Romme, USDA Forest Service General Technical Report RM-81, 42–45 (Fort Collins, CO: Rocky Mountain Forest and Range Experiment Station, 1980); White, *Wildland Fires*; White, "Fire and Biomass"; Masters, "Fire Frequency in Kootenay"; Johnson and Larsen, "Change in Fire Frequency."

21 Rogeau, Pengelly, and Fortin, "Fire Cycles in Banff."

22 Interestingly, forests up-valley from Moraine Lake near Lake Louise have been frequently burned, and are dominated by fire-dependent alpine larch. Possibly this is evidence that lightning-caused fires frequently crossed the continental divide from the Tokumn Creek valley, or perhaps that this area was a short-cut route for peoples travelling from the Columbia to the Red Deer watersheds, and was often human-burned.

23 Wierzchowski, Heathcott, and Flannigan, "Lightning Fire."

24 Johnson and Larsen, "Change in Fire Frequency"; E. A. Johnson and D. R. Wowchuk, "Wildfires in the Canadian Rocky Mountains and the Relationship to Mid-tropospheric Anomalies," *Canadian Journal of Forest Research* 23 (1993): 1213–1222.

25 Van Wagner, Finney, and Heathcott, "Historical Fire Cycles."

26 White, Feller, and Vera, "New Approaches for Testing Fire History Hypotheses."

27 White, *Wildland Fires*, 82–84.

28 C. J. Krebs, *Ecology* (New York: Harper Collins, 1996), 483–91.

29 See Krebs, *Ecology*, 483–511, for processes and examples of primary and secondary succession. For descriptions of succession after fire in northern and western ecosystems, see J. K. Brown, J. K. Smith, and L. J. Lyon, eds., *Wildland Fires in Ecosystems: Effects of Fire on Flora* (Fort Collins, CO: Rocky Mountain Forest and Range Experiment Station, 2000); S. R. Kessell and W. C. Fischer, *Predicting Post-Fire Plant Succession for Fire Management Planning*, USDA Forest Service General Technical Report INT-94 (Ogden, UT: Intermountain Forest and Range Experiment Station, 1981).

30 C. J. Heusser, "Postglacial Environments in the Canadian Rocky Mountains," *Ecological Monographs* 26 (1956): 263–302.

31 Luckman and Kavanagh, "Impact of Climate Fluctuations."

32 Forest regeneration after fires near treeline is often slow. In some areas current forest regeneration is attributed to climatic warming, but it could alternatively be due to a delayed post-burn recovery.

33 See B. Sveinbjörnsson, "North American and European Treelines: External Forces and Internal Processes Controlling Position," *Ambio* 29 (2000): 389–95; Luckman and Kavanagh, "Impact of Climate Fluctuations."

34 For more details on subalpine forest succession, see R. J. Day, "Stand Structure, Succession, and Use of Southern Alberta Rocky Mountain Forests," *Ecology* 53 (1972): 472–77; P. L. Achuff and I.G.W. Corns, "Vegetation," in *Ecological (Biophysical) Land Classification of Banff and Jasper National Parks. Volume 2: Soil and Vegetation Resources*, ed. W. D. Holland and G. M. Coen, 146–48 (Edmonton: Alberta Institute of Pedology, 1982); E. A. Johnson and G. I. Fryer, "Population Dynamics in Lodgepole Pine–Engelmann Spruce Forests," *Ecology* 70 (1989): 1335–1345. L. L. Sachro, W. L. Strong, and C. C. Gates, "Prescribed Burning Effects on Summer Elk Forage Availability in the Subalpine Zone, Banff National Park, Canada," *Environmental Management* 77 (2005): 183–93.

35 References for montane ecoregion forest succession include J. R. Habeck and R. W. Mutch, "Fire Dependent Forests in the Northern Rocky Mountains," *Quaternary Research* 3 (1973): 408–24; Tande, "Fire History"; Achuff and Corns, "Vegetation," 146–48; W. C. Fischer and B. D. Clayton, *Fire Ecology of Montana Forest Habitat Types East of the Continental Divide*, USDA Forest Service General Technical Report INT-141 (Ogden, UT: Intermountain Forest and Range Experiment Station, 1983); L. B. Nadeau and I.G.W. Corns, "Post-fire Vegetation of the Montane Natural Region of Jasper National Park," *Forest Ecology and Management* 163 (2002): 165–83; B. M. Wikeem and T. J. Ross, "Plant Succession in the Rocky Mountain Trench: Influence of Historic Factors," *Rangelands* 24 (2002): 17–20; White and Feller, "Repeat Photography of Trembling Aspen."

36 See Lothian, *History of Canada's National Parks*, 4:74–77, White, *Wildland Fires*, 82–84; P. J. Murphy, *A History of Forest and Prairie Fire Control Policy in Alberta* (Edmonton: Alberta Energy and Natural Resources, 1985).

37 R. E. Keane, K. C. Ryan, T. T. Veblen, C. D. Allen, J. A. Logan, and B. Hawkes, "The Cascading Effects of Fire Exclusion in Rocky Mountain Ecosystems," in *Rocky Mountain Futures: An Ecological Perspective*, ed. J. Baron, 133–52 (Washington, DC: Island Press, 2002).

38 Hart, *Battle for Banff*, 302–6; Rogeau, Pengelly, and Fortin, "Fire Cycles in Banff"; C. A. White, I. R. Pengelly, D. Zell, and M. P. Rogeau, "Restoring Heterogeneous Fire Regimes in Banff National Park," in *Mixed Severity Fire Regimes: Ecology and Management*, ed. L. Taylor, J. Zelnik, S. Cadwallader, and B. Hughes, 255–66 (Pullman: Washington State University Extension, 2005).

39 Parks Canada, *Regional Forest Management Strategy*, Environmental Screening Report (Banff: Banff National Park, 2002).

40 C. S. Churcher, "Pleistocene Ungulates from the Bow River Gravels at Cochrane Alberta," *Canadian Journal of Earth Sciences* 5 (1968): 1467–1488; B. Kurten and E. Anderson, *Pleistocene Mammals of North America* (New York: Columbia University Press, 1983); Flannery, *Eternal Frontier*, 155–69.

41 Contributors to P. S. Martin and R. G. Klein, eds., *Quaternary Extinctions: A Prehistoric Revolution* (Tucson: University of Arizona Press, 1989), provide a comprehensive overview of likely human-caused mass faunal extinctions; Pielou, *After the Ice Age*, 257–66, describes alternative extinction theories.

42 Kay, Patton, and White, "Historical Wildlife Observations."

43 See C. J. Krebs, S. Boutin, and R. Boonstra, eds., *Ecosystem Dynamics in the Boreal Forest* (Oxford: Oxford University Press, 2001), 18–23, for more information on boreal forest food webs.

44 Kay et al., *Long-term Ecosystem States*, 7.2–7.12, describe long-term human use of large mammals in the Canadian Rockies. Peacock and Turner, "'Just Like a Garden'," 133–79, describe traditional human use and low-intensity cultivation of plants. Langemann and Perry, *Banff National Park of Canada*, 19, argue for the importance of expanding knowledge of traditional use of plants for the Banff National Park area.

45 Ecological model described by White, Olmsted, and Kay, "Aspen, Elk, and Fire."

46 Cole, "Ecological Rationale," 420, 423.

47 Kay, "Are Ecosystems Structured."

48 For example, see J. G. Nelson, "Some Observations on Animals, Landscape, and Man in the Bow Valley Area: c. 1750–1885," in *Vegetation, Soils and Wildlife*, ed. J. G. Nelson and M. J. Chambers, 63–96 (Toronto: Methuen, 1969).

49 Kay, Patton, and White, "Historical Wildlife Observations."

50 M. Hebblewhite, D. H. Pletscher, and P. C. Paquet, "Elk Population Dynamics in Areas With and Without Wolves in Banff National Park," *Canadian Journal of Zoology* 80 (2002): 789–99.

51 Roe, *North American Buffalo*, 467–88.

52 Millar, *Game Preservation*, 30–46.

53 Hart, *Place of Bows*, 209–10, describes the return of bison to a small paddock in Banff. However, unlike several parks in United States (e.g., Yellowstone, Grand Teton, Theodore Roosevelt, Badlands, National Bison Range), Parks Canada has not restored partially or fully free-roaming herds in Banff and Jasper. Given the potential ecological significance of bison, and the demonstrated ease of "drift-fencing" mountain valleys to contain cattle or horses, bison restoration is receiving further consideration. See Parks Canada, *Banff National Park Management Plan*, 21–22; White et al., "Plains Bison Restoration."

54 Lothian, *History of Canada's National Parks*, 4:16–18; Hart, *Place of Bows*, 205–29; Binnema and Niemi, "'Let the Line Line be Drawn Now.'"

55 Graphic from data in C. E. Kay and C. A. White, "Long-term Ecosystem States and Processes in the Central Canadian Rockies: A New Perspective on Ecological Integrity and Ecosystem Management," *George Wright Society Annual Conference on Research and Resources in Parks and on Protected Lands* 8 (1995): 119–32. The interpretation of relatively low long-term abundance of elk in the Rocky Mountains, as indicated in archaeological sites and historical records, is controversial. See alternative viewpoints presented by Kay, "Aboriginal Overkill"; R. L. Lyman, "Aboriginal Overkill in the Intermountain West of North America: Zooarchaelogical Tests and Implications," *Human Nature* 15 (2004): 169–208; R. B. Keigley and F. H. Wagner, "What is 'Natural': Yellowstone Elk Population – A Case Study," *Integrative Biology* 4 (1999): 133–48.

56 Binnema, *Common and Contested Ground*, 37–54, provides a preliminary ecosystem model of historic landscape level interactions of humans and bison. Langemann, "Zooarchaeological Research in Support of a Reintroduction of Bison to Banff National Park Canada." *Conference of the International Council of Archaeolzoology* 9 (2002): 79–89, uses archaeology to interpret prehistoric bison habitat use patterns.

57 See Roe, *North American Buffalo*, 308–10; Kay et al., *Long-term Ecosystem States*, 11.7–11.11; White et al., "Plains Bison Restoration."

58 Spry, *Papers of the Palliser Expedition*, 258; Binnema, *Common and Contested Ground*, 42; Roe, *North American Buffalo*, 100–105.

59 N. V. Debyle and R. P. Winokur, eds., *Aspen: Ecology and Management in the Western States*, USDA Forest Service General Technical Report RM-119 (Fort Collins, CO: Rocky Mountain Forest and Range Experiment Station, 1985), 25–39.

60 Burns and Schintz, *Guardians of the Wild*, 22–24, 81–97; K. R. Jones, *Wolf Mountains: A History of Wolves along the Great Divide* (Calgary: University of Calgary Press, 2002), 108–40.

61 Cowan, "Overstocked Mountain Range"; D. R. Flook, *Causes and Implications of Observed Sex Differential in the Survival of Wapiti*, Canadian Wildlife Service Report Series No. 11 (Ottawa: Queen's Printer, 1970), 65–69; J. Woods, "Ecology of a Partially Migratory Elk Population" (PhD diss., University of British Columbia, 1991), 148–49; Burns and Schintz, *Guardians of the Wild*, 98–107.

62 L. E. Morgantini and R. J. Hudson, "Migratory Patterns of the Wapiti, *Cervus elaphus*, in Banff National Park, Alberta," *Canadian Field Naturalist* 102 (1988): 12–19; Woods, "Partially Migratory Elk Population."

63 Hebblewhite, Pletscher, and Paquet, "Elk Population Dynamics"; Parks Canada, *Elk Management*.

64 M. Hebblewhite, E. H. Merrill, L. E. Morgantini, C. A. White, J. R. Allen, E. Bruns, L. Thurston, and T. E. Hurd, "Is the Migratory Behavior of Montane Elk Herds in Peril? The Case of Alberta's Ya Ha Tinda Elk Herd," *Wildlife Society Bulletin* 34 (2006): 1280–1294, describes changing elk migratory patterns. M. Hebblewhite, "Linking Predation Risk and Forage to Ungulate Population Dynamics" (PhD diss., University of Alberta, 2006), evaluates how current human land use caused the change in annual elk movements.

65 White, Olmsted, and Kay, "Aspen, Elk, and Fire"; C. A. White, M. C. Feller, and S. Bayley, "Predation Risk and the Functional Response of Elk-Aspen Herbivory," *Forest Ecology and Management* 181 (2003): 77–97; Hebblewhite et al., "Human Activity Mediates a Trophic Cascade."

66 Nietvelt, "Herbivory Interactions"; Hebblewhite et al., "Human Activity Mediates a Trophic Cascade."

67 D. Hamer, "Buffaloberry (*Shepherdia canadensis* [L.] Nutt.) Fruit Production in Fire Successional Bear Feeding Sites," *Journal of Range Management* 49 (1996): 520–29; D. Hamer, "Forest Fires Influence on Yellow Hedysarum Habitat and its Use by Grizzly Bears in Banff National Park, Alberta," *Canadian Journal of Zoology* 77 (1999): 1513–1520; Hurd, "Moose Numbers," 42–43; M. Hebblewhite, *Ya Ha Tinda Elk and Wolf Project: Third Quarter Progress Report, 30 September 2004 to 31 December 2004* (Edmonton: University of Alberta, 2005), 4.

68 L. K. Shepherd, "Caribou Habitat Selection in Relation to Lichen and Fire in Banff and Jasper National Parks" (master's thesis, University of Alberta, 2006).

69 Hebblewhite, "Linking Predation Risk," 288–89, and Hebblewhite et al., "Conditions for Caribou Persistence," describe the relationship between elk populations and regional wolf abundance, and hence caribou decline. Hebblewhite recommends that human use should be reduced on the Ya Ha Tinda Ranch to allow wolf predation to decrease resident elk numbers. Another option would be to increase human predation on elk to reflect traditional First Nations use patterns, thus reducing habituation levels to people, increasing elk movements, and favouring wolf predation of elk in areas off of the ranch, resulting in fewer elk and eventually wolf population declines.

70 Alberta Woodland Caribou Recovery Team, *Caribou Recovery Plan*; Parks Canada, *Ya Ha Tinda Ranch*, 82–94.

71 Effects of Canadian Rockies highways are described by R.T.T. Foreman, J. Bissonnette, A. Clevenger, C. Cutshall, V. Dale, L. Fahrig, C. Goldman, K. Heanue, J. Jones, D. Sperling, F. Swanson, T. Turrentine, and T. Winter, *Road Ecology: Science and Solutions* (Washington, DC: Island Press, 2002), 151–53, 356–58; Clevenger and Waltho, "Wildlife Underpasses."

72 For a history of dams in the upper Bow River watershed, see Armstrong and Nelles, "Bow River Waterpowers"; Bella, *Parks for Profit*, 48–58, Hart, *Place of Bows*, 242–43; Hart, *Battle for Banff*, 78–81, 140–42; McDonald, *Where the River Brought Them*, 490–93, describes the Bighorn Dam on the North Saskatchewan River.

73 The Mica Dam is the most upstream impoundment of several dams built and managed under the Columbia River Treaty between Canada and United States. These dams eliminated one of the world's longest and largest salmon migrations. Prior to the completion of the Grand Coulee Dam in 1941, salmon migrated over 2,000 kilometres from the Pacific Ocean to Lake Windermere and Columbia Lake at the headwaters of the river. See D. D. Goble, "Salmon in the Columbia Basin: From Abundance to Extinction," in *Northwest Lands, Northwest Peoples: Readings in Environmental History*, ed. D. D. Goble and P. W. Hirt, 229–63 (Seattle: University of Washington Press, 1999).

74 D. W. Schindler and C. Pacas, "Cumulative Effects of Human Activity on Aquatic Ecosystems the Bow Valley of Banff National Park," in *Ecological Outlooks Project: A Cumulative Effects Assessment and Futures Outlook of the Banff Bow River Valley*, ed. J. Green, C. Pacas, L. Cornwell, and S. Bayley, chap. 5 (Ottawa: Department of Canadian Heritage, 1996).

75 Selected references on the ecological effects of the rapid rate of industrial development on Alberta's east slopes outside the national parks include: H. G. Kariel, "Land Use Alberta's Foothill Country," *Western Geography* 7 (1997): 20–46; I. Urquhart, ed., *Assault on the Rockies: Environmental Controversies in Alberta* (Edmonton: Rowan Books, 1998), i–vii; D. W. Schindler, "The Eastern Slopes of

the Canadian Rockies, Must We Follow the American Blueprint?" in *Rocky Mountain Futures: An Ecological Perspective*, ed. J. Baron, 285–89 (Washington, DC: Island Press, 2002); B. Stelfox, S. Herrero, and D. Ryerson, "Implications of Historical, Current, and Likely Future Trajectories of Human Landuses and Population Growth to Grizzly Bears in the Alberta Portion of CRE," in *Biology, Demography, Ecology, and Management of Grizzly Bears in and around Banff National Park and Kananaskis Country*, ed. S. Herrero, 202–22 (Calgary: Faculty of Environmental Design, University of Calgary, 2005); S. E. Nielsen, S. Herrero, M. S. Boyce, R. D. Mace, B. Benn, M. L. Gibeau, and S. Jevons, "Modelling the Spatial Distribution of Human-Caused Grizzly Bear Mortalities in the Central Rockies Ecosystem of Canada," *Biological Conservation* 120 (2004): 101–13; Timoney and Lee, "Environmental Management."

76 Hart, *Place of Bows*, 253–76.

77 Bella, *Parks for Profit*, 121–27; *Battle for Banff*, 133–58.

78 These changes in land use are similar throughout the Rocky Mountains. See W. R. Travis, D. M. Theobald, and D. B. Fagre, "Transforming the Rockies: Human Forces, Settlement Patterns and Ecosystem Effects," in *Rocky Mountain Futures: An Ecological Perspective*, ed. J. Baron, 1–24 (Washington, DC: Island Press, 2002).

79 Travis, Theobald, and Fagre, "Transforming the Rockies," 9–12.

80 Stelfox, Herrero, and Ryerson, "Implications ... Human Landuses," 202–22.

INDEX

E

F

G

H

I

J

K

L

M

N

O

P

R